D0205372

The purpose of the Cambridge edition is to offer translations of the best modern German edition of Kant's work in a uniform format suitable for Kant scholars. When complete (fourteen volumes are currently envisaged), the edition will include all of Kant's published writings and a generous selection of his unpublished writings such as the *Opus postumum, Handschriftliche Nachlass,* lectures, and correspondence.

This volume contains four versions of the lecture notes taken by Kant's students in his university courses in ethics given regularly over a period of some thirty years. The notes are very comprehensive and expound not only Kant's views on ethics but many of his opinions on life and human nature as well.

Much of this material has never before been translated into English. As in other volumes in the series, there are copious linguistic and explanatory notes and a glossary of key terms.

THE CAMBRIDGE EDITION OF THE WORKS
OF IMMANUEL KANT

Theoretical Philosophy, 1755–1770
The Critique of Pure Reason
Theoretical Philosophy after 1781
Practical Philosophy
Aesthetics and Teleology
Religion and Rational Theology
Anthropology, History, and Education
Natural Science
Lectures on Logic
Lectures on Metaphysics
Lectures on Ethics
Opus postumum
Notes and Fragments
Correspondence

IMMANUEL KANT
Lectures on ethics

THE CAMBRIDGE EDITION OF THE WORKS
OF IMMANUEL KANT

General Editors: Paul Guyer and Allen W. Wood

Advisory Board: Henry Allison
Lewis White Beck
Reinhard Brandt
Mary Gregor
Ralf Meerbote
Charles D. Parsons
Hoke Robinson
Eva Schaper
J. B. Schneewind
Manley P. Thompson

IMMANUEL KANT

Lectures on ethics

EDITED BY

PETER HEATH

University of Virginia

AND

J. B. SCHNEEWIND

Johns Hopkins University

TRANSLATED BY

PETER HEATH

CAMBRIDGE
UNIVERSITY PRESS

PUBLISHED BY THE PRESS SYNDICATE OF THE UNIVERSITY OF CAMBRIDGE
The Pitt Building, Trumpington Street, Cambridge CB2 1RP, United Kingdom

CAMBRIDGE UNIVERSITY PRESS
The Edinburgh Building, Cambridge CB2 2RU, United Kingdom
40 West 20th Street, New York, NY 10011-4211, USA
10 Stamford Road, Oakleigh, Melbourne 3166, Australia

First published 1997

Printed in the United States of America

Typeset in Ehrhardt

A catalog record for this book is available from the British Library.

Library of Congress Cataloging-in-Publication Data
Kant, Immanuel, 1724–1804.
[Essays. English. Selections]
Lectures on ethics / Immanuel Kant; edited by Peter Heath and
J.B. Schneewind; translated by Peter Heath.
p.   cm. – (The Cambridge edition of the works of Immanuel Kant)
Includes bibliographical references and indexes.
ISBN 0-521-56061-6 (hc)
1. Ethics. I. Heath, Peter Lauchlan, 1922–   . II. Schneewind,
J. B. (Jerome B.), 1930–   . III. Title. IV. Series: Kant,
Immanuel, 1724–1804. Works. English. 1992.
B2794.E892E5   1996
170 – dc20   95-50944
CIP

ISBN 0-521-56061-6 hardback

Contents

General editors' preface

Within a few years of the publication of his *Critique of Pure Reason* in 1781, Immanuel Kant (1724–1804) was recognized by his contemporaries as one of the seminal philosophers of modern times – indeed as one of the great philosophers of all time. This renown soon spread beyond German-speaking lands, and translations of Kant's work into English were published even before 1800. Since then, interpretations of Kant's views have come and gone and loyalty to his positions has waxed and waned, but his importance has not diminished. Generations of scholars have devoted their efforts to producing reliable translations of Kant into English as well as into other languages.

There are four main reasons for the present edition of Kant's writings:

1. Completeness. Although most of the works published in Kant's lifetime have been translated before, the most important ones more than once, only fragments of Kant's many important unpublished works have ever been translated. These include the *Opus postumum*, Kant's unfinished *magnum opus* on the transition from philosophy to physics; transcriptions of his classroom lectures; his correspondence; and his marginalia and other notes. One aim of this edition is to make a comprehensive sampling of these materials available in English for the first time.

2. Availability. Many English translations of Kant's works, especially those that have not individually played a large role in the subsequent development of philosophy, have long been inaccessible or out of print. Many of them, however, are crucial for the understanding of Kant's philosophical development, and the absence of some from English-language bibliographies may be responsible for erroneous or blinkered traditional interpretations of his doctrines by English-speaking philosophers.

3. Organization. Another aim of the present edition is to make all Kant's published work, both major and minor, available in comprehensive volumes organized both chronologically and topically, so as to facilitate the serious study of his philosophy by English-speaking readers.

4. Consistency of translation. Although many of Kant's major works have been translated by the most distinguished scholars of their day, some of these translations are now dated, and there is considerable terminological disparity among them. Our aim has been to enlist some of the most accomplished Kant scholars and translators to produce new translations, freeing readers from both the philosophical and literary preconceptions of previous generations and allowing them to approach texts, as far as possible, with the same directness as present-day readers of the German or Latin originals.

In pursuit of these goals, our editors and translators attempt to follow several fundamental principles:

1. As far as seems advisable, the edition employs a single general glossary, especially for Kant's technical terms. Although we have not attempted to restrict the prerogative of editors and translators in choice of terminology, we have maximized consistency by putting a single editor or editorial team in charge of each of the main groupings of Kant's writings, such as his work in practical philosophy, philosophy of religion, or natural science, so that there will be a high degree of terminological consistency, at least in dealing with the same subject matter.

2. Our translators try to avoid sacrificing literalness to readability. We hope to produce translations that approximate the originals in the sense that they leave as much of the interpretive work as possible to the reader.

3. The paragraph, and even more the sentence, is often Kant's unit of argument, and one can easily transform what Kant intends as a continuous argument into a mere series of assertions by breaking up a sentence so as to make it more readable. Therefore, we try to preserve Kant's own divisions of sentences and paragraphs wherever possible.

4. Earlier editions often attempted to improve Kant's texts on the basis of controversial conceptions about their proper interpretation. In our translations, emendation or improvement of the original edition is kept to the minimum necessary to correct obvious typographical errors.

5. Our editors and translators try to minimize interpretation in other ways as well, for example, by rigorously segregating Kant's own footnotes, the editors' purely linguistic notes, and their more explanatory or informational notes; notes in this last category are treated as endnotes rather than footnotes.

We have not attempted to standardize completely the format of individual volumes. Each, however, includes information about the context in which Kant wrote the translated works, an English-German glossary, an index, and other aids to comprehension. The general introduction to each volume includes an explanation of specific principles of translation and, where necessary, principles of selection of works included in that volume. The pagination of the standard German edition of Kant's works, *Kant's Gesammelte Schriften*, edited by the Royal Prussian (later German) Academy of Sciences (Berlin: Georg Reimer, later Walter deGruyter & Co., 1900–   ), is indicated throughout by means of marginal numbers.

Our aim is to produce a comprehensive edition of Kant's writings, embodying and displaying the high standards attained by Kant scholarship in the English-speaking world during the second half of the twentieth century, and serving as both an instrument and a stimulus for the further development of Kant studies by English-speaking readers in the century to come. Because of our emphasis on literalness of translation and on information rather than interpretation in editorial practices, we hope our edition will continue to be usable despite the inevitable evolution and occasional revolutions in Kant scholarship.

PAUL GUYER
ALLEN W. WOOD

Acknowledgments

The editors wish to thank Paul Guyer and Allen Wood for helpful advice. Terence Moore of Cambridge University Press gave us useful guidance at the start of the project, and cheerfully accepted our proposal to include the whole of the Vigilantius notes. Werner Stark kindly provided information about the general state of the student lecture notes. The translator is greatly indebted to Eusebia Estes for her skilled typing of the manuscript of the translation. Kathleen Much of the Center for Advanced Study in the Behavioral Sciences provided expert editorial advice about the Introduction; and the Center itself was an ideal place in which to write it. We are both most grateful to Natalie Brender for her invaluable assistance in preparing the Explanation of Names and in readying the typescript for publication.

Introduction

by J. B. Schneewind

Kant began to teach at the Albertina University in Königsberg in 1755, when he was thirty-one years old. He taught there for more than four decades, carrying what seems today an astonishingly heavy load. Usually he gave four or five courses each semester, meeting classes four or five hours a week. He taught logic, metaphysics, physical geography, anthropology, and many other subjects. (He even taught the rudiments of making fortifications to the officers of the Russian army that occupied Königsberg in the late 1750s.) Among his more frequent offerings were courses on ethics: He taught the subject in one form or another nearly thirty times.[1] In 1924, on the occasion of the bicentennial of Kant's birth, the German scholar Paul Menzer published for the first time a full transcript of student notes from one of Kant's lecture courses on ethics.[2] New copies of lecture notes have come to light since then, and some previously known manuscripts have disappeared or become unavailable.[3] In this volume we present student notes covering Kant's ethics courses from near their beginning to the last time he taught the subject.

The importance of these notes differs from the importance of the student notes on subjects, such as logic or physical geography, on which Kant published little or nothing. Kant's published books presented his mature thought on morality quite fully. Some of the early writings yield information about the development of his views, and a number of essays shed further light on his theory and its applications. The student notes on moral philosophy are valuable as supplements to these much discussed texts. They richly repay study, each in a different way.

I

We begin with selections from the notes taken by Johann Gottlieb Herder (1744–1803). Herder, who later became one of the most influential critics of the Enlightenment, studied medicine and theology in Königsberg between 1762 and 1764 and attended several of Kant's courses.[4] His notes on the ethics course are fuller than any of his other surviving notes. They are of great interest because Kant wrote so little on moral philosophy during these early years. Herder was a profoundly original thinker, incom-

xiii

parably more gifted than anyone else whose notes on Kant's ethics lectures survive. Later Herder and Kant came to disagree seriously on several vital issues, but in 1762–4 Herder was an enthusiastic admirer of Kant as philosopher and as teacher. At the same time he was beginning to work out his own views. Partly because he may have allowed his own thoughts to interpret Kant's, Herder's notes are not altogether reliable. He worked them over at home, and he may have put words into Kant's mouth.5 Given the scarcity of other material on the development of Kant's moral thought, however, they remain an important resource for understanding how Kant came to his mature position.

None of Kant's early published essays center on moral philosophy, but from some of them we can learn a little about the development of his thought on the subject.6 The *New Elucidation of the First Principles of Metaphysical Cognition* (1755) shows him thinking about freedom along the lines worked out by Christian Wolff. In the *Inquiry Concerning the Distinctness of the Principles of Natural Theology and Morality* (1764, but written in 1763), Kant uses ideas drawn from Crusius, Wolff, and the British "moral sense" thinkers in explaining his position. His 1765 *Announcement of the Programme of His Lectures for the Winter Semester 1765–1766* mentions Shaftesbury, Hutcheson, and Hume in a paragraph on ethics that draws heavily on Rousseau. The *Dreams of a Spirit Seer Elucidated by Dreams of Metaphysics* (1766) contains a mocking sketch of an imagined but impossible relation between a spiritual and a natural world that turns out to foreshadow features of the moral relation between the noumenal and phenomenal worlds discussed in Kant's later work.7 More than any of these essays, the *Observations on the Feeling of the Beautiful and the Sublime* (1764) shows Kant exploring issues directly connected with moral philosophy.8

Our best insights into the main steps Kant took on the way to his mature theory come from the unpublished *Notes* he wrote, probably around the time of the lectures Herder attended, in his copy of his *Observations on the Feeling of the Beautiful and the Sublime*. The *Notes* show that he had been giving a great deal of thought to the deepest issues of moral philosophy.9 By the time he wrote them he had come to think that morality centers on laws that bind us regardless of our desires and ends, and that moral laws are different in principle from any directives that may guide us in our search for happiness.

In the Herder notes we see Kant presenting only some of the ideas sketched in the *Notes*. Morality as feeling, worries derived from Rousseau about the corruption of the natural man in society, putting oneself in the place of another as a test of morality, and the priority of natural ethics to any religious morality are all touched on. Kant does not expound the distinction between moral and prudential imperatives in the terms he later used. But he talks to the class about a matter that remained central to all his moral thought, the issue of the relation between morality and God's will. He has yet to come to terms with the question of the role of the will in constituting morality, but he is already certain that the doctrine, usually called "voluntarism," that what is right is so only because God wills it is untenable because of the servility it requires. It is typical of the later Kant to reject such a doctrine on essentially moral grounds.

If Herder was recording Kant accurately, then it seems that the course was not very carefully organized. But the notes convey something of the pleasure it must have been to hear Kant talking, rather informally, not only about theory but also about substantive moral issues: friendship, the importance of truthfulness, toleration. We also glimpse a number of Kant's other opinions, including his biases against women, Jews, and Catholics.

II

We next give a complete translation of lecture notes from a notebook owned by a student named Georg Ludwig Collins, who attended the university in 1784. We supplement Collins in two or three places (indicated in the text) with material from a notebook owned by another student, named Mrongovius, who started his studies at the Albertina in 1782 and whose notebook indicates that he attended the course earlier than Collins did. The Collins notes are almost indistinguishable both in order and in content from the notes Paul Menzer published. Menzer, however, based his published text not on Collins but on a notebook (which seems now to have disappeared) owned by a student named Brauer. He supplemented it with material from Mrongovius's notebook and from a third notebook, owned by one Kutzner. The striking similarity among the many surviving sets of notes calls for explanation, but scholars are not wholly agreed on what the explanation is.[10]

It is not at all likely that the notebooks carrying the names of Brauer, Collins, and Mrongovius, or any of the other sets of almost identical notes, were actual transcriptions made during class. The notes are too full, too grammatical, and above all too similar to one another to be records of classes unless Kant had read the same lectures year after year for transcription. And there is good reason to believe that Kant did not encourage note taking. "Those of my students who are most capable of grasping everything," Kant wrote in a letter dated October 20, 1778, "are just the ones who bother least to take explicit and verbatim notes. . . . Those who are most thorough in note taking are seldom capable of distinguishing the important from the unimportant."[11] Kant probably did not alter his material radically from year to year during the period covered by these very similar notes. But aside from the notebooks we have relatively little evidence for what he said in class. His marginal annotations in the copies of the textbooks he always used tell us something;[12] but the evidence suggests that Kant did not teach from full lecture notes that might be used to check on the accuracy of what the student notebooks contain, and if he ever prepared such notes they have not been located.

Whether Kant liked it or not there was, plainly, a good deal of note taking in his classes, and class notes, perhaps made by a hired professional note taker, must be behind the material that has come down to us. The various notebooks are probably copies of an original put together outside the classroom – perhaps by several students, perhaps over several years. It was not uncommon for a text like this to be made, copied, and sold or passed on. Sometimes the notebooks passed from student to student; sometimes they were sold by people with only a commercial interest in them. Menzer says that "we do not know how the original text of such notebooks came into being or what alterations it underwent."[13] And the differences among the various versions make the question of alterations quite puzzling. The variations are not simply those that would naturally arise from careless copying. Whole phrases and sentences vary, sometimes in philosophically important ways, and the length of treatment of some topics varies from notebook to notebook. It is, of course, possible that in making a new copy from an older one, a student might have inserted material from the actual lecture he was attending, or deleted things he found unclear or uninteresting. But we do not know enough about the matter to be sure.

Scholars are divided on the question of how well the notebooks represent Kant's actual teaching.[14] Given the way the notebooks were created, they probably do not allow us to know what Kant said in class year by year. Menzer was of the opinion that the text he published conveys faithfully what Kant taught in his ethics courses from about 1775 to 1780 or so.[15] The notes we give after the Collins notes show that in 1784–5 Kant gave his class at least some quite different material. But if Menzer is right about the reliability of his text, then we can probably take it that Collins represents the basics of Kant's teaching for the nine years from 1775 until 1784.

The Collins notes show Kant coming remarkably close to his mature views without actually presenting the most characteristic of them. He clearly rejects voluntarism, various forms of egoism in ethics, and the basic formula of Wolffian perfectionism. He speaks of moral law and argues that religion alone cannot give it to us, because knowledge of the moral law on purely rational grounds is presupposed by any knowledge of God as a moral being. All this remains central in his later theory. Yet in Collins he never formulates the categorical imperative, and although he stresses the importance of believing that rational awareness of moral rightness can move us to act, he also seems at times unsure that such motivation can be sufficient.

Those who think of Kant's ethics as mainly a matter of various formulations and applications of a single basic moral law will be surprised by the rich discussions in Collins of the ways in which morality requires us to improve our own character as well as our relations to others. Kant begins with careful discussion of the grounds and nature of proper religious worship. He next treats duties to oneself: abstinence from suicide and from self-abasing attitudes, control of our passions, attention to the body's needs to keep it fit for its tasks, caution about sexual indulgence, and the importance of having enough wealth to be independent are just a few of the matters that receive thoughtful treatment. One is reminded that Kant's audience consisted largely of unsophisticated boys, younger than present-day college students, usually away from their rural homes for the first time, and for the most part ill-educated. When Kant turns to duties to others, he also covers a broader range of topics than we might expect. Not only justice and the rights of man but also friendship, the avoidance of revenge, envy, and slander, and the importance of truthfulness receive full and sometimes eloquent treatment. Kant ends with a stirring exhortation to his students to strive toward the final vocation of the human race, perfection insofar as that is the work of individual freedom.

III

Anyone who has studied or taught Kant's *Groundwork of the Metaphysic of Morals* must have wondered how even Kant could make such difficult thoughts clear to beginners (which his students usually were).[16] The third set of lecture notes suggests an answer – a not very encouraging one. The *Groundwork*, the result of over twenty years of brooding on the subject, was published in April 1785. Kant had sent the manuscript off for publication in the early fall of 1784, but the printer's delays held the book back. The first public presentation of Kant's mature moral philosophy was, therefore, the one he gave in the winter semester of 1784–5. Mrongovius, a faithful follower who had attended an earlier set of lectures on ethics, attended this set as well. In Mrongovius II we have his notes on part of it – the part that was new. His notebook breaks off as it seems Kant is about to revert to material he presented in earlier years. It is possible that these notes were taken in the class itself. We present excerpts showing how Kant explained his main theses to students for the first time.[17]

We have, of course, no record of how much Mrongovius and the other students understood of what Kant said. It seems fairly clear, however, that Kant taught his ethics no better than we do. He explains the categorical imperative only briefly, and in showing its use he gives examples as misleading or difficult as the famous ones in his book. He mourns the fragility of innocence and sounds other themes with which every student of Kant's ethics is familiar. He goes beyond the *Groundwork*, however, in remarks about the way in which morality needs God; and in one or two other matters he shows that he has already come to the main theories that are to appear only in the second *Critique* and in the *Metaphysics of Morals.*

IV

So far no ethics lecture notes have been found for courses between that recorded in Mrongovius II and the last material we include, the notes on a course given in 1793–4 on "The Metaphysics of Morals." The notes were taken by a lawyer who served Kant in a professional capacity and who was also a good friend and a frequent guest in Kant's house, Johann Friedrich Vigilantius (1757–1823). His notes coincide with the latter parts of Collins to some extent but much less with the early part. The German text is printed from a reedited version worked over by the Kant scholar Emil Arnoldt. Although Vigilantius wrote the notes himself, the section numbers (which we include) are the German editor's, not his.[18]

In Vigilantius we see how Kant expounded his mature system, including not only the main lines of thought of the *Groundwork* and the *Critique of Practical Reason* (1788) but also some anticipations of the last work he published on ethics and politics, the *Metaphysics of Morals* of 1797. Despite the name Kant gave to the course, it is not as closely related to the book as we might expect. There is much more about the foundations of morality in §§1–63 than there is anywhere in the *Metaphysics of Morals.* Like the first division of the book, entitled "Doctrine of Right," although much more briefly, §§66–70 of the lectures deal with matters of external legality. Kant, we should remember, frequently taught a separate course on the doctrine of right; here he is concisely indicating how to understand our duties to others insofar as they are enforceable. In §§72–112 the lectures consider duties to oneself; and in §§113–37, the unenforceable duties to others involved in virtue. These topics receive more attention here than in the *Metaphysics of Morals.* The lectures conclude, in §§138–48, with an examination of our duties to God. But the book ends with a section strikingly entitled "Religion as the Doctrine of Duties to God Lies beyond the Bounds of Pure Moral Philosophy."

Kant's *Metaphysics of Morals* is not easy to understand. Because the Vigilantius lecture notes are expansive on many of the same topics, they provide us, despite their divergences from the book, with a substantial amount of much needed help.

V

Kant was a popular teacher. From the first, he attracted a large number of students. Often between fifty and seventy hearers, and sometimes as many as a hundred, attended his lectures. As the whole student body at the

Albertina numbered only about five hundred during most of Kant's career, these numbers attest to striking success as a teacher.[19] Not all his auditors were students. Sometimes the younger students were accompanied by their tutors; civil servants, military officers, intellectuals like Herder, lawyers, doctors, and merchants from the town often came as well. In 1770, when Kant obtained a professorship, a poem in his honor was read in the name of the students, praising him for combining wisdom with virtue and for practicing what he taught. Until the 1790s, his lectures were reported to be witty, somewhat rambling, full of life and feeling, with scattered references to current events and to books. In his early and middle years at least, if not toward the end of his life, Kant answered questions and held discussions during the lecture hour.[20] And as we have noted, he did not want his students to spend their class time taking notes. He wanted to teach them "not philosophy, but to philosophize; not thoughts to repeat, but thinking . . . thinking for themselves, investigating for themselves, standing on their own feet."[21]

However much Kant might stray from the topic of the moment, the students could always know where he was supposed to be (and what he was returning to when he called himself back). The Prussian government insisted that professors should use textbooks, and Kant always did. (He was excused from the requirement for his course on physical geography because in his lectures he was inventing the subject and there were no textbooks.) His textbooks in ethics were, it seems, always or almost always the same: two works by Alexander Gottlieb Baumgarten (1714–62).[22]

Baumgarten achieved a degree of lasting fame with a textbook on the philosophy of art, to which he gave the title *Aesthetica*. As a result the term "aesthetics," which until then had referred to the study of feelings generally, has become the common term for Baumgarten's subject, on which his own views are of interest. In metaphysics, on which he also wrote a text that Kant used, as well as in ethics, he was less original. In these subjects he closely followed Leibniz and Christian Wolff. It helps in reading Kant's lectures on ethics to know a little about Baumgarten's moral philosophy and about the textbooks in which he expounded it.

The philosophy itself is a form of perfectionism, the view that the first task of rational agents is to improve themselves. Baumgarten's version of perfectionism rests on the rationalist belief that all the contents of the mind are representations or cognitions, some of them clear and distinct, others confused and indistinct. In this view, the perceptions of the five senses, as well as feelings, desires, passions and even pleasures and pains, are in the same basic category as abstract thoughts. Our thoughts are *clear* when we see the parts that are contained in them. They are *distinct* when we are aware of how a whole compound thought, as well as its simpler elements, differs from other thoughts. Clarity and distinctness are matters of degree. Emotion, sensory perceptions, and bodily feelings are vastly less clear than, say, our idea of a triangle. God's thoughts are completely clear and distinct. Unlike him, we always have room for improvement.

Since the mind does and can do nothing but think, or represent the way things are, mental improvement can be nothing but improvement in thinking. We increase the perfection of our minds each time we change from having obscure thoughts whose connections with one another we do not notice to having carefully distinguished thoughts whose implications stand out markedly. Obviously our bodies affect our minds, and therefore we must improve our bodily condition in order to think better. And since all our behavior is determined by our thoughts, we must improve our minds if we wish to improve our conduct. These duties to ourselves are prior to our duties to other human beings, since we cannot behave properly toward others unless we know what to do, and we cannot have this knowledge without first increasing our own perfection. It is no use, according to this view, protesting that feelings are enough to guide us, because feelings are themselves simply indistinct representations. They will be better guides if they are perfected by being made more distinct.

By virtue of their inner constitution, all our thoughts ultimately relate to God. When we begin life we are unclear about this connection. We learn only gradually about our total dependence on God, and then we begin to see that to have a proper grasp of any of our thoughts we must first see how through that thought we are related to God. To think about God with proper attention is to begin to worship him, and therefore duties to God are prior to duties to ourselves. Without attending to God, we cannot improve even our own thoughts, let alone our behavior toward other people.

The more we know of God, the more we will see of his infinite perfection. Our own perfection will increase as we improve the clarity and distinctness of our ideas. As we achieve better knowledge of others, we will improve our grasp of the perfections with which God has endowed them. Now the feeling of pleasure is nothing but a confused awareness of an increase in perfection. The more our own perfection increases, therefore, the more we enjoy life. As we come to be more perfect, we also come to be more directly concerned for the perfection of others, and therefore to take more and more pleasure in their happiness. The perfections of the universe are thus all harmonious. And since the awareness of perfection always generates love, clarification of our ideas of God, self, and others will lead us increasingly to love as we ought: God above all, and our neighbor as ourself.

The central concept Baumgarten used to spell out this essentially Christian moral teaching was that of being obligated or obliged. Following Wolff, he thought that the concept has the same meaning in all practical discussions. When we think that we are obligated to do something, we are thinking that we have to do it. But the "have to" here is special. If we have to do something because we are compelled by someone – for instance, a robber with a gun – we do not act freely. There are some cases, however, where we act freely in doing what we have to do. These are cases where our own ideas show us clearly that one course of action will bring about so much more perfection – and, therefore, so much more happiness – that we cannot bring ourselves to do anything else. It is, as Baumgarten would say, morally necessary to do what (we think) is best. But we are free in acting for the best, because we are doing what we clearly see to be the most nearly perfect action; and as we always love most what is most nearly perfect, we are doing what we most want to do. What is freedom if not that?

The earlier of Baumgarten's textbooks, the *Initia philosophiae practicae primae* (Introduction to Practical First Philosophy), was first published in 1740. Kant used the third edition, published in 1760.[23] The *Initia* is abstract and general, explaining the fundamental ideas not only of ethics as we understand the subject but of political theory, jurisprudence, and economics as well. In all these areas of practice, there are better and worse courses of action. Hence everyone engaged in them needs to understand obligation, rules or laws, punishment and reward as consequences of disobedience and obedience, degrees of responsibility, and the means, such as conscience, by which we learn what we ought to do. In his analyses of these concepts and their various implications, Baumgarten took himself to be laying the foundations of general practical philosophy.

Kant used two editions of Baumgarten's second text, *Ethica philosophica* (Philosophical Ethics), that of 1751 and that of 1763.[24] Unlike the *Initia*, it is devoted to detailed presentation of particular precepts pertaining to the guidance of individual life. The discussions are general, their author claiming, somewhat implausibly, that they do not rest on any unique features of any particular society. Baumgarten produces, among many others, precepts about how to worship, increase our control over our lower appetites, and cope with boredom. He considers the proprieties of helping others to worship properly as well as to enjoy life, and instructs us in appropriate concern for our material well-being and for our reputations. He also provides brief reflections on proper treatment of nonhuman beings, due respect for those, like the learned, who enjoy special social standing, and the requirements and benefits of friendship.

In his German compendium of morality, Wolff says that "the rule 'Do what makes you and your condition more perfect, and omit what makes you and your condition less perfect' is a law of nature. Because this rule covers all free human actions, there is no need for any other law of nature, but all special laws must be derived from it."[25] Baumgarten does his best to spell out the special laws that follow from Wolff's fundamental principle.

VI

In the section following this, we provide translations of the tables of contents of Baumgarten's two texts. A comparison of the two with the table of contents of Collins will indicate the extent to which Kant followed the order of Baumgarten's presentation. Kant used the same textbooks in the other courses represented in this volume, and those notes also reflect, if not always as obviously, a similar dependence on them. Even in Vigilantius, where Kant finally breaks with Baumgarten's placement of duties to God as the first topic of ethics, he treats somewhere or other almost every issue Baumgarten raises.[26]

Kant disagreed with Baumgarten on many fundamental philosophical matters, as well as on various points of morality. One might well wonder, therefore, why Kant used his books for so many years. A full answer would require a detailed discussion of the philosophical relations between Kant's thought and Baumgarten's, which cannot be given here.[27] We should, of course, keep in mind that Kant's initial orientation in philosophy was perfectionist, and that he never wholly abandoned certain aspects of the Wolffian view. He never doubted that we have duties to ourselves, he took them to constitute a major portion of the subject matter of ethics, and he developed his own version of the requirement that we should perfect ourselves. In addition to sympathies with parts of Baumgarten's view – and an unwillingness to write his own text – there are two further considerations that would have led Kant to think Baumgarten's books useful.

First, the *Initia* enabled Kant to discuss the issues he himself took to be central to moral theory, such as the nature of obligation and its relation to self-interest, the moral law, and moral motivation. The *Ethica* gave him reason to discuss another theoretical matter close to his heart, the relations between religion and morality. Although Kant sometimes summarized his "Author," he far more often criticized him or simply presented his own views instead. Kant never finished thinking out a subject. His texts, therefore, presented him with regular occasions to work out what he was rejecting and what he was still prepared to accept from the basic general outlook with which he himself had begun.

Second, in the *Ethica* Baumgarten brought up a large number of topics that contemporary teachers of practical philosophy usually discussed.[28] There was nothing original about Baumgarten's thoughts on how to live. They were the commonplaces of the time. Kant's theoretically based, and personally felt, respect for the moral beliefs of ordinary people made him reluctant simply to dismiss such opinions. What he usually did in the lectures was not to reject the precepts propounded by his author but, rather, to put them on a footing entirely different from the one Baumgarten provided. He gave a Kantian rather than a Wolffian account of the main topics of commonsense morality as systematically presented. He rejected the Wolffian view that our duties to ourselves and to others all rest ultimately on the moral necessity of pursuing increased perfection in everything we do. The new way in which he accounted for these duties required some amendment of the precepts themselves, but Baumgarten's range was wide enough to enable Kant to show the bearing of his own outlook on every aspect of our practical attitudes to ourselves and others.

Kant's procedure recalls the way Hobbes describes his relation to Aristotelian moralists, at the end of Chapter 15 of *Leviathan*. Hobbes remarks that those who wrote on moral philosophy before him agreed with him about what the virtues are. But they did not understand "wherein consisted their Goodnesse"; so they praised them as showing "mediocrity of passions" rather than as means to peaceable living, which is what Hobbes himself has shown them to be. In similar fashion, Kant is arguing, against Baumgarten, that the common virtues and vices are so not because of their relation to perfection and consequent happiness achieved or missed, but because of their relation to our unique status as free rational agents.

VII

Here, finally, are the tables of contents of Kant's two standard textbooks.

A. G. Baumgarten, *Introduction to Practical First Philosophy*
Prolegomena to Universal Practical Philosophy:

Ch. I. Obligation
    I. Obligation in general
    II. Moral Constraint
Ch. II. What Obligates
    I. Law
    II. Skill in Law
    III. Principles of Law
    IV. Legislator
    V. On Rewards
    VI. Punishments
    VII. Imputation of Action
    VIII. The Author
    IX. Degrees of Imputability
    X. Imputation under Law
    XI. Forum
    XII. External Forum
    XIII. Conscience

A. G. Baumgarten, *Philosophical Ethics:*[29]

Prolegomena
I. General
  A. Religion
     1. Internal Religion
     2. True Knowledge of God
     3. Clear Knowledge of God
     4. Certain Knowledge of God
     5. Knowledge of the Life of God
     6. Inner Worship of God
     7. Inner Prayer
     8. Pious Habits
     9. External Worship of God
     10. Confession of God
     11. Studying to Promote Religion
     12. Pious Example
     13. Pious Ceremonies, etc.
  B. Duties toward Oneself
     1. Knowledge of Oneself
     2. Judgment of Oneself
     3. Duties toward Conscience
     4. Love of Oneself
     5. Duties toward the Soul[30]
     6. Intellect
     7. Enjoyment and Boredom
     8. The Appetitive Faculty
     9. The Lower Appetitive Faculty
     10. The Will
     11. The Body
     12. Occupation and Leisure
     13. Chastity
     14. Necessities and Conveniences of Life
     15. Work
     16. One's Faculties
     17. External Delights
     18. Reputation
  C. Duties toward Others
     1. Universal Love
     2. Love of Mankind
     3. Pursuit of Peace
     4. Vices Opposed to Philanthropy
     5. Candor
     6. Judgment of Others

NOTES

1. There is some uncertainty because occasionally lectures were announced but not actually given. The fundamental study is Emil Arnoldt, "Möglichst vollständiges Verzeichnis aller von Kant gehaltenen oder auch nur angekündigten Kollegia," in his *Gesammelte Schriften* (Complete Works), ed. Otto Schöndörffer, Vol. V, Berlin, 1909, pp. 173–344. I refer to this hereafter as Arnoldt.

2. Paul Menzer, ed., *Eine Vorlesung Kants über Ethik*, Berlin, 1924, referred to hereafter as Menzer. This has been translated by Louis Infield as *Immanuel Kant: Lectures on Ethics*, London, 1930, reprinted various times. The studies of the development of Kant's moral philosophy by Kuenberg, Schilpp, Schmucker, and Ward all use the Menzer lecture notes.

3. For information see the "Einleitung" by Gerhard Lehmann, the editor, to Vol. XXVII of Kant's *Gesammelte Schriften*, Berlin, 1970, p. 1041 ff., and his remarks in Vol. XXVIII, Berlin, 1972, pp. 1348 ff.

4. For a brief sketch of Herder's views, see Lewis White Beck, *Early German Philosophy*, Cambridge, Mass.: Harvard University Press, 1969, pp. 382–92. Frederick C. Beiser, *The Fate of Reason*, Cambridge, Mass.: Harvard University Press, 1987, contains a helpful fuller discussion; see especially Ch. 5.

5. See Lehmann in Vol. XXVIII, pp. 1353–4.

6. Schmucker (1962) supersedes all earlier work on this subject although it needs supplementation by later studies of Kant's development, such as Werner Busch, *Die Entstehung der kritischen Rechtsphilosophie Kants 1762–1780*, Berlin: Walter de Gruyter, 1979; Richard Velkley, *Freedom and the End of*

Reason, Chicago: University of Chicago Press, 1989; Marie Rischmüller, ed., *Kant's Bermerkungen in den "Beobachtungen über das Gefühl des Schönen und Erhabenen,"* Hamburg: Felix Meiner Verlag, 1991; and Alison Laywine, *Kant's Early Metaphysics and the Origins of the Critical Philosophy,* Atascadero: Ridgeview, 1993.

7. For these works, see Immanuel Kant, *Theoretical Philosophy, 1755–1770,* translated and edited by David Walford and Ralf Meerbote, Cambridge: Cambridge University Press, 1992.

8. GS II. 207–256; translated by John T. Goldthwait, Berkeley: University of California Press, 1960.

9. First published in full in *Bemerkungen zu den Beobachtungen über das Gefühl des Schönen and Erhabenen,* in *Kant's Gesammelte Schriften,* Vol. XX, Berlin: Walter de Gruyter, 1942. This edition is superseded by Marie Rischmüller's excellent annotated edition of the notes, mentioned in note 6.

10. For discussions of these issues, see Erich Adickes, *Untersuchungen zu Kants physischer Geographie,* Tübingen, 1911; the essays in Reinhard Brandt and Werner Stark, eds., *Kant-Forschungen,* Vol. I, Hamburg: Felix Meiner Verlag, 1987; and the essays by Werner Stark listed in the Bibliography.

11. Kant, *Philosophical Correspondence, 1759–99,* edited and translated by Arnulf Zweig, Chicago: University of Chicago Press, 1967, p. 91.

12. See in particular GS XIX, which contains the marginal notes Kant wrote in one of the ethics textbooks by A. G. Baumgarten that he regularly used for his classes.

13. Menzer 1924, p. 323. See also Stark, "Kant als akademischer Lehrer," p. 52.

14. For some warnings, see Werner Stark, in Brandt and Stark, pp. 136–7.

15. For this and the material from Menzer in the previous paragraph, see Menzer, pp. 323–7.

16. The Philosophical Faculty of which Kant was a member had as its main task the preparation of students for work in the faculties of theology, medicine, or law. It was during study with these faculties that students were trained for careers; the Philosophy Faculty was a transitional, often remedial stage of their education.

17. See the remarks by Gerhard Lehmann in Vol. XXIX, pp. 651–2.

18. We add section numbers 6 (27.488), 7 (27.491), and 92 (27.627) where the text omits them and we conjecture that they belong.

19. Students at German universities then and for a long time thereafter paid their teacher directly. There are manuscript notes of letters from Kant requesting payment from parents whose sons (no daughters attended) were in arrears; there are also records indicating his remission of fees for needy students and some others.

20. Beginning perhaps in the late 1780s, Kant felt himself less able to teach well, and was in fact less successful in attracting students.

21. Karl Vorländer, *Immanuel Kant: der Mann und das Werk* (1924), Hamburg: Felix Meiner Verlag, 1977, I., p. 83, from a report by a former student, but the same idea in almost the same words is in Kant's announcement of his lectures for the winter semester 1765–6, GS II 306, Walford and Meerbote,

p. 292. I have drawn on Vorländer and Arnoldt for the material in this paragraph. Vorländer discusses Kant as teacher in several places; see esp. Vol. II, pp. 54–65. See John Ladd, "Kant as Teacher," in *Teaching Philosophy* 5.1, January 1982, pp. 1–9, and Werner Stark, "Kant als akademischer Lehrer," for further discussion and references.

22. It is not certain when Kant started using the two Baumgarten texts. Stark conjectures that it may have been as early as 1760, the date of publication of Baumgarten's *Initia Philosophiae practicae*. The first announcement of lectures on ethics is for 1756–7; for 1765–6, Kant announced that he would use the Baumgarten texts. See Werner Stark, *Nachforschungen zu Briefen und Handschriften Immanuel Kants*, Berlin: Akademie Verlag, 1993, pp. 326–7.

23. The text of the *Initia* is published in Kant's *Gesammelte Schriften*, Vol. XIX, Berlin, 1934, to show the text to which Kant's handwritten annotations relate.

24. Both editions of the *Ethica philosophica* are printed in GS XXVII, Berlin, 1975.

25. Christian Wolff, *Vernünftige Gedancken von der Menschen Tun und Lassen zu Beförderung ihrer Glückseeligkeit* (Reasonable Thoughts about the Actions of Men, for the Promotion of Their Happiness) (1720) 1733, reprinted Hildesheim: Georg Olms, 1976, Part I, Ch. 1, §19.

26. Bernd Ludwig, in *Kant's Rechtslehre*, Hamburg: Meiner, 1988, pp. 54–6, gives a careful comparison of Vigilantius with Baumgarten.

27. The fullest recent discussion is in Josef Schmucker, *Die Ursprünge der Ethik Kants*, Meisenheim: Verlag Anton Hain KG, 1961, Ch. 5.

28. And the order in which he treated them – duties to God, duties to self, duties to others – was also commonplace.

29. Baumgarten prefixed an elaborate outline of his treatment of issues to the 1751 edition of his book, giving outline numbers and titles to single paragraphs or small groups of paragraphs. There was no table of contents in the 1763 edition. What follows is a list of the main section headings used within the texts (the same in both editions).

30. Baumgarten entitles this section "Officia erga analogon rationis," or "Duties toward the Analog of Rationality." He himself glosses the Latin as meaning "duties toward the soul." In his *Metaphysics*, §468, Baumgarten explains that we have many mental powers, such as wit, sensory memory, and taste, which represent the connections of things, though unclearly and indistinctly. They are, therefore, the part of the mind that is the analog of reason. We might consider what we call common sense to be an analog of reason.

PART I
Kant's practical philosophy

NOTES TAKEN BY J. G. HERDER

... Do I have, not merely a self-interested feeling, but also a disinterested feeling of concern for others? Yes – the weal and woe of another touches us directly: the mere happiness of another pleases us in the telling: even that of fictional persons whose tale we know of, or in distant ages – this common concern is so great that it collides with the self-interested feeling. The sense of it is indeed a noble feeling, nobler than the self-interested one. Nobody despises it: everyone wishes for it, though not all have it in the same degree; in some it is great, and the greater it is, the more it is felt as a perfection. It is universal, though seldom so great that it inspires active exertions – in misers, for example, with whom self-interest has become very strong. As needy beings the creator gave us self-interest in our own perfection. As beings who have the power to be of service to our fellows, He gave us a disinterested concern for the perfection of others. The concern for others ranks high, since even the concern for self can be subordinated to it, but not *vice versa.* The more self-interested, the poorer (at least in thought), and hence the more to be despised. The disinterested feeling for the welfare, etc., of another has our own perfection, not as an end, but as a means.

Hobbes followed the plan of Lucretius and Epicurus, whose principles were of less nobility, by far, than those of the Stoics. And likewise the majority of Germans relate everything to self-interest, since it is fine to derive everything from a single *principium,* however little they may do this in metaphysics, etc. It was argued (1) that here we put ourselves in the other's shoes, and the deception of fancy creates this pleasure, which arises, not directly, but indirectly, from the other's pleasure. This false ordering of the matter comes about because, in the disinterested feeling, we always envisage the other's joy, and such joy as we may have in his person. But if we had no disinterested feelings, this would not occur, because we do not *convince* ourselves that *we* are in his person – imagine yourself, too, in the shoes of a *wealthy* idler; you will not take any pleasure in him. This putting of oneself in the other's shoes is thus necessary, indeed, but is merely a means to vivacity, which presupposes the disinterested feeling. I have no pity for Damien's misfortune, though I do for that of Julius Caesar, since Brutus, his friend, murdered him. (2) It is said that the pleasure we have in [the welfare of others] is merely our own end, and a more refined self-interest. *Responsio:* the pleasure itself presupposes (1) a power of having it; (2) I cannot explain pleasure by means of pleasure. I *will* pleasure means, merely: I have pleasure in pleasure, and thus already presupposes a certain feeling. So there are merely lower grades of it. This feeling also constitutes a great beauty of our nature. A self-interested feeling presupposes our own imperfections, which can be acquired (so are not God-given), and imply neediness. A disinterested feeling presupposes our own perfections: the grounds for it may lie in the acquisition of other perfections, and it presupposes perfection. The disinterested feeling is like a force of attraction, and the self-interested feeling like a force of repulsion. The two of them, *in conflictu,*[a] constitute the world.

Free actions are good (1) in virtue of the consequences, and (to that extent) physically good; (2) in virtue of the intention, and (to that extent) morally good. The measuring-rod is very different in the two. Small will and great capacity is less morally good even in great benefactions. Great will and small capacity is morally better, even in benefactions that are small. We also esteem moral acts, not by their physical effects, but for their own sake, even when they are self-interested, and not always when disinterested (as Hutcheson mistakenly believes). Morally good actions must be directed to a physical good, but not measured by this. Physically good actions are always indifferent; they may be free effects, or necessary ones, for the good lies in the effect, and is measured by the consequences; the good is no greater than the effect. But morally free actions have a goodness which is assessed, not by the effect, but by the (free) intent; otherwise, the morally good would be less than the physically good. But this contradicts feeling and emotion. Free actions may be immediately good (give pleasure), not as means to consequences, so that their value is not to be measured by the results, and they are not equivalent to the physical causes that produce the same effect.

Pleasure in free actions directly is called moral feeling. We have a moral feeling, which is (1) universal (2) unequivocal. At neglect of another I feel displeasure, hatred; not because he has to starve, but because of the neglect, for at privation through sickness I feel pity. A great disproportion, which enhances self-interested feeling till the other feeling is outweighed, does not abolish the latter; for when we hear morally good things of another, we are touched with pleasure. A direct pleasure at the other's misfortune is devilish, and not to be thought of among us (though there can certainly be an indirect pleasure, and displeasure, and likewise direct displeasure). The moral feeling is unanalysable, basic, the ground of conscience. . . .

27:5

The feeling inspired by morality (without profit) is beautiful or sublime; my joy at the perfected in myself (feeling of self-esteem, of one's own worth) is noble; my joy at satisfaction (feeling of goodwill) is beautiful. Here the division of all actions according to these classes is completely reconstituted.

Sources of morality:

27:6

Morality as such. Moral beauty (not obligation, right and wrong) – In morality perfection is never the transcendental; not what belongs merely to the essence, for the essence might be better still.

Solely from the fact that it is in accordance with *our* nature, it is not perfection merely, for I can have a better nature, e.g. angel; thus death is

---

[a] in conflict

good. Hence the supreme law of morality is: act according to your moral nature. My reason can err; my moral feeling, only when I uphold custom before natural feeling; but in that case it is merely implicit reason; and my final yardstick still remains moral feeling, not true and false; just as the capacity for true and false is the final yardstick of the understanding, and both are universal.

In order not to err in logical matters, I must seek out the 1st *propositio* of the true.

In order not to err in moral matters, I must seek out the 1st *propositio* of the good.

The natural feeling is here opposed to the artificial; the feeling of modesty, for example, is almost artificial; Spartan children went naked up to 14 years old; Indian women never cover up the breasts, in Jamaica they go stark naked – and yet the feeling is very strong; Caesar, Livia, when dying would not uncover themselves.

Spartan women thrown naked on the street, worse than capital punishment.

Yet artificial, as with showing the fingers among the Chinese.

Thus marriage with a sister is artificially abhorred; but sacred with the Egyptians. To distinguish the artificial from the natural, we must therefore push back to the origin, as we do to distinguish prejudices (maxims) from certainty. One would have to investigate the feeling of the *natural* man, and this is far better than our artificial feeling; Rousseau has looked into it. . . .

71. Can we, even without presupposing God's existence and His *arbitrium,* derive all obligations from within? *Responsio:* not merely in the affirmative, for this, rather, is *ex natura rei,*[b] and we conclude from this to God's choice.

27:9

1. From the *arbitrium divinum*[c] I cannot myself obtain the relevant concepts of the good, unless the concept of the morally good be assumed beforehand; apart from that, the sheer *arbitrium* of God is good merely in a physical sense. In short, the judgement as to the perfection of God's *arbitrium* presupposes the investigation of moral perfection.

2. Supposing the *arbitrium* of God to be known to me, where is the necessity that I should do it, if I have not already derived the obligation from the nature of the case? God wills it – why should I? He will punish me; in that case it is injurious, but not in itself wicked; that is how we obey a despot; in that case the act is no sin, in the strict sense, but politically imprudent; and why does God will it? Why does He punish it? Because I am obligated to do it, not because He has the power to punish. The very application of the *arbitrium divinum* to the *factum*, as a ground, presup-

[b] from the nature of the case
[c] divine choice

poses the concept of obligation; and since this constitutes natural religion, the latter is a part, but not the basic principle, of morality. It is probable that, since God by His *arbitrium,* is the ground of all things, this is also the case here; He is indeed the ground of it, but not *per arbitrium,* for since He is the ground of possibility, He is also the material ground (since in Him all things are given) of geometrical truths and morality. In Him there is already morality, therefore, and so His choice is not the ground.

27:10

The quarrel between reformers and Lutherans over *arbitrium divinum* and *decretus absolutus*[d] is based on the fact that even in God, morality must exist; and every conception of the divine *arbitrium* itself vanishes, if morality is not presupposed; this cannot, however, be demonstrated from the world (where it is merely possible), since the good things of the world may merely be physical consequences. How dreadful, though, is a God without morality. The *jus naturae*[e] *divinum,* and even *positivum,* vanishes, if there be no morality as ground of the relation and conformity of my *arbitrium* and that of God. Without the prior assumption of obligation, punishments come to nothing; what God displays is merely ill-will; the physical consequences I can avoid, and thus the action is no longer a transgression. Morality is more general than the *arbitrium divinum.*

3. For one who has not wholly fulfilled his obligation, morality is incomplete, if all grounds of obligation are not included, and in that case, the *arbitrium divinum* is a ground of external obligation for our morality. So the *arbitrium divinum* should never be left out, as an external obligating ground; thus our moral perfection becomes incomplete, if it arises solely from inner morality, and is considered without reference to God's *arbitrium.* In the absence of the latter, my action is already still moral, indeed, but not so completely good, morally, as when it conforms to all grounds. Those who attend solely to the *arbitrium Dei* are considering merely their liability to the *jus naturae divinum;* but we should attend also to the inner morality, and consider obligation as well. *Ethica rationalis:*[f] the one without the other is not universal morality, and indeed far less than this; we are virtuous already from the nature of the case, pious only in having regard to the *arbitrium divinum.* To disregard the one is wicked; to disregard the other, godless; the former are moral errors, the latter, sins; the former concern the moral teacher, the latter, the preacher; the one wishes to have people morally good, the other wants their moral goodness to be complete. In education, we have first to awaken the moral feeling, and then must apply it to God's *arbitrium;* without that, religion is a prejudice, and hypocrisy. He who has a notion of the external obligation, without the inner, sees the motivating grounds as tasks, which do not

[d] absolute decree
[e] divine/positive law of nature
[f] rational ethic

6

make him moral at all, but merely politically crafty. If an immediate divine inspiration and influence are added to this, then (in that case only) the *arbitrium Dei* is sufficient. Thus cultivation of the moral feeling takes precedence over the cultivation of obedience.   27:11

Can an atheist be tolerated in society? There is the atheist *in sensu privationis*,[g] ignorant in the knowledge of God, who never thinks about the matter; and the atheist *in sensu contradictorie*, who errs in the knowledge of God, though well acquainted with the subject. The former are to be tolerated, because obligation remains – apart from the new motivating ground that is derived from God's *arbitrium*, and morality is still present. Such are many nations, who are, in a fashion, civilized folk; for example, the Hottentots, now informed by the Dutch that God is called a great commander – they possess moral feeling, nonetheless; their Hottentot ditties of ungrateful Holland are evidence of this. The *atheist* may be one who denies God from wantonness and lack of respect for the better conviction; or one who does so, not from wantonness, but because he thinks himself incapable of a better conviction. The former has a moral ground for his atheism, and is very dangerous to society. The latter has a logical ground for it, and is not so dangerous. Should the former have received the idea of the divine as a mere premise of his education, it is at least worthy already of respect and consideration. Since he has now been able to overcome this strong and weighty feeling, he may be presumed to have great moral wickedness in his principles. The majority of *wanton* atheists are in Rome, Paris, etc., where there is also the greatest hypocrisy; on them, too, theism has been imprinted, but because of certain errors, totally rejected – because of trifles, a feeling so worthy of veneration, and venerable even as a delusion, has been mocked; what wickedness, and what will that come to in regard to obligation towards other, lesser beings? Atheism may first occur with misgivings – without any show of proof, merely by imitation; but at once the misgivings are repressed, and people acquire an actual readiness to be atheists, for they think that others may have proved it, or could if they thought more about it. Atheists by reasoned conviction are dangerous simply because of the consequences, since others, from a desire to imitate, may follow their example. Because of their careful investigation, it is presumed that their morality is good. Hence they are not to be punished, and need, rather, to be persuaded, or their example removed, as with Spinoza, for example. He is not to be execrated, but deplored. He was honorable, with a very high degree of morality, but extremely speculative, and supposed that with the new Cartesian philosophy he might perhaps find out something altogether new; and   27:12
as Descartes had destroyed everything, so he, Spinoza, also destroyed the concept of God, and thought he had demonstrated this. . . .

[g] in the privative/the contradictory sense

7

27:13 §1. *Ethics, the science of inner duties*, is ranked under general practical philosophy, and alongside law, the science of outer duties.

The *jus naturae* and ethics are thus quite different, since the one demands liabilities, the other, obligations.

The topic of observation is in each case society, and for us, society in the *state of nature*, insofar as mankind does not impose on it the combination with others, and still less politics and economic laws.

Moral perfection is moral as end, and not as means; by that very fact it touches and satisfies us, not by relation to the effect, but immediately in itself. Nor is the action measured by the quality of the effect, but by the intention; for example, the death of a man, as effect, is of very small account, in regard to contingency and the whole; but the killing of a man is in itself of much importance, and is avenged.

Since the distinction between liability and obligation is very subtle, let us state it more clearly:

Ethics: the science of actions that are validly imputable before no other *forum* save the *internal* one. For example, even cases that partly belong before the *forum externum* (*jus*), fall into *ethics*, insofar as they belong before the *forum internum*. The principles of all that pertains to the *forum externum* are presented in natural law. The principles of all that pertains to the *forum internum* are presented in ethics.

Ethica est scientia imputabilitatis actionum liberarum coram foro interno.[h] We shall therefore not require to cast even a glance at any possible *forum externum*.

Ethics explained by a *doctrine of virtue* is good inasmuch as virtue belongs solely before the inner tribunal; but since virtue entails, not just *morally good* actions, but at the same time a great possibility of the opposite, and thus incorporates an inner struggle, this is therefore too narrow a concept, since we can also ascribe *ethics*, but not virtue (properly speaking) to the angels and to God; for in them there is assuredly holiness but not virtue.

§2. *Philosophical* ethics is ethics insofar as it is known *philosophically*, and thus not from the testimony of others, such as sages, for example, but on the basis of the matter itself.

27:14 §3. *Utility*, and *perfection* are in themselves clear.

§4. Morality is *laxa* or *rigida*, depending on whether it contains *pauca* or *multa motiva ad pauca* or *multa moleste apparentia;*[i] for example, if it impels men merely to kindness, sobriety and moderation, it is too feeble; if it impels them also to self-sacrifice, to greater goods, it is serious; for the one coddles men, and presents them with easy duties, while the other represses the deceptive joys of the lower faculties of desire. The greater

---

[h] ethics is the science of the imputability of free actions before the inner tribunal
[i] few or many motives to few or many irksome tasks

the moral perfection of the action is to be, the greater must be the obstacles, and the struggle, and hence the more needful, in that case, is the *strict* ethic. The other never constitutes true virtue, though it often produces moral *goods* as well; but the satisfaction of the strict ethic is serious, and is a *noble* morality.

§5. The ethic of our author is *blandiens,*[j] since he always wrongly presupposes the broad concept of obligation, to which he attributes motivating grounds of utility, merely, in an improper sense of the term 'ethics'. For only he performs a morally good action, who does it from principles, not as a means, but as an end. By *sensitive jucunda*[k] I can certainly *motivate,* as by practical means, but cannot oblige, as by moral motivating grounds. Likewise by *sensitive molesta;* and so if it is to be *philosophia ethica,* it has to be *moral,* and the ethical motivating grounds should always be moral and not merely practical as physical means; even though the latter may become *mediately* motivating grounds, they would properly be a part of politics, which should, moreover, have been written down. All these subjectively motivating grounds are very good, and often preparatory to ethics, and hence, too, we have appended them; but they must always be distinguished from *ethical* grounds, since the latter must be drawn solely from noble, virtuous and free choice. The tender-hearted ethic makes for a beautiful morality; the strict and serious ethic for a sublime one. Thus the charities of a rich man, *qua* consequence of kindliness, are morally beautiful; but as a consequence of principles and a sense of obligation, they are *sublime.*

Everyone, to be sure, has need, in part, of *sensitive jucunda,* and in part of *sensitive molesta,* even for *moral* actions. For our moral feelings are so buried away under the sensuous, and the sensory motivating grounds thus make it easier for the soul subsequently to make its decisions on principle. By those principles which outweigh the sensory motives, we are brought nearer, as it were, to the domain of morality. This extends, not merely to the teaching of ethics, but also to education and religion. . . .

27:15

§8. Should the Christian ethic be given priority over philosophical ethics, or *vice versa?* One must certainly be explained from the other, as theoretical physics is explained from experimental physics; but the *natural* ethic must rightly be given priority, (1) since the other is related to it; (2) since the natural ethic contains also a ground of the other's truth; (3) since the natural ethic shows us many obligations which are impossible *secundum quid,*[l] and thus leads to the Christian ethic; the former creates the contradiction in man, that he *imputes* to himself something which he cannot omit; it creates the collision between impotence and the moral ordinance, which

27:16

[j] coaxing
[k] pleasing/displeasing to the senses
[l] by derivation

the Christian ethic reconciles. (4) The revealed ethic, if it is to be practical, must ground itself upon the motives of the *natural* ethic. Like any revelation, it presupposes natural powers, e.g. capacities of the soul that are fit for the purpose. Otherwise, it would be at most a miraculously transforming book; but in fact it is a book that *lays obligations* upon us, and presupposes instruments and receptivity in the face of revealed religion.

§10. *Perfice te ut finem,* and *ut medium,*[m] are the two major rules of our author.

By this perfection is meant either moral perfection, and in that case the latter is already presupposed, so that this rule is not a basic one, for it presupposes a ground; or else by this perfection is meant something undetermined, e.g. health, etc., and again it is not a basic rule, on account of its instability. If I am to seek perfection as a rule, this amounts to saying: Desire all perfections, a proposition quite certain, indeed, subjectively speaking, whereby we always act; but objectively speaking an empty proposition, since it is wholly identical. The sole moral rule, therefore, is this: Act according to *your moral feeling!* In *philosophia practica prima* this feeling is defined merely negatively, viz., that it is not the physical, as means to an end; so merely as a relationship. This distinction is bungled by Baumgarten throughout his entire book, which is otherwise the *richest in content,* and perhaps his best book; though everything he says may make for great practical perfection, it does not constitute moral perfection. The latter he omits to define, according to the taste of the philosophy of Wolf, which continually based perfection on the relation between cause and effect, and thus treated it as a means to ends grounded in desire and aversion. With us, both moral and physical feeling are always combined. For God, in His goodness, has for the most part laid down the same rules for practical and moral perfections. So let us set forth, not only the difference, but also the consensus, between the two. . . .

27:17   All morally good actions are thus, in their highest stages, religious acts; but this is not the first stage from which we begin. On the contrary, moral beauty (weak morality) is made prior to the moral nobility of actions in terms of what is right, and this new and higher morality is only brought in afterwards. It contains a relationship to the greatest supreme rule, which is the ground of everything, and thus constitutes the greatest harmony. Meanwhile, I must first abstract my actions from the divine will, in order even to recognize the goodness of that will. But once I have perceived it with sufficient abundance, exactitude and vividness, it becomes the supreme basis, (1) because the knowledge is then noble, and (2) because it provides the highest degree of vividness. But if my knowledge of God does not yet have life enough, I must concern myself with other beings;

---

[m] perfect yourself as to the end/as to the means

otherwise, all this knowledge of God would remain merely dead, and fail of its purpose. We begin, then, with moral beauty, and with moral liability – these are grounds of morality that are sensuous and vivid. When a man then rises to the highest level, that shows him as God's supreme instrument; but if he begins at that point, there arises from it a hypocritical religion; our author's method is therefore incorrect, since it begins from religion, whereas it ought to have started from a morality, which would then be increasingly purified.

27:18

Obligation towards God (religion) is not merely a practical necessity of making use of God, as of a means to certain ends. Our author, however, puts the use of God as a means before His immediate goodness. Yet *obligatio* should merely have explained morally good actions in direct relation to God as an end; if I follow God's will, because he has coupled my best interests with those of others, then this is a borrowed God, and it is merely the *practical* attitude of a self-interested agent. The highest degree of connection with God as a means is when we utilize the divine will as a means to the betterment of our own morality. Julie says, for example:* Our good actions are noticed by witnesses: – she uses God's will to better her morality; but to use it merely as a means to happiness is ignoble, and no religion. . . .

§14–22. The man who acts from motives of *welfare* is thereby subtly self-interested, and is not acting from religion, since he does not act from morality, and the sole motivating grounds of religion are those of *blessedness;* to entice us to our duties, as physical goods, from *happiness,* and thus derive all motivating grounds from *pleasure,* but yet make blessedness the motive to morality, and happiness the motive to welfare. That is mere *misbinding,* but since *happiness* and *blessedness* require one way, they do not actually conflict, on the whole, though they have to be distinguished. Even self-interest prepares us for religion, though without constituting it.

27:19

§19. Perhaps the image of God consisted in the immediately clear sensation of the divine presence – not symbolic, but intuitive; not from inference but from sensation; and in that case, how vivid the effect upon morality and the ground of blessedness. With us, perhaps, the broadest and vaguest concept thereof still resides, even now, in conscience. If we directly improve our moral feeling, we approach the divine presence in sensation; so maybe such people again develop the image, although their spiritual utterances sound fanatical; and religion elevates us to the highest degree of such sensation.

§21. This is true morality; a part of it already precedes all religion, but a part is greatly enhanced by religion, and since religion enhances the whole *summa* of morality, this is a *truly* binding ground of motivation. . . .

*[Rousseau: *La Nouvelle Héloïse,* Pt. III, Letter XVIII – Tr.]

27:22 §44. All enthusiasm is hard to prevent, lest we fall at once into the opposite vice of coldness. But in drawing conclusions from speculation it must be avoided, since passions do not confute or confirm opinions, but in regard to the *truth* are always blind; though in regard to the practically *good* they may be useful.

27:23 §45. When pietists make the idea of religion dominant in all conversation and discourse, and it has to be inferred from their constant behaviour that this idea has lost the light of novelty, then they are mere twaddlers. But were this state of mind *ours* in this world, it would be the most blessed of all.

§46. Try especially to always couple the idea of God with your morality; first with your *natural* moral feeling, so that your immediate liking for the good becomes, in the light of God, religion. Try also to make the idea of God *dominant* in the *depths* of the soul. This is difficult, but if it always predominates in clear ideas, then it will also pass over into the obscure ones. . . .

27:25 §72. Thou shalt love this or that, is not said apodeictically, since it is no more of a duty than to *hold* something *to be true;* for it is not a *voluntary* action, but a mere arousal of feeling. So the command is merely: Do everything that can be a means to this. Nevertheless, though I perceive the appropriateness of love, it cannot always be in my power, any more than it often is when I would like to be rid of it. But when I perceive myself in the *defective* state of *cold-heartedness,* whether towards God, or my benefactor, or my brother who loves me, then I try to impress on myself the moral qualities that arouse one to love. For example, consider especially that God loves you (the very remark already inspires love), and that men may be *moved* at receiving your love; so love them as objects of one of the gentlest of impulses.

§73. To feel the *concursus divinus,*[n] suppose yourself in possibly worse circumstances, and you will then feel your own to be that much the better.

§75. Insofar as we regard all acts of God as the best means, to the best end, of happiness, we may be completely at ease. The great mutability of things, and the storms of my passions, can best be comforted by the thought that I am placed in the world, and placed there by supreme goodness, not for my own benefit; and however uncertain the order of nature may be, it is nevertheless under the supreme being; and in this way, then, *religion* alone may be completely reassuring. For even a naturally
27:26 good and moral man must always tremble before *blind fate.*

§77. Since all God's acts (1) cannot be self-interested, and (2) are aimed at happiness, and thus are real *benefactions,* they arouse, by that very fact, *thankfulness;* and anyone insusceptible to any disinterested benefi-

---

[n] divine reinforcement

cence, will also be insusceptible to gratitude, and *vice versa;* for if he does not feel the *nobility* of well-doing in his own actions, how will he do so in the case of another? And nobody will feel gratitude even for God's bene-factions, who does not himself feel the *beauty* of well-doing; for example, the magnificence of a summer's evening will itself have an effect upon the benevolent.

That love is [not] tender, which seeks to please the object of love; the latter is in fact *amorous* love. *Amor* is, in fact, *tener, quo quis amatum laedere, admodum reformidat;⁰* amorousness does not presuppose esteem, but *tender-ness* does. That which does not merely wish to make the other into an object of desire, as amorousness does, but presupposes, rather, something *noble* in the way of thinking, does not offend, of itself, by a want of love, since it merely takes away something *beautiful.* But he who regards tender-ness as a *duty** incumbent on him, and so fears to withdraw it, gives offence. Amorousness occurs also among the foolish, and is often very *pleasing,* but there is a want of esteem in it; the *tender* lover shows respect, and desires to preserve his own esteem, and is therefore not so laughing, not merely pleasing.

In love towards God, the amorous, and even the *tender* elements must disappear, since both are very anthropomorphic, and always presuppose a secret *grace* and *favour.* These are, however, simply the greatest of duties, and thus the highest degree of tender love, albeit without the name. Resignation to the divine will is necessary, in that we must trust God to have the utmost wisdom and benevolence. Thus Socrates told the praying Alcibiades: Cast your eyes down, and say, Give me, O God, what is best, whether I ask for it or not.

Love for the *creature* is always good, insofar as it is considered to be a creature; and idolatrous creature-love is merely the excessive degree of it.

If we walk upright in our inmost soul, then we shall not, perhaps, find love, but the esteem and reverence that arise from greatness, and bring 27:27 fear rather than love as their consequence. The *moral beauty* of God, and His benevolence, are far less vivid in us, (1) because we are accustomed, as grumblers, to attribute our ills to God; and (2) because we have a dim idea that God's benefactions may perhaps have cost Him very little love – for we take our *own virtue,* which always has obstacles to *overcome,* as a measure; and since that is not so with God, we also perhaps concede him little benevolence. The world cost Him but a word, etc., etc., and since the return of love always presupposes love, our *natural* love towards God is therefore so laboured and small; nevertheless, through the agreeable feeling that, without our earning it, so much bounty streams upon us, we are seized by something akin to love. Only revealed religion discloses to us

---

*[Reading *Pflicht* for *Recht*–Tr.]
⁰ love is tender when it shuns entirely anything harmful to the beloved

a love, on God's part, that cost Him an effort, and so, properly understood, can arouse love in return.

Mistrust in God: If I had no other evidences of God's benevolence
beyond the course of nature, the judgement to that effect would inspire
little confidence, since in human life I perceive a constant entanglement,
and the opposite of good. It is not, therefore, from *individual* cases that I
seek to determine the *general* concept of *benevolence as such;* for in that case
I merely regard each action, in isolation, as a touchstone of benevolence,
but cannot therefore conclude to the total happiness of my existence as a
whole. And it is likewise possible to be without *mistrust* of God, if I do not
attribute to Him the fulfillment of individual wishes. Despite my honesty,
I can, for example, perhaps be unlucky for a long time. *Trust in God* is felt,
therefore, merely in regard to the *whole* of our life, but not with respect to
the *externals* of particular specific cases; otherwise, it can become a *tempting* of God. As the most benevolent of beings, God will, in total, at the end
of it all, make everything good; without specifying the cases in which He is
to evince benevolence, precisely in accordance with our own presumptions. In short, I shall one day be able to regard my whole existence with
confidence; that is trust in God.

It is extravagant if, in individual cases, I rely upon God's goodness, as
determined by my own intent; and it is for this reason a tempting of God,
that I think myself able, by my own wish, to determine precisely the case
where God's goodness is to display itself. A marriage with an uncertain
27:28   outcome cannot be settled by trusting to God, for He might be no less
wise and benevolent, were He even to let me starve. I see this in such a
case, because if my wish proves false, I could not stupidly declare that His
goodness has been . . . [unfinished].

27:31   Awe presupposes reverence, and the latter, the feeling for the sublime in
moral perfections, just as love presupposes the *intuitus*[p] of morally beautiful perfections. The sublime is a perfection that is distinguished from the
beautiful, and in both, the perfections may move us either morally or *non-
morally.* To be moved by a morally perfect sublimity is reverence; it does
not always presuppose *love,* for the grounds of the two are very different,
and reverence, indeed, can actually suppress love, if the moral sublimity of
the other seems greatly to collide with our own qualities, and we have not
credited him with suitable goodwill in regard to ourselves. Thus a grave
clergyman, who evokes our reverence, often arrives very inopportunely in
a gathering where the beautiful predominates. Love wishes for closer
union; sublimity frightens us away. Thus for the most part we have the
greatest love for those we revere less, for example, the female sex, whose
very weaknesses we forgive for the sake of their beauty, and are even

---

[p] intuition

14

delighted to win. So also there can be reverence for God, without loving   27:32
Him, just as a miscreant may perhaps have great respect for his *upright*
judge, but never loves him. Awe is a higher form of reverence, and thus in
itself not mingled with love; but since reverence is commonly coupled
with an anxiety not to offend its object, there arises from this the true
concept of *awe*, which is also quite wholly distinct from *fear*, since we are
guarding, not against the *evil* that he might visit upon us, but against that
which we do ourselves. The *fear of God* is thus quite different from
fearfulness towards God, the latter being a *servile* fear, which by no means
increases reverence, but in fact diminishes love; for as soon as we see
somebody against us, a degree of love is eliminated; who loves anyone,
insofar as he punishes us? The *fear of God* (i.e. awe) is childlike, and that
can coexist with love, because it is much on guard against the other's
displeasure; and the *childlike fear* of God is thus an *awe coupled with love*.
We guard against God's displeasure because of His beautiful and sublime
qualities; but not, to that extent, from fear; it is ourselves we are in fear of,
for we would in contrast be hateful in our own eyes.

§89. Deficiency, here, may thus be either want of *fearfulness towards
God*, or a lack of the fear *of God;* the two are very different and have to be
separated. The former is much the worse; the *servile* fear recoils from
actions because of punishment, and I would fear someone in servile
fashion, were I to shun him because of an evil to be apprehended. This
destroys love, and is to be guarded against, therefore, in tender minds,
since the frightful always engraves itself far more deeply, and even afterwards is not wholly softened in the presence of *beautiful* qualities. *Human
fear* is again either fearfulness *towards men*, or of them; the one fears the
evil of men more than that of God, the other holds men more greatly in
awe than God. For example, to prefer the displeasure of God to that of an
awe-inspiring ruler, is the latter kind of human fear; and a reprobate who,
as La Mettrie tells us, is frightened only of torture and authority, evinces
fearfulness towards men. The latter is no *moral* defect, but a political one;
just as the opposite fearfulness [towards God] presupposes, not morality,
but mere calculation. The former kind of fear is moral, however, just as is
the awe at moral qualities.

§90. Not everyone, who fulfils a command, *obeys* it on that account, if
he does not fulfil it *just because* it has been commanded. Thus men fulfil
many divine commands from their own impulses – through their own   27:33
moral feeling – and yet with the *false lustre* of one who obeys. Indeed,
often the judgement concerning the divine command is superfluously
added in this way, being entertained, *per subreptum,*[q] even prior to the true
ground. Universal obedience seems to be impossible for us, so long as the
knowledge of God is not the dominant idea in us; and in a future state,

[q] surreptitiously

perhaps it will be like that, since everything else will then be very easily subordinated thereto. . . .

27:36 *Wisdom* and *prudence* are different. A man of much prudence may choose ends, for which he selects his means in the best way possible, without in fact being *wise*, i.e., having chosen a good end. Wisdom chooses ends, and the want of it makes men dolts; *prudence* chooses means, and without it, on the contrary, they are fools. Womenfolk have little wisdom, but much prudence, and more than men; for keeping their own secrets, finding out those of others, and conducting embassies, women would be better. But men (if they have not, by laxity, become womanish) are able to choose better ends, and avoid doltishness. But feelings often make dolts of us, even though we may display the utmost prudence in the process. Passions, for the most part, run counter to wisdom, since they choose silly ends. *To seek honour* is not doltish; but to seek it overmuch is silly, because this end, though natural in itself, bulks too large in comparison with others. The *puffed-up person*, on the other hand, is a fool, because in this he has no proper end, though he may well choose good means for it. Any intention which, in regard to itself, is nothing, makes a man a dolt. An intention that is relatively of no importance makes him silly. An intention unattainable by any means makes him a fool.

So, too, in religion. A man shows himself a dolt, if he does not sufficiently subordinate the lesser intentions to the main one; for example, an old man, who instead of regulating his passions, wishes to provide for his children. *Prudence* is evinced in religion, if I select the appropriate means; he who errs in his ends, errs the more grossly; for a good end at least makes the morality good. The error of a dolt is morally the greater; that of a fool, logically the greater. The one is immediate, the other mediate, since the means are not well chosen. The nature of the end determines the morality. . . .

27:39 *Self-abasement* is the opposite of self-esteem. He who so *grovels* that he lowers himself, does not feel his own worth, though the other is distinguished only by an empty title, which depends merely on illusion.

Humility presupposes a *correct estimation* of self, and keeps it in bounds. We have more reason to observe imperfections than perfections, since they are more numerous, and the contemplation of perfections can very easily do harm. *Humility* is therefore not a *monkish virtue*, as Hume believes, but already needful even in natural morality. A vain science, such as geography or stargazing, can give us less distinction than moral worth. The latter will balance off imperfection with perfection; it is by rules of morality, not well-being, that I must be humble. Such humility will not be mingled with hypocrisy, but will be felt in that I perceive that I am not higher than others; and in fact, all men are not so far apart in that respect.

16

The educator should implant self-esteem and humility, so that respect is evoked by achievements only, and not by illusion. The spoiling of the upper class is attributable to the middle class, and subjugation,* luxury and pomp are the result. Here I also begin to reform myself, and then Rousseau's ideas become attractive. If I compare myself with others, and form a lesser opinion of them, this should not arise from self-esteem. The latter compares itself with itself. In humility we compare ourselves with others to our disadvantage; otherwise the imperfections of others would give me occasion for rejoicing, and this is morally evil. To despise others is also in this respect a bad method, that it evokes hatred instead. To be sure,   27:40 I may compare my imperfections with the better circumstances of others, if I perceive the possibility of a greater perfection; but I should not always be taking notice of this. I should not take note of relative imperfection – that doesn't matter; *whether I am inferior* to the other – the comparison is harmful, as it is in ranking perfection and imperfection; just so long as I go on, in addition, to frame my self-estimate as a whole, and also feel my imperfections, but not imperfection as calculated against the other. His worth remains the same, whether it be above mine or below it. From this comes hypocritical humility, which extenuates itself; and even an upright man despises such a person, not because of his imperfection, but because he declares it. That he feels it, is good for himself; but that he declares it – what is the good of that? It is useless. Humility is that honest self-esteem which is also aware of one's perfections, and must be sharply distinguished from self-abasement, which merely inspires contempt. . . .

§171. *Pride* is an inclination to think highly of oneself *in comparison with*   27:41 others. It asks, not what one is worth, but how much more one is worth than another. It cannot well be *mistaken*, if it merely finds its own worth in the fact that others are imperfect. Thus this imperfection of theirs is the reason for its own joy, and that makes it a moral *defect*. It may be outwardly evinced, and is then called self-conceit.

The *vain man* seeks merely the *opinion* of others; he is wholly turned outward from himself, and does not judge by his own feeling: Frenchmen.

The *proud man* already believes in his own worth, but esteems it solely by the lesser stature of other people, and is thus at fault: Spaniards.

The *self-assured man* does not compare himself at all, and is inwardly good; but outwardly he must then be of sober mien.

The *man of pride,* who allows it to be very conspicuous, is also externally at fault, and is said to be *puffed-up;* disdain (Dutchmen).

Haughtiness is pride in display (since there is pride in the whole demeanour). Germans are vain and haughty.

Self-estimation is either *absolute* or relative; the latter is *inadequate,* since the other person may be very wicked, and so this does not determine

*[Reading *Unterwerfung* for *Unterweisung* – Tr.]

that my own state is a good one; it is also *evil*, because it presupposes an inclination to take pleasure in the moral imperfection of another.

And thus humility, too, is strictly *absolute*, though the relative form can certainly help out the absolute one; it must never become ignoble, however, in that I become vexed at the virtues of others. Thus even the signs of humility are *absolute*, in that I should display them modestly, on the whole, and not *relatively* to others, since by the moral rules they are *needless*, and could be evil, in that they may make us self-abasing, and other people proud. As against this, the civil order demands outward marks of precedence, which emphasize relative merit; but this is absurd, since by such boasting absolute esteem is diminished. This relative worth is plainly false, since it changes with the circumstances. How does a prince figure among peasants? And how before his king? A man who dwells merely on that is *indoles abjecta*. I esteem a person of note hypocritically, on account of his rank; truly, on account of his inner worth, when he has risen (on his merits) into the middle class; and the more highly, because he has had so many obstacles to overcome. . . .

27:42

Conscience is *logica*,[r] in that I am aware of some property; and *moralis*, in that I couple this with my moral feeling. Defects are therefore *logical*, in the want of consciousness concerning one's actions, as with frivolous people, or young folk; and *moral*, in the want of moral feeling concerning one's actions, as with old scoundrels, who have been prevaricating for so long, that in time that feeling is stifled, and a sham version takes over; for example, a *shopkeeper's catechism*.

The falsified conscience *adultera*[s] is (1) *erronea*, when it is logically falsified; (2) *prave*, when it is morally so. The one goes astray, by intellectual error (*errores*); the other feels wrongly, by emotional defect (*depravitates*).[t]

To distinguish the natural from the acquired conscience is often difficult. Much that is acquired is taken to be *natural*. The parental curse that we might incur through a marriage that we do not seek to contract in the proper way, is an *acquired* conscience. Since, by natural law, the father would retain parental control only until such time as the son is able to govern himself, all duty of obedience (other than gratitude) would have lapsed, and does so here, since it has been acquired only through custom. But when Voltaire holds *all* conscience to be *acquired*, and demonstrates it by various examples drawn from different nations, he goes too far; the Eskimoes, who kill their parents as a loving service to them, are to some degree justified, since they foresee a more ignominious death for them in the hunting that is *necessary* for survival.

27:43

[r] cognitive/moral
[s] corrupted/errant/depraved
[t] viciousness

To what degree our conscientious feelings are acquired, in particular cases, is hard to say. Our relationships with friends are perhaps acquired – the feelings are too greatly enhanced; as they also are in moral concepts.

Of *bad* actions, conscience judges far more strongly and correctly *after* the deed than before, and *beforehand,* more strongly than in course of the act. This is exemplified in the *pangs of conscience* that are bound to result after a lustful act. The reason: any passion draws attention to the gracious side, and clouds the other – and once the passion is there no longer, then the cloud also falls away.

If we men here in the world are not always in a state of passion, we are nevertheless the prey of impulse; in a state of mind such that passion has to judge of things; and thus throughout life, our judgement is never wholly impartial. It is *itself* the judge in its own case. Debarred from passion after death, we are then impartial judges upon ourselves, and on our morality; the judgment upon our life will then be far more vivid and truthful, and we shall perceive the abhorrent aspects more clearly still. So long as passion remains, however, the judgement becomes even more partisan. The fiercer the passions, the more clouded the moral feeling, and even the physical one, so that physical evil is also left over. If *conscience* is silent before the deed, or if it *grumbles* ineffectually, it is a bad conscience, and in the latter case a pedant that fails to restrain, and yet plagues us. Yet there is one hope for a more lively impression: the conscience that speaks *long beforehand* is stronger than the one that immediately precedes, since the former, from a long perspective, presupposes a greater impression. Otherwise, however, the conscience that immediately precedes is the stronger. Hence one who is caught with dagger in hand is not punished with death. The *conscientia consequens*[u] is thus the strongest, but bad when the *conscientia antecedens* does not precede it; to be sorry afterwards is no reparation. 27:44

Since our life is a whole in its existence, one part of it cannot be sacrificed to another; the pleasure of the one must also be the pleasure of the other, and happiness a whole. Foresight, a daughter of affluence, is the source of unhappiness; enjoyment of the present, with attention to our morality, is our happiness. We have to enjoy these things in *this world,* and the all-too-abundant talk of eternity must not tear us away *from time;* eternity should serve merely to diminish the evil of this world, but not to lessen its joy. Man engineers downright robberies of himself; robbing himself of youth, in order to secure enjoyment of old age, of which he then deprives himself, through getting set in his habits. A part of life should not be sacrificed to the whole.

I can employ the higher powers of mind for utility's sake, and that is good; or for the sake of appearances, and that is bad. The motive for

[u] conscience after and before the act (pangs/qualms)

enhancing my powers is largely the good *opinion* of other people. But this is either an actual lie, or if truthful, is nevertheless (if it serves no useful purpose) chimerical when regarded immediately in itself, since it does not promote the best in me. Apart from that, since all show is far easier than substance, honour is wholly false; and therefore is harmful to the human race. The philosopher throws a veil over his own weaknesses, just as the Chinese were unwilling to accept the calendar, so as not to run into mistakes. The teacher, who perceives the falsity of his views, is still happy to let himself be honoured, and does not admit his errors. Should not Crusius, over so many years, have recognized the untruth of his insistent utterances? But he does not say so. The pursuit of honour is more harmful to morality than any other passion; all others have something real about them, but this one is a phantom of the brain. I depart entirely from my inner state of moral goodness, and try to improve it with something external; and what harm the sciences do then. The pursuit of honour will perhaps be totally suspended in beings somewhat higher than ourselves; with us, it is still useful as a counter to great immorality, and to stiffen our resolve against extreme laziness, and thus it is needed for the lesser morality of mankind. Self-esteem, however, is rooted in morality; not in calculating on the opinion of other people. Thus people seldom marry on their own account; always with a view to others.

27:45 Suspension of judgement can occur from moral motives or logical ones. Prudential planning decides, up to a point, with certainty, yet indicates the uncertainties, the want of assurance, the uncompleted matters that are merely set aside. In social matters, the suspension of judgement is very necessary, and a sign of humility, that should be achieved still more in practical affairs than in writing. Of all people, however, the scholar is the most covetous of honour, and thinks of nothing else; works for it, apportions it himself, and is the trumpet of fame. Knowledge as such is splendid, and without the highest insight, the highest of beings would not be the most perfect; but man must learn to recognize his limitations, not merely in logic, but in morals as well. In themselves, mathematics or numismatics are well worth knowing; but not, perhaps, for us; such eagerness for knowledge can eventually throw us entirely out of our orbit. All these attractions cause us, thereafter, to become stuck in the mud, so to speak; the child hastens, in prospect, ahead of the man; the earth-dweller has his eyes on eternity; and thus he is unfit for either state.

Learn to shun the impulses that diminish morality; pursue the moral use of your powers of cognition. They may also be greatly cultivated in other things, but prematurely so; between the sublimest human spirit and the lowest man there is no true difference of merit, save in regard to morality.

At present, mere scientific acumen must serve to compensate the defects of the sciences; otherwise there would be no need of them, for the *analogon rationis*[v] is a surer guide in morality than reason is, and the good man's feeling more reliable than the reason that makes palpable errors in its inferences. Since the *analogon rationis* is actually given for our guidance, reason, equipped as it is with many needless adornments, must certainly not acquire many privileges. Confined by the law of necessity, and by human folly, we must therefore not be puffed up; to despise the useful guide, yet take the long way round to get home, is self-destroying.

A readiness in all circumstances to posit good ends for oneself, or to choose the best means, is *presence of mind.* Womenfolk are able to select good means, but not good ends. By long reflection we must accustom ourselves to presence of mind *in ancipiti.*[w] Young people should first accept counsel, therefore.

That man alone is blessedly happy, who has the highest enjoyment of   27:46
pleasure that he is capable of in the circumstances. So this life is to be distinguished from that to come. Blessed happiness consists:

1. of happiness; non-moral good; physical well-being. Since this depends on external factors, it can be very defective, and very changeable.
2. of blessedness: the morally good.

The longing for mere well-being must therefore, by the law of mutability, already make for unhappiness, since all physical things relate to the whole, and cannot always affect us favorably. The morally good, in which we are the ground, is thus immutable, and fruitful in physical goodness, so that everything which comes about *through* me must come from moral goodness. If I am to make myself indifferent towards evil, am I also so towards the good?

If I am to make myself receptive to the good, am I also so towards evil?

Responsiveness to physical good often becomes a ground of aversion, and one must therefore try to make oneself impervious to certain things. This costs us deprivations, indeed; though they are not painful, since the feeling about them simultaneously *diminishes,* and a much finer moral feeling awakens for them instead. The savage, moreover, is in a state of *indifference* about many things. Virtue calls for *maxims* and principles, which are very different from instincts, and even from morality; and thus there can be forms of conduct that are abhorrent, without being *vices,* because they actually presuppose *maxims,* and are only *figuratively* called vices – just as actions from *good* instincts are only figuratively called *virtues.*

The motivating ground for acting according to principles is the constancy that remains ever the same, whereas *good instincts* depend on im-

[v] analogue of reason (i.e. good sense)
[w] in danger

pression and variable circumstances. These latter, in fact, are provided by human society. *Maxims*, on the other hand, are actually universal *principles*, under which particular cases can be subsumed, plus the skill of subsuming such cases. Moreover, there are indeed maxims that are *analogous* to virtue, for example, maxims of honour; and how many have acquired great lustre from these alone.

Self-conquest: No victory gives more evidence of personal activity than this, and hence it is the most satisfying. . . .

27:48 Of the sexual impulse we must judge, not merely in accordance with our civilized state, but according to the natural condition of man. And then, this impulse was very powerful, in order to sustain the species. Those who hold God's end to be always the principal one should consider here, whether the natural man has the providential intention to sustain the human race, or merely an inclination to immediate pleasure. The former is indeed the main end, but not the only one, and the remainder must certainly not conflict with it, but they can nevertheless be non-injurious to it; and it is thus altogether too scrupulous to forbid married couples those intimacies which are not immediately connected with propagation.

The sexual impulse would not have developed so early, but only once the powers of the body had matured, for it would not have been accelerated by instruction. The impulse satisfied itself merely by immediate pleasure, and there would probably not have been a permanent bond. But since, no doubt, the man will have felt that the impulse would recur, he would allow the woman to follow him into the forest; she became his companion, and both would have cared for the children. He would have had to help her while she was suckling them, and thus arose monogamy,

27:49 since there are as many women as men. The impulse would not have been so rampant then, since the fantasied pleasures of the civilized were lacking. Moreover, this impulse is covered with the veil of shame, which is also found among the majority of savages, and is quite unlike any other form of shame, and restrains the impulse. There is much truth in the objections of the cynic: we should be ashamed only of what is dishonourable; but for all that, there is a genuine shame-instinct, which has indeed no rational cause, and is strange, but whose aims are (1) to restrain the untamed sexual impulse; and (2) to maintain the attraction of it by secrecy. The male sex, which has more principles, possesses this shame in a lesser degree; for want of principles, the woman has a great deal of it, and it dominates her; and where this shame has already been uprooted in women, all virtue and respectability have lost their authority, and they go further in shamelessness than the most dissolute of men. Such shame, moreover, has an *analogon* with an act that is intrinsically dishonourable, and this has produced the stupid *shame of monkishness*. It is not, however, in itself the mark of an unpermitted act, but the veil of an honourable one, which *propagates* mankind. In addition to the sexual impulse, the female sex has many other qualities, which all focus on beauty, and are therefore charms and allurements. The male sex has friendship and devotion; the female, roguishness, kindness, etc.

The man has an acute judgement of beauty; coarse male kisses and matrimony are not so disgusting to womenfolk, and this is the wisest arrangement. This impulse is nowadays the source of so many vices, and plunged into such indecencies – so how, then, is it possible, amid such general corruption, where so many inhuman vices have sprung up, to effect an improvement? The Spartans let girls up to nine, and boys up to thirteen, go naked in the years before puberty. Our artificial virtues are chimeras, and become vices, if the hidden is regarded as vicious. As soon as chastity of speech, clothing and demeanour increases, true chastity is thrust aside. Where one side of a thing is shown, the other side tempts us from out of the chimerical land of fantasy. Perhaps Rousseau has hit upon the best method. The precocious sexual urge must be confined, lest it hamper our growth and development, and enervate normal bonding, to our subsequent regret; yet this is to be accomplished, not by hiding the impulse, but by holding up to the young man an image of the beauty that he is one day to make happy, and which will wish to have him pure. In that case, he will not throw himself away, but will travel with this image, and save it up for his happiness. The quite total removal of the concept never achieves this effect; it is rather by the following principles: As I summarize the duties of the man in the words: Be a man, so there is also a plan for womanly duties: Be a woman, etc. Unity and union are altogether different; the friendship between two men, from the concept of the sublime, can have unity, as can the friendship between women, from the concept of the beautiful. But in matrimony there must be not mere unity, but union, for a *single* purpose, the perfection of the marriage. Now to this end nature has endowed the pair with different gifts, whereby one has dominance over the other. The woman allures, the man arouses; the woman admires, the man loves; and so each prevails over the other, and there is union without tyranny on the husband's part, or servitude on that of the wife, but by way, rather, of mutual dominance. Thus the ultimate goal of the bond between the two sexes is marriage. But if the *husband* becomes *womanish*, or the *wife mannish*, the marriage is inverted and not perfect. Imagine a learned lady, bold and robust: she is then a competitor to my worth; I cannot prevail over her, and the marriage will not be perfect. Imagine a bejewelled man, a feeble, dressy fellow: he is then a competitor to the woman's beauty: she cannot prevail over him, and again the marriage is imperfect. On the contrary, she will be more pleased with a man of natural dignity and self-confidence, with a plain, unaffected style of dress. The two sexes should not be mixed up; *womanliness* is no reproach to a woman, but manliness is, and in our country, owing to their lesser education, the

27:50

womenfolk are closer to nature than those amazons in France, for example. Thanks to their delicacy of feeling, they are still able to make the difference quite clear. . . .

27:53   *Endeavouring to please others:* The motivating ground of utility is nonmoral; the inclination to please is moral – it does more to bring men together. Complaisance is a species of it, and the opposite of self-will, since I adjust myself to the will of another. It is a slippery quality – may be praiseworthy, but soon invites censure and contempt, since it shows that a man has no will of his own, and is without moral worth. It is a quality of weak souls. The noble prefer self-will, and the faults that result from it are not so grave as those due to complaisance, which in many people is often a cause of idleness. The young must still try to please, since as yet they have few principles. In trifles (and human life is so full of them that it almost seems to be a trifle itself, compared with the whole of what exists) self-will tends to separate us, etc.; but in morality it is worthy of praise.

Honourableness: Rousseau's conception of honour is purely internal, and such, also, is honourableness; a *true* self-esteem for one's inner worth. The judgement of others is merely an *accessorium.* It takes *personal* fortitude to overcome the constraints of conventional morality.

Egoismus moralis has two forms: that which breaches the limits in self-esteem, or in love of benevolence; since I am constantly promoting my own interest.

Self-abasement may be to oneself, or to others. The latter makes others puffed-up, and oneself into a worm. It proceeds from the former, and often makes our perfection useless, as when I do nothing for myself out of honour, but do it instead out of contempt.

Love towards others already indicates a lesser need in oneself for other things; self-love must take precedence, since the love for others simply rests upon it. That he, who thus loves others, enlarges his own happiness, is a property of dependents, and hence of created beings. He who enlarges the system of his love, also enlarges the well-being of his fellowmen. How love is extended, is a practical question; I cannot say, as an absolute injunction, Thou shalt love! This love is that of wishing well, or of pleasing well. The latter is also non-moral, but wishing well presupposes a morality of beauty: the idea of the *beautiful* in the action is the means thereto.

Affability is a sign of our love, and is not a real and efficient quality, i.e., readiness to be of service is symbolic, since we show the inclination to it,
27:54   e.g. in our demeanour. Rules are very difficult – affable friendliness requires greater equality.

Indifference, as a moral quality, is the opposite of human love; but even by this cold-bloodedness I may understand a very good trait, if it holds the love inspired by sympathy in check, and gives it due measure. If the sympathetic inclinations are blind and serve no purpose, the stoic must say: If you cannot be of help to others, then what business is it of yours, pray?

Friendship is very complex; it already presupposes the *alter ego,* and does not always exist where I love another and he loves me; for (1) I shall not, on that account, simply disclose my secrets to him; and (2) I am not convinced, either, that he will sacrifice something for my sake. We have to be able to assume that his efforts on his own behalf will be made also for us, and ours for his; but that is a great deal to expect, and so friends are few. If I multiply friends, I diminish friendship, and hence it is already much, to have but one true friend. Between different persons there can certainly be sincere human love, though not in the degree of friendship; for the latter is the highest form of that love, and presupposes an identity of personality. Yet some people come reasonably close to this, and are also said to be friends. Friendship proper is in part impossible (owing to the number of our own requirements), and in part needless (since my security is already manifestly looked after by many others). . . .

Compassion. The ability to put ourselves in the position of another, is not 27:58
moral only, but also logical, since I can project myself into the standpoint of another, e.g. of a follower of Crusius. So too in moral matters, when I project myself into another's feelings, to ask what he will be thinking about it. If I put myself, by a fiction, into another's shoes, this is a *heuristic* step, in order the better to get at certain things. It can be quite skilfully done, yet not moral, since I am not actually in his position; except in the case of true *sympathy,* where we really feel ourselves to be in his place. The *feeling of pity* would not be sufficient for morality. In the savage state, instincts are enough; everyone looks after himself; few are in need, and in that case pity is adequate. In civil society, where the needy have multi-plied, it would often – however widespread – be futile to be merely sorry for them, and hence the feeling is much weakened, and evinced only to those in the *direst* necessity. In the common man, however, whose needs are fewer, and who can thus be the readier to share, the nearer he is to simplicity, these compassionate instincts will be greater. The civilized man is much constrained by self-serving artificial desires, so that pity is here replaced by the concept of what is *right,* what is *seemly.* This can never be futile, because I shall not be bound to the *impossible;* here virtue becomes calm and rational, and no longer remains a mere animal instinct, though such instincts certainly operate pretty regularly in the state of nature. In general, however, civil motives are insufficient. . . .

Lying is simply too restricted, as an injury to the other; as untruth, it 27:59
already has an immediately abhorrent quality, for (a) this most *trenchantly* separates human society, of which truth is the bond; *truth* is simply lost,

and with it, all the happiness of mankind; everything puts on a mask, and every indication of civility becomes a deceit; we make use of other men to *our own* best advantage. The lie is thus a higher degree of untruth. (b) So soon as the lust for honour becomes a prevailing principle, it already sets no bounds to the lie. Self-interest cannot be so strong a reason, for lying is not an *enduring* means of advantage, since others shun the liar. The greediest shopkeepers of all are the *most honourable* in their dealings, simply from self-interest, and this is thus often a reason for truthfulness, etc. The lust for honour makes *lying* easier, since here the inner content is not so apparent; religion and well-being, for example, can easily be simu-

27:60   lated, and not so readily exposed. (c) The longing for imaginary perfec-tions, that perhaps were not thought suitable before; for example, a disin-terested zeal to serve is a *fantasy* too high for us. But since we can indeed be of service to a person in certain matters, there is the wish, in fantasy, to sacrifice ourselves; and since this cannot actually *be*, there is the *wish*, at least, for it to *seem* so. Second example: The fantasied desire for infinite knowledge, that is impossible to us, creates the *semblance* of this knowl-edge. In the indulgence in knowledge and enjoyment, do we therefore find the *lie* that is most abhorrent of all to the *natural man*?

Value of the love of truth: It is the basis of all virtue; the first law of nature, Be truthful!, is a ground (1) of virtue towards others, for if all are truthful, a man's untruth would be exposed as a *disgrace*. (2) of virtue to oneself, for a man cannot hide from himself, nor is he able to contain his abhorrence.

The *feeling of shame* (which is *later* made subject to delusion, and envelops even the best actions), seems to be a natural means (*pudor,*[x] not merely *pudicitium* in the pursuit of pleasure) of promoting truthfulness and betraying falsehood. If we wanted to use such shame, simply to betray the lie, it is very *practicable*. Providence would certainly not have furnished it to delude us, for it is the greatest of tortures; it is given, rather for betrayal – *involuntary* betrayal. It has never been there to cause us anxiety, but rather to betray *something* which nature did not want to hide. To thus make use of this shameful feeling as an antidote against lying, we must not employ it for any other purpose, e.g. to show up a child. Here I use merely the means for imitation; if he has behaved or spoken stupidly, I simply persuade, and *as a child* there is much that becomes him, which is not becoming to the *man*. But supposing that, regardless of his love of truth, he has *but once* told a lie, from self-interest, because the love of truth is not so lively as physical feeling; in that case I do not talk to him of *obedience* (of which no child has the *concept*, nor is of an age to do so), but simply of *untruth*. In the end he acquires as much abhorrence for it as he has for a spider. *Incest* with a sister is abhorrent, not because God has forbidden it,

[x] shame/modesty

but because the wrongness of it has been imprinted since childhood. Such is the power of ideas of dreadfulness; and if a son were to see his father's abhorrence of lying, he would by moral sympathy perceive the same himself. Suppose him now grown up, then everything would go better. I would openly declare my intention, for example, that I am working, not for the benefit of science, but from self-interest; I would yearn only for an official position that I am capable of filling. Nowadays, however, there is *untruth,* not merely in the world, but also before God, in solitude, since we cannot stand even before Him without pretence. To be truthful, we would now have to forfeit a great deal, and so each of us shies away from the truth, and most of all in a nightshirt. Untruth may end by deceiving itself, and so self-examination becomes equally slippery; the good side of kind-heartedness, for example, is put before its reprehensible aspect, and men eventually become deceivers even towards God: for example, Job's comforters. Certain untruths are not called lies, because the latter are *strictly untruths* that are contrary to *duty;* not, however, as our author thinks, merely to the duty *to myself,* but also to that *towards others.* The importance of the love of truth is so great that one can almost never make an exception to it.

Untruth, to the great *advantage of another,* still has something *sublime* in it, that is near allied to virtue. Yet to speak *truth,* to the *disadvantage of oneself,* is sublimer still, and to speak untruth to *one's own advantage* is doubtless always immoral. But since the *highest morality* is not on a par with the *moral level* of man, this is not, indeed, quite settled. Yet because the bounds of a man's strength and obligation are hard to determine, this *human ethic* of untruth will be as confused as the *logica probabilis.ʸ Every coward* is a liar; Jews, for example, not only in business, but also in common life. It is hardest of all to judge Jews; they are cowards. Children, for example, that are brought up cowards, tell lies, since they are weak in conquering themselves, etc. But not every liar is a coward, for there are inveterate scoundrels as well.

With us, in many cases, a small untruth does not seem untoward, for weak persons; the case is often complicated; if another asks him something, a man cannot remain silent, for that would be to assent, etc., etc. In short, we should investigate the degree of morality that is suited to men. As with all fine inclinations, we can also enlarge the desire for holiness; but not all can be moral men, when they are weak or needy, since in few cases are we able to attain to holiness. If our untruth is in keeping with our main intent, then it is bad; but if I can avert a truly great evil only by this means, then . . . etc. Here goodness of heart takes the place of sincerity. To obtain a great good by untruthfulness is far less excusable than to ward off a great evil by that means; for (1) our inclination to our happiness is

27:61

27:62

ʸ logic of the probable

27

often fanciful, and morality should not be sacrificed on that account; (2) the taking away of what I have is a greater denial than a withdrawal of what I might have. A white lie is often a *contradictio in adjecto;*[z] like pretended tipsiness, it is *untruth* that breaches no *obligation,* and is thus properly no *lie. Joking* lies, if they are not taken to be *true,* are not immoral. But if it be that the other is *ever* meant to *believe* it, then, even though no harm is done, it is a lie, since at least there is always deception. If untruth presupposes cleverness and skill, we get *artful* lying and repute; courtiers and politicians, for example, have to achieve their aims by lying, and everyone should flee any position in which *untruth* is indispensable to him.

The inclinations of men in nature are to be distinguished from those that evolve from artificial motives; a primary piece of self-knowledge. An ethic for man, *determined* in his nature, by his knowledge, powers and capacities, has yet to be written. For by reason we can also discern rational perfections that are suitable, indeed, for a higher being, but not for him. We here have to investigate his limitations; and to become acquainted with the *natural man,* let us adopt this as our rule, that we take those *parts* that are unalterable by any art; and what is contrary to them will be artificial. Such regular inclinations of nature are: (1) *self-preservation,* and (2) the inclination to preserve the species; these may be increased or diminished by reflection, but reflection does not produce the urge. We must also, reflection notwithstanding, eat and cover ourselves; the sexual impulse is purely a lustful thing. The *arrangements* of nature are ancient, original, irresistible *reflection.*

(a) *Freedom* is also an urge, because anyone wishes to follow his *own will,* and against physical hindrances he knows of means for this; but not against the will of another. This he considers to be the greatest misfortune, and so it is, since in part it is far more vexatious, and in part 27:63   irremediable. Hence all animals are *equally free.* From freedom there arises

(b) the desire for *equality,* especially in strength (or else by cunning), since this is the . . . [unfinished].

From the urge to *equality* there arises

(c) the urge to *honour;* if the other would take power over me, he must be made to think that I am equal to him. That is *honour,* and it takes two forms:

1. to preserve myself; to have *strength,* and to show it, in order not to become a serf.

2. to preserve one's kind; the man, being stronger, covets the trust of the woman, so that he may *preserve* and defend her. He will choose a wife, and must ensure that he is *pleasing to her;* and since she is *weak,* she sets

---

[z] contradiction in terms

store by valour. This second urge to honour is more effective than the first. Hence Rousseau extols the sexual impulse. The first he can defy, but this one is strong in its effect.

The *urge to know* does not lie in *nature;* to us, indeed, it is now indispensable, but simply through long practice. The reason for it, in ourselves, is merely *tedium.* The scientific urge for purposes of *self-preservation* depends merely on the contingency of our condition; *immediate honour* is never the source, but always the end.

A thing cannot lie in nature, if (1) it can never be satisfied, and (2) it is out of proportion to the shortness of life, and to great desire.

In general, a thing is *unnatural* if it is contrary to the urges of nature; the scientific impulse is not merely somewhat at variance with the urge to self-preservation; it is particularly adverse to the sexual urge.

However, I am simply to know the *natural man,* not in the present connection, *to be one.* My heart may not yearn for that, indeed, but I must *nevertheless adapt* myself to it. So let *ambition* be no passion; since I despise it, it plagues me not; but I still need it as a goal, in order to be effective. Science, and the like, must not therefore be a blind thirst (so I must not be bored without it; not unsociable; not contemptuous of the unlearned, but gladly cherishing them); yet I still need it *externally,* as a goal. One can never attain to inner virtue in any other way. For the *moralist* or *cleric* already (1) presupposes comforts, honour, etc., though that is unnatural; (2) extends duties contrary to nature, e.g. by deriving marriage, not from the sexual impulse, but from the command of God. People also fabricate false virtues; those that are *appropriate* to the *natural* man are too *elevated* and hyperbolical for the *artificial* one. The happy man is he who is good without virtue (by feeling, without concepts; the *man does,* the philosopher *knows it*). The happy man is he who is knowledgeable without science. Both of those things are mere glitter, etc.

Plan of judgements of the *common* judgement. Examination of nature and art; thence to judge projects. One should look first to the median; otherwise the *height* is never reached, since our life is commonly too short, and the project too fanciful.

§348. Relationship of men; towards a concept of the system of human love: the love of *well-wishing* (of the other's greater welfare) is either active or wishful. The merely *yearning* or *wishful* love comes *either* from the degree of weakness, or from the disposition, in that it is merely fanciful. For a degree of love that is all-too-elevated for my practical capacity is just as ineffectual as a *want* of love. *Excessiveness* in the way of life also creates such wishes and yearnings, and is not good, since it is (1) *useless;* (2) *deceptive,* in that it squanders time and actually impedes practical love; for the love that is *too little practical* has the love that is all-too-greatly *fanciful* as its cause. So to enquire into them both, let us note (1) that a person does not actively *love* another *until he is himself in a state of well-being;* since

27:64

he is the *principium* of the other's good, let him first better himself. He should be at ease with himself, and thus the more there is of excess, the less there is of practical human love. For by excess we multiply in fancy our own needs, and thus make practical love *difficult,* i.e., *eo ipso rare.* To make itself practical, it puts itself *at ease* with itself, making do with little; and from this comes practical love, etc. All other motives produce fanciful urges, and hence in a condition of simplicity there will be much practical love, and in a state of luxury, little; but more of the fanciful kind, and since this cannot be satisfied, for in that case the entire human race would be before me, *I merely wish,* and have simply thought up the fancy for myself, because practical love is wanting in me.

27:65 Transfer a man of nature (not a man of the woods, who is perhaps a chimera, but a simple man) into the midst of artificial society; a man whose heart is not set on anything. The man whose love is *real,* loves *in a more limited way,* and his love cannot be extended to *everyone,* without his *forgetting,* for his own part, to take note of his *own position.* Thus a natural man has a care for himself, without informing himself much about the well-being of others. Our professions of sympathy, as compliments, seem foolish to him. Nevertheless, his love will be practical, e.g. for one who is suddenly in danger. Here this instinct cannot be eradicated by wickedness; it unites the whole human race, and is powerful, since it often does not wait upon reason. Yet this truly practical instinct is directed, not so much to the increase of good, as to the *prevention of great and sudden harms;* and as soon as they are too much for his powers, wishings and pityings strike him as too foolish; he would have to divert his attention *from himself,* and so he is perfectly ready to turn his thoughts elsewhere. In present-day civil society, since the needs multiply, the *objects of pity* mount up; the capacity of men itself declines, since in part *really,* and in part through illusion, they are weak and thus miserable; for the evils of illusion, which make me *in imagination,* and a thousand others *in reality* similar, are on the increase. What must *human love* be here? *A topsoil,* an imagined human love, a yearning of the fancy, is the natural consequence. So it now spreads abroad, and corrupts *the heart.* Since, through morality, the fanciful love of humanity is so widely diffused in people by instruction, it remains a matter of speculation everywhere in life, a topic of romances, such as Fielding's, etc., that has no effect, since (1) it is too exalted, and (2) does not get rid of the obstacles.

True love is (1) rectitude: It is the love we have by nature, the fundamental love, for it is founded upon a living feeling of *equality; otherwise, favour,* etc., will come of it, but here, *rectitude;* that I *owe* nothing. Equality means that the natural man is equal to all others, and they to him, and since *moral sympathy* is imprinted on all, he has to put himself in the other's place; and from this there follows *living rectitude.* From it there arises the *obligation* to alleviate the woes of others, which is equivalent to rectitude. Take, for example, one who fails to give me warning of a ditch; you would require this of others, so you must do it yourself. Without love of humanity this rectitude would be merely a semblance. Man in the civil state is called on to have *love of rectitude* only towards a few; yet truly the *whole human race* has an obligation to it for every single person; not, however, *each* individual, because *his possibilities* are lessened. From *love of humanity, favour* will arise, since it *selects people*, without special compulsion or desert. The love due to *favour*, if it is not to be artificial, too extreme, too overpowering, has to be built upon love of humanity. Here we must examine how far the duties of society can be grafted on to *love of humanity* and the *obligation* towards it; on to *rectitude* – such is the indispensable goal of moral theory, and *rectitude* is based on the *exalted feeling of equality*. There exists in man a moral *sympathy*, to put oneself in the other's place; it is the basis of *righteous* love, and holds it to be an *obligation*, etc., and the opposite hateful. *Righteous* love differs from *kindly* love, in that absence of the former is hateful, while absence of kindly love means that one is not to be praised in a higher degree. Actions to which I am bound by the rule of rectitude are *obligations*. The boundaries between the two cases, where someone must hate the other, and simply does not love him, are very distinct, but hard to discriminate. Anyone who puts something before an *obligation* to himself, would find himself *hateful*. Nature has not framed us to be *generous*, but to be self-sustaining; sympathetic, indeed, to the woes of others, yet in such a way that the sum shall not be zero; that I not sacrifice as much as I redeem, but preserve myself and my kind. 27:66

In the state of nature, obligations are few, and the sense of them is great.

In the civil state, there are more obligations, and the sense of them is small.

In the one, men have little to do with one another, but the helpful actions they do encounter, have a bearing on their natural state: natural evils, and not the fabricated ills of delusion.

In the other, the *commercium* is greater. Many helpful actions are needed, even on account of the numerous invented evils, and hence there are many grounds for giving aid, but more obligations upon oneself. Many people live unjustly at the expense of others, and therefore incur so many debts that no room is left for kindness. They are a major reason for acts of violence towards others; and to such people their ill-fortune is not indifferent to them, as in the state of nature; rather, they have brought it on themselves. Hence there are many obligations; and here we have the first axiom: *All men are equal to one another*. To the savage, it is a principle; but to us, who have strayed so far from it, it is a thing to be proved, and the basis of *ethics*. *Every man* has an equal right to the soil. Thus *obligations* multiply, but the *sense* of them diminishes. For, (1) the sense of *equality* declines; I feel my superiority, though others yet rank above me, and I 27:67

think myself willing to take after God. Yet I still am under *obligation*, for (2) there is a decline of *moral sympathy;* a cause of the harshness of superior folk, and of the misfortune of the poor. Their oppressions continue, since the others do not even claim responsibility for them.

Acts of goodness. Man fancifully exaggerates his moral capacity, and sets before himself the most perfect goodness; the outcome is nonsense; but what is required of us? The Stoic's answer: I shall raise myself *above myself,* will become a *savage,* rise superior to my own afflictions and needs, and with all my might be *good,* be the *image of godhood.* But how so, for godhood has no obligations, yet you certainly do; anyone has a right upon me, on my work and help. Now the god departs, and we are left with *man,* a poor creature, loaded with obligations. *Seneca* was an impostor, *Epictetus* strange and fanciful. All *goodness* is not, in itself, *obligation;* from this it follows that our education, and mutual education, must be such that our sympathies do not become *fanciful,* but remain confined to the *practical.* I must be *upright,* and attend to my obligations; but the exalted pretension of wanting to love the whole of mankind is a fraud. He who loves the Tartar, loves not his neighbour. Loving *all,* we love *none,* and our love is therefore less. In place of rendering assistance to everyone, there should be simple *courtesy,* which is (1) not hatred, and (2) a mere *calm* willingness to assist in emergencies, according to *our powers.* Out of *rectitude* (but not *ardent desire*) there may be sacrifice; to that I am not obligated, though I am to courtesy, which has beauty because it springs from *equality,* and goes with self-esteem. To inferiors we owe, not *favour* merely, but a courteous attitude; to superiors, not hatred, but courtesies; for *they are simply equals.* All *favour* is offensive; here I shall neither cringe nor despise; with no *lofty ideas of virtue,* I shall be *honourable,* without wishing to be a great *saint.* . . .

27:73 §368. The doctrine of *tolerance* is generally well known, and much invoked by the persecuted; its limits, however, are still very indefinite. It is (1) *moral tolerance,* as a duty that one person bears to another, without constituting them members of a state. Since all true religion is internal, and lies in the relationship of the human heart towards God, a man may judge of the signs thereof in another, but not of the religion itself. The external practice of religion can be imitated, without anything within. In Rome, the majority are atheists, including even popes. Now since the signs are so ambiguous, it is a *duty* not to deny somebody a religion, because in signs he differs from myself; for I *cannot* have insight into an inner religion. It is thus (1) possible with difficulty only, and (2) also unnecessary, according to the concerns of nature; because the judgement upon others, the presumptions of doing this, calls for great authority, if it is not to be an offence. Now in the state of nature there is no such authority, since religion is a relationship to God; to myself it can only represent a form of conduct, which religion admittedly elevates, but which can be sufficient for me even without religion. For example, the Talapoins of Pegu;* if they receive me, I *ought* not to trouble myself at all, for my own part, about their religion. I have a concern for what may be conformable to my welfare, but religion plays no part in that. Why should I not have a concern for it, out of a *general love of mankind? Responsio:* It is certainly worthy of note, but afterwards. In short, a moral code can exist without religion. But now if I detect in it a religion that may be very injurious to my own interests, for example, the vindictiveness that springs from religion, then it does concern me. A *persecuting* religion can be an object of suspicion, even in a state of nature, that I may guard myself against it, and keep out of its way.

27:74

(2) *Civil Tolerance.* In the state of nature there is less occasion for religion, than there is for it as a means to civic well-being. Religion is for our eternal well-being, and for this and other reasons it is a major motivating ground to many human duties. But how if there be no religion? Is it always equally necessary, with regard to our welfare in the present? *Responsio:* No, and it is the less necessary in a state of nature, because there are fewer occasions for those departures from human duties, to which religion is held to be an antidote. Peoples that possess no other religion than some ancient traditional fancies, have much that is good among them, and little that is bad; warfare excepted, and that, too, is just a customary habit.

So since here there is little occasion for it, the other's religion is likewise of little concern to me. But as soon as the *interest* grows, and perfections have ascended to the fanciful level, moral feeling is no longer so sure a guide. In the end, that feeling becomes too weak to resist fervour; the love of humanity cools off; here the moral grounds of motivation are too feeble to provide defence against everything; higher grounds are called for, and thus religion becomes ever more needful (in the civil state; it can never be so in the natural one), and finally we get superstitious religion, in the degree to which extravagances increase. For things that I can do without, I shall not lie, and still less perjure myself; but, attracted by many things, to which I cleave, I have to be bound by oath against such major sources of temptation. There is an ever greater need for fantastical ceremonies, which in fact mean nothing, but are able to conquer rampant immorality. Here, religion is a police-force; morally, its boundaries are defined, but in civil society they become vague, because already we are at a loss to provide means sufficient to preserve us from ruin.

In regard to civil tolerance, religion is a matter of indifference to the natural man; there is already morality in his heart, before he has religion; so long as, in the state of simplicity, there are forces that impel him to be

*[Buddhist monks, in Burma – Tr.]

33

good, and no incentives are required for the avoidance of evil, he does not need religion. But when many of his comforts turn into necessities, his impulses gain the upper hand, so that morality becomes too weak, and the religion of nature does not suffice. For this, more understanding and philosophical reflection are required, than can be expected of the whole human race. So it has to be complemented by a revelation, either pretended or true.

27:75

The Pulserro bridge of the Persians produces many noble deeds, so Chardin tells us. Pure morality asks for no rewards, etc., but this pure morality is nowadays not present in the human heart; nor can the religion of nature provide aid to morality. Without basing itself on reason, a revelation at least offers a pretence of doing so. All civilized nations have a revelation of their own, and the barbarous ones a myth. India has one of the most ancient. The dispute as to which is the true revelation, cannot be decided here. In religion of this kind, to be suitable to the most considerable portion of men, much must be symbolic, to make the duties of nature venerable by many solemnities; certain ceremonies must make the matter worthy of respect. A custom once adopted must not be impeached, for till now it has been the foundation of the state, and if it is changed (though only fractionally) and for the better, we finally come to think that, since something has been altered, it could all of it be false. Hence republics are at their strictest concerning the old religion.

Can a government protect a multiplicity of religions? *Responsio:* Yes; insofar as any one of them is already established, it is far better to protect it, instead of wishing to improve it; because eventually an indifference to all religion would result. The multiplicity of religions creates an attachment to your own, and the civic utility is very much the same; for, as experience shows, Holland, for example, is a well-governed state. To be sure, were the principles, if pursued, to be adverse to the state, as with the Jews, for example, who are permitted by the Talmud to practice deceit, then the natural feeling rectifies this false article of religion. Such evil freedoms are not followed; the principles of the Catholics, for example, would in practice be adverse to the state, but this does not actually occur. The improvements of religion relate, therefore, merely to the political, for example, monastic orders. If a customary traditional religion, that is not based on rational demonstration, is generally accepted, anybody ought to be prohibited, on the state's account, from impugning it, even when errors are perceived therein. Nor can anybody deprive me of my ability to *think for myself,* and that should not be permitted. But since I take the greatest of

27:76

pleasure in imparting my opinion to my fellow-citizens, is it not injustice to forbid me from doing this? Yes indeed; however, the general welfare is not possible without these simple injustices, where luxury is concerned. In a state of perfect tolerance, a particular moral beauty must prevail; if everyone states his opinion, then every part will be put in a special light, and *truth* will be suppressed by coercion. Nor is any given error ever a moral transgression, even though it be an offence against the state. A universal tolerance is possible, but only if we again return to the first state of things; in that case, we are also morally good without God. Why should I not state my opinion of religion? In regard to this world, the decision concerning tolerance is solely a matter for authority; not for anyone else, and not for any clergyman. The latter is interested only in truth or falsity, not in what is useful or harmful; and the truth he is unable to decide. The cleric and his adversary are both citizens, about whom only authority has anything to say. But what degree of freedom do they have? To give no freedom at all is just as injurious as to give too much. Precisely because of a total lack of freedom, clever men become indifferentists. For this tolerance, the most subtle question is, whether there are errors worthy of respect.

So let us have *moral* tolerance, for it is in no way a form of doubt. Yet many religions foster a real hatred among men, when they set up their opponents as devils rather than men. Moral tolerance is called for in everything. Let us look upon the other with love; he *errs*, yet I do not hate him on that account, but have pity for him, that through error he should go astray. No individual who is morally intolerant is guilty of a crime, for the state has no concern with him. With luxury, religion proliferates in ceremonies; with profusion it declines; and one day complete tolerance may be possible.

Should authority, too, be concerned with the cure of souls? *Responsio:* This question must extend to all nations. Can the authority that is convinced of its religion forbid all others? *Responsio:* No, for if every nation, which also believes itself persuaded of its own religion, likewise totally denies entry to arguments from the other side, then all access to the truth would be closed off. Each thinks it has the truth, and if this *belief* is a reason for prohibition, then all nations possess such a right. Thus authority can certainly practice intolerance for political reasons, but not for the sake of salvation hereafter. However righteous a religion may be, and however great the conviction of it, there follows from this no right to deny   27:77 entry to other opinions, for salvation's sake; for it is hard to distinguish between true and false conviction. Can an authority proselytize for a religion? *Responsio:* Yes, the propagation of a truth by argument is morally always useful (though it may often be politically harmful, since it frequently promotes zealotry as well); but it is also man's prerogative to require arguments. This method is reasonable, and the compulsion to declare something true, that one did not hold before, is very unjust and offensive, extremely damaging and never useful, save perhaps to do away with certain other injustices.

Arguments for coercion. As soon as I regard a religion as the *sole* means of blessedness, then it is plainly a matter of humanity to snatch men from perdition, and here, assuredly, all means are good, for even small evils in this life are nothing to those that are eternal. So means of compulsion are not unjust if they are means; but physical coercion never produces conviction, as with the Saxons under Charlemagne. *Objectio:* But much consideration needs also to be given to the descendants, who, even if their ancestors were merely made hypocrites by coercion, will perhaps have good and true conviction, through a better education.

All this seems plausible; but in brief, (1) no means that is adverse to the supreme prerogatives of mankind, is a good one. Now men are all equal, and should mere inequality, coercion, be the means of eternal happiness, it is a means of injustice, which already presupposes force. (2) The whole of mankind rises up against *having* to maintain something. From all this it follows that, in regard to the hereafter, authority must avail itself merely of the prerogatives of mankind: the arguments, in which every man has a share.

The common man, who never uses or misuses reason, must admittedly be guided, and this, therefore, for the most part, in a historical way. The less noble portion, which uses and misuses arguments, should not be taught merely by authority, but supported by grounds of reason. If education has been *rightly* conducted, there is no injustice required in securing tolerance.

1. The subject will be brought up tolerant, with error distinguished from crime.

27:78 2. It will not be harmful to him, since he is being educated by means of reason.

To coerce other into *opinions,* or into *silence,* is in this way harmful as a moral intolerance, that one can thereupon never guard against the evil consequences of abhorrence:

1. Every man wants to have his own opinion as the general one; the *causes* of which are:
2. that he supposes all morality to be based on religion, and thus hates the other, for he sees in him wickedness rather than error. It is the clergyman's duty to expel this intolerance from the heart. Education should be made into the seed-bed of moral tolerance.
3. a man's intolerance is often *founded upon great ignorance.* Since he cannot answer by reason, he thinks of it as an enemy that will expose his nakedness. He who has no arguments to offer is hostile to counter-arguments. A clergyman, who has examined himself (we may suppose), will have no hatred, even for the ignorant theologian.

Moral intolerance, to be sure, is in itself already an absurdity, and if a proper education were to be universal, then political tolerance could be universal too. At present, however, authority must be vigilant *everywhere....*

PART II
Moral philosophy

FROM THE LECTURES OF PROFESSOR KANT
KÖNIGSBERG, WINTER SEMESTER, 1784–5
GEORG LUDWIG COLLINS
(ON BAUMGARTEN)

TABLE OF CONTENTS

[On universal practical philosophy]

PROEM

All philosophy is either theoretical or practical. Theoretical philosophy is the rule of *knowledge,* practical the rule of *behaviour* in regard to free choice. 27:243 The difference between theoretical and practical philosophy is in the object. The one has theory for its object, and the other practice. Philosophy is otherwise divided into speculative and practical. Sciences are in general called theoretical and practical, be the objects what they may. They are theoretical if they are the ground of concepts of the objects, but practical if they are the ground of exercising knowledge of the objects; thus there is, for example, a theoretical and a practical geometry, a theoretical and a practical mechanics, a theoretical and a practical medicine, and a theoretical and a practical jurisprudence: the object is always the same. So if, regardless of the object, the sciences are nevertheless theoretical and practical, it has to do merely with the form of the science, the theoretical being for judgement of the object, and the practical for producing it. But in the present case there is a difference between theoretical and practical in regard to the object. Practical philosophy is practical not by form, but by the object, and this object is free acts and free behaviour. The theoretical is knowing, and the practical is behaving. If I abstract from the particular matter in hand, the philosophy of behaviour is that which gives a rule for the proper use of freedom, and this is the object of practical philosophy, without regard to particulars. So practical philosophy treats of the use of free choice, not in regard to particulars, but independently of all of them. Logic gives us rules in regard to the use of understanding, and practical philosophy in regard to the use of willing, which are the two powers from which everything in our minds arises. Now if we take the ruling powers of knowledge and motor capacity, the first is the ruling capacity for knowledge, or understanding; and the second the ruling capacity of desire, or free choice. We now have two forms of instruction for the two powers, namely logic for the under- 27:244 standing and practical philosophy for the will. The lower powers cannot be instructed, because they are blind.

So here we are considering a being that has free choice, who may not be a man only, but also any rational being. And we are examining the rule for the use of freedom, and that is practical philosophy in general. It thus has objective rules for free behaviour. Any objective rule says what ought to

41

occur, even if it never does. The subjective rule says what actually does occur, for even among the wicked there are rules by which they act. Anthropology is concerned with subjective practical rules, it observes solely the actual behaviour of man; moral philosophy seeks to bring his good behaviour under rules, namely of what ought to occur. It contains rules for the right use of the will, just as logic contains rules for the correct use of the understanding. The science of the rules of how man ought to behave is practical philosophy, and the science of the rules of his actual behaviour is anthropology; these two sciences are closely connected, and morality cannot exist without anthropology, for one must first know of the agent whether he is also in a position to accomplish what it is required from him that he should do. One can, indeed, certainly consider practical philosophy even without anthropology, or without knowledge of the agent, only then it is merely speculative, or an Idea; so man must at least be studied accordingly. People are always preaching about what ought to be done, and nobody thinks about whether it can be done, so that even the admonitions, which are tautological repetitions of rules that anyone knows already, strike us as very tedious, in that nothing is said beyond what is already known, and the pulpit orations on the subject are very empty, if the preacher does not simultaneously attend to mankind; and in this Spalding is preferable to all others. So one must know of man whether he can also do what is required of him. Consideration of rules is useless if one cannot make man ready to follow them, so these two sciences are closely connected. But it is the same as when theoretical physics is combined with experiments, for we also make experiments with man. For example, we test a servant to find out if he is honest. So in examining a preacher, we should look just as much to his character and heart as to his knowledge of dogma.

27:245

So practical philosophy is practical, not by its form, but by its object. It is a doctrine of doing. Just as logic is a science of reason, so the object of practical philosophy should be *praxis*. It is thus a science of the objective laws of free choice, a philosophy of the objective necessity of free actions, or of the will, that is, of all merely possible good actions, just as anthropology is a science of the subjective laws of free choice. Practical philosophy, like logic, does not deal with any particular kind of practices but with free actions as such, regardless of all such practices. The practical rules, which lay down what is to occur, are of three kinds: rules of skill, rules of prudence, and rules of morality. Any objective practical rule is expressed in the imperative, but the subjective practical rule is not; for example, the old are given to saying, that is so, yet it should not be so. For instance, one should not save so much in old age as in youth, since when old one no longer needs so much, having not so long to live as when young. There are thus three kinds of imperative, of skill, prudence and morality. For every imperative expresses an ought, and thus an objective necessity, and this a necessity of free and good choice, for that pertains to the imperative mood, and necessitates objectively. All imperatives contain an objective necessitation, and this under the condition of a free and good choice. The imperatives of skill are problematic, those of prudence pragmatic, and those of morality ethical. Problematic imperatives say that under any rule a necessity of the will is indicated to some given end. The means are assertorically stated, but the ends are problematic. Thus practical geometry gives such imperatives. If a triangle is to be constructed, for example, or a square, or a hexagon, we must proceed according to the following rules. There is thus an arbitrary end, by prescribed means. Hence all practical sciences in general, such as geometry, mechanics etc., contain imperatives of skill. They are of great utility, and must precede all other imperatives, for one must be in a position to fulfil ends of any kind, and have means of achieving them, before one can 27:246 fulfil appointed ends. The imperatives of skill instruct us only hypothetically; for the necessity of using the means is always conditioned, namely in an acceptance of the end. Practical philosophy contains, not rules of skill, but rules of prudence and morality. It is thus a pragmatic and ethical philosophy, pragmatic in regard to the rules of prudence, and ethical in regard to those of morality.

Prudence is readiness in the use of means to the universal end of man, namely happiness, and thus here the end is already determined, which is not the case with skill. For the rule of prudence there are two requirements: to determine the end itself, and then the use of means to this end. It therefore involves a rule for judging what pertains to happiness, and the rule for using means to that happiness. Prudence is thus a preparedness to determine adequately both the end and the means. The determination of happiness is the primary thing in prudence, for many still dispute as to whether happiness consists in preserving or acquiring. The man who has no means, but also nothing of what can be obtained through these means, seems to be happier than he who has many means, but also many needs. Hence determination of the end of happiness, and what it consists of, is the first task of prudence, and the means to it the second. The imperatives of prudence do not enjoin under a problematic condition, but under an assertoric universally necessary one, found in all men. I do not say: 'Insofar as you wish to be happy, you must do this and that', but 'Because everyone wishes to be happy, which is presupposed of all, he must observe this'. It is thus a subjective necessary condition. I do not say: 'You are to be happy', for then it would be an objective necessary condition; I say, rather: 'Since you wish to be happy, you must do this and that.' We can, however, conceive yet another imperative, where the end is laid down with a condition that commands us not subjectively but objectively, and that is the moral imperative; 'You shall not lie', for example, is not a problematic imperative, for then it would have to run: 'If it does you no harm, then you should not lie'; rather, it commands categorically and absolutely 'You shall not lie'. So this imperative commands either unconditionally, or under an objectively necessary 27:247

condition. In the moral imperative the end is quite undetermined, nor is the action determined by the end, for it relates only to free choice, be the end what it may. Hence the moral imperative commands absolutely, without looking to the end. Our free acting and refraining has an inner goodness, and thus gives man an immediate inner absolute worth of morality. The man, for example, who keeps his word, always has an immediate inner worth of free choice, be the end what it may. But pragmatic goodness gives man no inner worth.

OF THE ETHICAL SYSTEMS OF ANTIQUITY

All ethical systems of the ancient world were founded on the question of the *Summum Bonum* and what it consists of, and the systems of antiquity are distinguished according to their answers to this question. This *Summum Bonum* I call an ideal, that is, the maximum case conceivable, whereby everything is determined and measured. In all instances we must first conceive a pattern by which everything can be judged: the *Summum Bonum* is scarcely possible, being merely an ideal, that is, a pattern, Idea or archetype of all our concepts of the good. What does the highest good consist in? The most perfect world is the highest created good. But the most perfect world involves the happiness of rational creatures and the worthiness of these creatures for such happiness. The ancients saw perfectly well that happiness alone could not be the one highest good, for if all men might secure this happiness, without distinction of the just from the unjust, then there would indeed be happiness, but no worthiness of it, and if the latter is included, then that is the highest good. Man can only hope to be happy insofar as he makes himself worthy of it, for that is the condition of happiness demanded by reason itself.

They also perceived that happiness rests on the goodness of the free will, on man's willingness to make use of everything that nature so abundantly bestows on him. Of a rich man with ample resources, the question is, what notion he has of making use of them. So the nature and perfection of the free choice which contains the ground of worthiness to be happy is moral perfection. Physical good or well-being, which involves health, wealth, etc. does not constitute the highest good. Imagine this: If the world were full of such rational creatures, who were all well-behaved, and thus worthy of happiness, and they were in the neediest circumstances, surrounded with sorrow and trouble, they would then have no happiness, and there would thus be no highest good there; while conversely, if all creatures were surrounded with happiness, and there was no good behaviour, no worthiness, there would then be no highest good either. In antiquity the ideal of the highest good took three forms:

27:248

1. The Cynic ideal, that is, the sect of Diogenes.
2. The Epicurean ideal, that is, the sect of Epicurus.
3. The Stoic ideal, that is, the sect of Zeno.

These sects are distinguished by concepts:

The Cynic ideal is that of innocence, or rather simplicity. Diogenes said the highest good consists in simplicity, in the sufficiency of the enjoyment of happiness. The Epicurean ideal was that of prudence. Epicurus said the highest good consists solely in happiness, and that good behaviour would only be a means to happiness. The Stoic ideal was that of wisdom; it is the reverse of the foregoing. Zeno said the highest good consists solely in morality, in worthiness, and thus in good behaviour; and this happiness would be a consequence of morality. He who behaved well would already be happy. The Cynic sect said the highest good would be a thing of nature and not art: For Diogenes the means of happiness were negative. He said that man is by nature content with little; because man, by nature, has no needs, he also does not feel the want of means, and under this want he enjoys his happiness. Diogenes has much in his favour, for the provision of means and gifts of nature increases our needs, since the more means we have, the more our needs are augmented, and the thoughts of man turn to greater satisfactions, so that the mind is always uneasy. Rousseau, that subtle Diogenes, also maintained that our will would be good by nature, only we always become corrupted; that nature would have provided us with everything, if we did not create new needs. He also argues that the education of children should be merely negative. Hume is opposed to this, for he claims that it is a matter of art and not nature.* Diogenes says: You could be happy without abundance, you could be moral without virtue. His philosophy was the shortest way to happiness; through sufficiency we live happily, in that we can do without everything. His philosophy was also the shortest way to morality, for if one has no needs, one also has no desires, and then our actions coincide with morality; for such a man, it costs nothing extra to be honest, and so virtue would be only an Idea. And simplicity is thus the shortest way to morality. The Epicureans maintained that the highest good would be a matter of art and not nature, as the Cynics said. So here was the difference between the two sects, in that the second was the opposite of the first. Epicurus said that even if we have no vice by nature, we do have an inclination to it, so that innocence and simplicity are not assured; art must be added to them, and in this Zeno agreed with Epicurus, since he also saw it as a matter of art. Thus if, for example, an innocent peasant girl is free from all ordinary vices, this is because she has no opportunity for indulging in them, and a farmer who lives on plain fare, and yet is content with it, does not do so

27:249

*[*Treatise of Human Nature*, Br. I, Pt. III, Sec IX. – Tr.]

45

because he sees it as all the same to him, but because he has nothing better, and if he were given the opportunity of living better, he would also covet it. So simplicity is merely negative. Thus Epicurus and Zeno accepted art, but it was different for each of them. The two elements of the highest good are: physical good and moral good – well-being and behaving well. Since all philosophy endeavours to bring about unity in our knowledge, and to reduce it to the fewest principles, the attempt was made to see if one principle might not be put together out of these two. Yet we call everything after the end and not the means. So on Epicurus' theory, happiness was the sole end, and worthiness merely a means, and thus morality would be a consequence of happiness. Zeno also sought to combine the two principles, and on his view morality would be the end. Worthiness and virtue, [however, would be in themselves the supreme good, and happiness therefore,] would be merely a consequence of morality.* The ideal and pattern of Diogenes is the man of nature; the pattern of Epicurus is the man of the world; the pattern or archetypal Idea of Zeno is the sage, who feels happiness within himself, who posseses everything, and who has in himself the source of cheerfulness and righteousness; he is a king, in that he rules over himself, and cannot be constrained, in that he constrains himself. Such a sage they ranked above the gods, for not much pertained to their gods, since divinity had no temptations or obstacles to overcome; but a sage of that kind would have attained to such perfection by his strength in overcoming obstacles. We can even conceive of a mystical ideal, in which the highest good consists in man seeing himself in communion with the highest being; this is the Platonic ideal, which is of a visionary character. The Christian ideal is that of holiness, and its pattern is Christ. Christ, too, is a mere ideal, an image of moral perfection who is holy by divine aid. But this must not be confused with the people who call themselves Christians, for they merely seek to come closer to this pattern or ideal.

27:250

Epicurus and Zeno were at fault, in that Epicurus wanted to give virtue motives and no value; the motive was happiness, and the value worthiness. Zeno extolled the inner value of virtue, and located the highest good in it, and took away the motives to virtue. The highest good of Epicurus was therefore happiness, or, as he called it, pleasure, that is, an inner contentment and a cheerful heart. One must be secure against all reproaches from oneself or others – but that is no philosophy of pleasure, and he has thus been poorly understood. We still have a letter from him,† in which he invites someone to dine, but promises to receive him with nothing else but a cheerful heart and a dish of polenta, a sorry meal for an epicure. Such pleasure was thus the pleasure of a sage. So he took away the value from virtue, in that he made morality into a means of happiness.

---

*[The passage in brackets is interpolated from Mrongovius, 27:1402, 29–31. – Tr.]
†[Letter to Menoikeus (see Diogenes Laertius, *De Vitis Philosophorum X, 130*). – Tr.]

Zeno did the opposite, locating happiness in value, and assigning no motive to virtue. Motives are all those grounds of our will which are drawn from the senses. The consciousness of worthiness to be happy still does not silence the desires of man, and if a man does not fulfil his desire, even though he feels in himself that he is worthy, he is not yet happy. Virtue pleases above all else, but does not satisfy, for in that case all the virtuous would be happy. Just because of this virtue, the desires of a virtuous man are all the stronger in their yearning for happiness; the more virtuous and the less happy a man is, the more painful it is for him, that he is not happy, though he is worthy of it; and then the man is content with his behaviour, but not with his condition. 27:251

Epicurus promised man contentment with himself, if he would only contrive that his condition be happy. Zeno promised man contentment with his condition, if he would only contrive that he be contented with himself.

Man can be contented or discontented with himself either pragmatically or ethically. But he very often confuses the two. He often thinks he has pangs of conscience, although he is only afraid of a tribunal of prudence. If we have offended someone in company, we reproach ourselves about it at home, yet these are the reproaches of a tribunal of prudence, in that we now have to reckon upon an enemy. For every reproach of prudence is for an act whereby harm arises. If we know that the other has not observed it, we are content; so it is a reproach of prudence, and yet we take it for a reproach of morality. Now Epicurus said: If you so conduct yourself that you have no reproaches to expect from yourself or others, you are happy. The ideal of holiness,* as philosophy understands it, is the most perfect ideal for it is an ideal of the greatest purely moral perfection, but because such a thing is unattainable by man, it is based upon a belief in divine assistance. It is not only worthiness to be happy that has the greatest moral perfection in this ideal, for it also has the greatest incentive, and that is happiness, but not in this world. Thus the ideal of the gospels has the greatest moral purity, and also the greatest incentive, namely happiness or blessedness. The ancients had no greater moral perfection than that which could come from the nature of man; but since this was very defective, their moral laws were also defective. So their ethical system was not pure; they accommodated virtue to human weakness, and hence it was incomplete. But in the gospel ideal everything is complete, and we there find the 27:252 greatest purity and the greatest happiness. The principles of morality are presented in all their holiness, and now the command is: You are to be holy; but because man is imperfect, this ideal has an adjunct, namely divine assistance.

*[Reading *Heiligkeit* for *Klugheit;* cf. Mrongovius, 27:1404, 3 – Tr.]

OF THE PRINCIPLE OF MORALITY

Now that we have considered the ideal of the greatest moral perfection, we need to see what the principle of morality consists in. No more has been said of it beforehand, than that it rests upon the goodness of free choice; but we have to inquire what the principle of morality actually is. It is in general very difficult to establish the first principle of any science, especially if it has already attained some magnitude. Thus it is hard, for example, to establish the first principle of law, or of mechanics. Yet since we must all have a principle of moral judgement, whereby we can unambiguously decide about what is morally good or bad, we perceive that there must be a single principle emanating from the ground of our will. It is now a matter of ascertaining this principle in which we situate morality, and whereby we can distinguish the moral from the immoral. Even if a man has many good talents and capacities, it still remains to ask what his character is like. Even if he possesses all kinds of goodness, we still want to know about his moral goodness. Now what, then, is the supreme principle of morality whereby we judge everything, and in what way does moral goodness differ from every other sort of goodness? Before we decide these questions, we must first set forth the division of the various viewpoints whereby the principle is specified in different ways. The theoretical conception of morality (which does not specify a theory, but only a concept from which a theory can be constructed) consists in this, that morality rests either on empirical or intellectual grounds, and must be derived from either empirical or intellectual principles. Empirical grounds are those that are derived from the senses, insofar as our senses are satisfied thereby. Intellectual grounds are those where all morality is derived from the conformity of our action with the laws of reason. So *systema* 27:253 *morale est vel empiricum vel intellectuale.*[a] If a system of ethics is based on empirical grounds, it rests either on inner or outer grounds, drawn from the objects of inner and outer sense. If morality rests on the inner grounds, then this is the first part of the empirical system; if it rests on outer grounds, then it is the second part of that system. Those who derive morality from the inner grounds of the empirical principle, postulate a feeling, a physical and moral feeling. The physical feeling consists in self-love, which takes two forms, vanity and self-interest. It aims at one's own advantage, and is a self-seeking principle, whereby our senses are satisfied. It is a principle of prudence. The authors who uphold the principle of self-love include, among the ancients, Epicurus, in that he employed, in general, a principle of sensuality, and among the moderns, Helvétius and Mandeville. The second principle of the inner ground of the empirical system arises if the ground is posited in the moral feeling whereby we can

---

[a] the moral system is either empirical or intellectual

48

discriminate what is good or bad. The leading authors are Shaftesbury and Hutcheson.

The empirical system of the theoretical concept of morality includes, secondly, external grounds. Those who posit morality therein say that all morality rests on two things: on education and on government. All morality would be merely a custom, and we judge by custom concerning all actions, by rules of education or by laws of the sovereign authority. So moral judgement arises by way of example or legal prescription. Montaigne took the first view. He says: In different parts of the world we also find that men differ in regard to morality; thus in Africa, theft is allowed, in China parents are permitted to throw their children on the street, the Eskimos strangle them, and in Brazil they are buried alive. The second view was taken by Hobbes. He says: the sovereign can permit all acts, and also forbid them, so actions cannot be judged morally by reason; we act, rather, by example of custom and by order of authority, so that there can be no moral principle other than what is borrowed from experience.

However, if the principle of morality rests on self-love, it rests on a contingent ground, for the nature of actions, whereby they bring me pleasure or not, rests on contingent circumstances. If the principle rests on a moral feeling, where the action is judged by the satisfaction or dissatisfaction, by the sensation or in general the feeling of taste, it also rests on a contingent ground. For if someone finds a thing congenial, another may have an aversion to it; thus savages, for example, spit out the wine that we drink with pleasure. And so it is also with the external grounds of education and government. Under the empirical system, the principle of morality rests on contingent grounds. 27:254

The second *systema morale* is the intellectual one. On this, the philosopher judges that the principle of morality has a ground in the understanding, and can be apprehended completely *a priori*. For example: You are not to lie; if this were to rest upon the principle of self-love, it would run: You are not to lie only if it brings harm your way, but if it profits you, then it is permitted. If it rested on the moral feeling, then anyone not possessed of a moral feeling so fine as to produce in him an aversion to lying would be permitted to lie. Were it to rest upon education or government, then anyone educated or living under a régime where lying is permitted, would be at liberty to lie. But if it rests on a principle that resides in the understanding, then the injunction is absolute: You are not to lie, whatever the circumstances may be. If I consider my free choice, it is a conformity of free choice with itself and others. It is thus a necessary law of free choice. But those principles which are supposed to be everywhere, always and necessarily valid, cannot be derived from experience, but only from pure reason. Yes, the moral law expresses categorical necessity, and not a necessity fashioned from experience. All necessary rules must hold good *a priori*, and hence the principles are intellectual. The judgement of morality does not take place at all through sensuous and empirical principles, for morality is no object of the senses, but rather an object merely of the understanding. This intellectual principle can take two forms:

1. Insofar as it rests on the inner nature of the action, so far as we apprehend it through the understanding.
2. It can also be an external principle, insofar as our actions have a relation to a being other than ourselves.

The latter is the theological principle of morality, and just as we have a moral theology, so we also have a theological morality. But this theological principle is also erroneous, for the difference between moral good and evil does not consist in relationship to another being; the intellectual moral principle is internal. Now what this inner intellectual principle consists in, it will be our aim in morals to determine, though it can only be extracted gradually, over time.

All imperatives are formulae of a practical necessitation. The latter is a making-necessary of free actions. But our actions, though, can be necessitated in two ways; they can either be necessary according to laws of free choice, and then they are practically necessary, or according to laws governing the inclination of sensuous feeling, and then they are pathologically necessary. So our actions are necessitated either practically, i.e. by laws of freedom, or pathologically, i.e. by laws of sensibility. Practical necessitation is an objective determination of free actions; pathological, a subjective one. So all objective laws of our actions are in every case practically and not pathologically necessary. All imperatives are mere formulae of practical necessitation, and express a necessity of our actions under the condition of goodness. The formula which expresses practical necessity is the *causa impulsiva* of a free action, and since it necessitates objectively, is called a *motivum*. The formula which expresses pathological necessitation is a *cause impulsiva per stimulos*,[b] since it necessitates subjectively. So all subjective necessitations are *necessitationes per stimulos*.[c]

The imperatives express objective necessitation, and since they are of three kinds, there are also three kinds of goodness.

1. The problematic imperative says that something is good as a means to any given end, and that is *bonitas problematica*.[d]
2. The pragmatic imperative is an imperative by the judgement of prudence, and says that the action is necessary as a means to our happiness. Here the end is already determined, so this is a necessitation of the action under a condition, but one which is necessary and universally valid, and that is *bonitas pragmatica*.[d]

---

[b] impelling cause due to stimuli
[c] necessitations by stimuli
[d] goodness for something/for happiness/moral goodness

3. The moral imperative expresses the goodness of the action in and for itself, so that moral necessitation is categorical and not hypotheti-   27:256
cal. Moral necessity consists in the absolute goodness of free actions, and that is *bonitas moralis.*[d]

From these three imperatives there arises the following:

All moral necessitation is an obligation, and the necessity of acting from rules of prudence, or pragmatic necessitation, is not. The obligation is thus a practical, and indeed moral one. All obligation is either from duty or coercion, of which more will be said hereafter.

All obligation is not merely a necessity of action, but also a constraining, a making-necessary of the action, and is thus *obligatio necessitatio,* and not *necessitas.*[e] In regard to morality the divine will is necessary, whereas the human will is not necessary, but constrained. Hence practical necessity, in the eye of the supreme being, is no obligation; He necessarily acts morally, but has no obligation. Why do I not say: God is duty bound to be truly holy? Moral necessity is an objective necessity, but if it is also a subjective necessity, it is no necessitation. It is an objective necessitation and an obligation only if the subjective necessity is contingent. All imperatives express the objective necessitation of actions which are subjectively contingent. For example, You should eat, if you are hungry and have food; this is a subjective constraint, and also an objective one, and therefore is no necessitation or obligation. So in the case of a perfect will, in which moral necessity is not only objectively but subjectively necessary, no necessitation or obligation arises; but in the case of an imperfect will, where moral good is objectively necessary, necessitation and constraint, and thus also obligation, do arise. Hence moral actions must be merely contingent if they are to necessitate, and those who have a morally imperfect will are bound in this way, and these are men. All obligation is, however, a *necessitatio practica,* not *pathologica,*[f] an objective and not a subjective constraint. A pathological necessitation occurs where impulses arise from the senses and the feeling of the pleasant and unpleasant. One who does something because it is pleasant is pathologi-   27:257
cally necessitated; one who does a thing that is good in and for itself, is acting from motives, and is practically necessitated. So the *causae impulsivae,* insofar they are drawn from the good, come from the understanding, and one who is moved to action by them is necessitated *per motiva;* but so far as they are drawn from the pleasant, they come from the senses, and one who is moved to action by them is necessitated *per stimulos.* Hence all obligation is neither a pathological nor a pragmatic necessitation, but a moral one. The motives are drawn either from pragmatic grounds, or from moral grounds of inner goodness.

[e] constraining obligation, not necessity
[f] a practical, not a pathological, necessitation

All pragmatic motives are merely conditioned, insofar as the actions are means to happiness, so here there is no ground for the action itself, but merely qua means. Hence all *imperativi pragmatici hypothetice necessitant et non absolute.*[g] But *imperativi morales necessitant absolute* and express a *bonitas absoluta,* just as the *imperativi pragmatici* express a *bonitas hypothetica.* So on grounds of prudence, truthfulness can be mediately good – in commerce, for example, it is as good as ready cash – but regarded in the absolute sense, to be truthful is good in itself, and for every purpose, and untruth is in itself vile. Hence moral necessitation is absolute, and the *motivum morale* expresses *bonitas absoluta.* How it is possible for an action to have *bonitas absoluta,* cannot yet be explained: but it must be noted in advance that the subjection of our will under the rule of universally valid ends is the inner goodness and absolute perfection of free choice, for then it is in conformity with all ends. This can easily* be shown in the present case; for example, truthfulness is in accordance with all my rules, for one truth concurs with another, and is thereby in conformity with all ends, and the willing of others, so that everyone can be guided by it. But lies contradict each other, and do not concur with my ends and those of others so that everyone can be guided by them. Moral goodness is thus the governance of our choice by rules, whereby all acts of my choice concur with universal validity. And a rule which is the principle of the possibility of conformity in all free choice, is the

27:258   moral rule. All free actions are determined neither by nature nor by any law, so that freedom is a terrifying thing, since the actions are not determined at all. Now in regard to our free actions a rule is needed whereby all actions concur, and this is the moral rule. If my actions are in accordance with the pragmatic rule, they do indeed concur with my own choice, but not with that of others, nor even always with my own, for they are drawn from well-being; but because we can have no *a priori* insight into well-being, it follows that we can give no *a priori* rule of prudence, but only an *a posteriori* one. Hence there can be no rule for all actions; if it were to be that, it would have to be *a priori.* Thus the pragmatic rules are in agreement neither with the choice of others, nor with my own. There must therefore be rules whereby my actions hold good universally, and these are derived from the universal ends of mankind, and by them our actions must agree; and these are moral rules. The morality of actions is something quite special, which differs from all pragmatic and pathological actions, so that morality must be expounded in a quite subtle, pure and special way. So although, if moral motives do not avail for moral goodness, pragmatic and even pathological *causae impulsivae* are taken, yet if it is a question of the goodness of actions, we do not ask what moved us to that goodness, but what the goodness of the actions consists of, in and for itself. The moral motive must therefore be consid-

---

*[Reading *leicht* for *nicht* – Tr.]
[g] pragmatic imperatives necessitate hypothetically and not absolutely

ered quite purely, in and for itself, and separated from the motives of prudence and the senses. In our hearts we are skilled enough by nature to distinguish moral goodness very accurately and subtly from problematic and pragmatic goodness, and then the action is as pure as if it came from heaven. And a pure moral ground has greater impulsion than when it is intermingled with pathological and pragmatic motives; such motives have more power to move at the sensuous level, but understanding looks to* the power that moves with universal validity. Morality is indeed unprepossessing; it is not so pleasing and enjoyable; but it has reference to universally valid satisfaction, and must thus be pleasing to the supreme being, and that is the highest motivating ground. 27:259

Prudence calls for good understanding, and morality calls for good will. Our free conduct rests solely on good will, if it is to have moral goodness, and thus our will can be good in itself. In prudence it is not a matter of the end, for all such action has the same end, namely happiness; it is a matter of the understanding, insofar as it perceives the end and the means of attaining it, and in this one person can be more prudent than another; so for prudence we need a good understanding, and for morality a will that is good in itself. For example, the will to become rich is good in relation to the end, but not in itself. We are now about to explain the nature of that will, absolutely good in itself, on which moral goodness depends.

The moral motive must not only be distinguished from the pragmatic; it cannot even be contrasted with the latter. To see this better, let it first be noted as follows.

All moral motives are either merely *obligandi*, or else *obligantia; motiva obligandi*[h] are grounds *ad obligandum*, to oblige a person; but if these grounds are sufficient, they are *obligantia*, binding grounds. *Motiva moralia non sufficientia non obligant, sed motiva sufficientia obligant.*[i] Thus there are moral rules of obligation which do not, however, bind, for example, to help a person in distress. But there are also intrinsically moral rules which oblige absolutely, and are thus not merely incumbent on me, but also binding, and make my action necessary, for example, You shall not lie. If we combine pragmatic and moral motives, are they homogeneous? No more than honesty, if a person lacks it, can be replaced by his having money, or than an ugly person acquires beauty if he possesses ample funds, can pragmatic motives be inserted into the series of moral motives and compared with them. Their necessitating powers can, however, be compared with one another. It seems as if, at the judgement-seat of the understanding, it is more expedient to prefer advantage over virtue.

*[Reading *nach* for *nicht* – Tr.]
[h] obliging/binding motives
[i] non-sufficient moral motives do not bind, but sufficient motives do

But moral perfection and advantage simply cannot be compared at all, any more than a mile can be compared with a year; for there is a difference here. But how does it come about that we do in fact confuse them? For

27:260 example, there is an unfortunate, and another says, You can indeed help him, but not to your detriment. Here, if understanding judges, there is no difference between the moral and the pragmatic motive, though there is between the moral and the pragmatic action; for it is not only prudence that tells me to look to my advantage; morality also enjoins me that I can best expend only the surplus of my resources on the unfortunate. For if a man gives away his means, he puts himself in want, and must himself then try to beg charity from others, and finds himself in no position to be moral. So objectively a moral motive cannot be set in contrast to the pragmatic one, because they are unlike.

DE OBLIGATIONE ACTIVA ET PASSIVA

Obligatio activa is an *obligatio obligantis*, and *obligatio passiva* an *obligatio obligati*, though the difference is unimportant. All obligations to generous actions are *obligationes activae;* I am constrained to the action, although it is a service. Acts whereby we can put others under obligation, if we perform them, are services. We are constrained to the action towards a person, without having an obligation to the person himself. *Obligati sumus ad actionem ita ut et illi non obligati sumus.*[j] We are obligated to the action, not to the person. If I am under an obligation to help the unfortunate, and thus to the action but not the man, that would be *obligatio activa*. But if I owe a debt to someone, I am obligated, not only to the act of payment, but also to the creditor, and that is *obligatio passiva*. It seems, however, that all *obligatio* is *passiva*, for if I am obligated then I am constrained. Yet with an *obligatio activa* there is a constraint of reason, I am constrained by my own reflection, so there is nothing passive about it; and *obligatio passiva* must come about through another, whereas if a man is necessitated by reason, he rules himself. The distinction of obligation is therefore correct. *Obligatio passiva est obligatio obligati erga obligantem, obligatio activa est obligatio erga non obligantem.*[k]

The author says: Obligations can be larger and smaller, and cannot conflict, for where something is morally necessary, no other obligation can make the opposite necessary. For example, the obligation to the creditor of

27:261 paying a debt, and of being grateful to one's father. If the one is to be called an obligation, the other is not; to my father I am conditionally obliged, but to my creditor, categorically so. So the one is an obligation,

---

[j] we are obligated to the action as such, and not to the person
[k] passive obligation is that which is owed to the recipient; active, that which is not owed to him

and the other not. In the one case there is a necessitation, and in the other not. We are thinking, therefore, of a conflict of motives, but not of duty.

Many obligations arise, grow and then cease. When children are born, an obligation arises, and as they grow, so do the obligations; when the child becomes a man (but not as a child) there is an end of the obligation that he owed as a child; he is still obligated indeed, yet not as a child, but to the benefits received from his parents. The more a labourer works, the more the obligation grows; once he is paid, the obligation ceases. Some obligations can never be discharged. For example, towards the benefactor who was first to show kindness to me; however much he is repaid for it, he still remains the first to have done me a favour, and I am permanently under obligation to him. Yet in one case the obligation terminates, namely if my benefactor plays me a scurvy trick, though this seldom happens, if only one is grateful to the benefactor.

The act whereby an obligation arises is called an *actus obligatorius.*[1] Every contract is an *actus* of that sort. An *actus obligatorius* can give rise to an obligation to myself, but it can also engender an obligation to another; for example, the begetting of children is an *actus obligatorius*, whereby the parents have imposed on themselves an obligation to the children. But I do not think that by procreation the children are obligated to the parents, for existence is no obligation, since to exist is no happiness in itself, and to be utterly unhappy one must, after all, exist; the children are, however, indebted to the parents for support. Where actions are simply not free, and nothing personal is involved, there is also no obligation; thus a man, for example, has no obligation to stop hiccuping, for it is not in his power. So for obligation we presuppose the use of freedom.

Obligation is divided into *positiva* and *naturalis*. The former has arisen by a positive and voluntary choice; the latter from the nature of the action itself. All laws are either natural or arbitrary. If the obligation has arisen   27:262 from the *lex naturalis,*[m] and has this as the ground of the action, it is *obligatio naturalis;*[n] but if it has arisen from *lex arbitraria*, and has its ground in the will of another, it is *obligatio positiva.* Crusius believes that all obligation is related to the will of another. So in his view all obligation would be a necessitation *per arbitrium alterius.*[o] It may indeed seem that in an obligation we are necessitated *per arbitrium alterius;* but in fact I am necessitated by an *arbitrium internum*, not *externum*, and thus by the necessary condition of universal will; hence there is also a universal obligation. All *obligatio positiva* is not directed immediately to the action; rather, we are obligated to an action which is in itself indifferent. Hence all *obligatio positiva* is *indirecta*

[1] obligating act
[m] natural law
[n] obligation of nature
[o] by the choice of another

55

and not *directa*. For example, if I am not supposed to lie because God has forbidden it, but has done so because it pleased Him, then He could also have not forbidden it, had He so wished. But *obligatio naturalis* is *directa:* I must not lie, not because God has forbidden it, but because it is bad in itself. All morality, however, rests on the fact that the action is performed because of the inner nature of the act itself; so it is not the action that makes for morality, but the disposition from which I do it. If I do a thing because it is ordained or brings advantage, and omit a thing because it is forbidden or brings harm, that is not a moral disposition. But if I do it because it is absolutely good in itself, that is a moral disposition. So an action must be done, not because God wills it, but because it is righteous or good in itself; and it is because of this that God wills it and demands it of us.

Obligatio can be *affirmativa* and *negativa,* and the latter is thus opposed, not to *positiva* but to *affirmativa,* as is likewise already assumed in law. A man has negative obligation *ad omittendum,*[p] and affirmative *ad committendum.* The *consectaria*[q] of an action are either good or bad, and can be *naturalia* or *arbitraria,* as well as *physica* or *moralia.* Our author takes *consectaria* to be *naturalia* or *arbitraria.* The former are those which flow from the action itself; the latter, those which flow from the will of another being, e.g. punishments. Actions are either directly good or bad in themselves, or are good or bad indirectly, or contingently.

27:263

The goodness of the action is thus either internal or external.

Moral perfection is either subjective or objective. The latter resides in the action itself; subjective goodness consists in the conformity of the action to the will of another. So *moralitas objectiva*[r] lies in the action itself. The supreme will, which contains the ground of all morality, is the divine will; so in all our actions we can consider either objective or subjective morality. There are objective laws of action, and these are *praecepta;*[s] the subjective laws of action are maxims, and seldom coincide with the objective laws. We can regard all objective morality as the subjective morality of the divine will, but not as that of the human will. The dispositions of the deity are morally good, but those of man are not. The dispositions or subjective morality of the divine are therefore coincident with objective morality, and if we act in accordance with the latter, we also act in accordance with the divine will, so that all moral laws are *praecepta*, since they are rules of the divine will.

In regard to moral judgement, all grounds are objective, and not one must be subjective. But in regard to moral impulses, there are subjective grounds. So grounds of decision are objective, but grounds of execution

[p] to abstain/to perform
[q] consequences
[r] objective morality
[s] precepts

can also be subjective; the distinction of what is morally good or bad must be judged by the understanding, and thus objectively, but in order to perform an action there can also be subjective grounds. The question of whether something is moral is one which refers to the action itself. Moral goodness is thus an objective thing, for it does not consist in conformity with our inclinations, but subsists in and for itself. All subjective laws are derived from the constitution of this or that subject and are also valid only in regard to this or that subject; they are restricted to him. But moral laws ought to be valid universally and as such of free actions, without regard to the diversity of the subject. In the divine will the subjective laws of that will are identical with the objective laws of the universally good will, but   27:264
God's subjective law is no ground of morality; it is good and holy because His will is in conformity with this objective law. So the question of morality has no relation at all to subjective grounds; it can only be framed on objective grounds alone. If we divide morality into objective and subjective, that is utterly absurd; for all morality is objective, and only the condition for applying it can be subjective.

The first moral law of our author is: *Fac bonum et omitte malum.*[t] The express meaning of the phrase is: *Fac bonum.* The good must be distinguished from the pleasant; the pleasant refers to sensibility, the good to the understanding. The concept of the good is a thing that satisfies everyone, and hence it can be judged by the understanding. The pleasant satisfies only according to private predilection. So the statement might mean: Do what your understanding presents to you as good, and not what is pleasant to your senses. The [implied] 'ought' always signifies the excellence of the good, and not of the pleasant, and so it is actually tautological. But in this statement the differentiation of goodness might already have been made. Do what is morally good. But in that case there ought to have been another rule, to tell us what moral goodness consists in. So it can in no way be a principle of morality. Not all imperatives are obligations, as the author thinks; thus *imperativi problematici*[u] are not obligations, as we saw above.

But obligation, according to our author, is the coupling of the most superior grounds to my action, for he says that the good contains impelling grounds to act, and the superior good has superior impelling grounds to act. But the statement *Fac bonum et omitte malum* can be no moral principle for obligation, for the good can be good in a variety of ways for any given purpose, since it is a principle of skill and prudence; only if it is good for moral actions would it then be a moral principle. It is therefore a *principium vagum.*[v] And besides that, it is also a *principium tautologicum.* A

[t] do good and abstain from evil
[u] problematic imperatives
[v] a vague principle

57

tautological rule is one which, when called upon to decide a question, gives an empty answer. If the question is, What am I to do in regard to my obligation?, and the answer is, Do the good and abstain from the bad, that is an empty answer, for *fac* means, in effect, It is good that it be done; so the statement runs: It is good that you do the good, and is therefore a tautology. It tells us nothing of what is good, saying merely that I should do what I should do. There is no science so filled with tautologies as ethics; it supplies for an answer, what was actually the question, and question and answer to the problem form a tautology. For to have what was implicit in the problem or question explicitly asserted in the answer, is tautological; and ethics is full of such statements, and many a one thinks he has done everything, once he has explained and pointed out the principles of ethics to his pupil in that way. If someone is costive, for example, and the doctor were to say: See that your bowels are loose, perspire freely and digest well, what he says is just what the patient wanted information about. These are tautological rules of decision.

But the question is, What are the conditions under which my actions are good? Our author says: *bonorum sibi oppositorum fac melius,*[w] so this follows from the previous tautology. Abnegation here means the sacrifice and self-denial where we make renunciation in regard to a small good in order to obtain a greater one. Sacrifice means tolerating an evil, so that a greater evil does not arise. Abnegation can be pragmatic or moral. I may forgo an advantage, where a greater is obtainable, and that is *abnegatio pragmatica.*[x] But if I forgo an action on moral grounds, in order to perform a greater, that is *abnegatio moralis.*[y]

The author's statement, as the ground of obligation: *Quaere perfectionem quantum potes,*[z] is indeed less indefinitely expressed; it is not a total tautology, and so has a degree of usefulness. What, then, is perfect? The perfection of thing and man is different. The perfection of a thing is the sufficiency of all that is needed to constitute the thing, so in general it means completeness. But the perfection of a man does not yet signify morality. Perfection and moral goodness are different. Perfection here is the completeness of the man in regard to his powers, capacity and readiness to carry out all the ends he may have. Perfection can be greater or less; one man can be more perfect than another. But goodness is the property of making good and proper use of all these perfections: So moral goodness consists in the perfection of the will, not the capacities. Yet a good will needs the completeness and capacity of all powers to carry out everything willed by the will. So we might say that perfection is indirectly

27:265

27:266

---

[w] of opposing goods, do the better
[x] practical self-denial
[y] moral self-denial
[z] seek perfection as much as you can

necessary to morality, and to that extent belongs to it, and that the proposition is indirectly a moral one. Another of the author's moral principles is: *Vive convenienter naturae.*[a] This is a Stoic principle. Where there are already many principles in ethics, there are certainly none, for there can only be one true principle. If the proposition is also stated as: Live according to the laws which nature gives you through reason, then it is still tautological, for to live according to nature would mean to direct one's action according to the physical order of natural things, and would thus be a rule of prudence, and so not a moral principle; and in fact not even a good rule of prudence, for if it tells us: Direct your actions so that they conform to nature, I do not know whether it is a good thing if actions conform to nature. Still less is it a principle of morality. The final principle is: *Ama optimum quantum potes.*[b] This statement is of no more use than its predecessors. We love everything that pertains to perfection and contributes anything to it, and to that extent everybody loves it. But there are two ways of loving anything: from inclination and from principle. Thus a rascal also loves the good on principle, but the bad by inclination.

So none of these statements are principles of morality.

OF MORAL COMPULSION

We begin by noting of compulsion in general that the necessitation is of two kinds, objective and subjective. Subjective necessitation is the idea of the necessity of actions *per stimulos,* or through the *causae impulsivae* of the subject. Objective compulsion is the constraining of a person through that which has the greatest constraining and moving power in his subject. Compulsion is therefore not a necessity, but a constraint to action. But the being who is constrained must be one who would not do this action without constraint, and would, indeed, have reasons against it. So God cannot be constrained. Compulsion is thus the constraining of an action unwillingly   27:267 performed. This constraint can be objective or subjective. Thus we forgo a thing unwillingly from one inclination, though we do it according to another; as a miser, for example, forgoes a small advantage if he thereby secures a greater; but unwillingly, since he would sooner have both. All compulsion is either pathological or practical. Pathological compulsion is the necessitation of an action *per stimulos;* practical is the necessitation of an unwillingly performed action *per motiva.* No man can be pathologically compelled, because of freewill. Human choice is an *arbitrium liberum,*[c] in that it is not necessitated *per stimulos;* if a man, for example, is forced to an

[a] live according to nature
[b] love the best as much as you can
[c] free choice

action by numerous and cruel tortures, he still cannot be compelled to do these things if he does not will it; he can, after all, withstand the torture. Comparatively speaking, he can be compelled, indeed, but not strictly; it is still possible to refrain from action, regardless of all sensory incentives – that is the nature of *arbitrium liberum*. Animals are necessitated *per stimulos*, so that a dog must eat if he is hungry and has something in front of him; but man, in the same situation, can restrain himself. Hence a man can be pathologically compelled, but only comparatively speaking, e.g. by torture. An action is necessary if one cannot resist it; grounds are necessitating if human powers are not adequate to resist them. But man can be practically compelled *per motiva*, and then is not compelled but moved. The compulsion, then, is not, however, subjective, for otherwise it would not, of course, be practical, and it takes place *per motiva* and not *per stimulos*, for stimuli are *motiva subjective moventes.*[d]

In a free being an action can be practically necessary, and that in a high degree, which simply cannot be surpassed – and yet it does not contradict freedom. Thus God must necessarily reward men whose behaviour is in accordance with the moral law, and then He has acted according to the rules of His own good pleasure, for the behaviour conforms to the moral law, and so also with the divine choice. Thus an honourable man cannot lie, but he refrains of his own will. So actions can be necessary without conflicting with freedom. This practical necessitation can occur only in

27:268 man, and not in God; for example, no man willingly gives away his possessions, but if he can save his children no otherwise than by the loss of what he has, then he does it, and is here practically necessitated. Hence a person constrained by motivating grounds of reason is constrained without it conflicting with freedom. We perform the actions reluctantly, indeed, but we do them nevertheless, because they are good.

OF PRACTICAL NECESSITATION

All necessitation is not only pathological, but also practical. Practical necessitation is not subjective, but objective, for if it were subjective it would be a *necessitatio pathologica*. No other necessitation save practical necessitation *per motiva* is compatible with freedom. These motives can be pragmatic and moral, the latter being drawn from the *bonitas absoluta* of the freewill.

The more a man can be morally compelled, the freer he is; the more he is pathologically compelled, though this only occurs in a comparative sense, the less free he is. It is strange: the more anyone can be compelled, in a moral sense, the more he is free. I compel a person morally through *motiva objective moventia*, through motivating grounds of reason, whereby

---

[d] subjectively moving motives

he is maximally free, without any incentive. Hence it takes a greater degree of freedom to be morally compelled, for in that case the *arbitrium liberum* is more powerful – it can be compelled by motivating grounds and is free of stimuli. So the more a person is free of stimuli, the more he can be morally necessitated. His freedom increases with the degree of morality. In God there is no *necessitatio practica*, for in Him the subjective laws are one with the objective. But in man there is a *necessitatio practica;* for he acts reluctantly, and so must be compelled. But the more he accedes to the moral ground of motivation, the more free he is.

The less obligation a man has, the freer he is. So far as anyone is under obligation, he is not free; but if it ceases, he becomes so. Our freedom is therefore diminished by obligation, but in God it is not diminished by moral necessity, nor is he obligated thereto; since such a will intrinsically wills what is good, He cannot be obligated, but men, because their will is evil, can be. So a man is not free if he has accepted favours. Yet, comparatively speaking, we can have more freedom in one case than in another.

27:269

A person under *obligatio passiva* is less free than one under *obligatio activa.* We cannot be compelled to any act of magnanimity, yet we are, however, obligated to such acts, and are therefore under *obligatio activa.* To the payment of debts we can be compelled, and are then under *obligatio passiva;* now anyone under *obligatio passiva* to a person is less free than he who can put him under obligation.

We have *obligationes internae erga nosmet ipsos,*[e] in regard to which we are outwardly quite free; anyone can do what he chooses with his body, and that is no concern of anyone else; but inwardly he is not free, for he is bound by the necessary and essential ends of mankind.

All obligation is a kind of compulsion; if this compulsion is moral, then we are either compelled from without, or we compel ourselves, and this is a *coercio interna.*[f] But a person can be morally compelled from without by others, if another exacts from us, according to moral motives, an action that we do with reluctance. If, for example, I am in debt to someone, and he says: If you wish to be an honest man, you must pay me; I will not sue you, but I cannot let you off, because I need it – then this is a moral compulsion from without, by the choice of another. The more a man can compel himself, the freer he is. The less he can be compelled by others, the more inwardly free he is. We still have to distinguish here between the capacity for freedom and the state of being free. The capacity for freedom can be greater, although the state is worse. The greater the capacity, and the more the freedom from stimuli, the freer a man is. If man were not in need of self-compulsion, he would be wholly free, for his will would then be entirely good, and he might willingly do all that is good, since he would

[e] inner obligations to ourselves
[f] inner compulsion

61

be in no need of compelling himself; but that is not the case with man. Yet one man may approach it nearer than another, if, that is, the sensory drives, the stimuli, are stronger in the second than the first. The more a person practises self-compulsion, the freer he becomes. Many a one is already by nature disposed to magnanimity, forgiveness and well-doing, and can thus the better compel himself, and is all the freer. But no man is above self-compulsion.

27:270

All obligation is either internal or external. *Obligatio externa est necessitatio moralis per arbitrium alterius.*[g] *Obligatio interna est necessitatio moralis per arbitrium proprium.*[h] A volition is a desire that I have in my power. But a wish is a desire that I do not have in my power. Necessitation by the will of another is *necessitatio moralis externa,* for the other has it in his power to compel me, and the obligation arising from this is *obligatio externa.* The *necessitatio moralis* that occurs, not through another, but of my own choice, is *necessitatio moralis interna,* and the obligation that arises from it is *obligatio interna.* I am obliged for example, to help another, but that is internal. Requital for an injury is morally necessary at the behest of another, and that is *obligatio externa.*

External obligations are greater than internal, for they are simultaneously internal, whereas the latter are not simultaneously external. *Obligatio externa* already presupposes that the action as such is subordinated to morality, and is therefore *interna;* for the *obligatio externa* is an obligation because the action is already one in the internal sense. For in that the action is a duty, that makes it an internal obligation, but because I can still compel a man to this duty at my own behest, it is also an *obligatio externa.* In *obligatio externa* I have to conform my action to the choice of another, and to this I can also be compelled by others. *Obligatio externa* can also be pathologically compelled by another; if he does not let himself be morally compelled, he is also entitled to compel pathologically. In general, every right entitles the possessor to compel pathologically.

Internal obligations are imperfect, because we cannot be compelled to them. But external obligations are perfect, since besides the internal obligation, there is a further external constraint thereto.

The motivating ground whereby we fulfil an obligation is either internal, and is then called duty, or external, and is then called compulsion. If I

27:271

satisfy my obligation by my own choice, then the motivating ground is internal, and I do the action from duty. The man who fulfils an obligation from duty, and he who does so from compulsion, have both fulfilled their obligation, but the former acts from internal grounds of motivation, and the latter from external. The sovereign is unconcerned as to what sort of motivating ground the obligations towards him are discharged from,

---

[g] external obligation is moral necessitation by another's choice
[h] internal obligation is moral necessitation by one's own choice

whether they are done out of duty or compulsion; it is all one to him. But parents demand obligation from children out of duty. So when our author divides obligations by whether they are done out of duty or compulsion, that is false. Obligation cannot be divided in that way, for compulsion does not make an obligation; obligations must be distinguished in themselves, namely insofar as they arise *ex arbitrio alterius,* in which case they are *externae,* or *ex arbitrio proprio,* in which case they are *internae,* as above. However, the *motiva satisfaciendi*[^i] for all obligations, whether they are *externae* or *internae,* can be distinguished as follows: If the motivating grounds are internal and flow from my choice, they are duties; if they flow from the choice of another, it is compulsion. But the obligations can be as they please. Objective motivating grounds are grounds of the disposition and determination of the will to satisfy the rule. As to their objective grounds the obligations are internal and external; as to their subjective grounds they are duty or compulsion.

All obligations whose motivating grounds are subjective or internal are ethical obligations. All whose motivating grounds are objective or external are, strictly speaking, juridical; the first are obligations of duty, the second of compulsion. The difference between law and ethics does not consist in the kind of obligation, but in the grounds that motivate us to fulfil the obligations. Ethics deals with all obligations, whether they be of charity, generosity and goodness, or of indebtedness, and considers them all together, only insofar as the motivating ground is internal; it discusses them as arising from duty, and the inner nature of the thing itself, and not from compulsion. But law considers the satisfaction of the obligation, not from duty but from compulsion; though attention is given to the springs of compulsion. Obligations are considered as they relate to compulsion. 27:272

We have obligations to God, but He demands, not only that we perform them, but that we should do so gladly, from inner grounds of motivation. We do not fulfil obligations to God when we do so out of compulsion, but rather out of duty. If I do a thing gladly, out of goodness of heart, I do it from duty, and the action is ethical; but if I do a thing out of compulsion, it is juridically correct. There is thus a true distinction of obligations, if they are divided into *internae* and *externae,* but the difference between ethics and law does not lie here, but rather in the motivating grounds to these obligations; for we can fulfil obligations out of duty and out of compulsion. The choice of another can constrain me to an external obligation, although he does not compel me, and then I do it out of duty; but if he does compel me, I do it out of compulsion. *Obligatio externa* is not such because I can be compelled by it. From the obligation there flows a title to compel; it is a consequence of the obligation.

[^i]: motives to performance

OF LAWS

Any formula which expresses the necessity of an action is called a law. So we can have natural laws, where the actions stand under a general rule, or also practical laws. Hence all laws are either physical or practical. Practical laws express the necessity of free actions, and are either subjective, so far as we actually abide by them, or objective, so far as we ought to do so. Objective laws are again of two kinds: pragmatic and moral. It is the latter that concern us here.

Law, so far as it signifies authority, is the agreement of the action with the rule of law, so far as the action does not conflict with the rule of choice; or is the moral possibility of the action, if it does not conflict with moral laws. But law, considered as a science, is the totality of all the laws that make up the Law. *Jus in sensu proprio est complexus legum obligationum externarum, quatenus simul sumuntur.*[j] *Jus in sensu proprio est vel jus late dictum, vel jus stricte dictum.*[k]

27:273 *Jus late dictum* is the law of equity. *Jus stricte dictum* is the strict Law, so far as it has authority to compel others. So there is free Law and compulsory Law. Ethics stands in contrast to *jus strictum*, and not to *jus* in general. It relates to laws of free action, so far as we can be compelled thereto. *Jus stricte* is either *positivum seu statutarium,*[l] or *jus naturale.*[m] *Jus positivum* is that which arises from human choice, whereas *jus naturale* arises insofar as it is discerned by reason from the nature of the actions. *Jus positivum est vel divinum vel humanum.*[n] *Jus positivum* contains commands within it, but *jus naturale* laws. Divine laws, however, are also at the same time divine commands, so that *jus naturale* is at the same time the *jus positivum* of the divine will, not insofar as such laws lie solely in His will, but in that they lie in the nature of man; not the other way round, however: All divine laws are natural laws, for God can also give a positive law. *Jus positivum*, no less than *jus naturale*, can be either free Law or compulsory Law. Many laws are merely rules of equity. The *jus aequitatis*[o] is less cultivated, however, than could be wished, albeit not because the courts ought to judge by it, since there they are only required to judge *valide*. The *jus aequitatis* is not, however, an external Law, but only holds good *coram foro conscientiae.*[p] In *jus positivum* and *naturale* we are always referring to *jus strictum*, and not to *jus aequitatis*, since the latter pertains only to ethics. All duties, even compulsory ones, if the motivating ground for fulfilling them is drawn from inner nature, belong at once to

[j] law in the proper sense is the complex of external legal obligations, so far as they are taken together

[k] law in the proper sense is either broadly or strictly construed

[l] positive or statute law

[m] natural law

[n] positive law is either divine or human

[o] law of equity

[p] before the bar of conscience

ethics. For in content laws may belong either to *jus* or ethics, but they need not do so by content alone, since they may also belong to *jus* or ethics in virtue of the motivating ground. The sovereign does not require that a subject pay his taxes willingly, but ethics does demand this. Both he who pays willingly and he who pays from compulsion are equally subjects, since they have both made payment.

The disposition cannot be required by the sovereign, since it is not known, in that it is internal. But now ethics tells us to act from a good disposition. The observance of divine laws is the sole case where *jus* and ethics coincide, and both, in regard to God, are compulsory laws, for God can compel us to ethical and juridical actions; but He requires the actions, not out of compulsion, but from duty. So an action can have *rectitudo juridica*[q] so far as it accords with compulsory laws, but the conformity of the action to the laws out of dispositions and duty – that possesses morality, which consists, therefore, in the disposition to act from goodwill. Hence the moral goodness of the action is to be distinguished from its *rectitudo juridica*. *Rectitudo* is the genus; if it is merely juridical, then it has no moral goodness. Thus religion can have *rectitudo juridica*, if the divine commands are done from compulsion and not from a good disposition. But God desires, not the action, but the heart. Heart is the *principium* of moral disposition. So God desires moral goodness, and this is worthy of reward. Hence the disposition to performance of duties is to be cultivated, and this is what the teacher of the gospels says: that we should do everything from the love of God. But to love God is to do His commands gladly. 27:274

Leges can also be *praeceptivae*, whereby something is commanded; *prohibitivae*, whereby actions are forbidden; and *permissivae*, whereby actions are allowed. *Complexus legum praeceptivarum* is *jus mandati;*[r] *complexus prohibitorum* is *jus vetiti;*[s] and one might also conceive of a *jus permissi* as well.

OF THE SUPREME PRINCIPLE OF MORALITY

We first have to take up two points here: (1) The principle of appraisal of obligation, and (2) the principle of its performance or execution. Guideline and motive have here to be distinguished. The guideline is the principle of appraisal, and the motive that of carrying-out the obligation; in that they have been confused, everything in morality has been erroneous.

If the question is: What is morally good or not?, that is the principle of appraisal, whereby I judge the goodness or depravity of actions. But if

[q] legal rectitude
[r] the complex of preceptive laws is mandatory law
[s] the complex of prohibiting laws is interdictory law

the question is: What moves me to live according to this law?, that is the principle of motive. Appraisal of the action is the objective ground, but not yet the subjective ground. That which impels me to do the thing, of which understanding tells me that I ought to do it, is the *motiva subjective moventia*. The supreme principle of all moral judgement lies in the understanding; the supreme principle of the moral impulse to do this thing lies in the heart. This motive is the moral feeling. Such a principle

27:275 of motive cannot be confused with the principle of judgement. The latter is the norm, and the principle of impulsion is the motive. The norm is the understanding, but the motive is in the moral feeling. The motive does not take the place of the norm. Where motive is lacking, we have a practical fault, and where judgement is lacking, a theoretical one. We are now going to show briefly, in a negative way, what the principle of morality does not consist in. The *principle of morality* is not *pathological;* it would be so, if it were derived from subjective grounds, from our inclinations and feelings. Morality has no pathological principle, for it contains objective *laws of what we ought to do,* and *not of what we want to do.* It is not a species of inclination, but a caution against all inclination. The *pathological* principle of morality would consist in *giving satisfaction* to all one's inclinations; that would be a brutish Epicureanism, though it is not yet the true Epicureanism.

We can, however, envisage two *principia pathologica* of morality; the first aims at the satisfaction of all inclinations, and this is physical feeling. The second aims at the satisfaction of an inclination directed to morality, and would thus be grounded on an intellectual inclination, as to which, however, we shall show at once that an intellectual inclination is a contradiction. For a feeling for objects of the understanding is in itself an absurdity, and hence a moral feeling out of intellectual inclination is likewise absurd, and thus not possible. I cannot hold a feeling to be anything ideal;* it cannot be something both intellectual and sensory. And even if it were possible that we should have a sensation for morality, no rules could be established on this principle, for a moral feeling says categorically what ought to happen, whether it pleases us or not; and is hence no satisfaction of our inclination. Were it so, there could also be no moral law, and everyone might act according to his feeling. Supposing the feeling were present in all men to the same degree, there would still be no obligation to act according to the feeling; for in that case it could not be affirmed that we ought to do what pleases us, but only that anyone might do such a thing himself, because it pleases him. The moral law, however, commands categorically; so morality cannot be based on a pathological principle, either of physical or moral

27:276 feeling. This method of appealing to feeling in a practical rule is also

*[Reading *Ideales* for *Reales* – Tr.]

wholly contrary to philosophy. Any feeling has a private validity only, and is not accessible to anyone else, and is also in itself pathological; if someone says he feels it so in himself, that cannot hold good for others, who do not even know how he is feeling, and once anyone appeals to a feeling he is giving up all grounds of reason. The pathological principle therefore does not occur. Hence there has to be a principle of morality that is intellectual, insofar as it is borrowed from the understanding. This consists in the rule of the understanding, either so far as the latter gives us the means to hand of so framing our actions, that they coincide with our inclinations, or so far as the ground of morality might be immediately known through the understanding. The first is indeed an intellectual principle, so far as understanding furnishes us with the means, but still it is obviously rooted in the inclinations. This intellectual pseudo-principle is the pragmatic principle. It rests on the aptitude of the rule to satisfy our inclinations. This principle of prudence is the true Epicurean principle. So when it is said that you ought to promote your happiness, this amounts to saying: Use your understanding to discover the means of satisfying your inclinations and taste for pleasure; such a principle is intellectual, inasmuch as the understanding is supposed to draw up the rule for using the means to promote our happiness. Hence the pragmatic principle depends on the inclinations, in that happiness consists in the satisfaction of all inclinations. But morality is not grounded on any pragmatic principle, since it is independent of all inclinations. If it were so grounded, there could be no agreement among men in regard to morality, since everyone would seek his happiness according to his inclinations. But morality cannot rest on the subjective laws of human inclinations, and so its principle is not pragmatic. It must, indeed, be an intellectual principle, but not mediately, as the pragmatic is; it has, rather, to be an immediate principle of morality, insofar as the ground of morality is immediately known through the understanding. It is thus an utterly pure intellectual principle of pure reason. Such a principle cannot, however, again be tautological, and consist in the tautology of pure reason, like that put forward by Baron Wolff: *Fac bonum et omitte malum*, which, as seen above, is empty and 27:277 unphilosophical. A second tautological principle is that of Cumberland, which consists in truth. We all seek perfection, he says, but are betrayed by illusion; morality, however, shows us the truth. A third is Aristotle's principle of the mean, which is consequently tautologous. This pure intellectual principle must not, however, be a *principium externum*, so far as our actions relate to another, and so it does not depend on the divine will; nor can it say: Thou shalt not lie, because it is forbidden. Thus the principle of morality, since it cannot be external, cannot be tautological. Those who think otherwise are saying that we must first have God, and then morality afterwards, which is a very convenient principle. Neither ethics nor theology is a principle of the other, although theology cannot, indeed, exist without ethics, or ethics without theology. But the question here is not whether theology is a motive to ethics, which it undoubtedly is, but whether the principle of moral appraisal is a theological one, and this it cannot be. If that were so, then all peoples would first have to know God before they could have the notion of duties; and thus it would have to follow that all peoples having no proper conception of God would also have no duties, which is, however, false. Peoples have perceived their duties correctly, and recognized the odiousness of lying, without having any proper notion of God. Other peoples, moreover, have created merely pious and false conceptions of God, and yet still had correct ideas of their duties. The duties must therefore be borrowed from another source. The cause of this derivation of morality from the divine will is as follows: Because moral laws run, Thou shalt not, it is supposed that there must be a third being, who has forbidden it. It is true that any moral law is an order, and they may be commands of the divine will, but they do not flow from such a command. God has commanded it because it is a moral law, and His will coincides with the moral law. It also seems that all obligation has a relation to one who obliges, and thus God appears to be the obligator of human laws. In performance, to be sure, there must indeed be a third being, who constrains us to do what is morally good. But for the making of moral judgements we have no need for any third being. All moral laws

27:278 can be correct without such a being. But in execution they would be empty if no third being could constrain us to them. It has therefore been rightly perceived that without a supreme judge all moral laws would be without effect, since in that case there would be no inner motive, no reward and no punishment. Hence the knowledge of God is needed in the execution of moral laws. How, then, do we know the divine will? Nobody feels such a will in his heart, nor can we know the moral law, either, from any revelation, for if so, those who had none would be totally ignorant of it; whereas even Paul himself says* that such people also are guided by their reason. So we know the divine will through our reason. We conceive of God as possessing the holiest and most perfect

[27:1425] will.† [Now the question is, which is the most perfect will? We are shown this by the moral law, and thus we have the whole of ethics. We now say that the divine will is in accordance with the moral law, and that is why His will is the holiest and most perfect. We therefore recognize the perfection of the divine will from the moral law. God wills everything that is morally good and appropriate, and that is why His will is holy and most perfect. What is in fact morally good, is shown to us by ethics.

*[Romans 2:12–15 – Tr.]
†[The rest of this section is from the text of Mrongovius, 27:1425.32–1430.11. – Tr.]

All theological concepts are the more corrupt, the greater the corruption of the moral concepts. If the concepts of morality in theology and religion were pure and holy, there would be no endeavour to please God in a manner that is human and highly unsuitable to Him. Everyone conceives of God according to the notion that is most familiar to him. E.g., as a great, powerful and mighty ruler, who is something more than the mightiest ruler on earth; and thus everyone also frames for himself a concept of morality that matches the concept he has already fashioned of God. Men therefore try to please God by glorifying and praising Him, and extol Him as a lord so great that He is nowhere to be found; perceiving their faults, they believe that all men have such failings, that none is able to do anything good; hence they gather all their sins into a heap and lay them at God's feet, and sigh, and think thereby to honour Him, and do not see that a praise so trifling, from such worms as we are, is a slur upon God, and that they simply cannot praise Him. To honour God is to do His bidding gladly, not to exalt Him with laudatory phrases. But if an honest man tries to practise the moral law from pure motives, because of the inner goodness of the actions, and does God's bidding with gladness, he honours God. If, however, we are to carry out His commands because He has ordained it, and because He is so mighty that He can make us do it by force, then we act under orders, from fear and terror, and simply fail to perceive the justice of the injunction; nor do we know why we ought to do what God has commanded, and why we should be obedient to him; for the *vis obligandi*[t] cannot consist in force, since one who threatens does not obligate, but extorts. So if we are to abide by the moral law out of fear for God's punishment and power, and this because it has no ground other than that God has commanded it, then we do so not from duty and obligation, but from fear and terror, though that does not better the heart. If, however, the act has arisen from an inner principle, and if I do it, and do it gladly, because it is absolutely good in itself, then it is truly pleasing in the sight of God. God wishes to have dispositions, and they must come from an inner principle, for if we do a thing gladly, we do it also from a good disposition.

[27:1426]

Even if the divine revelation should be well expounded, it must be done according to the inner principle of morality. To act morally is not piety, therefore, as it would be on the theological principle; to act morally is virtue, though if it occurs according to God's beneficent will, then it becomes piety.

Having shown what the principle of morality does not consist in, we now have to show what it does consist in. The principle of morality is *intellectuale internum;*[u] it must be sought through pure reason in the action

---

[t] obligative power
[u] internal to the mind

itself. What, then, does it consist in? *Morality* is the conformity of the action to a universally valid law of free choice. All morality is the relationship of the action to the universal rule. In all our actions, that which we call moral is according to rule – this is the essential part of morality, that our actions have their motivating ground in the universal rule. If I make it the basis for my actions, that they conform to the universal rule which holds good at all times and for everyone, then they have arisen from the moral principle. For example, to keep one's promise as a means of procuring happiness is not moral, for if everyone wished to keep his promise as he might choose, then in the end it would be of no use at all; but if I judge by the understanding whether it is a universal rule, and keep my promise in that I perceive that everyone else ought to keep their promises to me, then my action is in conformity with the universal rule of all choice. Or take the act of benevolence. Suppose someone is in the utmost need, and I am in a position to help him, but am quite indifferent to his situation, and would actually prefer to use the money for my own pleasure; I now examine this according to my understanding, as to whether it can be a universal rule, and whether it would also be my choice, in such need, that another should be equally indifferent to me; if I then find that it does not accord with my choice, then the action itself is not moral. Every man who is against morality has his maxims. A precept is an objective law, by which we ought to act; but a maxim is a subjective law by which we actually do act. Everyone sees the moral law as something he can openly profess. But everyone sees his maxims as something that must be kept hidden, because they are contrary to morality, and cannot serve as a universal rule. A person, for example, has the maxim of becoming rich, since otherwise he would not attain his goal, if he made it known to anyone; were this to become a universal rule, then everyone would want to become rich, and since all would know it, and all be striving to that end, it would then be impossible to become rich. The examples of duties to oneself are rather harder to discuss, since they are the least known, and it must strike us as strange that those duties which most nearly concern us are the least familiar to us; they are confused, moreover, with the pragmatic rules of promoting one's well-being, of which more anon. For example, can a person, for the sake of profit, do harm to himself in his own body? Can he sell a tooth, or offer himself for money to the highest bid? What does morality consist in here?

I examine by the understanding whether the intention of the action is so constituted that it could be a universal rule. The intention is to magnify one's advantage, and I now see that in such a case the man is making himself into a thing, and an instrument of animal gratification; but as men we are not things, but persons; so here one dishonours humanity in one's own person. So it is also with suicide; by the rule of prudence there might be cases where to escape from all one's troubles one may kill oneself; but

[27:1427]

it is contrary to morality, for the intention is, by sacrificing one's condition, to abandon at a stroke all the pains and hardships of life; but in so doing, humanity is subordinated to animal nature, and my understanding is under the sway of animal impulse; and if so, I contradict myself when I demand to have rights of humanity. [27:1428]

In all moral judgements we frame the thought: What becomes of the action if it is taken universally? If, when it is made into a universal rule, the intention is in agreement with itself, the action is morally possible; but if not, then it is morally impossible. For example, lying, in order to obtain a large estate, becomes impossible to achieve if practised universally, since everyone knows the aim already. An immoral action, therefore, is one whose intention abolishes and destroys itself if it is made into a universal rule. The understanding is the faculty of rules; if our actions are consistent with the universal rule, they are consistent with the understanding, and then they have motivating grounds in the understanding. So if the action is done because it concurs with the universal rule of the understanding, it has come about *ex principio moralitatis puro intellectuali interno.*[v] Now since the understanding is the faculty of rules and judgement, morality consists in the subordination of the action as such to the principle of the understanding. But how the understanding might contain a principle of actions is somewhat difficult to see. In no sense does it contain the end of the action; the morality of the action consists, rather, in the universal form of the understanding (which is purely intellectual), assuming, that is, that the action is taken universally, so that it can exist as a rule. It is here that we have to bring in the already-mentioned distinction between the objective principle of the appraisal of the action, and the subjective principle of its performance. Of the former we have just been speaking, but the subjective principle, the motive, is the moral feeling. We now come again upon the feeling, which in another connection we have previously rejected. The moral feeling is a capacity for being affected by a moral judgement. When I judge by understanding that the action is morally good, I am still very far from doing this action of which I have so judged. But if this judgement moves me to do the action, that is the moral feeling. Nobody can or ever will comprehend how the understanding should have a motivating power; it can admittedly judge, but to give this judgement power so that it becomes a motive able to impel the will to performance of an action – to understand this is the philosophers' stone. The understanding pays regard to everything that eliminates the possibility of rules; it accepts everything that accords with the use of its rule, and opposes itself to everything that is contrary to that rule. Now since immoral actions are contrary to rules, in that they cannot be made into a universal law, the understanding is resistant to them, because they run counter to the use of its rule. Hence,

---

[v] from a pure principle of morality internal to the mind

in virtue of its nature there resides in the understanding a moving force.

[27:1429] Actions have therefore to be so constituted that they accord with the universal form of the understanding and can at all times become a rule; if so, the action is moral. Which, then, is at fault, if the action is not moral – the understanding or the will? If the understanding is lacking, i.e., if it is not well instructed in the appraisal of the action, then it is morally imperfect, although the badness of the action does not lie in the appraisal and therefore is not to be imputed to the understanding, but rather to the motive of the will. When a man has learnt to appraise all actions, he still lacks the motive to perform them. The immorality of the action consists, therefore, not in the want of understanding, but in the depravity of the will or the heart. The will is depraved when the motive power of the understanding is outweighed by sensibility. The understanding has no *elateres animi*,[*w*] albeit it has the power to move, or *motiva;* but the latter are not able to outweigh the *elateres* of sensibility. A sensibility in accordance with the motive power of the understanding would be the moral feeling; we cannot, indeed, feel the goodness of the action, but the understanding resists any action that runs counter to the rule, and this antagonism of the understanding is the motivating ground, if it could move sensibility to concur and to motivate, that would be the moral feeling. What, then, is the condition for a man to have moral feeling? Anyone can see when an action is abhorrent, but only he who feels this abhorrence has a moral feeling; the understanding does not abhor, but it sees the abhorrency and is averse to it; only the sensibility, however, must abhor. When, therefore, sensibility abhors what the understanding considers abhorrent, this is the moral feeling. It is quite impossible to bring a man to the point of feeling the abhorrency of vice, for I can only tell him what my understanding perceives, and I do indeed bring him also to the point of perceiving it; but that he should feel the abhorrence, if his senses are not susceptible to it, is impossible. Such a thing simply cannot be produced, for man has no such secret organization, that he can be moved by objective grounds. Yet we can indeed produce a *habitus*,[*x*] which is not natural, though it replaces nature, and becomes habitual through imitation and frequent exercise.

All methods, however, for making vice abhorrent to us, are false. We should instil an immediate abhorrence for an action from early youth onwards, but not a mediate one, which has only a pragmatic use; we must represent an action, not as forbidden or as harmful, but as inwardly abhorrent in itself. For example, a child who tells lies must not be punished, but shamed; we must cultivate an abhorrence, a contempt for this act, and by frequent repetition we can arouse in him such an abhorrence

[27:1430] of the vice as can become a *habitus* with him. But if he is punished for it in

---

[*w*] mental springs of action
[*x*] habitual response

school, he thinks that once out of school you are absolved of punishment and also of the act, and will thereafter try to avoid punishment by trickery. Many people also think this way, and form the intention of undergoing conversion shortly before their end, and making everything right again, which is accordingly just as good as if they were to have lived morally all their lives; so in this connection they consider sudden death to be unlucky. Education and religion should therefore set out to instil an immediate abhorrence of evil in actions, and an immediate delight in their morality.] Our author continues with 27:279

DE LITTERA LEGIS

The coupling of the law with the causes and grounds on which it rests is *littera legis*. We can discern the meaning of the law when we discern the principle from which it is derived, though we can define the meaning even without discerning the principle.

The meaning that words have in the law is the *anima legis*. Such words already have a meaning, but they may also have another which departs from the common usage, and that is *anima legis*. For example, in the divine positive law of the sabbath, the meaning is not just rest, but ceremonial rest.

But *anima legis*, if it actually means the spirit of the law, does not signify the meaning, but the motivating ground. In every law the action itself, which takes place according to it, conforms to the *littera legis*. But the disposition from which the action proceeds is the spirit of the law. The action itself is *littera legis pragmaticae;*[y] but the disposition is *anima legis moralis.*[z] The pragmatic laws have no spirit, for they require no dispositions, only actions, but the moral laws have a spirit, for they require dispositions, and the actions only have to evince the dispositions. So one who performs the actions without good dispositions is fulfilling the law *quoad litteram,*[a] but not in spirit. Divine and moral laws can be fulfilled, in a pragmatic sense, merely *quoad litteram.* For example, a person nearing his end, thinks that if there is a God, He must reward all good actions. So if he has money, he cannot employ it to any better advantage than by doing good deeds with it, with the intention, merely, of being rewarded by God; the Bible* calls this the mammon of unrighteousness, and says that the children of darkness are wiser than the children of light, because one of them has now done what the moral law requires to be done, but without disposition, so that he has fulfilled it *quoad litteram.* However, the *anima*

---

*[Luke 16:8–9 – Tr.]
[y] the letter of a pragmatic law
[z] the spirit of a moral law
[a] as to the letter

legis moralis was not fulfilled, since it requires morally proper dispositions. It is not all one, and a matter of indifference, what sort of motivating ground the action is done from. The moral law is thus the only one to have spirit; in general, an object of reason has spirit, but now my advantage is not an object of reason, so that an action which proceeds from that
27:280 intention also has no spirit.

In explaining *jus,* our author is so discursive that he merely illustrates words, and takes the ethical along with the juridical. Obligation is ethical, if the ground of obligation lies in the nature of the action itself; but juridical, if that ground lies in the choice of another. The difference of ethics from law therefore consists in this:

1. that its laws have no relation at all to other people, but only to God and oneself;
2. that if it relates to other laws, the obligation to action has its ground, not in the *arbitrium* of another, but in the action itself;
3. that the motivating ground of its obligation to fulfil is, not compulsion, but free disposition or duty.

The outer motivating ground is compulsion, and the action is juridical; the inner is duty, and the action is ethical. In juridical obligation we do not ask about the disposition, which can be what it will, so long as the action takes place. In ethical obligations the motivating ground must be internal; one must do the action because it is proper, I must pay my debt, not because the other can compel me, but because it is proper so to do.

Our author also speaks here of the transgression or violation of laws, of their observance, and of the persons against whom we act, or of injury. The law is not injured, but violated; it is the person who can be injured. Injury does not arise in ethics, for I injure no man if I fail to perform ethical duties towards him. So *oppositio juris alterius*[b] is an injury. Antinomy or conflict can occur among laws, if they merely enunciate the ground of obligation; but if they oblige in themselves, they cannot conflict.

The author presents three propositions which he takes to be axioms of morality: *Honeste vive;*[c] *neminem laede;*[d] *cuique suum tribue.*[e] We shall show what they mean, so far as they are supposed to have validity as moral axioms. The first proposition, *honeste vive,* can be regarded as a universal principle of ethics, since the motivating ground of satisfying its obligation
27:281 is taken, not from compulsion, but from inner motivation. *Honestus* means that behaviour and characteristic of a man, when he does anything, which is honorable. The proposition could also run: Do what makes you an

[b] contravention of another's right
[c] live honestly
[d] harm nobody
[e] render to everyone his due

object of respect and esteem. All our duties to ourselves make such a reference to respect in our own eyes, and approval in that of others. A person is of little account, the less inner worth he has in himself. The infamy of another excites hatred, the worthlessness evokes contempt. We should therefore, on this principle, so act as to be worthy of honour, to deserve respect and esteem from all, if it were generally known. For example, unnatural sins are such that they dishonour humanity in one's own person. Such a man is unworthy of honour, and if it becomes generally known, he is treated with contempt. That man is worthy of positive honour, whose actions are meritorious, and contain more than they are due to contain. But that man is merely not unworthy of honour, who has abstained from anything shameful; he is merely honest, though that is no merit, but the minimum of morality, since so far as there is any deficiency in it, one is already a rogue. Hence the state of that country is very poor, where honesty is held in high regard; for it is very unusual and rare there, which is why it is much esteemed. But only those actions are ethical which contain more than due performance requires. If I act in such a way as to do no more than what I am liable for, I have merely lived honestly, but deserve no honour on that account. But if I do more than I am liable for, that is an honourable action, and only such actions appertain to *honestas.* Hence this principle of ethics is still possible in that sense. The other two propositions: *Neminem laede* and *suum cuique tribue,* can be regarded as principles of juridical obligation, since they relate to compulsory duties. For to give everyone his own is as much as to say that you must allow to everyone what he can demand from you under compulsion. Both propositions can be combined, for if I take his own from somebody, I injure him. I can injure a person, either by omission, when I fail to give him his own, or by commission, when I take his own away from him. So I can take his own from a person either negatively or positively. The negative is the more important, since there is more involved in taking his own from another than in not giving it to him. So injury consists in an action which is contrary to the law of another. For if I injure a person, he has a right to 27:282 demand from me what is necessary by universal laws of choice. In ethics the laws have a relation to the will of another. *Ethice obligans respectu aliorum est felicitas aliorum, juridice obligans respectu aliorum est arbitrium aliorum.*[f] But the first condition of all ethical duties is this, that requital is first given to the juridical obligation. The obligation which arises from the right of the other must first be satisfied, for if I am also under juridical obligation I am not free, since I am subject to the other's choice. But if I now wish to perform an ethical duty, I wish to perform a free duty; if I am not yet free from the juridical obligation, I must first discharge it by

[f] the ethically obliging, with respect to others, is their happiness, the legally obliging, with respect to others, is their choice

fulfilling it, and only then can I perform the ethical duty. Thus very many neglect the duties they are bound to, and wish to perform those that are meritorious. Thus a man who has done much injustice in the world, and deprived many of their possessions, ends by making bequests to the hospital. But it is a penetrating and brazen voice that cries out at that point, that one's debts are not yet paid, nor can such a person silence it by all his dutiful actions; and such meritorious acts are an even greater transgression, since they are given as bribes and presents to the supreme being, to make good the offence. So happiness is not, therefore, the chief motivating ground for all duties. Thus a person cannot make me happy against my will; if so, he does me wrong. Hence the practice of compelling others to be happy in your own fashion is a use of force – for example, the pretext used by the gentry towards their inferiors.

OF THE LAWGIVER

Moral and pragmatic laws need to be distinguished. In a moral law it is dispositions that are referred to; in a pragmatic law it is actions. Hence governments oblige us to actions only, and not to dispositions. Pragmatic laws can be given, as is easy to see, but whether anyone can give moral laws, and command our dispositions, which are not in his power – that must be looked into. Anyone who declares that a law in conformity with 27:283 his will obliges others to obey it, is giving a law. The lawgiver is not always simultaneously an originator of the law; he is only that if the laws are contingent. But if the laws are practically necessary, and he merely declares that they conform to his will, then he is a lawgiver. So nobody, not even the deity, is an originator of moral laws, since they have not arisen from choice, but are practically necessary; if they were not so, it might even be the case that lying was a virtue. But moral laws can still be subject to a lawgiver; there may be a being who is omnipotent and has power to execute these laws, and to declare that this moral law is at the same time a law of His will and obliges everyone to act accordingly. Such a being is then a lawgiver, though not an originator; just as God is no originator of the fact that a triangle has three corners.

The spirit of moral laws lies in the dispositions, and such laws can simultaneously be regarded as divine commands, since they conform to His will. They can also, however, be seen as pragmatic laws of God, insofar as we merely look to the actions that are ordained in the law. For example, the moral law tells us to promote the happiness of all men, and God wills this also; if I now act in accordance with the divine will, and practise well-doing to obtain rewards from God thereafter, I have not done the action from any moral disposition, but by reference to the divine will, in order to be rewarded later on. Insofar as a man may have fulfilled the divine law in a pragmatic sense, he has at least satisfied the law, and may to that extent expect good consequences, in that he has, after all, done what God wanted, even though the disposition was impure. But God wills the disposition; morality is what conforms to His will, and as laws of that kind they already oblige absolutely. If an action is done in accordance with morality, we then have the greatest conformity with the divine will. We have therefore to regard God, not as a pragmatic lawgiver, but as a moral one.

OF REWARDS AND PUNISHMENTS

A *praemium* must be distinguished from a *merces.*[g] *Praemia* are either *auctorantia* or *remunerantia.*[h] The former are those rewards where the actions are motivating grounds, and are done merely for the sake of the promised rewards; *remunerantia* are those rewards where the actions are not motivating grounds, being performed from a good disposition alone, from pure morality. The former are incentives, the latter requitals. Hence *praemia auctorantia* cannot be *moralia,* though *praemia remunerantia* can be. The former are pragmatic, and the latter moral. If a person performs an action on grounds of physical welfare, purely for the sake of the promised reward, his act possesses no morality, and he thus can expect no *praemia remunerantia,* but only *praemia auctorantia.* But actions done solely from good disposition and pure morality are capable of receiving *praemia remunerantia. Praemia auctorantia* include many purely natural consequences and expectations; health, for example, is a *praemium auctorans* of temperance; but I can also be temperate on moral grounds. Honesty, likewise, if it is practised for the sake of advantage and approval, has a *praemium auctorans.* One who practises it on moral grounds is eligible for a *praemium remunerans.* Such *praemia* are larger than the other kind, since here the action is in accordance with morality, and that confers the greatest worthiness to be happy. Hence the *praemia moralia* must also be greater than the *pragmatica.* The former have an infinite goodness. The morally disposed agent is eligible for an infinite reward and happiness, because he is always ready to perform such acts of goodness. It is not good when *praemia auctorantia* are introduced in religion, and we are urged to be moral because we shall be rewarded for it hereafter; for nobody can demand that God should reward him and make him happy. He may anticipate reward from the supreme being, who holds him innocuous, due to the performance of such acts; but the reward must not be the motivating ground for performing the action. Man can hope to be happy, yet that must not move, but only console him. The man who lives morally can hope to be rewarded for it, but this cheerful mood does not arise from the

27:284

---

[g] payment
[h] reward as incentive/as requital

motivating ground of the reward; for men still have no proper conception of the happiness to come, and nobody knows what it will consist in, since providence has carefully hidden it from us. If man were to know that happiness, he would wish to arrive at it without delay. But nobody does that; every man wishes to linger here longer and longer, and however highly the happiness to come may be commended to him, over his present miserable existence, nobody is in a hurry to get there, for he thinks he will reach it soon enough, and it is also natural that we should all have more taste for this present life, since it can be known and felt more clearly. It is futile, therefore, to represent the *praemia* as *auctorantia,* though they can well be conceived as *remunerantia,* and that, too, is every man's hope; for the natural moral law already carries such promises with it, for a subject having morally good dispositions, and provided nobody has cried up and commended these *praemia remunerantia* to him. Every upright man has this belief; he cannot possibly be upright, without hoping at the same time, on the analogy of the physical world, that such righteousness must also be rewarded. From the very same grounds on which he believes in virtue, he also believes in reward.

27:285

Merces is a payment that may rightfully be demanded of someone. It must therefore be distinguished from reward. If a man expects his payment, he demands it from another in accordance with the latter's indebtedness. From God we can ask no payment for our actions, since we have, after all, done nothing to benefit Him, but have merely done for our own good everything that was incumbent on us to do. But while we can expect no payment from God for our services, we can in fact expect *praemia gratuita,*[i] which might well be regarded as payment, especially with respect to other people, to whom we have behaved well. We can now look upon God as one who pays all human debts, in that He repays those deserving acts that we have performed towards others, which we had no obligations to do for them. Thus we really do have deserving acts, not towards God, indeed, but to other people. Such a person is thereupon indebted to me, and cannot in any way discharge that debt; but God pays it all for him, as is also said in the Gospels:* "Inasmuch as ye have done it unto one of the least of these, ye have done it unto me," etc. etc. The doer has thus earned a payment from others, for which God, however, repays him. We must not adopt here an imagined purity of morals, and strike out all deserving actions. For God wills the happiness of all men, and this by human agency, and if only all men together were unanimously willing to promote their happiness, we might make a paradise in Novaya Zemlya. God sets us on a stage where we can make one another happy; it rests entirely upon us. If men are wretched, it is their own fault. Thus a man is often in distress, but

27:286

*[Matt. 25, 40 – Tr.]
[i] gratuitous rewards

not because God wills it. Yet God leaves him in distress as a sign to those who allow him to suffer, though together they could help him. God does not wish a single one of us to fare ill. He has determined us all to unite in helping one another. Hence our author's statement: Do that which procures you the most reward, is obviously contrary to morality. The motivating ground there, is the reward that offers most. However, Do what is worthy of the greatest reward, would be correct.

Punishment in general is the physical evil visited upon a person for moral evil. All punishments are either deterrent or retributive. Deterrent punishments are those which are pronounced merely to ensure that the evil shall not occur. Retributive punishments, however, are those pronounced because the evil has occurred. Punishments are therefore a means of either preventing the evil or chastising it. All punishments by authority are deterrent, either to deter the transgressor himself, or to warn others by his example. But the punishments of a being who chastises actions in accordance with morality are retributive.

All punishments belong either to the justice or the prudence of the lawgiver. The first are moral, the second pragmatic punishments. Moral punishments are imposed because a sin has been committed; they are *consectaria* of moral transgression. Pragmatic punishments are imposed so that sin shall not be committed; they are means of preventing crime. Our author calls them *poenae medicinales,* and they are either *correctivae*[j] or *exemplares.*[k] The *correctivae* are imposed in order to improve the criminal, and are *animadversiones.* The *exemplares* are given as an example to others. All the punishments of princes and governments are pragmatic, the purpose being either to correct or to present an example to others. Authority punishes, not because a crime has been committed, but so that it shall not be committed. But every crime, in addition to this punishment, has a property of deserving to be punished, because it has taken place. Such punishments, which must therefore necessarily follow upon the actions, are moral in character, and are *poenae vindicativae;*[l] just as a reward follows upon a good action, not so that further good actions should be done, but because there has been a good action done. If we compare punishments   27:287 and rewards, we notice that neither ought to be regarded as motivating grounds of the actions. Rewards should be no inducement to do good actions, and punishments no inducement to refrain from bad ones, since both engender a low habit of mind, namely *indoles abjecta.*[m] In those moved by reward to perform good actions it is called *indoles mercennaria,*[n] and in

[j] corrective punishments
[k] exemplary punishments
[l] retributive punishments
[m] submissive character
[n] mercenary character

those restrained by penalties from bad ones, *indoles servilis;* but both go to make up *indoles abjecta.* The motivating ground should be moral. The ground for doing a good action should not be made to lie in the reward; the action should be rewarded because it is good. Nor, either, should the ground for refraining from bad actions be made to lie in the punishments; the actions should be refrained from, because they are bad. Rewards and punishments are merely subjective motivating grounds; if objective grounds no longer avail, the subjective serve merely to replace the want of morality. The subject must first be habituated to morality; before coming primed with rewards and punishments, the *indoles erecta* must first be excited, the moral feeling first made active, so that the subject can be actuated by moral motives; if they do not avail, we must then proceed to the subjective motivating grounds of reward and punishment. A person rewarded for good actions will again perform them, not because they are good, but because they are rewarded, and a person punished for bad actions hates, not the actions, but the punishment. He will do the evil deed anyway, and try, with Jesuitical cunning, to evade the punishment. It is therefore not good in religion to preach the avoidance of evil-doing on the motivating grounds of eternal punishment, for everyone will then do the evil, and think in the end to escape all punishment by a hasty conversion. Yet rewards and punishments can indeed serve indirectly as means in the matter of moral training. A person who does good actions for the sake of reward becomes afterwards so accustomed to them that he later does them even without reward, simply because they are good. If a person refrains from bad actions because of the punishment, he gets used to this, and finds that it is better not to do such things. If a drunkard abstains from tippling because it is doing him harm, he gets so used to this that he subsequently does without, even in the absence of harm, and merely because he sees that it is better to be sober than a drunkard. Rewards are in better accordance with morality, since I do the action because its consequences are agreeable, and will be able to cherish the law which promises me reward for my good deed; but I cannot so love the law which threatens punishment. Love, however, is a stronger motivating ground for doing the action. Hence it is better in religion to begin with rewards than with punishments. The latter, moreover, must be in keeping with *indoles erecta,* with an honourable attitude; they must not be contemptuous or abusive, for then they produce an insensitive state of mind.

27:288

DE IMPUTATIONE

All imputation is the judgement of an action, insofar as it has arisen from personal freedom, in relation to certain practical laws. In imputation, therefore, there must be a free action and a law. We can attribute a thing to someone, yet not impute it to him; the actions, for example, of a

madman or drunkard can be attributed, though not imputed to them. In imputation the action must spring from freedom. The drunkard cannot, indeed, be held accountable for his actions, but he certainly can, when sober, for the drunkenness itself. So in imputation the free act and the law must be conjoined. A deed is a free action that is subject to the law. Now if I attend to the deed, that is *imputatio facti,* if I attend to the law, it is *imputatio legis.*[o] In *imputatio facti* we find *momenta in facto,* i.e., the manifold in the deed, which forms the ground of imputation. *Momenta* are elements of the ground, parts of the sufficient reason, and are thus, *in facto, momenta* of the imputation. They do not yield any imputation, but are the ground of it. *Momenta* are either *essentialia* or *extra essentialia.* The former must first be collected; if all the *momenta essentialia in facto*[p] are stated, that is *species facti,*[q] which expressly belongs to the *factum.* The *extra essentialia facti*[r] are not *momenta facti,* and so do not belong to the *species facti.* In 27:289
imputatio facti the *imputatio legis* must not simultaneously enter; e.g., a man may indeed have killed another, but yet not murdered him. The first question is whether the action was done by him. If the *factum* is to be directly imputed under the law, then there are likewise two imputations. *Imputatio legis* is the question whether the action falls under this or that practical law. It is the question whether one may impute to someone what he had to do in virtue of the law, to a general, for example, the death of so many foes left on the battlefield. Their death, to be sure, not their murder. But here he is considered insofar as his action was not free, but compelled by law, and in that sense it cannot be imputed to him. As a free action it would be ascribed to him, but as a legal action not to him, but to whoever gave the law. All imputation that takes place generally is made either *in meritum,* as a merit, or *in demeritum,*[s] as a fault. The consequences and effects of actions can be either imputed to a person, or not.*

[OF IMPUTATION OF THE CONSEQUENCES OF ACTIONS

The consequences and effects of action may be imputed to somebody, or [27:1438]
not. As to the imputation of consequences, the following should be noted: If my well-doing is more or less than is required of me, that may be imputed to me in regard to the consequences, but if I do neither more nor less than is due, it cannot be so imputed. If I do no more good than is

*[The section that follows is translated from the text of Mrongovius, 27:1438, 12–43; a better version at this point. – Tr.]

[o] imputation of fact/of law

[p] key elements in an act

[q] type of act or situation

[r] inessential features

[s] imputation of merit/of fault

required, the outcome cannot be imputed to me as a merit or service; for example, if I discharge my debt, and the other has thereby achieved a great stroke of fortune, this good consequence of the action cannot be imputed to me as a merit, since the thing had to be done as a matter of liability, and no overplus is therefore laid to my credit; but if I also do no less than I have to, the outcome cannot be laid to my discredit either. On the other hand, however, all the consequences of actions may be laid to my account, insofar as my well-doing is more or less than I am liable for. If I do more than I have to, the result is attributed to me as a merit; for example, an advance payment that I have made to somebody, and by which he has achieved a great stroke of fortune, can be imputed to me with all its consequences, since I have done more than I had to. And the result of my action is also imputed to me as a demerit, if I do less than I am required to; for example, if I do not pay my debt on time, and the other goes bankrupt in consequence, the outcome is imputable to me.

So if I merely do what is requisite, nothing can be ascribed to me in demerit, or merit either; for example, were someone to say: "If only you had then advanced me so much, I would not have got into difficulties", his troubles cannot be imputed to me, since I was not called upon to do it. For insofar as a man does what he has to, he is not free, because he has done the action in that he was necessitated by the law. But if he acts contrary to his obligation, it is imputed to him, because there he is acting freely, and contrary, indeed, to the law that necessitates him to the action; he is thus misusing his freedom, and here all the consequences can legitimately be imputed to him. For to act contrary to obligation is still an exercise of freedom.

27:289   *Juridice*, the consequences of an act to which a person was constrained, are not imputed to him *in demeritum*, since in that case he was not free; he is responsible for the *factum*, indeed, but not for the wrongness of it. In

27:290   regard to the performance of ethical actions, man is free, and hence all consequences can be imputed to him; but those consequences that arise from the non-performance of ethical action cannot be imputed, since it cannot be regarded as an action when I leave undone what I had no liability to do. So ethical omissions are not actions; but juridical omissions are, and can be imputed, for they are omissions of that to which I can be necessitated by law; but to ethical actions I cannot be necessitated; nobody can compel me to acts of benevolence. So the key to all imputation in regard to consequences is freedom.]

OF GROUNDS OF MORAL IMPUTATION

Imputatio moralis can occur in connection with both juridical and ethical laws, and consists in *meritum* and *demeritum*. The observance of juridical laws, and the violation of ethical laws can be imputed neither *in meritum*

nor *in demeritum.* Conversely, the violation of juridical laws, and the observance of ethical laws must at all times be imputed *in demeritum* and *in meritum.* So in the observance of juridical laws there is no *meritum,* either of reward* or punishment. But in the observance of ethical laws, every action is a *meritum,* since they are not compulsive laws, and their violation is also no *demeritum.*

A *meritum* always has positive consequences, either of reward or punishment. All observances of juridical laws, and all violations of ethical laws, are without positive consequences. The observance of juridical laws has only negative consequences, e.g., if I pay my debt, I shall not be taken to court. But the violation of juridical laws, and the observance of ethical ones, always have positive consequences. Everything said about imputation here holds only in regard to other men, not in regard to God.

DE IMPUTATIONE FACTI

Facta juridice necessaria[1] cannot be imputed, since the action is not free. *Facta* which are contrary to the juridical law can be imputed, since the action is free. In ethical action it is the other way about. Hence the action that is imputed in the juridical context is a bad one, and in the ethical context a good one; for ethical laws are not compulsive, though juridical ones are.

27:291

OF DEGREES OF IMPUTATION

Degrees of imputation depend on the degree of freedom. The subjective conditions of freedom are the ability to act, and further, that we know what pertains thereto, that we are aware of the motivating ground and the object of the action. In the absence of these subjective grounds there is no imputation. Thus when children destroy something useful, it cannot be imputed to them, because they know not what they do; one can, indeed, impute actions in a certain degree; everything is imputable that pertains to freedom, even though it may not have arisen directly through freedom, but indirectly nevertheless. E.g., what a person has done in a state of drunkenness may well not be imputed; but he can be held accountable for having got drunk.

The same causes which bring it about that a thing cannot be imputed to somebody may also be imputed to him in a lower degree. We have impediments and conditions to imputation. The more an action has impediments, the more it can be imputed, and the less an action is free, the less imputable it is. The degree of morality in actions must not be con-

*[Reading *Belohnung* for *Belobung* – Tr.]
[1] acts required by law

fused with the degree of imputability of the *factum*. If a person kills somebody in a fit of passion and wrath, he has not incurred so much evil as one who deals another a fatal thrust in cold blood, though the *factum* of the first is the greater. The action to which I have to force myself, and where I have many impediments to overcome, is the more imputed, the more wilfully it is performed, and the less, also, is its omission imputed. If a hungry man steals food, for example, it is not so harshly imputed to him, since he would have had to restrain himself severely. The appetites demand self-restraint; but if they should be thought to alter the degree of imputation, what would be the consequences of that? Yet natural appetite and greediness must be distinguished, the one being not so harshly imputable as the other. Greediness can be eradicated, and must not take root; hence it cannot be so much imputed to a person, if he does a thing under pressure of hunger, as if he did it from lust. Of natural inclination it should be noted, however, that the more a man struggles against it, the more he is deserving of credit; hence virtue is more to be imputed to us than to the angels, since they do not have so many impediments thereto. The more a person is compelled to an action from outside, the less it is imputed to him. Yet if he overcomes the compulsion and actually refrains from the action, that is all the more imputed to him. There are *merita* and *demerita conatus*,[u] and *merita* and *demerita propositi*[v] can also be added in here. People consider it to their credit, if they had the intention of doing a thing. Where there is *propositum*, no action can be imputed, since it is not yet an action, but where there is *conatus*,[w] there can be such imputation, since that is already an action; in the subject everything is sufficient for action, and his powers are being applied; but because they are not adequate, the effect does not come about.

27:292

Now since we only conclude to the sufficiency from the outcome, and so cannot tell whether the *conatus* was already present and there was merely a deficiency of power, the courts of justice do not impute the *conatus* in the way that ethical laws do; for example, a person bent on killing someone in the room, and caught with the dagger, is not considered a murderer under juridical laws, although the *conatus* was present. The reason is that the *conatus* often cannot be regarded as an *actus*. A person may have the intention, and be entertaining such wickedness in his heart, but when he would proceed to the action, he is horrified by its atrocity, and so changes his intention. Hence judges adopt the surest method of protecting the innocent, since there is, after all, no proof. But morally speaking, a complete *propositum* is as good as the deed itself. Though it has to be such that it might also persist in the execution as well.

[u] merits/demerits of attempt
[v] merits/demerits of intention
[w] endeavour or attempt

A *consuetudinarius*[x] is one who makes the action necessary to himself out of habit. Habit makes for ease in the performance, but in the end it also produces necessity. This necessity from habit lessens the imputation, since it has fettered our choice; although the *actus* whereby the habit has been acquired is imputable. So habit reduces the degree of imputation; for example, if a person has been reared among gypsies, where the habit of evil-doing has become a necessity, the imputation must be lessened. Yet habit is a proof of the frequent repetition of the action, and so is all the more imputable. If someone has often repeated a good action, and it has therefore become a habit with him, this is all the more imputed to him. And the same applies to ill-doing. Innate passions are therefore not so imputable as those acquired by custom, which through repeated arousal have come to be a necessity.   27:293

We now come, in conclusion, to two points which might be regarded as grounds of imputation, namely the weakness of human nature, and its frailty.

The weakness of human nature consists in its want of sufficient moral goodness to make the action adequate to the moral law. But its frailty consists, not only in its want of moral goodness, but also in the prevalence therein of even the strongest principles and motivations to ill-doing. Morality consists in this, that an action should arise from the motivating grounds of its own inner goodness, and this pertains to moral purity, known as *rectitudo moralis.* The latter, therefore, is the highest motivating ground to an action. But although the understanding is well aware of this, such a motivating ground still has no driving force. Moral perfection meets with approval, to be sure, in our judgement, but since this motivating ground of moral perfection is produced from the understanding, it does not have a driving force so strong as the sensory one, and that is the weakness of human nature, when it lacks moral goodness and *rectitudo.* However, let us not brood upon the weakness of human nature, and wonder whether it be incapable of moral purity; for the endeavour to find all one's actions impure is apt to cause a man to lose self-confidence in his ability to perform good and morally pure actions, and to believe his nature too weak and incapable for that; we have to believe, rather, that *rectitudo moralis* might be a strong motivating ground for us. The human soul is not totally devoid of all motivating grounds from pure morality; if a destitute person, for example, himself begs us for something, we are moved by pity towards him, and give him a trifle, which we would not have done if he had not been present himself, and had merely made his request in writing. Or if, on a journey, we see blind people lying at the roadside and give them something, we do not, in that case, have any other motivating ground, of honour or self-interest, since we then have to move on from

[x] creature of habit

there; we do it, rather, from the inner morality of the action; so there is something morally pure in our heart; it just does not have a wholly sufficient driving force, on account of our sensory impulses. However, the judgement as to the purity of morality brings with it numerous motivating grounds of purity, by way of association, and pushes our actions on more, and we grow accustomed to this. So we must not seek out the flaws and weaknesses in the life of a Socrates, for example, since it helps us not at all, and is actually harmful to us. For if we have examples of moral imperfection before us, we can flatter ourselves at our own moral imperfection. This desire to hunt for faults betrays something ill-natured and envious in seeing the morality that shines in others, when we do not possess it ourselves.

The principle we draw from the weakness of human nature is this: moral laws must never be laid down in accordance with human weakness, but are to be presented as holy, pure and morally perfect, be the nature of man what it may; this is very worthy of note.

The old philosophers demanded no more of men than they were able to perform; but their law lacked purity. Their rules were thus accommodated to the capacity of human nature, and where they elevated themselves above this, the motive for doing so was not pure moral judgement, but pride, honour, etc. in the exercise, for example, of extraordinary bravery or magnanimity. Only since the time of the evangelists has the complete purity and holiness of the moral law been perceived, though it lies in our own reason. The law must not condone anything; on the contrary, the utmost purity and holiness must be displayed in it, and in virtue of our weakness we must look for divine aid to make us able to fulfil the holy law, and to replace whatever purity is lacking in our actions. But the law must in itself be pure and holy. The reason is that the moral law is the archetype, the yardstick and the pattern of our actions. But the pattern must be exact and precise. Were it not so, by what are we supposed to judge everything? So the highest duty is therefore to present the moral law in all its purity and holiness, just as the greatest crime is to subtract anything from its purity.

In regard to the frailty of human nature, we observe that it is indeed correct, that our nature is frail, and not only possesses no positive good, but in fact has even positive evil. Yet all moral evil arises from freedom, since otherwise it would not be *moral* evil, and however prone we may also be to this by nature, our evil actions still arise from freedom, on which account they are also debited to us as vices.

The principle, therefore, in regard to the frailty of human nature, is this, that in judging action I must not take this frailty into consideration. The law must be holy, and the sentence within us, in accordance with this law, must be just, that is, the penalties of the law must be applied with all precision to the actions of men.

Fragilitas humana[y] can therefore never be a ground, *coram foro humano interno,*[z] for diminishing imputation. The inner tribunal is correct; it looks at the action for itself, and without regard to human frailty, if only we are willing to hear and feel its voice; suppose, for example, that I have insulted someone in company, by my words, and return home; it then troubles me, and I wish for an opportunity of repairing the situation. By no means must I rid myself of these inner reproaches, however many plausible excuses I may have, which would certainly be sure to weigh with any earthly judge. One is a man, after all, and how easily a word can escape one; but all this counts for nothing before the inner judge, who attends not at all to the frailty of nature, but examines the action as it is in itself. From this it is also clear that motivating grounds of pure morality do exist in human nature, and that we have no need to inveigh so much at its weakness. *Fragilitas* and *infirmitas humana*[a] can only be taken into account when judging the actions of other people; in regard to my own actions, I myself must not count on them, and thereby excuse what I do. Man, as a pragmatic lawgiver and judge, must take *fragilitas* and *infirmitas humana* into consideration when dealing with others, and remember that they are only human; but in regard to himself he must proceed with complete strictness.

Imputatio valida[b] is a legally effective imputation, whereby the *effectus a lege determinato*[c] is set in train by the *judicium imputans.*[d] We can pass judgement on all men, and anyone may do so, but we cannot sentence them, since our *imputatio* is not *valida,* which is to say that my judgement does not have the authority to set in train the consequences *a lege de-* | 27:296
terminata. The judgement which is authorized to bring about the *consectarium* that the law has determined is a legally effective imputation; but in order that the judgement may bring about the consequences determined by the law, it must have power. So without power there is no legally effective judgement. He who has authority to judge with legal effect, and also the power to carry it out, is a magistrate. The office of magistrate therefore contains two parts: The authority to judge with legal effect according to the law, whether a *factum certum*[e] is a *casus datae legis;*[f] but also the ability to apply a law *valide* to the *factum;* so he must have power to fulfil the law.

Judex is that person (*vel physica,* if he is only one, *vel moralis,*[g] where

---

[y] human frailty
[z] before the inner human tribunal
[a] human infirmity
[b] legally effective imputation
[c] effect determined by law
[d] sentencing authority
[e] ascertained fact
[f] case under a given law
[g] a single or collective judge

there are several, though they are seen as one), who has the authority and power to judge action with legal effect. Different persons belong under different *fora*, just as different actions also do. *Judex non competens*[h] is one who either does not understand how to judge at all, or does not have the authority to judge, in that he has been deprived of it, through having been deposed; or he may also be an authentic judge, though the *factum* does not belong under the law that he has to preside over; or he is also *non competens* if he cannot procure justice for anyone.

The *forum* is of two kinds. *Forum externum*, which is the *forum humanum*, and *forum internum*, which is the *forum conscientiae*.[i] With this *forum internum* we couple, at the same time, the *forum divinum*;[j] for in this life our *facta* can be imputed before the *forum divinum*, no otherwise than *per conscientiam;* hence the *forum internum* is a *divinum* in this life. A *forum* is required to exercise compulsion; its judgement has to have the force of law; it should be able to compel the execution of the *consectaria* of the law.

We have a faculty of judging whether a thing is right or wrong, and this applies no less to our own actions than to those of others. This faculty resides in the understanding. We also have a faculty of liking and disliking, to judge concerning ourselves, no less than others, what is pleasing or displeasing there, and this is the moral feeling. Now if we have presupposed the moral judgement, we find, in the third place, an instinct, an involuntary and irresistible drive in our nature, which compels us to judge with the force of law concerning our actions, in such a way that it conveys to us an inner pain at evil actions, and an inner joy at good ones, according to the relationship that the action bears to the law.

27:297

It is thus an instinct for us to judge and pass sentence on our actions, and this instinct is conscience. Hence it is not a free faculty. If it were a voluntary capacity, it would not be a tribunal, since in that case it could not compel. If it is to be an inner tribunal, it must have power to compel us to judge our actions involuntarily, and to pass sentence on them, and be able to acquit and condemn us internally.

Everyone has a faculty of speculative judgement, though that is at our discretion; there is, however, something in us which compels us to pass judgement on our actions. It sets the law before us, and obliges us to appear before the court. It passes sentence on us against our will, and is thus a true judge. This *forum internum* is a *forum divinum*, in that it judges us by our very dispositions, and we cannot, indeed, form any concept of the *forum divinum* other than that we must pass sentence on ourselves according to our dispositions. All dispositions and actions, therefore, which cannot be known from without, come before the *forum internum;* for

[h] an inept or inappropriate judge
[i] bar of conscience
[j] divine tribunal

88

the *forum externum humanum* cannot judge by dispositions. Conscience is thus the representative of the *forum divinum*. No ethical actions belong *coram foro externo humano*, for the latter has no authority to compel externally, which only an external judge possesses. But everything belongs *coram foro externo humano* which can be externally enforced, and hence all external compulsory duties do so. The authority and the proof of the *factum* must be externally valid. But the external grounds for imputation are those that are valid according to the external universal law. Those imputations which have no externally valid grounds whatever belong, not to the *forum externum*, but to the *forum internum*. Now *in foro externo*, in those matters where there are no externally valid grounds, people try whether one might not use the *forum internum* in the *forum externum*. A person is compelled to step up before the *forum divinum* (though in fact this has already occurred within him); he is constrained to find himself subject to penalty before this forum, if there is wrong-doing, and he is compelled to declare it openly; and this is an oath. The *forum internum* is already present, and he will already find the deed punishable within himself, without first having to declare it, yet the declaration makes a greater impression on him. The man may think that if he does not declare it, he will also not be punished before the *forum divinum;* but, whether he declares it or not, he will still be punished. It is, however, quite absurd to swear, and to say: I will that this or that may happen if it be not true, since that does not depend on us. Hence the gospel very properly says on this point: 'Swear not by heaven, for it is not thine', etc. Yet be that as it may, it is nevertheless appropriate to human nature. The man pictures to himself the perils of the divine will.

27:298

Our author here goes on to speak of several matters which only need to be looked up: e.g., of trial and sentencing. The trial is a methodical *imputatio legis*, where *per actionem civilem*[k] I merely seek to establish my right in the *forum externum*. The *summa* of all imputations are legal acts. The sentence is the judgement.

Finis
Philosophiae practicae universalis

[k] by a civil action

[On religion]

OF ETHICS

All actions are indeed adjudged to be necessary, but a motivating ground is also needed in order to perform these actions. Now if this motivating ground is derived from coercion, the necessity of the actions is juridical; but if it is derived from the inner goodness of the actions, the necessity is ethical. Ethics treats of the inner goodness of actions, jurisprudence of what is legally correct – it refers, not to dispositions, but to authority and coercive power. Ethics, however, refers solely to dispositions. It does indeed extend also to juridical laws, but demands that even those actions to which one can be compelled should be done from inner goodness of the dispositions, and not from coercion. Hence juridical actions, insofar as the motivating ground is ethical, are also included under ethics. It therefore represents a major difference, whether we consider the necessity of actions ethically or juridically; and so ethics is not a science which should include no coercive laws and actions; on the contrary, it also extends to coercive actions, though the motivating ground is not coercion, but the inner quality. Ethics is thus a philosophy of dispositions, and hence a practical philosophy, for dispositions are basic principles of our actions and serve to couple actions with their motivating ground. It is hard to explain what we understand by a disposition; a person who pays his debts, for example, is not yet on that account an honourable man, if he does it from fear of punishment, etc.; yet he is nonetheless a good citizen, and his action has *rectitudo juridica*, though not *ethica*. But if he does it because of the inner goodness of the action, his disposition is moral and has *rectitudo ethica*. There is much need for this distinction in religion, for example. If people look upon God as the supreme legislator and regent, as one who demands the fulfilment of His laws, and does not look to the motivating ground from which the action proceeds, then here, between God and a worldly ruler, there is no other difference save merely this, that God discerns the outer action better than the worldly judge, and that one

cannot so easily impose on Him as on the latter. Now if someone fulfils His laws, the action is certainly good, but it possesses only *rectitudo juridica*, in that he does it from fear of punishment. If, however, a person abstains from an evil action, not from fear of punishment, but because of its atrociousness, his action is ethical. It is this that the teacher of the

Gospels especially recommends us to practise. He says we must do everything from love of God. But to love God is to do His bidding gladly, from a good disposition. Of which more anon.

Ethics is also called theory of virtue, for virtue consists in *rectitudo actionum ex principio interno.*[1] A person who complies with coercive laws is not yet virtuous. Virtue does indeed presuppose respect and punctilious observance for human laws, but it refers to the disposition from which arises the action that possesses *rectitudo juridica.* We must not yet infer, therefore, to the dispositions from the outer actions that possess *rectitudo juridica.* If I discern the moral necessity of the action that is juridical, I can do it in a juridical and also an ethical sense. In the first case the action conforms to the law alone, not to the disposition, and for that reason we also say of juridical laws that they lack morality. Morality is employed of ethical laws alone, for even if juridical laws have moral necessity, their motivating ground is still coercion and not disposition.

Virtue, however, does not express quite accurately the notion of moral goodness; it means strength in mastering and overcoming oneself, in regard to the moral disposition. But here I am considering the original source of the disposition. There is something that goes unperceived here, and is only cleared up in what follows, for ethics has only the disposition as its topic. The word *Sittlichkeit* has been adopted, to express morality, although *Sitte*, custom, is the concept of decorum; for virtue, however, we require a certain degree of customary goodness, a certain self-coercion and self-command. Peoples can have customs but no virtue, and others virtue but no customs (*conduite* is the propriety of customs). A science of customs is not yet a theory of virtue, and virtue is not yet morality. But because we have no other word for morality, we take *Sittlichkeit* to signify morality, since we cannot take virtue to do so.

In spirit, the moral law ordains the disposition, in its letter the action. We shall therefore see in ethics how the moral law is exercised in spirit, and will not be adverting to the action at all.   27:301

"Ethics can propound laws of morality that are lenient, and adjusted to the weakness of human nature. It can accommodate itself to man, so that it requires of people only so much as they can perform. But on the other hand it can also be rigorous and demand the highest level of morality, perfection. The moral law must also be strict, and enunciate the condition of lawfulness. Whether man can accomplish it or not, the law must not be lenient and accommodate itself to human weakness; for it contains the norm of moral perfection, and this must be exact and rigorous. Geometry, for example, lays down rules that are strict; it pays no heed to whether man can observe them in practice or not; the centre-point of a circle, for example, is too gross to be a mathematical point. Now since ethics also

---

[1] rectitude of actions on an internal principle

propounds rules which are meant to be the guide-line for our actions, they must not be adjusted to human capacity, but have to show what is morally necessary. An indulgent ethics is the ruin of moral perfection in man. The moral law must be pure. There is, however, a theological and moral purism, whereby a man ponders on things of no consequence and tries by subtlety to express something therein. Ethics has no such purism. But purity with regard to principles is another matter. The moral law must have purity. The Gospel has such purity in its moral law, as did none of the ancient philosophers, who even at the time of the evangelic teacher were merely brilliant pharisees, holding strictly to the *cultus externus,*^m of which the Gospel often says that it is not a matter of that at all, but rather of moral purity. The Gospel does not allow the least imperfection; it is altogether strict and pure, and adheres without any leniency to the purity of the law. A law such as this is holy; nor does it demand too much, so that in practice it would be content with a half-way observance. On the contrary, everyone perceives that the ground of it lies in his understanding, and the proof can be drawn from the understanding of anyone. This punctiliousness, sub-

27:302   tlety, rigour and purity of the moral law, which is called *rectitudo,* is evidenced among us in all cases. We have only to offend someone unwittingly, for example, among strangers, and even though we might certainly be assured, through an impending journey, against all evil consequences, we still continue to reproach ourselves for it. He who considers the moral law a lenient affair is a *latitudinarius.*ⁿ Ethics must be precise and holy. The holiness attaches to the moral law, not because it is revealed to us; on the contrary, it can also attach thereto by reason, since it is an original principle whereby we judge even the revelation; for holiness is the highest, most perfect moral good, which we nevertheless derive from our own understanding, and from ourselves.

Our author [Baumgarten] divides ethics into the ingratiating and the morose. The motivating grounds of proper behaviour must be in keeping with morality, and the incentives thereto must be so linked that they are becoming to it, i.e., they must match its dignity. It is not a matter of the actions taking place, but of what sort of source they came from. Ethics is ingratiating to a person who considers virtuous conduct to be an elegant way of living well. It is true that virtue is also a rule of prudence, and that one feels at ease with it. Thus many dispense good works on this account, that they then find satisfaction in the happiness of the poor; but there the motivating ground is not moral. Many boast of having done much good, even though it may stem from improper grounds. But a good thing must not be supported on grounds that are false. Virtue, however, is a good thing; so one must not support it on false grounds,

---

^m outer religion, ritual
ⁿ a lax moralist

e.g., that even in this life it brings many amenities with it, which is false; for the virtuous disposition may increase the pain of this life still further, in that a man might think he is virtuous, and yet things go badly with him; if he were not virtuous, he could endure it better, for he would have deserved it. Ethics must not, therefore, be commended by such cajoleries. If it is set forth in its purity, it brings with it respect, and is an object of the highest approbation and highest wish, and the ingratiating arguments merely diminish the incentives, whereas they ought to increase them. Morality must not debase itself, it has to be recommended on its own account; everything else, even heavenly reward, is as nothing in comparison, for by morality alone do I become worthy of happiness. The morally motivating grounds must be set forth quite distinctly, and all others, even from motives of benevolence, kept separate. The reason 27:303 for the lesser effectiveness of morality is that it has not been presented purely. Till now all moralists, even of the clerical type, have failed to commend it in pure fashion. It gains more if it is recommended for its inner worth, than if it is accompanied by sensuous attractions and inducements. The ingratiating ethic dishonours itself more than it can serve to recommend itself, just as happens with amorousness in general. A quiet modesty is far more engaging than any ingratiating charms. In moral teaching itself, no attractions or sensuous urges are to be brought in; only after the lessons of morality have been grasped in full purity, and the pupil has first learned to value them highly, can such motives be brought into play, not so that the action should be done for that reason, for in that case it would no longer be moral, but in order to serve merely as *motiva subsidiaria,*[o] to overcome the inertia our nature has towards motives, relating to such intellectual concepts as exist for the understanding; but once these sensory motives have done their work, the correct motivating grounds must again take over. Hence they serve merely to remove sensory obstacles, so that the understanding can again prevail; but to mix up everything together is a grave corruption, to which many are still very prone. This purely moral concept produces an uncommon effect upon him who possesses it; it attracts him more than any sensory impulses. There lies in this a major aid in recommending morality to men, which should already be attended to in education; we would thereby become capable of pure judgement and sound taste in matters of conduct. Just as a person cannot relish pure wine, if it is mixed with other drinks, so also in morality all other obstacles must be removed if its purity is to be discerned.

The ingratiating ethic is contrasted to the morose, which latter is also called the misanthropic. Such an ethic sets morality in opposition to all pleasures, just as the ingratiating ethic confuses the two. This morose

[o] subsidiary motives

ethic ranks all pleasures of life, all amenities of the senses, below morality. Though it may seem at first that this morose ethic harbours a greater error than the other, nothing could be less true, for since it relates to man's pride, it can bring about sublime actions. Man is enjoined by it to sacrifice all conveniences of life to a single act of sublimity.

27:304

The ingratiating ethic links all amenities of life with morality; but the morose sets the latter in opposition to them, which is certainly an error, though in this way morality at least is distinguished from the amenities, and this is a great service. So if any error is to be admitted into ethics, it would be better to permit the error of the morose view. Many amenities are admittedly sacrificed by this ethic, but to a more refined taste they might also not even fit together, and drop away by themselves. Even this misanthropic ethic has something in it that is worthy of great respect. It looks to the rigour and precision of morality, although it goes astray by setting up pleasures as the opponent. To correct it, we must note that morality and happiness are two elements of the highest good, which are different in kind, and therefore have to be distinguished, but are yet in a necessary relation to one another. Happiness has a necessary relation to morality, for the moral law carries with it a natural promise. If I have so conducted myself as to be worthy of happiness, I can also hope to enjoy the latter, and such are the springs of morality. I can promise no one that he will achieve happiness without morality. Happiness is no ground, no *principium* of morality, but a necessary *corollarium* thereof. Here the ingratiating ethic has the advantage, in that it links happiness with morality, though the one is only a natural consequence of the other. The morose ethic, though, has something proud about it from this angle, that it renounces all claim to happiness. But though the renunciation of all happiness distinguishes it from morality, it is from that viewpoint unnatural, since it is transcendental.

Our author goes on here to speak of the *ethica deceptrix.*[p] This consists in the fact that it realizes an ideal. Everything which contains an illusion that is contrary to truth is fraudulent. The deceiving ethic must, however, be so constituted that the deception is in itself moral, but yet deceiving in that it is simply not appropriate to human nature; is perfect, indeed, but not adequate to ourselves; for example, the consciousness of oneself, as the *principium* of the well-being of all mankind, occasions a great joy, though nobody can attain it. The moral ground of perfection naturally does not occur among men. We posit the highest perfection in the supreme being, and communion with that being would be the highest perfection that we could attain. But this is an ideal that cannot be reached. Plato made this ideal a reality. This may also be called the ethic of fantasy and enthusiasm.

27:305

[p] deceiving ethic, cant

OF NATURAL RELIGION

Natural religion should properly furnish the conclusion to ethics, and set the seal on morality. The Idea of moral perfection should there be thought out and brought into being, and with this the completion of all our morality should be attained in regard to its object. But it has pleased our author to deal with it beforehand, and since not much depends on this, we shall follow him, seeing that the concept of ethics, so far as it is needed, has already preceded in any case.

Natural religion is no rule of morality; religion, rather, is morality applied to God. So what religion must be made the basis in natural religion? Natural religion is practical, and contains natural indications of our duties in regard to the supreme being. So morality and theology in combination constitute religion. Without morality, no religion is possible. There are, however, religions without morality, and people think they have religion, though they lack any morality. Such religion consists only in the external *cultus* and observances; there is no morality in that, merely the attentiveness and assiduity of a prudent course of conduct towards God, whom one is seeking to please by such observances. There is no more religion in that than in compliance with civil laws and observances towards the monarch.

So since religion presupposes theology, and religion should possess morality, the question is, what theology must be made the basis of religion? Whether God be a spirit, and how He is omnipresent, so that He fills all space, is not part of theology insofar as it ought to be the basis of natural religion, but belongs, rather, to speculation. Thus an Egyptian priest fashioned a ceremonial image of God, and when he was forbidden this notion, he lamented, weeping, that he had been robbed of his God, since before he might have been able to picture God to some extent, but now no longer. In the observance of duties, the representation of God is no obstacle, whatever the image employed, if only it is a sufficient ground for morality. The theology which is the basis of natural religion includes the condition of moral perfection. We must therefore represent to ourselves a supreme being, who is holy in His laws, benevolent in His government, and just in His punishments and rewards. Now this, in one being, is the concept of God that is needed for religion, as the basis of natural religion. These, then, are the moral attributes of God; the natural attributes are needed only insofar as they give the moral ones a greater perfection, and can produce a greater effect in religion. So the moral attributes arise under the condition of the omniscience, omnipotence, omnipresence and unity of the supreme being. The most holy and benevolent being must be omniscient, so that He may perceive the inner morality that resides in the disposition. Hence He must also be omnipresent; and the wisest will can only be a single one. Hence His unity, since without this condition the *principium* of morality

27:306

95

might be fabricated. And this, then, constitutes the essence of the theology of natural religion. Its sources should be drawn, not from speculation, but from pure reason. Speculative knowledge is needed only to satisfy our curiosity, but if religion is at issue, and what is needful for acting and omitting, we no longer require anything more than what can be discerned and perceived through sound reason. How does theology arise? If morality is expounded, the very concept of it brings us to belief in God. By belief, here, from a philosophic viewpoint, we mean, not the trust one should have in revelation, but the belief arising from the use of sound reason. This belief, arising from the *principium* of morality, if it is practical, is so powerful that no speculative grounds are needed to extract it from the moral feeling. For in morality it is a matter of the purest dispositions, but these would be lost if no being were there who might perceive them. It is impossible that a man should possess and feel such moral worth, without believing at the same time that it might be perceived by such a being. For why, then, should we cherish pure dispositions that nobody except God can perceive? One might, after all, perform the same actions, but not with honest intent. We might perform good deeds, but only from honour or pleasure; the action would remain always the same and the analogues of morality produce a like effect; hence it is impossible to cherish morally pure dispositions without believing at the same time that they are linked to a being who observes them. And it is equally impossible to turn to morality without a belief in God. All moral precepts would count for nothing, therefore, if there were no being to oversee them. And this, then, is the representation of God from moral concepts. So one may believe that a God exists, without knowing it for certain, and natural religion therefore has, as its main feature, simplicity, which means that in such theology as is necessary to natural religion the ordinary man is as well-versed as the speculative thinker. Everything else, then, that we have in theology, serves no other purpose but to assuage our curiosity. Morality must be combined with religion, which the old philosophers did not appreciate. Religion is not the origin of morality, but consists in this, that the moral laws are applied to the knowledge of God. If we imagine a religion prior to all morality, it would still have to have a relation to God, and then it would amount to this, that I picture God as a mighty lord who would need to be placated. All religion presupposes morality; hence this morality cannot be derived from religion. All religion gives force, beauty and reality to morality, for in itself the latter is an ideal thing. If I imagine how beautiful it would be if all men were to be honest, such a state of affairs might induce me to be moral; but morality says, thou shalt be moral as such and for thyself, be the others what they may. The moral law then begins to become ideal in me; I am to follow the Idea of morality, without any hope of being happy, and this is impossible; hence morality would be an ideal, if there is no being who carries out the Idea. So there must be one who gives force and reality to the moral laws. But this being

27:307

must then be holy, benevolent and just. Religion gives weight to morality, it should be the motive thereof. Here we recognize that he who has so con- ducted himself as to be worthy of happiness may also hope to achieve this, 27:308 since there is a being who can make him so. And this is the first origin of religion, which is possible even without any theology. It is a natural progres- sion from morality into religion. Religion has no need of any speculative acquaintance with God. Thus morality carries with it natural promises, since otherwise it could not bind us. For to one who cannot protect me, I also owe no obedience; but morality cannot protect us without religion. The proposition: We are obligated to blessedness, is an ideal one; for all our actions obtain *completudo*[q] through religion. Without religion, all obligation is without a motive. Religion is the condition for conceiving the binding force of laws. Yet there are, indeed, men who do good without religion. It is found very convenient to tell the truth and be honourable, for then we do not need to reflect, but have merely to tell the thing as it actually is. Such men do good, therefore, not from principles, but from sensory intentions. However, if we are in trouble, if vice shows itself in a morally pleasing light, and then religion is not present, things are very bad. The best is knowledge of God through moral need.

Our author speaks of inner religion. The distinction of religion into inner and outer is very bad. Outer actions can be either means to inner religion, or effects thereof. But outer religion is nothing. Religion is an internal matter, and consists in the disposition. So there might be a dual religion, of disposition and observances. But true religion is that of the disposition. Outer actions are not acts of religion, but means or effects thereof. Religious actions take place within myself. Men can be religious in all their actions, if, that is, religion accompanies everything they do. So inner religion constitutes the whole of religion. *Piety is good conduct* from the motivating ground of the divine *will*, and pious *actions* are those that *arise from this motivating ground.* But if the motivating ground has sprung from the *inner goodness* of the actions, it is *morality or virtue.* So piety and virtue differ, not in actions, but in their motivating grounds. Piety does not exclude virtuous motivating grounds; rather, it demands them. But the 27:309 true motivating ground of actions must be virtue itself, for God obliges us to that because in itself it is really good. The motivating ground is moral- ity, therefore, and not the divine will, for the former is directly addressed to the inner goodness or disposition. That the action be done without regard for the motivating ground is not the intent of religion; it is that the action be done from a good disposition. The divine will is a motive, but not a motivating ground. A pious man would be one with a proper regard for the observances, the means of religion. But a God-fearing man already signifies something more, namely a certain punctiliousness in observing

[q] fulfilment

the means of religion. A scrupulous man is one who pictures to himself a divine judge.

Actions that are virtuous from religion are pious actions; but those that are vicious from religion are godless actions.

Supernatural religion can be distinguished from supernatural theology. Theology can be supernatural or revealed, and yet religion can be natural, if, that is, it contains only the duties that I discern through reason in regard to the supreme being. So a natural religion is possible in conjunction with a supernatural theology. If we only look into the matter, we shall find that with a supernatural theology men still retain a natural religion. If they had a supernatural religion, supernatural counsel would also have to be met with among them. But we see that men only practise those duties which they can naturally discern through reason. Natural religion is to be distinguished from supernatural, but not because they are in opposition to one another; natural religion, rather, is the use of the knowledge of God, so far as it is possible through reason, and is conjoined with morality. Supernatural religion is the supplementing of natural religion by a higher divine counsel. If, even in supernatural religion, there is much that can make up for the frailty of man, the question arises: What, then, can be imputed to man? Everything can be imputed to him that is brought forth naturally by him, through his own powers. By such conduct, and by

27:310   proper use of his natural powers, he can now make himself worthy of every supplementation of his frailty. Natural religion is therefore not opposed to supernatural; the latter, rather, is a supplement to the former. Natural religion is a true religion, only incomplete. By means of it we have to recognize how much we might do from our own powers, and how much can be imputed to us; and if we so conduct ourselves, we make ourselves worthy of being made whole. What makes us capable of securing the completion and fulfilment of our perfection, the supernatural means of religion? Nothing but the proper use of natural religion; so the supernatural presupposes the natural. The man who does not behave as he naturally ought to, can hope for no supernatural assistance. One cannot, therefore, simply accept supernatural religion, and be forthwith supported by divine assistance, and let natural religion go by the board. Still less could one dispense with natural religion and promptly go over to supernatural or revealed. Natural religion, on the contrary, is the necessary condition under which we can become worthy of fulfilment, since the supernatural is a supplement of the natural. Only our good behaviour makes us worthy of divine assistance, for natural religion is the totality of all moral actions, and supernatural the fulfilment of the incompleteness of those actions. Were we to abandon natural religion, the supernatural would be a passive thing, and man would have to let God do what He pleased with him, and would thus have nothing to do, since everything would have to proceed in a supernatural way. But if there has to be morality in actions, natural religion must precede. So in every man there has to be a natural religion, which can be imputed to him, and whereby he makes himself worthy of fulfilment.

OF ERRORS IN RELIGION

Errors in religion are to be distinguished from errors in theology. The latter relate to the knowledge of God, but the former to the corruptibility of morality. The errors affecting morality are heresies, but those having to do with theology are merely false doctrines.

There can be theological errors which do not affect religion, and the religion can be very good, although the knowledge of God is very anthro-   27:311 pomorphic. A religion can be good, even though it be incomplete, and natural religion can always be good. But to get rid of natural power altogether, and abandon oneself to the supernatural, is the religion of the underling. Ignorance partly affects theology, and partly religion. In theology we are all too ignorant. The reason is that the concept of God is an Idea, which has to be regarded as the limiting concept of reason, and the totality of all derived concepts. To this concept I seek to attribute all properties, so long as they are suitable. Now to define this, we are greatly at a loss. Ignorance in theology can be great, but in regard to morality it should be considered of no account.

As to the errors in theology, men have at all times gone astray when they speculated, though such error has not affected religion at all, being entirely separated from that. Yet in those cognitions of God where the influence on our conduct is great, it has to be ensured that the error does not also impinge on religion. Hence, in regard to theological errors, we are very wary, since they can affect religion, and are therefore to be avoided as much as possible. The household remedy for this is not to judge dogmatically at all, and then we fall into no errors; for example, I simply do not meddle with the enquiry as to how God is omnipresent; suffice it to know merely that He is the pattern of moral perfection, and that since He is benevolent and just, He will also apportion our destinies in accordance with our behaviour; we then fall into no error, and need have no recourse to dogmatic judgements.

Among errors in theology, the first to be listed is atheism, which takes two forms: godlessness and denial of God. The first is when we know nothing of God; the second, when it is dogmatically asserted that there is no God. But of a person devoid of the knowledge of God we can say that he simply does not know that a God exists; were he to know it, he might still have religion. Godlessness, therefore, is still remediable. But on the other hand, again, we may have a man so wicked that, although he knows that a God exists, he still lives as if there were none; it would be better for him if he did not know that there is a God, for then he would still be excusable; the acts of such a man are contrary to religion, and not devoid of it.

27:312

Atheism can reside in mere speculation, while in practice such a person can be a theist or venerator of God, whose error extends to theology, but not to religion. Those persons who have fallen into atheism through speculation should not be so readily condemned for wickedness as the custom is; only their understanding was corrupted, not their will; Spinoza, for example, did what a man of religion should do. His heart was good, and could easily have been brought to rights; he merely had too much trust in speculative argument. Atheism is a theological error of the kind that has an influence on morality and religion, for in such a case the rules of good conduct have no motive power. There are still other theological errors, but we pass them by, since they belong more to *theologica naturalis*[r] than to ethics. But on the theoretical side, we shall point out two kinds of mistaken aberration: (1) in regard to knowledge, ratiocination and superstition; (2) in regard to the heart, scoffing at religion and fanaticism. These are the limits of aberration. As to ratiocination, it consists in wishing, by reason, to deduce as necessary the knowledge of God that underlies religion, and to apprehend and prove the necessity of this. But that is not needed. In religion, the knowledge of God may be founded only on faith. So far as we merely regard God as the *principium* of morality, and know Him as a holy law-giver, benevolent world-ruler and just judge, that is sufficient for faith in God, insofar as it is meant to be the basis of religion, without being able to prove such a thing by logic. So ratiocination is the error of accepting no other religion but that which rests on such theology as can be discerned through reason. But there is no need for a man to discern and prove this, if he merely requires theology for religion; for atheism, Spinozism, deism and theism are equally little capable of proof. There is need, therefore, merely for a rational hypothesis, whereby I can sufficiently determine everything by rules of reason. This is a necessary hypothesis; if it is set aside, then one can frame no concept of anything, and understand neither the order of nature, nor yet the purposive, nor even the reason why one should be obedient to the moral law. If I presuppose this necessary hypothesis, and assume a holy law-giver, etc., etc., I shall involve myself in no speculative controversies nor even read such books as attempt to maintain the opposite; for this is no help to me, and can dissuade me not at all from this faith; for if such a thing were made controversial to me, I would have no fixed principle, and what is one to do then? This is equivalent to my deciding to lay aside all principles of the moral law, and become a villain; but the moral law still commands, and I also perceive that it is good to obey it, though without a supreme ruler it would have no worth or validity; so I shall consult, not speculative grounds, but my own needs, and can satisfy myself no otherwise than by accepting it.

27:313

[r] natural theology

Thus ratiocination in religious matters is dangerous. Were our religion to rest on speculative grounds, it would be but weakly assured if one wanted to demand proof of everything, for reason can go astray. So in order for religion to stand firm, all ratiocination must be done away with.

On the other hand, superstition is again an irrational thing. It consists, not in principles, but in a method. If one assumes as the *principium* of judgement and religion something that is based on fear, or old report, or regard for persons, these are sources of superstition, on which religion is very insecurely and unreliably founded. Superstition is always creeping into religion, because men are not inclined to follow the maxims of reason, when they derive from sensibility* what has to be deduced from an intellectual principle; for example, when the observances which are only a means to religion are adopted as principles, religion becomes superstitious. Religion is a thing that is grounded on reason, but not on ratiocination. So when I depart from the maxims of reason, and allow myself to be guided by sensibility, that is superstition. But the guidance of knowledge by mere speculation in religion is ratiocination; both are harmful to religion. Religion is based solely on faith, which needs no logical proofs, but already suffices to presuppose itself as a necessary hypothesis.

On the other hand, there are two kinds of dispositional aberration adverse to religion, namely scoffing and fanaticism. The first is when a man not only fails to treat religion seriously as something important, but   27:314 regards it even as an absurdity deserving of contempt. Since religion is an important matter, it is not a topic for ridicule; for example, if a judge has a malefactor before him, he will not make mock of him, since the matter is important, and could cost the man his life. All religion, therefore, even if it contains such absurdity, is in no way an object of mockery, for the man who possesses it has an interest in it, and his future weal or woe depends on it, so that he is rather to be pitied than laughed at. However, to scoff at religion generally is a fearful transgression, since it is far more important. Nevertheless, one should not at once treat a person who talks humorously about religion as a scoffer, for such people have religion inwardly, and are merely giving free rein to their humour and wit, which extends, not so much to religion, but rather to certain persons. Such conduct is not to be approved of, indeed, but nor should it be considered scoffing. It is more frequently due to thoughtlessness, vivacity and want of sufficient trial.

Fanaticism is a condition whereby one runs into excesses above and beyond the maxims of reason. Superstition extends within those maxims, but fanaticism beyond them. The former is grounded upon sensual principles, but the latter on mystical and hyperphysical ones. Scoffing is directed, partly to superstition, and partly to fanaticism. It is not becoming indeed,

*[Reading *Sinnlichkeit* for *Sittlichkeit* – Tr.]

but nevertheless a means of snatching such people out of their folly, and bemusing them in their giddy fit of sensory intuition. Ratiocination (*rationalismus*) stands in contrast to superstition, but if we are to contrast two things in the practice of religion, they would be piety and zealotry (bigotry). The latter, like ratiocination, signifies a game, and is thus to be distinguished from devotion. Piety is a practical thing, and consists in observing the divine laws because they proceed from the divine will. Zealotry consists in endeavouring to revere God by using words and expressions that indicate submission and devotion in order to procure favour for oneself by such external tokens of respect and laudatory ejaculations. It is a hateful and repulsive thing to adopt this mode of honouring God, for in that case we think to win Him over without being moral, merely by flattery, and picture

27:315   Him to ourselves as a mundane ruler whom we try to please by submissive acts of service, hymns of praise and sycophancy.

Devotion is the mediate relation of the heart to God, and the attempt to practise this, and make the knowledge of God effective upon our will. It is therefore not an act, but a method of making oneself ready for actions. True religion, however, consists in actions, in practising the moral law, in doing what God would have us do. But to be adept at this, we need the habit of it, and this is devotion. We seek by means of it to acquire a knowledge of God, which makes such an impression on us that we are thereby impelled to be practical, and to follow the moral law. We should therefore [not]* look askance if a person is devout, in order to prepare himself thereby for the performance of well-disposed actions. But if a man is setting about to make his knowledge of God fruitful, and there comes along a needy unfortunate begging him for help, but he is unwilling to be disturbed from his devotions by this, that is altogether absurd; for devotion is training oneself to perform good actions; and here is the very situation, where a good action needs performing, for which he has trained by being devout. Devotion, as a mere occupation and a separate pursuit, is in itself quite needless; for if, by the practice of good actions, we have arrived at a point where we can believe that the knowledge of God is sufficiently strong in us to impress us with the need of performing further good actions, then no devotion at all is required, since here we have merely the true fear of God, where the effect is at all times shown by good actions; hence the fear of God can only be exercised in actions, and not by being devout.

OF UNBELIEF

Our author already talks of unbelief, though he has not yet spoken of belief. We shall explain this notion, so far as it is needed here in ethics. Belief can be taken in two senses. First, it signifies a readiness to give

*[Omitted in text. – Tr.]

102

assent to evidence, and then it is historical belief. Many are unable to have historical belief, due to mental incapacity, if they cannot discern the evidence. In many people historical judgement differs even though the data are the same, and it is impossible to convince a man of something in which he has no belief, e.g., newspaper reports. In historical belief, therefore, there are discrepancies, for which we can no more supply reasons, than we can for discrepancies of taste. Thus Bulenger believes that the seven kings in Rome represent the seven planets. So even in regard to the historical, there is a tendency to unbelief. Man is more inclined to doubt than to agreement. He finds it safer to postpone judgement. But this is based on the understanding, and also on the fact that one has often been imposed on by reports on other occasions, so it is not done from any evil intent, but merely to guard against error; though this is the road to ignorance, if we cut off all access to knowledge. Here, however, we are not concerned with historical belief, since it has its strength in the understanding and not the will, and here we are speaking only of what lies in morality. Belief in the other sense is when we believe in the reality of virtue.

27:316

Moral unbelief, then, is when one does not believe in the reality of virtue. It is a misanthropic attitude to suppose it an Idea. It is a conceit to satisfy one's inclination; a man can go far in it, and actually carry it so far that he is not even considered a righteous man, and then he will also never even try to become one. It is not good to cast suspicion on virtue and the seeds of belief in man, which many learned men have done, in order the better to demonstrate to man his corrupted state, and to take away from him the idea that he is virtuous. That, however, is very odious, for man's imperfection is already sufficiently shown thereafter, by comparison with the purity of the moral law. Anyone who seeks out the seed of evil in man is virtually an advocate of the devil. Thus Hofstede attempted, against *Bélisaire*, to undermine virtue; but how could that do anything for religion? It is, on the contrary, far more useful, when I hear the character of a Socrates, for example, whether it be fancied or true, depicted as perfectly virtuous, to seek to render this image more perfect still, rather than that I should hunt about for flaws in it. It elevates my soul, after all, to the emulation of such virtue, and is an incentive to me. But anyone who preaches such a lack of belief in virtue and the seed of goodness in man is thereby implying that we are all of us rascals by nature, and that nobody is to be trusted if he be not enlightened by the grace and counsel of Christ. But such people do not consider that a society of radically evil persons would be utterly unworthy of divine aid. For the idea of devilish evil, where there is no seed of good at all, not even a good will, is just as pure in its way as the goodness of angels, on the other hand, is pure of evil. In that case it is also quite impossible for such people to receive assistance; God would have to make them anew, not lend them support. Man, therefore, possesses virtue; though any self-conceit at his virtue is already put down

27:317

by the purity of the moral law. Hence one must believe in virtue. If this were not so, the vilest thief would be as good as his neighbour, in that the latter already has the seeds of stealing in him, and only circumstances have brought it about that the one, but not the other, is a thief. Many have maintained that in man there are no seeds of good, only of evil, and Rousseau alone proclaims the opposite. This, then, is moral unbelief.

The second form is religious unbelief: the want of belief in the existence of a being who both rewards good dispositions adequately, as it pleases Him, and also assigns appropriate consequences to our good behaviour. We find ourselves enjoined by a moral law to good dispositions, as principles of our actions, and by its holiness we are admonished to keep the law with absolute precision, so that we have a holy law. But we cannot practise this law so purely; our actions are very imperfect by comparison, so that they are even blameworthy in our own eyes, if only we do not stifle our inner tribunal, which judges according to this law. Anyone noticing this would eventually have to give up observing such a law, since he could not face up to so holy and just a tribunal, that judges by this law. So man finds himself very defective in terms of the moral law. But belief in a heavenly supplement to our incompleteness in morality makes up for our want. If only we cultivate good dispositions, and bend all our efforts to fulfilment of the moral law, we may hope that God will have the means to remedy this imperfection. If we do this now, we are also worthy of divine assistance. If anyone has this belief, it is religious belief in regard to our

27:318   conduct, and the first part of such belief. The other is merely to be seen as a consequence, namely that if we have so conducted ourselves, we may hope for reward.

There is thus an unbelief in natural religion, and it is the cause of all ceremonies in religion, since people think they can replace morality by trying to win God over through non-moral* actions. So if true religious belief is wanting, the result is, that because a man finds deficiency in himself, and ought therefore to believe in a heavenly supplement to it, he resorts instead to ceremonies, pilgrimages, chastisements, fasts, etc., whereby he seeks to remedy his imperfection himself; and thus omits the very thing that could make him worthy of divine assistance.

Edification means the fashioning of an active disposition, so far as it springs from devotion. People can be devout without edifying themselves. To edify means the same as to build something. We thus have to erect a special edifice of disposition and moral conduct. This is founded on the knowledge of God, which imparts emphasis, life and motive force to the moral law. Edification is thus an effect of devotion, the perfection of a voluntarily active disposition of the heart, to act in accordance with God's will. So when it is said that the preacher has delivered an edifying address,

*[Reading *nichtmoralisch* for *moralisch* – Tr.]

that does not mean that he has thereby built anything; only that it is thereby possible to erect an edifice, a system of active dispositions, though it is not yet built, for there is still nothing there. The hearer can only infer the truth of his edification from his subsequent life, and the preacher from just those consequences that his edifying has brought about. The edifying-power of the preacher does not consist, therefore, in words, gestures, voice, etc.; he has it insofar as his sermon has the power to establish in his hearers a God-fearing frame of mind. To edify is therefore as much as to say how it is shown forth and fashioned, when a fabric of piety is created in anyone.

Our author goes on to speak of the theoretical and practical knowledge of God, of which we have already said something above. Speculation in regard to God has much to do with many things, but nothing to do with religion, whose knowledge must be practical. Theology can certainly contain speculative knowledge, but to that extent the latter does not belong to religion. The righteous teacher will therefore omit speculative knowledge 27:319 from religion, so that man may become all the more attentive to the practical. Brooding and subtlety in matters of religion can be regarded as obstacles thereto, in that they divert us from the practical.

Now in order to know what pertains to religion, and what to speculation, the following test must be applied: That which makes no difference to my actions, whether it be answered this way or that, belongs, not to religion, but to speculation. So if the rule of conduct remains the same, the issue belongs to speculation and not to religion.

Our author talks of contentment with the divine will. One may be patient of necessity, since one cannot alter things, and it is useless to complain. This seeming contentment is not conjoined with moral goodness and the divine will; contentment with the divine will consists, rather, in enjoyment of, and pleasure in, divine rule. Since this contentment is universal, it must be met with in all circumstances that one may run into, whether they be good or bad. But is such contentment possible? We must not make man hypocritical. It is contrary to his nature to be in trouble and want, and still to thank God for it, is very difficult. For if I thank God for it, I am content, and then there is no trouble; but how are we to be thankful for something that we wish had never happened? Nevertheless, it is still possible, under all want and affliction, to retain one's peace and contentment. We can be sad and yet content, although not through the senses. We can perceive by reason (which also gives us a basis for belief), that the ruler of the world does nothing that would have no purpose, and may thus have comfort in the evils of life.

We can be thankful to God for a thing in two ways: either in respect of His extra-ordinary guidance, or His universal providence. The first is a prying of our judgement into His rule and purposes, whereas the judgement whereby we attribute a thing to God's universal providence is appropriate to the dutiful modesty that we have to observe in passing judgement on God's ways. The ways of God are divine intentions which determine the governance of the world. These we must not define in detail, but are to judge of them in general that holiness and righteousness prevail

27:320 therein. It is presumption to wish to know the particular ways of God, and it is equally presumptuous to wish to define the good that specially befalls us with reference to ourselves; we have won in the lottery, for example, and wish to ascribe this to God as a special dispensation; it is, indeed, a part of divine providence in general, but to think it a proof of my having been picked out by God as fortune's favourite, is presumptuous. God has universal intentions and purposes, and a thing can be a side-effect of a grander intention; but not something specially intended. Those persons, accordingly, who attribute all special cases to God's providence, and say that God has heaped benefits and happiness upon them, believe themselves to be God-fearing on that account, and suppose it an adjunct of religion that one should have reverence for God, which they take to consist in ascribing everything directly to His special guidance. But everything lies in universal providence, and it is actually better in our discourse to abstain from trying to determine anything of God's intentions. In the course of the world, taken as a whole, everything is founded upon a kindly providence, and we may hope that everything in general takes place in accordance with God's foresight. The generality of nature should evoke our gratitude, and not particular circumstances, which admittedly touch us more nearly in our own regard, though it is not so noble to dwell on them.

Renunciation (resignation) in regard to the divine will is our duty. We renounce our own will, and leave things to another, who understands the matter better, and means us well. Hence we have cause to leave it all in God's hands, and let the divine will take control; but that does not mean that we ought to do nothing, and let God do it all; rather, we should resign to God what does not lie in our power, and do those things of ours which are within our compass. And this is resignation to the divine will.

OF TRUST IN GOD UNDER
THE CONCEPT OF FAITH

We take faith here to mean that we should do the best that lies in our power, and this in the hope that God, in His goodness and wisdom, will make up for the frailty of our conduct. So faith means the confidence that,

27:321 so long as we have done everything possible to us, God will supply what does not lie in our power. This is the faith of meekness and modesty, which is associated with resignation. Such faith prescribes nothing, but does what duty requires to the best of its ability, and hopes, without defining it, for support; and of such a person one may say that he has an unconditional faith, and that it is practical. So practical faith does not consist in believing that God will fulfil our intentions, if only we trust firmly in Him; it lies in this, that we in no way prescribe anything to God through our will, but resign the matter to His will, and hope that if we have done what lies within our natural capacity, God will repair our frailty and incapacity by means that He knows best. Fleshly trust consists in the firm confidence whereby we try to move God to satisfy our carnal inclinations. Fleshly intentions relate to any fulfilment of those inclinations of ours which are directed to the sensual. Fleshly trust is when we ourselves determine the worldly ends of our inclinations. It is then impossible for us to believe that our confidence, in regard to the satisfaction of our inclinations, should be a motivating ground for God to grant us our wishes. The purposes of deity must be determined by God, and we cannot determine any of the world's purposes.

The sole object of spiritual trust is in the pure morality, the holiness of man, and then his eternal blessedness under the condition of morality. On that we may repose our trust with all certainty, a trust that is also unconditional in this regard. To have fleshly trust in God, our author calls *tentatio dei*, which is to say, trying whether our trust in God cannot be a motivating ground for Him to fulfil our carnal intentions. I cannot, in reason, have trust that God will do anything, save what is included in the universal plan of His wisdom. Now since I cannot know this, it is presumption to determine the purposes of the divine world-government, and to believe that my foolish wish has a place in the scheme of the divine wisdom. So anyone who tries to move God, through temporal wishes, to depart from the supreme plan of wisdom, is enticing God, and it is actually an insult to Him. What, then, are we to say of those who consider this to be the true faith? Hence, in order that our trust may coincide with the plan of wisdom, it must be a wise trust, and unconditional, so that we believe in general that God, in His goodness and holiness, will both lend us His aid in regard to acting morally, and also allow us to participate in blessedness. Our conduct towards God is of three kinds. We may reverence, fear and love Him. We revere God as a holy law-giver, love Him as a benevolent ruler, and fear Him as a just judge.

27:322

To revere God is to regard His law as holy and righteous, to respect it and seek to fulfil it in one's dispositions. We may honour a person outwardly, but reverence springs from the disposition of the heart. The moral law is in our eyes estimable, treasurable and worthy of respect. If, then, we consider God to be its author, we must also honour Him in terms of the highest moral worth. There are no other cases for practical reverence towards God. We can marvel at Him, indeed, and fall into astonishment at His greatness and immeasurability, and also recognize our own littleness in comparison with Him, but we can revere God only with respect to morality. We can also revere a man only for his morality;

his skill and industry we are only able to admire. We can also love God only as a benevolent ruler, not on account of His perfections, since they are for Him, and are worthy merely of admiration, but not of love. We can love only one who is in a position to confer benefits upon us, and so in God we love only His benevolent will. The fear of God is directed simply to the righteousness of His justice. The fear of God has to be distinguished from fearfulness towards Him. The latter is when we find ourselves guilty of a transgression. But the fear of God is the disposition, so to proceed, so to act, that we can stand before Him. Thus the fear of God is a means of avoiding fearfulness towards Him. If the fear of God is coupled with love of Him, we are said to fear Him as children, since we do His bidding gladly and from a good disposition; fearfulness towards God, on the other hand, is a slavish fear, and arises when our obedience with respect to God does not gladly follow his commandments; or we are also fearful of Him if we have either already violated His commands, or have an inclination to do so. The imitation of God is a poorly-chosen idea. When God says: Be thou holy, that does not tell us that we should imitate Him, but that we are to pursue the ideal of

27:323   holiness, which we cannot reach. A being distinct in that respect cannot possibly be imitated, but we can follow after, and be obedient. Such an archetype should not be imitated, but we must try to conform thereto.

OF PRAYER

It seems to be generally supposed that praying to the supreme being is needless, since He knows our requirements better than we do ourselves. All explanation in regard to our wants seems otiose, since God is manifestly aware of our needs, and the nature of our dispositions. The setting forth of our dispositions in words is equally useless, since God sees what is innermost in us. Objectively, then, prayers are quite unnecessary. An explanation is needed only for the benefit of a being who does not know what we require. But subjectively prayer is needed, not so that God, who is the recipient of it, should learn anything, and thereby be moved to grant it, but rather for our own sakes. We men cannot make our ideas comprehensible other than by clothing them in words. We therefore put our pious wishes and trust into words, so that we may picture them to ourselves more vividly.

On the other hand, there are topics of prayer that do not have the intention of inducing moral dispositions in us, by means of the praying, but are aimed at our wants, and then prayer is never necessary; for example, we are in distress and then prayer is objectively needless, for God knows that I am in trouble; and it is subjectively needless too, since I here have no need to bring the idea vividly to mind. Prayers are needed, indeed, for moral purposes, if they are to set up a moral disposition in us;

but never for pragmatic purposes, as a means of gaining what we require. They serve to kindle morality in the innermost heart. They are means of devotion; but the latter consists in so training ourselves, that the knowledge of God makes an impression in regard to our acts and omissions; prayers, then, are such exercises of devotion. It is in general an absurdity, to wish to talk with God. We can only talk to somebody we can see; but since we cannot intuit God, but can only believe that he exists, it is utterly absurd to talk with someone who is not intuited. Prayer, therefore, has 27:324 only a subjective use. It is a weakness of man, that he has to express his thoughts in words. He speaks, then, when he prays, to himself, and expresses his thoughts and words so that he does not go astray, and on that account, too, it is absurd; but nevertheless it is still a subjectively necessary means of giving strength to his soul, and power to his dispositions towards action. Ordinary people often cannot pray except aloud, in that they lack the ability to reflect in silence, and praying aloud provides greater emphasis for them; but anyone who has trained himself to unfold his dispositions in silence should not pray aloud. So if the moral, God-fearing disposition in a person has strength enough, such people then employ, not the letter, but the spirit of prayer. A person already accustomed to having ideas and dispositions does not require the medium of words and explanation. So if I subtract this from the prayer, the spirit of it remains behind, i.e., the God-fearing disposition, the direction of the heart to God, so far as we put trust in Him, by faith, to take away our moral frailty and grant us blessedness. The spirit of prayer subsists without any letter. The letter has no purpose, in regard to God, in that He sees the disposition directly, but the letter of prayer is not to be censured on that account; on the contrary, if solemnly uttered, in church, for example, it has a great effect on everyone; but in and for itself, the letter is dead.

Whence comes it that men, in praying, alter the postures that they otherwise have in ordinary life, and are ashamed if they are caught doing so? Because it is absurd to declare one's wishes to God, since He knows them already, and because it is a weakness in man to clothe his dispositions in voice and words. But this use of the medium is appropriate to human weakness.

What it all comes down to, is the spirit of the prayer. The gospel* inveighs against praying aloud in public on the streets. The prayer that is clothed in a formula teaches us that we should have no verbose prayers, and contains only the most necessary of our requirements; prayers should be directed only to dispositions. None should be a definitive prayer, save that which has regard to moral dispositions. As to these, I can beg categorically and unconditionally; but for everything else only in conditional 27:325 terms.

*[Matt. 6:5–7 – Tr.]

But why do I need to propose a condition, whereby I admit, after all, that my request might be stupid and detrimental to myself? Reason tells us, therefore, that our prayers should contain absolutely nothing definitive, rather that in regard to our requirements generally we should leave it to God's wisdom, and accept what it provides. But because men are weak, the gospel gives permission to make conditional requests in worldly matters. Conditional prayers are to be regarded as intrusive, for their self-conceit is perverse. I would myself be alarmed, if God were to grant me particular requests, for I could not know whether I might not have called down misfortune on myself. Specific prayers are unbelieving prayers, for I am asking under a condition, and do not believe that a thing will quite certainly be heard, since otherwise I would not pray with a condition attached. But prayers offered in faith are not determinative at all, and he who blithely wishes that things might go for him exactly as he wants, has no confidence in God. The spirit of prayer, which makes us skilled in performing good actions, is the perfection that we seek; the latter, however, is merely a means of arriving at the spirit. Prayers, therefore, must not be regarded as a special way of serving God, but merely as a means of awakening dispositions devoted to Him. We serve God, not by words, ceremonies and grimaces, but when we express in our actions the dispositions that are devoted to God. So a person who has prayed has not yet done anything good thereby; he has merely schooled himself to express good in his actions. We have to remove everything from it that is practically good, and seek out the purest concept. The result is, then, that prayer has the goodness of a means. So when prayers that have only the value of a means are taken for special ways of serving God, for an immediate good, that is a false illusion of religion. An error in religion is more excusable than an illusion there; for erroneous religion can be put right, whereas illusion is not only without content, but is also, in fact, adverse to the reality of religion.

Prayer seems to awaken a presumption and mistrust of God, as though we had no confidence in His knowing what is useful to us. On the other hand, persistent, unremitting petition seems like a temptation of God, whereby we are seeking, therefore, to move Him to satisfy our wishes. The
27:326 question arises, then, as to whether such persistent prayer is effectual. If it has been offered in faith, and the petitioner has the spirit and not the letter of it, such trust in God is a motivating ground for granting the request, but specification of the object of prayer is no such ground. The object of prayer must be general and not specific, so that God's wisdom can be exercised to its fullest degree of adequacy. Generality is achieved, however, when we ask to be worthy of all the benefits that God is ready to bestow on us, and only a prayer of that sort can be granted; for it is moral, and hence conformable to God's wisdom. But in temporal matters the specific plea is needless, for in that case one always has to add: so far as may seem fitting to God; but the

condition already does away with the specificity. Now although specific requests are needless, therefore, man is nonetheless a helpless and incapable creature, who is beset with ignorance of his future destiny, so that he cannot be blamed for making specific requests, e.g., in peril at sea. It is an expression of the neediness of a helpless creature in the utmost distress. Such a plea is heard to this extent, that its trustfulness can be a motivating ground for God either to grant the request or provide aid in some other fashion, even though the petitioner can have no firm belief that God will grant him just what he asks. To pray in faith is to ask of God that of which it can reasonably be hoped that He will grant it. But only spiritual objects are of this kind. If, then, I beg for these from a pure disposition, my prayer arises from faith, and in that case I am also worthy of redress for my moral shortcomings; but if I beg for temporal favours, I cannot reasonably hope that God will grant them to me, and hence I cannot pray for them in faith. The spirit of prayer must be distinguished from the letter of it. The letter is needed, in our case, only insofar as it awakens in us the spirit of prayer. But the spirit is a disposition devoted to God. To pray is thus an act of devotion. If the practice of it, in life, is directed so that prayer awakens in us active dispositions that find expression in action, then our prayer is devout.

Our author speaks of the purity of religion. Purity is contrasted either to the mixed, or to the stained. Pure religion, insofar as it is opposed to the mixed, means a religion solely of dispositions towards God and containing morality. Mixed religion, insofar as it is mingled with sensibility, represents merely a means to morality. We may say, then, that with man no pure religion is possible, since he is a sensory being; yet sensory means in religion are not to be censured. However, the pure Idea of religion has to be an archetype for us, and serve as the basis; for this is the goal, and so is strongly looked to, here in morality. 27:327

Our author goes on to speak of religious zeal. Zeal is an inflexibly decided will to attain the end with unchangeable resolution. Such zeal is valuable in all circumstances; but if, in religion, it denotes a passion directed to promoting everything in religion, then it is blind, and if there is anywhere that we should have our eyes open, it is in religion. Hence there should be no zeal there, but rather an inflexible seriousness. Pious simplicity, insofar as it is opposed to the affected kind, denotes precision in the use of means, whereby the action is accurately suited in magnitude to the end. In religion we should attend only to what is directed to the end. Theology requires learning, but religion simplicity. A practical atheist lives in such a way that one would take him to maintain that there is no God. Those who live thus are called practical atheists, though that goes too far. The practical atheist is the godless man, for godlessness is a kind of shameless wickedness which bids defiance to the punishments that the idea of God inspires in us. Ratiocination, zealotry and superstition are three deviations from religion, of which we have already made some mention above. Zealotry is when the letter of religion is mistaken for its spirit. Superstition consists in the notion whereby we adopt as the ground of reason what is essentially contrary to the maxims of reason. Religious superstition is for the most part religious illusion. Religious fanaticism is a delusion of inner sense, whereby we believe ourselves to stand in a communal relation with God and other spirits.

DE CULTU EXTERNO

27:328

Just as we have distinguished from one another the fear of God and the service of God, so we also distinguish religious acts into the God-fearing and the God-serving. Anthropomorphism is the cause of our picturing duties towards God on the analogy of duties to man. We think we are performing acts of service to God when we tell Him of our submissiveness and humility by worship, praise-giving and declarations. We can indeed render a service to any man, however great he may be. Among services there are some which consist merely in assurances of being ready to do anything the other may require. That includes paying court, where we merely present our person as ready to perform any services desired. A prince covets respect, and hence this provides a service to him. But now men are inclined to apply such acts of service to God, and to render Him services, and pay court to Him with submissiveness and humility, and by such tokens of reverence they think they have already done Him a service. Hence the impression has arisen that the deity, to keep men in practice, has issued commands that are in themselves empty, whereby men would grow accustomed to attend to commands and be kept always serviceable. Thus certain religions have fasts, pilgrimages and chastisements, whereby their members demonstrate that they are ready to obey orders. These are mere observances, which have no goodness whatever and are no help to anyone. All religions are full of them. The totality of actions having no other purpose than to demonstrate assiduity in the performance of God's commands is called the service of God. But the true service of God does not consist in outward observances, but in sanctified dispositions actively displayed in life by our actions. The God-fearing man is he who venerates God's most holy law, and whose fear of God accompanies all his actions; so acts of service to God are not special actions, since in all my actions I can serve God; and that is an incessant service of God, extending throughout the whole of life, and does not consist in special actions that have only to be observed at certain times. The fear and service of God are not special actions, but the form of all actions. In religion, though, we have actions by which men imagine they are serving God directly; but in fact we can perform no actions save those whose effects extend to this world. We can have no effect upon God at all, save only in dedicating devout dispositions to Him. Hence there are no religious acts whatever, addressed to

God, whereby one might show Him a service, and devotional exercises are in no way intended to please Him and elicit a service, but only to strengthen the dispositions of the soul in us, so that in our lives we become pleasing to God through our actions. This includes, for example, prayer and all sensory means, which are merely preparations for making our dispositions practical. The true service of God consists in a course of life that is purified by the true fear of God. So we are not going to serve God, when we go to church; we go there only to school ourselves, so that we may thereafter serve Him in our lives. On coming out of church, we have to practise what we have trained for inside it, and so serve God only in our lives. The *cultus* consists of two parts: that which belongs to it as a moral training, and that which is mere observance; examples of the former are prayer, responses and the sermon, and also certain physical acts, which are meant to enhance belief in us, and lend more emphasis to our moral actions. But the more the *cultus* is overloaded with observances, the emptier it is of moral training. It has value only as a means, and God is not directly served by it at all; its only purpose is to exercise a man's mind in dispositions, and to keep him conformable in life to the supreme will. Men are inclined to mistake what has the value of a means for the thing itself, and hence to look upon observances as real acts of service to God. This is the greatest evil, inherent in all religions, and comes not from their constitution, but from the inclination that is so inveterate in all men. But to serve God, and take on dispositions devoted to Him, is in fact very difficult, for men have to curb their inclinations thereby, and they need constant cultivation. But specific numbers of prayers, fasts or pilgrimages are things that impose no unceasing duty upon us; they merely last for a time, and then we are free again, then we can do as we want; maybe even cheating a little once more, and then again putting it right by keeping observances and submissively declaring our remorse. Well may men practise a cult, in place of moral dispositions, for the latter bear heavily upon them, and must be observed without ceasing, so that they would sooner make a system out of the cult. Hence it has come about, that men have held religion to be a plaster for their conscience, whereby they have thought to make good the sins committed against God. The *cultus* is thus an invention of men, and then having two ways of pleasing God, by morality and by *cultus,* they resort to the latter to replace the former; for if men are not punctilious in regard to morality, they are all the more so in regard to the *cultus.* It is needful, therefore, for teachers of the common people to try to eliminate and root out such things. *Cultus* and observance are thus of no value at all in regard to God; they have value only for ourselves, as a means of strengthening and awakening the dispositions that should be expressed in actions from love towards God. But when does a man know that he is using the *cultus* merely as means? When he pays heed in his life as to whether moral dispositions and the fear of God are to be met with in his actions.

27:329

27:330

External religion is a contradiction. All religion is within. There may well be external actions, but they do not constitute religion at all, nor can we serve God at all by means of them; on the contrary, all these actions directed to God are but means of reinforcing the dispositions devoted to Him. The *cultus externus* comprises outward means, intended to inspire the soul to good dispositions, that are to be displayed in life and action. So there really are outward means which strengthen the inner dispositions, ideas and convictions, and lend life and emphasis to them, for example, in a whole congregation of the people, to dedicate holy dispositions unanimously to God. But anyone who thinks he has already done God a service thereby, is suffering from the most appalling delusion. A source of misunderstanding on this point has done great harm in religion. Because men are exceedingly frail in all acts of morality, and not only what they practise as a good action is very defective and flawed, but they also consciously and wilfully violate the divine law, they are quite unable to confront a holy and just judge, who cannot forgive evil-doing *simpliciter*. The question is, can we, by our vehement begging and beseeching, hope for and obtain through God's goodness the forgiveness of all our sins? No, we cannot without contradiction conceive of a kindly judge; as ruler he may well be kindly, but a judge must be just. For if God could forgive all evil-doing, He could also make it permissible and if He can grant it impunity, it rests also on His will to make it permitted; 27:331 in that case, however, the moral laws would be an arbitrary matter, though in fact they are not arbitrary, but just as necessary and eternal as God. God's justice is the precise allocation of punishments and rewards in accordance with men's good or bad behaviour. The divine will is immutable. Hence we cannot hope that because of our begging and beseeching God will forgive us everything, for in that case it would be a matter, not of well-doing, but of begging and beseeching. We cannot therefore conceive of a kindly judge without wishing that on this occasion He might close His eyes, and allow Himself to be moved by supplications and flatteries; but this might then befall only a few, and would have to be kept quiet; for if it were generally known, then everyone would want it so, and that would make a mockery of the law. So begging can bring about no remission of punishment; the holy law necessarily entails that punishments should be appropriate to actions. But is man, then, to be left without help, seeing that he is frail, after all, in regard to morality? He cannot, indeed, hope for any remission of punishment for his crimes from a benevolent ruler, since in that case the divine will would not be holy; but man is holy insofar as he is adequate to the moral law; he can, therefore, hope for kindness from the benevolent ruler, not only in regard to the physical, where the very actions themselves already produce good consequences, but also in regard to the moral; but he cannot hope to be dispensed from morality, and from the consequences of violating it. The goodness of God consists, rather, in the aids whereby He can make up for the deficiencies of our natural frailty, and thereby display His benevolence. If, for our part, we do everything we can, we may hope for a supplementation, such that we may stand before God's justice and be found adequate to the holy laws. How God brings about this supplementation, and what sort of means He employs for it, we know not, nor do we have any need to know; but we can hope for it. In that case, then, instead of a lenient justice, we have a supplementation of justice. But because men have believed that, however far they might go in well-doing, they would still always be defective in their own eyes, far more than in those of God, they have supposed that God must do everything in them, or pardon all their sins; and hence they have employed external means, to solicit this from God and obtain His grace, and thus have gone over to begging. Their religion was thus a religion of courting favour. And so there is a religion of courting favour, and a religion of leading the good life, which consists in endeavouring to observe the holy law punctiliously, from a pure disposition, and in hoping that a supplementation will be granted to one's frailty. Now a person of that sort has a religion, not of courting favour, but of leading a good life. The religion of courting favour is harmful and altogether contrary to the concept of God, and is a system of make-up and disguise in religion, where, under the appearance of religion and outward service to God, whereby men think to make good all that has gone before, they thereupon later go back to sinning again, in the hope of making it good once more by similarly external means. But of what use to a shop-keeper, for example, are all his morning and evening devotions, if straight after early service, he cheats an unsuspecting customer in marketing his wares? And then goes on to thank God for it with a couple of pious ejaculations as he passes a church door? That is simply trying to impose on God by Jesuitical subterfuges. Reason is in complete agreement here with the gospels, which present the example of the brothers,* of whom one was a *complementarius,*ˢ who courted favour, and promised at once to obey the will of his father, but failed to do so, whereas the other made difficulties, yet still did his duty towards his father. Such religion is more harmful than every kind of irreligion, since there is no longer any remedy for it. A godless man can often be set on the right road with a word, but not the hypocrite. All these remarks are intended to bring out that the external side of religion, the *cultus,* has the value of a means only, in regard to ourselves, but counts for nothing directly, in regard to God; and that we should not believe that our moral imperfections are made up for by the *cultus externus,* but rather that they are made adequate to the holy law by means known only to God.

27:332

*[Matt. 21:28–32 – Tr.]
ˢ a hypocrite

115

OF EXAMPLE AND PATTERN IN RELIGION

27:333

An example is when a general proposition of reason is exhibited *in concreto* in the given case. Of *a priori* propositions we must have it proved that they also occur *in concreto*, and do not merely reside in the understanding; for otherwise they are reckoned among *fictiones;* for example, a plan of government conceived by reason must also be proved possible *in concreto* by means of an example. It may be asked, therefore, whether examples should also be permitted in morality and religion. What is apodeictically *a priori* needs no example, for there I perceive the necessity *a priori*. Mathematical propositions, for instance, need no examples; for the example serves, not as a proof, but as an illustration. Of concepts, on the other hand, that are drawn from experience, we cannot tell whether they are possible until an example is presented *in concreto* in the given case. All cognitions of morality and religion can be set forth apodeictically, *a priori*, through reason. We perceive *a priori* the necessity of behaving so and not otherwise; so no examples are needed in matters of religion and morality. There is thus no pattern in religion, since the ground, the *principium* of behaviour, must lie in reason and cannot be derived *a posteriori*, and even if experience furnishes me with not a single example of honesty, uprightness and virtue, still reason tells me that I ought so to be. In religion, indeed, the examples themselves must be judged by universal principles, as to whether they are good or not. The examples, therefore, must be judged by moral rules, not morality and religion by the examples. The archetype lies in the understanding.

So if saintly figures are presented to us as a pattern in religion, I am not to imitate them, however holy they may be, but rather to judge them by universal rules of morality. There are examples, indeed, of righteousness and virtue, and even of holiness, such as that set forth to us in the gospels, yet I do not make this example of holiness fundamental, but judge it by the holy law. Only if it agrees with the latter, do I then perceive that it is an example of the holiness. Examples serve us for encouragement and emulation, but must not be used as a pattern. If I see a thing *in concreto*, I recognize it all the more clearly. The reason why men would gladly imitate in matters of religion is that they fancy that if they behave as does the great majority among them, they will thereby constrain God, in that He cannot, after all, punish everybody; so that if He forgives everyone, He will also forgive themselves. Men are happy, moreover, to cling to the belief of their

27:334

forefathers; for in that case they think, even though it be false, that they are absolved from blame; it was their ancestors who impelled them to it, and if a man can only shift the blame to others, he is content, and thinks thereby to shield himself from responsibility. But a person who alters the religion of his elders and forefathers, and adopts another, is accounted a foolhardy fellow, who is embarking on something very dangerous, since in that case he is taking all the blame on himself. If we accept what is universal in religion, and must prevail in every religion, namely to please God by inner dispositions, and to practise His holy law, and to hope by His benevolence for a supplement to our frailties, then anyone may always follow the religion of his fathers; it can do him no harm, so long as he does not believe that by the *cultus* of his own religion he is more pleasing to God than by the *cultus* of some other one. The observances may be as they will, if only they are regarded as means whereby godly dispositions are to be awakened; but if they are held to be an immediate service to God, this is a major fault in a religion, and in that case one religion is as harmful as another.

OF STUMBLING-BLOCKS

An example is not for copying, though it is certainly for emulation. The ground of the action must be derived, not from the example, but from the rule; yet if others have shown that such an act is possible, we must emulate their example and also exert ourselves to perform such moral actions, and not let others surpass us in that respect. Men like, in general, to have examples, and if none exists they are happy to excuse themselves, on the ground that everybody lives that way. But if examples are available, to which appeal can be made, then it encourages people to emulate them. A bad example, however, is a stumbling-block and gives occasion for two evils; for imitation as a pattern, and for excuse. Thus men of high position or spiritual standing give occasion, by their example, for imitation, though in religion there should be no imitation whatever; but it happens, nevertheless. If, however, an example furnishes an excuse, it is also a *scandalum.*[t] No man will readily be wicked on his own, any more than he will gladly do a duty on his own; he always appeals to others. And the more examples of the kind are available, the happier he is at being able to appeal to a number of them.

27:335

All *scandala* are either *data* or *accepta.* The first are those which inevitably constitute a necessary ground of evil consequences for the morality of others. The second, those which merely represent a contingent ground. It cannot be accounted to me, if another makes a misuse of my actions, which may then have evil consequences in regard to his morality, albeit none for mine; for I might have seen the matter differently, so that it is in full agreement with my own moral convictions. Although, therefore, I cannot help it if another makes a perverse use of my actions, one is nevertheless constrained to provide no occasion for it. However, if I need to avoid the occasion for such a *scandalum acceptum*[u] by having to behave

[t] a bad example
[u] a necessarily bad/a dangerous example

affectedly in my actions, and even against my conscience, then I do not need to avoid it, if no other way remains open to me; for all my actions should be upright and unaffected, and if I am persuaded in my conscience of the opposite viewpoint, I would be obliged, in seeking to give no offence to the other, to act against my own conscience. If I am convinced, for example, in my conscience, that to prostrate oneself before images is idolatry, and I am in a place where this is going on, then if I did it in order to give no offence to others, I would be acting against my conscience; yet this must be holy to me. I can, indeed, feel sorry that anyone should be offended thereby, but it is no fault of mine.

Religion has two parts: to honour God and to love God. I can honour someone in two ways, practically, when I do his will, and in a flattering manner, by outward marks of esteem. I cannot honour God by flattering Him, through assurances of esteem, but only in a practical way, by actions. So if I practise the holy law from a sense of duty and reverence towards God, as the law-giver, and readily obey His commandments, which are worthy of respect, I do honour to God.

To love God in a practical sense is to obey his commandments gladly, because they are worthy of love. I love God when I love His law and fulfil it from love. The false interpretation of doing honour to God has brought forth superstition, and the false love of God, fanaticism.

27:336   What is it to praise God? To form a vivid idea of God's greatness, as a motivating ground of our will, to live in accordance with the will of God. The endeavour to discern God's perfection is a necessary part of religion, which is meant to strengthen and reinforce our will to live according to the holy will of God. But on the other side we may ask: What does the praise of God contribute to that? The praise of God, expressed in words and psalm-singing, which are the medium for our concepts, serves only to magnify within us the practical reverence for God, and thus in our own regard has a subjective, not an objective use; for by praise we give no immediate gratification to God. We praise God only when we employ His perfections, and the glorification of them, as a motivating ground to awaken good dispositions of a practical kind in ourselves. We cannot admit God to have any inclination to be praised by us. Our knowledge of Him is also very inadequate to His greatness, and those concepts whereby we think to praise Him are very erroneous, so that our hymns of praise are utterly out of keeping with His perfections. Their usefulness is therefore merely subjective, and objective indirectly, by means of that. It would be better if man were schooled as to how he should feel true reverence for God in his soul, rather than letting him express in words and formulae a variety of laudatory utterances that he does not actually feel. But how can we instil a concept of God that evokes such reverence in the soul? That is not done by expressions and mechanically repeated formulae uttered in praise of the divine perfections, and those who regard the formulae extolling God's goodness and omnipotence as praise of Him, are much mistaken. But in order for us to feel within us the greatness of God, we must be able to intuit it; it would be a very good thing, therefore, if in religion the community were not instructed by way of general concepts exalting God's omnipotence, but rather that they should be brought to realize the might of God – a thing all men are capable of – exemplified in the infinite frame of the universe, containing a multitude of worlds that are populated with rational creatures. Such picturing and intuiting of God's greatness produces far more effect in our soul than any amount of psalm-singing. But men believe that such encomia are directly pleasing to God. Observances, however, are no part of religion, but merely means to it. True religion is the religion of fearing God, and of the course of life. If a man shows no sign of it in his actions, he has no religion, let him talk as he will. 27:337

The signs of religion are of two kinds, essential and ambiguous. The first include, for example, conscientiousness in the conduct of life. The second, for example, observance of the *cultus*. But although the *cultus* is an ambiguous sign, it need not on that account be rejected; it is a sign that men are trying, by means of the *cultus*, to awaken in themselves dispositions devoted to God. But in judging them both, the *cultus* is an ambiguous sign. For others cannot see that in a man. The man can feel within himself that he is observing the *cultus* to awaken in himself, by means of it, dispositions devoted to God; but he can only demonstrate this to others, in life, by actions.

OF SHAME IN REGARD TO DEVOTION

No man seems to be ashamed of piety and the fear of God, unless he be in such company as is wholly wicked, and bids defiance to everything; and then he is ashamed of having a conscience, just as one is ashamed, among rascals, of being an honest man. But among morally cultivated men, nobody will be ashamed of being devout. We point this out merely for consideration, and not as pertinent to religion. The more upright a man is, the more readily he is ashamed if surprised in an act of devotion. A hypocrite will not be ashamed, but on the contrary, will let himself be seen. When the gospel tells us:* When thou prayest, go into thy chamber, this is merely to avoid the appearance of being a hypocrite; for a man is ashamed if another thinks any ill of him, even though he has committed no fault. For example, if something is found missing in a group of people, and inquiries are made, and someone is looked at, he blushes. The first reason for shame, therefore, is lest one be taken for a

*[Matt. 6:6 – Tr.]

hypocrite. The second, however, is this: We know God, not by intuition, but through faith. We are thus able to speak of God, as of an object of faith, to the effect that: If God in His goodness were so to guide the children in their upbringing, that they, etc., and one will not then be in the least ashamed of such a wish, and we may thus also speak of it in company. Suppose, though, that someone in the company were to lift his 27:338 hands and pray, even if he said nothing, it would strike us very much. What is the reason for this? The object of faith is being made into an object of intuition. To be sure, faith is just as strong as intuition; but, after all, God, once again, is an object, not of intuition, but of faith, and hence I must address Him as such. So why, then, do we pray? If I pray by myself, I can imitate an intuition and compose my soul. But in church, prayer has something pathetic about it, in that the object of faith is turned into an object of intuition. Even a preacher, though, can pray to God, as to an object of faith, given that in such an assembly the *pathema*[v] may quite well be aroused. In other company, however, it would be highly fantastic.

OF THE CONFESSING OF RELIGION, AND TO WHAT EXTENT ANYTHING IS A *STATUS CONFESSIONIS*,[w] AND THE CONDITIONS UNDER WHICH THE LATTER OCCURS.

This can best be seen in examples. In foreign countries, where there is a superstitious religion, there is no need for a person to declare his religion. If I believe that ceremonies and prostration before saints are a hindrance to religion, and if a case occurs where in my presence everyone prostrates himself before a holy image, it does me no harm to join in, and I have no need to declare my own religion, for God looks to the humbled heart, and not to the humbled body. But if I am forced, on peril of my life, to comply with the local religion or customs, as Niebuhr relates of the travellers who go to Mecca to witness Mahometan practices, that they must either lose their lives or let themselves be circumcised – which actually happened to a Frenchman – then this, too, is no *status confessionis*; I can always let myself be circumcised, it does no harm, especially if I can thereby save my life. But if someone is forced to declare his dispositions, and accept by swearing and protestation what he considers false, and to abjure what he is obligated to hold in high esteem, then that is a *status confessionis*, and in that case I can say: Your customs I am always willing to adopt, but at once to frame new dispositions – that can't be done, and so in that regard I 27:339 must declare nothing. If I believe that ceremonies and prostration before

[v] religious feeling
[w] commitment to religious belief

saints are a hindrance to religion, and if a case occurs where in my presence everyone . . .*

Anyone who denies his religion is either a renegade or an apostate. One can be an apostate without being a renegade, that is, one may forsake a religion of one's own accord, as Spinoza, for example, renounced Judaism, but one has not yet become a renegade on that account. The name of God can be misused in the practice of hypocrisy and impiety. But one should not at once take people to be impious, when they swear for instance; often they are the kindliest of men, and it is merely a matter of habit with them. As with a commanding officer, for example; such people do it merely to lend emphasis to their words, though they know full well that they cannot so command the divine thunder, that their soldiers should be stricken by it.

Here ends the section on natural religion, and now we come to morality proper.

*[Repetition and a break in the text at this point. – Tr.]

On morality

I. OF DUTIES TO ONESELF

Having hitherto dealt with everything that pertains to natural religion, we now proceed to morality proper, and to our natural duties toward everything that exists in the world.

The first topic, however, is our duties to ourselves. These are not considered by the law, for the latter deals only with the relationship to other people. I cannot observe the law in regard to myself, for what I do to myself, I do with my own consent, and am committing no breach of public justice when I take action against myself. We shall be talking here of the use of freedom in regard to oneself. By way of introduction, it should be noted that no part of morals has been more defectively treated than this of the duties to oneself. Nobody has framed a correct concept of such duties; it has been considered a trifling matter, and mentioned only at the end, as a supplement to morality, in the belief that once a man has fulfilled all his duties, he may finally also think about himself. In this portion, therefore, all philosophical systems of morality are false. But Gellert hardly deserves mention here, since he never even gets to the point of discussing the case of duties to oneself. He talks merely of benevolence and good behaviour, the poet's hobby-horse, though finally, not to forget himself altogether, he thinks of himself, just as an innkeeper, who has already fed all his guests, finally does the same. Hutcheson also belongs here, though he has otherwise thought in a more philosophic spirit. It all comes of the fact that people have had no pure concept on which to base a duty to oneself. The thought has been that self-regarding duty consists in promoting one's own happiness, as Wolf also defined it; it now depends on how everyone determines his happiness, and then duty to oneself would consist of a general rule directing us to satisfy all our inclinations and promote our own happiness. This would, however, be a great hindrance thereafter to
our duty to others. It is by no means the principle, though, of self-regarding duties, and the latter have nothing to do with well-being and our temporal happiness.

So far from these duties being the lowest, they actually take first place, and are the most important of all; for even without first explaining what self-regarding duty is, we may ask how, if a man degrades his own person, anything else can be demanded of him? He who violates duties toward himself, throws away his humanity, and is no longer in a position to perform duties to others. Thus a person who has performed his duties to others badly, who has not been generous, kindly or compassionate, but has observed the duty to himself, and lived in a seemly fashion, may still in himself possess a certain inner worth.

But the man who has violated the duties to himself has no inner worth. Thus the infringement of self-regarding duties takes all his worth from a man, and the infringement of duties to others deprives him of worth only in that respect. Hence the former are the condition under which the others can be observed. We shall first illustrate the violation of self-regarding duties with a few examples: A drunkard, for instance, does nobody any harm, and if he has a strong constitution, does no harm even to himself. But he is an object of contempt. A fawning servility is likewise not indifferent to me; such a man dishonours his own person, for one should not fawn, and a man degrades his humanity in doing so. Or if a person, for the sake of profit, lets himself be used in everything, like a ball, by someone else, he is throwing away his worth as a man. The lie is more an infringement of duty to oneself than to others, and even if a liar does nobody any harm by it, he is still an object of contempt, a low fellow who violates the duties to himself. Indeed, to go further still it is already a breach of the duty to oneself if one accepts favours; for he who accepts favours creates debts that he cannot repay; he can never even the score with his benefactor, since the latter first did him the kindness of his own accord; if he returns the favour, he does it only insofar as the other preceded him in this, and thus remains forever owing thanks to him; but who will incur such debts? A debtor is at all times under the constraint of having to treat the person he is obliged to with politeness and flattery; if he 27:342 does not, the benefactor soon lets him know of it, and often he has to circumvent the latter with many detours and greatly burden himself. But he who pays promptly for everything can act freely, and nobody will hamper him in doing so. Then again the timorous man, who complains of his fate, and sighs and weeps, is in our eyes an object of disdain; we try to get away from him, rather than having to commiserate with him. But the man who shows a steadfast courage in his misfortune, feeling pain at it, to be sure, but making no abject complaints, and knowing how to handle the situation, is the man who evokes compassion from us. Yet again, the man who throws away his own freedom, and barters it for cash, is acting contrary to his manhood. It is not life that is to be treasured, but rather that one should live it throughout as a man, not, that is, in a state of well-being, but so that one does not dishonour mankind; as a man one must live worthily, and whatever deprives us of that makes us fit for nothing and abolishes us as men. So those who expose their bodies to the mischief of others, in order to gain something, and also those who pay them, are behaving with equal vileness. Nor can persons give themselves up to satisfying the desires of another – even if they might thereby at once save parents and friends from death – without casting their person away. Still less can it be done for money. If somebody does it to satisfy their own inclination, that is still, indeed, natural, though it is very lacking in virtue and runs counter to morality; but if done for money, or any other purpose, it throws away the worth of humanity, in that it allows one to be used as a tool. So it is too with the offences against oneself that are called *crimina corporis,*[x] which are also deemed indecent for that reason. Nobody is harmed by them, yet it is a dishonouring of the worth of humanity in one's own person. Suicide is the supreme violation of the duties to oneself. Now what, then, does the abominable nature of this act consist in? With all such duties, one must not look for the ground in any prohibition on the part of God, for suicide is not abominable because God has forbidden it; on the contrary, God has forbidden it because it is abominable. If it were otherwise, suicide would be abominable only by God's prohibition, and then I would not know why He should have forbidden it, if it were not abominable in itself. So the reason for regarding suicide and other transgressions of duty as abominable must be derived, not from the divine will, but from their inherently abominable nature. Now the latter resides in the fact that a man uses his freedom to destroy himself, when he ought to use it solely to live as a man; he is able to dispose over everything pertaining to his person, but not over that person itself, nor can he use his freedom against himself. In this case it is very difficult to recognize the self-regarding duties, for a man has, after all, a natural revulsion from suicide, yet if he starts to think over the matter, he may believe it possible to lay hands on himself and exit from the world, and thereby be rid of all his troubles. This has a very plausible air, and by the rules of prudence* it is often the surest and best method, yet suicide is in itself abhorrent. Here enters the rule of morality, which surpasses all rules of prudence and reflection, and commands us, apodeictically and categorically, to observe the duties to oneself; for the man is here employing his powers and freedom against himself, to make himself a carcase. A man can indeed dispose over his condition, but not over his person, for he himself is an end and not a means. It is utterly absurd that a rational being, who is an end whereto every means exists, should use himself as a means. A person can, indeed, serve as a means for others, by his work, for example, but in such a way that he does not cease to exist as a person and an end. He who does something, whereby he cannot be an end, is using himself as a means, and treating his person as a thing. To dispose over his person as a means is not a choice open to him, and of this there will be more to say later on. Self-regarding duties do not depend on the relation of actions to the ends of happiness, for in that case they would rest on inclinations and

27:343

* [Reading *Klugheit* for *Freiheit* – Tr.]
[x] crimes of the body

be a rule of prudence. But rules which only show the necessity of the means in satisfying inclinations are not moral rules, and nor, in that case, could they impose a duty. Self-regarding duties, however, are independent of all advantage, and pertain only to the worth of being human. They rest on the fact that in regard to our person we have no untrammelled freedom, that humanity in our own person must be highly esteemed, since without this, man is an object of contempt, which is an absolute fault, since he is worthless, not only in the eyes of others, but also in himself. The self-regarding duties are the supreme condition and *principium* of all morality, for the worth of the person constitutes moral worth; the worth of skill relates only to one's circumstances. Socrates was in a sorry state, which had no value at all, but his person, in this condition, was of the greatest worth. Even if all the amenities of life are sacrificed, maintenance of the worth of humanity makes up for the loss of them all, and sustains approbation, and if all else is lost we still have an inner worth. Under this worth of humanity alone can we perform our other duties. It is the basis for all the rest. He who has no inner worth has thrown away his person and can no longer perform any other duty. On what, then, does the *principium* of all self-regarding duties depend? 27:344

Freedom, on the other hand, is the capacity which confers unlimited usefulness on all the others. It is the highest degree of life. It is the property that is a necessary condition underlying all perfections. All animals have the capacity to use their powers according to choice. Yet this choice is not free, but necessitated by incentives and *stimuli.* Their actions contain *bruta necessitas.*ʸ If all creatures had such a choice, tied to sensory drives, the world would have no value. But the inner worth of the world, the *summum bonum,* is freedom according to a choice that is not necessitated to act. Freedom is thus the inner worth of the world. But on the other hand, insofar as it is not restrained under certain rules of conditioned employment, it is the most terrible thing there could ever be. All animal acts are regular, for they take place according to rules that are subjectively necessitated. In the whole of non-free nature we find an inner, subjectively necessitated *principium,* whereby all actions in that sphere take place according to a rule. But if we now take freedom among men, we find there no subjectively necessitating *principium* for the regularity of actions; if there were, it would not be freedom, and what would follow from that? If freedom is not restricted by objective rules, the result is much savage disorder. For it is uncertain whether man will not use his powers to destroy himself, and others, and the whole of nature. Given freedom, I can imagine every kind of lawlessness, if it is not objectively necessitated.

These objectively necessitating grounds that restrict freedom must lie

---

ʸ animal necessity

27:345 in the understanding. The supreme rule is therefore the proper use of freedom. What, then, is the condition under which freedom is restricted? The general law is as follows: Behave in such a way that in all your actions regularity prevails. What, then, will it be that is to restrict freedom in regard to myself? It is: Not to follow my inclinations. The prime rule whereby I am to restrict freedom is the conformity of free behaviour to the essential ends of mankind. I shall therefore not follow my inclinations, but bring them under a rule. Anyone who allows his person to be governed by his inclinations is acting contrary to the essential end of mankind, for as a free agent he must not be subject to his inclinations, but should determine them through freedom; for if he is free, he must have a rule; and this rule is the essential end of mankind. In animals the inclinations are already determined by subjectively necessitating grounds. There can therefore be no lawlessness among them. Now if man freely follows his inclinations, he is lower even than the animals, for in that case there arises in him a lawlessness that does not exist among them. But if so, he contravenes the essential ends of mankind in his own person, and is acting against himself. All the evils in the world spring from freedom. Animals act according to rules because they are not free. But free beings can act in a regular fashion only insofar as they restrict their freedom by rules.

 Let us consider those actions of a man that relate to himself, and contemplate freedom there. They arise from impulses and inclinations, or from maxims and principles. It is therefore necessary for a man to resort to maxims, and restrict his free self-regarding actions by rules, and these are rules and duties that are directed to himself. For if we consider a man in regard to his inclinations and instincts, he is not bound in that respect, and is not necessitated by either of them. In the whole of nature there is nothing that would be injurious to man in the satisfaction of his inclinations. Everything harmful is the product of his invention and the use of his freedom, for example, all strong drink, and the many dishes for his palate. Now if he follows without a rule the inclination he has devised for himself, he becomes the most abhorrent of objects, in that by means of his free-

27:346 dom he can remodel the whole of nature in order to satisfy his inclinations. It may certainly be conceded to him, that he should discover many things to satisfy his inclination; but he must have a rule to avail himself of them. If he has none, freedom is his greatest misfortune. So it has to be restricted, not, though, by other properties and faculties, but by itself. Its supreme rule is: In all self-regarding actions, so to behave that any use of powers is compatible with the greatest use of them. For example, if I have drunk too much today, I am incapable of making use of my freedom and my powers; or if I do away with myself, I likewise deprive myself of the ability to use them. So this conflicts with the greatest use of freedom, that it abolishes itself, and all use of it, as the highest *principium* of life. Only under certain conditions can freedom be consistent with itself; otherwise it comes into collision with itself. If there were no order in nature, every-thing would come to an end, and so it is, too, with unbridled freedom. There are doubtless evils in nature, but the true wickedness, vice, resides solely in freedom. We pity an unfortunate, but hate a villain and rejoice at his punishment. The conditions under which alone the greatest use of freedom is possible, and under which it can be self-consistent, are the essential ends of mankind. With these, freedom must agree. The *principium* of all duties is thus the conformity of the use of freedom with the essential ends of mankind.

We shall show this by means of examples. Thus a man is not entitled to sell his limbs for money, not even if he were to get 10,000 thalers for one finger; for otherwise all the man's limbs might be sold off. One may dispose of things that have no freedom, but not of a being that itself has free choice. If a man does that, he turns himself into a thing, and then anyone may treat him as they please, because he has thrown his person away; as with sexual inclinations, where people make themselves an object of enjoyment, and hence into a thing. There is thus also a degradation of humanity in it, and people are ashamed of it as well. Freedom, therefore, is the basis for the most dreadful vices, in that it can contrive a multitude of things – a *crimen carnis contra naturam,*[z] for example – to satisfy its inclination, just as it is also a basis of the virtue that does honour to mankind. Some crimes and vices arising from freedom evoke horror, as suicide does; others disgust, indeed even when they are so much as mentioned. We are ashamed of them, in that we thereby put ourselves below the beasts. They are still viler than suicide, for though that cannot be mentioned without horror, these cannot be spoken of without disgust. Suicide is the most abominable of the crimes that inspire horror and hatred, but the object of disgust and contempt is more repellent still.

27:347

The *principium* of the self-regarding duties does not consist in self-favour, but in self-esteem; our actions, that is, must be in keeping with the worth of humanity. Just as the law tells us: *neminem laede,* so here we might also say: *noli naturam humanam in te ipso laedere.*[a]

We have in us two foundations for our actions: inclinations, which are animal in nature, and humanity, to which the inclinations have to be subordinated. The self-regarding duties are negative, and restrict our freedom in regard to the inclinations that are directed to our well-being. Just as the precepts of the law restrict our freedom in our dealings with other people, so the self-regarding duties restrict our freedom with re-spect to ourselves. All such duties are founded on a certain love of honour consisting in the fact that a man values himself, and in his own eyes is not unworthy that his actions should be in keeping with humanity. To be

[z] unnatural sex offence
[a] do not injure human nature in yourself

worthy in his eyes of inner respect, the treasuring of approval, is the essential ingredient of the duties to oneself.

The better to appreciate such duties, if we picture to ourselves the evil consequences of violating them, we shall find out how injurious it is to a man. It is not, indeed, the consequences that are the *principium* of these duties, but rather the inner vileness; yet the consequences help, nonetheless, to provide a better insight into the *principium*. Since we have the freedom and ability to satisfy our inclinations by all manner of devices, men would bring about their own downfall, in the absence of restraint. One might, indeed, consider this a rule of prudence, but our prudence can only be fashioned from the consequences. So there has to be a *principium*, that men restrict their freedom to prevent self-conflict, and this *principium* is a moral one.

27:348   We shall now be going on to the particular duties to ourselves, and this in regard to our condition, insofar as we consider ourselves to be intelligent beings.

Man has a general duty to himself, of so disposing himself that he may be capable of observing all moral duties, and hence that he should establish moral purity and principles in himself, and endeavour to act accordingly. This, then, is the primary duty to oneself. Now this entails self-testing and self-examination, as to whether the dispositions also have moral purity. The sources of those dispositions must be examined, to see whether they lie in honour or delusion, in superstition or pure morality. The neglect of this does great harm to morality. If people were to inquire what lies at the bottom of their religion and conduct, the majority would discover that there is far more honour, compassion, prudence and habit in it, than there is morality. This self-examination must be constantly pursued. It is, to be sure, a special act, which cannot always be carried on, but we should pay constant attention to ourselves. In regard to our actions a certain watchfulness is in order, and this is *vigilantia moralis.*[b] This watchfulness should be directed to the purity of our dispositions, and to the punctiliousness of our actions.

Moral fantasies may relate either to the moral law itself, or to our moral actions. The first such delusion is to fancy of the moral law that it is indulgent in regard to ourselves. But the other is to fancy of our moral perfections that they are in conformity with the moral law. The first is more harmful than the second, for if a man fancies that his perfections are compatible with the moral law, it is still easy to dissuade him of this, by pointing to the purity of the moral law. But if a man frames for himself the idea of an indulgent moral law, he has a false law, whereby he also creates maxims and principles such that even his actions can then have no moral goodness.

[b] moral vigilance

OF PROPER SELF-ESTEEM

This self-esteem includes, on the one hand, humility, yet on the other a true noble pride. The opposite of this is meanness. We have reason to harbour a low opinion of our person, but in regard to our humanity we should think highly of ourselves. For if we compare ourselves with the holy moral law, we discover how remote we are from congruity with it. This low opinion of our person arises, therefore, from comparison with the moral law, and there we have reason enough to humble ourselves. But in comparison with others, we have no reason to entertain a poor opinion of ourselves, for I can just as well possess worth as anyone else. This self-esteem, then, in comparison with others, is noble pride. A low opinion of one's person in regard to others is not humility; it betrays, rather, a petty soul and a servile temperament. Such imagined virtue, which is merely an analogue of the real thing, is a monkish kind of virtue, and that is quite unnatural; for the man who so humbles himself towards others is actually proud thereby. Our self-esteem is reasonable, for we do the other no harm by it, if we deem ourselves equal to him in worth. But if we wish to pass judgement on ourselves, we must compare ourselves with the pure moral law, and there we find reason for humility. We must not compare ourselves with other righteous men, for they are but copies of the moral law. The gospel does not teach us humility, but it makes us humble. 27:349

We can have self-esteem out of self-love, which would be partiality and favour to oneself. This pragmatic self-esteem by rules of prudence is reasonable and possible, insofar as it seeks to provide assurance. Nobody can demand that I should abase myself, and consider myself lower than others; though we all have the right to insist that the other should not exalt himself. However, moral self-esteem, which is founded on the worth of humanity, must never be based on a comparison with others, but only on comparison with the moral law itself. People are very much inclined to take others as the measure of their own moral worth, and if they then believe themselves superior to some, it would be self-conceit to think thus; but the latter is far greater if one believes oneself to be perfect in comparison with the moral law. I can always think that I am better than others, although if, for example, I am better than the worst, I am still by no means very much better; and so this is really not moral self-conceit. If moral humility, then, is the curbing of self-conceit in regard to the moral law, it never implies any comparison with others, but only with that law. 27:350 Humility is thus the curbing of any high opinion of our moral worth, by the comparison of our actions with the moral law. Such a comparison makes us humble. Man has reason to have a low opinion of himself, since his actions are not only in contravention of the moral law, but also lacking in purity. Out of frailty he violates the law and acts against it, and out of weakness his good actions fall short of its purity. A person who conceives the moral law to be indulgent can have a high opinion of himself and possess self-conceit, since the standard by which he measures his actions has been incorrect. All the concepts of the ancients concerning humility and all the moral virtues, were impure and inconsistent with the moral law. The gospel was the first to present us with a pure morality, and as history shows, nothing else came near it. This humility can, however, have injurious consequences, if it is wrongly understood. For it brings timorousness and not courage with it, if a man believes that owing to the defectiveness of his actions they never comply with the moral law, from which inertia arises thereafter, in that he ventures to do nothing at all. Self-conceit and timorousness are the two rocks a man runs into, if he departs, in one direction or the other, from the moral law. On the one hand a man must not despair, but believe he has the strength to follow the moral law, even if he fails to comply with it. On the other, however, he can fall into self-conceit, and build far too much on his own powers. Yet this self-conceit can be averted through the purity of the law; for if the law is presented in its full purity, nobody will be such a fool as to think he can fulfil it quite purely by his own efforts. On this side, therefore, there is not so much danger to be feared, as when a man never ventures anything, from faith. The latter is the rule of the lazy, who wish to do nothing at all themselves, but leave everything to God. To remedy such timorousness, bear in mind that we may hope that our weakness and frailty will receive a

27:351 supplement through divine aid, if we have but done as much as we were able to, knowing our capacity; yet under this condition alone may we hope, for it is thereby only that we are worthy of divine aid. It is not good that certain authors should have sought to deprive man of good dispositions, and thereby thought to convince him of his weakness; by which he was meant to be driven into humility and the beseeching of divine assistance. It is right and proper, indeed, for man to recognize his weakness, but not to be deprived of his good dispositions. For if God is to give him aid, he must at least be worthy of it. The lessening of the worth of human virtues must necessarily have the damaging effect that man thereafter considers both the righteous man and the evil-doer to be on a par; for in that case the righteous man has no good disposition either. Thus everyone will feel in himself that, once at least, he has performed a good action from good dispositions, and that he is capable of doing yet more of them; though they are still always very impure, and will never be fully in keeping with the moral law, they may nevertheless approximate ever closer to it.

OF CONSCIENCE

Conscience is an instinct, to direct oneself according to moral laws. It is not a mere faculty, but an instinct, not to pass judgement on, but to direct oneself. We have a faculty of judging ourselves according to moral laws.

But of this we can make use as we please. Conscience, however, has a driving force, to summon us against our will before the judgement-seat, in regard to the lawfulness of our actions. *It is thus an instinct, and not merely a faculty of judgement.* Moreover, it is an instinct to direct and not to judge. The difference between a magistrate and one who judges is this: that the magistrate can judge *valide,* and actually put the judgement into effect according to the law; his judgement has the force of law, and is a sentence. A magistrate must not only judge, but also either condemn or acquit. If conscience were an impulse to judge, it would be a cognitive faculty, like others, such as the urge to compare oneself to other people, for example, or to flatter oneself; these are not impulses to direct. Everyone has an urge to award praise to himself for his good actions, according to rules of prudence. And conversely, he also reproaches himself for having acted imprudently. So everyone has an impulse to flatter or blame himself by rules of prudence. This, however, is not yet conscience, but only an analogue of it, whereby a man apportions praise or blame to himself. People are often liable to confuse this analogue with conscience. A criminal in the condemned cell is angry, levels the severest reproaches at himself, and is greatly agitated, but mostly over the fact that he has been so imprudent in his actions as to have been caught in them. These reproaches that he now levels at himself he confuses with the reproaches of conscience against his morality; but if only he had extricated himself without trouble, he would never have reproached himself at all, though had he a conscience, this would still have occurred. So the judgement by rules of prudence must assuredly be distinguished from the judgement of conscience.

27:352

Many people have an analogue of conscience, which they take to be conscience itself, and the repentance often displayed on a sick-bed is not remorse for their behaviour in regard to morality, but because they have acted so imprudently that, now that they are to appear before the judge, they will not be able to stand upright. He who abhors his past wickedness, whose consequences torment him at every moment, these torments themselves being evidence of his culpability, does not know whether he is abhorring his wickedness because of the torments, or because of the culpability. He who has no moral feeling, no immediate abhorrence, that is, of the morally evil, and no liking for the morally good, is without conscience. He who must fear accusation because of an evil deed is not reproaching himself for the atrocity of the action, but because of the evil consequences he has thereby brought upon himself; and such a one has no conscience, but only an analogue thereof. But he who feels the atrocity of the acts themselves, be the consequences what they may, does have a conscience. These two things must in no way be confused. Reproaches because of the consequences of imprudence must not be taken for reproaches because of the violation of morality. In life a teacher, for exam-

27:353 ple, must look carefully to see whether a man rues his act out of a true feeling of abhorrence, or whether he is only reproaching himself because he now has to appear before a tribunal where he will not be able to stand upright, on account of his actions. When repentance appears only on the death-bed, there is surely no morality there, for in that case the cause is merely the proximity of death. If there were no fear of this, the man would hardly be repenting his actions. In this case he is like a luckless gambler. As the latter rages against himself and is vexed at having acted so imprudently, and beats himself over the head, so here, too, the man is not abhorring his crimes, but the consequences arising from them. One has to guard against extending comfort to such a man in virtue of this analogue of conscience. Prudence leads us to self-reproach, but conscience accuses us. If a man has once acted imprudently, and does not long torment himself with prudential reproaches, but keeps them up only so long as is necessary to learn better, this is itself a rule of prudence, and does him honour, in that it shows strength of mind. But the accusation of conscience cannot be dismissed, and neither should it be. Here it is not a matter of willpower. In the very dismissal of the accusation, and of the prick of conscience, we can look for no strength of mind; it is infamy, rather, and theological obduracy. He who can dismiss the accusation of his conscience as he pleases, is a rebel, just as is the man who can dismiss the accusation of his judge, when the latter has no control over him. Conscience is an instinct, to judge with legal authority according to moral laws; it pronounces a judicial verdict, and just as a judge can only punish or acquit, but not reward, so conscience, too, either acquits or declares us to deserve punishment. *The judgement of conscience is legitimate if it is felt and exercised. Two consequences arise from this. Moral remorse is the first outcome of the legally binding judicial verdict.* The second outcome, without which the sentence would have no effect, is *that the act be done in accordance with the judicial verdict.* Conscience is idle if it produces no endeavour to carry out what is required in order to satisfy the moral law, and however much remorse a man may display, it is of no avail if he does not perform what is incumbent on him in accordance with the moral law. For even *in foro*

27:354 *humano,* guilt is not assuaged by remorse, but by payment. *Preachers at the sick-bed must therefore see to it, that people do indeed repent the transgression of self-regarding duties, since these can no longer be remedied, but that if they have wronged another, they genuinely try to make amends; for* in foro divino, *whining and blubbering are of no more use than* in foro humano. But never yet have we had an example of such active repentance on the death-bed, and this, too, is at the same time evidence of the neglect of an element that is essential here.

The inner tribunal of conscience may aptly be compared with an external court of law. Thus we find within us an accuser, who could not exist, however, if there were not a law; though the latter is no part of the civil positive law, but resides in reason, and is a law that we can in no way corrupt, nor dispute the rights and wrongs of it. Now this moral law underlies humanity as a holy and inviolable law. In addition, there is also at the same time in man an advocate, namely self-love, who excuses him and makes many an objection to the accusation, whereupon the accuser seeks in turn to rebut the objections. Lastly we find in ourselves a judge, who either acquits or condemns us. There is no deceiving him; it would be easier for a man not to consult his conscience at all; but if he does so, the judge pronounces impartially, and his verdict falls regularly on the side of truth, unless it be that he has false *principia* of morality. Men, to be sure, are more ready to listen to the defender; but on the death-bed they harken more to the accuser. The first attribute of a good conscience is the purity of the law, for the accuser must be on the watch in all our actions; in the judgement of actions we must have probity, and finally morality and strength of conscience in regard to carrying out the judgement in accordance with the law. Conscience should have *principia* of action, and not be merely speculative, and hence must have authority and strength to execute its judgement. For what judge would be content merely to admonish and pronounce his judicial verdict? The latter must be carried into effect.

The difference between the correct and the errant conscience lies in this, that error of conscience takes two forms, *error facti* and *error legis.*[c] He who acts according to an errant conscience is acting conscientiously and if he does so, his action may be defective, but cannot be imputed to him as a crime. There are *errores inculpabiles* and *errores culpabiles.*[d] In regard to his natural obligations, nobody can be in error; for the natural moral laws cannot be unknown to anyone, in that they lie in reason for all; hence nobody is guiltless there in such error, but in regard to a positive law there are *errores inculpabiles,* and there one may act in all innocence, because of a *conscientia erronea,*[e] whereas in regard to the natural law there are no *errores inculpabiles.* But now if a positive law requires one to act contrary to natural law, for example, as in certain religions, to rant and rave against adherents of other religions, which law is one to follow? Supposing someone were to be taught, by the Jesuits, for example, that one might perform a good action by rascally means, such a person is not acting according to his conscience; for the natural law is known to him, viz., that he should engage in no wrong-doing for any purpose, and since here the utterance of the natural conscience is contrary to the instructed one, he has to harken to the former. The positive law can contain nothing that is in conflict with natural law; for the latter is the condition of all positive laws. It is a bad thing to find excuses in an erring conscience; on that score,

27:355

[c] error of fact/of law
[d] errors, blameless or culpable
[e] an erring conscience

much can be shuffled off, but such errors must also be taken into the reckoning. Our author calls conscience a natural thing, and perhaps wishes to distinguish it from what is revealed. But all conscience is natural, though it can be founded on either a natural or a revealed law. Conscience represents the divine tribunal within us: first, because it judges our dispositions and actions according to the purity of the law; second, because we cannot deceive it; and last, because we cannot escape it, since, like the divine omnipresence, it is always with us. It is thus the representative within us of the divine justice, and hence must on no account be injured. The *conscientia naturalis* might be contrasted to the *conscientia artificialis*. Many have contended that conscience is a product of art and education, and that it judges and speaks in a merely habitual

27:356 fashion. But if this were so, the person having no such training and education of his conscience could escape the pangs of it, which is not in fact the case. Art and instruction must admittedly bring to fruition that to which nature has already predisposed us; so we must also have prior knowledge of good and evil, if conscience is to judge; but though our understanding may be cultivated, conscience does not need to be. It is therefore nothing but a natural conscience. A distinction can be made between conscience before and after the act. Before, it is still strong enough, indeed, to deflect a man from the act, but in action it is stronger, and afterwards strongest of all. Prior to action, it cannot yet be so strong, because the deed has not yet been done, and the agent does not feel so powerful yet, and because inclination is still unsatisfied, and is thus still strong enough to withstand conscience; in the course of action, conscience is already stronger, and inclination, since it is already satisfied by then, is already too weak to withstand conscience, which is then, subsequently, at its strongest. On satisfaction of the strongest inclination arising from passion, man at once experiences a revulsion, because a strong feeling, once satisfied, becomes quite languid, and offers no resistance, and then conscience is at its strongest. At that point comes remorse, but the conscience which merely stops at that is still incomplete; it has to give the law its due. The *conscientia concomitans,*[f] or accompanying conscience, at length becomes weak through habituation, and in the end one becomes as accustomed to vice as to tobacco-smoke. Conscience eventually loses all respect, and then, too, the accusation ceases, having become superfluous, since nothing is any longer decided or carried out in the courtroom. If conscience is burdened with many small scruples on matters of indifference (*adiaphora*)[g] it becomes a micrological conscience, and the questions laid before it are the subject of casuistry, e.g., whether one should tell lies to a person, to make an April fool of him? Whether in certain rituals one

[f] conscience that monitors the act
[g] trifles

should perform this action or that? The more micrological and subtle the conscience is over such trivialities, the worse it is in practical matters; such people are chiefly given to speculating over questions of positive law, and in all else the door is left open. A lively conscience exists when the agent can reproach himself for his misdeeds. But there is also a morbid conscience, where he seeks to impute evil in his actions, when there is really no ground for it; but this is needless. Conscience should not be a tyrant within us. We can always be cheerful in our actions, without offend- 27:357 ing it. Those who have a tormenting conscience eventually weary of it entirely, and finally send it on vacation.

OF SELF-LOVE

The love that takes pleasure in others is the judgement that we delight in their perfection. But the love that takes pleasure in oneself, a self-love, is an inclination to be well-content with oneself in judging of one's perfec- tion. *Philautia*, or moral self-love, is to be contrasted with arrogance, or moral self-conceit. The difference between them is that the former is only an inclination to be content with one's perfections, whereas the latter makes an unwarranted pretension to merit. It lays claim to more moral perfections than are due to it; but self-love makes no demands, it is always merely content with itself and devoid of self-reproach. The one is proud of its moral perfections, the other is not, believing itself merely to be blameless and without fault. *Arrogantia* is thus a far more damaging de- fect. *Philautia* tests itself against the moral law, not as a guiding-principle but by way of examples, and then one may well have cause to be self- satisfied. The examples of moral men are standards drawn from experi- ence; the moral law, however, is a standard set by reason; if the first of these is used, the result is either *philautia* or *arrogantia*. The latter arises if the moral law is thought of in a narrow and indulgent fashion, or if the moral judge within us is partisan. The less strictly the moral law is taken, and the less strictly the inner judge passes judgement upon us, the more arrogant we tend to be. Self-love differs from esteem. The latter refers to inner worth, love to the relationship of my worth in regard to well-being.

We esteem what has an inner worth, and love what has worth in a relative sense; understanding, for example, has an inner worth, regardless of what it is applied to. The man who observes his duty, who does not degrade his person, is worthy of esteem; the man who is companionable is worthy of love. Our own judgement can represent us as worthy either of 27:358 love or respect. The man who believes that he is kind-hearted, that he would be glad to help everyone, if only he were rich, and even if he actually is rich, thinks that if he were still richer, like so-and-so, he would do it, though what he has he sorely needs – the man who believes this, as all misers do, considers himself worthy of love. The man, however, who believes, in regard to himself, that he fulfils exactly the essential ends of humanity considers himself worthy of respect. If a man thinks himself kind-hearted, and promotes the well-being of all mankind by empty wishes, he lapses into *philautia*. That a man bestows everything good upon himself, is certainly natural; but that he cherishes a good opinion of himself, is not. Men fall into *philautia* or arrogance according to the difference of their temperaments. Gellert's moral philosophy is filled with love and kindliness, and talks much of friendship, which is the hobby-horse of all moralists, and such a morality gives occasion for self-love. But man must be worthy, not so much of love, as of esteem and respect. A conscientious and upright man, who is impartial and accepts no bribes, is not an object of love; and since he is scrupulous in regard to his acceptance, he will also be able to perform few actions of magnanimity and love, and hence will not be found loveable by others; but his well-being consists in this, that he is held worthy of respect by others, and virtue is his true inner worth. Thus a person can be an object of respect but not of love, because he does not ingratiate himself. We can also love a bad man, while not respecting him in the least. Everything in moral philosophy that increases self-love should be rejected, and only that recommended which makes us worthy of esteem, e.g., the observation of the self-regarding duties to be upright and conscientious; and if then we are no object of love, we can look anyone in the eye with confidence, though not with defiance, for in that case we have worth. This is not arrogance, however, for here the measure of the law has not been misapplied. If I compare myself with the moral law, I am humble in regard to it, but in comparison with others I can hold myself worthy of esteem. Moral *philautia*, where a man has a high opinion of himself in regard to his moral perfections, is

27:359 contemptible. It arises when a man holds his dispositions to be good ones, and thinks by empty wishes and romantic ideas to promote the welfare of the world; he loves the Tartar, and would like to practise kindness towards him, but gives no thought to his closest neighbours. That whereby the heart only becomes flabby, is the *philautia* that consists in mere wishes, and is otherwise inactive. The lovers of self are weaklings, who are neither brave nor active; arrogance, however, is at least still active.

    In the moral courtroom of man, there is sophistry wrought by self-love. This advocate is a pettifogger when he expounds the laws sophistically to his advantage, but on the other hand is also deceitful in disavowing the *factum*. Thus man finds that his advocate, be he never so sophistical, enjoys little credit with him, and is viewed, rather, as a shyster. The man who fails to think this, and perceive it, is a weakling. This pettifogger expounds the law in all sorts of ways. He has recourse to the letter of the law, and in questions of fact looks, not to the dispositions, but rather to external circumstances. He deals in probabilities. This moral probabilism is a means whereby man betrays himself, and persuades himself that he has acted rightly, according to principles. Nothing is more crafty and repulsive than to fabricate such a law for oneself, whereby one may do evil under the aegis of the true law. So long as a man has violated the moral law, but yet knows it in its purity, he can still be redeemed, because he still has a pure law before him. But he who has fabricated a propitious and false law, has a principle for his wickedness, and in him there can be no hope of redemption.

Moral egoism is when a man thinks highly of himself only in relation to others. But we have to judge of our worth, not in relation to others, but in relation to the rule of the moral law; for the measuring-rod furnished by other people is highly contingent, and then a quite different worth emerges. If we find, on the contrary, that we have no such worth as others, we hate those whose worth is greater; and from this arises envy and ill-will. Parents produce this in their children, when they do not try to lead them by moral principle, but are always pointing out other children as a model, so that their own are then ill-disposed towards these children; for in their absence, they themselves would be the best. Moral solipsism is when we love only ourselves alone, in relation to others. But this belongs   27:360
not to the duties to oneself but, rather, to those that relate to others.

OF SELF-MASTERY

The general *principium* of self-mastery was that esteem for one's person in regard to the essential ends of human nature, and the self-regarding duties, are conditions under which alone the other duties can be performed. This is the *principium* of the self-regarding duties, and the objective conditions of morality. But what, now, is the subjective condition for the performance of duties to oneself? The rule is this: Seek to maintain command over yourself, for under this condition you are capable of performing the self-regarding duties. There is in man a certain rabble element which must be subject to control, and which a vigilant government must keep under regulation, and where there must even be force to compel this rabble under the rule in accordance with ordinance and regulation. This rabble in man comprises the actions of sensibility. They do not conform to the rule of the understanding, but are good only insofar as they do so. Man must have discipline, and he disciplines himself according to the rules of prudence; he often, for example, has the desire to sleep late, but compels himself to get up, because he sees that it is necessary; he often has the desire to go on eating or drinking, but sees that it is harmful to him. This discipline is the executive authority of reason's prescription over the actions that proceed from sensibility. It is the discipline of prudence, or the pragmatic discipline. But we have to have another discipline, namely that of morality. By this we must seek to master and compel all our sensory actions, not by prudence, but in accordance with the moral laws. It is in this authority that moral discipline consists, and it is the condition under which alone we can perform the duties to ourselves. Hence we may say that self-command consists in this, that we are able to subject all *principia* to the power of our free choice. This may be considered under two rules, namely those of prudence and morality. All prudence rests, indeed, on the rule of the understanding; but in the rule of prudence understanding is the servant of sensibility, providing it 27:361 with means whereby the inclination is satisfied, since in regard to ends it is dependent on sensibility. But the true self-mastery is moral in character. This is sovereign, and its laws hold a categorical sway over sensibility, and not as the pragmatic laws do, for there the understanding plays off one sensible factor against the rest. But in order for it to have a sovereign authority over us, we must give morality the supreme power over ourselves, so that it rules over our sensibility. Can a man rule over himself, if he will? This seems, indeed, to be so, since it appears to rest with himself, and we think it harder to gain mastery over others, than over oneself; but just because it is a mastery over ourselves, it is difficult, for there our authority is divided, and sensibility is in conflict with the understanding. But if we wish to have mastery over others, we marshal all our authority. Mastery over ourselves is also more difficult because the moral law has precepts, indeed, but no motives; it lacks executive authority, and this is the moral feeling. The latter is no distinction between good and evil, but a motive in which our sensibility concurs with understanding. Men may indeed have good powers of judgement in moral matters, but no feeling. They are well aware that an act may be, not good, but worthy of punishment, yet they commit it nonetheless. But now self-mastery rests on the strength of the moral feeling. We may have good command of ourselves if we weaken the opposing forces. But this we do when we divide them; hence we first have to discipline ourselves, i.e., to root out, in regard to ourselves, by repeated actions, the tendency that arises from the sensory motive. He who would discipline himself morally must pay great attention to himself, and often give an account of his actions before the inner judge, since then, by long practice, he will have given strength to the moral motivating grounds, and acquired, by cultivation, a habit of desire or aversion in regard to moral good or evil. By this the moral feeling will be cultivated, and then morality will have strength and motivation; by these motives, sensibility will be weakened and overcome, and in this way self-command will be achieved. Without disciplining his inclinations, man can attain to nothing, and hence in self-mastery there lies an immediate 27:362 worth, for to be master over oneself demonstrates an independence of all things. Where there is no such self-mastery, there is anarchy. Yet even if there is moral anarchy in a man, prudence still steps in to replace morality, and reigns in its stead, so that there shall not yet be total anarchy. Self-control according to the rules of prudence is an analogue of self-mastery.

The power that the soul has over all its faculties and the entire situation, to subordinate them to its free choice, without being necessitated to do so, is a monarchy. If man does not busy himself with this monarchy, he is a plaything of other forces and impressions, against his choice, and is dependent on chance and the arbitrary course of circumstances. If he does not have himself under control, his imagination has free play; he cannot discipline himself, but is carried away by it, according to the laws of association, since he willingly yields to the senses; if he cannot restrain them, he becomes their plaything, and his judgement is determined by the senses; without alluding to inclination and passion, let us consider merely his thinking state, which is very arbitrary if one does not have it under control. Every man must therefore see to it that he subjects his powers and his condition to the authority of his free choice. We have a double authority over ourselves, the disciplinary and the productive. The executive authority can compel us, in spite of all impediments, to produce certain effects, and in that case it has might. But the directing authority exists merely to guide the forces of our mind. If we have in us, for example, an impulse to indolence, it cannot be suppressed by the directing authority, but only by the compelling one. If I have prejudices, I am obliged, not merely to direct my mind, but to use force if I am not to be swept away by the tide. Men have the power of directing the mind, but not yet of mastering it. If nothing in the mind offers resistance, but there are simply no rules present, then it can only be directed. Yet there is something habitual in our powers, which resists the force and free choice we have as thinking subjects; sensual indulgence and laziness, for example, must not merely be directed, but also mastered. The autocracy is therefore the authority to compel the mind, despite all the impediments to doing so. It involves mastery over oneself, and not merely the power to direct. 27:363

In enumerating the duties to oneself, our author commits an error of which we must therefore say something at this point. He lists among such duties all the perfections of a man, including those that relate to his talents. He speaks of the perfection of the sensory powers, of the soul; in this fashion, logic and all the sciences which make the understanding more perfect and satisfy our curiosity might belong here; but there is nothing at all moral about that. Morality does not show us, of course, what we must do to become more perfect in regard to the dexterity of our powers; all such precepts are merely pragmatic, and rules of prudence, whereby we are bidden to extend our powers insofar as this conduces to our well-being. But if we are talking of morality, nothing will come into it, save how much we make ourselves more perfect in regard to our inner worth, and how we are to uphold the honour of mankind in regard to our own person; how we are to subject everything to our own choice, so far as our actions are directed thereby in accordance with the essential ends of humanity. All the propositions and rules of our author, in expounding the self-regarding duties, and all his definitions, are tautologies. Those practical propositions are tautological, from which no execution can follow, which state no means whereby one can carry out what is demanded, which contain conditions identical with the given conditions and requirements. It is a tautological resolution of the problem, if it contains the same condition as that contained in the requirement. All practical sciences *a priori* except mathematics contain tautologies; practical logic, for example, is full of them; it states the conditions set forth in theoretical logic, and that is what also happens in morality, when no means are given for satisfying the conditions required. This is a general error, which we cannot impute solely to our author; and if we cannot completely repair it either, we shall at any rate show what it consists in. How we are to notice the gaps in the sciences that might yet be filled up, though this could not happen were we to believe that there are no gaps, and that everything is perfect.

27:364   So the requirement to perfect one's talents does not belong among the self-regarding duties, as to which our author discourses at length in his guidelines [of psychology]. Even without speculation, and with feeble discernment, we can perform the self-regarding duties. All embellishments of the soul pertain, indeed, to its luxury and its *melius esse;*[h] but not to the *esse* of the mind. Yet the health of the soul in a healthy body is among the self-regarding duties. So far as the perfections of our mental powers are bound up with the essential ends of humanity, it is one of our self-regarding duties to promote them. All our states of mind and mental powers can have a bearing on morality. The autocracy of the human mind, and of all the powers of the soul, so far as they relate to morality, is the *principium* of the self-regarding duties, and thereby of all the others.

Let us go through the mental powers, insofar as they have a bearing on morality, and see how there may be autocracy in regard to them, or a faculty of keeping them under free choice and observation; and for this reason let us first take imagination. Our strongest imaginings and mental pictures we obtain, not from the attractiveness of objects, but from our imagination; and this we must have under control, so that it does not run riot and dictate involuntary images to us. The objects which create images in us are not always present to us, but the imaginings can always be so, and we constantly carry them with us; from this there arise major breaches and violations of the self-regarding duties, for example, if we allow free play to the imagination in regard to sensual pleasures, so that we actually endow it with reality, there arise in consequence the vices that run contrary to nature, and extreme violations of the self-regarding duties; thus our imaginings have enhanced the attraction of the object. Autocracy should consist, then, in a man's banishing his imaginings from his mind,

[h] well-being

so that imagination does not work its spell of presenting objects that are unobtainable. That would be our self-regarding duty in regard to imagination. With regard to the senses in general, since they dupe and also outwit the understanding, we can do nothing else but outwit them in turn, by trying to furnish the mind with another form of sustenance than that offered by the senses, and seeking to occupy it with ideal diversions, comprising all refined forms of knowledge. The relation of wit to morality does not fall among the self-regarding duties.   27:365

Our author includes among such duties the observation of oneself. But this must not consist in eavesdropping on oneself; we have, rather, to observe ourselves through actions, and pay attention to them. The endeavour to know ourselves, and tell whether we are good or bad, must be carried on in life, and we have to examine our actions to see if they are good or bad. The first thing here is to try to show yourself good and active in life by means of actions, not by pious ejaculations, but by the performance of good deeds, by orderliness and work, and especially by uprightness and active beneficence towards your neighbours; then it can be seen whether you are good. Just as you get to know a friend, not by talking, but by having dealings with him, so it is also not easy to acquire self-knowledge from the opinion you have of yourself, and in general, self-knowledge is not so easy to come by. Thus many do not know that they are brave, until they have a chance of finding out in practice. Again, a man is often disposed to something, but does not know whether he could also actually perform it; for example, a person often thinks that if he were to win a large prize in the lottery, he would do this or that generous action, but when the thing actually happens, nothing comes of it. So it is, too, with the evil-doer confronting his own death. He is thereupon possessed of a most honourable and upright disposition, which may even be quite genuine, but he does not know himself; he cannot tell whether he would exercise it, if rescued from his plight. In his present state he cannot imagine this, but were he subsequently to escape death, he would continue to be just such a rascal as he was before. He can change, indeed, but not all at once. So a man always has to get to know himself in a gradual fashion.

Let us now go on to that which approaches ever more closely to autocracy; and that includes *suspensio judicii*.[i] In such judgement we must have enough autocracy to be able to defer it if we will, and not be moved to declare our judgement on good persuasive grounds. The deferring of judgement indicates great strength of mind, be the decision what it may, for example, to put off one's judgement in a vote or decision until we are convinced, exhibits strength of mind; for example, if I receive a letter, and   27:366
it has at once aroused anger in me; if I answer right away, I let my anger be

[i] suspension of judgement

very plain; but if I can put it off till the following day, I shall view the matter from a different standpoint. *Suspensio judicii* is thus a major element in autocracy.

In regard to activity, we display autocracy by keeping our mind active and effective under the burden of work, by being content whatever the work may be, by being satisfied with ourselves on recognizing that we feel strong enough to perform such work without distress, and by having strength to overcome the hardship of our labours. We must therefore have the resolve to stick firmly to what we have undertaken, and to carry it through regardless of the arguments for procrastination. Presence of mind is also a part of autocracy. It is the union and harmony of the mental powers evinced in carrying out one's business. This is not, indeed, a thing for everyone, but depends on talent. Yet it can be strengthened by practice.

Let us now take the self-regarding duties pertaining to enjoyment, to desire and aversion, and to contentment and displeasure. Evil is the opposite of well-being, but wickedness the opposite of well-doing. Wickedness arises from freedom, and evil, too, completely from this source, but also from nature. In regard to evil* in the world, man should display a calm, equable and constant mind; but in regard to wickedness the case is altered; it will not do, there, for a man to be able to display a calm and equable mind, since that enhances his wickedness still further; it is the condition of an infamous mind and a vile character. The wickedness of the action ought, rather, to be accompanied by a consciousness of mental pain. But a calm and cheerful mind in the midst of evils and misfortunes enhances the worth of a man. It is contrary to human dignity to submit to the power of physical evil, and to depend on the play of chance. Man has within him a mental capacity to withstand all evils. The reasons for cultivating such constancy of mind are that we seek to remove the false appearance that lies in the supposed good things of life and in imagined happiness. The greatest source of happiness or unhappiness, of faring well or ill, of content or discontent, lies in the relationship to other people. For if everyone alike in the town is eating rotten cheese, I eat it too, with satisfaction and a cheerful mind, whereas if everyone else were well-fed, and I alone in sorry circumstances, I would deem it a misfortune. Thus all happiness or unhappiness depends on ourselves, and on the way our minds accept the situation. If we consider the happiness of this life, which consists only in illusion, and where often the beggar at the gate is happier than the king on his throne; if we assess the trifling nature of this happiness, in view of the shortness of life; if we notice how a great misfortune, at which everyone shudders, can be borne nonetheless, once it has already befallen us; if we bear in mind that we can make no claim to happiness, and only deem ourselves unfortunate because we were always happy be-

27:367

* [Reading *Übel* for *Urtheil* – Tr.]

fore, and have merely been coddled by this, and so now regard every diminution of happiness as a new misfortune; – we then see that we can do without much in a generous spirit, and amid all evils may still exhibit a virtuous and cheerful mind. Because here we can lay claim to no better fortune, in that God has set us down here on the stage of this world, where He has furnished us with all the materials for our comfort, and endowed us also with freedom to use such things as we please, so that it is simply a matter of how men distribute these gifts of fortune among themselves. Though men may spoil it all between them, let us take the good things of life as we have received them, and be content with the universal wisdom and care of God, and allow no misery or misfortune to weigh upon us. The man who is in need, but bears it with a calm and cheerful mind, who makes light of it, because it is simply there and cannot be altered, is not in need; the needy man is he who thinks himself to be so. The man who deems himself unfortunate is also malicious, for he envies others their good fortune. Thus a callous nobleman asserted that God hates the unfortunate man, since otherwise He would not let him languish in misfortune, and that we are furthering God's purpose if we seek to make such a man more unhappy than ever; but if we give this malign thought another turn, we may say that he who deems himself unfortunate deserves to be hated; but he who in misfortune still shows a cheerful and steadfast spirit, who maintains a firm courage, even when he has lost everything, still has that within him which possesses an intrinsic worth, 27:368 and such a man deserves compassion instead. To keep the soul free from the vice of envy, we must therefore try to bear every hardship, and, once it has befallen us, to extract from it the advantage that always resides in misfortune. It is up to us to put ourselves into a certain mood, which is a voluntarily chosen disposition, whereby we contemplate the world and its destinies, and from which we pass judgement upon them.

As to the direction of the mind in regard to the emotions and passions, we distinguish them here from the feelings and inclinations. One may feel something, and be inclined to it, without having emotion or passion over it. If the feelings and passions are so bound up with reason that their soul is in harmony with reason, they may accord with the self-regarding duties. In duty to ourselves, and for the dignity of mankind, the demand upon a man is that we have no emotions or passions at all; such is the rule, though it is another matter whether man can actually get as far as that. Man should be brave, orderly and steadfast in his work, and guard against falling into the fever-heat of the passions; for the state of a man in passion is always a frantic one; his inclination is then blind, and that cannot be in keeping with the dignity of mankind. Hence we must yield nothing to passion, and the demand of the Stoics was correct on this point. Religious passion is the most godless of all, for then, under the cloak of godliness, people think they can perpetrate anything.

The conclusion we draw from this is, that we hold the autocracy of the mind over all powers of the soul to be the prime condition for observance of the self-regarding duties. Our maxims must be well considered, and it is worse to do wrong from maxims than from inclination. But good actions must be done from maxims.

Our author goes on to speak of self-conquest. But if a man rules himself so well that he prevents any rebellion of the rabble in his soul and keeps peace within it (which here, however, is not contentment with everything, but good command and unity in the soul), and if he now conducts so good a government within himself, then no war will arise in him, and where there is no war, no conquest is necessary either. It is therefore far better if a man is so governed that he need gain no victory over himself.

27:369

OF DUTIES TO THE BODY, IN REGARD TO LIFE

We now come to the right that we have, to dispose over our life, and whether we have such a right. On the other side, there is the right to take care of our life. Let us note, for a start, that if the body belonged to life in a contingent way, not as a condition of life, but as a state of it, so that we could take it off if we wanted; if we could slip out of one body and enter another, like a country, then we could dispose over the body, it would then be subject to our free choice, albeit that in that case we would not be disposing over our life, but only over our state, over the movable goods, the chattels, that pertained to life. But now the body is the total condition of life, so that we have no other concept of our existence save that mediated by our body, and since the use of our freedom is possible only through the body, we see that the body constitutes a part of our self. So far, then, as anyone destroys his body, and thereby takes his own life, he has employed his choice to destroy the power of choosing itself; but in that case, free choice is in conflict with itself. If freedom is the condition of life, it cannot be employed to abolish life, since then it destroys and abolishes itself; for the agent is using his life to put an end to it. Life is supposedly being used to bring about lifelessness, but that is a self-contradiction. So we already see in advance that man cannot dispose over himself and his life, though he certainly can over his circumstances. By means of his body, a man has power over his life; were he a spirit, he could not make away with his life; because nature has invested absolute life with an indestructibility, from which it follows that one cannot dispose over it, as though it were an end.

OF SUICIDE

Suicide can be considered under various aspects, from the blameworthy, the permissible and even the heroic point of view. At first it has a seeming air of being allowable and permitted. The defenders of this view argue that, so long as he does not infringe the rights of others, a man disposes freely over the earth's goods. So far as his body is concerned, he can dispose over it in many ways. He can have an abscess lanced, for example, or ignore a scar, have a limb amputated, etc. and is thus at liberty to do anything in regard to his body that seems to him expedient and useful. Should he not, then, be also entitled to take his life, if he sees that this is the most useful and expedient course for him? If he sees that he can in no way go on living and may thereby escape so much torment, misfortune and shame? Although it deprives him of a full lifetime, he nevertheless escapes at once in this way from every calamity. This appears to be a very telling argument. But let us, on the other hand, consider the action simply in itself, and not from the religious point of view. So long as we have the intention of preserving ourselves, we can, under such a condition, indeed dispose over our body. Thus a man can have his foot amputated, for example, insofar as it impedes him in life. So to preserve our person, we have disposition over our body; but the man who takes his own life is not thereby preserving his person; for if he disposes over his person, but not over his condition, he robs himself of that very thing itself. This is contrary to the supreme self-regarding duty, for the condition of all other duties is thereby abolished. It transcends all limits on the use of free choice, for the latter is only possible insofar as the subject exists. 27:370

Suicide can also come to have a plausible aspect, whenever, that is, the continuance of life rests upon such circumstances as may deprive that life of its value; when a man can no longer live in accordance with virtue and prudence, and must therefore put an end to his life from honourable motives. Those who defend suicide from this angle cite the example of Cato, who killed himself once he realized that, although all the people still relied on him, it would not be possible for him to escape falling into Caesar's hands; but as soon as he, the champion of freedom, had submitted, the rest would have thought: If Cato himself submits, what else are we to do? If he killed himself, however, the Romans might yet dedicate their final efforts to the defence of their freedom. So what was Cato to do? It seems, in fact, that he viewed his death as a necessity; his thought was: Since you can no longer live as Cato, you cannot go on living at all. 27:371

One must certainly admit of this example, that in such a case, where suicide is a virtue, there seems to be much to be said for it. It is also the one example that has given the world an opportunity of defending suicide. Yet it is also but one example of its kind. There have been many similar cases. Lucretia also killed herself, though from modesty and vengeful rage. It is assuredly a duty to preserve one's honour, especially for the fair sex, in whom it is a merit; but one should seek to save one's honour only inasmuch as it is not surrendered for selfish and voluptuous purposes; not, however, in such a case as this, for that did not apply to her. So she ought rather to have fought to the death in defence of her honour, and would then have acted rightly, and it would not have been suicide either. For to risk one's life against one's foes, and to observe the duty to oneself, and even to sacrifice one's life, is not suicide.

Nobody under the sun, no sovereign, can oblige me to commit suicide. The sovereign can certainly oblige the subject to risk his life against the foe for the fatherland, and even if he loses his life in doing so, it is not suicide, but depends on fate. And on the opposite side, it is again no preservation of life to be fearful and faint-hearted in the face of death, with which fate inevitably threatens us already. He who runs away to save his life from the enemy, and leaves all his comrades in the lurch, is a coward; but if he defends himself and his fellows to the death, that is no suicide, but is held to be noble and gallant; since, in and for itself, life is in no way to be highly prized, and I should seek to preserve my life only insofar as I am worthy to live. A distinction has to be made between a suicide and one who has lost his life to fate. He who shortens his life by intemperance, is certainly to blame for his lack of foresight, and his death can thus be imputed, indirectly, to himself; but not directly, for he did not intend to kill himself. It was not a deliberate death. For all our offences are either *culpa*[j] or *dolus*.[k] Now although there is no *dolus* here, there is certainly *culpa*. To such a one it can be said: You are yourself to blame for your death, but not: You are a suicide. It is the intention to destroy oneself that constitutes suicide. I must not, therefore, turn the intemperance that

27:372   causes shortening of life into suicide, for if I raise intemperance to the level of suicide, the latter is thereby degraded in turn and reduced to intemperance.

There is a difference, therefore, between the imprudence in which a wish to live is still present, and the intention to do away with oneself. The most serious violations of the duties to oneself produce either revulsion with horror, and such is suicide, or revulsion with disgust, and such are the *crimina carnis*. Suicide evokes revulsion with horror, because everything in nature seeks to preserve itself: a damaged tree, a living body, an animal; and in man, then, is freedom, which is the highest degree of life, and constitutes the worth of it, to become now a *principium* for self-destruction? This is the most horrifying thing imaginable. For anyone who has already got so far as to be master, at any time, over his own life, is also master over the life of anyone else; for him, the door stands open to every crime, and before he can be seized he is ready to spirit himself away out of the world. So suicide evokes horror, in that a man thereby puts himself below the beasts. We regard a suicide as a carcase, whereas we feel pity for one who meets his end through fate.

[j] due to fault
[k] done with intent

The defenders of suicide try to push human freedom to the limit, which is flattering, and implies that persons are in a position to take their lives if they wish. So even well-meaning people defend it in this respect. There are many conditions under which life has to be sacrificed; if I cannot preserve it other than by violating the duties to myself, then I am bound to sacrifice it, rather than violate those duties; yet on the other hand, suicide is not permitted under any condition. Man has, in his own person, a thing inviolable; it is something holy, that has been entrusted to us. All else is subject to man, save only that he must not make away with himself. A being who existed of his own necessity could not possibly destroy himself; one who does not exist by such necessity sees his life as the condition of all else. He sees, and feels, that life has been entrusted to him, and if he now turns it against itself, it seems that he should recoil in trembling, at having thus violated the sacred trust assigned to him. That which a man can dispose over, must be a thing. Animals are here regarded as things; but man is no thing; so if, nevertheless, he disposes over his life, he sets upon himself the value of a beast. But 27:373 he who takes himself for such, who fails to respect humanity, who turns himself into a thing, becomes an object of free choice for everyone; anyone, thereafter, may do as he pleases with him; he can be treated by others as an animal or a thing; he can be dealt with like a horse or dog, for he is no longer a man; he has turned himself into a thing, and so cannot demand that others should respect the humanity in him, since he has already thrown it away himself. Humanity, however, is worthy of respect, and even though somebody may be a bad man, the humanity in his person is entitled to respect. Suicide is not repulsive and forbidden because life is such a benefit, for in that case it is merely a question for each of us, whether he deem it to be a major good. By the rule of prudence, it would often be the best course, to remove oneself from the scene; but by the rule of morality it is not allowed under any condition, because it is the destruction of humanity, in that mankind is set lower than the beasts. In other respects, there is much in the world that is far higher than life. The observance of morality is far higher. It is better to sacrifice life than to forfeit morality. It is not necessary to live, but it is necessary that, so long as we live, we do so honourably; but he who can no longer live honourably is no longer worthy to live at all. We may at all times go on living, so long as we can observe the self-regarding duties, without doing violence to ourselves. But he who is ready to take his own life is no longer worthy to live. The pragmatic motivating-ground for living is happiness. Can I then take my life because I cannot live happily? No, there is no necessity that, so long as I live, I should live happily; but there is a necessity that, so long as I live, I should live honourably. Misery gives no man the right to take his life. For if we were entitled to end our lives for want of pleasure, all our self-regarding duties would be aimed at the pleasantness of life; but now the fulfilment of those duties demands the sacrifice of life.

Can heroism and freedom be met with, in the act of suicide? It is not good to practise sophistry from good intentions. Nor is it good to defend virtue or vice with sophistry. Even right-thinking people denounce suicide without giving the proper reasons. They say that there is great cowardice in it; but there are also suicides who display great heroism, such as Cato, Atticus and others. I cannot call such suicide cowardly. Anger, passion, and madness are in many cases the cause of suicide, which is why persons who have been saved from the attempt at it are affrighted at themselves, and do not venture it a second time. There was a period among the Greeks and Romans when suicide conferred honour, and hence, too, the Romans forbade their slaves to do away with themselves, because they belonged, not to themselves, but to their masters, and were therefore regarded as things, like any other animal. The Stoic declared suicide to be a gentle death for the sage, who leaves the world as he might go from a smoky room to another one, because he no longer cared to stay there. He departs from the world, not because he has no happiness in it, but because he despises it. As already mentioned, it is very flattering to a man to have the freedom to remove himself from the world if he so wishes. Indeed, there even seems to be something moral in it, for anyone who has the power to depart from the world when he pleases need be subject to nobody, and can be bound by nothing from telling the harshest truths to the greatest of tyrants; for the latter cannot compel him by any tortures, when he can rapidly make his exit from the world, just as a free man can go out of the country if he chooses. But this illusion disappears, if freedom can exist only through an immutable condition, which cannot be changed under any circumstances. This condition is that I do not employ my freedom against myself for my own destruction, and that I do not let it be limited by anything external. This is the noble form of freedom. I must not let myself be deterred from living by any fate or misfortune, but should go on living so long as I am a man and can live honourably. To complain of fate and misfortune dishonours a man. If Cato, under all the tortures that Caesar might have inflicted on him, had still adhered to his resolve with steadfast mind, that would have been noble; but not when he laid hands upon himself. Those who defend and teach the legitimacy of suicide inevitably do great harm in a republic. Suppose it were a general disposition that people cherished, that suicide was a right, and even a merit or honour; such people would be abhorrent to everyone. For he who so utterly fails to respect his life on principle can in no way be restrained from the most appalling vices; he fears no king and no torture.

But all such illusions are lost, if we consider suicide in regard to religion. We have been placed in this world for certain destinies and purposes; but a suicide flouts the intention of his creator. He arrives in the next world as one who has deserted his post, and must therefore be seen as a rebel against God. So long as we acknowledge this truth, that the preservation of our life is among God's purposes, we are in duty bound to regulate our free actions in accordance with it. We have neither right nor authority to do violence to our nature's preservative powers, or to upset the wisdom of her arrangements. This responsibility lies upon us until such time as God gives us His express command to depart this world.

Men are stationed here like sentries, and so we must not leave our posts until relieved by the beneficent hand of another. He is our proprietor, and we His property, and His providence ensures what is best for us: A bondman who is under the care of a kindly master invites punishment if he defies the latter's intentions.

Suicide, however, is impermissible and abhorrent, not because God has forbidden it; God has forbidden it, rather, because it is abhorrent. So all moralists must begin by demonstrating its inherent abhorrency. Suicide commonly occurs among those who have taken too much trouble over the happiness of life. For if someone has tasted the refinements of pleasure, and cannot always possess them, he falls into grief, worry and depression.

OF CARE FOR ONE'S LIFE

As to the duty in regard to our life, of taking care of it, we have this to say: Life, in and for itself, is not the highest good that is entrusted to us, and that we ought to take care of. There are duties that are far higher than life, and that must often be performed by sacrificing life. By observation of experience we see that a worthless man values his life more than his 27:376 person. So he who has no inner worth sets great value on his life, but he who has more inner worth sets a far smaller value on it. A man of inner worth will sooner sacrifice his life than commit a disreputable act; so he puts the worth of his person above his life. But the man without inner worth would sooner commit a disreputable act than sacrifice his life. In that case he sets a value on his life, indeed, but is no longer worthy to live, because he has dishonoured humanity and its dignity in his own person. But how does it follow that the man who sets little value on his life has worth in his own person? There is something hidden here, though it is clear enough that that is the way of it. Man looks upon life, which consists in the union of soul and body, as a contingent thing; which indeed it is. But the *principium* of free action in him is such that life, the union of soul and body, is deemed of little account. So if certain persons, in all innocence, were to be accused of treason, though among them there were really a few men of honour, along with others of the baser sort, having no inner worth, and if all these people were together condemned to die, or to undergo a life-sentence of penal servitude, and each had to choose which of these punishments he preferred, it is perfectly certain that the honourable ones would choose death, and the worthless ones the penal servitude. The man of inner worth is not afraid of death, and would sooner die than be an object of contempt and live among felons in servitude. But the worthless man prefers servitude, almost as if it were already the proper thing for him. There are duties, therefore, to which life is much inferior, and in order to fulfill them we must evince no cowardice in regard to our life. The cowardice of man dishonours humanity, and it is very cowardly to set too much store by physical life. The man who on every trifling occasion is exceedingly fearful of his life, strikes everyone as very ridiculous. We must await our death with resolution. There is little worth in that which there is great worth in treating with disdain.

27:377 On the other hand, however, we ought not to risk our life, and hazard it from mere interest or private aims, for in that case we are not only acting imprudently, but also ignobly, e.g., if we wanted to wager a considerable sum on swimming across a lake. There is no good in the world for which we are liable, as a matter of duty rather than freedom, to put our life at risk. There are, indeed, circumstances in which a man risks his life from interest, e.g., as a soldier in war. But that is not a private aim, but for the general benefit. Because men are already so constituted that they wage wars, there are also those who devote themselves to soldiering. It is a very subtle question, how far we ought to treasure our life, and how far to risk it. The main point is this: Humanity, in our person, is an object of the highest respect and never to be violated in us. In the cases where a man is liable to dishonour, he is duty bound to give up his life, rather than dishonour the humanity in his own person. For does he do honour to it, if it is to be dishonoured by others? If a man can preserve his life no otherwise than by dishonouring his humanity, he ought rather to sacrifice it. He then, indeed, puts his animal life in danger, yet he feels that, so long as he has lived, he has lived honourably. It matters not that a man lives long (for it is not his life that he loses by the event, but only the prolongation of the years of his life, since nature has already decreed that he will some day die); what matters is, that so long as he lives, he should live honourably, and not dishonour the dignity of humanity. If he can now no longer live in that fashion, he cannot live at all; his moral life is then at an end. But moral life is at an end if it no longer accords with the dignity of humanity. This moral life is determined through its evil and hardships. Amid all torments, I can still live morally, and must endure them all, even death itself, before ever I perform a disreputable act. At the moment when I can no longer live with honour, and become by such an action unworthy of life, I cannot live at all. It is therefore far better to die with honour and reputation, than to prolong one's life by a few years through a discreditable action. If somebody, for example, can preserve life no longer save by surrendering their person to the will of another, they are bound rather to sacrifice their life, than to dishonour the dignity of humanity in their person, which is what they do by giving themselves up as a thing to the will of someone else.

Thus the preservation of life is not the highest duty; one often has to give up life, merely in order to have lived in an honourable way. There are 27:378 many such cases, and although the jurists say that preservation of life is the highest duty, and that *in casu necessitatis[1]* we are bound to defend our life, this is not a matter of jurisprudence at all; the latter has only to decide the rights and wrongs of the duties that we owe to others, not those that we owe to ourselves; nor can it compel any man to give up his life in such a case, for how does it propose to compel him? By depriving him of his life? The jurists have to regard preservation of life as the supreme duty, because only by threatening to deprive a man of life can they test him to the utmost. And so beyond it there is no other *casus necessitatis;* though where morality absolves me from concern for my life, no need, danger or hardship is any *casus necessitatis* for preserving it; for need cannot do away with morality. So if I can preserve my life only by disreputable conduct, virtue absolves me from the duty of preserving it; because here a higher duty beckons and passes judgement on me.

OF DUTIES IN REGARD TO THE BODY ITSELF

Our bodies belong to ourselves, and are subject to the general laws of freedom whereby duties are incumbent on us. The body is entrusted to us, and our duty in regard to it is that the human mind should first of all discipline the body, and then take care of it.

The body must first be disciplined, because in it there are *principia* by which the mind is affected, and through which the body alters the state of the mind. The mind must therefore take care to exercise an autocracy over the body, so that it cannot alter the state of the mind. The mind must therefore maintain supremacy over the body, so that it may guide the latter according to moral and pragmatic *principia* and maxims. This requires discipline, albeit of a merely negative kind; the mind has only to prevent the body from being able to necessitate it to anything; to prevent it from affecting the mind is doubtless impossible. Much depends on the body, in regard to our faculties of knowledge, desire and aversion, and appetite. If the mind 27:379 has no proper control over the body, the habits that we allow to the body become necessities, and if the mind does not repress bodily inclination, the result is a predominance of the body over the mind. This governance of mind over body, or of intellectuality over sensuality, may very well be compared to a republic, in which there is either good or bad government. The discipline can be of two kinds, insofar as the body has to be strengthened or weakened. Many visionary moralists think, by weakening and removing all the body's sensuality, to renounce everything that its sensuous enjoyment promotes, so that thereby the animal nature of the body would be sup-

[1] in a case of necessity

pressed, and the spiritual life, which they hope one day to attain, might already be anticipated here, and the body approach ever nearer to it by a gradual divestment of all sensuality. Such practices may be called mortification of the flesh, though that term was unknown to the pagan world; they did, however, call them *exercitia coelestica,*[m] by which they endeavoured to liberate themselves from the fetters of the body. But all such practices, which include, for example, fasting and chastisements, are fanatical and monkish virtues, which merely emaciate the body. The perfection of bodily discipline consists in a man being able to live in accordance with his vocation. The body must certainly be subjected to discipline, but it must not be destroyed by men, nor must its forces be impaired. So it will be a part of discipline to strengthen the human body, which may be accomplished by every useful toughening process, in which the body is cared for, indeed, but not pampered. We must therefore let none of the body's enjoyments become entrenched, but endeavour so to train it, that it is capable of doing without everything except necessities, of putting up with a poor diet, and of bearing up cheerfully under all exertions and mishaps. Man feels his life the more, the less need he has to sustain his vital forces. We must toughen our body like Diogenes, who had learnt nothing in slavery but resignation, and brought up his master's children to be inured to all life's hardships, though with a serene and cheerful mind, and imbued with the *principium* of righteousness. Just as the happiness of Diogenes also consisted, as was said at the beginning, not in superfluity but deficiency, and in doing without the good things in life.

27:380

While on the one hand we can and should discipline the body, we have a duty, on the other, to take care of it. This involves trying to promote its vigour, activity, strength and courage. As to bodily discipline, we have the following two duties to observe, namely moderation in its diversions, and sufficiency in regard to its genuine needs. We cannot deny necessities to the body, but it is better for a man to remain within these limits than to overstep them; better for him to deny the body something of what it needs, than to go too far the other way; for flabbiness represents an incapacity. As to moderation, there are two ways of going wrong, gluttony in eating and intemperance in drinking. Drinking to excess does not refer to quantity (nobody ever gets a passion for drinking large amounts of water), but to the refinement and quality of the beverage; but in eating, a man can be led into excesses even by bad food. Both departures from moderation are a breach of the self-regarding duties; they both dishonour a man, because both of them are beastly; for certain of man's vices are human, in that they accord with his nature, even though they are vices – for example, lying; but others are such that they lie outside humanity, and cannot be reconciled at all with the nature and character of man. Such

[m] corrective disciplines

152

vices are of two kinds, the beastly and the devilish. By his beastly vices, man puts himself below the beasts; the devilish vices have a degree of wickedness that goes far beyond the human, and we include among them the following three: envy, ingratitude and malice. Among beastly vices we have gluttony, drunkenness and the *crimina contra naturam*. All beastly vices are objects of the utmost contempt; but the devilish are objects of the utmost hatred. Which of the two beastly vices, gluttony or drunkenness, is the lower and more contemptible? The taste for drinking is not so low as gluttony; for drink is a means to sociability and talkativeness, and promotes a man's enthusiasm, and to that extent there is an excuse for it; 27:381 but if drinking goes beyond that stage, it becomes the vice of drunkenness. Thus, insofar as drunkenness is founded on social drinking, it remains, indeed, always a beastly vice, yet is not so contemptible as gluttony, which is far lower still, because it promotes neither sociability nor invigoration of body, but merely displays the animal in us. Drinking and drunkenness in solitude are similarly shameful; because there we no longer have the factor which raised them a little above gluttony.

OF THE DUTIES OF LIFE
IN REGARD TO OUR STATE

Man feels his life through action, not through enjoyment. The busier we are, and the greater our feeling of living, the more conscious we are of our existence. In idleness we not only feel that life is passing us by, but are actually aware of a lack of life in what we do; so it plays no part in sustaining our life. The enjoyment of life does not fill up time, but leaves it empty. Yet the prospect of an empty time fills the human mind with abhorrence, ill-humour and disgust. The present moment can, indeed, seem filled to us, but in recollection it still strikes us as empty; for if it is filled with play, etc., it actually seems full only so long as it is present, but in recollection is empty; for if a man has done nothing in his life, but has merely squandered time in that way, and then looks back upon his lifetime, he is at a loss to know how it has come to an end so quickly, since he has done nothing in it. Time, however, is filled only by actions; we only feel our life in occupations, and in enjoyment we don't feel content with it, for life is the faculty of spontaneity and the awareness of all human powers. The more we feel our powers, however, the more we feel our life. Sensation is only the power of perceiving impressions, and in it we are merely passive, and active only insofar as we pay attention thereto. But the more a man has acted, the more he feels his life, and the more he can remember of it, because he has done much in it, and the more he has had fullness of life when he dies. To have had one's fill of life, is not, however, to be satiated with it. Mere enjoyment makes a man satiated with life; but 27:382 he can only die in fullness of life if he has packed it with actions and occupations, and employed it rightly, so that he is not sorry to have lived. We die in fullness of life if throughout our life-time we have acted much and done much, and employed our life rightly. The man satiated with life is he who has done nothing; to him, it is as if he had never lived at all, but has only now wanted to start living. Hence we must fill up our time with actions, and then we shall not complain of the length of time, nor, taken as a whole, of the brevity of time when we look back upon it. For it is people who do nothing who grumble at the lengthiness of time. Every stretch of time is too long for them, in that they have nothing to do in it, and when they again think back on it, they know not what has become of the time. But for the man who is occupied, it is the other way round; to him, every portion of time is too short, he knows not what becomes of the time when he is busy, and the hours always strike too quickly for him; but when he looks around him, he sees how much he has already accomplished in the time. A man must therefore preserve his vitality, i.e., his activity, by much practice. Our human worth depends on the measure of our achievements. All idleness is thus a change in the degree of life. This is the condition of all duties, that we seek to maintain in ourselves an urge to activity, since otherwise all moral precepts are in vain; for if a man has no urge to activity, he will never even trouble to make a start with anything. So a man must be active and courageous, i.e., be resolute and vigorous even in difficult enterprises.

All occupation is either play or work, and it is better to have some occupation. Better to be occupied in play than with nothing at all, for in that way we at least continue to be active. If we are totally unoccupied, we lose a measure of vitality, and then become ever more indolent, so that it is harder thereafter to restore the mind to its previous activity. A man cannot live without occupation, and if he earns his bread, he eats it with more satisfaction than when it is dished out to him. Thus when mailing-day is over, the merchant goes happily to a concert or social gathering, and is more content than if there had never been one. If a man has done much, he is more contented after his labours than if he had done nothing whatever; for by work he has set his powers in motion, and so is that much better aware of them, and then, too, his mind is more aroused to enjoy diversions. But he who has done nothing has no awareness of his life and powers, and then, too, is not ready for enjoyment.

Rest is to be distinguished from idleness. To seek a restful existence is certainly appropriate, if it comes at the close of a life-time of work. One can, indeed, rest from the general business of the world, or of everyday routine, after having laid down one's position in the world, yet may still continue to be busy in private matters. This repose of the aged is no indolence, but a refreshment after toil.

So in order to be at rest, one must have been occupied; for he who has done nothing cannot rest. Repose can be properly enjoyed only after

27:383

exertion. He who has achieved much will be able to sleep well at night; but he who has done nothing does not find rest so agreeable.

A NOTE ON SHORTENING TIME

There are many expressions and means of shortening the time in which man exists. He who looks at the clock, for example, finds time long. But he who has something to do is not aware of time, and it appears all the shorter to him. If we direct our attention to objects, we do not notice time, and then it seems short to us, but as soon as we think about the measuring of time, and attend to it, it becomes empty for us. Our life is therefore the longer, the more filled it is. All miles in the proximity of a city seem shorter, and longer further off; for to anyone going there, and seeing nothing along the way, the miles appear long as he travels them; but once he has covered them, and thinks about it, they seem short to him, because in all that distance he has nothing to recall, since he did not perceive anything; whereas close to the city there is more to see and take note of, than farther away.

OF DUTIES TO THE BODY
IN REGARD TO THE SEXUAL IMPULSE   27:384

Man has an impulse directed to others, not so that he may enjoy their works and circumstances, but immediately to others as objects of his enjoyment. He has, indeed, no inclination to enjoy the flesh of another, and where that occurs, it is more a matter of warlike vengeance than an inclination; but there remains in him an inclination that may be called appetite, and is directed to enjoyment of the other. This is the sexual impulse. Man can certainly enjoy the other as an instrument for his service; he can utilize the others' hands or feet to serve him, though by the latter's free choice. But we never find that a human being can be the object of another's enjoyment, save through the sexual impulse. There is a sort of sense underlying this, which may be called the sixth sense, whereby one human being is pleasing to the appetite of another. We say that somebody loves a person, insofar as he is inclined to them. If we consider this love as human affection, if he loves this person from true human affection, he must make no distinction in regard to them. This person may be young or old, yet he may still love them from true human affection. But if he loves them merely from sexual inclination, it cannot be love; it is appetite. Love, as human affection, is the love that wishes well, is amicably disposed, promotes the happiness of others and rejoices in it. But now it is plain that those who merely have sexual inclination love the person from none of the foregoing motives of true human affection, are quite unconcerned for their happiness, and will even plunge them into the greatest unhappiness, simply to satisfy their own inclination and appetite. In loving from sexual inclination, they make the person into an object of their appetite. As soon as the person is possessed, and the appetite sated, they are thrown away, as one throws away a lemon after sucking the juice from it. The sexual impulse can admittedly be combined with human affection, and then it also carries with it the aims of the latter, but if it is taken in and by itself, it is nothing more than appetite. But, so considered, there lies in this inclination a degradation of man; for as soon as anyone becomes an

27:385   object of another's appetite, all motives of moral relationship fall away; as object of the other's appetite, that person is in fact a thing, whereby the other's appetite is sated, and can be misused as such a thing by anybody. There is no case where a human being would already be determined by nature to be the object of another's enjoyment, save this, of which sexual inclination is the basis. This is the reason why we are ashamed of possessing such an impulse, and why all strict moralists, and those who wish to be taken for saints, have sought to repress and dispense with it. To be sure, a person who did not have this impulse would be an imperfect individual, in that one would have to believe that he lacked the necessary organs, which would thus be an imperfection on his part, as a human being; yet such has been the pretension, and people have sought to refrain from this inclination, because it debases man. Since the sexual impulse is not an inclination that one human has for another, *qua* human, but an inclination for their sex, it is therefore a *principium* of the debasement of humanity, a source for the preference of one sex over the other, and the dishonouring of that sex by satisfying the inclination. The desire of a man for a woman is not directed to her as a human being; on the contrary, the woman's humanity is of no concern to him, and the only object of his desire is her sex.

So humanity here is set aside. The consequence is, that any man or woman will endeavour to lend attraction, not to their humanity, but to their sex, and to direct all actions and desires entirely towards it. If this is the case, humanity will be sacrificed to sex. So if a man wishes to satisfy his inclination, and a woman hers, they each attract the other's inclination to themselves, and both urges impinge on one another, and are directed, not to humanity at all, but to sex, and each partner dishonours the humanity of the other. Thus humanity becomes an instrument for satisfying desires and inclinations; but by this it is dishonoured and put on a par with animal nature. So the sexual impulse puts humanity in peril of being equated with animality.

Now since man, after all, possesses this impulse by nature, the question arises: To what extent is anyone entitled to make use of their sexual impulse, without impairing their humanity? How far can a person allow another person of the opposite sex to satisfy his or her inclination upon

27:386   them? Can people sell or hire themselves out, or by any kind of contract allow use to be made of their *facultates sexuales?*[n] All philosophers censure this inclination only for its pernicious effects, and the ruin it brings, partly to the body, and partly to the general welfare, and see nothing reprehensible in the act as such; but if this were so, if there were no inner abhorrency and damage to morality in employing the inclination, then anyone who could simply obviate these ill-effects might make use of his impulse in any way conceivable; for what is forbidden only by the rule of prudence is forbidden only in a conditional sense, and in that case the act is good in itself, and harmful only under particular circumstances. Yet here there is something contemptible in the act itself, which runs counter to morality. Hence conditions must be possible, under which alone the use of the *facultates sexuales* is compatible with morality. There must be a ground that restricts our freedom in regard to the use of our inclination, so that it conforms to morality. We shall be looking for these conditions, and this ground. Man cannot dispose over himself, because he is not a thing. He is not his own property – that would be a contradiction; for so far as he is a person, he is a subject, who can have ownership of other things. But now were he something owned by himself, he would be a thing over which he can have ownership. He is, however, a person, who is not property, so he cannot be a thing such as he might own; for it is impossible, of course, to be at once a thing and a person, a proprietor and a property at the same time.

Hence a man cannot dispose over himself; he is not entitled to sell a tooth, or any of his members. But now if a person allows himself to be used, for profit, as an object to satisfy the sexual impulse of another, if he makes himself the object of another's desire, then he is disposing over himself, as if over a thing, and thereby makes himself into a thing by which the other satisfies his appetite, just as his hunger is satisfied on a roast of pork. Now since the other's impulse is directed to sex and not to humanity, it is obvious that the person is in part surrendering his humanity, and is thereby at risk in regard to the ends of morality.

Human beings have no right, therefore, to hand themselves over for profit, as things for another's use in satisfying the sexual impulse; for in that case their humanity is in danger of being used by anyone as a thing, an instrument for the satisfaction of inclination. This method of satisfying the sexual urge is *vaga libido,*[o] in which the other's impulse is satisfied for profit; it can be carried on by both sexes. Nothing is more vile than to take money for yielding to another so that his inclination may be satisfied and to let one's own person out for hire. The moral ground for so holding is that man is not his own property, and cannot do as he pleases with his body; for since the body belongs to the self, it constitutes, in conjunction

27:387

---

[n] sexual capacities
[o] indiscriminate lust

157

with that, a person; but now one cannot make one's person a thing, though this is what happens in *vaga libido*. Hence this method of satisfying the sexual impulse is not sanctioned by morality.

Is it not permitted, though, to satisfy one's impulse by the second method, namely, *concubinatus?*[p] Where the persons mutually satisfy their desires, and have no thought of monetary gain, the one merely serving to gratify the inclination of the other? There seems to be nothing at all repugnant in this; yet one condition makes even this case impermissible. Concubinage occurs when a person surrenders to the other merely to satisfy inclination, but retains freedom and rights in regard to other circumstances affecting their person, viz., the concern for happiness and future well-being. But those who give themselves to another person, merely to satisfy inclination, still continue to let their person be used as a thing; for the impulse is still always directed to sex, merely, and not to humanity. Now it is evident that if someone concedes a part of himself to the other, he concedes himself entirely. It is not possible to dispose over a part of oneself, for such a part belongs to the whole. Yet by concubinage I have no right to the whole person, but only to one part of it, namely the *organa sexualia.*[q] Concubinage presupposes a *pactum*, but this *pactum sexuale*[r] relates only to enjoyment of one part of the person, not to the total state thereof. It is a contract, to be sure, but an unequal one, in which the rights of the two parts are not the same. Yet if, in concubinage, I enjoy one

27:388 part of the other, I thereby enjoy the whole person. Now since, under the terms of concubinage, I have no right to that whole, but only to a part of it, it follows that I am treating the whole person as a thing; hence this method of satisfying one's inclination is likewise impermissible on moral grounds.

The sole condition, under which there is freedom to make use of one's sexual impulse, is based upon the right to dispose over the whole person. This right to dispose over the other's whole person relates to the total state of happiness, and to all circumstances bearing upon that person. But this right that I have, so to dispose, and thus also to employ the *organa sexualia* to satisfy the sexual impulse – how do I obtain it? In that I give the other person precisely such a right over *my* whole person, and this happens only in marriage. *Matrimonium* signifies a contract between two persons, in which they mutually accord equal rights to one another, and submit to the condition that each transfers his whole person entirely to the other, so that each has a complete right to the other's whole person. It is now discernible through reason, how a *commercium sexuale*[s] may be possible without debasement of humanity or violation of morality. Marriage is

---

[p] concubinage
[q] sexual organs
[r] sexual contract
[s] sexual intercourse

thus the sole condition for making use of one's sexual impulse. If a person now dedicates himself to the other, he dedicates not only his sex, but his whole person; the two things are inseparable. If only one partner yields to the other his person, his good or ill fortune, and all his circumstances, to have right over them, and does not receive in turn a corresponding identical right over the person of the other, then there is an inequality here. But if I hand over my whole person to the other, and thereby obtain the person of the other in place of it, I get myself back again, and have thereby regained possession of myself; for I have given myself to be the other's property, but am in turn taking the other as my property, and thereby regain myself, for I gain the person to whom I gave myself as property. The two persons thus constitute a unity of will. Neither will be subject to happiness or misfortune, joy or displeasure, without the other taking a share in it. So the sexual impulse creates a union among persons, and only within this union is the use of it possible. This condition upon utilizing the sexual impulse, which is possible only in marriage, is a moral one. Were this to be worked out 27:389 further, and in a more systematic way, it would also have to follow that nobody, even in *matrimonium,* can have two wives; for otherwise each wife would have half a husband, since she has given herself totally to him, and thus has a total right to his person as well. There are therefore moral grounds that tell against *vagae libidines;* grounds that tell against concubinage; and grounds that tell against polygamy in *matrimonium;* so in the latter we only have monogamy. Under this condition alone may I employ the *facultas sexualis.* We can say no more on the subject at present.

We can, however, go on to ask whether there can be moral grounds that tell against *incestus* – sexual intercourse that violates the limits of the relationship, by reason of consanguinity – in all forms of the *commercium sexualis?* In regard to incest, the moral grounds are unconditional only in a single case, and elsewhere are merely conditioned. In civil society, for example, it is not allowed; but in a state of nature there is no *incestus,* for the first men must have married among their sisters. Yet nature, by itself, has already implanted a natural resistance to it; for nature wished us so to conjoin with one another, that in one society there should not be altogether too much of a bond, since where bonding and familiarity are all too excessive, the impulse produces indifference and disgust. So men have to restrain this impulse through modesty, lest they make it altogether too commonplace, and so that indifference shall not arise from associating too closely together. For this impulse is very delicate; nature has given it its strength, but it also has to be confined by bashfulness. Thus savages, who go completely naked, are quite cold to one another. And hence, too, the inclination towards a person one has known from youth upwards is very cold, while that towards a stranger is much stronger and more alluring. Thus nature has already by itself set limits to such inclinations between siblings.

The one case, however, where the moral grounds in regard to *incestus* are unconditional, is intercourse of parents with their children; for in regard to these two a respect is necessary that also has to endure throughout life; but respect rules out equality. This is the sole case where incest is unconditionally prohibited, and already so by nature; the other forms of it automatically forbid themselves, but are not *incestus* in the order of nature. Another reason for this alone being an *incestus* is that in sexual intercourse there is the utmost subordination of both persons, whereas between parents and children the subordination is all on one side; the children are merely subordinated to the parents, and hence there is no true intercourse.

OF *CRIMINA CARNIS*

The *crimina carnis* are contrary to self-regarding duty, because they run counter to the ends of humanity. A *crimen carnis* is a misuse of the sexual impulse. Every use of it outside the state of wedlock is a misuse of it, or *crimen carnis*. All *crimina carnis* are either *secundum*, or *contra, naturam.* ' The former are contrary to sound reason; the latter, to our animal nature. The former include *vaga libido*, which is the antithesis of *matrimonium*. It is of two kinds, either *scortatio*" or *concubinatus*. The latter is indeed a *pactum*, but *inaequale;* the rights are not reciprocal; in such a pact, the person of the woman is wholly subordinated to the man in sexual matters. Concubinage is therefore classified as a *vaga libido*. The second *crimen carnis secundum naturam* is *adulterium,*ᵛ which occurs only in marriage, when the marriage-vow is broken. Just as betrothal is the greatest of pledges between two persons, lasting for life, and is therefore the most inviolable, so, of all betrayals and breaches of faith, *adulterium* is the greatest, since there is no promise more important than this. Hence *adulterium* is also a cause for divorce; another cause for it is incompatibility and dissension between the parties, whereby unity and concord of will among them is impossible.

The question may be raised, whether *incestus*, which is in itself incestuous, but not under civil law, is a *crimen carnis secundum*, or *contra, naturam?* But here we first have to distinguish, whether the question is to be answered according to natural instinct, or according to reason. By natural instinct it is merely a *crimen carnis secundum naturam;* for it is, after all, an intercourse of both sexes, and not, therefore, *contra naturam animalium,*ʷ for animals make no distinction in the matter, and are promiscuous in their sexual habits; but by the judgement of the understanding, it is *contra naturam*.

' natural or unnatural
" prostitution
ᵛ adultery
ʷ contrary to animal nature, perverse

Crimina carnis contra naturam involve a use of the sexual impulse that is contrary to natural instinct and to animal nature; *onania*[x] is a case in point. It is misuse of the sexual faculty without any object, occurring, that is, when the object of our sexual impulse is totally absent, and yet even without any object the use of our sexual faculty by no means lapses, but is exercised. This obviously runs counter to the ends of humanity, and conflicts, even, with animal nature; man thereby forfeits his person, and degrades himself lower than a beast.

Second among the *crimina carnis contra naturam* is intercourse *sexus homogenii,*[y] where the object of sexual inclination continues, indeed, to be human, but is changed since the sexual congress is not heterogeneous but homogeneous, i.e., when a woman satisfies her impulse on a woman, or a man on a man. This also runs counter to the ends of humanity, for the end of humanity in regard to this impulse is to preserve the species without forfeiture of the person; but by this practice I by no means preserve the species, which can still be done through a *crimen carnis contra naturam,* only that there I again forfeit my person, and so degrade myself below the beasts, and dishonour humanity.

The third *crimen carnis contra naturam* is when the object of sexual inclination continues to be of the opposite sex, indeed, but is other than human. This includes sodomy, for example, the intercourse with animals. It also runs counter to the ends of humanity, and is contrary to natural instinct; by this I degrade humanity below the animal level, for no animal turns away from its own species. All *crimina carnis contra naturam* debase the human condition below that of the animal, and make man unworthy of his humanity; he then no longer deserves to be a person, and such conduct is the most ignoble and degraded that a man can engage in, with regard to the duties he has towards himself. Suicide is certainly the most dreadful thing that a man can do to himself, but is not so base and ignoble as these *crimina carnis contra naturam* which are the most contemptible acts 27:392 a man can commit. For this reason, too, such crimes are unmentionable, because the very naming of them occasions a disgust that does not occur with suicide. Everyone recoils from alluding to these vices; every teacher refrains from mentioning them, even with the good intention of warning his charges against them; yet in that they occur so frequently, we are here in difficulty, and at a loss to decide whether we should name them, to make them known, and thereby prevent them from happening so often, or whether we should avoid naming them, so as not to give occasion for some to learn of them, and thereafter to commit them all the more often. The reason for this diffidence is that mention of them creates a familiarity such that the revulsion against them is lost, and that by being alluded to, they

[x] masturbation
[y] with the same sex

become more tolerable; but if we are cautious in referring to them, and reluctant to do so, it seems as if we still retain an abhorrence for them. Another reason for this diffidence is that each sex is ashamed of the vices its members are capable of. So people are ashamed to mention things of which mankind should be ashamed, that it is capable of doing them. We have to be ashamed of being human, and yet capable of these things, for no animal is capable of any such *crimina carnis contra naturam.*

OF THE DUTIES TO ONESELF
IN REGARD TO OUTER CIRCUMSTANCES

We have already said earlier that man has a source of happiness in himself; this cannot, indeed, consist in the fact that he acquires complete independence of all needs and external causes, yet it may be such that he requires little. But to attain this, he must have an autocracy over his inclinations. He must curb his inclination to things that he cannot have, or can obtain only with much trouble, and then he is independent in regard to them. He must also have the principle of procuring for himself such amenities of life as he can have in his power; these are the permitted enjoyments, i.e., sufficiency and enhancement of mental pleasures. But as to external things, so far as they are the condition and means of well-being, they take two forms, as means either for requirements and necessities, or for amenities. The means for necessities serve only to support life, whereas those for amenity enable one, not to live, but to live comfortably. The natural degree of contentment is bound up with requirements, yet if I am content with the means to these, I still have no diversion. Contentment is a negative thing, amenity a positive one. So long as I take pleasure in living, I am contented, and if I take none, I am discontented: but now I take pleasure in living if I can but live needily, albeit I still have no amenities. The amenities are means of well-being that we find dispensable; but now where there is no dispensability, we already have a means of necessity. The question, then, is what we regard as a means of amenity, and what as a means of necessity, how much we account to amenity, and how much to necessity, and what we can dispense with, or not. All amenities and pleasures are to be enjoyed in such a way that we can also dispense with them; we must never make them into necessities. On the other hand, we must accustom ourselves to a steadfast endurance of all discomforts – for they are not yet a misfortune. Hence, in regard to diversions, we should get used to dispensing with them, and in regard to discomforts, to tolerating them. The ancients were expressing this when they said: *Sustine et abstine.*[z] We ought not to deprive ourselves of all amenities and pleasures, and enjoy none whatever; that would be a

27:393

---

[z] endure and do without

monk's virtue, to forgo everything that is proper to human life; but we must only enjoy these things in such a way that we can also do without them, and do not turn them into necessities; we have then become abstinent. On the other hand, we must get used to putting up with all the inconveniences of life, and to trying our strength in enduring them, and not losing our contentment in the process. We have strength of mind if we bear evils that cannot be altered with a cheerful spirit and buoyant mood, and this is the *sustine* of the ancients. We ought not to impose discomforts on ourselves, invite all evils, and punish ourselves with chastisements; that is a monkish virtue, which differs from the philosophic attitude, that goes cheerfully to meet those ills that fall upon us, and are unavoidable; for in the end, after all, everything can be endured. So here the *sustine et abstine* 27:394 is taken, not as a discipline, but as a willingness to do without, in regard to amenities, and as a tolerance of all inconveniences with a cheerful courage. There are true necessities of life, the forfeiture of which leaves us altogether discontented, for instance, to be without clothing or food. But there are also requirements, for lack of which we remain discontented, indeed, but which we can always do without. The more a person depends on such pseudo-necessities, the more he is a plaything thereof, in regard to his contentment. So a man must discipline his mind with respect to the necessities of life.

If we wish to differentiate among our needs, we may call excess in the enjoyment of diversion, luxury, and excess in the enjoyment of comfort, flabbiness. Luxury makes us dependent on a multitude of things, which we afterwards cannot procure, and whereby we are subsequently thrown into all kinds of distress, so that we may even proceed to do away with ourselves; for where luxury abounds, suicide is apt to be prevalent. If luxury takes over, it diminishes the well-being of our condition; and if flabbiness gains the upper hand, there is a total extirpation of manly strength. Luxury is lordly indulgence, flabbiness an indulgence in languor; the former is active, but the latter indolent. Active luxury is useful to a man's powers, for the forces of life are strengthened by it, and thus riding, for example, is a lordly indulgence. But all kinds of flabby indulgence are very injurious; the forces of life are weakened thereby, and thus to be conveyed in a sedan chair, or ride in a carriage, is flabbiness. A person inclined to lordly indulgence preserves his own activity, and also that of others; hence it is better to give way to refining one's enjoyment than to flabbiness. For lordly indulgence enhances our forces, and sustains activity in other people. In regard to both luxury and flabbiness we must also observe the rule of *sustine et abstine*. We must make ourselves independent of both, for the more a man depends on them, the less he is free, and the nearer he is to vice.

But nor again should we slavishly deprive ourselves of all diversions; we should merely enjoy them always in such a way that we can also do

27:395 without them. The man who violates neither his duties to himself, nor those he has to others, may enjoy as much pleasure as he has the ability and taste for. In so doing, he remains always well disposed, and fulfils the purpose of his creation. Nor, too, on the other hand, should we impose all manner of ills upon ourselves, and then endure them; for there is no merit in enduring evils that are self-imposed, and which we might have been spared; we must, however, bear with fortitude those evils that fate may send us, and which cannot be altered; for destiny can no more be arrested than an already collapsing wall. All this, however, is in itself no virtue, any more than its opposite is vice, for it is merely the condition of our duties. A man cannot fulfill his duties if he cannot dispense with everything, since otherwise the inducements of the senses overwhelm him; he cannot be virtuous if he is not steadfast in misfortune. He must, therefore, be able to endure, so that he may be virtuous. This is the reason why Diogenes called his philosophy the shortest way to happiness. Here, indeed, he was in error, in that he regarded it as a duty, since it only amounts to saying that even at that level a man can be contented. The philosophy of Epicurus is the philosophy, not of luxury, but of manly strength. He taught that one should be content even with polenta, and yet be happy and cheerful and capable of all the enjoyments of society, including all the amenities of life. So the two take happiness from opposite ends. The Stoic not only did not permit himself such things, but even denied them to himself.

Among the hardships we must get used to bearing and enduring is work, which is purposeful occupation having an object in view. There are also occupations, however, which are not work at all, but serve only for pleasure and involve no hardships. Such occupation is play. The loftier the purposes are, the more obstacles and difficulties the work contains, but however numerous they may be, we must still so accustom ourselves to the work that it, too, becomes play, and occasions us no hardship, but entertains and pleases us. But a man must be active and industrious, and undertake laborious tasks willingly and cheerfully, for otherwise the work bears the marks of coercion and not of ease. There are those who toil with 27:396 a purpose, and others who do so without one; but those who have no proper purpose are busy idlers, which is a foolish sort of occupation. We do indeed have occupation without purpose, for example play; but that is merely a refreshment from laborious work; to be constantly occupied without purpose is worse, though, than not to be occupied at all; for it still creates a delusion of being occupied. Man's greatest fortune is to be himself the originator of his happiness, when he feels himself enjoying what he has obtained himself. Without work a man can never be contented. One who wishes to sit down in peace, and free himself from all work, neither feels nor enjoys his life at all; but so far as he is active, he feels that he is alive, and only so far as he is industrious can he be contented. A man must be industrious, a woman only needs to have occupation. Occupation without a purpose is to be occupied in being idle, where we busy ourselves only for amusement. Occupation with a purpose in being occupied is business. Business under difficulties is work. Work is business thrust upon us, where we either compel ourselves, or are compelled by others. We compel ourselves if we have a motivating ground which outweighs all the hardships of the work. On the other hand, many things compel us to work, for example duty. One who is not compelled to his work by anything, but can work as he pleases, cannot occupy and fill up his time with voluntary work so well as he can if he has to do it from duty; for the thought arises: you don't have to do it, nobody is compelling you. So it is one of our needs, that we should have compulsory tasks. When work is executed, there is a feeling of satisfaction of which nobody is capable, save he who has done the work. There is likewise merit, approbation and self-praise to be accorded to oneself, if in spite of all difficulties one has nevertheless completed the work. Man must discipline himself; but the greatest discipline is to accustom oneself to work. This is an incentive to virtue. In working one has no time to contemplate vice, and it really brings about those benefits which another must maliciously think about obtaining through deceit.

Of luxury it remains to be said that it has long been an object of philosophic consideration. It has long been asked whether it ought to be approved or disapproved, and whether it conforms to morality or is opposed to it. A thing can be in conformity with morality, though it is indirectly a hindrance. In the first place, luxury multiplies our needs; it increases the enticements and attractions of inclination and thereby it becomes hard to comply with morality; for the simpler and more innocent our needs, the less we are liable to err in fulfilling them. Indirectly, therefore, luxury is an incursion upon morality. But on the other hand, it promotes all the arts and sciences; it develops all the talents of man, and thus it seems as if this state is what man is intended for. It refines morality; for in that regard we may look either to uprightness or refinement. The one is when we do not obstruct morality; but the other is when we also combine amenity with this, for example, in being hospitable to one another. So luxury develops humanity to the highest degree of beauty. It must, however, be distinguished from self-indulgence. Luxury consists in variety, but self-indulgence in quantity. We find intemperance in people who have no sort of taste, for example, when a wealthy skinflint for once gives a dinner-party, he piles up the food in great quantity, and pays no attention to variety, but only to the amount. Luxury, however, is found in people who do possess taste. So by means of variety it enlarges our judgement, gives occupation to many human hands, and enlivens the whole of communal existence. In that respect, therefore, there can be no objection to luxury from the moral point of view, save only that there must be laws, not to restrict it, but to furnish guidance. One should not go too

27:397

far in luxury, but only to the extent that it can be borne and paid for. The flabby kind of luxury must be restricted, and includes, for example, effeminacy of dress in men, delicacy in eating, and coddling of every kind. Thus even the ladies look more kindly upon a sturdy, active and industrious man than on a sugary, overdressed fop, provided the former does not exaggerate the limits of his attire all too much in the other direction, so that he thereby betrays his ignorance and indifference; if, however, he does but dress as befits his station, and in keeping with the times, his appearance is the more seemly. The other, though, who is so very limp and effeminate in his dress and deportment, is preoccupied more with himself, and cares more for himself than for the ladies. So a man must be manly, and a woman womanly. Effeminacy in a man is as little pleasing as masculinity in a woman. Such feminine luxury makes a man womanish. The masculine luxuries and pleasures include hunting, for example.

27:398

OF WEALTH

We call a man well-to-do if his stock of possessions is perfectly adequate to his needs; we call him a man of means if he has resources to spare, both for his needs and for any other purposes. A man is rich if his means also suffice to make others comfortable. Riches are a sufficient condition for luxury. On the other hand, a man is poor if he lacks resources for casual purposes; needy if he lacks them for necessary ones. Possessions are treasured, not only by the possessor, but also by others. A rich man is highly esteemed by others because of his affluence, and a needy one less so because of his penury. We shall soon see the reasons for this. All resources are called means, insofar as they are means to satisfy one's needs, intentions and inclinations. The excess of resources beyond one's needs or carnal purposes is wealth; this is already more than to have means. Wealth has two advantages: firstly it makes us independent of others, for if we have wealth we do not need others, or require their help; but secondly, wealth has power, for much can be bought. Everything that human forces can produce may be had for money. Hence money and goods are wealth in the true sense. By means of them I am independent; I do not have to serve anyone, or beg anything from anyone; for I can have it all for money; if I have money, I can subject others to myself through their self-interest, so that they serve me and are willing to serve me with their labour. A man, then, so far as he is independent of others and has resources, is an object of respect; for a man loses his worth if he depends on others. It is already natural to respect a person less if he depends on others; but if, in turn, he has others at his command, like an officer, that restores the situation. So a common soldier or a servant is less respected. Thus, in that money confers independence, one is the more respected; one has worth, needs no one, and depends on no one. But because money

27:399

makes us independent, we at length come to depend on money, and since money makes us free of others, it enslaves us once more to itself. This worth which arises from independence is merely negative; the positive worth conferred by wealth stems from the power it gives. By money I have the power to employ the energies of other people in my service. The ancients declared, indeed, that wealth is not noble. A rich man has influence in society and on the common weal. He keeps many people occupied. But his is not a nobility of person. Contempt for wealth does, however, ennoble the person. Wealth ennobles merely the conditions of a person, but not the person himself. Hence contempt for wealth is noble to the understanding, but wealth is noble in appearance.

OF THE MIND'S ATTACHMENT TO WEALTH, OR AVARICE

The possession of resources for any purpose is already pleasing in itself, and hence riches are intrinsically pleasing, because they relate to ends; but they are also pleasing before I have framed any ends, or if I renounce all ends, and merely feel that I have the wherewithal and power to attain them; for if only one has the means to hand, that is already pleasing, in that one can then already enjoy the outcome, if so desired; it merely rests on my will; for the money, after all, is already in my pocket, and so here one enjoys the power in thought, because it can actually be enjoyed if one wants to. People fret if they have to forgo what they have an appetite for, and it is not in their power; but it is easy for them to manage without, even when the appetite is present, if only it is within their power. Thus it vexes a young bachelor that he has to forgo the perquisites of a husband, and although this husband has just the same appetite, it is nonetheless easier for him to forgo it, since he has the thought: after all, you can always have it. So if a man has appetite for something, and no means of satisfying it, it pains him more strongly than it would if, given the same appetite, he were to renounce it when he does have the means. Hence there is something pleasing in the mere possession of the means, in that we can thereby have a thing, as and when we want. Thus wealthy people of a miserly habit go poorly clad; they have no regard for clothes, in that they think: I might always have such clothes, since I have the money for it; I have only to get a haircut, if I so wish, and have these clothes made for me. When they see a carriage and horses, they think: I could have all that just as well as this fellow yonder, if only I wanted to. So they nourish themselves on the thought of the enjoyment they have in their power; they all go about in fine clothes, ride in a carriage with six horses, and eat twelve-course dinners every day; but all this in thought, merely, for if only they wanted to, they could indeed have such things. Possession of the wherewithal serves them in place of the real possession of all pleasures; by merely

27:400

having the means thereto, they can enjoy these pleasures and also forgo them. A man who has enjoyed a pleasure is by no means so pleased as when he is still looking forward to it and keeping his money, rather than actually experiencing it and paying out cash. A miser who has money in his pocket argues thus: 'How will you be feeling, once you have paid out money for pleasure? You will be no wiser then than you are now; so better keep the money.' He is therefore not thinking of the pleasure he is to enjoy, but of how he will be feeling after having enjoyed it. The spendthrift, however, pictures his pleasure at the moment of enjoying it. He cannot imagine how he will feel afterwards, once he has enjoyed it, and does not advert to this.

In the attachment to worldly goods we encounter something that has a resemblance to virtue, and is an analogue of this. Such a person has self-command in his inclinations, and denies himself many pleasures; he thereby promotes his health, and is regular in everything. Hence, too, old people, if they are miserly, live longer than if they were not; for in saving money they live moderately, as they would not otherwise do if it were to cost them nothing; hence they can eat and drink heartily, when another is paying the bill, since their stomachs are in good shape.

27:401 Miserly folk are scorned and detested by others, and they cannot see why. Even persons who make no demand on them are scornful of them, and the more they deprive themselves of anything, the more despised they are. With all other vices we find that the culprit blames himself; everyone recognizes it to be a vice, and reproaches himself about it; only with the miser do we find that he does not blame the fault; he does not know that it is one, and cannot comprehend at all how it can be. The reason for this is as follows: A miser is a person who is stingy and hard only in regard to himself; to others he can always act properly, and takes nothing away from anybody, though he also gives them nothing either; so he simply cannot grasp why another person should despise him, since he is doing nothing to anyone else, and what he does in regard to himself occasions no harm to the other, nor is it anyone's business whether he prefers to eat much or little or not at all; it is of no concern to anyone whether he chooses to go about in smart clothes, or poorly and shabbily dressed. In this he is admittedly correct, and hence, too, he does not perceive it to be a vice. And one cannot be so downright in answering a miser, if only he is not otherwise unjust, which misers seldom are. They consider themselves free from any fault. They even have some excuse for saving, and say, for example, that they do it for their relatives; but this is only a delusion they create for themselves. If the miser's intention were to save for his relatives, he would support them during his life-time, in order to take pleasure in their well-being.

Miserly persons are commonly also very devout, for in that they do no entertaining, and never go into society, because it costs money, their minds are occupied with anxious cares. In such anxieties they wish to have comfort and support; and this they try to obtain from God, by means of their pieties, which, after all, cost nothing. They think, in particular, how very good and profitable it would be if they were to get God on their side; it could do no harm, and would be even better than an annual return of twelve per cent. Mean as the miser is in all his actions, he is equally mean in religion as well, and just as he wants to make gain out of everything, he also wants to gain the kingdom of heaven. He pays no heed to the moral worth of his actions, but thinks that if only he prays earnestly, which costs him nothing, he will already be on his way to heaven.

A miser is also very superstitious. He sees danger arising from every 27:402 circumstance, and therefore beseeches God to preserve all men from danger; but is chiefly thinking of himself. When a disaster has occurred in which many have come to grief, he loudly laments their plight, thinking that they will be asking for something from his purse. The miser is thus a stranger to himself; he does not know his own nature, and hence he is incorrigible, since he can in no way be persuaded of his fault. No miser can be reformed, though many another reprobate may be. Avarice is contrary to reason, and so no rational argument addressed to a miser is of any use; for if he were capable of grasping it, he would not be miserly. The reason avarice is irrational is that money has value as a means, but is not an object of immediate enjoyment. The miser literally takes an immediate pleasure in money, though it is nothing but a mere means. It is simply a crazy dream of possibility, to make use of it. The advantage of using the money is never realized. This dream cannot be corrected by reason, for it would already be a crazed man who would wish to speak prudently and rationally to the crazy one. If this vice were not confirmed by experience, we simply could not see the possibility of it, for it is utterly in conflict with reason. Avarice, indeed, swallows up all the vices, but that is why it is incorrigible.

Avarice begins, however, in the following way, for which reason already provides a foothold: If we see many objects and pleasures of life, we also wish to possess and enjoy them; but since funds are lacking, as the condition and means of obtaining them, we decide to acquire the necessary means, and thus get accustomed to doing without one thing after another. Now if this goes on for a long time, we wean ourselves entirely from all the pleasures, and their presence and enjoyment is a matter of indifference to us. Since we have got used to dispensing with all of them, in acquiring means, we also do so once we have already acquired them in actuality, and have them in our power. On the other hand, once we have again got used to hoarding, we keep on doing so afterwards when we no longer have any need to save and put aside.

The invention of money is also a source of avarice, for prior to that it cannot have been widely prevalent. Hence stinginess, the habit of being frugal with things that can be immediately enjoyed and used, such as 27:403

foodstuffs and old clothes. Money, however, gives occasion for avarice, since it is not an object of immediate enjoyment, but a means of obtaining everything possible for that; for if I am still in possession of a sum of money, I can have innumerable projects for procuring amenities and objects for myself, in all of which money is useful. Here, therefore, I can still employ the money for whatever purpose I please; I see all the amenities and objects of my satisfaction as things that I can still always have; but if I have already paid out money for one of them, then I am no longer free in regard to disposing of the money; now I can no longer buy anything else with it, and all the projects for procuring amenities and objects are thus at an end. But here we fall prey to an illusion. While still in possession of the money, we would have to expend it disjunctively, in that we could use it either for this or for that. But we think of it collectively, and fancy we could have everything in return. So long as a man still has money, he has the agreeable daydream of procuring every amenity for himself. Now he is happy to remain subject to this pleasing error, and so does not rid himself of it by reason. And since he takes money for a means of enjoying every kind of pleasure, he considers it the greatest of pleasures, seeing that all others reside within it, and he can enjoy them all if he wishes. Thus, so long as he has the money, he enjoys all pleasures in prospect; but once he has chosen to apply it to the object of a single pleasure, the illimitable prospect of all the others at once disappears. Hence the man sees money as the object of the greatest pleasure, in which all other pleasures and objects lie hidden. This game is daily played out in the miser's head – it is an illusion he suffers from. So when he sees how others enjoy all the amenities of life, he thinks: you can have all that too, of course, if only you wish it; it pains him, indeed, and he grudges it to others, but once the other has already enjoyed his pleasure, and the money for it has gone, then it is the miser's turn to gloat; for he still has his money in his pocket, and can laugh at them all, since they are now as prudent as he.

If we consider the circumstances of avarice in regard to station, sex and age, we notice that in respect of station the clergy are particularly accused
27:404 of being prone to it. But this reproach could be levelled against men of learning in general and thus also at clerics insofar as they are included among the learned, were it not that if a clergyman has a small income, and is thus accustomed to putting a high value on every trifle, he is then especially liable to avarice. However, the reason why this can be imputed to all scholars, as a class, is as follows: Learning is not an immediate acquisition of means, but only insofar as it is valued, and hence every scholar sees his métier as something that is not especially lucrative, not a business, as would be essentially the case with a livelihood by which one earns money directly, as with any other. He is thus more uncertain about all his revenues than another, who is all the time earning his bread by artistry and manual toil. This can then dispose a scholar to avarice and to

thinking highly of money. Moreover, people who have a sedentary occupation become used to avarice, since by not going out they grow unaccustomed to all the expenditures associated therewith. Remote as they are from all pleasures and amusements, they are also free from the costs involved, and in pursuing a sedentary occupation, they suit themselves with the pleasures that also suit their temper, and in doing so they likewise get used to abstinence. The shopkeeper will doubtless be more inclined to cupidity than avarice. But the military have no inclination to it at all, for since they know not when or how long they may enjoy their possessions, and are not very secure in them either, and are likewise in a calling that involves much conviviality, they have no motives for avarice.

In regard to sex, we notice that women are more exposed to avarice than men, which is doubtless also in keeping with their nature; for in that they are not the bread-winners, they also have to be more sparing, whereas he who does the earning can already be more generous.

In regard to age, we notice that the old are more inclined to avarice than the young, for youth still has the power to acquire everything, while age does not. But money empowers, in that it signifies attaining all the ends that one lacks. Money gives power. Thus in the end even thieves, once they have collected enough loot, attempt by money to secure themselves against punishment; they procure titles, for example, so that they 27:405 may not so easily be hanged. Old age therefore seeks to make up for its want of strength and power by the use of artificial resources. Another reason among the aged is the fear of future neediness and want; for if they have lost everything, they are no longer capable of acquiring more. But the young can do this; if one thing does not succeed, they can embark on something else; they can make new plans, whereas the old cannot, and so must amass funds whereby they are secured from want. Among the stingy, the cause of their avarice is mostly fear, though in some it is also merely to possess power and authority, which they can best obtain through money.

A CONSIDERATION OF THRIFTINESS, AND THE FORM IT MAY TAKE

Thrift is a habit of exactitude and carefulness in the expenditure of one's resources. It is not a virtue, for to be thrifty requires neither skill nor talent. If we compare it with extravagance, we see that it takes far more talent and skill to be a spendthrift of taste than to economize, for even the stupidest can put money aside. But to squander money on refined pleasures takes knowledge and skill; and hence those who acquire money by saving are very drab souls, whereas among the spendthrifts we find people of vivacity and intelligence.

If we ask: Which is more harmful to man in civil society, avarice or extravagance? – then we must first separate from both the factor whereby they may infringe upon the rights of others, namely cupidity in the miser, and the spendthrift's waste of other people's money. We then see that the spendthrift has enjoyed his life, whereas the miser has cheated himself, in that he has always wanted to enjoy it in prospect. So he departs from the world like a stupid dullard, who does not even know that he has lived. But if, on the other hand, we consider improvidence, then there is a lack of prudence in the spendthrift, since, after all, he does not know how long he will live, and so will subsequently have to do without everything, if he has previously squandered it, which the miser has no need to do. But the latter does no better; he deprives himself in the present, where the spendthrift does so in the future. It is harder, indeed, to have first enjoyed comfort, and later to be in want, than to forgo a thing earlier, and later to enjoy pleasure; the spendthrift, admittedly, has already had his enjoyment, and if the miser were also to have it in the end, then all would be well; but he never does have it, and is always postponing it; it always lies ahead of him, and he feeds merely on the hope of pleasure. A spendthrift is thus an amiable ass, but a miser a hateful fool. The spendthrift, moreover, has not destroyed his character, and may yet pluck up courage to live in misfortune; but the miser's character is always a bad one.

27:406

But if we ask, in regard to others: Which is the better, the spendthrift or the miser? – then we answer that so long as both are alive, the spendthrift is better, but that after death the miser is of more use to others. In misers providence even has a means of furthering its ends. They are machines that operate, in the order of things, in accordance with universal ends; they thereby take care of their posterity, which enters, by means of them, into full possession of their goods, and since the money is there all in one heap, great enterprises can thereby be undertaken, and by such undertakings the money is again returned to circulation. Thrift is no virtue, merely prudence; but frugality is a virtue. It is either moderation or abstinence, total renunciation. It is easier to renounce something entirely than to be moderate in its use. In renouncing it, one has not, after all, felt anything; but if one is to be moderate, one must already have enjoyed something beforehand, and thus the appetite has been whetted; so it is harder to refrain from what has already been partially enjoyed than to renounce it entirely. There is virtue in abstinence, but more in moderation. These virtues lead to mastery over oneself.

OF THE TWO DRIVES OF NATURE, AND THE DUTIES RELATING TO THEM

27:407

By nature we have two drives, whereby we demand to be respected by others, and to be loved. These drives relate, therefore, to the dispositions of other people. Which of these inclinations is the stronger? The inclination for respect, and this for two reasons. Respect is directed to our inner worth, but love only to the relative worth of others. One is respected because one has inner worth. The other reason is because respect confers greater security in regard to others than love does. By means of it we are more inviolable and better protected from offence. Love, however, can be present even where there is little esteem. It rests on the love of other people. It is up to others, whether they wish to love or reject or hate me. But if I have inner worth, I shall be respected by everyone; here it is not a matter of anyone's liking, for he who perceives my inner worth will also respect me. If we take the opposites of these two, contempt is more painful than hatred. Both are unpleasant, but if I am an object of hatred, I shall, after all, be hated only by one person or another, and even though I may have much trouble to expect from such hatred, I shall nevertheless, if others do but know my worth, find courage and means enough to bear the hatred, and stand up against it. Contempt, however, is unbearable. An object of contempt is despised by everyone. It takes away our worth for others, and also the consciousness of our own worth. If we wish to be respected, we must also have respect for other people, and for mankind in general. On the other hand, we are under a similar obligation, that if we wish to be loved, we must also display a love for mankind. Hence we must do to others what we demand they should do to us.

If we analyse further the respect that we are glad to receive from others, we find that providence dictates that we should not be indifferent to the judgement of others, but should be directly concerned with what they think of us. But we demand this respect from others, not for use, advantage or other purposes, since in that case we would not be honour-loving, but greedy or covetous for honour. With such intentions a shop-keeper will want to be thought rich, since it is useful to him. But things must be named, not from the means, but from the end. Thus he who sets aside money, to dissipate it later on showy display, is not miserly, but ambitious. Hence, too, the inclination to secure favourable opinions from others is not due to the thought of advantage, but is an immediate inclination directed solely to honour, and having no advantage as its object, and so cannot be said to covet honour, but to love it. Thus providence has instilled the inclination in us, and hence no man, even a great one, is indifferent to the opinion of others. To be sure, one man is more attentive to it than another, and so it seems, for example, that the nobleman is indifferent to the opinion of the peasantry or even the townsfolk, and the prince to that of all his subjects; but each will solicit the opinion of his peers, which is not indifferent to him. To the prince, for example, the judgement of another prince will not be indifferent although the respect of a subordinate seems not to be so considerable, since one has authority over such people, and so their respect has less value than that of those over whom one has no control. The love of honour seems, in fact, to have much to do with one's equals; thus a young woman of low degree, for

27:408

example, is more ashamed in front of her equals than her superiors, from whom she would sooner incur contempt than from those on her own level. Thus the respect of superior persons towards us flatters us more than that of the lowly; but he who is not indifferent even to the esteem of the humble, is one who honours mankind generally; to such a one, the opinion of the worst of men is no more indifferent than that of the highly born.

The intent of providence, in implanting this desire for respect from others, is that we should assess our actions by the judgement of others, so that such acts may not proceed solely from motives of self-love; for our judgement, on its own, corrupts these actions, whence the need that others should also be able to judge them.

The craving for honour must be distinguished from the love of it. Thus if we take the two together, the love of honour is a negative thing; our only concern is not to be an object of contempt. But the craving for honour yearns to be an object of high esteem to others. We might call the love of honour *honestas*, though it would then need to be distinguished from

27:409 respectability. But the craving for honour is ambition. We may love honour, even though we are not in the company of other people. For love of honour we may seek solitude, simply in order to not be an object of contempt. But we cannot crave honour in solitude, for we want to be highly esteemed by others. So this craving is a presumption, a demand upon others, that I am to be highly esteemed. The love of honour we approve on all occasions in anyone, but the craving we never do. It is modesty, if the love of honour does not become a craving. Out of such love, we wish for the respect of everyone, so that we shall not be despised; but out of the craving, we demand to be more highly esteemed than is commonly the case. Wishing to be exceptionally respected, we presume to compel the judgement of others to our own view. But since other people's judgements of us are free, the grounds for respecting us must be such that these outside judgements ensue without duress. The man who craves honour, though, is trying to compel others to respect him; he demands that they should do so, and thereby makes himself ridiculous; he is encroaching on the rights of all.

The man who craves honour we shall therefore at once resist; but he who merely loves it, and clings to respect only to avoid being despised, we also have respect for, and the more he deserves that respect, and the less he makes presumption to it, the more ready we are to bestow our esteem upon him. In the craving for honour there are two elements to be distinguished: vanity and the true craving. Vanity is a hunger for honour in regard to that which does not pertain to our person, as with those who seek honour in titles, attire, and so on. But the true craving is a hunger for honour in regard to what does pertain to the worth of our person. All such craving, though it is natural to man, must nevertheless be kept in check. Everyone craves honour, but nobody must push for it, for in that case the craving fails of its purpose, in that people at once reject the presumptuous claim on their favourable opinion; for they wish to be free in their judgement, and by no means want to be compelled. We can value a thing for what it is worth, but high esteem and honour we can give only to that which has merit. Average men are those who have such worth as can be demanded from everyone, without distinction. And on that account one deserves to be respected and valued, but not esteemed or honoured, if one is honest, upright and punctilious in the discharge of one's obligations, since that can be demanded of anybody. Because a person is honest, he can still demand no acclaim on that account, but only respect; for he has no exceptionally outstanding worth. In all periods where honesty commands acclaim, and is a target for ambition, and one is accorded merit for being honest, we already have corruption of morals and honesty is already rare; it is reckoned a merit, though it ought to be a commonplace attribute of anyone, for he who is only a mere fraction less than honest is already a rascal. Thus it is praised as a merit in Turkish judges, that they have not taken bribes, and when Aristides was called 'the Just', this was certainly praise for him, but an affront to his age, since in those days, since he was so famed for it, there were few just men. Meritorious actions include, however, magnanimity, kindness, etc., since this I cannot require of everyone; so such people are not only respected, but highly esteemed and honoured. We acquire respect in virtue of good conduct, but honour in virtue of meritorious actions. We forfeit respect by failure to perform duties incumbent on us. Nature bids us hide the sexual impulse, and keep it secret, though it is natural to all; yet this concealment serves to set limits to that urge and inclination, and to ensure that it is not so common and open, so that it may be the more strongly preserved. In just the same way, nature also requires a man to try to conceal his inclination to crave for honour; for no sooner is it expressed, than it is already an improper presumption. Man has an impulse towards honour, which is quite unselfish; the craving for honour is often selfish, to wit, when it seeks honour to better its condition, to procure an office or a wife thereby; but he who seeks honour, without any ulterior motive, merely in the approval of others, is truly a lover of honour.

27:410

If we take that impulse to honour which people evince in that they would be glad to retain the approval of others even after death, we see that there is nothing self-interested in that. Without this honour, nobody would trouble to devote himself to the sciences. If he were on a desert island, he would throw away all his books, and prefer to hunt for roots. One might ask whether this impulse to honour is a right or wrong motive to scientific inquiry. Providence has implanted that drive in us, so that our actions and practices might conform to the general judgement of others. For if we lacked it, we would not make our actions so acceptable to the community. We might go astray in our own judgement, so that our opin-

27:411

ions would often be much mistaken, if they were to rely solely on our own judgement. Hence this drive leads* us to compare our judgements concerning our knowledge with the opinion of others. This is the touchstone, that we subject our knowledge to the judgement of many heads. Universal reason, the judgement of all, is the tribunal before which our knowledge has to stand, for otherwise I could not tell whether I have erred or not, which might happen for many reasons. Another might doubtless go wrong himself, but not at the very point that I do.

We have, therefore, an honour-loving urge to refer our knowledge to the judgement of others. It is true that this impulse subsequently decays into the craving for honour, where we seek to deck out falsehoods and misinformation with specious arguments, to filch the approval of others and try to obtain honour; but in origin the urge is a pure and genuine one, though if it degenerates, the intent of providence is thereby frustrated too. The craving for honour is not so natural, save under certain conditions; but the love of it is. Without any such love, the sciences would have no motive.

This love of honour, in and by itself, without any self-interest, cannot be indifferent to us even after death, and may even be stronger still, since by then we can no longer cleanse any stain from it. But is it in keeping with the duties to oneself, or even itself an object of such self-regarding duty? The impulse, in fact, is not only in accordance with these duties, but also an object of our duty. Man must be honour-loving. A person indifferent to his honour is worthless. Honour is the goodness of actions in appearance. But men's actions must not only be good; they must also seem to be good in the eyes of other men. Morality, good will and disposition impart worth to the human race. Since this is also the moral bond, everyone must see that his actions not only furnish a negative example, in containing nothing evil, but also provide a positive one, in possessing an element of good. So our actions must not only be good, but also be seen as an example in the eyes of others. They must spring from a love of honour.

27:412

The question now arises: Should one, in matters of honour, be guided by the opinion of others, which they have drawn from what earns their approval or disapproval? Or should one be guided by one's own principle? The opinions of others are of two kinds: those based on empirical grounds, and there they have authority; and those founded on reason, where they have none. In regard to rectitude, which I perceive by my own reason, I can follow no opinion, but must be guided by my own principle, discerned through reason. But if it is a matter of custom, for example, I have to be guided by the opinion of others.

The craving for honour can also be of two kinds, depending on whether one takes the object of honour to be what people say of one, or

* [reading *abhängig* for *unabhängig* – Tr.]

what they think of one. Every one must consider it a matter of honour, what people think of him; it is already bad if he merely pays heed to what people say of him.

Honourability is the worthiness of behaviour to be honoured, i.e., not to be an object of contempt.

End of the section on self-regarding duties

II. OF DUTIES TOWARDS OTHER PEOPLE 27:413

Our author here commits an extravagance, in that he discusses duties towards inanimate things, animate but irrational creatures, and rational beings. We have duties, though, only towards other people; inanimate things are totally subject to our will, and the duties to animals are duties only insofar as they have reference to ourselves. Hence we shall reduce all duties to those towards other people. Among such duties we discern two main groups:

I. Duties of good-will, or benevolence
II. Duties of indebtedness, or rectitude

In the first case our actions are kindly, but in the second, righteous and required of us.

If we first take the duties of benevolence, we cannot say that we are bound to love other people and do them good; for he who loves another wishes him well, but without owing it to him; he acts, rather, from a willing disposition, gladly, and from his own impulse. Love is well-wishing from inclination. But there can also be benevolence on principle. Hence our pleasure and satisfaction in doing good to others may be either an immediate or a mediate pleasure. The immediate pleasure in well-doing towards others is love, the mediate pleasure of beneficence, where we are simultaneously conscious of having done our duty, is well-doing by reason of obligation. Well-doing from love arises from the heart; but well-doing from obligation arises from principles of the understanding. A man may act well to his wife, for example, from love; but where inclination has already departed it is done from obligation.

The question arises: Can a moralist say that we have a duty to love others? Love is well-wishing from inclination; but nothing can be laid upon me as a duty which depends, not on my will but on my inclination; for I cannot, of course, love at will, but only if I have an urge to it. Duty, however, is always a compulsion; either I have to compel myself, or I am compelled by others. What, then, is the source of the obligation to do 27:414 good to others on principle? Here we must survey that worldly stage upon which nature has set us as guests, and on which we find everything needed for our temporal welfare. Everyone has a right to enjoy the good things of this world. But now since each has an equal interest therein, though God has not parcelled out his share to anyone, but has left it to men to divide these goods among themselves, everyone must so enjoy these good things of life, that he is mindful also of the happiness of others, who have an equal interest in them, and must not preempt anything from his fellows. For since the provision made for us is universal, one must not be indifferent in regard to the happiness of others. If I find, for example, a table laden with food in the forest, I am not to suppose that it is solely intended for myself; I can partake of it, but must also be mindful of leaving something for others; nor should I devour some dish entirely by myself, since another might also have an appetite for it. On seeing, therefore, that the provision is universal, I have obligations to limit my consumption, and to bear in mind that nature has made these arrangements for everyone. This is the source of well-doing by reason of obligation.

If we now, on the other hand, take well-doing from love, and consider a man who loves from inclination, we find that such a man has need of other folk, to whom he can show his kindness. He is not content if he does not find people to whom he can do good. A loving heart has an immediate pleasure and satisfaction in well-doing, and finds more pleasure in that than in its own enjoyment. This inclination must be satisfied, for it is a need. This is a kindliness of heart and temper, but no moralist should seek to cultivate such a thing; it is benevolence from principle that must be cultivated, for the other is based on a man's inclination and need, which gives rise to an irregular sort of behaviour. Such a man will be beneficent, from inclination, to everyone, but when he is imposed on by some he will repent of it, and then he takes an opposite decision and makes it a rule henceforth to benefit nobody. His behaviour is therefore not governed by principle at all. Moralists, accordingly, must lay down principles, and commend and cultivate the benevolent life based on obligation; and once all natural obligation has also been set forth through religion, then the inclination, too, may be cultivated, but only insofar as it has to be subject to principles, and then they can be presented as motives to kindly actions from inclination.

27:415

We now proceed to the second type of duties towards others, namely those of indebtedness and justice. They arise, not from inclination, but from the rights of other people. Here we look, not, as before, to the needs of others, but to their rights; the other may be needy or not, he may be miserable or not, but if it is a matter of his rights, I am bound to give him satisfaction. These duties rest upon the universal rule of right, and the supreme duty of them all is respect for the rights of others. I am bound to uphold such rights and regard them as sacred. There is nothing in all the world so sacred as the rights of others. They are impregnable and inviolable. Woe unto him who infringes those rights, and tramples them underfoot! The right of the other should keep him secure in everything; it is stronger than any bulwark or wall. We have a divine ruler, and his sacred gift to us is the rights of man.

If we picture a man who acts only by right and not by kindness, he can always close his heart to any other man, and be indifferent to his wretched and pitiable fate, if he is but conscientious in observing his bounden duty to everyone, and does but accord to every man his right, as a sacred and most awesome trust that has been given to man by the ruler of the world. If he gives to no man a jot over his due, but is also punctilious in withholding nothing from him, he is acting righteously, and were we all to behave thus, and perform no act of love or kindness, but left the rights of every man inviolate, there would be no misery in the world, save that which does not arise from the mistreatment of others, e.g., sicknesses and misfortunes. The greatest and commonest of human miseries are due more to men's injustice, than to ill-luck.

But since respect for rights is a result of principles, whereas men are deficient in principles, providence has implanted in us another source, namely the instinct of benevolence, whereby we make reparation for what we have unjustly obtained. We thus have an instinct for benevolence, but 27:416 not for justice. By this impulse men take pity on another, and render back the benefits they have previously snatched away, though they are not aware of any injustice; the reason being, that they do not rightly examine the matter. One may take a share in the general injustice, even though one does nobody any wrong by civil laws and practices. So if we now do a kindness to an unfortunate, we have not made a free gift to him, but repaid him what we were helping to take away through a general injustice. For if none might appropriate more of this world's goods than his neighbour, there would be no rich folk, but also no poor. Thus even acts of kindness are acts of duty and indebtedness, arising from the rights of others.

Let us now, on the other hand, consider a man who pays no heed to the rights of others, but is accustomed to perform even his bounden duties from benevolence, who will hear nothing of rights and obligations, though he will frequently act out of kindness; if someone comes to him, asking for repayment of a debt, because he is in direst need and has obligations of his own to repay, and if this person employs the customary language of indebtedness, our man will assail him for being so uncouth, and wanting to have everything by enforcement, even though the other is perfectly entitled to require payment in that way. If he now refuses to pay off his creditor, and the latter thereby gets into difficulties, all the kindly and beneficent acts he has done over a lifetime will count for less than the one injustice he has done to this man; for this is a wholly different sort of reckoning, in which those acts have no place at all. He may practise benevolence with what he has to spare, but must not deny anyone his due.

If all men were willing to act from benevolence merely, there would be no 'mine' and 'thine' at all, and the world would be a stage, not of reason, but of inclination, and nobody would trouble to earn anything, but would rely on the charity of others. In that case, however, there would have to be the greatest abundance of everything, and it would all be passive, as when children enjoy something which one of them shares out to the rest, so long as it lasts. Hence it is a good thing that men have to tend their happiness by work, and that everyone must have respect for the rights of others. All moralists and teachers should therefore see to it that, so far as possible, they represent acts of benevolence to be acts of obligation, and reduce them to a matter of right. A man should not be flattered for performing acts of kindness, for then his heart inflates with generosity and he wants all his actions to be of that kind.

27:417

We have something more to say about the duties of well-wishing and benevolence. Well-wishing from love cannot be commanded, though well-wishing from obligation can. If, however, we do well by someone from duty, we get used to this, so that we subsequently do it from love and inclination as well. If we speak well of someone, simply because we see that he deserves it, we get used to this, so that we afterwards intone his merits in everything. Thus even love from inclination is a moral virtue, and might be commanded to this extent, that one should first practise well-doing as a duty, and later, through habituation, out of inclination as well.

All love is either love that wishes well, or love that likes well. Well-wishing love consists in the wish and inclination to promote the happiness of others. The love that likes well is the pleasure we take in showing approval of another's perfections. This liking may be either sensuous or intellectual. All such liking, if it is love, must first of all be inclination. The love that is sensuous liking is a delight in the sensuous intuition, due to sensuous inclination; sexual inclination is an example of this; it is directed, not so much to happiness, as to the mutual relation of the persons. The love based on intellectual liking is already harder to conceive. Intellectual liking is not difficult to envisage, but the love based on it is so. What intellectual liking gives rise to inclination? The good disposition of benevolence. If we are told: *Thou shalt love* thy neighbour, how is this to be understood? It is not with well-liking love that I am to love him, for with that I can also love the worst of villains; it is with well-wishing love. But moral good-will does not consist in merely wishing someone well, but in wishing that he might also be worthy of it, and that sort of well-wishing love we may also have for our enemies. Such well-wishing can always be heart-felt. I wish that he may come to himself, and may thereby make himself worthy of all happiness, and actually attain to it. A monarch may have such good-will towards one who betrays him. He may punish the man, indeed, and have him hanged, but may likewise pity him for being so unfortunate that such punishment has to be visited on him according to

27:418

law; and can also heartily wish of him, that he may make himself worthy of blessedness hereafter, and actually attain it. Thus well-wishing love to one's neighbour can be enjoined upon everyone. But well-liking love to one's neighbour cannot be generally commanded, since nobody can have such a liking where there is no object of which to approve. There is, however, a distinction to be drawn in a man between the man himself and his humanity. I may thus have a liking for the humanity, though none for the man. I can even have such liking for the villain, if I separate the villain and his humanity from one another; for even in the worst of villains there is still a kernel of good-will. There is not one of them unable to perceive or distinguish between good and evil, or who would not wish to be virtuous. So moral feeling and good-will are present there, and only strength and motives are lacking; for, villain though he be, I am still able to think: who knows what has driven him to it? Given his temperament, it may have been just such a trifle as a small transgression of my own. If I now enter into his heart, I can still find a feeling for virtue in him, and so humanity must be loved, even in him. Hence it can rightly be said that we ought to love our neighbours. I am not only obligated to well-doing, but also to loving others with well-wishing, and well-liking, too.

Since men are objects of well-liking love, in that we should love the humanity in them, even judges, in punishing crime, should not dishonour humanity; they must, indeed, penalize the evil-doer, but not violate his humanity by demeaning punishments; for if another dishonours a man's humanity, the man himself sets no value on it; it is as if the evil-doer had himself so demeaned his humanity, that he is no longer worthy of being a man, and must then be treated as a universal object of contempt.   27:419

The injunction to love others is thus equally applicable to love from obligation and love from inclination; for if I love others from obligation, I thereby acquire a taste for loving, and by practice it becomes love from inclination. About love from duty, and every duty, indeed, of the artificial kind, a man may wonder whether he is actually obliged to practise them; but inclination takes its own straight path; it has to travel straight, in fact, for it has no rule.

Affability is nothing more than a certain civility in our outward demeanour to others. It is an abhorrence of any offence that might be given to them. It arises from love of mankind, and moderates anger and vengefulness towards others. At bottom it is nothing* positive; for the affable do nothing to hamper the well-being of another, but nor are they generous in promoting it. Both should really be combined; but generosity, which is associated with bravery and strength of mind, is not compatible with affability, which consists only in mildness and gentility.

* [Reading *nichts* for *was* – Tr.]

To be humane is to interest oneself in the fate of other men; inhumanity is to take no interest in what happens to them. Why are some studies designated *humaniora?*[a] Because they refine people. In anyone who pursues these studies, even if he may not otherwise have acquired much learning, a corresponding refinement and gentility are therefore left behind; for the humane sciences, in occupying the mind, endow it with a polish that is afterwards peculiarly its own. Thus the merchant will judge how much a man is worth according to his fortune; but a studious man will already be judging by another standard.

Affability coupled with frankness is candid friendship, which is very much liked. Every show of friendliness, courtesy, politeness and civility is already the same virtue, though exercised only in little. But that the virtue itself should be exerted, with its strength, serviceability and sacrifice of personal happiness, is extremely rare. It is therefore not good to have a friend whom we burden with appeals for help in distress; we are thereby a trouble to him for he thinks at once that he will often be called upon in this fashion. We do better to endure hardships alone, rather than burden others. Those who complain of a lack of friends are self-serving folk, who would always be happy to profit from their friendships. I need as a friend, not one from whom I can extract something, but simply one whose company I can enjoy, and to whom I can unburden myself; but courtesy I expect from everyone. Social intercourse is already a cultivation of virtue, and a preparation for the surer exercise of it. Courtesy signifies that complaisance whereby we have nicety enough, even in the smallest trifles, to make ourselves congenial to another. Politeness is the removal of coarseness by attrition. Men polish and rub against each other until such time as they are mutually adjusted.* This aptitude shows delicacy of judgement in discerning what is pleasing or unpleasing to another.

A cold-blooded temper towards others is one that evinces no loving affection or stir of emotion. The man to whom such stirrings of good-will are unknown, is cold. Yet cold-bloodedness should not, on that account, be censured. The poets may rejoice at being steeped in warm feeling and affection, and heap abuse on cold-bloodedness; but if it is accompanied by principles and good dispositions, those who possess it are at all events people who can be relied on. A cold-blooded guardian who means me well, an advocate or patriot of that type, are people of steadfast character, who will surely do their utmost on my behalf. Whereas cold-bloodedness, in an evil-doer, is all the worse on that account, in a good man – though it may not sound so well – it is actually better than a warm feeling of affection, since it is more constant.

Frigidity is a want of love; but cold-bloodedness is a want of emotion in

27:420

* [Reading *passen* for *hassen* – Tr.]
[a] more humane

love. A cold-blooded love provides regularity and order; but frigidity is a lack of the feeling whereby the state of others affects us.

We ought to love others, because it is good to do so, and because we thereby become kind. But how can we love, if the other is not worthy of it? The love in this case is not an inclination to have liking for another, but an inclination whereby the other would be worthy of our liking. We should be inclined to the wish of finding the other worthy of love, and anyone who seeks in the man something that would be worthy of love will also certainly find it there, just as an unloved man who seeks in another for what makes him unworthy of love, also actually discovers it in him. We should wish for the happiness of the other, but also wish to find him worthy of love. Here there is also a rule to be noted: we must see to it that our inclination to love the other, and wish for his happiness, are not idle longings, or desires with no outcome, but practical desires. A practical desire is one that is directed not so much to the object as to the actions whereby this object is brought about. We should not only take satisfaction in the welfare and happiness of others, but this satisfaction should relate to the effectual actions that contribute to this welfare. In just the same way, I should not wish, when the other is in misery, that he might be rescued from it, but should attempt, rather, to rescue him. All human evils and misfortunes are objects of our aversion, not insofar as they are evil, but insofar as these evils are brought about by man. If a person has suffered injury in health or fortune, he has nothing more to say, if it came about through a general disaster, for such things can often happen in life; but if this evil was perpetrated by another man, it is an object of extreme aversion to us. If I now observe such a man sitting in distress, and see that I have no way of altering it, and cannot come to his aid in any fashion, I may turn away coldly and say, with the Stoic: What is it to me? My wishes cannot help him. But so far as I can extend a hand to help him, I am to that extent able to promote his happiness, and sympathize with his plight; but I show no sympathy whatever for his plight in harbouring passionate wishes for his deliverance. The heart, then, is only a good heart insofar as it is able to contribute something to the other's happiness, and not when it merely wishes for that. People pride themselves on having a kind heart, when they merely wish that everyone might be happy. But the only one to have a kind heart is he who contributes something to that happiness.

All moral instruction will therefore dwell upon this, that our satisfaction at the happiness of others should be felt only insofar as we find pleasure in promoting that happiness. Hence the other's happiness, in and for itself, is not an object of satisfaction, save insofar as we have rendered assistance to it. People think here that sympathy for another's plight, and kindness of heart, consist merely in feelings and wishes. Yet he who pays no heed at all to the wretchedness of others, where he can be of no help, and who is indifferent to all misfortune that cannot be altered, but takes

27:421

27:422

trouble only where he can do something and be of help, is in fact a practical man, and his heart is a kind one, because it is active, even though he makes no such parade of it as others, who sympathize by wishes, merely, and already see friendship in that.

OF FRIENDSHIP

This is the hobby-horse of all poetical moralists, and here they seek nectar and ambrosia. Men are actuated by two motives; one is drawn from within them, and that is the motive of self-love; the other is the moral motive, drawn from others, and that is the motive of the general love of mankind. In man, these two motives are in conflict. Men would love others and attend to their happiness, if they did not have to pursue the aims of their own self-love. On the other hand, they also see that acts of self-love have no moral merit, being merely permitted, as such, by the moral laws. It is, however, a great merit, if a man is moved by a general love of mankind to promote the happiness of others. But now a man clings especially to what gives worth to his person. Friendship evolves from this idea. Yet how do I now begin? Should I first care for my own happiness, from self-love, and later, when that is attended to, try to promote the happiness of others? But in that case the happiness of others is put second, and the inclination to my own happiness grows ever stronger, so that I never make an end of cultivating it, and that of others goes unattended. But if I first begin by looking after other people's happiness, my own is left behind. But if all men are so minded, that each looks out for the other's happiness, then each man's welfare will be nurtured by the rest; were I to know that others were caring for my happiness, as I would wish to care for theirs, I would be sure of not falling too short in any cultivation of my own happiness, for 27:423 it would be made good to me, in that I was cultivating that of others, and thus we would be making an exchange of welfare, and nobody would suffer any harm; for however well a man takes care of another's happiness, that other will be taking equally good care of his. It looks as if a man loses, when he cares for other people's happiness; but if they, in turn, are caring for his, then he loses nothing. In that case the happiness of each would be promoted by the generosity of others, and this is the Idea of friendship, where self-love is swallowed up in the idea of generous mutual love.

If we now take the other side again, where each looks out for his own happiness, and is indifferent to that of others, then everyone is admittedly entitled to take care of himself. This is certainly no more than the moral rule permits, but there is no merit in it; so long as a person has created no obstacle to other people's happiness in pursuing his own, he possesses no moral merit, indeed, but nor is he morally a transgressor. Were we now obliged to choose, what choice would we make? Friendship or self-love? On moral grounds we would choose friendship, but on practical ones, self-love, for nobody could take better care than I of my own happiness. But whichever one of the two I take, there is always something amiss. If I choose friendship, merely, my happiness suffers thereby; if it is only self-love, there is no moral worth or merit in it.

Friendship is an Idea, because it is not drawn from experience, but has its seat in the understanding; in experience it is very defective, but in morals it is a very necessary Idea. In this connection we may note what an Idea is, and what an Ideal. We have need of a measure, by which to estimate degree. The measure is either arbitrary, if the amount is not determined *a priori* by concepts, or a natural measure, if the amount is determined in that way. In regard to quantities, so far as they are deter-mined *a priori*, what is the specific measure by which we can assess them? Their measure is always the maximum; so far as this maximum is a measure in regard to other, lesser qualities, such a measure is an Idea; but so far as it is a pattern for them, it is an Ideal. If we now compare the affectionate inclination of people to one another, we find many degrees and proportions in regard to those who share out their love between themselves and others. The maximum of mutual love is friendship, and this is an Idea, since it serves as a measure by which to determine recipro-cal love. The greatest love I can have for another is to love him as myself, for I cannot love anybody more than that; but if I would love him as   27:424
myself, I can do it no otherwise than by being assured that he will love me as much as himself; in that case I am requited for what I part with, and thereby regain occupancy of myself. This Idea of friendship enables us to measure friendship, and see how far it is still deficient. So when Socrates said: "My dear friends, there are no friends", this was as much as to say that no friendship ever matches the Idea of friendship; and he was right about this, for it is not in fact possible. But the Idea is true, nonetheless. If I choose friendship only, and look solely to the other's happiness, in the assurance that he is similarly looking to mine, then this is indeed a recipro-cal love, whereby I am again requited. Here each would be tending the other's happiness from generosity; I do not throw away my happiness, but merely place it in other hands, while I have the other's happiness in my own; yet this Idea is valid only in reflection, and no such thing occurs among men. But if everyone looked out for himself only, without troubling about others, there would be no friendship at all, so the two things must be mingled together. Man cares for himself; and also for the happiness of others. But because the limits here are not defined, and there can be no indication of degree as to how far I ought to care for myself, and how far for others, the measure of friendly disposition is not determinable by any law or rule. I am obliged to care for my needs and for my comfort in life; if I cannot now care for the other's happiness, except by giving up my own needs and comfort, then nobody can oblige me, in that case, to care for the other's happiness, and exercise friendship towards him. But in that

everyone can increase his needs, and make as many things needful to him as he wishes, there is no means of specifying under what forfeiture of needs it is alone possible for friendship to occur; for many of our needs, that we have made into necessities, are such that we might largely sacrifice them for our friend.

27:425 Friendship is divided into friendship of need, taste or disposition. The friendship of need is that whereby the participants may entrust each other with a reciprocal concern in regard to their needs in life. This was the first beginning of friendship among men, but occurs, for the most part, only under the most primitive conditions. Thus when savages go hunting, and are friends, each stands up for, and tries to accommodate, the needs of his fellows. The fewer men's needs, the more they engage in such friendship; for if a man is in a state of luxury, where he has many needs, he also has many concerns of his own, and then is all the less able to occupy himself with those of others, since he has himself to look after. So in the state of luxury such friendship does not occur, and is not even wanted; for if one of the parties realizes that the intent of the other in friendship is to secure some attention to his needs, the friendship loses interest and is then broken off. If the friendship is active, in that one of the parties is actually caring for the needs of the other, it is generous; but the passive one, who aims at getting benefit from the other, is most ungenerous. Hence no man will cause trouble to a friend with his affairs, and each will prefer to endure his woes alone, rather than burden his friend with them. Once the friendship of two people is honourable on both sides, each will recoil from such behaviour, and neither will want to bother the other with his affairs. Yet in every friendship we must still presuppose this friendship of need, not in order to enjoy it, though, but to trust in it; I must, that is, have confidence in each of my true friends, that he would be able and willing to look after my affairs, and promote my interests; though in order to enjoy that confidence, I must never ask him to do it. He is a true friend, of whom I know and can presume, that he will really help me in need; but because I am also a true friend of his, I must not appear to him in that light, or impose such dilemmas upon him; I must merely have trust on that score, not make demands, and will sooner suffer myself than burden him with my troubles. And he must likewise have confidence in me, and be equally undemanding. Thus there is a presupposition of trust in the

27:426 other's good-will, and willingness to be a friend in need, though subject to the further principle, that we cannot misuse this trust. Because my friend is so generous as to be well disposed towards me, wishing me well, and being ready to aid me in any difficulty, I must be equally generous in my turn, and not demand it of him. The friendship that goes to the length of actually helping the other in his troubles is very rare, and also very delicate and fine. The reason is, that one cannot appear to the other in that light. The sweetest and most delicate aspects of friendship are the well-wishing dispositions; but these the other must not seek to diminish, since the delicacy of friendship does not reside in the fact that I see my friend's coffers to contain even a shilling for myself. The other reason, however, is that it alters the relationship. The relation of friendship is that of equality; but if one friend now helps the other in his troubles, he has become my benefactor, and I am in his debt; if so, that makes a blind man of me, and I can no longer look him so straight in the eye, and by then the true relationship is at an end, and friendship no longer exists.

The friendship of taste is an analogue of friendship, and consists in taking pleasure in the company and mutual association of the two parties, rather than their happiness. Between persons of similar station or calling a friendship of taste is not so common as it is between those of differing occupations; thus one scholar will have no friendship of taste with another, for the one can do what the other can; they cannot satisfy or entertain one another, for what one knows, the other knows too; but a scholar may well have a friendship of taste with a merchant or soldier, and so long as the scholar is no pedant, and the merchant no blockhead, then each can entertain the other on his own subject. For men are bound together only by what the one can contribute to the other's needs; not by what the other already has, but when the one possesses what supplies a want in the other; not, therefore, by similarity, but by difference.

The friendship of disposition and sentiment cannot be so readily expressed in German. It involves dispositions of feeling, and not those of actual service. The friendship of sentiment has the following basis: It is curious that, even when we engage in social intercourse and companionship, we still do not enter completely into society. In any company we tend to withhold the greater part of our disposition. We do not at once pour out all our feelings, attitudes and judgements. Everyone makes such judgements as are advisable in the circumstances; we are all under constraint, and harbour a mistrust of others, which results in a reserve, whereby we not only cover up our weaknesses, so as not to be ill thought of, but also withhold our opinions. If, however, we can get rid of this constraint, and impart our feelings to the other, then we are fully in communion with him. So that each of us may be free of this constraint, we therefore have need of a friend in whom we can confide, and to whom we may pour out all our views and opinions; from whom we cannot and need not hide anything and with whom we are fully able to communicate. On this, therefore, rests the friendship of disposition and fellowship. We thus have a strong impulse to unbosom ourselves and be wholly companionate. But this can be only in the company of one or two friends. People also have a need to confide, moreover, in that only so can their opinion be subject to reflection. If I possess such a friend, of whom I know that his disposition is upright and kindly, neither malicious nor false, he will already be helpful in rectifying my judgement, when I have

27:427

gone astray. This is the whole purpose of man, which allows him to enjoy his existence.

The question arises, whether, in such friendship, there is still a need for reserve? Yes, but not so much for one's own sake, as for that of the other; for everyone has his weaknesses, and these must be kept hidden even from our friends. Intimacy relates only to dispositions and sentiment, not to decorum; that must be observed, indeed, and one's weaknesses in that respect concealed, so that humanity should not be offended thereby. Even to our best friend, we must not discover ourselves as we naturally are and know ourselves to be, for that would be a nasty business.

To what extent are men the better for engaging in friendship? People do not favour everyone with their goodwill, but would sooner confine themselves, in that respect, to a small circle. They delight in joining sects and parties and societies. The earliest societies are those that arise from the family, and so some have dealings only within the family circle. Other societies are formed through sects, religious parties, and so on, whereby men band themselves together. This has a laudable appearance, for it looks as if they are trying, in combination, to cultivate their feelings, opinions, and so forth; but it has the effect, in a religious party, for example, of closing the human heart towards those who are outside the group. But that which diminishes the generality of good-will, and closes the heart towards others, impairs the soul's true goodness, which aspires to a universal benevolence. Friendship is thus an aid in overcoming the constraint that we harbour, from mistrust, towards those we associate with, and in opening up to them without reserve. But if we engage in such friendship, we have to guard against closing our heart towards others who are not of our company. Friendships are not found in heaven, for heaven is the ultimate in moral perfection, and that is universal; friendship, however, is a special bond between particular persons; in this world only, therefore, it is a recourse for opening one's mind to the other and communing with him, in that here there is a lack of trust among men.

When people complain of a lack of friendship, it comes about because they have no friendly heart or dispositions, and then they say that others are no friends; such people always have something to demand from their friends, or to burden them with. A person who has no need of that, withdraws from friendship with such people. However, the general complaint about lack of friends is like the general complaint about lack of money. The more civilized men become, the more universal their outlook, and the smaller the incidence of special friendships. The civilized man seeks a general friendship and amenity, without having special ties. The more savagery prevails in the habits of society, the greater the need for such ties, which are sought in accordance with one's dispositions and taste. Such friendship presupposes weaknesses on both sides, for which neither party is able to reproach the other; but where each has something

27:428

to excuse in the other, and neither need reproach himself, there is then equality between them, and neither can claim to be superior.

What, then, is the basis for that compatibility and bond of friendship? Identity of thought is not required for the purpose; on the contrary, it is difference, rather, which establishes friendship, for in that case the one supplies what the other lacks; but in one particular they must agree: they need to have the same principles of understanding and morality, and then they can fully understand each other; if they are not alike in that, they cannot get on at all together, since in judgement they are poles apart. Each of us seeks to be worthy of being a friend, and this he may do by uprightness of disposition, candour and trustworthiness, by conduct that is free from malice and falsity, and conjoined with vivacity, amiability and cheerfulness of mind. This makes us into objects worthy of a friendship. Having made ourselves worthy to be a friend, there will always be someone or other to conceive a liking for us, and choose us as a friend, till by closer association such amity constantly increases. 27:429

Friendship may also terminate, for men cannot see right into each other, and often fail to find in the other what they supposed and were looking for. In friendships of taste, the amity vanishes because in process of time the taste is lost, and alights upon new objects, and then the one displaces the other. The friendship of disposition is rare, because people seldom have principles. So friendship ceases, because it was not a friendship of disposition. In regard to all this, we must note as follows. The name of friendship should inspire respect, and even if our friend has somehow become an enemy, we must still venerate the previous friendship, and not show that we are capable of hatred. It is not only bad in itself to speak disparagingly of our friend, in that we thereby show that we have no respect for friendship, have acted badly in choosing him, and are now ungrateful towards him; it is also contrary to the rule of prudence, since those to whom we say such things will think that the same might happen to them, if they became our friends, and thereafter fell out with us; and hence they eschew our friendship. We must so conduct ourselves to a friend, that it does us no harm if he were to become our enemy; we must give him nothing to use against us. We are not, indeed, to suppose that he may become our enemy, for then there would be no trust between us. But if we give ourselves entirely to a friend, and entrust him with all the secrets which might detract from our happiness, and might well be divulged if he did become an enemy, then it is very unwise to tell him these things, since he could either give them away through inadvertence, or use them to our hurt if he became our foe. If we are friends with a choleric person, who in a fit of anger might well consign us to the gallows, but is all apologies the moment he calms down, we should never put a weapon in his hands. 27:430

It may be asked, whether one can be a friend to everybody? Universal friendship is to be a friend to man as such, to have general good-will towards everyone; but to be everybody's friend will not do, for he who is a friend to all has no particular friend; but friendship is a particular bond. One might, to be sure, say of some people that they are friends of everyone, if they are capable of establishing friendship with anybody. Such citizens of the world are but few in number; they are well disposed, and inclined to see the best side of everything. This good-heartedness, combined with understanding and taste, is what makes a universal friend, and it already represents a high degree of perfection. But people are still very much inclined to form special ties. The reason is, because man starts from the particular and goes on to the general; and besides, it is also an impulse of nature. Without a friend, a man is totally isolated. By friendship we cultivate virtue in little things.

OF ENMITY

Enmity is more than a lack of friendship. If a man has no friend, it still does not follow from that, that he is an enemy of everybody. He can always have a good heart, but be without the gift of making himself liked and sought after. He can also have upright dispositions, but know not how to become popular by making allowance for all faults; such a person may have no friends, but it does not follow that he therefore has to be ill-natured. Just as friendship consists in mutual good-will and liking, so 27:431 enmity consists in mutual ill-will and dislike. We may have dislike for somebody but no ill-will. We dislike him if we do not find in him the good qualities we look for; we cannot associate with him, nor can he be our friend; but apart from that, we still bear him no ill-will; we wish him the best, and would even, maybe, give him something, if he would stay away. Ill-will, however, we bear to a person, when we wish him no good: Now since enmity consists in ill-will and dislike, where we find a pleasure in the other's misfortune, we ought never to harbour enmity to anyone, for it is itself a hateful thing in a man, when he hates others and wishes them ill. A man is amiable in his own eyes, only when he finds himself amicable. We may also have an enemy, even when we are not an enemy to him; we may avoid him, and wish him to feel what it is like, to forfeit the approval of others; we may be sore and angry at him, without being his enemy, for we still do not seek, on that account, to make him unhappy. So true enmity we must bear towards none; we may, indeed, hate someone, if he has behaved to us in such a way as to do us harm by divulging our secrets, for he deserves our hatred, though he should not yet be an enemy for that reason; we should do him no evil on that account, for enmity is a declared disposition to do something harmful to the other.

A man is peaceable, if he abhors any kind of enmity. There are two ways of being a peace-lover: if we wish for our own peace, and if we institute peace among others; the latter is the more magnanimous. This peace-loving disposition differs from that of indolence, whereby we try to avoid all trouble and strife because of the inconvenience it causes, though not because of any gentleness of character; the peace-lover, on the contrary, acts from kindness and good-nature. To be peace-loving on principle, however, is still to love peace as a matter of principle, without regard for any gentleness of temperament.

Misanthropy is hatred of mankind, and takes two forms: aversion from men, and enmity towards them. In the first case we are afraid of men, regarding them as our enemies; but the second is when a man is himself an enemy to others. The aversive man shrinks from men out of temperament, he sees himself as no good to others, and thinks he is too unimportant for them; and since, for all that, he has a certain love of honour, he 27:432 hides and runs away from people. The enemy of mankind shuns his fellows on principle, thinking himself too good for them. Misanthropy arises, partly from dislike, and partly from ill-will. The misanthrope from dislike thinks all men are bad; he fails to find in them what he was seeking; he does not hate them, and wishes some good to all, but simply does not like them. Such people are melancholy folk, who can form no conception of the human race. But the misanthrope from ill-will is he who does good to nobody, and pursues their harm instead.

OF THE DUTIES ARISING FROM HUMAN RIGHTS

In *jus*, there is determination of what is right. It sets forth the necessity of actions from authority or compulsion. Ethics, however, sets forth the necessity of actions from inner obligation, arising from the right of another, insofar as one is not compelled thereto. We must first attend above all to what *principia* duties have sprung from. If we owe a person something, according to his right, we must not regard this as an act of kindness or generosity, nor treat the act of requital as an act of love. The titles of duties must not be altered. If we have taken something away from a person, and then do him a kindness when in need, that is not generosity, but a poor recompense for what has been taken from him. Even the civil order is so arranged that we participate in public and general oppressions, and thus we have to regard an act we perform for another, not as an act of kindness and generosity, but as a small return of what we have taken from him in virtue of the general arrangement. All acts and duties, moreover, arising from the right of others, are the greatest of our duties to others. All acts of kindness are permitted only insofar as they are not contrary to the right of another; if they are so, the act is morally impermissible. Thus I cannot rescue a family from misery and afterwards leave debts behind. There is nothing in the world so holy, therefore, as the right of another. Kindness is an extra. He who performs no kindly actions, but has also

27:433 never offended against the rights of others, can always be a righteous man, and if everyone were like him, there would be no poverty. But he who has spent all his life in acts of kindness, and has but infringed the right of a single man, cannot wipe this out by all his acts of kindness. Yet at the same time, the duties that stem from right and benevolence are not so binding as those towards myself. Duties arising from the right of another must not have compulsion as their motive; for they are but rascals who observe rights from fear of punishment; nor should the motivation be from fear of being punished by God.

OF EQUITY

Equity is a right, but one which gives no authority to compel the other. It is a right, but not a compulsive right. If anyone has worked for me, for agreed payment, but has done more than I required, then he has, indeed, a right to demand payment for his extra work, but he cannot compel me to it. If he wants to return things to their previous condition, he cannot do that either, if I will not let him, since nobody has any further right to interfere in my affairs; he thus has no authority to compel me, because it was not agreed upon. There has been no declaration. For in order for someone to be authorized to compel me, the action must firstly have originated from the right of the other himself; in that case, however, it also has to rest on sufficient external conditions for imputation of the right, and these are exhibited by externally adequate proofs. *Coram foro interno*, equity is a strict right, but not *coram foro externo*. Equity is thus a right where the grounds of outer imputation *coram foro externo* are not valid, though they are so at the bar of conscience.

OF INNOCENCE

In law a person is guilty, insofar as he has performed an action that is contrary to the right of another. But in ethics he is guilty if he has merely had the thought of committing it. Christ expresses this clearly, when he says, "Whosoever looketh on a woman to lust after her . . ." etc.* So if
27:434 someone does not reform his disposition, he continues always to be ethically guilty of the offences he has not committed, since, had there been an opportunity, they would have been, for the decision had already been taken in thought, and only circumstances prevented it. Purity in our dispositions rids us of the guilt of transgressing in our ethical duties. Without it, a man is considered, in the moral tribunal, as if he had done the actions; for even in an ordinary court he is held guilty of them, even though led astray by circumstances and opportunity. How many a man walks guiltless

* [Matt. 5:28 – Tr.]

of such crimes, only because he did not fall into similar circumstances; had he been brought into the same temptation, he would also have been guilty of the same offence. So it was due only to the outward circumstances. There is thus no virtue so strong, that temptation could not be found for it. We do not know our dispositions aright, until we have got into those circumstances in which we might exercise them; for every villain also wishes to be good, and to think himself such. But who can say that such and such a one has been under temptation to deceive his neighbour, and has not done so? To be morally innocent is to give practical evidence, at every opportunity, of the purity of our dispositions. A man has often plumed himself on his innocence, but has not withstood temptation, and we therefore have reason to guard against every temptation; whence Christ, too, in the Lord's Prayer – an entirely moral prayer, which even in asking for our daily bread displays modesty more than concern for sustenance – has taught us to pray that we be not led into temptation. For who knows the extent of our moral dispositions, and who has already withstood every test of them? Heaven has the best knowledge of our guilt; and who can say that he is morally innocent? We may be innocent enough *coram foro externo*, but not here.

OF INJURY

There is nothing to be said of this, since it already has to do with the rights of others. If anyone has defrauded or lied to me, then I do him no wrong if I defraud or tell lies to him in turn; but I have done wrong in general according to the universal laws of humanity. He himself can certainly not complain of me, but I am also in the wrong for having done it at all. Hence it is nothing, if we can plume ourselves on having done nobody any wrong; for we may still have done wrong in general. On giving offence, an excuse or reparation is needed; if that cannot be done, apologies must follow. If contrition is shown for the offence, and there is regret at having offended the other, but the injured party is not content with that, then it does a man honour if he offers an apology; so it is not degrading to apologize.

27:435

OF REVENGE

The desire for vengeance must be distinguished from the desire to have one's rights. Everyone is bound to uphold his rights, and to see that others do not trample them underfoot. This human privilege of having rights he must not abandon, but must fight for so long as he can, for otherwise, if he throws away his rights, he throws away his humanity. So all men have a desire to protect their rights, whence they also demand power to see the rights of others vindicated, if there is an assault upon them. When we hear of injustice done to someone, we are indignant, and anxious to let the culprit know what it means to violate the rights of others.

Suppose that we have done work for somebody, and he is not inclined to pay for it, but makes numerous objections, that is already a matter affecting our rights, which we must not allow to be played with. Here we are no longer concerned with a few thalers, but with our rights, which are worth more than a hundred thalers, or a thousand. But if this desire for our rights goes further than is necessary to defend them, then it is already a form of vengeance. It makes for implacability, and for the pain and evil we wish to be visited on anybody who has violated our rights; even though we thereby instil in him no further respect for them. This desire is already vicious, and is truly vengeful in nature.

27:436

OF THE SLANDERER

There is a distinction to be drawn, between a true and an insidious enemy. Fawning, secret and cunning enmity appears far baser than open malevolence, even when coupled with power; for the latter one may guard against, as one cannot against deceitful malice, which subverts all confidence in men, in a way that open enmity does not. He who openly declares himself an enemy can be depended on; but cunning and secret malignity, were it to become general, would put an end to all trust. We despise it more than the violent kind, for the deceitful one is utterly worthless and base, and has not a spark of goodness in him. The avowed villain can still be tamed, and his savagery taken from him; but he who has no good in him at all can be given none.

OF JEALOUSY, AND THE ENVY AND ILL-FEELING THAT RESULT

Men have two means of estimating themselves; when they compare themselves with the Idea of perfection, and when they do so in relation to others. If we estimate ourselves by the Idea of perfection, we have a good standard of measurement; but if we do so in comparison with others, we may often come to the very opposite conclusion, for now it is a matter of what sort of people they are, with whom we compare ourselves. If a man measures himself against the Idea of perfection, he remains far short of it, and must take great pains to achieve more likeness to it; but if he compares himself to others, he may still have great worth, in that those with whom he matches himself may be great rogues. Men may well be glad to compare themselves with others, and estimate themselves accordingly, for there they always have advantages. Even among those with whom they wish to compare themselves, they always choose the worst and not the best, for there they are most able to shine forth. If they compare themselves with those of greater worth, the resultant self-estimate comes out against them.

There are now only two ways left of getting even with the other's perfections. Either I seek to acquire those perfections of his for myself as well, or I try to diminish them. Whether I enlarge my own perfection, or lessen his, I always come out the better man. Now since the latter comes easiest, men will sooner diminish the other's perfections than enhance their own. This is the origin of jealousy. When men compare themselves with others, and find these perfections, they become jealous of every perfection they perceive in the other, and try to diminish it, so that their own may stand out the more. This is disparaging jealousy. But if I try to add to my perfections, making them equal to the other's, this is emulating jealousy. Jealousy is the genus, therefore, and is either of a disparaging or an emulating type. But because the latter is the more difficult, it is natural for men to relapse into the disparaging form.

In educating their children, parents should therefore be wary of trying to motivate them to good actions by emulation of others, for by this there arises in them a disparaging jealousy, and they will grow hostile towards, and later try to belittle, the one who is set before them as a model for emulation. So when a mother says: 'Look, child, at young Fritz next door, how well-behaved he is, and how industrious', the boy at once takes a dislike to Fritz next door, and thinks: 'If there were no such fellow, you would not be compared to him, and then you would be the best'. Now the boy may indeed make an effort to acquire the very same perfections as those of the neighbour's child, but because this is harder to do, he falls back on disparagement. So goodness must be commended to children in and of itself, whether others be better or worse; since if one were not better, then the other would have no motive to be better too. For just as the mother can say: 'Look, he's better than you', so the son might answer: 'Yes, that one is certainly better than I, but take a look at the others; there are more of them that are very much worse'. For if comparisons apply to me on the one side, they may equally well do so on the other.

These are errors in upbringing which subsequently become deep-rooted. The parents thereby cultivate a jealousy which they actually presuppose in their children, when they present them with others as a model, since otherwise the children might be wholly indifferent to such competitors. Since they now adopt the latter course, it being easier to destroy the other child's perfections than to raise one's own to such heights, a disparaging attitude results. Jealousy is indeed very natural to us, but that does nothing to excuse us for cultivating it, seeing that it is merely a *subsidium*, [b] a motive when maxims of reason are not yet present; but since we already possess such maxims, we have to limit that motive by reason. For in that

27:437

27:438

[b] a makeshift

we are designed as human agents, there are many motives given to us, such as ambition, and so on, and jealousy, too, is among them. But as soon as reason holds sway, we should not seek to become perfect on the ground that others surpass us, but must desire perfection for itself. Motives must then abdicate, and reason rule in their stead.

Jealousy is especially prevalent among persons of similar station and occupation; merchants, for example, are jealous of each other. But it is particularly common among scholars in a given field, for they cannot allow anyone else to surpass them there. Women are jealous of each other in regard to the opposite sex.

We grudge, when displeased at another's advantage; we are too much put down by his good fortune, and therefore grudge it to him. But if we are displeased at the fact that the other has any share of happiness, that is envy. So envy is when we wish imperfection and ill-fortune to others, not so that we might ourselves be perfect or fortunate in consequence, but so that in that case we might alone be perfect and fortunate. The envious man wishes to be happy when all around him are unhappy, and seeks the sweetness of happiness in this, that he alone enjoys it, and all others are unhappy. This is the envy of which we will soon be learning that it is demonic. Grudging is more natural, though it, too, should not be condoned. Even good-natured souls feel grudging; for example, if I am discontented, and every one else is in good spirits, then I grudge it to them. For it is hard to be the only one out of humour, when all around are in cheerful mood. If I alone have poor fare to eat, and everyone else is faring well, that vexes me, and I grudge it them; but if nobody in the whole town is any better fed, then I am contented. Death can be borne, for all men must die; but were all to live, and I alone should have to die, that would vex me greatly. We take our stand on the relativities of things, not on the things themselves. We are grudging, because others are happier than we are. But when a good-natured person is happy and cheerful, he wishes that everyone in the world might be equally happy and cheerful, and begrudges it to nobody.

27:439

It is grudging for a man to not even grant to another what he himself has no need for. This is already a malignity of spirit, but still not envy, for in refusing to grant the other some part of my property that I cannot use, I am not yet desiring that I alone should have something, and the other nothing at all; after all, I do not begrudge him his own property. There is already much of the grudging element in human nature that could turn into envy, but has not yet done so. We are more than willing to listen, in company, to the tale of another's misfortunes, though they still have to be bearable, or to hear of the downfall of certain wealthy personages, and though we show no satisfaction, it is still privately pleasing to us. When we sit by a warm fire at the coffee-table, during foul and stormy weather, and talk of those who are travelling or at sea in such conditions, we enjoy our good fortune the more for it, and it heightens our sense of comfort. There is thus a grudging element in our nature, though it does not amount to envy.

The three vices that may here be taken together, and which form the totality of the meanest and basest vices, are ingratitude, envy and malicious glee (*Schadenfreude*). On attaining their full height, these are devilish vices.

All men are ashamed at receiving favours, since they thereby incur obligations, and the other acquires calls and claims on the person he has shown favour to. So everyone is ashamed at being beholden, and a strong-minded man will therefore not accept favours, in order not to be bound. But this is already a motive to ingratitude, if the recipient of favour be proud and selfish, since from pride he will feel shame at being beholden to the other; and from selfishness he will not concede his indebtedness, and so becomes defiant and ungrateful. If this ingratitude increases so much that he cannot endure his benefactor, and becomes his enemy, that is the devilish degree of the vice, since it is utterly repugnant to human nature, to hate and persecute those who have done one a kindness, and since it would also cause untold harm, if all men were thereby deterred 27:440 from well-doing, and so became misanthropes, on seeing that they would be ill-used for their benevolence.

The second vice is envy. This is utterly detested, for the man of envy not only wishes for happiness, but wants it all for himself. He would like to enjoy it with misery all about him, and only so can he be fully content with his happiness. Such a man is thereby seeking to eradicate happiness throughout the world, and is thus an insufferable creature.

The third form of devilish wickedness is *Schadenfreude*, which consists in taking an immediate pleasure in the misfortunes of others; for example, by trying to stir up strife in a marriage, and suchlike, and then gloating at the parties' troubles. Here we must make it a rule, never to repeat to anyone what others may have told us to his disadvantage, unless our silence would be harmful to him; for by tale-bearing we create enmities which are disturbing to the others, and need not have occurred, had we held our peace; and in such a case, too, we also break faith with our informant. Our concern should be to behave in an upright manner, and then, though the whole wide world may say what they please, it is not by our words, but by our way of life, that we have to confute them. As Socrates put it: we must so behave, that people will not believe what is said against us.

All three, ingratitude (*ingratitudo qualificata*),ᶜ envy and *Schadenfreude*, are devilish vices, because they evince an immediate inclination to evil. That man should have a mediate inclination to evil is human and natural;

ᶜ aggravated ingratitude, hatred of a benefactor

the miser, for example, would like to acquire everything; but he takes no pleasure in the other having nothing at all. There are vices, therefore, that are evil both directly and indirectly. These three are those that are directly evil.

The question may be raised, whether the human soul contains an immediate inclination to evil, and thus a propensity for devilish vice. We call a thing devilish when the evil in man is carried to the point of exceeding the level of human nature, just as we call angelic the goodness that surpasses the nature of man. All happiness we refer to Heaven, all badness to Hell, and the middle ground to earth. There is reason to believe, however, that in the nature of man's soul there resides no immedi-27:441 ate inclination to evil, but that its tendency is evil only in an indirect fashion. Man cannot be so ungrateful as actually to hate his benefactor; he is merely far too proud to be thankful to him, and for the rest, wishes him every happiness; the only thing is, he would like to be well out of his way. Nor does he have any immediate urge, either, to rejoice at another's misfortune, save only that if, for example, a person has come to grief, we are pleased because he was puffed-up, rich and selfish; for men would like to preserve equality. Man therefore has no direct inclination towards evil *qua* evil, but only an indirect one. Yet *Schadenfreude* is often already strongly apparent in the young. Thus children, for example, are wont to catch a schoolfellow unaware, and give him a jab with a pin; they do it for a joke, merely, never thinking of the pain that the other must feel, and play similar tricks as well, such as inflicting distress upon animals, e.g., by twisting the tail of a cat or dog. We see already where that is going to lead, and such things must be nipped in the bud. It is, however, a sort of animality, whereby man retains something of the beast in him, which he cannot overcome. The source of it we know not, and for some of our characteristics we can adduce no reason whatever. Thus there are animals which have this tendency to carry off everything without making any use of it, and it looks as if man has inherited the same urge from the brute creation.

Of ingratitude, in particular, we still have the following to add: To assist someone in distress is an act of charity; to help him in regard to other needs is an act of kindness; and to aid him in matters of amenity is an act of courtesy. We may receive a benefit from someone, though the cost to him is not great, and our gratitude is measured by the degree of good-will that impelled him to the act. We regulate our gratitude by the self-denial it cost him to confer the benefit, and are thankful not merely for the good we have received, but also for the fact that the other is well disposed toward us. Gratitude is of two kinds: from duty, and from inclination. It comes from duty, when we remain unmoved by the other's kindness, but see that it behoves us to be grateful; in that we have, not a grateful heart, but principles of gratitude. We are grateful from inclination, insofar as we feel love in return. Our understanding has a weakness that we are often unaware of, inasmuch as we project a condition into things, though it is 27:442 actually a condition of our understanding; we estimate force no otherwise than by the obstacles it encounters; and thus we are also unable to estimate the degree of another's beneficence, save by the degree of its impediments. We are then quite incapable of perceiving the beneficence and love of a being who has no such impediments. If God confers a benefit on someone, he thinks that it has cost God no trouble, and that in giving thanks he would be fawning upon God. It is natural for a man to think thus. We are very well able to fear God, but it is not so easy for us to love Him from inclination, since here we encounter a being whose goodness arises from a limitless abundance, and who has nothing to stop Him from doing good to us. This is not to say that we ought to think thus, but that the human heart, when we search it, does indeed think this way. And hence many peoples even pictured their deity as a jealous God, and said that the gods were stingy with their benefits, and wanted only to receive many prayers, and that the one thing needful was to load the altars with many sacrifices; for people saw, after all, that it would cost God nothing to give them more; yet that is the way of it in the human heart. But if we summon reason to our aid, we see that a high degree of goodness must pertain to such a being, for Him to benefit a creature so unworthy as ourselves. The following can assist us here. We owe thanks to God, not from inclination, but from duty, for He is a wholly different sort of being, and cannot be an object of our inclination.

We should guard against accepting benefits, unless it be under the following two conditions: first, out of dire necessity, and then with complete confidence in our benefactor. The latter is no longer a friend, but a patron. To accept benefits indiscriminately, however, and to be constantly seeking them, is mean-minded, for we thereby incur obligations. If we are in direst need, we have to swallow our pride, and accept these things under pressure of necessity; or we may be convinced, of our patron, that he will not see them as imposing any obligation on us. But for the rest, we should sooner go without, then accept benefits. For beneficence creates a debt that can never be repaid. Even if I return to my benefactor fifty times more than he gave me, I am still not yet quits with him, for he did me a good turn that he did not owe me, and was the first in doing so. Even if I return it to him fifty times over, I still do it merely to repay the benefit and 27:443 discharge the debt. Here I can no longer get ahead of him; for he remains always the one who was first to show me a kindness.

The benefactor may impose his benefits on the other as an obligation, or as an expression of his own duty. In the first case, he inflames the other's pride, and thereby diminishes his gratitude; if he wishes to avoid such ingratitude, he must consider himself to have performed a human duty, and not impute it to the other as an obligation that he must think about repaying. The recipient, though, must still accept this benefit as a lien upon him, and be grateful to his benefactor; only so can there be benefits. A right-thinking man will not even accept a kindness, let alone favours. Grateful dispositions are extremely loveable, so that even at the theatre such impulses move us to tears; but generous dispositions are sweeter still. Ingratitude we hate amazingly, and even if not directed to ourselves, it still so rouses our wrath that we feel driven to intervene. This is because generosity is thereby decreased.

Envy does not consist in wanting to be the happiest, as with grudging, but in wanting to be the only one happy. This is the vilest thing about it, for why should not others be happy too, when I am? Envy finds expression also in some matters involving rarity; among the Dutch, for example, who in general are a nation given to envy, tulips were at one time worth hundreds of guilders apiece. A wealthy merchant, however, possessed one of the best and rarest, yet when he heard that someone else had one of them too, he bought it from him for 200 guilders, and trampled it underfoot, saying: What's it to me – I already have a specimen, and only wanted this one so that nobody else should have it but myself. And so it is also, in regard to happiness.

Schadenfreude has a different complexion. Such people laugh when others weep, and feel pleasure when others feel pain. To make other people unhappy is cruel, and if physical pain results it is bloodthirsty; collectively these things are labelled inhumanity, just as pity and sympathy are called humane, because they distinguish man from the beasts. It is difficult to explain how a cruel disposition can come about. It has to come

27:444 from the notion that others are evilly disposed, so that we hate them. People who believe themselves hated by others therefore hate them in turn, even though the latter may have good reason for their hatred. For if a man, by selfishness and other vices, becomes an object of hatred, and knows that this is why others hate him, though they do him no wrong, he returns their hatred. Thus kings, because they know themselves to be hated by their subjects, become crueller still. It is just as when a person, knowing that somebody loves him, loves the other in return; love tends to be reciprocated, and so, too, does hatred. For our own sakes, we must guard against being hated by others, lest we be affected in turn by hatred towards them. But this is more disturbing to the person who hates, than to those who are the objects of hatred.

OF ETHICAL DUTIES TOWARDS OTHERS, AND ESPECIALLY TRUTHFULNESS

In human social life, the principal object is to communicate our attitudes, and hence it is of the first importance that everyone be truthful in respect of his thoughts, since without that, social intercourse ceases to be of any value. Only when a person voices his opinions can another tell what he thinks, and if he declares that he wishes to express his thoughts, he must also do it, for otherwise there can be no sociality among men. Fellowship among men is only the second condition of sociality; but the liar destroys this fellowship, and hence we despise a liar, since the lie makes it impossible for people to derive any benefit from what he has to say. Man has an impulse towards holding himself back, and disguising himself. The former is *dissimulatio,* the latter *simulatio.*[d] Man holds back in regard to his weaknesses and transgressions, and can also pretend and adopt an appearance. The proclivity for reserve and concealment rests on this, that providence has willed that man should not be wholly open, since he is full of iniquity; because we have so many characteristics and tendencies that are objectionable to others, we would be liable to appear before them in a foolish and hateful light. But the result, in that case, might be this, that people would tend to grow accustomed to such bad points, since they would see the same in everyone. Hence we order our behaviour in such a way that in part we conceal our faults, and in part also put a different face on them, and have the knack for appearing other than we are; so other people see nothing of our sins and weaknesses beyond the appearances of well-being, and hence we habituate ourselves to dispositions that produce good conduct. Hence nobody, in the true sense, is open-hearted. Had it been as Momus wanted, that Jupiter should have installed a window in the heart, so that every man's disposition might be known, then men would have had to be better constituted, and have good principles, for if all men were good, nobody could hold anything back; but since this is not so, we must keep our shutters closed. When domestic nastiness is confined to the privy, and a person is not invited into the bedroom, where the chamber-pots are, though he knows we have them, just as he does himself, we refrain from these things lest we get into the habit of it and corrupt our taste. In just the same way, we conceal our faults, and try to give a different impression, and make a show of politeness, despite our mistrust; yet by this we grow used to politeness, and at length it becomes natural to us, and we thereby set a good example, at least to the eye; if this were not so, everybody would neglect these things, finding nobody the better for them. So by this endeavour to look well we actually end up doing so, later on. If men were all good, they could afford to be open-hearted; but not at present.

27:445

Reserve consists in not expressing one's mind. This can be done, in the first place, by complete silence. That is a short way of being reserved. But it represents a want of sociality. It robs a man of the pleasure of company, and such silent men are not only unwanted in social circles, but also incur suspicion, and everyone thinks he is watching them. For if he is

---

[d] concealment/pretence

asked his opinion of a thing, and says: I have nothing to say, that is as much as if he were to speak against it, for if he thought well of it, he could surely say so. Since silence always gives us away, it is not even a prudent form of reserve; but we can also be prudent in our reserve without it. For such prudence in reserve we need deliberation. We must speak and pass judgement on everything, save that on which we wish to keep our counsel.

27:446

Secretiveness is quite a different thing from reserve. I can hold a thing back, when I have no desire to speak of it, and am reserved about my misdeeds, for example, since nature by no means impels me to betray them; thus every man has his secrets, and these he can easily keep quiet about; but there are matters where it needs strength to preserve discretion. Secrets have a way of getting out, and it takes strength not to betray them, and this is secretiveness. Secrets are always deposits lodged by others, and I must not release them for the use of third parties. But since human garrulity is very interesting, the telling of secrets is what chiefly sustains it, for the other views it as a gift. How are secrets to be kept? Men who are not themselves very garrulous, generally keep secrets well, but better still are those who talk freely, but with prudence; from the former, something might yet be elicited, but not so from the latter, for they always know how to interpose with something else.

Just as practical taciturnity is an excess on the one side, so loquacity is on the other. The first is a male shortcoming, the second a female one. Some writer has said that women are talkative, because the upbringing of infants is entrusted to their care, and that by reason of their chattiness they soon teach children to talk, since they are able to keep babbling to them all day long; among men, however, it would take the children much longer to speak. Taciturnity is an odious habit. We are irritated by people who say nothing. They betray a sort of pride. Loquacity in men breeds contempt, and is unbecoming to their strength. All these were merely matters of pragmatic interest. We now turn to something more important.

If a man announces that he means to disclose his opinions, should he knowingly disclose them in full, or keep something to himself? If he says that he intends to speak his mind, but does not, and makes a false statement instead, that is a *falsiloquium,* or untruth. *Falsiloquium*ᵉ may occur, even though the other cannot presume that I shall state my views. One may impose on a person, without actually saying anything to him. I can make a pretence, and give expression to something, from which the other may deduce what I want him to; but he has no right to infer from my

27:447

utterance a declaration of intent, and in that case I have told him no lie, for I never declared that I was opening my mind to him; if I pack my bags, for example, people will think I am off on a journey, and that is what I want them to believe; but they have no right to demand any declaration of

ᵉ speaking falsely

will from me. That is what the famous John Law did; he kept on building, and when everyone was thinking: He'll never leave, off he went.

I can also, however, commit a *falsiloquium,* when my intent is to hide my intentions from the other, and he can also presume that I shall do so, since his own purpose is to make a wrongful use of the truth. If an enemy, for example, takes me by the throat and demands to know where my money is kept, I can hide the information here, since he means to misuse the truth. That is still no *mendacium,*[f] for the other knows that I shall withhold the information, and that he also has no right whatever to demand the truth from me. Suppose, however, that I actually state that I mean to speak my mind, and that the other is perfectly well aware that he has no right to require this of me, since he is a swindler; the question arises: Am I then a liar? If the other has cheated me, and I cheat him in return, I have certainly done this fellow no wrong; since he has cheated me, he cannot complain about it, yet I am a liar nonetheless, since I have acted contrary to the right of humanity. It is therefore possible for a *falsiloquium* to be a *mendacium* – a lie – though it contravenes no right of any man in particular.* Whoever may have told me a lie, I do him no wrong if I lie to him in return, but I violate the right of mankind; for I have acted contrary to the condition, and the means, under which a society of men can come about, and thus contrary to the right of humanity.

When one country has broken the peace, the other cannot do so in retaliation, for if that were allowable, no peace would be secure. And thus though something may not infringe the particular right of a man, it is still already a lie, since it is contrary to the right of humanity. If a man publishes a false report, he thereby does no wrong to anyone in particular, but offends against mankind, for if that were to become general, the human craving for knowledge would be thwarted; apart from speculation, I have 27:448 only two ways of enlarging my store of information: by experience, and by testimony. But now since I cannot experience everything myself, if the reports of others were to be false tidings, the desire for knowledge could not be satisfied. A *mendacium* is thus a *falsiloquium in praejudicium humanitatis,*[g] even when it is not also in violation of any particular *jus quaesitum*[h] of another. In law a *mendacium* is a *falsiloquium in praejudicium alterius,* and cannot be anything else there, but from the moral viewpoint it is a *falsiloquium in praejudicium humanitatis.* Not every untruth is a lie; it is so only if there is an express declaration of my willingness to inform the other of my thought. Every lie is objectionable and deserving of contempt, for once we declare that we are telling the other our thoughts, and fail to

---

* [Reading *keines* for *eines* – Tr.]
[f] a lie, with intent to deceive
[g] untruth damaging to humanity/to another person
[h] special right

do it, we have broken the *pactum*, and acted contrary to the right of humanity. But if, in all cases, we were to remain faithful to every detail of the truth, we might often expose ourselves to the wickedness of others, who wanted to abuse our truthfulness. If everyone were well disposed, it would not only be a duty not to lie, but nobody would need to do it, since he would have nothing to worry about. Now, however, since men are malicious, it is true that we often court danger by punctilious observance of the truth, and hence has arisen the concept of the necessary lie, which is a very critical point for the moral philosopher. For seeing that one may steal, kill or cheat from necessity, the case of emergency subverts the whole of morality, since if that is the plea, it rests upon everyone to judge whether he deems it an emergency or not; and since the ground here is not determined, as to where emergency arises, the moral rules are not certain. For example, somebody, who knows that I have money, asks me: Do you have money at home? If I keep silent, the other concludes that I do. If I say yes, he takes it away from me; if I say no, I tell a lie; so what am I to do? So far as I am constrained, by force used against me, to make an admission, and a wrongful use is made of my statement, and I am unable to save myself by silence, the lie is a weapon of defence; the declaration extorted, that is then misused, permits me to defend myself, for whether my admission or my money is extracted, is all the same. Hence there is no case in which a necessary lie should occur, save where the declaration is wrung from me, and I am also convinced that the other means to make a wrongful use of it.

27:449

The question arises, whether a lie that affects nobody's interests, and does nobody any harm, is likewise a lie? It is, for I promise to speak my mind, and if I fail to speak it truly, I do not, indeed, act *in praejudicium* of the particular individual concerned, but I do so act in regard to humanity. There are also lies whereby the other is cheated. To cheat is to make a lying promise. Breach of faith is when we promise something truthfully, but do not have so high a regard for the promise as to keep it. The lying promise is offensive to the other, and though it does not invariably cause offence, there is still always something mean about it. If I promise, for example, to send a person wine, but subsequently make light of it, that is already a cheat, for though he certainly has no right to demand such a gift from me, it is still cheating, in that it was already, as he saw it, a part of his* property.

Reservatio mentalis[i] is a form of dissimulation, and *aequivocatio*[j] of simulation. *Aequivocatio* is permitted, in order to reduce the other to silence and get rid of him, so that he shall no longer try to extract the truth from

---

* [Reading *seinem* for *meinem* – Tr.]
[i] mental reservation
[j] equivocation

us, once he sees that we cannot give it to him, and do not wish to tell him a lie. If the other is wise, he will also let it go at that. It is quite difficult, though, to employ equivocation when we state and declare that we are expressing our views, for in that case the other may infer something else from the equivocation, and then I have deceived him. Such lies, professing to achieve some good result, were called by the Jesuits *peccatum philosophicum*, or *peccatillum*,[k] from which comes the word 'bagatelle'. But the lie is intrinsically a worthless thing, whether its intentions be good or bad, because it is evil as to form; it is still more worthless, however, when it is also evil as to matter. For by lies something evil may always result. A liar is a cowardly fellow, for since he has no other way of obtaining something, or getting out of trouble, he starts to tell lies. But a bold man will love the truth, and never let a *casus necessitatis* arise. All such methods, whereby the other man cannot be on his guard, are utterly vile. Lying, assassination and poisoning are amongst them. A highwayman's attack is not so low, for there one may take precautions, but not so against the poisoner, since one does, after all, have to eat. Flattery is not always mendacity, but rather a want of self-esteem, where we do not scruple to demean our own worth 27:450 beneath another's, and elevate his, in order to gain something thereby. But one may also flatter from kindheartedness, and this is done by some kindly souls, who have a high opinion of others. So we have both well-meaning and false flattery. The former is weak, but the other low. When men do not flatter, they lapse into censoriousness.

Now if a man is often the subject of comment in society, he is criticized. But of a friend we should not always have good to tell, for others will then grow jealous and grudging, since, seeing that he, too, is only human, they will not believe it possible for him to have only good qualities; hence we must concede something to their grudging attitude, and mention some flaws in him; he will not think ill of me for that; in emphasizing his merits, I can grant him such faults as are common and inessential. Parasites are those who cry up others in company to gain something. Men are designed for the purpose of passing judgement on others, but nature has also made them judges, for otherwise, in matters outside the scope of external legal authority, we might not stand at the bar of public opinion as we do before a court of law. If somebody, for example, has brought shame upon a person, authority does not punish it, but others judge, and also punish him, although only insofar as it lies in their power to do so, and hence no violence is done to him. People ostracize him, for example, and that is punishment enough. But for this, the actions that authority does not penalize might go altogether unpunished. What does it mean, then, to say that we ought not to judge others? We cannot pass any complete moral judgement on another, as to whether he is punishable or not before the

[k] white lie

divine judgement-seat, since we do not know his disposition. The moral dispositions of others are therefore a matter for God, but in regard to my own, I am fully competent to judge. So as to the core of morality we cannot judge, since no man can know it. But in external matters we do have competence. In the moral sphere, therefore, we are not judges of men; but nature has given us the right to judge them, and determined us to judge ourselves in accordance with their verdict upon us. He who pays no heed to the judgement of others is low and reprehensible. There is nothing that happens in the world, on which we are not allowed to pass judgement, and we are also very subtle in the assessment of actions. The best friends are those who are exact in judging each other's actions, and only between two friends can such open-heartedness occur.

27:451

In judging a man, the next question to arise is: What are we to say of him? We should frame all our judgements so that we find mankind loveable, and never pass sentence of condemnation or acquittal, especially in regard to wickedness. We pronounce such a verdict when, in virtue of his actions, we hold a man worthy of being damned or exonerated. Though we are entitled to form opinions of others, we have no right to spy on them. Everybody has a right to prevent the other from investigating and spying out his actions; such a man is arrogating to himself a right over the acts and omissions of other people. Nobody should do that; for example, by eavesdropping when someone says something to the other in private; better to move away so as not to hear a word of it. Again, if we pay a call on a person, and are left alone, and there is a letter lying open on the table, it is a very disreputable thing to try to read it. A right-thinking man will even try to avoid any suspicion or mistrust; he will not care to remain alone in a room where there is money on the table, nor will he want to hear secrets from others, lest he fall under the suspicion of having let them out; and because such secrets always bother him, for even in the closest friendship, suspicion may always arise. The man who from inclination or appetite deprives his friend of anything, his intended bride, for example, is acting very basely in doing so; for just as he has taken a fancy to my intended, so he can also take a fancy to my purse. It is very mean to lie in wait for, or spy upon, a friend or anyone else; for example, if one tries to find out what he is doing from servants; in that case we have to lower ourselves to their level, and the servants, thereafter, will always consider themselves our equals. By everything that tells against candour, a man loses his dignity; for example, by doing something ill-natured behind the back, for this is a use of means in which a man cannot be open and honest, and all social life is destroyed thereby. All such furtive measures are far more vile than violent wickedness, since we can, after all, take precautions against that; but he who does not even have the courage to demonstrate his wickedness in public has no trace of nobility in him. A person who is violent, but otherwise abhors all pettiness, can still become good, however, if he is

27:452

tamed. Thus even in England, the attempt of a wife to poison her husband is punished by burning, because if that were to spread, no husband would be safe from his wife.*

Just as I am not entitled to spy upon another, so I also have no right to tell him his faults; for even if he should ask for this, the other never hears of it without offence; he knows better than I that he has such faults. He thinks, however, that others are not aware of them, and if they tell him, he learns that other people know of them. It is not good, therefore, for people to say: Friends must tell each other their faults, because the other can know them better; nobody, after all, can know my faults better than I do; the other, admittedly, can know better than I, whether or not I stand and walk upright; but who is to know better than I do myself, if only I choose to examine myself? It is forwardness in the other, if he tells someone his faults, and if it comes to that in a friendship, then the latter, too, will no longer last long. We must be blind to the other's faults, for otherwise he sees that we have lost respect for him, and then he also loses all respect for us. Faults must be pointed out if we are placed in authority over someone; in that case we are entitled to give lessons and indicate shortcomings, as a husband, for example, does to his wife; but here kindness, benevolence and respect must prevail; if displeasure alone is present, the outcome is censure and bitterness. But censure can be mitigated by love, good-will and respect. Nothing else makes any contribution to improvement.

The general duty of man includes affability, *humanitas*. What is it to be affable? '-able' means no more than a sort of propensity to an action, e.g., conversable. Affability is thus a habitual harmony with everyone else. If active it is complaisance. This is either negative, and then it consists merely in compliancy, or positive, and then it consists in helpfulness. This must be distinguished from courtesy. The latter is that whereby we incur no obligation to the other, and it extends only to matters of amenity. If 27:453 somebody, for example, sends his servant to accompany me, that is courtesy; but if he provides me with food, that is helpfulness, since it costs him some sacrifice. Negative complaisance is not of such value as helpfulness, in that it consists merely in compliancy. Thus there are people who will get drunk out of complaisance, being bidden to it by others, and not having enough strength to refuse. The man would be happy to see himself out of such company, but since he is already there, he complies. It shows a want of strength and manliness, if we have not enough courage and firmness to determine our conduct as we see fit. Such people lack character, and are incapable of acting according to principles.

The opposite of complaisance is self-will, which has only one principle, viz., never to accommodate oneself to the outlook of others. The complaisant man never pits himself against the other's views, and hence

* [The punishment was abolished in 1790 – Tr.]

he seems somewhat inferior to the self-willed man, who does at least have principles. One should rather try to be a little self-willed, than to show oneself wholly accommodating to the other's point of view. The determination of conduct by principles is no longer self-will; but if such determination relates to a private inclination, and not to what is generally pleasing, it is self-will, and a mark of stupidity.

The peaceable man has an abhorrence of discord and conflict with the views of others. He whose inclination is to fall in with such opinions of the others as are morally indifferent, is a peaceable man. There is no fear of any quarrel with such people. The indulgent man is he who also puts up with what is repugnant to him, just to prevent himself from falling into contention. He is one who does not hate others for their faults. The indulgent man is tolerant. The intolerant man is one who cannot endure the imperfections of others without hatred. We often find in society men who are intolerant because they cannot abide other people, and they become intolerant themselves, on that account, and others in turn will not suffer them. From this it follows, that tolerance is a universal human duty. Men have many faults, real and apparent, but we have to put up with them. Tolerance in regard to religion is found when a person can endure without hatred the imperfections and errors of religion in another; even though he does not like them. He who holds to be true religion, what according to mine is an error, is

27:454 nevertheless in no way an object of hatred. I ought to hate nobody, unless he be a deliberate author of evil; even insofar as he purposes to do good by way of evil and error, he is not an object of hatred.

Odium theologicum[l] is a hatred peculiar to the clergy, which occurs when the theologian turns some conceit of his own into a matter of divine concern, and conceives a hatred that is founded on pride, and believes that because he is a minister of God, he can claim to be a person empowered by God, whom the latter has sent as a deputy, vested with authority, to rule men in His name. *Odium religiosum* is directed upon a person when his errors are thought to be high treason against divinity, and the defects of his religion are declared to be *crimina laesae majestatis divinae.*[m] He who distorts and misrepresents the views of another, and draws many conclusions from that, so as to declare them *crimina laesae majestatis divinae*, is venting an *odium religiosum* upon him; one who does this is a *consequentarius,*[n] in that he infers from the other's opinion, what the latter never imagined; for if he gives him a name and says, for example, he is an atheist, then the other opens his eyes wide and says: 'What? An atheist? I would like to know anyone who looks like an atheist'; by using such a name the accuser becomes hated and insufferable to everyone.

[l] hatred on religious grounds
[m] disrespect to God, sacrilege
[n] a drawer of unjustified conclusions

The *crimen laesae majestatis divinae* is an absurdity for nobody will commit such a thing. The orthodox claim that their religion, such as they conceive it, should necessarily be universal. But who, then, is orthodox? If we were all to appear at Heaven's gate, and the question were asked: Who is orthodox? the Jew, the Turk and the Christian would all say: I am. Orthodoxy must not compel anyone. The dissenter is one who differs from others in matters of speculation, but is much the same in his practice. The peace-loving disposition consists in avoiding all enmity towards dissenters. Why should I hate a man who dissents? Syncretism is a sort of complaisance, a willingness to merge one's opinions with those of everyone else, simply to get along with them. This is very harmful, for anyone who merges his views with those of everybody else, has neither the one nor the other. Better to let men go astray, for, so long as they are able to distinguish, they can still also be liberated from the error. The spirit of covert persecution, where we pursue a man behind his back, talk about him, and make him out an atheist, is a very mean form of persecution. The more subtle form is when a man by no means pursues with hatred 27:455 those who are not of his opinion, but still has an abhorrence for them. The spirit of persecution for the sake of God's honour is at war with everything, and respects neither benefactor nor friend, neither father nor mother; everyone regards it as a merit to burn others at the stake in honour of God. In matters of religious truth, it is not force that must be used, but reasons. Truth can defend itself, and an error persists longer if force is employed against it. Freedom of inquiry is the best means of getting at the truth.

OF POVERTY, AND THE ACTS OF KINDNESS THAT ARISE FROM IT

A kind action is one that meets the needs of the other, and aims at his well-being. Such actions can also be magnanimous, by giving up advantages. If they relate to the dire need of the other, they are beneficent; if they aim at the extremest necessities of life, they are charities. Men satisfy, or think they satisfy, their duty to philanthropy, if they first seek to provide all their material needs, and thereafter think to pay off their tribute to the benefactor by giving something to the poor. If men were strictly just, there might be no poor, in whose regard we think to display this merit of beneficence and give alms. It is better to be conscientious in all our actions, and better still to help the needy by our conduct, and not merely by giving away the surplus. Alms-giving is a form of kindliness associated with pride and costing no trouble, and a beneficence calling for no reflection. Men are demeaned by it. It would be better to think out some other way of assisting such poverty, so that men are not brought so low as to accept alms. Many moralists try to soften our hearts, and to commend kind acts done from tenderness; but true good actions come from sturdy souls, and to be virtuous a man must be staunch. Beneficence to others must rather be commended as a debt we owe, than as a piece of kindness and generosity; and so it is in fact; for all acts of kindness are but small repayments of our indebtedness.

27:456

OF THE SOCIAL VIRTUES

Our author speaks here of approachability, conversability, politeness and polish, decorum, complaisance, insinuating or ingratiating – or rather, captivating – manners. In general we may observe that some of these are not reckoned among the virtues, since it calls for no great degree of moral resolution to bring them about; they demand no self-mastery or sacrifice; nor do they conduce to the happiness of others; they are not addressed to need, but merely to comfort, and there is no more to them than the pleasures and amenities of people in company. But though it be no virtue, it is still a practice and cultivation of virtue, when people conduct themselves in company in a civilized fashion; they thereby become gentler and more refined, and practise goodness in small matters. We often have no opportunity to perform virtuous actions, but are frequently called upon to exercise qualities of a sociable and courtly nature. Amenity in social intercourse often pleases us so much in a person that we overlook his vices. I need a person's honour and generosity less often than his modesty and courtesy in social matters.

It might be asked, whether there is also any value to books, which serve only for amusement, which exercise our imagination, and in regard to some passions, such as love, for example, may well go to lengths that exceed the normal limits? There is; although the charms and passions are much exaggerated therein, they still refine men in their feelings, by turning an object of animal inclination into one of more refined inclination; a man is thereby made receptive to the motive force of virtue on principles. They also have an indirect use, for in taming their inclinations, men become more civilized. The more we refine the cruder elements, the more humanity is purified, and man is rendered capable of feeling the motive force of virtuous principles.

27:457 Our author talks of the spirit of contradiction, of the cult of paradox, or crankiness in judgement. Paradox is good, if it does not entail acceptance of some particular point that is made. It is the unexpected element in thinking, by which men are often diverted into a new train of thought. The spirit of contradiction is evinced in company by dogmatism. But the object of social intercourse is entertainment, for the purpose of improving culture, and nothing of an important nature, where conflict of this sort often arises, should be taken up there. Such things should either be definitely decided, or dealt with playfully by telling of something new.

OF HAUGHTINESS

Our author calls it *superbia* – *arrogantia* is pride, when we presume to a value that we do not possess; but if we lay claim to precedence over others, that is haughtiness; in that case, we put down the other, and deem him lesser and lower than we are. The proud man does not think the less of others, but merely wishes to have the same merits; he will not bow and humble himself before them, and considers himself to have his own specific worth, which he does not yield to anyone. Such pride is right and proper, if only it does not overstep its limits. But if a man wishes to show others that he has such worth, this is incorrectly described as proper pride. Haughtiness is not a presumption to worth and esteem in virtue of equality with others, but a pretension to a higher esteem and superior worth in respect of oneself, and a lower estimation of other people. It is hated and derided, for the estimate is one's own. So if a person wants to be honoured by others, he must not begin by commanding it, or thinking the less of others; in that way he will arouse no respect for himself on their part, but will rather be laughed at for his pretensions. All haughty folk are therefore at the same time fools. They become an object of contempt, since they merely seek to display their superiority.

Fastus, or conceit, consists in wanting to outrank and take precedence over others, not in virtue of intellectual ability, or any genuinely superior merits, but simply to seem superior to others in regard to externals. Men are conceited when they always want to have first place. It is a vanity of seeking precedence in things of no account. Conceited persons look for 27:458 pre-eminence in trifles, and would as soon eat poorly, if only to have smart clothes and a fine carriage. They are concerned with titles and position, and try to appear genteel. People of true merit are neither haughty nor conceited, but humble, because the idea they have of true worth is so lofty that they fail to satisfy it and are never equal to it. They therefore perceive how far they are from worth, and are humble. Conceit affects chiefly the lower, and particularly the middle, rather than the upper classes, for since it signifies a climbing to the top, the conceited are those who wish to arrive there.

OF SCOFFING

Some people are backbiters (*médisant*), others mockers (*moquant*). Backbiting is vicious, but mockery frivolous, since its aim is to create amusement at the expense of other people's faults. Calumny involves malice. The cause of it is often a want of sociability, and it also nourishes our self-love, since in that case our own faults seem small. People are more afraid of raillery than backbiting. For slander and calumny work in secret, and cannot be introduced in every sort of company, nor can I hear it myself;

but raillery can be brought in anywhere. A man is more demeaned by it than he is by malice; for if we are a laughing-stock to others, we have no dignity, and are exposed to contempt. We have to see, though, what makes us an object of laughter to others. Often we may concede it to them, for if it costs nothing to either of us, we lose nothing thereby. A habitual scoffer betrays that he has little respect for others, and does not judge things at their true value.

OF DUTIES TO ANIMALS AND SPIRITS

Our author here goes on to speak of duties to beings that are above us and beneath us. But since all animals exist only as means, and not for their own sakes, in that they have no self-consciousness, whereas man is the end, such that I can no longer ask: Why does he exist?, as can be done with animals, it follows that we have no immediate duties to animals; our duties towards them are indirect duties to humanity. Since animals are an analogue of humanity, we observe duties to mankind when we observe them as analogues to this, and thus cultivate our duties to humanity. If a dog, for example, has served his master long and faithfully, that is an analogue of merit; hence I must reward it, and once the dog can serve no longer, must look after him to the end, for I thereby cultivate my duty to humanity, as I am called upon to do; so if the acts of animals arise out of the same *principium* from which human actions spring, and the animal actions are analogues of this, we have duties to animals, in that we thereby promote the cause of humanity. So if a man has his dog shot, because it can no longer earn a living for him, he is by no means in breach of any duty to the dog, since the latter is incapable of judgement, but he thereby damages the kindly and humane qualities in himself, which he ought to exercise in virtue of his duties to mankind. Lest he extinguish such qualities, he must already practise a similar kindliness towards animals; for a person who already displays such cruelty to animals is also no less hardened towards men. We can already know the human heart, even in regard to animals. Thus Hogarth, in his engravings,* also depicts the beginnings of cruelty, where already the children are practising it upon animals, e.g., by pulling the tail of a dog or cat; in another scene we see the progress of cruelty, where the man runs over a child; and finally the culmination of cruelty in a murder, at which point the rewards of it appear horrifying. This provides a good lesson to children. The more we devote ourselves to observing animals and their behaviour, the more we love them, on seeing how greatly they care for their young; in such a context, we cannot even contemplate cruelty to a wolf.

Leibnitz put the grub he had been observing back on the tree with its

27:459

* ['The Stages of Cruelty', 1751 – Tr.]

leaf, lest he should be guilty of doing any harm to it. It upsets a man to destroy such a creature for no reason, and this tenderness is subsequently transferred to man. In England, no butcher, surgeon or doctor serves on the twelve-man jury, because they are already inured to death. So when 27:460 anatomists take living animals to experiment on, that is certainly cruelty, though there it is employed for a good purpose; because animals are regarded as man's instruments, it is acceptable, though it is never so in sport. If a master turns out his ass or his dog, because it can no longer earn its keep, this always shows a very small mind in the master. The Greeks were high-minded in such matters, as is shown by the fable of the ass, which pulled by accident at the bell of ingratitude. Thus our duties to animals are indirectly duties to humanity.

The duties to other spiritual beings are merely negative. We should never meddle in such actions as imply a *commercium*, or intercourse, with other beings. All such actions are of a kind that makes men fanatical, visionary and superstitious, and are contrary to the dignity of mankind; for that dignity includes the healthy use of reason, and if one is given to things of that sort, the sound use of reason is impossible. There may always be such beings, and all that is said of them may be true, but we are not acquainted with them, and cannot have dealings with them.

In regard to evil spirits, the situation is the same. We have just as good an idea of evil as we do of good, and refer everything evil to Hell, as we attribute everything good to Heaven. If we personify this perfect evil, we have the idea of the Devil; and have only to imagine that such a being may have influence over us, that he appears at night and stalks abroad, to be plagued with phantoms that abolish the rational use of our powers. So our duties to such beings are negative.

Our author goes on to discuss duties to inanimate objects. These also allude, indirectly, to our duties towards men. The human impulse to destroy things that can still be used is very immoral. No man ought to damage the beauty of nature; even though he cannot use it, other people may yet be able to do so, and though he has no need to observe such a duty in regard to the thing itself, he does in regard to others. Thus all duties relating to animals, other beings and things have an indirect reference to our duties towards mankind.

OF SPECIAL DUTIES TO PARTICULAR
KINDS OF PEOPLE   27:461

Our author now points out special duties that we have to particular kinds of people, namely, duties in regard to differences of age, sex and station. But all these duties are deducible from the foregoing universal duties to mankind. Among differences of position, there is one that is founded on a distinction of inner worth, namely the status of the scholar, which appears to represent a difference of this kind. The distinctions of status elsewhere are those of external worth. The other avocations busy themselves with physical things, having reference only to human life. The scholar, however, has a role whose main concern is to extend knowledge, and this seems to represent a difference of inner worth. The man of learning seems to be the only one who contemplates the beauty that God has put into the world, and uses the latter for the purpose that God had in making it. For why else would God have put beauty into nature and its works, if not that I should contemplate it? Now since men of learning are alone in fulfilling the total purpose of creation, it seems as if in this respect they are alone in having inner worth. The cognitions they acquire are those for which God made the world. And indeed, the talents that reside in man are developed solely by the learned. It seems, therefore, that this station takes precedence over others, since it is distinguished from them by an inner worth. Rousseau, however, turns this around, and says that erudition is not the end of man; the learned thereby pervert the purpose of humanity. So the question remains: whether the scholar, because he contemplates the world's beauty, and develops talent, is fulfilling the end of creation, and has the world for his own? Because every individual scholar does not have the aim of immediately contemplating the beauty of nature, developing talent or promoting the total perfection of mankind, but seeks merely the honour he gets from this in communicating it to others, so the individual man of learning cannot, in fact, believe that he has any priority over every other citizen; although scholars as a class contribute collectively to the end of humanity, nobody can apportion himself a particular share in that, for every craftsman contributes something by his work to the purpose of humanity, just as much as any scholar does. From the general source of human actions, namely honour, there arises, therefore, a harmony of purposes in the world.

27:462 One may ask: Are men in general destined for learning, and should everyone try to become a scholar? No, life is too short for that; but it is part of the vocation of humanity that some should dedicate themselves to learning, and offer up their lives in its service. Nor is life long enough to be able to make use of the knowledge acquired. If God had willed that man should go far in the advancement of learning, He would have given him a longer life. Why must Newton die, at a time when he could have made the best use of his learning, and another have to start again from the ABC, and progress through every class, till he has again reached that point? And just when he is ready to apply it aright, he grows feeble and dies. Thus each by himself is not framed for knowing everything, but collectively the end of humanity is promoted thereby. The scholars are thus means to that end, and contribute something of value, but do not themselves have any superior worth thereby. Why should not a citizen, who is diligent and industrious in his calling, and otherwise does a good trade and keeps his house in order, have just as much worth as the scholar? Because the scholar's business is more universal? His status and destiny already provide for that.

Rousseau is correct to that extent, but is much in error when he speaks of the harm done by the sciences. No genuine scholar would make so arrogant a claim. The language of true reason is humble. All men are equal, and only he that is morally good has an inner worth superior to the rest. The sciences are *principia* for the betterment of morality. It takes knowledge and clarified concepts to discern moral notions. The spread of the sciences ennobles man, and the love of knowledge eliminates many a low inclination. Hume says there is no scholar who would not at least be an honourable man. On the other hand, morality serves the sciences in promoting integrity, respect for the rights of others, and of one's own person, and greatly advances the cognitions of the understanding. Honesty ensures that a man puts down his errors in writing, and does not conceal the weak points. Moral character thus has great influence on the sciences. He who lacks it treats the products of his understanding as a merchant does his wares; he will hide the weak points and deceive the public.   27:463

These are the duties that we have to observe in regard to learning.

OF THE DUTIES OF THE VIRTUOUS AND THE VICIOUS

Virtue is an Idea and nobody can possess true virtue. It is therefore just as uncommon to call a man virtuous as it is to call him wise. Everyone tries to come closer to virtue, as he does to wisdom; but in nobody is the highest degree attained. We can conceive of a mean between virtue and vice, a state of mediocrity, consisting only in the want of either. Virtue and vice are positive things. Virtue is an aptitude, on moral principles, for overcoming the inclination to evil. Holy beings are not virtuous, therefore, since they have no inclination to overcome; their will is adequate to the law. The man who is not virtuous is not yet vicious on that account; he is merely lacking in virtue. But vice is something positive. The want of virtue is mediocrity, but the contempt for moral laws is vice. Mediocrity consists merely in not obeying the moral law; vice, however, in doing the very opposite to it. The former is a negative thing, the latter a positive one. So there is a great deal that falls under vice.

One may have kindness of heart without virtue, for the latter is good conduct from principles, not instinct. Kindheartedness, however, is a conformity to the moral law from instinct. Virtue involves a great deal. Kindheartedness can be innate, but nobody can be virtuous without practice, for the inclination to evil has to be repressed according to moral principles and action brought into conformity with the moral law. It may

215

be asked, whether a vicious man can become virtuous? There is a malignity of temper that is incorrigible and remains permanent, but a bad character can always be transformed into a good one, because character acts according to principles, and can thus be gradually reshaped by good principles, so that it prevails over the malignity of temper. Thus it is said

27:464 of Socrates, that he was endowed by nature with a malign heart, which he nevertheless mastered by his principles. Men often betray in their faces that they are incorrigible, and have been well-nigh predestined already to the gallows; it is hard for such people to become virtuous. Just as an upright and honourable man cannot become vicious, and even if he lapses into a few vices, always returns to the path of virtue, because his principles have already become firmly rooted in him. Betterment must be distinguished from conversion. To become better is to alter our way of life, but conversion entails possession of fixed principles and a secure basis, such that we shall never live otherwise than virtuously. We often become better through fear of death, and know not whether we are improved or converted. Had we only hoped to live longer, the improvement would not have occurred. We are converted, however, when we firmly resolve to live virtuously, no matter how long we may live. Repentance is not a good term; it derives from penances and chastisements, where a man punishes himself for his crimes. Recognizing that he deserves punishment, he inflicts it on himself, and fancies that God will not punish him thereafter. But such contrition is of no help to anyone. The only thing that does help is inner contrition for our offences, and the firm resolve to lead a better life, and that is true penitence.

In regard to his vices, man can go astray in two directions, that of baseness, or brutality, where by violating duties to his person, for example, he demeans himself below the beasts; and that of wickedness, or devilry, where a man makes it his business to pursue evil, so that no good inclination survives. So long as he retains a good disposition, and the wish to be good, he is still a man; but if he commits himself to wickedness, he becomes a devil. The state of vice is one of enslavement under the power of inclination. The more a man is virtuous, the more he is free. He is obdurate, if he has no wish to become better. The fellowship of virtue is the kingdom of light, and the fellowship of vice the kingdom of darkness. However virtuous a man may be, there are tendencies to evil in him, and he must constantly contend against them. He must guard against the moral self-conceit of thinking himself morally good, and having a favourable opinion of himself; that is a dream-like condition, very hard to cure. It arises when a man tinkers with the moral law, till he has fashioned

27:465 it to suit his inclinations and convenience.

Virtue is the moral perfection of man. To virtue we attach power, strength and authority. It is a victory over inclination. The latter, in itself, has no rules, and it is the achievement of the moral man to subjugate it.

Angels in heaven may be holy, but man can only get so far as to be virtuous. Because virtue rests, not upon instincts, but upon principles, the practice of virtue is an exercise of principles, to give them a motivating power, so that they predominate and do not allow anything to divert us into departing from them. We must therefore have character, and such strength is the strength of virtue, indeed virtue itself. There are obstacles in the way of this virtue; but it must be coupled with religion and rules of prudence, calling for a contented outlook, peace of mind, and freedom from all reproach, true honour, respect for oneself and for others, indifference, or rather equanimity and steadfastness, in the face of all evil for which we are not to blame. These, however, are not sources of virtue, but merely aids to it. Such are the duties of the virtuous.

It seems vain, on the other hand, to speak to the vicious about duties; yet every vicious man still has seeds of virtue in him; he has the understanding to discern evil; he still has a moral feeling, for he who might wish, at least, to be good, is not yet a villain. Upon this moral feeling the system of virtue may be founded. But the moral feeling is not the first beginning of the judgement of virtue; the first thing, rather, is the pure concept of morality, which must be coupled with the feeling. If the man has a pure concept of morality, he can found virtue on that, and only then can he activate the moral feeling, and make a start in becoming moral. This beginning is again a wide field, to be sure; he must initially be negative, and first become blameless, and simply omit everything arising out of any sort of occupation that prevents him from such an inclination. A man can do this perfectly well, even though the positive task is a hard one.

OF DUTIES IN REGARD TO DIFFERENCES OF AGE 27:466

Our author has by no means hit on a good arrangement here; he could have divided up these duties with a view to differences in station, sex and age. The distinction of gender is not so minor as people think. The motivations among men are very different from those among women. In regard to sexual distinctions, one may look to anthropology, from which the duties can then be inferred. As to duties involving difference of age, we have duties to others, not only as human beings, but also as fellow-citizens, and civic duties arise there. Morality, in general, is an inexhaustible field. Our author discusses duties towards the healthy and the sick. In that fashion, we would also have duties towards the handsome and the ugly, the tall and the short. But these are not special duties, since they merely involve different circumstances under which the universal human duties have to be observed. Age may be divided into the period of childhood, when we cannot maintain ourselves; the period of adolescence, when we are able to maintain ourselves, and propagate our kind, but not to sustain them; and the period of manhood, when we can maintain ourselves, have issue, and sustain them too. The state of savagery is in accordance with nature, but the civilized state is not. In the latter condition one may yet be a child, able, indeed, to propagate one's kind, but still incapable of self-maintenance; but in the savage state one is by then already a man. A more far-reaching difference is to be found under discussion in anthropology. Because the civilized state is contrary to nature, but the state of savagery not, Rousseau holds that civilization is out of keeping with the ends of nature; but in fact it complies with them. The natural end of primitive man was to multiply the human race. Were we to come of age at thirty, such a time would correspond to the civilized state, but in that case the human race would not multiply so rapidly under conditions of savagery. For many reasons, the human race multiplies very poorly in the savage state, and so puberty has to be very early; but since, under civilization, such reasons no longer apply, the civil order compensates for this, in that we

27:467   cannot make use of our inclination at that age. The intervening period is, however, filled with vices. How, then, is man in the civilized condition to be trained for both nature and civil society? These are the two ends of nature, the education of man with respect to both the natural and the civil state. The rule of education is the chief end whereby man is formed under civilization. In education there are two parts to be distinguished: the development of natural aptitudes, and the superimposition of art. The first is the formative training of man, the second instruction or teaching. Anyone who does the first of these for a child might be called his tutor (or governess); but those who do the second are his instructors.

In formative training, we should try to ensure that it is merely negative, and that we exclude everything that is contrary to nature. Art or instruction may be of two kinds, negative and positive, or excluding and imparting. The negative side of instruction is to guard against the intrusion of errors; the positive, to make some addition to the store of information. The negative aspect, in both instruction and training of the child, is discipline; the positive aspect, in instruction, is doctrine. Discipline must precede doctrine. By discipline the heart and temperament can be trained, but character is shaped more by doctrine. Discipline amounts to corrective training; but by this the child is not taught anything new; there is merely a restriction of lawless freedom. Man must be disciplined, for he is by nature raw and wild. Only by art are human aptitudes conditioned to become civilized. In animals, their nature develops automatically, but with us it is by art, and so we cannot allow nature a free hand; otherwise, we rear men to be savages.

Discipline is compulsion; but as such it is contrary to freedom. Freedom, however, is the worth of man, and hence the young one must be subjected to compulsion by discipline in such a way that freedom is preserved; he must be disciplined by compulsion, but not of a slavish kind. Thus all education should be free, insofar as the pupil allows freedom to others. The chief ground of the discipline on which freedom is based is as follows: that the child should recognize its status as a child, and that its duties should all be derived from the consciousness of its childhood, age and capacity. A child, therefore, must exercise powers no greater than are commensurate with its years; and since, as a child, it is weak, it must not be able to obtain things by ordering and commanding, but must seek to secure everything by asking; if it wishes to obtain something by force, and is once allowed this, to placate it, it will do the same more forcefully and frequently, and forget its childish weakness. So a child must not be reared in habits of command; it should obtain things, not by will-power, but at the pleasure of others. This, however, it secures by itself seeking to please them; so if it gets nothing by coercion, it subsequently grows accustomed to obtaining everything by asking, and endeavouring to please. 27:468

If a child has had its own way at home, it grows up in the habit of command, and in social life thereafter meets with all kinds of resistance, to which it is quite unaccustomed, and is thus unfitted for society. The trees in a forest discipline each other, in seeking airspace to grow in, not near others, but up above, where they do not obstruct the rest, and thus grow straight and tall; whereas a tree in the open, where it is not confined by others, grows up quite stunted, and it is already too late to discipline it thereafter. So it is also with man; if disciplined early, he grows up straight with the rest; but if this be neglected, he becomes a stunted tree.

The earliest discipline rests on obedience, and can subsequently be applied to numerous ends, such as the body, the temperament, etc. If a child is given to tantrums, it must be strongly resisted; if it is lazy, we should likewise refuse to humour it. And so, too, with its habit of mind. This must be strongly resisted, especially where there are signs of malice, destructiveness, *Schadenfreude* and cruelty. In regard to character, nothing is more injurious than lying and a false, deceptive cast of mind. Falsity and lying are the character defects and marks of the coward, and must be closely attended to in education, to ensure their suppression. Bad behaviour still has its strength, after all, and needs only to be disciplined; but furtive, deceitful meanness no longer has any seed of good in it.

From discipline or correction we move on to instruction or doctrine. This is of three kinds: teaching by nature and experience, by narration, and by argument and disputation. Teaching by experience is the basis of everything. We must not teach a child anything more than it finds confirmed in experience and can observe. From this it must grow accustomed to observing for itself, whereby concepts ensue that are derived from experience. Teaching by narration already presupposes concepts and judgement. Argumentation must be adapted to the age of the child; at first it should be empirical, merely, and rely, not on *a priori* grounds, but on the effect in experience. If the child lies, for example, we should treat it as unworthy to be spoken to at all. 27:469

It is a matter, especially, of how education is adapted to the varying age of the child. In regard to age, there are three stages of education, for childhood, for youth and for manhood. The education always precedes, and is a preparation for the period to come. As a preparation for youth, education consists in giving the pupil reasons for everything; but in childhood this is not feasible; at that point, children are merely presented with things as they are, since otherwise they are forever asking questions, and during the answer are again thinking of new questions to ask. But the period of youth is already accessible to reason. When do we start preparing the child for youth? At the age when he is already by nature an adolescent, that is, in approximately the tenth year, for by then he is already capable of reflection. A youth must already know something of what is proper, but not so a child; the latter can only be told: that is not what is done. A youth must already be aware of the duties of civil society. Here he acquires the concept of steadiness, and of the love of man; now he is already capable of principles; from this point on, religion and morality are cultivated; and by then he is already refining himself, and can be disciplined by honour, whereas a child is disciplined only by obedience. The third stage is when the youth is being educated for entry into manhood, that is, when he is capable, not only of supporting himself, but also of propagating and supporting his own kind. At sixteen he is now on the verge of manhood, and then education by discipline comes to an end. At this stage he learns increasingly to recognize his vocation, and hence must get to know the world. At this entry into manhood he must be apprised of his real duties, of the worth of humanity in his own person, and of respect for it in others. Here doctrine must shape his character.

As to the situation in regard to sex, the greatest care must be taken, so that the affections, of which that of sexual inclination is the strongest, are not misused. Rousseau* says that at this juncture a father should give his son a complete account of the matter, and not keep it a secret; he must enlighten the boy's understanding, tell him the purpose of this inclination and the harm that comes from misusing it. He must show him here, on moral grounds, the abhorrent nature of such abuse, and set before his eyes the degradation of the worth of humanity within him. This is the last and most delicate point in education. Until the schools arrive at dealing with it, many vices will continue to be practised.

27:470

OF THE FINAL DESTINY OF THE HUMAN RACE

The final destiny of the human race is moral perfection, so far as it is accomplished through human freedom, whereby man, in that case, is capable of the greatest happiness. God might already have made men

* [*Emile*, II, IV, p. 106 – Tr.]

perfect in this fashion, and allotted to each his share of happiness, but in that case it would not have sprung from the inner *principium* of the world. But that inner principle is freedom. The destiny of man is therefore to obtain his greatest perfection by means of his freedom. God does not simply will that we should be happy, but rather that we should make ourselves happy, and that is the true morality. The universal end of mankind is the highest moral perfection; if only everyone were to so behave, that their conduct would coincide with the universal end, the highest perfection would be thereby attained. Every individual must endeavour to order his conduct in accordance with this end, whereby he makes his contribution such, that if everyone does likewise, perfection is attained.

But now how far has the human race progressed on the road to this perfection? If we take the most enlightened portion of the world, we find that all states are armed against each other, and that even in peacetime each is sharpening its weapons against the rest. The consequences of this are such as to prevent men from being able to approach the universal end of perfection. The Abbé de St Pierre's* proposal for a general senate of nations would, if carried out, be the moment at which the human race would take a great step towards perfection. The time that is now devoted to security could then be employed in measures that might further the end. But since the idea of law has no such power with princes as the 27:471 notions of independence, personal authority, and the craving to rule at one's own pleasure, we can hope for nothing of the kind from that quarter.

How, then, are we to seek this perfection, and from whence is it to be hoped for? From nowhere else but education. This must be accommodated to all the ends of nature, civil society and domestic life. But our education at home and in the schools is still very defective, not only in regard to discipline, doctrine and the cultivation of talent, but also with regard to the formation of character according to moral principles. We are more concerned with skill, than with the disposition to make good use of it. How else, then, can a state be ruled by persons who are not themselves better educated? But if education were so ordered that talents would be well developed, and character formed in a moral way, then it would ascend even to the throne, and princes would thereafter be educated by persons having just these skills. Till now, however, not a single ruler has ever contributed anything to the perfection of humanity, to inner happiness, or the worth of mankind; they have merely looked always to the prosperity of their domains, which for them is the primary concern. But after such an education, their mind would so broaden, as to exert an influence on concord and conciliation. And once the sources had already come into being, it would acquire permanence, and once generally diffused, would maintain itself through public opinion. But the monarch

---

* [*Projet de paix perpétuelle*, 1713 – Tr.]

alone cannot be trained in this fashion; all members of the state must be similarly educated, and then the state would have the required stability. Can we even hope for this? The Basedow* institutes of education create a small but fervent hope in that regard. Once human nature has attained to its full destiny and highest possible perfection, that will be the kingdom of God on earth, and inner conscience, justice and equity will then hold sway, rather than the power of authority. This is the destined final end, and the highest moral perfection, to which the human race can attain, and for which, after the lapse of many centuries, we may still have hope.

Finis, Königsberg, the 19th April, 1785.

* [J. B. Basedow (1723–90), educator and philanthropist – Tr.]

PART III

Morality according to Prof. Kant: Lectures on Baumgarten's practical philosophy

(WINTER SEMESTER)
C. C. MRONGOVIUS
JAN. 3, 1785

The faculty of knowledge, the feeling of pleasure and displeasure, and the faculty of desire, are the three powers of the human soul. In all three, understanding and sense can come into play. If understanding is present, then the following sciences are possible: (1) logic, in regard to the understanding; (2) aesthetic, the feeling of pleasure and displeasure in the understanding, which is taste; (3) practical philosophy, the faculty of desire in relation to the understanding. A man has taste, who so chooses, that his pleasure is universal to us, and can be universally communicated. So in feeling, we must therefore consider whether it be capable of universal communication (the understanding addresses the universal, and is therefore in play here). In all these sciences, the question is: Can anything be known *a priori* there? With the feeling of pleasure, etc., we get nowhere, for there it is a matter of how I am affected. But we can have cognitions and acts of will *a priori*, in regard to certain objects. There is no *a priori* science of taste. What things are to our taste can assuredly not be known *a priori*. A knowledge of objects *a priori* is possible, and the science thereof is metaphysics. Our will is free, and hence we may conceive of *a priori* laws that determine the will. The *a priori* laws that determine the free will are those of morality. Theoretical philosophy on *a priori* principles is metaphysics; practical philosophy on *a priori* principles is morality. All objective philosophy, that has to do with objects, consists of these two, metaphysics and morality. If the human will is free, then *a priori* laws can be prescribed to it. Practical philosophy and morals are not identical. General practical philosophy is related to morals as logic is to metaphysics. Logic abstracts from content, and treats of the laws whereby the understanding operates. Metaphysic deals with the pure use of reason. General practical philosophy exhibits the rules whereby the will is determined *a posteriori;* morals, the *a priori* rules whereby I ought to determine the will. Like metaphysic, morals is a pure philosophy of objects. Of objects, we have merely a pure philosophy in regard to the objects of knowledge, and a pure philosophy in regard to objects of the will. We might suppose there to be also a pure philosophy of the objects of the feeling of pleasure or displeasure. But this is not so. A metaphysic of the feeling of taste cannot exist, for feeling already indicates that I must feel and experience it. All pure philosophy consists, therefore, of metaphysics   29:598

and morals. Logic is not pure philosophy, for it is not knowledge of objects, but treats only of the form of knowledge alone.

Baumgarten and Wolff say that duty is the necessity of an action according to the greatest and most important grounds of motivation. Now to them it is all one, whether these grounds are from inclinations or from reason. It is thus no pure philosophy that they have in view here, but rather a general practical philosophy. The latter treats of concepts and all actions that proceed from willing. How we ought to act, it does not consider. It makes no mention of the determinations of our willing by pure motivating grounds of reason, but speaks in general of the determinations of the will. In general practical philosophy, nothing of morality must appear.

From what grounds are actions necessary? Every formula which declares here that my action is necessary according to reason, is an imperative. Now we can conceive of imperatives of skill, of prudence, and of morality.

The imperative of skill says that I must do this or that, if I wish to attain my end. That presupposes, however, that I desire to do something. Hence, an imperative of this kind is conditioned, as means to that end. We are looking here at the ground of motivation. The imperative of prudence assumes that we desire something, namely happiness, which in fact is true of everyone. Since you yourself wish to be happy, you must do this thing. The imperative of skill abstracts from all ends, whether we have them or not. The imperative of prudence establishes an end that is given to me *a posteriori*, since happiness is the maximal degree of satisfaction of all our inclinations. The imperative of morality abstracts from all inclinations. The motivating ground is not drawn from sense, or from happiness, but given solely from pure reason. The motivating grounds and the law itself must be *a priori*. In general practical philosophy it is undetermined, whether we have motivating grounds or not. Logic abstracts from our cognitions. General practical philosophy, from the grounds of motivation.

29:599 Moral laws cannot be empirically conditioned. The other practical laws are so. Morality, which discerns purely *a priori* the laws of freedom, is a metaphysic of freedom, or of morals, just as metaphysics is called a metaphysic of nature, since it contains *a priori* the laws of nature, as they are known *a priori*. General practical philosophy is included here, insofar as it furnishes a preparation. The metaphysic of morals, or *metaphysica pura*, is only the first part of morality; the second part is *philosophia moralis applicata,*[a] moral anthropology, to which the empirical principles belong. Just as there is metaphysics and physics, so the same applies here. Morality cannot be constructed out of empirical principles, for this yields, not absolute, but merely conditional necessity. Morality says, however, you must do it, without any condition or exception. General practical philoso-

---

[a] applied moral philosophy

phy is a *propaedeutica*. Moral anthropology is morality applied to men. *Moralia pura* is based upon necessary laws, and hence it cannot be founded upon the particular constitution of a rational being, such as man. The particular constitution of man, and the laws based upon it, come to the fore in moral anthropology under the name of ethics. In general practical philosophy, the metaphysic of morals, or *metaphysica pura*, is also presented in a mixed fashion.

The ancient Greeks concentrated the determining of the principle of morality on the question: What is the highest good? Among all that we call good, the major portion is good in a conditional sense, and nothing is good without restriction, save the good will. Understanding, bodily strength and prudence are good, but united with a bad will, are exceedingly harmful. Health, capacity, well-being and constant cheerfulness of heart are good only provided that the agent has a good will, in order even to make use of them. Thus a good will is simply good without restriction, for itself alone, in every respect and under all circumstances. It is the only thing that is good without other conditions, but it is also not completely good. A thing can be unconditioned, and yet not complete. It does not yet comprise the whole of goodness. The highest good is unconditionally good, and also comprises the whole of goodness. Were there a being in the world, such that his good will frequently led to his ruin, his good will would shine all the brighter. But the possession of virtue is not yet the whole of goodness. Virtue is the greatest worth of the person, but our state 29:600 must also be worth wishing for. The greatest worth of one's state is happiness. So virtue combined with happiness is the highest good. Virtue is the condition under which I am worthy of happiness; but that is not yet the highest good. . . .

We have to see that these two elements, not merely do not contradict each 29:602 other, but can also be united. The course of nature does not show us that. Reason prescribes laws to the former; to the latter they are also prescribed by our needs. Reason cannot satisfy my needs. If both are to be united, we have to postulate a universal world-ruler. The Stoics, too, had the concept of God, but only *in superfluo,*[b] for they thought that otherwise morality would lose its unity, and men act merely in their own interest. They said that, even if everything goes wrong for a sage, he still has a refuge, namely the hope of a future life. Thirdly, they also confounded the *principia* of morality, and how I ought to pursue it.

Objective *principia* are laws, and differ from subjective principles, or 29:603 from maxims by which I act. Objective *principia* are those in which morality consists, and subjective, those whereby I attain to morality; the ancients did not distinguish them.

[b] as an extra

A knowledge of the former must precede, but is much easier than knowledge of the latter, which is based on anthropology. We might attain to morality either naturally, through some cause that lies in our nature, or supernaturally, through the influence of a supreme being. Plato assumed a hyperphysical cause, the immediate intuition of God in his Ideas. The others take it to be natural, but are divided, in that Diogenes says that it rests on the simplicity of nature, whereas Epicurus and Zeno hold that it would need to be learnt, and that a major science therefore pertains to it. Rousseau, in modern times, has maintained that it does not need to be learnt, while Hume argues that it is a science. By nature we do not, indeed, have knowledge of right and wrong, but only a very small degree of culture is requisite for this, and our capacity is almost equal to it. Diogenes had to develop the concepts in his pupils by himself. He wholly rejected propriety, and thought it an obstacle to virtue. Among the ancients, we have the following ideals:

1. For Diogenes, the ideal of the most perfect man was the man of nature;
2. For Epicurus, it was the man of the world.

Epicurus has been poorly understood. We still have a letter of his, in which he invites someone to dine, but promises him no other welcome beyond a cheerful heart and a dish of polenta. This would make a sorry meal. Since he turned morality into the means to happiness, he deprived virtue of its worth.

3. For the Stoic, the ideal was the sage.

Plato's ideal is unthinkable, for it was a supernatural thing. The perfect man of Diogenes is good without virtue. Virtue is the strength of soul to withstand, out of duty, the onset of evil. Diogenes' perfect man has no need of virtue, for he has no concept of evil. It has not yet been engendered from his needs. He is happy without wisdom or prudence, and at the smallest price, since he needs the least for his happiness. The ancients called this the short way to virtue. Innocence is certainly desirable, only it does not last, and is easily led astray, for it contains no enduring principle. A man's desires keep on growing, and without realizing it he is out of his innocence. Rousseau has tried to bring it back again, but in vain. Epicurus founded his ideal on science though he said it was that in which contentment lies: the cheerful heart, for which virtue would be the means of attainment, and in which worth would consist. He called it *voluptas*,ᶜ and the term has been very damaging to his system. His pupils may well thereafter have taken it to mean sensual pleasure. That he did not intend by it any such thing, can be seen from the fact that he did not then demean himself.

29:604

ᶜ enjoyment

In the Gospel we also find an ideal, namely that of holiness. It is that state of mind from which an evil desire never arises. God alone is holy, and man can never become so, but the ideal is good. The understanding often has to contend with the inclinations. We cannot prevent them, but we can prevent them from determining the will. Holiness is purity of the will, even in thought. We can attain to virtue, i.e., to a moral preparedness to withstand all temptations to evil, so far as they arise from inclinations. The ancient philosophers never got to that point, though it has been said that they have enunciated all that is moral in the Bible. With these four ideals, the whole topic is exhausted.

The ideal of Christianity is hyperphysical, but it must nevertheless serve us as a model. An Idea is a concept that is universal, or the universal concept of a maximum, whose object cannot be presented *in concreto*. A practical Idea is a moral perfection whose object can never be adequately given in experience. It is intrinsic to moral perfection, that an action be done, without any advantage or self-interest, solely from the concept of duty. We shall be unable to name any action where such incentives have not been at work alongside morality. So to expound morality in full purity is to set forth an Idea of practical reason. Such Ideas are not chimeras, for they constitute the guideline to which we must constantly approach. They make up the law of approximation. We have to possess a yardstick by which to estimate our moral worth, and to know the degree to which we are faulty and deficient; and here I have to conceive of a maximum, so that 29:605 I know how far away I am, or how near I come to it. An ideal is the representation of a single thing, in which we depict such an Idea to ourselves *in concreto*. All ideals are fictions. We attempt, *in concreto*, to envisage a being that is congruent with the Idea. In the ideal we turn the Ideas into a model, and may go astray in clinging to an ideal, since it can often be defective. Mistakes in metaphysics are not so damaging as in morals, for the former remain acts of speculation, whereas in the practical sphere errors are dangerous. The ideal is a *prototypon* of morality. A natural man can never be the ideal, for he is still always subject to weakness. The ancients would certainly seem to have exhausted all the possibilities here. But if we ask: What is moral perfection, and on what principle is it to be judged?, we can and must enter upon new paths at this point.

All practical rules consist in an imperative which says what I ought to do. They are meant to signify that a free action, possible through myself, would necessarily occur, if reason were to have total control over my will. If reason has power enough to determine the will in accordance with its concepts, then it has full control. Do we even have such a reason? We are well aware of what a being with such reason would do; but we do it not, for we have inclinations that are hindrances. A being that, through reason, has total control over his will, has a naturally good will. Such a being has no need of any imperative, for *ought* indicates that it is not natural to the

will, but that the agent has to be coerced. Our will is not good of its own accord; only God's will is automatically good and perfect, and we cannot say of Him, as we do of men, that He ought so to act. With God, the objective practical law is also, at the same time, a motive. An objective practical law that is not, at the same time, subjective, is an imperative. Necessitation is an *actio* whereby a thing is made necessary, that was not so before. Every imperative is therefore a necessitation. Practical reason affects the will, and shows that we do not really, and by nature, act in that way, but that we must so act. With regard to ourselves, the moral laws are called commands, but not so with regard to God. All created beings are subject to commands, for they all have needs and inclinations which may
29:606 very well conflict with morality.

The imperative is either a command or a prohibition. Every imperative is a direction of my will by reason, as I picture how a reason, which had free control over my will, would act. Imperatives are drawn from the Idea of a perfect will, and hold good as rules for my imperfect will; duty is the Idea of a perfect will, as the norm for an imperfect one. God, therefore, has no duties. Reason is a use of our will that is fully imperative. Man must not only act in accordance with the willing of reason; he also has hindrances in willing, namely inclinations. Then is appended the *ought*, the Idea of a willing that is in accordance with the laws of reason, as a guideline to our own willing.

All imperatives are (1) hypothetical, i.e., the necessity of the action as a means to ends; (2) categorical, i.e., the practical necessity of the action in an absolute sense, without the motivating ground being contained in any other end. The latter has unconditioned, the former only conditioned practical necessity. The hypothetical imperative commands a thing either *problematically*, i.e., it enjoins a thing under the condition of a merely possible end; or *assertorically*, if it enjoins a thing under the condition of an actual end. The categorical imperative enjoins without any end. The problematic imperative occurs in all practical sciences; in geometry, for example, when I say: If you want to measure a tower, you must do thus and so. Those who have no wish to measure the tower, have no need to do these things. The imperative under a *problematic* condition is the imperative of skill. In youth, when we instruct him, we show the student all possible means to all possible ends, with the intention that, if he knows everything that is needed, it may be useful to him. He who knows the imperatives to very many possible ends, has a great deal of skill.

The imperative where I presuppose an assertoric end is the imperative of happiness, and this I can assume in everybody, since each of us automatically wishes to be happy. The imperatives which teach us how to attain happiness are those of prudence. *Skill* is dexterity in knowing the means to any desired ends. The influence of men is always directed here
29:607 to the particular skill, so that to utilize a man for one's own desired end is

prudence; for example, the clockmaker is skilled if he makes a good clock, but prudent if he knows how to dispose of it effectively; true prudence is the use of means to promote or nurture one's own happiness. That is the pragmatic imperative. That which makes us prudent is pragmatic, and that which makes us skilled is practical; or, the pragmatic is that which I can utilize for my freedom.

The categorical imperative is that which enjoins the necessity of such an action, without regard to any end. The hypothetical imperative tells us which action is good, either for any given end, or for an existing one; the categorical, on the other hand, tells us which action is good for its own sake. The questions now arise, (1) Are there indeed actions that are good for their own sake? And then (2) How is a categorical imperative possible? This is the hardest to answer: Everyone knows that nothing in the world is absolutely good without restriction, save a good will, and that this good will sets the limit to everything and for that reason is then good without limitation. The imperative that enjoins something through the good will can thus command. Even happiness in the bad will is nothing good. If a happy man does not have a good will, he laughs at the unfortunate, and does nothing to help. The good will is good without restriction, because everywhere it is itself the restriction. The categorical imperative sets forth the rules of a good will. The will that is intrinsically good cannot act in accordance with the hypothetical imperative, for then it would be good only insofar as the end is good, and no end is good without limitation; hence the good will must stand under a categorical imperative. Would the intrinsically good will indeed be good, if it always had a care only for its own greatest happiness? No. The rule that has objective necessity is necessitating, but for us it is not subjectively necessary. The rule of a good will, for my good will, is subjectively necessary. The divine will is perfect, and in accordance with the rules of a perfect will, but His will is not affected by these rules; it is impossible, rather, that He should will any- thing else. An imperative is categorical if it is the rule of a will itself intrinsically good; and this rule is imperative because it is addressed to an imperfect will, and is necessitating. The categorical imperative is thus the rule of a will intrinsically good. But that will is one that can in no circum- stances be bad. It is thus the rule of effecting that which, taken generally   29:608
as a rule, can always be the object of willing; and then it is in all circum- stances the same, and must in that case therefore be a good will. Lying can be good from many points of view, but from the subjective viewpoint it is not good, but useful; if truth, however, is made into an altogether general rule, I can always will it, and it is always good. Only the will that determines under the rule of the universal validity of its rules, is an absolutely good will. Only the will that wills action no otherwise, save insofar as it does not conflict with the universal validity of a rule, acts rightly.

Principles are objective rules of action, and *maxims* are practical principles, which make themselves, subjectively, into the very rule of their action. The will whose maxims can be objective principles is intrinsically good. I am never to will anything, unless I can also will that this maxim be at the same time a universal law; the will, in that case, is never in conflict with any other. Desire is that which conflicts with reason. An action is morally impossible if (1) its maxim cannot function as a universal law; (2) its maxim can indeed do this, but we simply cannot will it. It is therefore that of whose maxim we cannot possibly will that it be a universal law. There are actions such that, if we wanted to make their maxims into universal laws of nature, they simply could not hold.

If everyone might break a promise when it suited him, and this were to become a universal law, then nobody would trust to a promise, or therefore do anything because of it. In that case, promising would abolish itself, and thus automatically cease. Hence, it is subjectively possible, but morally impossible in practice. A man who fails to keep his promise, does not will that this should become a universal law; he merely wishes to exempt himself alone from this law. Here the action is not impossible because of the man's opinion; but if this maxim were made into a rule, it would be quite untenable. A maxim, qua universal law, whereby nobody gave anyone any help, but also did them no harm, would be able to hold, and so, too, could the world; but injustice, lying, etc. cannot subsist at all, and are therefore, in a strict sense, morally impossible. Although a man may recognize that loveless maxims are possible, and that nature could survive under them, it is nevertheless impossible for him to will it. The latter is a conditional, the former an unconditional, moral impossibility.

29:609

The maxim must be so constituted, that I can will at the same time that it become a universal law. If somebody is in distress, and I cannot help him here, then I cannot will that this action should become a universal law. The universalizing of a law that is strictly impossible, cannot occur, for it contradicts itself. Obligation is a moral necessity, namely the idea of the necessity of acting freely from the concept of a good will, whose principle it is that one can will that a maxim thereof should become a universal rule. *Duty (officium)*[d] is the necessity of an action from obligation. Perfect duty is that which conforms to the principle of the will, insofar as the opposite cannot become a universal law; imperfect duties, however, are those which originate from the *principium*, that we be able to will that the maxims of our actions should become a universal law. All perfect and imperfect duties are both inner and outer in regard to ourselves. With perfect duties, I ask whether their maxims can hold good as a universal law. But with imperfect ones, I ask whether I could also will that such a maxim should become a universal law. Perfect duties are strict duties. Were it to be a general rule, to take away his belongings from everyone,

---

[d] office or function

then mine and thine would be altogether at an end. For anything I might take from another, a third party would take from me. I cannot will that lovelessness should become a universal law, for in that case I also suffer myself. The will that is good under all circumstances must in no way conflict with itself, if I am to turn it into a universal law. The agreement of the will with its own general validity, or its accordancy insofar as it views itself as a universal law, is morality; and by this all men judge the morality of their actions. No man can call his acts good, if he considers them as subject to the universal law, but as an exception to it. That is the supreme canon, that the will should be in agreement with its own general validity. If the action is such that my will can have no general validity in the matter, then it is morally reprehensible. Here the will is considered in the light of its general validity, and in that case it is the intrinsically good will; and this, then, is the moral imperative: Act so that you can will that the nature of your will becomes a general rule. If my will can become such a general rule, then it agrees with itself in all circumstances, and is an intrinsically good will.

29:610

We are pleased by the thing we have an inclination to, but the inclination in itself does not please us, for if it did we should not have so many requirements. Inclination is never its own object, for to that we are subordinated; but moral will is its own object, for such a will is not conditional, but unconditioned. Inclination is merely conditioned. There are actions whose goodness depends merely on their effect. But moral actions are in no degree less good, even though no effect whatever comes to pass. Here the mere will has the worth. All other kinds of willing are good solely on account of the end. We must make all our decisions in such wise, as if we were legislating with the maxims of our will. Man sees himself, in a system of rational beings, as a legislating member thereof; otherwise we are mere instruments. It is impossible that a man should be able to judge the morality of his actions without moral principles, or consequently arrive at the point of taking no interest in them. Rascals are prepared to steal from others, but among themselves they still wish to be honourable fellows, for they see that otherwise they could not survive at all.

Perfect duties are those whose opposite cannot become a universal law; and imperfect duties are those where the opposite is possible, but I cannot will that it become such a law.

So morality, then, is now also divided thereby into two parts.

First part

Morality is the agreement of the will with its own possible generality. Now we have shown what it consists in, but not yet how it may be possible. Man must regard himself as a legislating member in the kingdom of ends, or of rational beings. Leibnitz also calls the kingdom of ends moral principles of the kingdom of grace. *Quid tibi non vis fieri, id alteri ne feceris*[e] is among these principles, and refers to the duty towards others. A moral law is the law of a good will, that determines itself no otherwise than by the principle of its own general validity. *The necessitation of an action by the moral law, is obligation; the necessity of an action from obligation, is duty.* Necessity and necessitation are different: the former is objective necessity. Necessitation is the relation of a law to an imperfect will. In man, the objective necessity of acting in accordance with the moral laws, is necessitation. Necessitation is making necessary. The persistent maxim of making his will conform to the moral law, is virtue. All creatures have virtue, but God does not, for He is holy. We can conceive of no creature that would not have hindrances to virtue.

29:611

Every man wishes to be virtuous, if only it had already come about. Necessity of action for the sake of the moral law is also applicable to God. Necessity of action from obligation is duty. Obligation is necessity of acting through the law, and the action that thereby becomes necessary is duty; so says our author. But the question arises, why is the education of children a duty? *Responsio:* The education of children is not a duty *from* duty, but duty is the ground of it. Duty is merely the necessity of the action from obligation.

Necessitatio of my *arbitrium* is either *pathologica* or *practica*. The former is *obligatio arbitrii bruti,*[f] but the latter, *liberi.* The former is necessitation through sensory impulses, but the latter, from motivating grounds. These grounds always have to do with free actions; but those impulses, with involuntary ones. For animals have no free choice, their actions being necessarily determined by their sensory impulses. Such impulses can be overcome by others that are stronger still. The human will is free when it is not determined or affected *per stimulos.* If this free will is nevertheless to

---

[e] do not do to others what you do not want done to yourself
[f] obligation of animal choice/of free choice

be necessitated, the necessitation must be practical, or *per motiva*. *Motiva* are all representations of the understanding, and of reason, that determine the will. They are set in opposition to the stimuli, and are called springs of the soul (*elateres animi*). If the *motiva* are to necessitate, the stimuli cannot do so; only free choice can be necessitated *per motiva*.

Practical *necessitatio* is either pragmatic or moral, related to the worth of our condition or our person. Pragmatic motives are those drawn from the worth of our condition, and in that case the *necessitatio* is *practica* but *non moralis*. Moral motives are drawn from the absolute worth of our person, and such worth gives us a good will, because everything else has only a conditional worth. *Necessitatio moralis* is *obligatio*. A man always sees, however, the great difference between the worth of his person, and that of his condition. Self-seeking always subordinates him to the worth of his total condition, but reason thinks otherwise. Even if our intention is merely to attain the sum total of happiness, this occurs through the understanding, and though motives are certainly there, they are pragmatic. Moral motives can necessitate the agent, but where *motiva pragmatica* necessitate conditionally only, *motiva moralia* do so unconditionally. Moral necessity is an objective necessity in relation to our will. And this is always obligation. . . . 29:612

Everything that contravenes the moral laws is transgression (*peccatum*), not sin. For the 'sin' is always linked to the concept of a transgression of divine laws. Transgressions are always *omissiones*, and *commissiones* are always actions that conflict with the moral law – are violations of it. Actions are related to the moral law in three ways: 29:615

1. Where there is agreement of the action with the moral law, *rectitudo actionis meritum*, which may be expressed by a plus.

2. Departure from the moral law, *pravitas actionis peccatum*,[g] which can be expressed by a minus. By the plus (+) we add worth to our person; by the minus (–) we diminish this worth.

3. What has no relationship to morality, is the *indifferentia actionis*,[h] *adiaphoron*, and is expressed by (o), for here there is neither merit nor aberration; this is also called *casuistry*, and is a sort of micrology in regard to the *rectitudo actionis*. Casuistry was at one time a major component in the teaching of scholars of the Jesuit order. It is so called, because it has to do with specific and particular cases. Are there, then, *adiaphora* as such? We have many actions that we perform merely for physical sustenance, and these are *adiaphora*. So if there are such, we also have actions whose worth is equal to nothing (zero).

Mala immortalia[i] are those that are *mala consectaria* even after the death

---

[g] culpable depravity of action
[h] indifference of action
[i] evils that outlive the perpetrator

of the *peccator*, and so, likewise, there are *bona immortalia*. All consequences of actions flow either from the nature of the act, or from the
nature of the agent, of soul and body. Our author plagues himself over
consectaria, and sees himself constrained, on his principle, to take the
consequences into account. We have no need to do that. I am in debt, but
29:616   do not pay, because my credit does not suffer greatly thereby, and I can
buy something else instead. How far can that go? The rules of prudence
are such that we have to look to the consequences. But not so with the
rules of virtue. It is also contrary to the passage in St. Paul* to do evil that
good may come of it (Buschings, Carl M.).

Morality can be divided into *objectiva* and *subjectiva*. The former can be
derived from the relation of an action to the *lex naturalis*, but the latter
only from its relation to a *lex arbitraria*. Subjective morality can again be
taken in two forms, as law *per arbitrium divinum*, and *humanum*. Can we,
however, regard *moralitas objectiva* as a morality that arises from the divine
will? Yes, for since the divine will is the idea of the most perfect will, we
can say that such a will commands it. But from this it does not follow that
it would have to be derived from the divine will; we could not, in that case,
perceive it to be necessary. Laws of a divine will, which imposes on us
actions that are morally indifferent, cannot be derived from nature. If we
live by an objective morality, then we have no need of a subjective one.
The *moralitas objectiva* cannot be derived from the subjective. If I can
discern, from the nature of the matter, that an action is moral, then I do
not need the divine will. Only the moral imperative designates an obligation. The pragmatic imperative, however, does not obligate. We say,
merely, that it is advisable to save money. The moral imperative is so
constituted, that it is incomprehensible, how a man so acute has been able
to speak lightly of such a thing. Make yourself perfect, he says, but that is
a tautology. Live according to nature; but that he has taken from the
ancients.

Necessitas actionis invitae[j] is a compulsion. For this it is required, not
only that our will be not morally good, but also that it have hindrances. A
compulsion always presupposes a hindrance in the will. A man often has
inclinations that conflict with the moral law. So duty we regard as a
compulsion. A compulsion occurs when we have an inclination to the
opposite of an action. The necessitation to an action, such that we have an
inclination to its opposite, is therefore compulsion. Here, however, we are
29:617   talking, not of pathological compulsion, for that occurs *per stimulos*, but
rather of the moral compulsion which alone arises through motives; for
example, if I owe someone money, and my creditor demands it of me, I
forgo a pleasure, simply in order to give him his due. Here I impose a

*[Romans, 7:19–Tr.]
[j] necessity of action against one's will

236

moral compulsion on myself; but if, on the other hand, I am led to it by fear of punishment, then the compulsion is a pathological one. The moral compulsion rests upon duty.

Can I really conceive of a pathological compulsion in man as well? Truly I cannot, for freedom consists in this, that he can be without compulsion in the pathological sense; nor should he be compelled in that way. Even if a man is so constrained, he can nevertheless act otherwise. Hence it is improperly called a compulsion, when we are necessitated by such impulses to do a thing, or leave it undone. The moral compulsion can be resisted. The more a man considers a moral act to be irresistible, and the more he is compelled to it by duty, the freer he is. For in that case he is employing the power he has, to rule over his strong inclinations. So freedom is all the more displayed, the greater the moral compulsion.

Moral compulsion can be external and internal. It is internal if duty makes the action necessary, against all the agent's inclinations, not by the will of another, but through his own will. External compulsion is possible, however, through another's will; thus it cannot be said, for example, that we were externally compelled into an act of kindness; rather, we compel ourselves. External and internal compulsion may be pragmatic, or also moral. The sovereign necessitates me pragmatically to observe his laws. Pragmatic compulsion also arises from reason, but the end, however, is always the satisfaction of pleasure. Moral compulsion presupposes that we do a thing with reluctance. To love God is to obey His laws abundantly, and most willingly; that is already more than to fear God. The latter is to do God's bidding, out of reverence for His holy law. Here the action can be reluctantly done.

Our obligations are of two kinds: (1) those to whose observance we may justly be compelled; (2) those to which we should not be compelled externally. The first are legal duties (liabilities), the others, duties of virtue. The former are also called, in a strict sense, perfect; the latter, imperfect duties. In the system of morality, all self-regarding duties are held to be imperfect; but they are no less perfect duties than those that we have towards others. 29:618 This comes about, however, because compulsory duties and perfect duties are taken to be identical. We can grant *latitudo* to a law, when it has exceptions. Thus the law of well-doing has *latitudo*, since I must first found my obligation in the reason for doing well to someone. The legal duty is a strict one, since here there are no exceptions.

Our actions are of two kinds: either (1) they relate simply to ourselves; or (2) to others. As to self-regarding duty, the question here is not whether we can be compelled to it; for since we have no external obligation thereto, from within us, we cannot be compelled to it, either, from without. But in regard to the duty towards others, there are some to which we can be compelled, and also others to which we cannot be. The duties towards others rest on two principles, namely either upon the other's freedom, or upon his particular ends. We may now say: the necessity of an action, under the condition by which alone a universal freedom can be self-consistent, is called a strict duty. The necessity in the action, by which alone the universal end, or happiness, can be attained, is imperfect duty, or the duty of well-doing. The consistency of an action with the freedom of others is necessary; but since these actions also concur with other ends, it is likewise a duty, though an imperfect one. The compulsion consists, therefore, in the limitation of freedom by the condition under which our own freedom may co-exist with the general freedom. Freedom consists in this, that everyone can act according to his own will, without being necessitated to act according to the will of another. The concept of legal order rests solely on that of freedom. To break my word to another would be self-contradictory, if it were to become a universal rule. In legal duties the question is always about human welfare. All teachers of morals and law have invariably added something to the concept of law that first needs to be proved. For they say that an action is legally binding, if it is so defined, that it is permissible to compel those who obligate themselves thereto, to carry it out. But the authority to compel a man to an action should by no means appear in the definition, but must first be demonstrated from that, 29:619 and this in the following way: Every action that is consistent with the condition under which freedom can be universal, may be compelled, i.e., it is not unjust to compel a man thereto. For the action that is contrary to freedom under universal laws, is no* evidence of universal freedom. And now since everything that counters a hindrance to universal freedom, promotes the latter, the compulsion is legitimate. I therefore do no wrong, if I compel someone who is acting wrongly.†

This serves to distinguish coercive from non-coercive duties. The former are simply the only kind of actions to which we can be compelled. Actions, whether appertaining to welfare or security, are all unjust, if they are contrary to universal freedom. To moral necessitation, a pathological or external sanction to obligation may be added, insofar as the action involves a liberty that cannot exist by universal laws, without the freedom of every individual being inhibited. If I act contrary to the general freedom, that is a hindrance to any general freedom, and if the latter is specifically impeded, the act is unjust, and the sanction therefore just. But that act is contrary to the general freedom, whereby, if it were to become a universal law, the freedom of everyone would have to suffer under it. In all actions, however, where the use of my freedom does not encroach upon the freedom of others, as in duties to myself and to others in regard to their welfare, there is no compulsion; for since there I do not limit the freedom of others, my freedom, too, should not be limited, i.e., I should not be compelled.

*[Reading *kein* for *ein* – Tr.]
†[Reading *unrecht* for *recht* – Tr.]

ON LAW IN GENERAL

We have imperatives of skill, under the condition that I will a problematic end; imperatives of prudence, or pragmatic imperatives, which enjoin under the condition of welfare; and categorical or moral imperatives, which enjoin absolutely. The moral imperative is opposed to the pragmatic, and commands in a different way. Pragmatic and moral imperatives are very often confounded with one another, which happens not only among the ancients, but also even nowadays among the moderns, though the two things are poles apart. Pragmatic imperatives are merely counsels; moral imperatives either *motiva*, rules of virtue, or *leges*, juridical laws. All   29:620 duties of virtue are meritorious, for we in fact do more than we are obliged to. Duties of law are incumbent on us. But we have a duty to both kinds of action. In duties of virtue to God we have no merit, but may possess it in regard to other men, for we do in fact make them obliged to us. In self-regarding actions there are also strict laws, i.e., *leges*, but they are not juridical. *Leges* determine strictly, but with *motiva* there are always exceptions. *Law is the totality of all our compulsory duties* (*leges strictae*). Ethics, the totality of all non-compulsory duties. To a disposition we cannot be compelled, even though one might be aware of it, since otherwise all freedom would cease; for only the externals of an action can be subject to coercion. Ethics has to do with the actions that are done from duty, and is thus applicable to all duties; whereas law is concerned with external actions. In questions of what is right, I look only to the action, and the latter is right if it conforms to the law; but in ethics I look only to the motivating grounds of actions. Juridical actions I may also consider in an ethical sense, if, that is, they are performed from moral dispositions. If I do a thing with an eye to the coercive law, then my action has legality, indeed, but not morality. The *leges praeceptivae* are either *prohibitivae* or *permissivae;*[k] the latter are called *jus mandati*, the former, *jus vetiti*. . . .

What, then, is the basis of morality? This question has been investigated in the modern age. The principle of morality, or the logical principle, is   29:621 that from which all moral laws may be derived. It is either subjective, if I show from what power of the soul I adjudge morality, or it is objective. This division, however, is often incorrect. So from what power does the principle come, and how does it run? The objective principle is: Act so that you can will that the maxims of your actions might become a universal law. It is the normative principle. The subjective or pragmatic principle consists in the direction of this principle. Here I show its possibility. This principle of morality has been sought (1) in empirical, and (2) in rational causes, in subjective and in objective concepts. Those who con-

[k] prescriptive laws that forbid or allow

struct it on empirical grounds, do so either (a) on internal, or (b) on external empirical grounds. The principle of morality from empirical grounds of inner experience is derived from sense in two ways, namely α. from physical, and β. from moral sense. Those who reduce the principle of morality to physical sense are the Epicureans, and their principle is that of self-love, and rests upon the comfort and safety of our condition. Those who assume a moral sense, whereby we are supposedly able, by feeling, to perceive the propriety or impropriety of our actions, have the principle of moral feeling. Shaftesbury introduced it, and had many Englishmen, including Hutcheson, among his followers. The moral and the empirical senses are both internal empirical grounds. Those who assume external empirical grounds as the principle of morality, base it on examples of custom and education. Through community with one another, men engender that which seems similar to a moral law. On top of that comes authority, which coerces us thereto with punishments.

This principle has been advocated by one Mandeville, and also by Montaigne. To prove it, they are at pains to show that moral judgement among peoples has long been very diverse. The Egyptians, for example, visited capital punishment upon all brigands except those who had a leader. But this came about because, in the Theban wilderness that lies between Egypt and the Red Sea, there are two Arab tribes a-wandering, called Bedouins, who live by robbing and plundering, and so it was also in those days. If one of their number was captured, he was not killed, but handed over to their Sheiks, who punished him; otherwise they might have become angered about the matter.

29:622

The rational grounds are also (1) internal, and (2) external. The former have been derived from metaphysical grounds, namely, from the concepts of unity, truth and perfection. Almost all writers have derived them from unity, because reason likes to have a rule. But we disapprove a thing on moral grounds, even though there is a rule. Cumberland has the principle of truth. A wicked man, he says, never tells the truth, because he cannot disclose his evil dispositions, without being at variance with himself. The principle of perfection, or of the harmonizing of the manifold into *one,* comes from Wolff. The principle of morality has also been derived from external rational causes. Inner rational grounds draw the morality from the constitution of the action itself; outer, from a being distinct from ourselves. This is the theological principle, or the principle of the divine will; it is rational, for we can discern the divine will only from reason. The principle of morality from external empirical grounds has but few adherents. The metaphysical principles are nowadays largely abandoned. A majority of writers has fallen back on the theological principle, because the metaphysical one has no force. The principle of morality has not yet been rightly discovered, because on it the worth, or otherwise, of moral conduct depends. We shall now go through all these principles, one by one.

1. The principle of morality from external empirical grounds. The claim is, that moral judgements among the various nations are also so diverse, that we can see from this, that it is a contingent matter. It arises, therefore, from education, government, example, etc.; but moral laws cannot be empirical, for they are necessary. Derived from other examples, they will not even have empirical generality. A crime would only be a crime under certain circumstances. But a crime remains always a crime. The Esquimaux, when their parents are decrepit, and no longer capable of working, strangle them; and the old also make preparation for this. But the children do it from true filial love, because in winter they are absent for many weeks out hunting, and during that time the old might starve. Nor have we learnt morality from examples and anecdotes; it is reason itself that teaches us. For if a father steals, for example, the son does not approve of it.

Then there are the inner empirical grounds, from self-love and the 29:623 moral feeling. The principle of the feeling for what is good for us, or the physical feeling, is the principle of happiness. The other is the principle that stems from the feeling for what is good as such. This is an invention of the modern age. Man is said to have a feeling for something that in no way affects his condition. The physical feeling is entirely natural, being satisfaction at our condition, insofar as it is agreeably affected. Hence

2. The principle of happiness. It seems that morality tells us to do nothing save what brings us happiness. But this principle is utterly false, totally adverse to morality, and cannot be applied at all; for

(a) We find in the world that virtue does not always make for happiness. Virtue has to do solely with the worth of our person, and not with our condition. It is said that consciousness of rectitude produces happiness; but it is the inner worth, that good conduct must already have beforehand, and without which one cannot be perfectly happy. The consciousness of our own rectitude does not yet make us happy by itself.

(b) Virtue, on the contrary, contributes much to human unhappiness. Inner worth gives man a consolation that will not let him sink entirely, but it is still no enjoyment. The Stoic believes that inner worth is already happiness. But in that case the wicked man would have to be always unhappy, and yet he is not. He is often in full enjoyment of happiness. It is said, however, that he is still tormented by conscience; but the greater the villain, the less does conscience plague him, for a tormenting conscience is still the remnant of a good disposition. Because of his punctiliousness, the virtuous man has a gloomy air, but the vicious man a cheerful one. It is also said that virtue is the best policy; but a prudent rascal arranges matters so, that to outward appearance he observes morality, and only permits himself exceptions when a great advantage may be hoped for. From this the falsity is apparent. Finally,

(c) This principle is totally at variance with the nature of moral conduct. We must not be virtuous for the sake of advantage; if so, all morality is totally lost. From morality we reap no benefit; on the contrary, it costs us. In the latter case, however, it gleams, for there the virtue rests upon its own inner worth. The rewards of virtue must not serve as motivating

29:624 grounds to the practice of it; not because we can dispense with all advantage, but because it would then be self-serving. Its inner worth must be its motivating ground. When the preacher tells of great rewards already accruing to virtue in this life, his hearer often thinks that the man is deceiving him, for he sees himself that this is often not the case. If men of vice and virtue are both in pursuit of advantage, but the virtuous man has the better of it, then they differ not at all in disposition, but only in their happiness, which is not, however, the case. Morality should be expounded in its pure inner worthiness, and merely linked with the possibility of reward; that would have a better effect than at present, where everything is mixed up together. The consolation of the virtuous is the shortness of life, and can we really call them happy, who wish, for that reason, that their life may be a short one? However much inner self-contentment a man may have, he will still always feel his external condition; divinity is independent of all outward circumstances, but man, on the contrary, is not. Conscious of his own worth, there is much that a man can do without, in that he finds a possession in himself; but such self-possession is not happiness. Regarded in itself, morality carries no promises with it; it is prior to religion, and the latter certainly carries a moral promise.

If virtue is always followed by happiness, it then has a price, and if vice then rested upon more advantages, we would have to prefer it to virtue. Both in this life, and in the next, happiness is at odds with morality, though the hope for a future life is also by no means so harmful, since it is uncertain; for he who has this hope must already have a tendency to morality. Virtue does not flirt or curry favour, but is honourable. Duty is not what I do for my advantage, but what I do for the sake of the law. The cast of mind which is won over only by reward, is called *indoles servilis;* that which acts only for the sake of duty, is *indoles erecta.* That act alone is morally good, which is done because it is a duty. Actions can be performed, that are outwardly in accordance with duty, though the heart is filled with vice. Virtue must have its own worth beforehand, if it is to be rewarded, and that is what makes it worthy. He who is virtuous from mercenary motives is not even worthy of reward; he enjoys the natural consequences of his actions. The more self-interest is appended, the

29:625 more virtue is deprived of its worth. But since we have need of happiness, a future life may supervene, to sweeten the ill-fortune of his life for the virtuous man.

3. The principle of moral feeling. This is null and void. From the feeling of a sensation that may be different in every creature, no generally valid law can be derived for all thinking beings, and that is how the moral

principle must be constituted. There is said to be an inner sense, whereby we become capable of satisfaction and dissatisfaction in moral actions. Hume even thought the moral feeling to comprise various lesser feelings. But morality simply does not admit of being felt. All rules derived from feeling are contingent, and valid only for beings that have such a feeling. Feeling is a satisfaction that rests on the constitution of a sense. So it would then be all one, if God had also framed in us a liking for vice, and then He might equally have done it in other creatures as well. Such laws are therefore merely arbitrary, and simply a childish game. Feeling, in man, is diversified, and that would also have to be so here. If morality rested on feeling, then many a one who is simply without tender feeling might attend to it less, and thereupon practise vice. If this were the principle of morality, then not everyone would have to be obligated in the same degree, for not everyone has the same feeling, and in degree the latter, in fact, is very varied. At bottom we have only one feeling, namely pleasure and pain, and this is the judgement upon our overall well-being. There are various kinds of sense, but only one feeling of pleasure. If there were several feelings, or a power of distinguishing by satisfaction, we could not distinguish feeling by degree. We compare with one another the pleasure at a fine speech and the pleasure of eating a dish.

Shaftesbury, a student of Locke, first proposed this principle. One might still grant the moral feeling, if it were a question of the mind's incentives to morality; but not as a principle for the judgement of moral action. It may be the receptivity of our will, to be moved by moral laws as incentives. The judgement of morality consists in objective principles, but the incentive is subjective; this makes the will practical. If reason itself can determine our will, then it has moral feeling. Reason attends either to the interest of the inclinations, or to its own interest. In the first case it is   29:626
subservient, but in the other, legislative. If reason determines the will through the moral law, it has the force of an incentive, and in that case has, not autonomy merely, but also autocracy. It then has both legislative and executive power. The autocracy of reason, to determine the will in accordance with moral laws, would then be the moral feeling. Man does really possess the force for this, if only he is taught to perceive the strength and necessity of virtue. He has within him the source for conquering everything. One of the ancient writers says: Were virtue to be conceived in a wholly pure form, it would have to be loved by all men. But this has never been done. If pragmatic motivating grounds are used for the purpose, then these are slippery, for often this does not occur. *Inventa lege inventa est fraus.*[1]

Moral feeling is inner reverence for the law. Sympathy is far more useful, but does not constitute moral dispositions; it is pathological, and

---

[1] by inventing laws you create offences

also to be found in animals. Moral feeling does not pertain to the giving of laws, but is the basis for their execution; a criterion for the good it cannot, however, be, for feeling is different in everyone, and one cannot contend about it, because nobody can communicate his feeling to another. The good, however, has to be universally valid. If someone says that he feels the truth, then the other can do nothing with him. It is a refuge of idiots to say that they feel it to be true. Morality must be based on *a priori* grounds.

4. The rational inner principles. These are drawn from perfection. The principle of perfection is not adverse to morality, but nor can it contribute anything thereto. It is an empty husk. Make yourself perfect, it says, or seek all the perfections in your person, which may serve as means to any sort of given ends. This was the postulate of Wolff and Baumgarten. It may also be so interpreted, that what is good without any restriction, is perfection regarded as an end; seek, therefore, perfection that is good in itself, or an end in itself; or seek absolute moral perfection. Here, however, is mere tautology. For if we want to know what the ground of this perfection is, and receive as an answer: Seek perfection, then it all comes to the same. To be sure, there are also perfections that are regarded as means; but to seek these would be pragmatic and not moral. All this is

29:627 good, but not without restriction, being good only if a good will is present.

5. The outer rational, or theological principle. If I conceive of a most perfect will, I can view all moral laws as commands of this will. Not as arbitrary commands, however, but as necessary ones. This principle of morality stemming from the divine will is the theological principle; that of self-love the pathological principle; while the inner rational is the transcendental or metaphysical principle. The rational principles have necessity, indeed, but not of a practical kind. The theological principle depends on a being whose existence is inferred from reason, but only insofar as the latter is made a ground for experience of the world. It, too, is a metaphysical principle.

It seems as though, in duty, the will of a legislator underlies, not anything we do by our own will, but what we do by the will of another. Yet this other will is not that of another being; it is only our own will, insofar as we make it general, and regard it as a universal rule. Such a will operates as a universal, not as a private will. My private will often fails to coincide with my will, taken as a universal rule.

People think that morality should not take precedence over the divine will, so that I cannot say that God tells us to perform actions because they are duties; they are duties, rather, because God tells us to do them. But in that case the moral laws would be arbitrary, and we should not perceive the slightest necessity in them. They would be *statuta*, having no power to bind on their own account, but acquiring it through the will of another. Transgression, too, would have no abhorrency in itself, and might even be made permissible in its turn, since the cause of it would lie, not in the action, but merely in God's will. By what means, however, are we to be obligated to obey the divine law? We would have, in that case, to know God's will, not from the nature of the action, because it does not reside there, but from revelation. A nation, therefore, that had no revelation, would thus be bound to no duties either; but even were God to have revealed Himself to everyone, the action would still have no morality. If actions are not grounded upon duty, the cause of their performance must be the authority of the overlord; yet that is not moral, but merely legal. Actions, in that case, will be based upon fear and hope. A created law is called *sanctio.*[*m*] Moral laws as *sanctiones* seem at first to be very desirable for morality; but if religion is made prior to morality, the first principle becomes: Obey the divine will, and with that the whole of morality is destroyed. You know the necessity of morality, and must also know that God is the supreme executor of its laws. Religion is nothing else but morality and theology combined. Prior to morality, theology is not possible. In morality there are laws, but there is no executor for them. At times the outward rascal is a better man than he who neglects to act, for fear of God. All religion, if morality is built upon it, rests on nothing but a currying of favours. If the law has been arbitrarily instituted by God, He can also, to be sure, dispense us from it.

29:628

The principle of morality is located in sensibility, either directly in the sensory pleasingness of an action, viz., in moral feeling; or in the consequences of actions, so far as they are in accordance with our inclination, viz., in pathological feeling; it is also placed in the understanding. If the understanding is to be practical, it cannot have amenities in view, but rather perfection, and this either our own perfection, i.e., the metaphysical principle, or the concept of a most perfect being, i.e., the theological principle. But we have seen that neither sensibility nor understanding furnish us the principle. The faculty of desire, that legislates, is the will, when I desire a thing under the conception of a rule. If the will simply remains over, and must be considered insofar as it is a law unto itself, then it is the principle; but it is not the principle of morality, insofar as it borrows the law from sensibility or understanding. The principle of morality is thus the Idea of a will, insofar as it is a law unto itself. The will, whose maxims can hold good as universal laws, is a law unto itself, for what it wills is always a universal law, and that is the good will. In this way the meanest human understanding can easily discern whether a thing be right or wrong, for it merely has to ask itself whether that thing could be a universal law. The agreement of an action with the principle of my will, as a universal legislator, is thus the principle of morality. If we cannot consider our will to be universally legislative, we reject the action. A principle of morality must at the same time be comprehensible to the meanest

[*m*] decree

understanding, because every man must possess it, and such is the case here. But how, then, is it possible for men to proceed so often merely according to their private opinions? The universality of the rule is holy to everyone, but we all want to retain for ourselves the right of being able, at times, to make exceptions to it, in that we always think that it could not do much harm.

The principles aforementioned are principles of heteronomy; but this is a principle of the autonomy of the will, in that, in all its actions, the will can regard itself as self-legislating. Autonomy is legislation of another sort, where there is neither feeling, nor inclination, nor speculative reason, nor another will; my actions, in this case, are good insofar as I can consider my will to be self-legislating therein. This gives to my morality an exalted worth. But why must I regard myself as universally legislative? If I picture to myself a kingdom of natural things, that are purposively ordered, even though the things themselves neither entertain the purposes, nor are causes of their existence, then that is the kingdom of nature under heteronomy. But I can also picture a kingdom of purposes with autonomy, which is the kingdom of rational beings, who have a general system of ends in view. In this realm, we consider ourselves as those who obey the law, but also as those who give laws. God is the supreme law-giver. Subordination under the law is duty.

The autonomy of our will greatly elevates our worth. The members of a kingdom of ends, whose ruler is God, are the true intellectual world. Augustine and Leibnitz called it the kingdom of grace. In the realm of ends, God is the supreme ruler; in the realm of nature, the ultimate cause. . . .

[OF JURISPRUDENCE]

29:631   . . . *Honeste vive, neminem laede, suum cuique tribue,* are formulae of Ulpian's, and also classical precepts of practical philosophy. *Honeste vive* is the principle of ethics, *neminem laede* that of law *in statu naturali,* and *suum cuique tribue* also that of law, but *in statu civili.*"

1. *Honeste vive* (live honourably), i.e. truly honour what universally has a worth. What necessarily has a worth for everyone possesses dignity, and he who possesses it has inner worth. A good will alone confers this dignity upon us. So the rule runs: So act, that in your actions you necessarily draw general respect upon yourself. Men are very discriminating, even in their commonest moral judgements. They separate off from morality everything that is alien, and recognize nothing to be moral, save what has been purified of this dross. They always ascribe the more worth to such an action, since the freer the agent is, in doing it, from sensory impulses, the

" in a state of nature/in the civil state

more he has acted simply from moral motivating grounds. That is also the only way to compel the esteem of others. This proposition is at the same time a principle of true ambition. If a man has many talents, but is immoral, he is nonetheless a worthless fellow. The formula also signifies as follows: Act so that you are worthy of honour in your own eyes. The motivating ground must be, not honour, but worthiness of honour. This principle also gives us the motivating ground for virtue. Ethics applies to all duties, in regard to motives, but is distinct from *jus.*

2. *Neminem laede.* The principle of freedom is the principle of external freedom; the restriction of freedom under the condition whereby alone it can co-exist with that of everyone else. All legal duties can be coerced. The principle *neminem laede* is a purely negative one; the other, affirmative though indirectly so. It tells us, not to avoid offending people, but never to injure anyone's rights. It is a *lex vetiti.* If I do what another can demand of me, as of right, I have rendered him nothing, but have taken away nothing that is his. Juridical laws are really just duties of omission. The whole of law contains merely negative duties.

3. *Suum cuique tribuere.* This is the *jus naturae publicum,* insofar as it is the principle of the possibility of a *status civilis.* It runs: Enter into the state of an external rectitude. In the *status naturae* we have inner laws, but there is no public law or authority there. Since no man is bound to act according to the judgement of others, there has to be an external tribunal, authority and law. *Tribuere* means, here, to determine what does or does not belong to the *suum alterius.*⁰ In the *status naturae,* nobody can determine what is his right or not. So this rule signifies: Enter into that state in which his right can be determined to everyone. Juridical actions have no honour, but are merely moral actions. Give to everyone his own, means nothing else but, allow him what is his. The *status naturae* has no public laws, tribunal or authority. There is no certain human law there. Hence the rule says: Enter into the condition, or *status,* of *justitia distributiva;* accord to others a guarantee for the security of their right in the *status civilis.* 29:633

Among *leges* of every kind, there is, moreover, a *lex perfectiva,* which runs: Act according to the laws of the greatest duty, or what is perfectly suited to your duty; do what is best. *Leges* are either *stricte obligantes,*ᵖ in which there are no exceptions, or *late obligantes,* where exceptions are possible; the latter, indeed, are really no *leges,* for they do not determine *a priori* what, and how much, needs to be done. How much I could do without, and what part of my resources I might therefore employ in charities, cannot be determined. He who regards all the laws of morality as *late obligantes* is called a *latitudinarius.* People also say: *Nulla regula sine*

⁰ possession of another
ᵖ strictly/broadly obligating

exceptione,[q] but that is false. If the rule is empirical, the statement holds, since my experience does, indeed, not extend to all possible cases, and thus may have exceptions. So there are such rules, which are general but not universal. We are happy, indeed, to make rules, though experience only yields generality. But moral laws are not empirical, and thus they have no *latitudo.* If a moral rule contains merely grounds for acting (*rationes obligandi* but *non obligantes*),[r] it is a law that has *latitudo,* and is better called a *praeceptum* or *norma. Lex* is that to which there are no exceptions. Moral *latitudinarii* are dangerous people.

[q] no rule without exceptions
[r] grounds of obligation, but not to an obligator

PART IV

Notes on the lectures of Mr. Kant on the metaphysics of morals

(BEGUN OCTOBER 14, 1793)
NOTES TAKEN BY
JOHANN FRIEDRICH VIGILANTIUS

§1. Philosophic and even scientific knowledge from rational concepts either has to do with the form of thinking, viz. logic, as the formal part of philosophy, or relates to objects themselves, and the laws under which they stand; the latter constitutes the material part of philosophy, whose objects must reduce *absolutely* to *nature* and *freedom* and their laws, and is thus divisible into

27:479

a. The philosophy of natural laws, or physics;
b. The philosophy of moral laws.

The former, in a more general sense, might be called physiology, and the latter eleutheriology. But the last-mentioned is actually concerned with developing the Idea of freedom (cf. the treatise on this subject by Prof. Ulrich of Jena, 1788). Both are based on pure or rational concepts, and hence not only the underlying laws of nature here, but also the moral laws, are founded on *principia a priori;* whence the two topics constitute that part of philosophy we call metaphysics, in that it assesses them according to pure principles (independent of all experience), whereas the historical sciences are assessed by empirical, *conditioned* principles, given in experience.

N.B. The metaphysic of nature is distinct from empirical physics, in that it develops the laws of nature purely *a priori*, as they exist independently of all experience, and is separated forthwith into the philosophic part, or metaphysic of nature *in specie*, i.e. that which is concerned with pure rational concepts; whereas the mathematical part at least has corresponding objects of experience as its subject-matter, insofar as it requires the construction of concepts in the imagination.

Metaphysics properly means *omne, quod trans physicam est;*[a] the *oppositum* of physics can therefore be concerned only with truths that are founded on *principia a priori*, or on supersensible principles, whose supersensible Idea is that of right and duty; it being understood that while, *in concreto*, we can certainly attach to these truths the corresponding objects in experience, we nevertheless develop such truths purely *in abstracto*, and thereby vault up into the boundless, so far as the limits of reason permit.

27:480

§2. The metaphysic of morals is concerned especially with the use of the freedom of the human will, according to rules of law. Now here

a. *Freedom of the will as such* is the accountability, or mode of human action that can be imputed to the agent, and *morals* is the name for the use of freedom according to the laws of reason.
b. The principle of freedom is independent of all experience, because reason imposes on man the laws of obligation.

---

[a] everything that is beyond physics

    c. He therefore neither can nor should look for them in experience, nor should he test the extent to which they correspond with experience. So conflict with experience does not abolish the law of reason, nor does experience, on the other hand, make right what is actually observed and brought about in consequence of it. And hence, too,

    d. The concept of what is right, or the rational Idea of obligation, on which the metaphysic of morals must be erected, is founded on reality; for since reason enjoins it unconditionally, it must be possible in itself.

It is thus a stupid opinion of the empiricists, that metaphysic of morals can have no influence on the constitution of the state, because (they say) experience shows both that in the history of all peoples the latter, whether savage or civilized, invariably maintain a defensive posture, and also that the application of this metaphysic is impossible; for it comes down solely to this:

    a. whether in state-craft principles of reason are fundamental and must be employed, and

    b. whether, if this must be done, these principles are authentic.

27:481

Now it can be shown *a priori* with apodeictic certainty, that duty and justice are the foundation of the political constitution, since otherwise force and injustice would have to determine the fortune of the state. But the metaphysic of morals has the laws of justice as its principle, so its applicability is beyond doubt. That we find in experience no constitution that does not have fundamental maxims deviating from this (e.g., that there has never yet been a state founded on a purely peaceful state-system) is not a valid objection; and likewise we can completely abstract here from the fact that application is not possible. The principle of the metaphysic of morals does not become a chimera, for all that, but retains its reality, since the latter attaches, not only to such principles as have an object corresponding to them in experience, but also to those of which it can be shown that they ought necessarily to be applied; and the latter is the case here.

    c. Now the laws of freedom are either

      1. *purely necessary*, or *leges objective mere necessariae.*[b] These are found only in God. or

      2. *necessitating, necessitantes.* These are found in man, and are objectively necessary, but subjectively contingent. Man, that is, has an urge to trespass against these laws, even when he knows them, and thus the legality and morality of his actions are merely contingent. Necessitation by the moral law, to act in accordance with it, is

[b] laws objectively necessary as such

obligation. The action itself, by the moral law, is *duty,* and the theory of duty is the foundation of moral philosophy, or the doctrine of ethics.

N.B. The laws produce the causality in actions, i.e., the property whereby the agent becomes the cause of the action, e.g., man, when he acts according to laws of freedom. The necessity of action according to laws of freedom constitutes duty. It is quite otherwise with the laws of nature, with the cause whereby the effect of nature is brought about, than it is with the effect of freedom. The accountability in the latter case is altogether absent in the former; e.g. the effect of the wind, and an exhalation on the part of a man.

§3. The ancients comprehended the whole of moral philosophy as a genus under the term *ethics,* and took it to cover both morals and the doctrine of justice. The two differ as the legality and morality of an action, depending, that is, on whether the motive to it is either the coercion or punishment associated with the law, or the law itself, and the resultant conception of fulfilling a duty, e.g., whether I pay governmental taxes from fear of execution, or do so, even without being required, from a duty to support the state. Nowadays we understand by ethics only the doctrine of the morality of our actions in particular, and under theory of justice that of their legality. Cicero, on the other hand, deals, in the *De officiis,* with the whole of moral philosophy. In the modern age we divide philosophy into (a) theoretical, and (b) practical philosophy, i.e., the science of the laws of things, and likewise of the laws of actions. The former embraces logic, as the formal, and physics as the material part. The latter, on the other hand, is split up into 27:482

(1) the *morally-practical,* i.e. the doctrine of duties or moral philosophy, ethics and theory of virtue, and

(2) the *technically-practical;* the latter signifies the *teaching of skill,* including that of utilizing the things of nature for our purposes, but particularly covers the *technically-practical doctrine of prudence,* i.e., the skill of using free men for our purposes. This is interwoven, even by Cicero, into his ethics. We might also give this subsection of practical philosophy the name of pragmatic philosophy; it includes, for example, history, if we employ the latter as a means to prudence in our conduct.

§4. The ancient philosophers, especially the Greek sects, when they made enquiry into ethics, reduced everything to the question: What is the *summum bonum?* By this they meant the highest good attainable in the world, to which we must nevertheless approach, even if we cannot reach it, and must therefore approximate to by fulfilment of the means.

They thus separated the Idea of this highest good from the notion that it could be apportioned to the human race in any other fashion than by human powers. On *a priori* principles they assumed that the Idea of the highest good would have to be sought in the totality of human ends, i.e., in the final end of all mankind, and could thus be attained only by fulfilling all human purposes with a view to the purpose of the whole.

27:483 Now in order to be able to define the *summum bonum* in this fashion, there appeared, on closer examination, to be two elements, namely

a. The principle of happiness, and
b. The principle of morality.

Since the latter consists in the worthiness to be happy, it was undoubtedly the supreme condition of happiness and its existence, and thus the prime requisite for the highest good. To be happy, it is of course necessary that man behave in a manner adequate to the moral laws, just as it is certain that every deviation from the law is a violation of his duty, and thus an action contrary to the end of man. There is also imprinted in man, moreover, an urge to change his condition, and hence a need in him to satisfy the ends of mankind, and to that extent he requires the state of happiness, in order, by the practice of virtue, to participate in the hope of enjoying the good fortune and welfare that he promises himself; for should it be impossible, by fulfilment of virtuous duties, to obtain any enjoyment, his endeavours would be pointless, and virtue an empty delusion.

But instead of unifying the two principles, so as thereby to define the highest good, the sects in fact separated them from one another, in that they proceeded by reason's maxim, to the effect, that a thing may only be derived from a single principle (*entia, i.e., principia praeter necessitatem non sunt multiplicanda*),ᶜ and subordinated one to the other, viz.:

a. for some, the principle of morality to that of happiness, and
b. for others, the principle of happiness to that of morality.

I. Epicurus was the founder of the doctrine of happiness, in which he located the highest good. For him, in other words, the latter was *voluptas*, i.e., well-being and enjoyment of life, while observing the necessary prudence. It was not merely sensual enjoyment; on the contrary, he thought it a duty to sacrifice that to the performance of virtuous actions. Pure mental enjoyment was the pleasure that arises from the performance of virtuous acts. An adequacy of conduct was for him the means of attaining the highest good. Wisdom, as he saw it, was the capacity for being able to attain that good, and this he founded on the knowledge of it, and of all means leading thereto, which may afford this pleasure, and on the use of it

27:484 for that purpose. The foundation of it was thus a great enlargement of the knowledge of all means of pleasure, and the end could be attained only by employing them, so it was a positive principle, and coupled with activity.

Diogenes and Antisthenes proceeded likewise from the principle of

---

ᶜ entities, i.e., principles, are not to be multiplied beyond necessity happiness, but in a totally opposite direction; they posited the greatest good in the *abstine*, i.e., the pleasure of being able to do without, and thus in the enjoyment of life under the fewest possible requirements, where the Epicurean, by contrast, could not pile up enough in order to feel enjoyment. Hence their symbol was the club of Hercules, signifying strength of mind with self-sufficiency. Also Diogenes' tub, i.e., a container made of clay, or hewn out of the rock, for living in, and the throwing away of the potsherd, as soon as Diogenes perceived that he might scoop up water with his hand.

Rousseau comes closest to this principle in the modern age.

Professor Kant thinks that the principle, were it attainable, would be preferable on the system of Diogenes even for the Epicurean, since there is more pleasure contained in doing without than in the burden of all the means acquired for the purpose; save that to set out the principle of the highest good on *this footing alone* is in both cases objectionable, since morality is quite necessarily required here as a special foundation.

II. The sect of Zeno, or stoicism, like that of the Platonists, proceeded, on the other hand, solely from the principle of morality; they assumed that the highest good was to follow the rules of wisdom and virtue, to despise all evil, and to be content solely with the feeling of righteousness; hence the maxim, that we should wrap ourselves in virtue, as if in a cloak. But to abstract from all enjoyment is contrary to nature, since there are so many natural needs that call for satisfaction. Plato, in particular, apart from the principle of morality he derived from the power of reason in man, assumed also a mystical principle, which he located in the influence of a supreme being on the human mind.

If we take these different opinions together, the result would be as follows:

None of the assumed principles is sufficient by itself; they have to be united, and this by a supreme being, as sovereign ruler of the world, and hence by belief in a deity, and in His power to accord man morality and happiness in due proportion.   27:485

Thus the highest philosophical ideal would be a theological one.

§5. The subject-matter of morals is the rules of duty. These rules are never theoretical, containing only those conditions under which a thing is; they are at all times purely practical, stating only those conditions under which a thing ought to come about, i.e., those rational laws which contain the sufficient reason determining to action, and which would also effect the latter in accordance with rational laws, if reason had sufficient free power to operate.

The distinction among practical rules refers to the fact that some of them are natural laws, and others moral ones. The former never indicate that such-and-such ought to happen; they point merely to the conditions under which a thing does happen. Moral laws, on the other hand, always have to do with the will and its freedom, and essentially these laws are so marked out by reason, that if they alone had influence, and contained the only ground for the reality of the action, no deviation from them would ever result. Thus everyone would pay his debts, for example, without a reminder. Now because man is prevented from giving free and unhindered attention to the laws of reason, insofar as contrary inclinations, sensory urges and the ends that are coupled to his actions make him inclined to transgression, it therefore becomes necessary for practical rules among men to be at all times imperatives; rules, that is, to which his will must be subjected, in order to determine what should happen. And this is why the moral acts of men, precisely because they are indeed subject to the laws of reason, whereas man does not follow reason quite unconditionally, are described as *objectively necessary*, but *subjectively contingent*. It is therefore necessary that he be *constrained* to morally free action; this constraint (*necessitatio*) is the determination of the human will, by means of which the action becomes necessary, and it is a *moral* constraint, because it comes about through moral rules. This *necessitatio moralis*, which is always expressed by an imperative, is therefore what we call *obligatio*.

27:486

In God the nature of action is likewise that it accords with the moral laws which are formed by the concepts of the highest reason; save only that since no subjective possibility of contravening such laws is possible in His case, His actions being morally necessary both objectively and subjectively, no imperative is appropriate to Him either, since however He acts, He does so in accordance with the moral laws, and will at all times act freely and unconditionally. Human actions, on the other hand, if they are to be moral, have need of practical imperatives, i.e., of practical determinations of the will to an action, in virtue of its objectively necessary but subjectively contingent quality; and these objectively necessary determinations of the will are expressed by an *ought*, or *necessitation*.

All imperatives, then, are either (I) Conditioned, and these are

a. Problematic, i.e., imperatives of skill;
b. Pragmatic, i.e., imperatives of prudence;

or (II) Unconditioned or categorical, i.e. imperatives of morality and duty. Categorical imperatives differ essentially from the problematic and pragmatic, in that the determining ground of the action lies solely in the law of moral freedom, whereas in the others it is the associated ends that bring the action to reality, and are thus the condition of it.

Problematic imperatives differ in turn from pragmatic, in that the ends in the former are possible and optional, whereas in the latter they are determinate.

The problematic include, for example, all mathematical problems, in which the laws for solving the problem constitute the imperative, in that they prescribe what has to be done should one wish to solve it, e.g., divide a straight line into two equal parts. The determination fundamental to fulfilment of the task is in this case conditionally necessary, since it comes in only if I wish to make use of it. The purpose itself is one of technical skill, and is not so determined as to preclude the existence of similar imperatives for any other given purpose of skill as well; the imperative itself has only a possible end in view. All means, therefore, of promoting culture are problematic imperatives, in that by the given rules of skill only the fitness for achieving all possible ends is supposedly attained to; all actions which take place on that footing lead merely to possible intentions, since it depends on the individual whether he wishes to employ such actions, and indeed whether he wants to obtain the skill; they rest, therefore, on conditioned problematical fulfilment. Pragmatic imperatives, on the other hand, have only the general happiness of mankind as their object, and state the means of employing other people to promote one's happiness. The end is therefore generally determined, namely to create the greatest amount of well-being, and the rules of the skill needed for that purpose are pragmatic imperatives. They are merely conditioned, however, because they are needed only if one wishes to attain this well-being in human life, and so they cease to be operative if one abstracts from that.

27:487

Finally we have, by contrast, human actions that are necessary without any end, and for whose existence no intention or purpose provides the motive. These are the moral actions, whose imperatives therefore have no regard either for skill, or prudence, or happiness, or any other end that might bring the actions into effect; for the necessitation to act lies purely in the imperative alone. These are the categorically unconditioned imperatives, e.g. to keep one's promise or speak the truth. A witness who in giving his testimony consults, on the one hand, the claims of friendship, or on the other, his fear of punishment or revenge, is already determining himself to bear witness in a manner that conflicts with duty, since instead of determining himself by the imperative of duty, he is looking merely to the outcome, as it affects the future state of his happiness, though this should have no influence on the categorical imperative. It is therefore a false opinion of certain philosophers, to have thought the happiness of a man necessary to his end and motive in the performance of moral actions.

In and for itself alone, the rule of my will must at the same time be the sufficient reason for determining it; the act must rest solely on this unconditioned imperative, without being coupled to any end, whether it be of advantage or disadvantage, gain or loss; such material grounds of willing have nothing whatever to do with its (so-called) formal grounds of determination in moral actions.

27:488

The concept of duty, like that of virtue, rests on the necessitation to an action that is bound up with moral necessity. An action having regard to duty and virtue requires a categorical imperative, because even though such actions are in themselves objectively necessary, since they are coupled with an imperative, they will nevertheless be undertaken by the agent according to his decision, merely, i.e., with subjective contingency, unless there be present in him principles of reason that have enjoined upon him the moral necessity of acting; and these rational principles are the categorical imperative that necessitates him to act.

[§6.]   Morality

N.B. All practical rules contain the determination under which a thing exists, and have as their object either nature or freedom. Hence

    a. Natural *laws*, which determine the existence of a thing, and that it comes about in a necessary manner. For example, the influence of the moon on the weather follows in necessary fashion by laws of nature. But here there is never an *ought*, such as freedom always demands of action, although Lichtenberg remarks, wholly in jest, that the moon ought really not to have this alleged influence (i.e., so far as we know the rules of nature).

    b. *Rules* of free action and free choice, whereby the action becomes possible by free choice and is objectively necessary, i.e. rules which determine that a thing *ought* to happen. But this ought in actions is precisely that which should indicate that, even when it does not occur, it would always come about nonetheless, if the rules of reason were the sole determining ground of the action.

The formulae here employed are called imperatives, by which we mean all practical rules of freedom, both technically-practical as well as morally-practical, in that they collectively presuppose an *ought* or a *necessitation*.

27:489
Every ought, that is, expresses an objective necessity, which is nonetheless at the same time subjectively contingent, i.e., it implies (1) that I will something; (2) that the determining ground to action, and the act itself, would only be in accordance with the laws of reason if it lay solely with me in reason; (3) that, notwithstanding the action ought to occur by rational laws, it nevertheless does not always result from them, owing to its subjective contingency, rooted in the impulses of human nature. – These conflicting qualities of the action together contain, under the term 'ought', the necessitation to act, which would cease to operate as such, if the subject were not deflected from following the laws of reason. Now insofar as this necessitation results from the moral law, i.e., in that the action, which would not have occurred from any impulse of the subject's own, is made necessary by the moral law, and he is thereby constrained to obey it, it is obligation, engagement, and the act to which he is necessitated by the moral law is duty. So a necessitation is conceivable only where a contravention of moral laws is possible, and hence a thing can be morally necessary without being a duty, which would happen if the subject were at all times

to act without necessitation in accordance with the moral law; for then a duty or obligation so to act would not be present; hence this does not hold of a morally perfect being, in that such a being acts solely from holiness, i.e., from the congruence of his willing with the moral law, and his acts are simply objectively necessary, and never subjectively contingent. Where there is no necessitation, there also no moral imperative, no obligation, duty, virtue, ought or constraint is conceivable. Hence the moral laws are also called *laws of duty*, because they presuppose an agent subject to impulses of nature. Thus God may be thought of, by contrast, as a being that is *alone holy*, i.e., has the property that He follows the moral laws without necessitation, His will being already congruent with them; that is *alone blessed*, i.e., is in complete possession and satisfied enjoyment of all good; and that is *alone wise*, i.e., not only perceives the relation of his action to the ultimate and final end, but also makes the latter the determining ground of what He does.

Like an angel, a being of this kind can in no way be thought of as existing, but to the philosopher is merely an Idea. For if not, it would have to possess needs, impulses and unsatisfied urges in accordance with its physical nature; these urges would have to be in conflict with the moral laws, and then necessitation would be required. Such is man, and hence it is only to him that the moral laws apply, as subject, in the form of laws of duty. In him, too, is virtue alone thinkable, therefore, since only where necessitation is the ground can we suppose, in consequence, a steadfast determination in obeying the moral laws. 27:490

But from this it is also certain that every obligation is forthwith associated with a moral constraint, and that it is contrary to the nature of duty to *enjoy* having duties incumbent upon one; it is necessary, rather, that man's impulses should make him disinclined to fulfil the moral laws, and that these impulses should be overcome only through the authority of the latter, without it being possible to say that these laws demand respect in the manner of painful or despotic commands. Assuming that man's fulfilment of the moral laws can be accomplished only under a necessitation, it cannot therefore be claimed, as Schiller does in his *Thalia*, where he takes issue with the Kantian critique of reason, that such fulfilment also has a certain *charm* about it, though otherwise, by man's nature, the necessitation requires obedience to the moral laws; if we wish, with Schiller, to assume a worth arising therefrom, it is nothing more than man's respect for the moral law, and that provides no ground for supposing a charm that attracts us to fulfilling it. That is contradicted by the authority of the laws, which enjoins absolute obedience, and awakens resistance and struggle, which we perceive in fulfilling them. The opposite view gets no confirmation from the attraction we feel, after fulfilment of a duty, for the action itself; that is derivable, rather, from the same source as the cheer experienced on getting through work that has cost trouble, and is evidence, rather, of the burdensomeness of duty. It is true that we can find pleasure in virtue and the contemplation of it, but only by the time, and for the reason, that we have already become equipped to fulfil duties, and it is thus easy for us to follow the prescriptions of reason; we thereby take satisfaction in our actions, and in the strengthening of our will to comply with the prescriptions of reason; we contemplate the future with a cheerful heart, and this also improves our physical condition. Finally, even psychological experience tells against Schiller's view: *We would do many things, if only they did not have to be done from duty;* women especially insist that no coercion should be evinced towards them, that it should seem as if they were doing a kindness, when duty tells them to act. It would be good if men were so perfect that they fulfilled their duties from a free impulse, without coercion and law; but this is beyond the horizon of human nature.

27:491

All conditioned or hypothetical imperatives are technically-practical in nature, i.e., they rest on an artistry employed for a purpose, and a skill to be observed in doing so; thus they always say merely what I should do *if I will* this or that. They differ merely in the type of end associated with them. If the latter has to do with the general purpose of humanity, namely happiness, then the rules of action for attaining this general goal are pragmatic imperatives, which are likewise founded on a skill, and *in specie* are called rules of prudence, because here we make use of our skill to employ other people for our ends. But if the intention relates to any arbitrary end, then the rules of the actions for attaining all possible ends, i.e. that men are even capable of having, are called problematic; for example, the art of so clothing our testimony, that we thereby cover up what is detrimental to a friend, without, however, speaking directly contrary to the truth, is problematic; a testimony, on the other hand, which is meant to procure me a benefit, is pragmatic. Technically-practical imperatives stand in contrast to the morally-practical, or imperatives of morality, which determine what must absolutely be done, without any regard for ends.

[§7]. An action, therefore, which is effectuated through the necessitation brought about by the moral law, is *duty.* But now since a man's sensory inclinations are the ground whereby he is affected in such a way as to act contrary to the moral law, and whereby his actions therefore become moral in a subjectively contingent fashion, it is clear that God, who has no animal nature, incurs no duties, since in Him there is no necessitation, and His actions have, on the contrary, only pure objective and subjective necessity. That man, moreover, should act in accordance or adequacy with the moral laws, can occur only insofar as he has repressed and conquered, through the moral law, the inclination he harbours to deviate or do the opposite. The struggle of inclination with the moral law, and the constant disposition (*intentio constans*) to carry out his duties, therefore constitutes what we call *virtue.* The very Latin

27:492

260

word *virtus* originally signifies nothing else but courage, strength and constancy, and the symbol for it indicates the same: a Hercules, with lionskin and club, striking down the hydra, which is the symbol of all vice. So man, by the most steadfast obedience to his duties, can never attain to holiness in his being, nor does he need this in order to be adequate to the moral law, in that by virtue of his subjective constitution he has to be necessitated by that law to fulfil his duties. Were he a holy being, however, he would have no motive for transgressing the moral law; he would have no duty, for want of necessitation, and would in fact be guided to it solely through the objective necessity of his actions, recognized by reason; and it would thus be impossible for him to violate the moral laws.

§8. The concept of duty is closely connected with that of *obligation,* or the dependence of choice on a necessitating law as its proximate cause. The latter, in fact, is necessitation by the moral law; the acting subject can, however, be either

- a. himself necessitated to action thereby, giving rise to *obligatio passiva* or *actio obligati;*[d] or
- b. he may necessitate another to moral action through the law, and then arises *obligatio activa* or *actio obligantis,*[e] which is also expressed through the power of putting the other under obligation. Furthermore, the moral laws express their law-like power to oblige, either
  - a. immediately towards every subject, insofar as the resultant obligations have their ground in the intrinsic nature of mankind; these are *obligationes internae,* e.g. to respect oneself; or
  - b. with respect to one subject, *vis-à-vis* another; these are *obligationes externae.*

§9. To have an obligation anywhere, or be bound to something, is not yet duty; for *rationes obligationis*[f] must be distinguished from duty and its grounds, in that the former are not yet *obligantes,* and do not yet create a duty.   27:493

So if there is thought to be a conflict (collision) of duties, this says no more than that *rationes obligandi* are in conflict with an obligation, or among themselves, and contradict each other; for it is impossible that duties themselves could contradict one another, since two *opposita* cannot both be necessary together; a duty, however, is always so far necessary that another conflicting duty is not simultaneously conceivable; but the grounds of a dutiful action may be exposed to a contradiction, e.g. a brother as witness; in his case, truth is in collision with kinship.

---

[d] the act of one obligated
[e] the act of one who obligates
[f] grounds of obligation

§10. The determining ground of choice (*causa determinans arbitrium*) is *causa impulsiva* to the action, the motivating cause.

N.B. every *causa impulsiva* or trigger of the mind to action is called, *in genere, elater animi,*[g] whether it be *motivum* or *stimulus.*

This motivating cause is called either *motivum* or *stimulus*. A distinction well worth noting, in view of the dual nature of man. For he has both a natural being and a free being.

1. A *motivum* is always a *moral causa impulsiva*, or a determining ground that determines man's *arbitrium tanquam liberum,*[h] i.e. according to the laws of freedom, and thus treats him as a free being. Conversely, the stimulus is the determining cause that determines man's *arbitrium* according to the laws of nature, and is the sensory impulse. We call it a natural cause, or inclination, when, for example, a person is brought by hunger and physical hardship to obey his parents, or to be diligent. Even among animals, these *causae determinantes* operate to possible ends, for taming them, and man is like them in that respect.

N.B. The *causa impulsiva moralis* therefore determines a man to act according to laws of duty, and is thus an objectively necessary determination of the fact that an action *ought* to take place, even if it does not always do so. Conversely, the inclination, the sensory impulse, the *causa impulsiva* according to natural laws, determines merely the action that does take place. In the former, therefore, the ground of determination lies in understanding and reason, in the subject himself, and not in external causes, and hence the action, too, is founded on self-activity (spontaneity), or the ability of man to determine himself through reason. The stimulus, on the other hand, affects man in such a way that he cannot avoid the impression and allure of it, and can only impede or prevent its effect.

2. As a natural being, man can be affected *per stimulum*, though as a free being this means is altogether fruitless. Hence man, insofar as sensory drives are operative upon him, is also quite passive, merely; he has to endure these impulses, since he is totally unable to avoid them. Conversely, motives occur only insofar as man is considered as a free being; they contain his activity, and are thus totally opposed to the state that depends on inclinations. They take their ground from the spontaneity of human willing, which is guided by rational conceptions, quite independently of all determining causes of nature, and thus solely by the moral law.

3. Man can only be affected by the stimulus, never determined to action; as a free being, it is therefore also possible for him to omit all actions to which the impulse of nature attracts him, and which he would undertake as a man of nature.

27:494

[g] generically, a spring of mental action
[h] choice so far as free

4. The stimulus may therefore be called *arbitrium brutum,* and the motive, on the other hand, *arbitrium liberum.* This distinction now leads

§11. to the concept of freedom, which *negatively* consists in the independence of choice from all determination *per stimulos;* so often, that is, as reason is determined by itself, independently of all sensory drives; *positively,* however, it consists in spontaneity, or the ability to determine oneself by reason, without the need for triggers from nature.

The proof that man's actions should occur solely according to the law of freedom will follow below.

§12. Since understanding and reason are to determine the imperative to moral action, the question is: Insofar as it lies in reason, what is the action's determining ground, from which there arises a moral necessitation as the ground of obligation?   27:495

The underlying categorical imperative is a morally practical one, i.e., a law of freedom, and the determining cause a *causa moralis.* Thus the latter cannot, like a natural law, lead man to action in a wholly passive way; he must determine himself and his choice through his reason. Now were he, in acting, to have regard to ends, or means of reaching them, and were the imperative called upon to prescribe them, then the matter of the law expressed in the imperative, and the object of the law as it is given for the action, would be the determining ground of the action, since the *action's end or means* constitutes *the matter of the law.*

N.B. Or rather, every determining ground of choice or willing, that is independent of any conception of law, may reside in some other ground.

This is not possible, since the categorical imperative carries with it an unconditioned moral necessitation, which is founded not at all on the end or purpose of the action; so all that is left is the *form of lawfulness,* which is the determining ground of free action; moral actions, that is, must be performed in compliance with the form of lawfulness, subject as they are to the condition that their maxims be in accordance with lawfulness. The *maxim* of an action differs, that is, from an objective principle in this, that the latter occurs only insofar as we consider the possibility of the action on certain rational grounds, whereas the former includes all subjective grounds of action whatsoever, insofar as they are taken to be real.

N.B. The principle is always objective, and is called a maxim *quoad subjectum.*[i] It is understood as the rule universally acknowledged by reason, while the maxim is the subjectively practical principle, insofar as the subject makes the rule by which he is to act into the motive of his action as well. It is the maximum in determination of the grounds of action.

The formula of the universal imperative would thus be as follows:

[i] as to the subject

You are to act according to that maxim which is qualified for universal legislation, i.e., you are so to act, that the maxim of your action shall become *a universal law*, i.e. would have to be universally acknowledged as such.

In other words, act so that you may present yourself, through the maxim of your action, as universally legislative, i.e., so that the maxim of your action is suitable for universal legislation. In this form of moral action lies, then, the determining ground of obligation, whereby it acquires the force of law.

The qualification of the maxim for universal legislation rests, however, on the agreement of the action with the imperative of reason; for example: You shall absolutely speak the truth, is an imperative of reason, and in application a maxim which reason converts into a universal law. For suppose that someone were to have the maxim, that he might tell an untruth whenever he could thereby obtain great advantage, the question arises, whether this maxim could stand as a universal law. We would then have to presuppose that nobody will tell the truth to his disadvantage, and in that case nobody would continue to have any trust; the liar could thus never succeed in deceiving anyone by lying, and the law would therefore automatically destroy itself. So it is with all perfect duties; if the opposite were to occur, it would so determine the action as to bring about a contradiction with itself, which could never become a universal law. This is inherent in the nature of the unconditioned necessitation of the law, which enjoins fulfilment of duty without end or purpose, and regardless of advantage or disadvantage. Hence, too, *every action is impermissible* whose maxim is unqualified for universal legislation. With so-called imperfect duties, the situation is quite different. Here the action does not straightway abolish itself by the law that contradicts it, for such actions rest on conditioned maxims; it simply can never become man's will, that the action become a universal law. For example, the duty of philanthropy by relieving those in distress; were we to act by a maxim founded on indifference to the suffering and needs of others, it could not be said that such a law was in contradiction to the moral freedom of man. A man might achieve all his aims, while making no claim upon the assistance of others. But since every

subject may fall into a similarly needy condition, this provides the reason why nobody will want to make this maxim into a universal law.

Now if, therefore, the determining ground of moral actions lies, not in the *material part of the law*, namely its end, but in the form of its universal lawfulness, then it is quite wrong to locate it

a. in the personal happiness of the agent; for in that case

1. the categorical imperative of morality would be conditioned and hypothetical, in that it would have to take account of the end of universal happiness, and of the means of obtaining this, but then it would be an imperative of prudence and artifice. In that case, however, it would not say

that a thing ought to happen, unconditionally and absolutely, without regard for the end, and yet this the categorical imperative must do, if it is otherwise to produce duty and obligation, and necessitate thereto. It cannot therefore be enunciated in a conditioned manner.

2. This principle in fact subsumes under it the principle of self-love, so that the artifice we resort to constitutes the means for us, as the end associated with it, to make ourselves happy thereby. But the state of happiness consists in consciousness of enjoying and possessing the means to procure for ourselves all ends that are even possible, and thereby to satisfy all wishes. It is natural that, however diverse the ends may be, the practical rules must be equally diverse as well, viz. as inclination, type of experience and tendency require. Any universality of the principle cannot, in that case, be thought of at all, though that is what we are looking for.

3. To be happy is the universal will of men; but the decision whether a person wills to be pleased or happy also depends, in the first instance, purely on his own decision and willing. So here we lack the ground of duty, moral necessitation; we lack an unconditioned imperative, no coercion can be thought of here that enjoins immediate obligation; the imperative itself can at all times refer only to the means of procuring happiness.

b. The relation of our choice to the *moral feeling* can equally little be the ground of duty; on the contrary, this feeling presupposes such a ground. For man is said to be drawn to a certain material part of the law, namely the well-being that is nevertheless neither happiness nor duty, but moral in character. Now the will becomes affected by the feeling of pleasure and pain, and here, indeed, since the action is to be moral, by the moral law; the agent is supposed, then, to feel pleasure or pain after he has fulfilled or transgressed the law; this effect, therefore, cannot be conceived without presupposing an idea of the concept of duty as its ground. So the agent must have knowledge of the law and its binding character, before he can be filled with pleasure or pain on obeying or violating it, and before he then couples self-satisfaction or dissatisfaction with his action (for these are surely the feelings of pleasure and pain). The *moral feeling*, or consciousness of procuring self-satisfaction for oneself by following the moral law, is thus an end, and hence not the ground of duty. 27:498

N.B. or explained by causes: does there exist in the domain of feeling a pleasure or pain from the act that complies with, or is contrary to, the laws? It is altogether a fiction.

c. Finally, even the *divine will* cannot be regarded as the supreme principle of morality; on the contrary, even this presupposes knowledge of our duty,

N.B. and yet that will is all that would be left, if the supreme principle were neither the principle of happiness, nor that of moral feeling, nor even that of the form of lawfulness in our action.

Here, indeed, the will of God can be thought of no otherwise than as binding upon us. Yet should it obligate us, there would still have to be the *idea of a duty there already, in order for us to know thereby* that a thing is in accordance with God's will,

N.B. and it is only because a thing is recognized as a duty that we can actually infer it to be in accordance with the divine will.

Should this not be God's purpose and will, then the stricter the command that would be coupled with the principle of happiness as His end, and the supreme principle of morality would in that case have to be derived from the principle of happiness, to which God as creator of happiness would have ordained the means. But through reason we recog-27:499 nize only duties, and should these be founded in the divine will, then God's commandments do indeed present us with our duties; but now we cannot, as would have to happen, discern God's commands in the absence of, and prior to, our duties; on the contrary, we first have to recognize our duties, before we discern God's commands; so the latter would be based upon the former, and could not be the first principle. It is, indeed, undoubtedly very congenial to human nature, to think of duties in conjunction with consciousness of the existence of a supreme being who *wills* them; but such willing is not the principle of the *ought*, and this consideration can have influence only in passing judgement on the consequences of our actions.

§13. Now if moral actions are to be grounded in the form of lawfulness, the moral laws must have their basic determination in a law-giving power which (so Kant says) constitutes legislation. Moral legislation is the law-giving of human reason, as which it is the law-giver in regard to all laws, and is so through itself. This is the autonomy of reason, whereby, that is, it determines the laws of free choice through its own law-giving, independently of any influence, and the principle of the autonomy of reason is thus the individual legislation of choice by reason. The opposite would be heteronomy, i.e., legislation that is founded in like fashion on grounds other than the freedom of reason.

Thus if, for example, the principle of universal happiness were to be the basis for determination of the moral laws, it would be a question of how far our needs were satisfied in their entire totality by following these laws; but here laws of nature are involved, and the moral laws would have to be subject to them, so that reason would have to obey the laws of nature and sensibility, and that in a necessary fashion (for in the physical order this is so anyway). But this would obviously put an end to the autonomy of reason, and thus be heteronomy.

But that the determining grounds of laws of duty cannot be built upon natural laws is already evidenced by the quality of these laws of duty, namely that they must be necessary and universally valid. Now the laws of 27:500 nature as ground, would admittedly bring necessary consequences and

266

effects in their train, but universally valid they would never be, and to that extent would not be objectively necessary and unconditioned either; for determination of the means to procure our happiness, and the satisfaction of our needs, is obviously founded upon experience; the principles derived therefrom would thus be empirical, and since empirical principles can never give rise to more than the natural quality of things, and are unable to yield the basic determinations under which they are possible, they would never become universal laws of moral duty. Experience itself contradicts the idea; for example, the means to happiness are too diverse to be determinable in advance, so long as there is no agreement on the ways in which a person may seek to become happy; and thus a different method is needed for the miserly, the restlessly busy, or the phlegmatically calm, etc. Still less are the moral feeling, or the principle of the divine will, qualified to give universal laws of morality; this principle is founded, rather, in reason alone, and is the autonomy of reason.

All autonomy of reason must therefore be independent, (a) of all empirical principles, such as the principle of personal happiness, which may be called the physiological principle; (b) of the aesthetic principle, or that of moral feeling; and (c) of any alien will (the theological principle).

§14. But now how is a categorical necessitation to duty possible, and how can it be demonstrated? Not so easily as the conditioned imperatives and their *principia*, for whether these be problematic or pragmatic, the necessitation rests in every case on the end to be attained, to which the imperatives prescribe the means; thus, once it is established that I aspire to this form of cultivation or that, or wish to seek my happiness in this or that way, it follows automatically that I must employ the means that lead there. But the categorical principle is unconditioned, excludes all objects of choice that can yield only the condition of my action, is to be founded purely on the authority of reason, and must determine the action only according to the form of lawfulness. This cannot, indeed, be proved in any way, nor illustrated, and yet every being that is conscious of his freedom must also think that he necessitates himself to duty through the autonomy of his reason. Whence this comes, and how it happens, can not, indeed be determined; but that it is so, can be illustrated in the following way. 27:501

1. If we presuppose, that is, that a being has freedom of the will, or free choice, then this choice, too, must be capable of determination by the mere form of lawfulness of his actions. For *ex adductis*[j] it cannot be assumed that the principle of the choice to be determined lies in an object of purposiveness, sensibility or alien will, without perpetrating a heteronomy; it is supposed, after all, to be independent of any object of choice, and must therefore lie in the autonomy of reason; but the latter determines itself categorically, and hence the principle of duty is coupled, by a

[j] from what has been stated

categorical principle, with this freedom of the will, and the necessitation to duty results *absolutely* and unconditionally through the autonomy of reason. Even freedom must, of course, be determined by grounds that are present, but they cannot be natural laws, since these contain the matter of the laws, to which, however, the choice of freedom pays no heed; such choice must therefore determine itself without an object, i.e., through itself, and this determination must rest solely on form.

2. But conversely, in this way man, if he stands under the moral law, i.e., if the determining ground of his action and willing is simply the form of lawfulness, must be absolutely free. For the moral law demands a categorical imperative, and is thus unlike any material laws, such as natural laws would be, and man is thus independent of natural laws in regard to the determination of his morality – his dutiful determinations result, therefore, from reason, and moreover from himself, and hence are free.

§15. But man is also at the same time a natural being, and to that extent subject to the determining grounds of nature. He is, in fact, implicated in his actions with grounds of nature, which as man of nature he must follow; for example, his needs require ends and actions undertaken in accordance with them; the grounds of nature determine him thereto.

This relationship in which man is placed, to the means, effects and causes of nature, is mechanism, or natural necessity. In this connection his actions are guided by natural determining grounds, and proceed from him, *qua* man of nature, in a necessary manner, since every action here results merely as an effect, which, like everything in nature, must have its cause, and the latter are simply the *causae determinantes a natura positae*,[k] the natural determinations of his actions; in the end, all the actions that he undertakes *qua* man of nature are predetermined, i.e., are to be regarded as effects of preceding causes. They are thus incapable, too, of being imputed to him; man finds himself in a perpetual state of receptivity, which has determined his every action, the latter being wholly lacking in spontaneity, and therefore no more avoidable by him than imputable to him. For example, a man strikes another dead; if he is considered merely as a man of nature, his action is exactly like the effect when a roof-tile takes away a man's life. He is acting solely by laws of nature; he can thus, moreover, introduce, execute and conceal the fatal blow in the subtlest manner; and thus even his reason, as subjected to the laws of nature, can be considered devoid of all freedom; he is guided solely by the purpose he wishes to attain by the blow, for example, the victim's money, and is using his reason in accordance with this purpose. The ground of his action is thus mere physical incentive, and the effect has to be regarded like any other effect of its cause, insofar as his physical strength has concurred with it, and has been set in motion by avarice, poverty, etc. These causes,

27:502

[k] determining causes posited by nature

of course, such as need, poverty or hot temper and savagery, likewise have their physical ground in the want of cultivation of his mental powers, and the latter in faulty or defective education; so we see that, already from the agent's youth onward, there begin the causes that have produced their effects, and that the latter have in turn become causes of subsequent effects, right up to the final deed. On this relationship of cause to effect by natural determination there rest the predetermined consequences, as an effect of causes, and to that extent we may assume that this man had to strike the other dead.

The philosophers' idea of determinism is, on the contrary, erroneous. They distinguish, that is, from a system of freedom, the doctrine whereby man is regarded as an unfree being, but quite falsely set up *determinism*, as the opposing relationship in which man is considered under laws of nature. But every act of man must be determined, only with this difference, that if this ensues according to the law of free choice, it must come about quite independently of all preceding circumstances; but apart from that, and *in* 27:503 *opposito*, man is determined with respect to the time-order, as to the manner in which causes and effects follow, and actions are undertaken for the attainment of all possible ends; the action and the man appear as phenomena; but this must be called predeterminism, and not determinism.

All actions can be regarded either as occurrences in nature, or under the condition that we have a certain obligation to them, and only in the latter case can they be accounted to us. An occurrence in nature is the determination of things insofar as they follow in time according to laws of nature, in which case, that is, the actions follow each other from moment to moment, and thus really take place. But nothing really takes place which does not have a cause, and so has its determination in past time; this is the universal law of all occurrences in nature, and actions, as effects that in virtue of this cause succeed in time, stand under the mechanism of nature. For were the action not to have its determination in the preceding cause, by virtue of this law of necessity, it would have to be an accident, and this is impossible. If, on the other hand, there is an obligation to the action, it can be imputed. For this to happen, however, it is requisite that somebody can be regarded as the originator (*auctor*) of the action, i.e., as its complete first cause. In this case the agent cannot be determined by other, external causes; he must be independent of all predetermining causes, and cannot stand under the law of natural necessity.

It is further assumed, indeed, e.g., by Wolf and Baumgarten, that the agent is independent of all natural necessity, insofar as his actions have been governed by motives, and thus determined by understanding and reason; but this is false. Man is not set free from the mechanism of nature by the fact that in his action he employs an *actus* of reason. Every act of thought or reflection is itself an occurrence in nature, in which the understanding seeks out the connection of things' causes with their effects, and chooses the means of acting accordingly; though this *actus* is an inner occurrence, since it takes place in the man himself; this is commonly the case, for example, when we consider the advantages, disadvantages or other consequences of the action, no less than its cause, e.g., the cunning and craftiness of the thief or swindler, the means of carrying out the deed, concealing it, and so on; it is certain that more activity and understanding are often involved in swindling, murder, robbery, etc., than in placidly conforming to the moral law. So the fact that a man is determined to action on grounds of reason and understanding does not yet release him from all mechanism of nature; a man, for example, is led from youth onward to have an eye to the main chance in every action; he will be covetous of the property of others; at first the difficulties and evil consequences restrain him, but he finds a plan for achieving his design unnoticed, and steals. The whole course of the matter in its linkage is natural mechanism, notwithstanding that the action depended on much use of rational grounds. The grounds of action lay in the past, and he was thereby led to the action itself. The grounds of action, which gradually determined him, obviously did not lie in his power, since he could not undo their occurrence; to that extent he was not acting freely, therefore, since he was simply subject to the mechanism of nature. The same must be assumed of the maxims on which the grounds of action are erected; he has witnessed stealing in his youth, for example, and has become handy in the use of tools.

§16. All actions stand, therefore, under the principle of determinism, though we can only call them predetermined, if the grounds of action are to be met with in the preceding time; but we have to assume the opposite, if the grounds of action are not predetermined, and the agent is the originator and complete cause of his act. In the first case the action is not in his power, in the second the agent determines himself to the action solely by himself, without the entry of external causes. Now in man, both grounds of determination are present in his actions. Thus to think of man as free, he has to be considered either

a. as a sensory being. Here he knows himself, not as he is, but as he appears to himself. This side of him is called phenomenon. He is attended to here, insofar as he is conscious of himself, his existence and actions, both through his outer senses and by means of his inner sense. The conditions of his sensibility and the constitution of his inner sense yield the measure of his agency here.

b. as an intelligible being, i.e., as a being who must be declared independent of all influence from sensibility, and considered in that light. This side is called noumenon. In this respect the determining grounds of his action are independent of all time and space, and the causality of his actions exists through mere reason. In this respect only can he be free, since it is only to that extent that he has absolute spontaneity, that his

27:504

27:505

actions are founded on the autonomy of reason, and that their determination is categorical.

Now the reason why we attribute freedom to an action that rests on motives lies in this, that we perceive in it a visible spontaneity, and this is an essential criterion of freedom. Supposing, now, that every action a man undertakes by the use of his reason were to be grounded, simultaneously, in the time preceding, then it would surely take place only with respective, not absolute spontaneity; for though it lay with reason in the first place, the latter was determined in the time preceding, and thus unconditioned self-activity would not be present in it. But it was this that was demanded of man *qua* noumenon or intelligible being, and hence a self-intrinsic determination through reason is impossible to human nature; only as an intelligible being does he emerge completely from the world of the senses. In that world, he can be considered, with Leibniz, as a piece of clockwork, an *automaton spirituale*, which another being than he is himself must therefore have wound up. If we follow up the determining grounds of human actions, they are linked to one another in a chain; if we go back to the source, the only possible outcome is that we must arrive at an external cause, a being that is outside the agent.

Freedom cannot, therefore, be made comprehensible, and so in itself there is no freedom; only the belief that we are free is capable of explanation. But to picture man as free has this great difficulty, that we have to think of him in the world of sense, and in relation to his natural necessity. There seems to be a manifest contradiction in the fact that a man is supposed to determine himself on his own account, and yet be already predetermined. Nor would this contradiction be removable, were we not necessitated to view man from two sides, namely as phenomenon, i.e., as an appearance through his inner sense, and as noumenon, i.e., as he 27:506 knows himself, in himself, through the moral laws. It is an additional question, whether we can be taught that we are free by empirical psychology, merely, or whether we can learn of this only through morally practical principles and our consciousness of them. From principles of the first kind we should know ourselves merely in the world of sense; moreover, if we had no moral laws, or categorical imperative of duty within us, and our actions stood merely under conditions of nature, and our grounds of determination were purely hypothetical, there would be no obligation, and all actions would be based simply on technico-practical laws. Morality, therefore, is the sole means of obtaining consciousness of our freedom.

That this consciousness of freedom should be immediately present in us, is impossible; for were I to possess it, without any preceding cause and the nature of it having led me to freedom and the consciousness thereof, I would be necessitated to moral action without knowing anything of duty or the principle of morality. Thou shalt do thus and thus, for example; this presupposes, after all, that I know the duty and obligation whereby I am to act; this duty is by its nature absolute, unconditioned and necessary; but what is necessary must certainly be possible; the consciousness of dutiful performance of action must therefore be inferred, not immediately, but through a moral imperative of freedom, and the moral consciousness must be derived by me from that. Just to become aware of freedom on its own, without acquaintance with duty, would be so utterly impossible that we would declare such freedom to be absurd; for in that case reason would determine something for which no determining cause would be present; so the moral law that presents an action as necessary must also provide a cause for it; now we do, indeed, never know this, and yet *ex adductis*, it must at all times be potentially present. For example, the case involves my having to speak the truth; but it also involves, on the other side, injury to my friend, physical pain, advantage that I may gain; regardless of all evil, all physical force, there is a necessitation here to a truthful testimony, notwithstanding all the physical incentives that induce me to the opposite. I now determine myself through my reason; this is freedom, but this reason of mine is determined by a moral law, the very law that necessitates

27:507   me to overcome the motives of nature. If the determination of my statement now results accordingly, I act freely, not from immediate consciousness, but because I have decided, from the categorical imperative, how I ought to act. There is thus within me a power to resist all sensory incentives, as soon as a categorical imperative speaks. The position, then, is that freedom is known by an inference (namely from the moral law) and not immediately felt. To be sure, it cannot be proved by experience that we are free, and become conscious of the fact, solely through awareness of the categorical imperative and in obeying the moral law. For no man is in a position to determine in advance whether, *in casu dato*,[1] he will despise all physical evil and absolutely speak the truth; he knows only that he ought to obey the categorical imperative; he must therefore also be able to, and for this a ground must be present, not an immediate consciousness. Hence it is also not possible to know freedom in a psychological manner; it is possible only through the moral law. So it is not worth the trouble, either, to refute all the objections levelled against freedom. In this determination of the consciousness of freedom, namely through the categorical imperative, the main question is always the one already illustrated: How is such a categorical imperative possible? This is the most difficult point, since it can neither be proved nor rendered comprehensible; the possibility rests solely on the presupposition of freedom.

If man is free, then, he does not depend on natural necessity; yet there must nevertheless be a ground that determines his moral actions, and this must be a law of reason that enjoins him immediately, and is thus categorical. For if, apart from freedom or the power of reason, an additional

[1] in the given case

purpose or sum of all purposes were to underlie the action, the imperative in that case would lie in an object of sensibility, and thus be sensuously conditioned; but that is the *oppositum* of the moral imperative. The latter, however, is the only one which can have as its consequence the possibility of freedom, so it must be a categorical imperative that necessitates man to action. And it likewise follows necessarily from this, that if a categorical imperative is presupposed in the action, man must be free.

Sundry obligations considered, as to their nature and form.   27:508

§17. Obligation is a moral necessitation, resulting from laws of freedom, and likewise a necessitation of our choice, inasmuch as it is free. In every obligation, therefore, (1) Choice is necessitated, (2) to act by laws of freedom, i.e. in accordance with them. The seeming contradiction between choice and necessitation falls away, as soon as we consider ourselves as having free will in our choice, and coupled with that, the power to act under and according to the moral law. As already said (§8), we predicate of the subject in a dual sense, *that he has an obligation to something,* in that we understand by this both *obligatio obligantis erga obligatus,*[m] or active obligation, and *obligatio obligati erga obligans,*[n] or passive obligation.

In obligation it is

1. already certain by §9, that a mutual *collisio* of several obligations is never conceivable or possible, it being admissible only that *rationes obligandi inter se collidere possunt;*[o] because duty, as moral action, is morally necessary, and it is thus impossible that omission of the dutiful act could simultaneously be a duty as well. Duty always contains a *ratio obligans,* or sufficient reason obligating to the dutiful act; directly opposed to this, however, is *ratio obligandi,* i.e., any other reason, insufficient though it be, and the statement that, on collision, *causa moralis potior vincit* (the stronger moral cause wins) means only that the ground of obligation that is not sufficient still yields no obligation. That the insufficient reasons nevertheless determine me contingently to the actual action, is naturally not a decisive objection; for example, if testifying is injurious to a father or benefactor, and the latter withholds my benefits, these relationships, of filial duty, and of gratitude, are merely *rationes obligandi* running counter to the duty of truth-telling, and to plain rectitude as *ratio obligans.*

2. It is likewise inadmissible and impossible that, in case of collision between them, a *causa impulsiva sensitive* should be set on a par *cum causa morali* in an act of duty; for this conflict of *stimuli cum motivis,* which is

---

[m] obligation of an obligator to one obligated
[n] obligation of one obligated to his obligator
[o] grounds of obligation may clash with one another

properly called *luctus facultatum inferiorum cum superioribus*,[p] would of course make the imperative of duty dependent on sensory inclinations; but now the former is categorical, so that in face of its unconditioned command the latter simply cannot come into play as *rationes obligandi*, nor can they even be counted in with it when the sensory urges create obstacles, or lie in the way as objections, to drive the agent into acting contrary to the moral law. This is nevertheless to be understood objectively only, as a matter of determining in which particular case the action is to be done solely from reason and laws of freedom, and where the only question to arise is what our duty is, *in casu*. Subjectively speaking, on the other hand, experience confirms that stimuli, or the laws of natural necessity, are much in conflict with our motives; but then the only question to be asked is whether it is hard or easy for man to do his duty. It is by no means contrary to the law of morality, that sensory impulses should be thrown up here in opposition to the performance of duty, when bodily pain and impairment of capacity are coupled with it; the law cannot prevent these natural feelings; but it does not follow from that, that they alone must be obeyed, for in spite of it all, the law absolutely commands the performance of duty. These grounds of determination, emanating from the power of sensibility, are therefore mere *rationes impellentes*,[q] and not to be regarded as *rationes obligandi*.

3. An *actus obligatorius* is any action whereby something is altered in regard to obligation, whether the latter either arises thereby, or ceases to exist. Thus an obligation may cease or expire without an *actus*, and through an *actus obligatorius*.

For example, the duty to feed a child arises as soon as it is born. The birth seems certainly to be the means, not a *causa obligatoria*. *Pereunte re, perit jus, absque actu*.[r] The debt is paid; the satisfaction of the duty is an *actus* whereby it ceases. An expired duty may revive again (*reviviscit*), for example, a payment of taxes, which is made annually, and again becomes due every year.

4. In every duty we have to suppose a *persona obligans*, even when he does not perform an *actus* that establishes the other as an *obligatus*. This will be shown hereafter; meanwhile the following question must be viewed as problematic: Whether, for an obligation, two persons are required, the one *obligans* and the other *obligatus*, and who the *obligans* may be?

Although the obligation is established by reason, it is nevertheless assumed that in the performance of our duty we have to regard ourselves as passive beings, and that another person must be present, who necessi-

[p] struggle of the lower faculties with the higher
[q] impelling grounds
[r] when the matter ends, the duty expires, without action

tates us to duty. Crusius found this necessitating person in God, and Baumgarten likewise in the divine will, albeit known through reason, and not positively, and on this principle a particular moral system has been erected. If, however, we pay heed to self-regarding duties, then man is presented in his physical nature, i.e., insofar as he is subject to the laws of nature, as the obligated, and rightly so; but if the obligator is personified as an ideal being or moral person, it can be none other than the legislation of reason; this, then, is man considered solely as an intelligible being, who here obligates man as a sensory being, and we thus have a relationship of man *qua* phenomenon towards himself *qua* noumenon. The situation is similar in obligations towards others.

§18. The division heretofore of obligation into *naturalis et positiva*, according to the *source of the obligation*, is not based on any existing relationship. Here it is actually necessary to distinguish *inter obligationem naturalem et statutariam.*[s] Thus although every law must be rational, there is nonetheless a distinction between laws of reason, i.e., which are known purely *a priori* from reason and the nature of the case, and statutory laws, i.e., which are known solely from the will of another, and emanate from another's choice, and, depending on difference in this choice, are called *leges divinae et humanae.*[t] The term *positiva* doubtless comes *a positione alterius*, i.e., from the fact that such laws have their ground in the choice of another.

We see, then, how obligation can be derived and known solely from the nature of the action by laws of freedom, or solely from the choice of another. These types of obligation are by nature necessarily distinct. Natural laws are often expressed through the will of another; the Mosaic ten tables, for example, contain nothing but natural laws. Thus they do not yet   27:511
become statutory, because it must then be impossible to know them through reason, but rather because the source of obligation must lie solely in the choice of the other, and be derivable from that; e.g. the ban on eating any animal having a cloven hoof. Hence natural and statutory laws, depending, that is, on whether the ground of duty is known from the legislation of reason alone, or from the other's will.

§19. The division between *obligatio affirmativa* and *negativa* is quite unthinkable from a moral point of view. The moral law is the motive which necessitates absolutely to action according to the principle of freedom; it is unthinkable, therefore, that the action might be omitted, without a transgression of the moral law. Nor can this transgression occur otherwise than by acting contrary to the motive of the law, the imperative, and hence by offering resistance, and an active employment of force, against the law itself. From the moral viewpoint, therefore, in every trans-

---

[s] between natural and statutory obligation
[t] divine and human laws

gression of the obligation to omit something, the command disobeyed is the same as when the obligation to do something is violated. The point at issue is not the acting according to laws of physical nature, but rather the disposition involved.

From the physical viewpoint, on the other hand, every *obligatio ad committendam actionem*[u] is *affirmativa* and every *obligatio ad omittendam actionem* is *negativa;* whereas, morally considered, even the act that from the physical viewpoint is a mere *omissio,* must be regarded as a *commissio.*

N.B. *Obligatio affirmativa* must never be confused with *obligatio positiva,* since the latter stands contrasted only to *obligatio naturalis,* or at least has been set in contrast to it; otherwise, positive and affirmative might be synonymous.

This provides a rectification of the term *suum cuique,* the principle that serves to ground all duties relating to the rights of others against us. This cannot mean *suum cuique tribue,*[v] for I cannot give the other anything – he already has what belongs to him; the meaning, rather, is that you are to leave the other his own, take nothing, abstain from all actions whereby you would detract from his rights. Thus all *obligationes* founded on this principle are negative. (Right, however, differs from ethics, which tells us to give.)

27:512

Again, in terms of physical forces, the payment of a debt is nothing else but an *actio commissiva,* though by the moral law the latter is not commanded; only the withholding of what belongs to the other is forbidden, and hence it follows that from the moral standpoint an *actio* can be *omissiva,* which *in jure* is *commissiva. Adiaphora* are contrasted to both, and are defined as those actions which produce neither affirmative nor negative obligation.

From the physical viewpoint, an *adiaphoron* is a state of inactivity which lies in the middle between pain and inclination, and is equally plus and minus. Thus whether one lives, i.e., the *factum* of vitality, is indifferent; to live happily, or unhappily, are opposing possibilities. From the practical viewpoint, the *adiaphora* are all those actions which are not accompanied by any obligation, for example, whether I decide to walk about in my yard, or sit still. They have no relation to any moral law that would determine the use of freedom. Such a prescription would bring duty in its train; but where reason leaves the entire action to our free choice, there is no obligation. These actions are therefore no object of morality, but too much has been inferred from this by those who assume, on the contrary, that morality permits no *adiaphora,* and that our actions will always have moral reward or punishment as their consequences. For there is no denying that we exist under natural laws.

---

[u] obligation to perform/to omit an action
[v] give everyone his due

§20. Considered as free actions, the actions of man stand under moral laws, i.e., they must be related to such laws. In this connection they are *good or bad.* Such a division from the logical standpoint, as depicted below, becomes more natural if it is gathered up into a three-fold division, resting on positive and negative good, or plus *a,* and the opposite minus *a,* and the zero or null point of equality, lying in the middle, which is the *adiaphoron.*

Thus an action is:

a. Good in the positive sense when it agrees with certain *leges obligantes,* and in the negative sense when it does not conflict with the law of duty, and is thus neither bad nor positively good. It is the negatively good, then, and the negatively bad, that the *adiaphora* really belong under.

b. Bad, on the other hand, when it either fails to conform to, or conflicts with, the law of duty.

According to this, then, all actions stand either

1. under commands, or *leges praeceptivae,*[w] or are
2. forbidden, under *leges prohibitivae,* or are in the middle,
3. under *leges permissivae,* laws that allow, to which belong all actions that do not contravene the law, and are called permitted actions – good in the negative sense, or indifferent, or *adiaphora.* If we disavow the latter, the whole classification falls apart, in that without exception all actions conform to the laws, or do not, and in the latter case are not actions, since they must at all times be accommodated to the law. However, from the fact that actions are to be especially accommodated to the moral laws, it does not yet follow that they must also be moral actions, since the laws do not determine something in regard to all human actions, and it would also be a cruel restriction, if every action were to be founded on a command or prohibition which determined to me what I *ought* to do; for example, it is morally indifferent, surely, what I eat, so long as it agrees with me; nor am I able to know, of course, whether it will upset me. Here, then, there is no moral law in operation, to which the action is subordinated. It is, though, another intricate question that Hufeland has proposed: whether there be *leges permissivae secundum jus naturae?*[x] Professor Kant says no to that

[w] prescriptive, prohibitory or permissive laws
[x] permissive laws in accordance with natural law

question, for insofar as a moral law runs concurrently, to determine what is allowed or not, there can no longer be an indifferent action involved, e.g., whether it is permitted to me as the stronger, when we are alike in mortal peril, to push another off a floating plank, in order thereby to save my own life.

27:514   N.B. That *leges permissivae* have to be accepted in *jus statutarium* is beyond dispute. For all *leges prohibitivae* contain general determinations which cannot, however, rule out *exceptiones*, and therefore make *leges praeceptivae* necessary. That to some extent a *lex permissiva* might arise from this in *jus naturae,* cannot be rejected out of hand; e.g., in the case of emergency alluded to, we cannot reject the possibility of a *lex necessitatis*, that would give authority to do something forbidden, once we have fallen into a predicament where danger to life is involved. Morality provides a decision on this, yet it must be noted beforehand that all coercive or juridical laws are prohibitive, and rely on the principle of not withholding from the other what belongs to him (*neminem laede*).*ʸ* (For the fact that both commissive and omissive actions are equally necessary for the performance of actions in a physical sense, makes no difference, since all commissive actions are omissive, *in sensu juris*.) From this it follows that if there are *leges permissivae,* they have to be accompanied with a prohibition. But prohibitive laws are some of them *universales*, valid under all circumstances, so that an exception is therefore impossible, and a permissive law not to be thought of here at all; others are *generales*, i.e., where the prohibition holds good in the great majority of cases (in general). Here, exceptions are conceivable, and in regard to them the rule is that what is not forbidden is *eo ipso* permitted, i.e., action is no more bidden or forbidden than abstention. So *contra legem prohibitivam generalem*ᶻ there are permissive laws as exceptions. For example, might must not replace right is a prohibitive, which is subject to an exception when all men are put into a condition where, by equal resistance to one another, they would despoil themselves of all rights and abolish the very existence of laws; e.g. *in statu naturali,*ᵃ where each takes himself to be defending the legitimacy of his own actions. Here, between them, they erase the possibility of passing over into a condition of legal order, and only the power of the stronger is then left, and thus might replaces right. This was probably how all political constitutions originated – as to which Professor Kant remarks in passing that the tales of King Romulus and King Numa are probably not historical truths, but fictions. In idea there was a progress from Romulus (signifying power) as the natural condition, to one of legal order under Numa, who symbolizes law.

ʸ injure nobody
ᶻ as against a law that prohibits in general
ᵃ in a state of nature

The same power applies to the case where two men are fighting for one 27:515
plank in a shipwreck.

Bearing this in mind, Professor Kant thinks that the question: *an datur
lex permissiva in jure naturae?*[b] cannot be answered absolutely in the negative, and that in resolving the problem it is a matter of whether the
conditions exist, under which we may assume that might replaces right, in
which case he lays down a naturally permissive law.

For if it be the case, that without might no right can be instituted, then
might must precede right, whereas rule by right has to be the basis of
power. If we take men *in statu naturali*, they are *ex leges*, under no legal
order, and have no laws, only external power to keep them upright. Each
exercises his own choice, without acknowledging any general freedom. At
length one man must remain, who lays claim to supremacy, and has the
intention of instituting a general legal order, for the purpose of organizing
his rule. He would have no such order, beforehand, to determine what
right and law should be, and it would thus proceed from his choice and
come about from his power; so here might replaces right, i.e. precedes it,
and is exercised to set up a legal order which did not previously exist, and
could not, indeed, be made actual without this power. Should a prohibitive law be now issued, whereby it was not permitted to employ force, so
that men might come into enjoyment of a *status civilis*, this would continue
to uphold the state of lawlessness, and a condition, therefore, in which
there would be no law, or no acknowledgement thereof. But this is a state
of affairs in conflict with the universal imperative of morality, and we thus
have to assume that nature allows us, in this fashion, to bring man's free
choice into agreement with general freedom, by means of universal law;
and so here there is a natural law in effect, to permit the force employed.
It follows, in regard to the manner in which political constitutions are
originally set up, that if we should have to assume (and generally assumed
it must be), that the existing legal power and legitimate order in the state
have been instituted *absque titulo*[c] by the founder, and the state established
by arbitrary decision, then no right thereby accrues to the subjects, to
repudiate the power of the law. For it is wholly contrary to the choice of
men, spontaneously and by their own determination to regulate their
actions by free decision, and so nor will they voluntarily enter, either, into 27:516
a restriction of their *arbitrium brutum,* and thereby subordinate themselves
by general consent to the command of a superior. By their own decision,
therefore, no *status juridicus* would have come about, though it can indeed
be brought about by force according to the permissive law; hence there is
no reason to do away with it again, in order to revert back into a *status
naturalis.* (Revolution and reform do not appear to be ruled out by this.)

[b] whether there is a permissive law within the law of nature
[c] without any right

Now the foregoing condition is enough to decide the existence of a permissive law, in the case where preservation of life for two people would depend on possession of a thing. Can the other deprive a man who is already in possession of the thing, to ensure his own survival at the price of the other's life? By right of nature this is never so, precisely because the one to be despoiled already has possession, and is thereby protecting his life; the other's need can never give a coercive right, insofar as the ground of the action did not already rest beforehand on a legally valid right to coerce; for otherwise the other would already have had to possess the coercive right, and this is impossible. But the case is altered, if neither of the two was yet in possession of the thing, and both were endeavouring to seize possession of that whereby the life of one of them can be saved. In that case, no right subsists between them, whereby one could be coerced by the other, nor is there any means of preventing the natural urge to use force; if no concession is made, both lose their lives, whereas by the universal law the life of at least one of them should have been preserved; it is impossible, though, for either one to decide on employing the means to act in accordance with the principle; so force must be permitted, in order thereby to institute a right to preserve life. Here, too, therefore, the underlying maxim is that to institute a right, might precedes right, in accordance with a permissive law.

Rectitudo actionis[d] rests on the moral goodness of the action, and in ethics, therefore, every action that does not conflict with duty is *actio recta;* but it is called *actio justa,* insofar as it does not conflict with a *legal duty.* Every action that does conflict with duty is thus *actio minus recta.* It is also called *peccatum,* although in pure Latin this term designates every departure from a rule, e.g., a rule of grammar. A *peccatum immortale* is presumed, when the *consectaria*[e] of the action persist even after the death of the *peccans,* for example, dangerous maxims in the writings of an author.

Elsewhere, *peccatum* in the theological sense is confined to the violation of a duty ordained by the divine will

§21. In his practical philosophy §39–46, Baumgarten has put forward various formulae which, as imperative, are supposed to serve for the general principle of all obligation, though Professor Kant rejects every one of them.

a. He censures the definition given in §39, of what an imperative is here, for Baumgarten extends it to every binding norm in the practical disciplines, whereas Kant refers a binding norm to that class only where a moral necessitation or obligation can gain entry, in that only there is it categorical, and thought of in application to a finite being, though the

27:517

---

[d] rightness of an action
[e] consequences

effect is thereby to make the subjective contingency of the action objectively necessary.

b. The formula *fac bonum, omitte malum*[f] is tautological, since if it has to be commanded that an action should occur, the transgression of the moral law by inaction or contrary action is self-evident. The formula *fac, quod optimum, etc.*, is likewise identical with the formula *fac bonum;* in that – reckoned against a greater good – the lesser is always an evil that could not be commanded.

c. *Quaere perfectionem, quantum potes*[g] – a formula that contradicts the nature of duty. Perfection is a variable concept. By perfection in general we understand everything we take to be complete, e.g. a perfect liar, a complete villain, who endeavours to exterminate, not only his enemy, but also the latter's family, and even to ruin them morally before murdering them. It is in general typical of man, to think always of *extrema opposita* under the concept of perfection, so that in order to think of a god, for example, he must simultaneously fashion a devil. Portional perfections contain, as such, a conformity to an end, and thus lead to a fitness on man's part for all possible ends, for example, the capacity for quick wit, good address in conversation, the ability to state a thing clearly, taste, etc. – in short, there is nothing at which a man might not try to become perfect and make himself happy. Indeed, even moral ends might be counted in here, if only the imperative of duty could be directed to an end; but it is so unconditional, that in fact it restricts the desire to attain them.   27:518

d. *Vive convenienter naturae.*[h] This might mean: Live like an animal – in the physical sense we thereby compare human behaviour with that of animals, sometimes to their gain and sometimes to their loss. If it were to mean: Live according to the precepts of reason, it tells us no more than to do our duty because it is duty, and is thus a tautology.

Professor Kant believes that the categorical general principle of morality set forth by himself:

So act, that by the maxim of your action you may present yourself as a universal legislator,

conveys the essential character of a moral principle, and incorporates within itself all others that have hitherto been devised. For (a) the principle of purposiveness and perfection is subordinated to the morality of the action; (b) morality can rest only on the law of reason; (c) the action can therefore relate, not to itself, but only to the form; (d) this must be the form of lawfulness; for it must conform to the universality of the faculty of reason, and only under this form can it be morally good; (e) the action is

[f] do what is good, refrain from what is bad
[g] seek perfection as much as you can
[h] live according to nature

merely to be tested according to this principle, without the agent expressly willing thereby that the determining ground of his action should also be law; (f) the conformity discovered serves only as a motive for him to act. We perceive very vividly from this, that the ground of duty is bound up with freedom.

§22. Moral necessitation is not yet moral compulsion (*coercitio*). It simply presupposes in the subject the possibility that all sorts of incentives may be present merely in the faculty of desire, which tend to make him strive and act in opposition to the moral law. This possibility, on which the subjective determining grounds to action may always alone rest, makes it necessary for him to be necessitated to duty, i.e. put under obligation. If the moral will were the moral law for the agent, he would have nothing else but readiness to fulfil the law; the latter would indeed be his own will; no subjective motives to transgress the law would run counter to it – he would be a holy being, even God himself, in whom a human free will is unthinkable, because subjective inclinations are impossible for Him, seeing that He wills only what the law prescribes. In every finite being, including man, it is, on the other hand, not only possible, but a fact, that he possesses *causae impulsivae* to offer resistance to the moral laws, and that all the inclinations present in him, the sensory impulses, bent, and the maxims derived therefrom operate counter to those laws, and impel him to act in opposition to them. This, then – should he obey the moral law – is the ground of the compulsion. It consists in the necessitation to an action that he undertakes with reluctance, a *necessitatio actionis invitae*.[i]

A thing is *done reluctantly* by a free being, insofar as (1) there is present in him an inclination to the opposite of what he *wills* to do and (2) he nevertheless does what he *wills* as a free being. This is *actio invita* in the moral sense. Elsewhere, to be sure, we also call *actio invita* an action done *without willing, or not done wilfully*, which has the name *actio involuntaria.* Here, then, there is an absence of will itself, i.e., the free choice and decision to act, on grounds of reason, which is the true *causa determinans;* the action is done unwillingly, only because of the motives to the contrary that lie in the physical nature of man. Instead of this, in *actio involuntaria* we have an absence or unawareness of the moving cause to action; it therefore does not belong among free actions, and *actio invita* must never be understood in that sense; for example, if a person forgets to pay a debt, he says he did not do this wilfully; or he stumbles and knocks others over. Things are very different in the chastisement of a son, which a father finds necessary, though paternal love tells against it.

Now this compulsion may be (a) moral, i.e., compulsion by the mere idea of the moral law. For whereas all moral actions rest solely on the one ground of duty, this being every action to which we can be obligated, and

---

[i] necessitation of action against one's will

whereas this obligation has its ground in the moral law, and the latter can be known solely through reason, it follows that the ground of all compulsion is the idea of the moral law. There can thus be no moral compulsion, 27:520 where no fulfilment or transgression of a law of duty can be presupposed; for example, all the other constraints, physical or ideal, employed in compelling a person morally through honour; or when we say it was morally impossible to win the battle; in both cases, the inducements of honour, and the laws of probability, lie outside the domain of morality. Hence

(b) Insofar as this compulsion results by the law of any kind of inclination, and is drawn, therefore, from sensory impulses and personal inclinations, whereby other inclinations conflicting with morality are overcome and weakened, where *stimuli* are set in motion *contra stimulos;* we call such a compulsion pathological. It is also called physical compulsion; only in that case it should not be confused with any mechanical compulsion.

§23. Man is no being sufficient unto himself; he depends, rather, on needs, and that, in fact, is what constitutes the ground and efficacy of his sensory impulses. Now these operate on man's will in so insistently self-preoccupied a fashion that they stand in no connection with the moral law. The latter is simply an Idea of his reason, and hence we no more find a necessary agreement of sensory urges and inclinations with the moral law, than we do a contradiction, since there is no linkage at all between them. Inasmuch as man can be regarded, for all that, as a being in whom the law of sensibility is operative, he is tempted to act contrary to the law of reason; he must therefore also have the power to determine himself in opposition to the law of sensibility, and this is called *self-compulsion*. It is therefore certain that man can compel himself to duty. We call it inner compulsion, *coercitio interna.*

This capacity is necessary, on account of his sensory inclinations. But it also follows from this, that we cannot possibly say that a man should do his duty with complete gladness; for in virtue of the stimuli by nature necessarily present in him, this is impossible. It is certain, on the other hand, that by self-compulsion man actually proves himself free, in that he thereby demonstrates an *independentia arbitrii liberi a determinationibus per stimulos,[j]* and thus gives evidence of his freedom. But from this there follows something else, viz.:

§24. A person may be compelled to duty by others, and even in that 27:521 case, may act freely. This happens when the other, having a right to do so, confronts the subject with his duty, i.e., the moral law by which he ought to act. If this confrontation makes an impression on the agent, he determines his will by an Idea of reason, creates through his reason that conception of his duty which already lay previously within him, and is only

---

[j] independence of free choice from determination by stimuli

quickened by the other, and determines himself according to the moral law. Here there is no sensory impulse employed in order to compel him, and he acts, therefore, of his own free will; he is thus also to that extent free in his action. But this moral compulsion on the part of another is

1. possible only insofar as the subject is wholly good and well disposed, i.e., has unreserved reverence for the moral law, and the fulfilment of his duties, and is so firmly convinced of their worth, that the sensory impulses, and all maxims framed thereby, are precluded from having any influence on the determination of reason. It is

2. thus possible only to the extent that the agent is free, since he must at least have the appropriate degree of firm knowledge of duty that is required, in order to overcome the full strength of the inclination that pulls the other way.

It is altogether different, when another is to be compelled pathologically. He can then be necessitated, indeed, but never obligated; for otherwise a man would also have to be acting freely when he is forced into an action by cudgelling or imprisonment. He does his duty, not from any conception of the moral law, but because of the painful feelings that assail him. Pathological means of compulsion relate to the idea of the consequences associated with an action, and operate

a. *per placentia, sive per illecebras,*[k] though compulsion by something that pleases is not in fact called compulsion; e.g., because it tastes so good.

b. *per minas,*[l] in regard to all disagreeable consequences. *Placentia* and *minae* are also called *extorsiones*, because we are trying by the idea to engender in the agent that degree of inclination, of which we believe that his freedom would not have power enough to counter it. Properly speaking, no *actio* can be extorted, since in an absolute sense the will concurs 27:522 thereto, though it is free, so that an action in accordance with its determination cannot become impossible. But in extortion we understand only in a comparative sense a relative counteracting of the impelling causes, whereby sensibility is determined.

Take, for example, one who has already adopted in his actions a maxim that he regards as a rule. To make profits and a living from wine-dealing, he finds it expedient to mix in sugar of lead and other sweeteners, and is thus deliberately acting on a principle that is a motive of his subjective inclination, and never a moral principle, if only because he is not unhappy to practise it. By notions of law, or by the moral route, it will never be possible to compel him, since he is convinced of the opposite. He must therefore be compelled pathologically. A constraint will be needed to counterbalance his maxim of selfishness, and destroy his motive for adulterating the wine. We put him in fear of the strictest controls, and of punishment.

[k] by what pleases or allures
[l] by threats

In general, if the countermeasures are adequate to weaken the inclination, and enliven his sensory feeling by another contrary feeling in collision with it, we are then in a position to ensure that continuing habituation will weaken the power of inclination, and thereafter moral grounds have an impact, so that by removal of the obstacle he is thus made free, and can be brought, by this pathological expedient, to a recognition of his duty.

§24.* Now in order to recognize properly the quality of the action, and the fact that one can be compelled to it, depending on whether or not it stands under juridical laws, we must know beforehand what the legitimacy of compulsion rests on.

1. An action that contradicts an obligation (i.e., a *necessitatio moralis*, not the *officium* or duty, viz., the action incumbent on the agent), is *illicita*, and one that does not contradict it is *licita* – permitted, or not permitted.

2. The possibility of an action, insofar as it is permitted, is the licence to act, *facultas moralis*, to which there corresponds the concept of a *res mere facultatis*, i.e., an action in which both doing and omitting are permitted, and in which, therefore, nothing contradicts the obligation to do or omit. This is really *actio adiaphoron morale,*^m is the object of the licence, and includes within it every permitted action.

3. The agreement of the action with the licence to act (*facultas moralis*) is the *legitimacy of the action: rectitudo actionis*. The latter includes that legitimacy of action which simultaneously agrees with a coercive duty, and is called *justitia actionis*. The difference here rests on outer and inner coercion. There is *outer* coercion, that is, when the necessitation to duty stems from an outer object; I can be coerced, for example, by others into payment of a debt, albeit only through the idea of the binding law. *Inner* coercion, on the other hand, is that which rests on the mere Idea of duty, independent of any other compulsion, and in which such compulsion is not even recognized; for example, remission of a debt owed me by an impecunious debtor; the action results from my own observance of the law of duty. Now *obligations* (N.B. taken for acts of duty), which contain no element of compulsion, are *coercive freedoms;* thence are drawn all duties to oneself, and likewise the legitimacy of an action as such, and thus the action itself, insofar as it is thought of as coinciding with duty. Obligations, on the other hand, that rest on external compulsion, or contain it, are *coercive duties,* and these always concern the relationship with other people, and thus duties to others; and to that extent an *actio* is only to be called *justa,* which really has to be *recta.* But not every *actio recta* is *actio justa,* any more than a wrong yet constitutes an injustice to others.

[4]. We therefore have knowledge of the legitimacy of our concepts. *Leges justi,* that is, are juridical laws, and are bound up with compulsion,

27:523

---

*[This section number has been repeated by the German editor – Tr.]

^m a morally indifferent action

i.e., the legitimacy of the action has its ground in the compulsion. *Leges honesti* are laws of virtue, and determine without compulsion, i.e., they have their determining ground in the inner constitution of the action, without any motive to it having arisen from compulsion.

Since all obligation also rests on freedom itself, and has its ground therein insofar as freedom is regarded under the condition whereby it can be a universal law, Professor Kant calls all moral laws (i.e., those that lay down the condition under which a thing should happen, as opposed to *leges naturae, physicae*, which merely state the condition under which a thing does happen) *leges libertatis*, laws of freedom, and includes thereunder the afore-mentioned *leges justi et honesti* (*ethicae*), though only inasmuch as they impose on the action the restrictive condition of fitness to be a universal law; on this he grounds the distinction between *jus* and *ethica*, the theories of law and virtue (which on his view must therefore be untenable).

5. Between *having the right* to do this or that, and *having a right* to something, Professor Kant distinguishes as follows. A subject may be granted licence to do a thing, and yet it may contain merely the possibility (namely, where the right appears by reason of the object, as opposed to any actual object of right); but in that case the subject still does not *possess the right to do* anything. This is equivalent to the term *jus illi competit*, i.e., he has permission to act, i.e., he does no wrong in engaging in the action, e.g., to take possession of a thing that belongs to nobody. But a subject *has a right* as soon as he has something in regard to whose use he can do or omit as he wills. Here an object is present, and not merely the right to act thus, in and for itself. To have a right therefore already presupposes an acquisition, and thus the possession of a thing, or a promise on another's part, over which promise or thing I am able to dispose and of which I can make use, as with something loaned to me. Of this we say *jus possidet*, he has a right. Klein has noticed this distinction, but not explained it.

Now on this depends the distinction among rights of coercion, coercive laws, as *leges praeceptivae, prohibitivae* and *permissivae*, viz.

6. *Leges praeceptivae*, whose totality makes up the *jus mandati*,*[n]* and *leges prohibitivae*, whose totality comprises the *jus vetiti*, contain between them the *leges permissivae*, on which are founded the mere authorizations of others.

Now this determines the right of coercion, i.e., the authority that others have, in respect of their obligation to their fellow-men, to compel according to the laws of freedom, depending on the applicability of this general formula:

Everyone can resist the freedom of another, so soon as it infringes that freedom of his own, which is able to co-exist with the freedom of everyone else,

[n] law that commands, or forbids

and the freedom from coercion, which stands in opposition to the right to coerce, is defined thus:

Act so, that your freedom can co-exist, *according to general laws*, with the freedom   27:525
of everyone else.

N.B. This means that the maxim underlying the use of your moral act of coercion must be so constituted, that it qualifies as a general law. For example, I have promised to deliver grain; on the presumption of a high price, I am unwilling to keep my unconditionally given word to the other, since on delivery the price will have fallen. The coercive right of the other agrees with the duty arising from a promise, and the fulfilment that everyone can demand, with universal freedom.

The agreement of the action with the universal laws of freedom is thus the measure by which to determine whether anyone possesses a coercive right, and the other can be subject to it; and I can thus have authority to coerce the will of the other's person, against his freedom, only insofar as my freedom agrees at the same time with the general freedom, according to universal laws. An action is therefore *right or wrong*, only insofar as it accords or conflicts with the condition, that the agent's freedom can coexist with that of anyone else, by universal laws, or is contrary to them; and the right to resist the other's freedom, or to coerce him, can only hold good insofar as my freedom is in conformity with universal freedom. The reason for that is as follows: the universal law of reason can alone be the determining ground of action, but this is the law of universal freedom; everyone has the right to promote this, even though he effects it by resisting the opposing freedom of another, in such a way that he seeks to prevent an obstruction, and thus to further an intent. For in the coercion there is presupposed the rectitude of the action, i.e., the quality that the agent's freedom accords with universal freedom. The other, however, obstructs the action by his freedom; the latter I can curtail and offer resistance to, insofar as this is in accordance with the laws of coercion; so *eo ipso* I must thereby obstruct universal freedom by the use of my own. From this it follows that I have a right to all actions that do not militate   27:526
against the other's right, i.e., his moral freedom; for to that extent I do not curtail his freedom, and he has no right to coerce me. From this it also follows that the right to coerce the other consists in resisting his use of freedom, insofar as it cannot co-exist with universal freedom according to universal law; and this is the right of coercion.

N.B. No right of coercion can therefore be based on the fact that the other need expect no harm from the limitation of his freedom, whereas I can expect advantage from the use of my own; I have no right, for example, to compel the other to give me a melon that he wants to throw away.

The outcome is, that the right to coerce, and the rectitude of the act (*justitia facti*), derive their justification from the extent to which they coincide with the universal law of freedom, and it has thus been, till now, an unproved assumption of the law, to consider the right to coerce as a legal axiom. For that right has been taken to be a basic concept of the law, and has been lodged in the very definition thereof. But since nobody can exercise a right to coerce, who has not obtained a right thereto from a higher ground, which consists, however, in one's own freedom and its congruence with the freedom of everyone according to universal law, it is clear that the right to coerce can only be derived from the Idea of law itself.

Within this universal moral law are comprehended both legal and ethical laws, though with this difference, that in the former actions are considered merely in regard to their form, whereas in the latter they are considered with respect to their end, as their object.

§25. It has been noted already, that all juridical laws pertain to rights of coercion, and are utterly negative, insofar, that is, as they are considered solely with respect to the form of freedom. For they amount to this, that they carry with them no benefit (and hence no end or matter), but merely prevent a theft of what is mine, whether it be a physical object or my right. For in that I exercise my right, I am not indeed first acquiring what is mine, since it is already presupposed to be that; I am merely preventing the other from taking it away from me. The corresponding legal duty can thus consist only in not depriving the other of what is his. In this sense, however, we have to view, in the abstract, all *actiones physicae* which consist *vel in committendo, vel omittendo*. Without giving, I cannot pay the debt, but by the law of freedom the principle here is only that of not depriving the other of his claim to the money lent; whence my right to resist him in this, were he to want it.

27:527

Ulpian: *Digests* 1, 1, 10., *De justitia et jure,* adopts the *tria praecepta stoicorum* as basic rules of law.

1. *honeste vive.*[o] This is the principle of ethics, which can determine affirmative acts of duty, since it is directed to ends; e.g., promote the happiness of others according to your powers, seek to perfect yourself. But the rightness of all such acts rests only on this, that we cannot be externally compelled to them, and that therefore an inner compulsion alone occurs in them, the outer being absent, and hence that every agent coerces himself, no less than in an external action the judge would deter him from the wrongness of it. We may call them actions of honour, insofar as the latter rests upon this, that no other ground deters us from transgression of the moral law, save the consciousness that this act would be contrary to the law. But this rests ultimately on our own judgement of the action; so *honeste vive* means, on this showing, live so as to be worthy of honour. For from our very own observance of the law the respect of others

[o] live uprightly

towards us must also spring. This phrase of Ulpian's therefore contains the whole *complexus* of ethical duties, which he thereby segregates from those of law.

2. *Neminem laede, suum cuique tribue.* Both appertain to *law.* Ulpian distinguishes between them in this fashion, that he construes all obligations *ad actiones commissivas* under *suum cuique,* and *ad actiones omissivas* under *neminem laede.* But in the spirit of the law, the two mean the same: to withhold from nobody what belongs to him. It cannot be supposed, without contradiction, that I do not give the other his due, and yet ought not to withhold it from him. *In sensu morali,* the difference in the physical action does not come into it, for the failure to deliver is harmful, the delivery accomplished merely the *factum* needed to satisfy the condition of not withholding.

However, another distinction can be discovered here, in respect to   27:528
whether man is considered *in statu naturali* or *civili. In statu naturali,* everyone exercises his own private right; he determines his own rights, and those of other men, according to his own judgement, and seeks to obtain them by his own power; here there is a want of any public system of justice, which assures to each his own, or any public power that delivers it to him. Here we may invoke the principle of *neminem laede.* If anyone violates it *in statum civilem,* he is at once obliged to submit to the public judiciary, which, since he cannot be his own judge, determines his rights instead of him, and delivers them under public enforcement; here we may invoke the *suum cuique tribue,* and this would run: subject yourself to the public judiciary, or to a state of affairs in which everyone is protected in his rights by a public law. Hence *jus in statu naturali* and *jus in statu civili,* which latter can therefore also be affirmative.

§26. Since a coercion is unthinkable without a right, and indeed this right must come first, before I can have a right to coerce, so the relevant division, founded on the right of others, *inter obligationes perfectas et imperfectas*[p] is to that extent false, when used to distinguish whether the other has a right of coercion in my regard or not; for by that test, no right at all would exist in the latter case, though this should not be assumed, for it is only a right of coercion that is held not to exist; but where a right exists in itself, there is also a resultant power of coercion present. We must therefore define this division thus:

Obligatio perfecta, an obligation where the agent can be necessitated to an act of duty by another's choice.

Obligatio imperfecta, is any ethical duty to which the agent can be necessitated only by his own moral principles.

The term *perfecta* has doubtless been drawn from the idea of subjection that occurs in every obligation, and to that extent it was more completely

---

[p] between perfect and imperfect obligations

present than with *imperfecta;* from a moral viewpoint, however, the truth is that where my own law necessitates me, the obligation is far greater than where the choice of another can do so.

§27. In §18 it was indeed assumed that *lex statutaria* is known solely through the choice of another, and *lex naturalis* by reason, from the nature of the case; yet this does not exclude the necessity, that all laws, whether they be natural or statutory, are founded on the universal laws of nature; on the contrary, it is by this that the true ground of the law's obligation, the moral necessitation to observe and obey it, is defined, and the person obligated made capable thereby of recognizing the binding force of the law. By the choice of another, therefore, the obligations underlying the law, i.e. the extent to which it is qualified to be a binding law, cannot be recognized; for natural laws, namely the universal grounds of obligation, are the general principle of the latter, and have no other laws above them, but give to laws all their binding force. Even with statutory laws as well, there must always be a universal ground, whereby everyone can be bound thereto, and made obedient to the same. So it must be known, in fact, from reason alone, that (*in statu civili*) a sovereign of the legal constitution is present in the assumed subject, before I can determine myself to obedience, and also that the duty ordained by the law is in accordance with the universal law of morality. Even *divine* laws are built upon this universal law of nature, and there could be no thought of my being bound thereto, were there no acknowledgement on my part that I have an obligation towards the divine will.

Divine laws are those revealed to us through the declared will of God; as natural laws they can be made positive by this will, and then they hold at the same time as positive laws, which are acknowledged, indeed, as binding by reason, but are called positive on the basis of promulgation, and the enhanced force they thereby acquire through the divine will; they must already be in accordance with nature, because God, as the supreme lawgiver, can ordain nothing else but the duty known by reason. It is also possible that God might have ordained such laws as have their ground merely in His *arbitrium,* and are thus actually statutory laws; yet even these, in themselves, would have to be knowable by reason; man must indeed be capable in himself of knowing them, only he would not have learnt them so early, had he not been led to their necessity empirically, and the declared will of God may perhaps be held to give greater emphasis to their force.

It is assumed, indeed, that the binding force of moral laws lies in the divine will, and God has been viewed as the moral legislator. But this cannot be construed to mean that the divine laws, and the binding force of the divine will, can be discerned and known no otherwise, than through the positive divine will; this is impossible. On the contrary, we must first have discerned through reason that the divine will is in accordance with

27:529

27:530

the concept of a moral law, i.e., that it coincides with the universal laws of nature, before we acknowledge the universal will as a binding law and subject ourselves to it. The binding force of the law lies, therefore, in the principle as it is known to reason; on the other hand, we can and must attach to this hypothesis the sense that God, as a moral and omnipotent being, is the supreme executor of all inner and outer moral laws, that He adds to their force the efficacy that is needed to manifest it, and that we, therefore, when we observe or transgress the laws, are subject to God's judgement-seat, in that we have acted according to His will, or against it, and must expect the consequences. By reason alone, therefore, the moral law can be demonstrated and known, and doubtless followed as well; yet there is no denying that if, apart from the binding efficacy of the law itself, our free choice is further supported by the idea that our action conforms to the will of a higher external cause, this hypothesis is a good, one might even say a necessary, accompaniment to human nature. The atheist, that is, if he belongs to the *sceptical order,* and merely maintains that he cannot be persuaded of God's existence, in an objective sense, himself adopts the maxim that, though God's existence may be unprovable, it is best after all to presuppose it as a hypothesis, since the moral laws find a surer entry thereby, and are more easily followed. For if God is not regarded as executor of the moral laws, then the only thing left is the inner nature of the obligation, albeit to the same end, namely to impel us to the observance of our duties; if, however, the existence of a higher being is so presupposed, that it determines the accounting of our actions, this idea of a higher power allies itself to reason as a helpful means of strengthening us in observance of the laws, and of assuring all the more our rights towards each other.

27:531

N.B. To be a sceptical atheist, an unbeliever, is not punishable. For his doubts are guiltless. The certainty of God's existence is impossible to bring to conviction, in the logical sense. Such a person cannot, therefore, persuade himself of theism, or the reality of God; though the impossibility of God is equally incapable of demonstration. It is therefore incumbent on him merely to assume the possibility of a God, and this all the more so, because it is such an excellent means of reinforcing the laws of duty. The dogmatic atheist, on the other hand, does not accept even the possibility. But now since, by the latter, the morality of actions can be so much improved, this is really a wrong and even dangerous contention, since he robs his fellow-men of an efficacious means whereby duties to one another are protected by a higher hand, and everyone is determined to the fulfilment of duty without enforcement by others; one may say, indeed, that for observance of the moral rules in them, well-nigh the majority of religions set out by taking as their guide-line in actions, not the laws of duty, so much as the approval or disapproval of God. The atheist himself must likewise acknowledge his obligation according to the laws of reason, but has to maintain, of course, that the imperative of duty is categorical, and needs no recourse to the condition of a higher power. He therefore has no reason to proclaim aloud his rejection of a divine being; the state, rather, is authorized to forbid such corrupting affirmations of a paradox.

The dogmatic atheist, on the other hand, or he who absolutely denies the existence of God, must indeed accept an obligation deriving from the nature of the case, and can only deny that moral laws could be regarded as God's will, because he does not assume a being above the nature of man; in so doing he loses the above-mentioned supports in the fulfilment of our duties, and it is undeniable that to that extent he cannot be regarded as a good citizen, and damages the obligating power of the laws, which this idea makes effective.

27:532 §28. All laws of right, i.e., laws concerning rights towards others, have their determining ground solely in freedom, and hence in the form of actions, i.e., in those determinations under which all actions must be set up, to attain any possible end.

They never, therefore, take notice of objective conditions of the matter of laws, or the universal end of happiness, as is the case with ethical laws, which have as their goal all the well-being that is possible to man. For so often as dutiful actions towards others are in question, then the action, even if a goal is to be reached by it, must be one which does but will to be directed, absolutely unconditionally, by the maxim that the freedom of the action should accord with the freedom of everyone, according to universal law.

Hence all such laws of right are also nothing else but laws of freedom, since they conform to the universal law of freedom. All ordinances of a sovereign must be so determined, that by the standards of universal freedom, the freedom of any subject suffers no abridgement thereby. So should laws of right have regard to the principle of happiness, it would then be inevitable, since this is subject to such infinitely varying definition by men, that the freedom of those obligated would suffer abridgement, and be restricted, in that it would then be left to the other's choice, just as his plan of happiness might demand; who, for example, would wish to adopt as a universally valid law of freedom: You need not repay to a rich man the money advanced, if it is a burden to you, and he thereby incurs no significant loss? In that case, of course, nobody would lend to another; this, then, is a contradiction of the action with the law itself, and this outcome is the true criterion of a morally free action.

§29. The laws of right rest either on *jus strictum* (strict right), i.e. all the laws of coercion, or on fairness, *aequitas*. The latter is a subtle concept, not yet sufficiently developed. It consists in the right to compel another, insofar as the latter is implicated in an undeclared condition. The condition for coercion is therefore present only insofar and under such circumstances as have not been outwardly acknowledged, but which, if they were so, would establish the right to coerce; for example, the wage of a servant has been settled, but during his period of service the real worth of the currency is devalued, and he cannot defray his expenses with the amount in question. This circumstance, as a ground for the right to demand compensation from his employer, has not been openly or outwardly acknowledged between master and servant, i.e., is not *in stipulatione,* but would, by strict right, bring about a rise in the wage if it were so; the master is therefore obligated merely *ex aequitate.* A right *ex aequitate* is not just an ethical right stemming from one's own duty, but bases an obligation on the right of another, only with this difference, that fairness is never accompanied by a right of coercion against the other, nor ever can be, because only the openly declared disposition of the entitled and obligated parties constitutes the condition from which external necessitation can accrue to the former, and all that is thought and not said, that is intended only, cannot be subsumed under the obligation; so had the servant determined that, and how much, there was need of money to defray his expenses, a stricter ground for compensation and the right to compel it would have been present; *in casu,* there are no data for any external imputation.

§30. *Anima* and *littera legis* are different, depending on whether they are taken from a statutory law or a *lex naturalis.* In the former, *anima legis* is the determination of that action which ought to occur according to the law, in order to satisfy an obligation; it is therefore *lex pragmatica,* since it determines the mode of performing the duty, e.g., to what extent payment of a debt should be made in hard cash, or with goods, and in what manner.

Littera legis is the meaning of words, as it is directly attached to them, without taking note of the intention of the legislator, and testing the law by that. Now since the rule is that, where an ambiguity occurs, the law must be so interpreted that the *littera legis* coincides with the *anima legis,* it is the principle of a legal quibble, an act of chicanery or pettifogging, if to suit one's purpose the *littera legis* is alone made fundamental.

The legal quibbler applies the law with sophistical subtleties, and therefore differs from the legalist, who has merely a historical knowledge of the law, according to its letter, but no rational awareness of its spirit.

Now natural law admittedly has no expressly enunciated rules, so that by *littera legis* here we mean the action that is undertaken in accordance with the express law of reason, and by *anima legis moralis* the condition upon the agent, that the law itself and alone be the motive of that action which has been undertaken in accordance with the law; it therefore excludes all actions which comply with the law, but for reasons of advantage or disadvantage, fear of punishment, etc. The determination to action, and obedience to the categorical law of duty, are necessary. *In lege statutaria,* obedience to the law is sufficient, and we cannot and should not

27:533

27:534

look to the motivating and determining grounds of the action – whether the agent has done his duty from intentions and purposes, or from absolute recognition of his obligation. It follows from this that the *littera legis naturalis* pertains solely to *jus*, but the *anima legis* wholly to ethics. On this, too, there rests the morality and the legality of an action, since the latter consists in its conformity with the law, whereas the former requires that, apart from that, duty alone was the motive to the action, and to that extent it can be accounted to us.

§31. A *juris peritia*[q] seems to be a contradiction, since the concept of law can be known solely from reason and is not to be gathered from experience. Nor, therefore, can it be limited to knowledge of the laws, and must, indeed, presuppose them; for a practical jurist, moreover, there is a need to combine with legal theory a knowledge of the application of laws; this rests upon the ability to distinguish the *casus datae legis,* and to what extent the *casus* is comprehended under the law. Such skill is attained only by frequent application of theory to the endless variety of cases, and this is a matter of testing by experience. The English are therefore advocating a legal compendium, that might one day be compiled from their monstrous accumulation of parliamentary verdicts, so that these precedents, through the limitless multiplicity of cases, might yield a certain norm, whereby the *anima legis* could be determined thereafter in each case. Professor Kant thinks it proper to use compilations of practical cases on law in application to particular cases under a general legislation, just as it exercises the power of judgement to become acquainted with them. For laws rest on principles of reason, from which they are derived. But experience often demonstrates that they are too indeterminate to be easily applicable in each case. In particular cases, therefore, closer determinations have been sought, and these are contained in the precedents. We thereby ascertain how far the principles adopted are in conformity with experience, and such precedents therefore facilitate and support the drafting of general laws, since the principles acquire greater reliability through the endless empirical modifications. And likewise they serve to exercise the power of judgement. This capacity of the soul is still so largely undeveloped, that it would be well worth the trouble of further cultivation. It is impossible for it to be taught, i.e., that rules could be given it, for applying the laws of understanding to each individual case, or for subsuming the particular under the general; for such a rule would have to be needed in each individual case, since if it were to be general, i.e., applicable to numerous cases of the judgement, *in casu quovis*[r] other rules would be needed in order to determine its applicability. Hence it can only be *exercised.* It is therefore possible that a large understanding, with knowledge and discern-

27:535

---

[q] practical knowledge of law
[r] in any given case

294

ment of a wide-ranging mass of rules, may yet be coupled with a small degree of judgement. Thus it also follows that a *juris sciens* is by no means yet a *juris peritus* or *juris practicus.*

The *juris scientia*, objectively understood, is in fact a science or systematic knowledge of the law; since law must be derived from reason, and thus from principles, this science has, indeed, not only a perception of the general outline of the principles of law as a whole, but also a knowledge of the individual parts (differing therein from the subjective knowledge of a *vasta congeries* of rules, which hangs together only by way of their affinity); but if the science is at the same time *juris practicus*, it has an ability to subsume the *casus sub legibus.*

N.B. The outline of the whole is needed, in the same way as was said of the painter: *nulla dies sine linea*, i.e., no day must go by, without making a sketch of the entire human body. One must therefore be at pains to study the interconnection of all law, i.e., the possibility of the ground to its consequences.

We may distinguish two types: he who through experience is *shrewd*, i.e., negatively clever, and has gained a knowledge of his erroneous principles, and he who is intelligent and has become clever through experience, i.e., combines scientific knowledge and consciousness of the rules *in abstracto* with a practised judgement. A *jure consultus* is only that man in whom *juris scientia* and *juris peritia* are united.

§32. *Rationes legis* are *vel historicae, vel legales.*[5] The historical refer to a specific *factum*, that has given rise to the law. Such historical facts can never occur in regard to pure laws of reason, but only insofar as statutory laws are concerned.

A law has legal grounds, where its ground must be sought in another law. This certainly happens with statutory laws, insofar as these, too, rest on principles of reason; for example, the ban on polygamy in the Mosaic law is based on the relationship of women to the male sex. It is certain that more males are born, but also die off earlier in youth, so that the surplus of women over men amounts to a twentieth part, who cannot now be withdrawn from the specifically female functions, such as midwifery, nursing of children, etc.

§33. Laws determine the obligation to an action both *stricte* and *late. Leges stricte determinantes* are those which determine not only the nature of the obligation, but also the degree of it, i.e., whether, when and how much needs to be done; as in buying and selling, for example. All laws of right are of this type. Here the person under obligation has no choice left to him; though some part of the obligation, or even the whole of it, may be remitted.

Leges late determinantes, on the other hand, determine only the nature,

27:536

[5] reasons of law are either historical or legal

not the degree, of obligation to the action, so that in the fulfilment itself a certain latitude is left open, in which the owner of the duty is allowed freedom to do or omit; for example, the duty of well-doing determines only that I should support the other out of my means, but how much remains absolutely reserved to the measure of my needs, my resources, and the other's distress. All ethical duties, insofar as they are purely ethical, are of this type. Here the degree of obligation is wholly undetermined. So too with the duty of furthering one's perfection; everyone, to be sure, must cultivate himself, or enlarge his understanding and fortitude of mind, or improve his fortunes, insofar as that may be consistent with his other duties; yet in so doing the aim and sphere of operation are too diverse to admit of anything definite being laid down about them.

27:537

Here is the case where departures from the rule, or so-called *exceptiones,* occur, whenever the law does not have true generality or absolute necessity (and this would surely not be so in any ethical law); well-doing, for example, lapses if my own poverty or family needs have to be dealt with. This case is associated with conflict of duties, whenever another obligation clashes with the first, and the rules are therefore in contention. This is called an *antinomia legum,* though, needless to say, it is not the laws (*stricti juris,* nor the rules *lati juris*) that are here themselves in conflict, for this would be a contradiction among duties. Laws and rules could not be universal, and thus necessary, if the opposite were not impossible; so two universal duties cannot contradict one another; it is only the grounds of duty, the *rationes obligandi,* that are in conflict here, because each of them would only be an insufficient ground for determining the act of duty; for example, a friend has shown me kindness, and falls into distress; as such, I certainly owe him gratitude, but *in quovis casu* this duty is only an *obligatio late determinans.* Suppose the money I might give to be already earmarked for payment of a debt; this is a greater obligation, since it binds absolutely, and though its *ratio obligandi* – reciprocation – may here come into conflict, even in respect of fairness, with the creditor's affluence, and the fact that it would do me no harm not to pay him now, and other *rationes obligandi,* it is nevertheless easy to decide which *rationes* lose their weight – duty settles the matter.

The rule here is: *Lex fortior vincit; regulae si collidunt, a minore fit exceptio.*[1] So imperfect duties always succumb to perfect ones, just as several imperfect duties outweigh a single one; for example, the distress of another, were it even to be mortal, could not compel me to contract debts or be grateful, when my parents would starve. Now we can never say here that it is absolutely impossible to fulfil both duties, and the duties remain, even though they are not fulfilled; for, as we have said, laws and rules can never contradict one another; there is, rather, a contrary action of the

_____

[1] the stronger law prevails; if rules conflict, make an exception to the lesser

grounds of one duty against those of the other, and this brings it about that the two cannot co-exist, since the ground of the one binds more strongly than that of the other, e.g., duty over gratitude. 27:538

§34. The *principia* of duties of right may be *domestica,* i.e. grounds of duty such that they belong solely to the *principles of morality* itself; these must be drawn from the science itself, and thus here, where they are supposed to determine our conduct, or our free choice according to laws of reason, they have to be derived, through reason, from the idea of freedom.

Otherwise, such *principia* are *peregrina,*[a] if the ground of duty is taken from other sciences, or merely from practical reason; for example, if the ground of duty is posited in the divine will, it is either drawn from metaphysics, namely *theologia naturalis,* insofar as the divine will is known through reason, or else derived from *theologia revelata,* and in that case it is empirical. Even human statutory laws can likewise give occasion to *principia;* and *in statu civili* they will also be *domestica,* since they are drawn from civil legislation, whereas *in statu naturali* they are *peregrina. Principia peregrina* are *propaedeutica (praeliminaria),* insofar as other sciences provide principles which are useful for a better understanding of moral principles and facilitate their use, for example, metaphysics; psychology, since it rests on experience, cannot explain theoretical morality or legal doctrine, since their concepts are purely metaphysical, i.e., abstracted merely from reason without the aid of experience, and the latter, indeed, can never become a criterion for the right and wrong that are elevated above it; in ascetic morality, on the other hand, many doctrines are explicable through the natural character of mankind. Such *principia peregrina* are, alternatively, *episodica,* as principles borrowed, in the form of *lemmata,* from other sciences, e.g. the history of morality. *Corollaria practica* drawn from moral principles are *porismata.*

The *propaedeutica* differ from the *episodica* in this respect, that the former yield a constitutive *principium* in practical philosophy, in order to derive one doctrine or another from that; the *episodica,* on the other hand, are only contingently in a position to contribute to the elucidation of a part of the science, and this only in regard to the application and use of the same.

§35. The theory of law is at the same time pragmatic, if it is furnished with instructions for the application of its use, i.e., contains rules of prudence as to the best use of means to the attainment of all the given subjective ends that we can but propose to ourselves. Insofar as we look to the agreement of the action with its end, it is a doctrine of prudence, and differs in that respect from the theory of law as a doctrine of wisdom, which, insofar as it is pragmatic, restricts the use of means to the objective 27:539

[a] foreign, extraneous

end of the action, i.e. the end we ought to have, and demands, in other words, that choice should determine itself solely according to the law of reason. Hence the rectitude of the action points to its agreement with the right of man as such, and permits no given end if it is contrary to the right of mankind in general, to which, indeed, the doctrine of prudence may also be opposed, but only insofar as the intent of the action would not be consistent with this.

§36. The *principia juris* must be sharply distinguished from the *principia ethicis*, which Baumgarten has neglected to do, just as the determination of the supreme principle of distinction, which in itself is very difficult, has never till now been worked out.

Professor Kant locates the supreme *principium juris*

in the limitation of anyone's freedom, through reason, to the condition that the freedom of each concur with the freedom of everyone, according to universal law.

He deduces from this, as *corollarium,* the authorization to resist, or a right of coercion, insofar as the freedom of the other's action would violate the supreme principle of right, i.e., that the other's freedom would infringe upon your freedom, which coincides with the freedom of everyone according to universal law; whence he sets forth all actions, with respect to right and duty, only upon a negative determination of the rights themselves, and also concludes that, so long as this *principium* is not violated, i.e., so long as my action (the freedom of my action, that is) is directed according to universal law, and thus effects no abridgement of universal freedom, no further reference is needed to any material quality of the action, whether it is consistent, for example, with the happiness, the wishes, the contentment or the need of the other, or runs counter to his ends as much as it pleases; thus the supreme principle of right has no matter of the action as its topic, but only the determination of the form thereof; every end you please, every object without distinction, can be coupled with it; the action can be self-serving, but righteous nonetheless.

27:540 Kant posits, accordingly,

What is *mine*, in every object of my choice, whose free, voluntary (self-interested) use can co-exist with the freedom of everyone.

What is mine presupposes only a coupling of the subject with the object, of such a kind that it becomes possible for him to exercise a choice upon it, and then requires nothing further, save that the subject satisfies the principle of universal jurisprudence – *neminem laede.* Such a principle as: Give to the other of what is yours, is here totally inapplicable, for since all principles of universal right enjoin categorically, there can be no thought of any right to demand something from the other, whatever the conditions may be. It is quite another matter if one puts oneself under the public law principle, *suum cuique tribue,* by subjection to a condition of legal order; here it can be determined, whether and when a thing should be given to another from my own store. But these voluntary determinations thereafter make even the legal relationships very complicated. Thus Professor Kant maintains that in the State, a poor man has gained the right to demand support from the wealthy; for if it were left to his unrestricted choice, it would be perfectly open to him to earn so much for himself that he could make provision for hard times; but the State has now limited his wages and possible earnings by taxation, whereby the rich man gets more advantages than he could in a state of equality; thus the poor man earns only enough for his current needs, and his savings are taken away from him.

In a *status naturalis*, on the other hand, it is also possible to conceive of a situation in which nobody can earn more than is required to meet his necessities, and since here, already, he can give nothing away, a duty to do so can never be categorically adopted. Professor Kant believes that if there is respect only for a universal law, such a situation might very well be realized. He cites the Greenlanders, especially the widows, who have to go hungry like everyone else; the children would sooner do away with their parents, seeing that it is impossible for them to make a living by catching fish.

It lies, moreover, in the nature of this principle, that we must be wholly indifferent to all well-wishing, or other intentions towards us.

N.B. The *principium* of ethics, on the other hand, divides into   27:541

1. The *principium ethicum*, which is purely formal, since it has to do only with the disposition from which the action is supposed to arise. It is called the general principle of virtue, or of virtuous duty, the action conforming thereto, and consists *generaliter* in this:

Act according to law for the law's sake, or do your duty from duty. Act, that is, not only according to the law's imperative, but perform the act also, merely because the motive of your action is the law itself. This principle of action is subjective; it refers to the motivating ground of the agent, which is supposed to be the law. The principle of right, on the other hand, views itself as objective, because the action is determined from the right of the other, and what right ordains must be done, whatever sort of motivating ground the agent may choose to have. Hence the difference between the legality and the morality of the action.

2. The *principium ethices*, which is material, since it itself determines the action that is to be done, and thus has to do with the performance of virtuous duties. It runs:

Act so towards other men, that you *can will* that the maxim of your action might become a universal law.

Here, then, the object is not universal freedom, but will in relation to the universal will. This universal will consists in the universal end of all men, and is called love for others, the principle of well-wishing, directed to the universal end of happiness.

It is, in fact, impossible for a man to will that the universal law of freedom should exist and be exercised, when it would run counter to the universal end of mankind. His own will compels him, in that case, to make no use of his legitimate freedom, since otherwise, by his own law, he would have to deprive himself of universal co-operation. He can thus will morally only that which is in accordance with the universal end of man, namely happiness, as the universal end of his action; yet he can only *will* this, and for that very reason, this will cannot have unconditioned obligatoriness; the limits of well-wishing cannot be determined, and hence moral laws are only *late determinantes*, only *generales*, never *universales;* they are therefore – as this general principle also is – a rule and not a law.

27:542

Now to determine by this the ethico-legal spirit of our actions, Professor Kant develops the formal and material principle of dutiful actions in the following way:

In regard to the determining ground of our dutiful acts, we may consider duties in relation to form and matter.

If we consider the use of our freedom merely under a formal condition, the action is lacking in a determinate object that might essentially contribute a determination thereto, or we abstract from all objects. The determinate form points to a limitation of freedom, namely to the universal legitimacy of the action, in that in the latter *requisitum* there lies the form of the dutiful act, viz. that it must be determined according to universal right, and by the condition that the maxim of the action can at the same time be universally legislative. For this formal condition has reference to strict duty, or duty of right, but according to universal right without regard for whether it concerns duty to others or duty to myself, right against myself, or right against others. In this sense universal right is a genus with respect to external relationships of right, as a sub-species.

This quality of rectitude in actions also includes their ethical form, i.e., that the form of all our knowledge of duty rests on this, that not only is the action done according to law, but that the law itself is the action's motive; that the agent determine himself, therefore, not only to a duty towards himself, but also in regard to another's rights against him, without any coercion and solely out of respect for the law and the right resulting from this.

Both things, that the action accord with the law, and be done for the sake of it, constitute the essential condition of the form of the action, and have as their consequence that an action that would have to be done from coercive duty, now comes about without compulsion. This formal condition of choice in human actions might be called the spirit of the action.

If, on the other hand, we consider duties and their grounds of determination in regard to matter, then the action has need of an object to which it is related. This object, or the matter in this determination of duty, is the end of the action. Though the latter is undetermined in its limits, there is nevertheless an end that we *ought* to have in view when performing our

27:543

duties, and which must thus be so constituted that the condition of universal rectitude can coexist with it. So in this principle also, right and obligation are present, but if the action is judged solely according to the material principle, the latter stands *in opposito* to strict right in the purposiveness of the action. Apart from the freedom of the action, there is thus another principle present, which in itself is enlarging, in that, while freedom is restricted by the determination according to law, it is here, on the contrary, enlarged by the matter or end thereof, and something is present that has to be acquired. Universal moral right now divides up, accordingly, into formal duty and material duty according to strict right. (Here *ethico-legale*, not *legale in sensu civili*),

    a. In regard to the rectitude of the action

      1. into the right of humanity in my own person, and
      2. into the right of other men towards myself.

The former presents in man only a personified person, who determines his inner use of freedom, is wholly inviolable and so unconfined that here no end of the action can be articulated, nor constitutes an exception. There is no talk here of rights against others, or of others against me; everything, rather, has to do with strict duty and strict right in one's own person. It can never, therefore, be adopted according to laws of right, but only ethically; a proof that even ethics is not essentially coupled with ends, but carries with it strict right in the universal sense.

    b. In regard to purposiveness, i.e., insofar as moral duty relates to ends in its determining ground, this is either

      1. the end of humanity in my own person, or
      2. the end of other men,

and to this end, therefore, my acts should have a relation, a congruence.

The end of humanity in my own person is my perfection, and the duty relating thereto, that of cultivating all the talents to be found in me. This is a duty, since it rests on necessitation, in that it is not attained without resistance from sensory impulses; the end of humanity in regard to other people is to promote their happiness. This is likewise a duty of our external relationships, by universal right, and to this end the earlier one is at the same time a means, in that if a man perfects himself, he makes himself fit for all desired ends, i.e., creates the inner means for all possible purposes; for the more a man gathers knowledge, and cultivates understanding and imagination, and the more he is in a position to direct the lower faculties of the soul, the fitter he becomes to attain ends. The rules that pertain to this are stated as follows:

      1. So act, that the maxim of your action may be a rule for everyone, in regard to the ends of your humanity; and
      2. in regard to the ends that can be attributed to all men.

27:544

Although 'end' is equivalent in meaning to the concept of what brings happiness, actions, with respect to the end, should not, however, be subjected to a duty in regard to our own happiness, but should rather promote, in fact, the universal end of all men, namely, happiness; because nobody can be compelled to promote his own happiness; only he can will this, only he can procure it for himself, and we cannot prescribe to him the ways of attaining it.

§37. Baumgarten, in §100, explains a legislator as *auctor obligationis quam lex enunciat,*[v] a definition which Professor Kant amends as follows: an *auctor legis* can be supposed only of a law that has no binding power of its own, but possesses it merely *ex voluntate vel arbitrio alterius.*[w] Since an *auctor* is *causa per arbitrium liberum,* and therefore everything depends on his choice, it can only be applied to a *lex statutaria.*

Were we to conceive of the legislator as an *auctor legis,* this would have reference only to statutory laws. But if we ascribe an *auctor* to laws that are known, through reason, from the nature of the case, he can only be author of the obligation that is contained in the law. Thus God, too, by the declared divine will, is *auctor legis,* and precisely because natural laws were already in existence, and are ordained by Him. Now the law is accompanied by consequences arising from it, whose result would not have been known to man by reason alone; for example, that acts of beneficence will also be coupled with the agent's contentment. If, now, the laws are presented as express commands, man assumes that their outcome will promote his happiness; he views the law-giver as creator of his happiness, and hence, as soon as we think of God as law-giver, we make claim to his *benignitas* and regard Him as a benefactor; for He thereby works towards the universal necessary end of all men. He has their happiness in His hands, as the universal end, and the assumption of such a creator is also the basis of the willingness to follow His laws. Hence, too, it is not contrary to reason to assume the possibility of God's existence in this respect; for reason is otherwise sufficient to think of this being as creator of the laws, and from the fact that God serves only as creator, a binding force of the laws does not actually follow, since the existence of man is not by itself a *factum* that produces any obligation. But that the reality of a God should be demonstrable from reason is impossible. If one wished to conclude from the morality of actions to an originator of moral laws, this, regarded as a requirement, would be to determine oneself by oneself; it can indeed also be inferred, from the purposiveness that we perceive everywhere in nature, that in regard to the moral nature of man a similar ordering of things is possible; but this ground can function as a motive to moral actions only insofar as the law is already known by reason. There is,

27:545

---

[v] author of the obligation that is stated by the law
[w] from the will or choice of another

however, no denying that if, over and above the moral law, we go on to think of a being who is able to unite with the law the consequences appropriate to the action, who is author of our happiness, who knows and gauges our worthiness to fare well, or our moral worth, then by this there arises an Idea very useful to man's disposition, which steels him in his moral conduct against all the obstacles he may encounter. Even if there be no objective duty to assume a positive divine will, it is nevertheless subjectively possible, accordingly, to think of a divine command present in our fulfilment of duty – an idea that was first openly associated by Anaxagoras with the ground of morality, and subsequently adopted by Plato. Now just as the author of a natural law can be thought of only as the originator of obligation according to the law's imperative, so a person under sanction, if he is to conceive an *auctor legis*, whether it be God or an earthly legislator, can really only suppose this for positive or contingent laws, which become 27:546 binding rules merely *ex voluntate superioris*, and in this way only can he understand the *declaratio* of the law-giver's will as that of an *auctor legis*. It is in this way, specifically, that we understand the sanction of punishments attaching to observance of the law, and call them *sanctio poenalis*. Punishments, as such, can also be appended to natural laws, but in that case, like the *sanctio* itself, they are merely contingent.

The term 'law-giver', in Kant's view, should designate only that man who is *necessitator*, in order to determine the will to observance of a law which the other knows, indeed, but would not have obeyed without this necessitation; the person, therefore, who employs coercion. Professor Kant goes on to maintain, *contra* Baumgarten, that the moral law does not make it a condition to acknowledge a God and assume that the laws are His commands. Religion, in that sense, is not moral, since it rests on the disposition to carry out all duties as divine commands. In that case they would merely be statutory laws, if it was only through knowing them that we obtained knowledge of what our duty is; but since it is the other way round, duties are founded solely on natural laws, which are merely co-ordained through God's declared will to the same effect. The *potestas legislatoria*[x] rests entirely on benevolence towards those who are to be obligated through the law-giving will.

It is impossible for man to obey, or have any duty to comply with, a law that would totally abolish his happiness. For the opposite, however, there is a *consensus* to obedience, because compliance represents a promotion of the general welfare. And thus it is, too, with the general consent of mankind to the divine commandments, which have been acknowledged because they are appropriate to man's welfare. We are similarly disposed in regard to the willing voiced by human legislators, which has a natural law as its basis; but it is called statutory law, because of the

[x] power to legislate

consequences that are annexed to fulfilment or transgression of the obligation. Now insofar as we conceive, in a legislation, the relation of a superior with an inferior, we are contemplating a state of inequality. Yet this cannot run counter to the moral freedom of man; for once it is established that man determines himself only through his own laws, 27:547 determined by his free choice, and if it is only in such a fashion that we can understand how man may be bound, then this inequality must also be derived from equality; the law, that is, must be given with his own agreement, or at least must be capable of being seen as though it sprang from the united will of the *subditi.*[y] And were this authority not ascribable to him as a free man, no moral obligation could be imputed to him; only his physical nature would be coercible, he would be *res in patrimonio* like the *servus romanus,*[z] and would also have no right to coerce. Even if we ask whether man can be regarded as *mancipia divina,*[a] we would have to deny this as well.

God himself can give man no other laws, save those that can coexist with the freedom recognized by reason; the happiness that He is alone in a position to provide us must be appropriate to this freedom. He can command only as a man may do, save with this difference, that He surveys the law to its utmost extent. It is impossible to conceive of God as an absolute ruler, since without subjecting Him to the condition of moral freedom, the latter is no longer thinkable, and nor is any moral obligation either. He can thus be no despot, and man no slave. He is, to be sure, unlimited only in this, that no moral necessitation can be supposed in Him, in regard to the determination of His will, since He lacks the limitation imposed on human nature, of an inclination to contravene the laws; but from this it does not follow that He has an unconditioned will.

§38. *Praemia* and *poenae. Praemia* are rewards, or a physical good apportioned to someone because of a moral good.

Poena, punishment, is the physical evil apportioned to someone because of moral evil. Since rewards follow because of moral good, they do not lie in the nature of the action, but are merely contingent, and conjoined with it, indeed, through the will of a third party.

N.B. The morally good is any fulfilment of one's moral duty, so that a good action and a righteous one are the same. Any morally good action is therefore subject to moral necessitation by the law; only when actually 27:548 committed do actions divide into:

a. *Debita* or incumbent duties, which become necessary through the right of other men, and are thus coupled with a right to coerce. *In sensu morali* these are negatively good – not punishable.

[y] subjects
[z] a chattel like the Roman slave
[a] the property of God

b. *Merita* or deserving duties, whose performance is not absolutely necessary, their fulfilment, and how and in what manner this is to occur, being left to the agent. *In sensu morali* these are positively good, capable of reward,

Laws of right, or coercive laws, can therefore never grant *praemia*, in that the most perfect fulfilment of them lies in their nature, and they have an *oppositum* only in punishment. Reward, therefore, presupposes no coercive duty, but an ethical one, along with the will of another person; just as *merces* differs again from that, in that it requires an action to which I would not have been obliged without a reward, and to which I therefore incur the obligation through the reward. An action is thus undertaken for the sake of payment, i.e., the commitment to it results only because of a bettering of my welfare, the enjoyment of a good, which I expect to follow; for example, when, to encourage silkworms, the sovereign offers a reward for planting mulberry trees, or some other action, which he cannot expect by means of a coercive law. For the sake of payment, the agent does more than is incumbent on him, and in that case can regard his action as a *meritum* or service, relative to his appointed tasks, for which he demands the *merces* as a *debitum*.

The *merces* is also reckoned among the *praemia*, seeing that here, too, a physical good is at least the ground of the act of duty; and it is distinguished thus, that

praemium gratuitum is called the reward, and
praemium debitum the *merces ab effectu.*[b]

§39. *Praemia* are divided into

a. *naturalia*, or all good outcomes from our dutiful actions; for example, moderation in physical life is rewarded by health, loyalty and truth in conduct by respect and honour, and so with every benefit that arises from our good actions. These are *praemia ethica*, which are also called *arbitraria divina*, because God is thought of as the source of order in nature; and into: 27:549

b. *arbitraria*, or benefits arbitrarily bestowed.

§40. The nature of duty does not allow of being coupled with the idea of reward. So reward can never be the motive of a moral act of duty, since the latter must be presented through the law itself. On ethical principles, therefore, an action undertaken in the hope of reward could never have morality, though it might well have legality. Apart from that, if the reward would also constitute a ground for the obligation to pay for the action, or a *debitum intuitu dantis,*[c] it would become a *meritum intuitu agentis*, and thus

---

[b] payment for services rendered
[c] a debt in the eyes of the giver/a fee in the eyes of the agent

a recompense. The *animus* with which the action was undertaken would be *animus servilis*[d] (*mercenarius*), and not *animus ingenuus*, an *indoles erecta*, as a dutiful action requires it to be.

The worthiness to be happy, that is attained by the fulfilment of all duties, can indeed expect the reward of also being happy; but it follows from the above that the happy state resulting should in no way be coupled with the fulfilment of duties, since it does not depend on that; the agent cannot therefore expect it, as *merita debita*,[e] in virtue of his action, but only as *gratuita merita*. Now the idea that in a future life we expect a reward that would be commensurate with our morally good acts in this world, can be joined with the dutifulness of our actions in this way only, that we think of it as a means for reconciling the wisdom of the creator, in world-history, to the order of things. For wisdom, here, is the agreement of morality with a happiness of man commensurate thereto. To conceive this gives respect for the moral law, and this is the spirit of morality. If we reverse the order of things (and this seems to happen in the world), then by that, and the removal, as condition, of the necessity for a proportionate happiness, morality seems to suffer a blow; there seems then to be a visible deficiency, which declares all our moral worth to be a glittering delusion. So to rescue the latter from an objection of reason:

27:550   Act as you please, the consequences may equally well be good or bad for you,

we have need of the hypothesis, that this purposeful harmony between ground and consequence will be manifested in the life to come. Furthermore, this idea of a future happiness is coupled with a notion of disinterestedness; the creator is thought of as a law-giver, who cannot require obedience and docility save by virtue of His benevolence, whereby He seeks, through His commands, to make His subjects happy as well, and who absolutely cannot be indifferent to their welfare; in a future life, therefore, He will bestow on us a happiness commensurate with the morality of our actions. This leads us to decide, here and now, to regulate our actions in accordance with the moral laws.

§41. What the law commands, it puts no price on; that is contrary to the nature of a prohibitive law, such as all *leges naturales* are, since their negative quality is inconsistent with the idea of gain.

Every payment presupposes a *pactum bilaterale loc. cond. operarum*,[f] in that by the constitution of the payment the obligation to the action is established, and by the latter, the obligation to pay; thus a contract of *do-facio* and *des-facias*.[g] The recipient earns the money, therefore, as *debitum*

---

[d] mean-minded and mercenary, not open and upright

[e] a recompense due/a payment freely bestowed

[f] a two-sided pact contingent on performance

[g] I give, I do . . . you give, you do

dantis.[h] Now by the nature of duties, nobody is bound to give anything to the other. The law-giver merely commands, absolutely, by his will, to withhold nothing that already belongs to the other; no contract forms the basis of the law, under whose condition fulfilment is supposed to ensue, and so the agent can have no *meritum* for himself that he could seek to found on a *debitum* of the law-giver. The *praemium* that he may expect can therefore only be *gratuitum*, insofar as he wishes to link his welfare with the act. A *praemium gratuitum* therefore constitutes a *debitum* of the receiver, and a *meritum* of the giver, because the law obliges absolutely, so that here there can be no thought of a *debitum merens* – a service in the act. It is well-doing from grace, and so the *meritum*, too, is mere gracious acknowledgement.

§42. Professor Kant therefore comments as follows on the statement of Baumgarten (§111): *Committe quod plurima maxima praemia spondet, omitte hujus oppositum;* Do that which is worthy of the greatest reward, i.e., observe the moral law through your own commitment to duty, so that you may be able to bring your physical state into agreement with your moral state. Do, therefore, what conforms to the law, so that you may become worthy of happiness. To that extent the author is correct; but reward cannot be a motive to the action, and there lies in the word *spondet* (promises) a connection between happiness and the worthiness to be happy, which is taken to hold as a condition of the action, and this is false.

§43. In punishments, likewise, a voluntaristic element has been supposed, in that, from the power of natural laws, a similar personification has also been made of things in nature, to the effect that they seek to determine a state of physical nature in keeping with man's moral conduct.

All punishments are divided into:

1. *Poenae vindicativae sive morales in sensu stricto*[i] – retaliatory punishments, i.e., those that are inflicted because some crime has been committed (*quia peccatum est*).
2. *Poenae correctivae sive pragmaticae,* i.e., that are imposed *ne peccetur,*[j] and thus provide a means of preventing transgression.

These are

a. *Animadversiones sive castigantes poenae,*[k] which fall upon the agent himself, to inhibit him from moral evil.
b. *Exemplares,* whose purpose is that others shall be kept from transgression.

[h] a debt of the giver
[i] punishments vengeful or moral in the strict sense
[j] punishments corrective or pragmatic, lest an offence be committed
[k] animadversions, or punishments by rebuke

27:551

N.B. The first are truly the *poenae justitiae*, because they are immediately necessary according to the principles of justice – the others are *deterrentes*, insofar as the punishment is viewed at the same time as a means; in *castigationes*, as a means of improving the *peccans*, and in *exemplares*, as a means of preventing further crime by others. A distinction is therefore made between *justitia et prudentia poenitiva;* the latter merely determines the amount of coercion the transgressor of the law may encounter; since every punishment must be based on justice, it is therefore subordinated also to *justitia poenitiva,* and must furthermore be so framed at all times, that it is in a position to promote morality, or at least not to restrict it. Hence the penal laws of Joseph II were just but not prudent, since they did away with motives of honour.

27:552   In punishments, a physical evil is coupled to moral badness. That this link is a necessary one, and physical evil a direct consequence of moral badness, or that the latter consists in a *malum physicum, quod moraliter necessarium est,*[1] cannot be discerned through reason, nor proved either, and yet it is contained in the concept of punishment, that it is an immediately necessary consequence of breaking the law; for if we take it that punishment serves only to frighten others away from crime, or to deter the criminal himself from further moral badness, then we are looking upon punishment merely as a way of achieving other intentions, or as a means; for it is a means, an act of graciousness or clemency, if I seek to improve the criminal himself, or an act of prudence, if I attempt thereby to prevent further wrong-doing. Punishment, however, should follow *quia peccatum est,* and thus be tied to the act itself. The question here is whether this is necessary, i.e., whether the morality of the action stands coupled, here, with the physical evil, seeing that they are two heterogenous things; here we can find only a propriety, which has its basis in the impropriety of a discrepancy between the consequences and the action itself. Our idea of justice requires that the moral worth of the action be recognized. We think it quite contrary to the order of things, that a morally bad action should by its nature be coupled with impunity, and punishment depend merely on arbitrary chance; reason at all times connects the rectitude of moral conduct with worthiness for happiness, and considers the transgressor as unworthy of the latter; the judicial office, by virtue of its law-giving power, is called upon by reason to repay, to visit a proportionate evil upon the transgression of moral laws. Otherwise, there lies nothing else in nature, save that moral badness is necessarily recognized as morally bad; that it also has to be punished by action, is supported by no *a priori* proof, and nor can it be inferred *a posteriori* either; for example, one man debauches himself and falls sick, another's strong constitution keeps him in health.

---

[1] physical evil that is morally necessary

§44. Now from this it is evident that an essential *requisitum* of any punishment is that it be *just*, i.e., that it is an immediately necessary consequence of the morally bad act; and this, indeed, is what its quality consists in, that it is an *actus justitiae*, that the physical evil is imparted on account of the moral badness. Hence its justice does not follow, if it is inflicted to improve the criminal, or as an example to others. This would simply have to do with its usefulness, and then it would be merely a means to that intent, for example, if somebody is flogged, whether guilty or not, in order to frighten people by his outcry, and create an impression. It is also intrinsic to justice that the transgressor knows within himself what his action is worth. But if the punishment is just, then the degree and nature of it, and whether a physical penalty is needed, are decided as prudence and mercy may dictate. Here justice, which rests in itself on wholly indispensable principles, does have a certain *latitudo*. If punishment had reform as its object, it would be doubtful, after a man's death, whether punishment could have occurred. For the criminal, it would be too late to reform, since in such a case his actions would have been decisively judged, and others are so little acquainted with the punishment, and the future is so uncertain, that it could not make any impression on them. The sole means of defence consists in this, that we find it incompatible with God's justice, and the order of things, that anyone might commit a crime with total impunity, that even in the next world no settlement should ensue, in accordance with the worthiness of actions.

27:553

We say of the human law-giver, when soliciting pardon from him, that he should *temper justice with mercy*. Now since the law demands absolute adherence, a universal justice can admit of no curtailment, and *ex stricto jure* the judge may in no case depart from punishing the action as it deserves. No remission is to be thought of, therefore, where a universal law is the guideline, whose suspension on behalf of any individual would establish a general claim to the same effect. But where, on the other hand, a statutory law is in question, depending solely on the whim of the law-giver, and in which only the person of the law-giver, and his private interest, are affected, so that private interests, and not those of the state, are at issue, then in that case the law-giver, by his own will, may relax the obligation that he imposes. For here we have no law that can be generally invoked, but only a *statutum*.

§45. It seems to be inherent in the idea of penal law, that it be persistent in its demand for punishment. We can never presuppose reformation among men, and are too weak to discern the inner motivations of crime. A merchant of morally upright conduct and blameless principles was beheaded at Marseilles, because 20 years previously he had for a time been a camp-follower in the Cartouche gang, and only later came under criminal investigation on that account. It seems, then, that crimes can never lapse from the record, and even after the longest time-span, when a complete

27:554

reform of life has been effected, would still contain no claim on that account to remission of punishment.

§46. The question arises, as to how far, by undergoing punishment, the breach of the moral law may be taken to be nullified for the transgressor.

To some extent, we regard the endurance of physical evil as a discharge of the debt that was owed to justice; so, *poenam dare, solvere.*[m] There is no denying that justice is satisfied with that, and in the eyes of others, the liability to punishment is annulled by its infliction; but we cannot conclude from this, that before the tribunal of his reason the criminal now becomes free of all reproach, once he has satisfied the demands of justice; he must first of all have become a better man, before he can absolve himself. So that man is declared infamous, whom the law holds to be no longer corrigible, and the *salva fama*[n] indicates reserve as to the moral improvement to be expected.

§47. Though there may be punishments that could be threatened, without seriousness, by the law-giver, it is then such threats, as employed, for example, by theologians in regard to *aeternae divinae poenae,* that would be the means of deterring men from crime; at the same time, however, the punishment itself, since its full execution is not linked to the offence, would likewise be a deception that can never be accepted.

§48. Whether a man can actually punish himself?

There was a sect of ascetics, the flagellants, who from supposed religious principles inflicted bodily evil upon themselves, by scourgings and chastisements; but the source of this was either fanaticism or despair, which misled them into repression of their own self-respect. And in this there lies a contradiction; for a punishment should surely be a coercion that is set in opposition to transgression of the laws of freedom, and it rests, moreover, on an external source of law. Now since every man is himself free, he cannot, of course, coerce himself, and so cannot punish himself, either, by his own penances. Among the flagellants, the motivating-ground may well be looked for in this, that by self-chastisement in amounts of their own choice they wished to escape the more apposite and severe penalties of the law. Yet it is strange, nonetheless, that when once we acknowledge our act to be worthy of punishment, we straightway think of someone who has the authority to punish us, and for this reason, and because we cannot punish ourselves for our offences, there naturally follows the idea that we think of God as the moral judge, who will deal out evils appropriate to our own unlawful actions, as to those of other men.

§49. The principle of all penal laws is none other than the *jus talionis*[o] albeit under the condition that consideration be given to the spirit of the

27:555

---

[m] to punish is to exonerate
[n] but for his reputation
[o] law of retaliation in kind

action. It is therefore to be assumed that he who kills, abuses or robs another, kills, abuses or robs himself to exactly the same degree; in general all evils that are inflicted on the other under the law of coercion, he inflicts, by universal laws of freedom, on himself; for he can only offend the other to just the extent that the other can compel him to desist from the offence, or not to use his right; but this, by universal laws of freedom, is equal and unconditioned for everyone.

This *jus talionis* admits of so little exception, that it is not even allowed to the judge, to substitute one punishment for another, since he must absolutely comply with what justice requires; so he who kills another must die in his turn, and it is out of the question to suppose that any substituted punishment could here be just. All substituted means of punishment are lacking in proportion, and degenerate into mere arbitrariness; if on abolition of capital punishment, for example, we were to choose, *gradatim,* all corporal evils, labour under close confinement, bad food, want of light and air, warmth and clothing. The result is, that for a man of feeling, all punishments associated with public disgrace are more unendurable than death itself, whereas for the mean-spirited, they stand far lower in the scale than death. The man of honour chooses death, the knave the tumbrel. Thus in the [Scottish] conspiracy on behalf of the Young Pretender, Lord Lovat would have chosen the second, and Lord Balmerino the first.*

All means of punishment, therefore, which merely aim at protecting   27:556 the person and property of men, are but means and signs of the punishment itself. From the man who robs me of my honour, I am entitled to compel an admission, that he is himself as unworthy as he deems me to be. The man who steals from me, I have the right to punish only by depriving him of his freedom, because more would plunge him into a state of penury. No punishment should be coupled with cruelty, i.e., it must not be so framed that humanity itself is thereby brought into contempt, the worth of the person abolished and turned into *a thing,* e.g., the streetsweeping and boat-hauling of Joseph II, in regard to persons, whole classes. All cruel tortures are also needless, for since death is the most dreadful, it may be assumed that anyone undaunted by capital punishment is also superior to all other torments as well.

§50. The promising of a *reward* (as in *leges brabeuticae,* compensatory laws), insofar as it is regarded as a motive to action, seems to involve an *animus mercenarius;* for since the act is supposed to be undertaken, uncon-

*[Both, in fact, were beheaded, after the Jacobite rising of 1745, but Kant is not much mistaken in his estimate of Lord Lovat. The German editors, having misread his name as 'Laval', are, however, mistaken in identifying him as Gilles de Laval, Baron de Retz, a fifteenth-century villain who – whatever his other crimes – had nothing to do with the 1745 rising. – Tr.]

ditionally, for the sake of the law itself, it would be self-serving, insofar as the ground of determination lies in the payment. Yet this does not so straightforwardly follow, and it is possible that the agent may nevertheless feel obligated to the action spontaneously, the only effect of the reward being that the agent loves the legislator, and this love reinforces respect for the law itself, and determines him, furthermore, to gratitude. It is quite otherwise in regard to punishments. These invariably damage morality; the victim believes that if the law had not been there, he would not suffer the physical evil; thus the law brings about an aversion towards it on his part, and he is thereby hampered from passing a free judgement on the morality of his action. In order not to feel this hindrance, the *animus servilis* must already be large, and the punitive law is at least a misleading guide to this.

Punitive laws also injure even those who have no inclination whatever to break them, because they are, after all, being held capable of doing so. This was the case with the punishments threatened by Joseph II. So penal laws must therefore be coupled to natural duties only in the most extreme emergency.

§51. Fear for the law must not be fear for the corporal evil threatened, since it would then be pathological. It consists, rather, in apprehension lest we displease the law-giver by breaking the law. God is ultimately taken to be the judge, and then fear of God in the purely moral sense would be a childlike fear, not dread at God and His punishments.

27:557

If, alternatively, we take determination to action through reason as the basis, the agent must feel convinced that if he were to take upon himself the endurance of corporal evil, he would appear contemptible to himself; and he must do the action because, by the opposite, he would be displeasing to himself; and must put the fear of this before the corporal evils.

§52. Are there such trifles as could be seen as transgressions, but which, on account of their unimportance, would not be accountable, and thus might even be permitted? But there are absolutely none such, though in Jesuit casuistry they are accepted *sub voce* peccadillo (from which we get the word 'bagatelle'). For though, in the individual case, the consequence and effect may certainly be a small evil, the maxim adopted by the agent to perform the action, in his determination by the laws of freedom, still remains a large one, and unlimited in its consequences. It is an established fact, that nobody starts off with the grossest crimes, but has been seduced into them by steps which had their basis in subjective principles. It is a small thing when a child thoughtlessly hits another, but habit implants a lack of sensitivity here, and the offender no longer feels anything. From this come steps to acts of violence, and with other maxims concurring in the process, the child can become a murderer. It is already necessary to block the early sources.

By cajolery a liar can secure unfounded trust from people – who lose by giving him credit, etc.

All moral actions are already regarded, in and for themselves, as acts of duty, and arise, therefore, solely from moral necessitation by the law of freedom. The latter enjoins *absolute*, so any transgression of duty must, therefore, since the agent acts freely, be imputable, and precisely for that reason, any excuse to the effect that it came about through sensory impulses is totally unacceptable; we must presuppose, rather, that even the transgressor acts with consciousness of the moral law, since he recognizes freedom through reason. If he now acts against the law, this can only happen because he adopts the opposite of the law into the maxim of his action, and this must be followed by the most extended consequences. 27:558

To what extent, though, is one breach of duty larger or smaller than another, when a person acts disobligingly, merely, or callously, or brutally? Since all breach of duty arises from the habitual maxim, containing the opposite of obligation itself, there is in fact no degree, in regard to the source of the breach; on the contrary, all such actions are alike, and to that extent the Stoics were correct when they made the practice of virtue an absolute demand, and maintained that every violation was an iniquity, and every iniquity like another. Yet this always refers only to obligation, considered as sufficient reason for the action, to which, in transgression, the maxim serves as *oppositum directum;* things are very different, however, with the insufficient obligating grounds, which may simultaneously determine the agent to perform the action, and then again to abstain from it; *in casu collisionis* of these grounds, therefore, it is certainly possible to assume a degree among them, whereby one is larger than the other, and has to be so, since the action must, after all, occur or not. If the agent abstains, then, or does an action, regardless of whether the contrary binding force of the law was larger or smaller, his fault also is larger or smaller, by the measure of the motivating ground that thereby remained unfulfilled; thus the degrees of transgression are determined merely in regard to the objects of duties.

§53. Imputation rests on the concepts of *meritum* and *auctor circa factum.*[p]

Meritum or service is the quality of an action, whereby more good occurs in the course of it than the agent was liable for under laws of right; or, a law-abiding action, such that it could not have been compelled, however, in the measure to which it actually took place; e.g., when beneficence and philanthropy are coupled thereto. A *demeritum* or fault, on the other hand, is a breach of obligation, in which less than the *debitum* is delivered. *Auctor* is an originator of action. Originator means that in regard to its determining grounds the action can, in its first beginnings, be derived from him. Hence he is regarded as the effectual first cause, i.e., the determining ground of the action can be sought nowhere else in 27:559

[p] originator as to the fact

313

nature; he pushes another into the water, for example, and that person drowns. If it was a dizzy spell, then the cause was merely physical and a matter of natural necessity; it rested on no originative cause in the agent. If he was drunk, however, it was his doing to have gotten so; he knew the power of drink, and could have envisaged the possibility of evil consequences; he was thus the effectual cause, and it all began with him.

As originator, he starts on each occasion a series of actions, whose beginning and cause lay in himself, not in nature. The ground of the fact that man is an accountable being, lies

a. not simply and solely in the fact that he is a rational being; accountability will, indeed, be founded *a posteriori* on that, but *a priori* it can still be separated therefrom. The idea is acceptable *a priori* that man, by virtue of his rational capacity, can reflect upon the grounds and consequences of his action, without its morality having to be connected with that; whether the action be good or bad is contingent in both cases. The motive to the action may lie in him, and not in nature. He wants, for example, by his testimony or his actions, to gain advantages, even though it be highly damaging to the other; the deceiver therefore has need of much prudence and foresight, in order not to be unmasked. He can even act *greatly,* because he employs much strength and freedom of mind in his relation to the honest man. It is

b. absolutely necessary in addition, that he act with freedom, indeed it is only when considered as a free being that he can be accountable. For it is from laws of freedom that the duties arise, which he can fulfil or violate, and only to that extent is his action independent of nature. The effect of his powers is an action insofar as it relates to a law, and is called *factum;* and only an action engaged in under the law is accountable. Imputation consists then, *generaliter,* in the *judicium, aliquem esse auctorem alicujus vel boni vel mali.*[q]

It thus has regard to the law that determines whether a thing is good or bad, and contains the judgement that the agent is *causa libera vel auctor actionis (facti).*[r]

27:560 §54. Now for it to be determinable, which actions can be imputed or not, we have to distinguish the action in relation to duty, as to whether it has observed or violated the latter; and the result of that is, that all imputation must be grounded on a *meritum* or *demeritum,* and that all permissive laws carry no imputation with them, since the actions are *adiaphora,* and so do not fall under duty or coercive right.

Thus only those actions can be imputed, which fall under a duty of right or a duty of love.

Now in *omissiones et commissiones actionibus,* the *modus* is:

---

[q] judgement that a person has done something, either good or bad
[r] free cause or author of an action (or fact)

1. The observance of juridical duty is the performance of what is owing. There is therefore no *meritum* connected with it, and so none of the good consequences accruing to the other party can be accredited to the agent.

Observance of the law of right is unconditionally enjoined; here the agent cannot and should not pay heed to the advantages or disadvantages that ensue for others, when he carries out the law. He has no choice, but to follow it; he is under a duty, and is thus not *causa libera* (*auctor*) of his action; the creditor, for example, has the opportunity to employ to great advantage the loan that is repaid to him *in termino*.⁵ The debtor gets no merit from this.

*Imputationes vel ponens vel tollens.*¹ Under the latter *modus* we define the cases where the consequences of action cannot be imputed, namely in part the good consequences of an action due, and in part also the bad consequences of a meritorious act omitted. The *modus ponens*, on the other hand, determines the case of imputation, namely all evil consequences of a due action omitted, and the good consequences of a meritorious action. For actions from duty and the right of another do not proceed from freedom, as do good and meritorious acts of duty; and likewise due actions omitted infringe the other's freedom, but the omission of meritorious acts does not.

2. The omission of a duty of love (ethical) is no *demeritum*. The agent was not bound to the action *absolute*, since the fulfilment of this duty involved only *latitudo* and not *jus strictum*. Fulfilment of the duty itself therefore countenances permitted exceptions, where it does not have to be   27:561
followed, and so the evil consequences resulting cannot be imputed to the agent either; for example, I pay no heed to a case of distress that I had no obligation to relieve.

3. The omission, however, of a duty of right, like the observance of a duty of virtue, is always imputed in regard to all its consequences; I help someone in distress, for example; the outcome, whether it be large or small, is beneficial, and I am therefore entitled to reckon on gratitude.

The relief of distress was a *meritum*, since fulfilment of the duty was not necessary; but the action itself is free, since it arises from the law of freedom, to help others; I am its *causa libera*. Now from this it follows:

a. that insofar as law-abiding actions can be *merita*, they can also, to that extent, be imputed to us in regard to their good consequences.

b. that insofar as illegal actions can be *demerita*, they can also, to that extent, be imputed to us in regard to their bad consequences.

⁵ on time
ᵗ imputations that either affirm or deny

315

The transgression of a strict law is certainly *demeritum;* the transgression of an ethical law is not *demeritum,* but its fulfilment is *meritum.*

A person often, to be sure, imputes to himself as a *meritum* a thing of which he is not, in fact, *causa libera,* it being only a *meritum* of the course of nature; this seems to be a contradiction, since nature can engender no *meritum;* but, precisely because of this contradiction, it is called a *meritum fortunae;*[u] in a scuffle, for example, someone pierces another with a dagger, but strikes an abscess, by the lancing of which the other regains his health.

§55. *Imputatio,* then, is

a. *vel facti,* i.e., it presupposes that an action can be considered as a *factum.* For an action (*actio*) is either the effect of a *causa naturalis qua talis* (results from natural causes), and is then physical; or it is the effect of a *causa libera qua talis* (chosen with free will, from the law of freedom). It is then *factum,* and *causa facti libera qua talis, sive quoad ex libertate profundit*[v] determines the *auctor facti.*

27:562
Causa actionis makes the *factum,* and *causa facti* the action (*actio*). That property of the action, whereby somebody can be regarded as *auctor facti,* is called the *imputatio facti.*

b. *vel legis.* This presupposes, (a) that the action is subject to a law, whether it be *lex prohibitiva, praeceptiva* or *permissiva,* and (b) that the action can be subsumed under this law. *Imputatio legis* is thus the *applicatio legis ad factum sub lege sumptum.*[w]

In a syllogism, the *imputatio facti* always constitutes the minor premise, and the law the major; the *imputatio legis* is then inferred from them, e.g.:

lex (major)	The abuser shall restore his honour to the abused.
imp. facti (minor)	He has abused me.
∴	He must make amends.

Thus the law is always founded upon a certain *factum;* if such a *factum* is present in the case, the law is applied. From this it follows that, since the minor premise has first of all to be determined by a judgement, it is necessary to establish whether the case governed by the law is present; hence *indagatio facti,*[x] also known as *quaestio facti,* whereby we examine: (1) whether an action exist that is to be regarded as an *eventus causae liberae;*[y] (2) whether, if an action is present, such action be a *factum,* or have causality; (3) whether this person be *auctor* of the *factum.*

From this we see that, for purposes of imputation here, only such

---

[u] accidental benefit
[v] cause of the fact, either free as such or insofar as based upon freedom
[w] application of law to the fact subsumed under it
[x] investigation of the fact
[y] outcome or effect of free causes

circumstantiae deserve attention as stand connected with the action, either as main or contributory cause, and indeed as *effectus causae liberae*. These are the *varia attendenda in facto,*^z which are called *momenta in facto*. For apart from that, every effect is bound up with chance determinations that stand connected in space or time; but they do not yet qualify on that account to be fit for consideration as causes of an action to be imputed. 27:563 Thus the *quaestio facti* rests on the *indagatio momentorum in facto*. These too, as with *error et ignorantia* in regard to them, would be *essentialis*, and pertain to the *essentialia*, in that *essentialia facti* and *momenta in facto* are all one; and the opposite, or *extraessentialia*, have reference to everything that has no bearing on the *quaestio in facto* itself, and cannot be regarded as a *momentum* therein.

From this there now arises the *species facti*, or *enumeratio omnium momentorum in facto,*[a] just as in a *delictum* we have the *corpus delicti,*[b] or (1) the certainty of the existence of a *delictum*, and (2) the outward signs indicating that a *delictum* has occurred. But the concept of *species facti* is broader than that of *corpus delicti*.

In ascertaining the *circumstantiae in facto* it is already necessary, for finding the *momenta in facto*, to have regard to the law; for even though the law is not yet imputed here, it still contributes to the more complete determination of the *factum* itself; and here it is also apparent that *circa imputationem facti* the *momenta* have their degrees, and are *graviora et debiliora.*[c] Indeed, owing to the differing capacity for action, it can absolutely be maintained that: *duo cum faciunt idem, non est idem.*[d]

The *consectaria facti libera sive moralis,*[e] those that spring, that is, from the freedom of the agent, are alone imputable; the *oppositum* comprises all *eventus inevitabiles*, and in *delicta*, the *delicta fortunae*, of which we are not the cause, or which we have no insight into, or do not have in our power, because (1) they exceed a man's powers, or (2) could not have been foreseen by him, or (3) have been prevented, or (4) were such that he was not morally permitted, or authorized, to prevent them. To all these circumstances, the rule applies: *ultra posse nemo obligatur,*[f] and they are not imputable.

Yet this impotence to act or forbear from acting, which is here taken to be absolute, is unimputable only insofar as the agent is not *causa libera* of this impotence, or it did not arise merely through a condition residing in himself. *Causa causati est causa causae.*[g]

---

^z details to be attended to in the fact
[a] listing of all factors in the case
[b] substance of the offence
[c] more or less weighty
[d] when two do the same, it is not the same
[e] free or moral consequences of the deed
[f] nobody is obligated beyond what he can do
[g] the cause of the outcome is the cause of what caused it

With proper foresight he might, for example, have realized what would happen; the proximate cause was admittedly an accident, but the remoter ones lay in himself.

27:564   A *judicium imputatorium*, or judgement whereby somebody is declared to be *auctor facti*, must always, if it involves an *imputatio demeriti*, be based on certainty. It is otherwise *invalidum*, the accused suffers injustice and is injured, if no certain answer is given to the question, whether anything, permitted or forbidden, took place, and whether he did it or not. For to base a judgement, even with probability, on the plight of the accused, is probabilism; such is the case with torture; such it is with all methods of extracting the truth by violence; in this way certainty can never be attained.

N.B. Since it is easier for a man to refute the arguments of others than to convince them of his duty, this gives rise to the prudential rules: *si fecisti nega,*[h] whereby the *imputatio facti* is rejected, and *fac et excusa,*[i] whereby the accuser has to prove the wrongness of my presumptively legitimate action, and whereby I exculpate myself from the *imputatio legis;* e.g., *beati possidentes.*[j]

Mere good will, it is said, can be accounted to nobody for his deed. That is true, so little do *volitio sola,*[k] or even *conatus,*[l] constitute the action (*factum*) itself; for they are still insufficient grounds of action, so that a person is not yet *auctor actionis* on that account. Yet their influence in the action should not be underestimated, for (1) good will can certainly mitigate a neglect of duty, and (2) bad will, malice aforethought, is the more imputable, the closer it approaches to *conatus,* and already, in and for itself, belongs to the *momenta.*

§56. Now the object of imputation is determined under the following considerations: (1) nothing can be imputed, save what is subject to laws, and in respect of which we are obligated *ad aliquid omittendum vel committendum*. For only an action that rests on freedom is imputable, and freedom itself is nothing more than the capacity to be held accountable (*receptivitas imputationis*).

Hence the *factum* is also called *actio libertatis*, in contrast to an *eventus* that was due to an *actio physica*.

To *hold accountable* is therefore to be distinguished also from *ascribing* an *eventus* to someone, insofar as the action rested on a *mera facultas,*[m] and 27:565   not on a duty of law; for example, that the servant to whom I gave money spent it on drink, picked a quarrel, etc.; to be sure, it depended on my freedom, not to give him the money, but there was no duty to that effect.

[h] it was not my doing
[i] I was entitled to do it
[j] happy are the possessors
[k] mere intent
[l] trying
[m] mere capacity

318

(2) Imputation requires a *factum*. The *eventus*, indeed, does not have to be completed; even the *conatus* is already imputable, for it is the beginning of the *factum*. It contains a sufficient determination to the action, whose reality is only interrupted, like the tendency of a body to fall, which is inhibited by a support. It rests on a decree of the will, i.e., *voluntas consequentis*, i.e., the resolution and decision of and to the action. But there is a great difference between this and *voluntas antecedens* or *volitio incompleta*. The latter contains no action, since it presupposes grounds still insufficient for decision; on the contrary, it is mere inclination, a mere entertaining of the action, a preliminary intention of willing, a will willing that its will should one day determine itself to an action. Here no imputation is to be thought of, since laws are not directed to inclination and desire.

They come into consideration only if an action is supposed to occur, and through this inclination a possibility has to be looked into, that someone is the *auctor*. To this, moreover, must be added all intentions that are decided upon without a view to carrying them out; for example, all good intentions. Men are full of these, but from this it does not follow that they will be executed, as actions *resolved upon* are.

(3) The *effectus* of an *actio libera* may be as remote from it as they please, yet can still be imputed. Thus a person may be mediately or immediately *auctor* of the action, provided a *causa libera* picks him out; for example, the teacher, who has helped to bring about fortune or misfortune through the knowledge he imparted, must admit to being held accountable. Once an *actio libera* has occurred, the agent must allow its remotest effects to be attributed to him, for it is impossible not to take the action as cause of the effect; thus Calas, for example, probably met his death because, instead of disclosing his son's suicide, he alleged that it was due to a stroke.* Hence imputation is also levelled against every effort having its ground in a *culpable* lack of knowledge or capacity. The agent was certainly under circumstances where he could have averted the consequences of the action, by removal of the obstacle or neglect through which he incurred them; through excessive drinking, for example, a person suffers from gout, and this makes him unfit to hold office; or somebody blunders through ignorance of a law, which it was necessary to know for the business in hand. This holds good of all actions, whether permitted or forbidden, whether *merita* or *demerita*, insofar as they are subject to law.

(4) The *factum* itself, for the man who wishes to impute it, and claim that the accused is its *auctor*, must have the utmost moral and logical certainty; the presumption must rest upon objectively sufficient grounds, and the imputation, since its judgement is based upon that, must agree in

27:566

*[Jean Calas (1698–1762), executed for the murder of his son, Marc Antoine, but later rehabilitated through the efforts of Voltaire. – Tr.]

this with the underlying requirements of duty, i.e., the *factum* itself must be in keeping with duty; this permits of no lower grade, that might allow of departure or relaxation from the *requisitum* of logical certitude. A presumption that rests on *objectively insufficient* grounds, or belief, or even simply on mere subjective grounds, or opinion, is inadequate and unacceptable here as a basis on which to ground an imputation. For even the highest degree of probability, if it were to play the part of moral certainty, would be bound at the same time to include subjective grounds of conduct, and thus to be accompanied by the risk of injuring the other's rights; the imputation would be staked on such a risk. But here the slightest gamble is at all times disallowed. In deciding about a *demeritum*, let us adopt the view that a high degree of probability replaces certainty in those cases where persuasion from the legally insufficient grounds adduced is nevertheless so strong, that we think ourselves fully ready to venture, on one throw, everything at our disposal, e.g., to wager our whole fortune on it, and then go on to declare for a *poena extraordinaria.*" Since this presupposes the case, that no moral certainty exists as to whether someone committed the crime, it still differs greatly from that in which the crime is not morally certain in every particular, but yet is so as to one part of it. A *poena extraordinaria* is then legitimate. But in the previous case the whole imputation is defective.

Persuasio, therefore, can never suffice for an imputation, since it rests on a presumption, without our being convinced, as to the quality of its grounds, whether they are subjective or objective; if a person presumes, for example, that the man did it, but does not know whether he concludes this from objective evidence, or from the personal characteristics of the accused, demeanour, clothing, his other actions, etc., then he is simply persuading himself of the fact.

27:567

This is also why the judge is forbidden to accept any kind of presents, because he will thereby be tempted, quite involuntarily, in the case before him, to pay close attention to all the grounds that tell in the donor's favour, and to discount the evidence against him.

So it follows from the above that, in order to impute a *demeritum*, it is absolutely necessary for total certainty to be present.

§57. The entire action can either be imputed to a single *auctor*, and then he is *solitarius*, or else it may have taken place *in concursu aliorum.*° We then have *coauctores* to one and the same *factum*, and this in turn (a) as *pro indiviso*, i.e., where the act can be wholly imputed to every one of them, or (b) as *pro diviso*, where only a part of it can be assigned to each.

The *consulens*,ᵖ along with the *consentiens*, are to be taken as *coauctores;* it

---

" special penalty
° in concert with others
ᵖ accessories/consenting parties

being necessary for all that they be connected with the action, not *physice*, but through their freedom.

§58. The degrees of imputation depend on the degree of freedom with which the action has come about; so the less free the agent is, the less the action can be attributed to him. For since freedom of action consists in the determination thereto of free choice, independent of all impulses of nature, the degree of imputation can be defined only in relation to the counteracting obstacles, whether from the physical or the moral side. So *generaliter* we now have the following norm here:

1. *The greater* our assessment of the physical hindrance, or obstacle confronting the action from the side of natural impulse, and likewise *the smaller* the moral hindrance, i.e., to the action in relation to the law of duty, the more the action performed in accordance with the moral law is accredited to the *auctor* as a merit; for example, if a man has by nature a choleric temperament, and yet restrains himself in face of an insult, it would be a merit on comparing him to a cold-blooded man, who did not have to overcome the physical hindrance. A man who himself has to overcome hardships, yet supports a person in need, has merit beyond that of a rich man, or one who pays his debts on time; for the well-doing is much less of a duty than the legal obligation arising from the right of another, even when it is difficult for the debtor.

27:568

So the greater the duty incumbent on the agent, even in overcoming the greatest of natural obstacles, the smaller the merit.

Wherever, then, there would be no grounds of obligation at all from the moral side, and the needs of nature put all possible obstacles in the way, there would have to be the greatest merit in the action. And so

2. the greater the want of physical impulses from nature, and the greater the moral hindrance, the less can the action be accounted as a merit.

For example, a man can support from his resources his parents, his brothers and sisters, and his benefactors, or else he can pay his debts; here it occasions him no difficulty to overcome the obstacles and determine himself by free choice in accordance with the law; so the smaller the degree of freedom that is present, the less the merit in the action. Even the magnitude of the duty deprives him of the incentive to act with freedom. If, on the other hand, with no obligating grounds, he acts well towards the other, simply because he wanted to, then the duty is smaller, and more merit is accounted to the act.

3. The smaller the physical obstacles to a man's fulfilment of duty, yet the greater the duty transgressed by his neglect to perform it, the more must his offence be held to his account; if a rich man, for example, withholds a poor man's property from him, the decision to violate the law of duty must cost much expenditure of reason, and his freedom has all the more unrestricted play when he does not have to contend with natural

hindrances; the greater, therefore, is the *demeritum*. As with a thief, who steals when not in need. From this it also follows:

4. That an action with intent, i.e. undertaken after prior consideration, with awareness of the law forbidding it, will have to be imputed far more than if it does not occur *deliberato animo.*[q] For here the direct action is open to imputation, whereas in the second case it can only be imputed *indirecte;* for example, whether a person wounds another after making preparations, and in a state of sobriety, or does so when drunk. In the first case, too, the action is the more imputable if it is done gladly, than when it is *actio invita*,[r] i.e., motivating grounds were present that could have led him to stay his hand. And likewise the imputation as *meritum* is greater if the action results, notwithstanding it was *actio invita*, owing to the greater freedom in both cases. But even if the action did not occur *ex proposito animo*,[s] it can nevertheless be held accountable for its contingent consequences, if a breach of duty was involved; though admittedly it is less imputable than when the agent could and should have foreseen the outcome of his act. Thus in practice even actions of this type are punished, not because of their inner criminality, but for the sake of example, so that others may be brought thereby to greater foresight and reflection.

5. The state of mind in which the agent finds himself does not come into consideration, to remove his accountability, if otherwise that state has been voluntarily incurred. The imputation is smaller, therefore, insofar as it was simply a natural propensity that engendered this state in him; e.g., natural ebullience, producing rage, that is nourished nevertheless.

6. Given an action to which a man must already compel himself, because of his natural impulses, the omission of it is less imputable to him, than when it costs him no trouble to do it, and he omits it nonetheless. For in the first case, self-mastery has far less free play, since it has to contend with the natural impulses, though it still rests upon an independence from sensory urges.

7. Since the *conatus* to perform a good action really cannot be regarded as a *meritum*, it follows that, strictly speaking, all imputation of desert to it also lapses, though it is commonly held to be not totally lacking in that respect.

8. The habit in certain actions, consisting in a necessitation thereto from an acquired tendency and readiness, makes the imputation all the stronger, the more and the longer the agent, in case of *demerita*, has condoned this tendency and way of acting, before he plucked up courage to overcome it. Yet the case allows of an exception, as and when the agent, at the time of acquiring the habit, does not realize its evil consequences; if

27:569

---

[q] intentionally
[r] an unwilling or reluctant action
[s] of set purpose

his tendency to drunkenness, for example, has its source in a bad upbringing by parents, who taught him the use of strong drink in early life, then the affection on the part of sensory urges is so great that it costs him a high degree of freedom to break his drunken habit, and his *demeritum* up to then becomes the less, precisely because of the greater difficulty in achieving self-mastery.

§59. The endeavour is made, albeit only in appearance, to exonerate men from imputation, when they transgress, by two natural means of defence, namely

a. *ex infirmitate naturae,* or because of an innate weakness in man, whereby we are said to be too feeble to attain in our actions to the full idea of duty, i.e., the entire degree of conformity to duty in our actions, that they are called on to possess.

It relates only to the attainable ground of the duty to be fulfilled, when the latter finds its goal in the uprightness (or integrity) of man, i.e., in the complete congruence of actions with duties. Now were this unattainable, it would involve a general exclusion of all imputation. Yet the infirmity (or impurity) of human nature set against this does not permit us to assume such a universal exculpation, since the existing freedom of man, or his independence of necessitation *per stimulos,* runs counter to it, in that by virtue of this active power he is at all times in a position to gain the upper hand, or act virtuously.

Because of this innate want of strength, he is said to be incapable of the persistence and firm resolve that steady observance of his duties requires, since he is too easily diverted from it by nature. On this view, accordingly, since human nature exerts its influence at all times, virtue would be a mere ideal, and hence unattainable. In presupposing, however, the conquest of all sensory influence on our moral conduct, it would also have to be assumed that a habit of acting well gets ingrained in us and that this would have become mechanical on our part. But virtue consists, precisely, in the strength of the resolve to perform our duties, and to strive against the constant enticements to do otherwise which sensory feelings inspire. Now if we had to suppose here an overmastering or preponderance, with total repression, there would no longer be any virtue at all; not only does experience contradict that, but the possibility of virtue is already sufficiently shown through the natural feeling of freedom, whereby we compare our duties with the natural temptations to violate them, and endeavour to resist the latter. To that extent, too, the utterances of the Stoics have full weight, and the descriptions of fiction-writers do not have to be taken for unattainable ideas. What follows from the constant clashing of the sensory and moral natures of man is simply that morality is not inborn, but only the capacity for arriving at it, and creating principles for ourselves; self-mastery, however, must be acquired, in that we constantly

27:570

27:571

resist our temperament or disposition by the laws of reason, and form principles of action; and this acquisition gives a man character. It follows also that the actions occurring contrary to morality cannot be so heavily charged to our account as they would if firmness of intention already lay in our nature, and had no difficulties to overcome. In that case, man would do good simply by a dutiful following of the law, and evil simply as a source of evil, and a true imputation would not be thinkable. It is no more possible to eliminate imputation

b. by the *fragilitas humanae naturae,* or fragility of human nature. Man, in other words, is said (and this is indeed true) to possess already by nature a tendency to evil, which is thus not only a hindrance to him in embracing the firm resolve to goodness, but also, as an inner positive ground to evil, constantly arouses in him an inclination towards it.

It is just because he possesses by nature a nevertheless conquerable tendency and propensity to evil, so that he harbours the possibility of being easily drawn away from good into transgression, that duty is coupled, in his case, with moral necessitation, and the latter needed for virtue.

Now man, when he judges himself, in whatever situation he may be, finds that he is never without faults, and always has grounds for self-improvement; he finds, therefore, a form of his actions whereby they have become ill-natured, whether he be otherwise cultivated or not; so from this it follows that such a tendency to evil is already implanted by nature; but it is clear *ex adductis* that it can also be repressed; so it is certain that, as soon as the tendency is not repressed, but nourished, a degree of imputation arises from this, which is greater than could be occasioned by that tendency previously implanted by nature.

27:572

It is this, too, which may distinguish man from a devil, who views himself as governed only by evil itself, and as author of the same, and who therefore, without struggle or inducement, engages in no actions other than bad ones.

Thus an inborn vice does not exist, and wickedness, as free action, is avoidable and hence imputable; and the supposed lessening of imputation in such a case can relate only to the degree that is based on the natural tendency to evil.

§60. *Imputatio legis* requires at all times *subsumptio facti sub lege,* and contains a syllogism. The constituents are:

a. *Lex et factum,* whose criterion rests on the *ars interpretandi leges;*[1] whether, that is, the law is that under which the *factum* belongs, either as an observance or transgression of the law; and whether the *factum* has such components that it can be brought under the law. If the express wording of the law is made the basis, then interpretation is *secundum*

[1] art of interpreting the law

litteram legis; but if recourse is had to the legislative intention associated with those words, interpretation is *secundum animam legis,* and *sophista* or *rabula*[u] is the name given to those who expound the meaning of the law against the wording of it.

b. *Forum sive judex,*[v] namely that physical or moral person having the authority to impute *leges* in a valid manner, to apply laws legitimately to the *factum,* and to impute the *effectus* connected therewith, or determined *a lege.* The *arbiter, quoad casum singularem,*[w] is similar in this respect, since he also determines with legal authority that the action shall have the consequences that are linked to it by the law.

The *forum* in question is *internum sive conscientia,*[x] since inner actions can be known to no external judge, and thus do not have one, for they can be judged only by the agent himself. Now insofar as another cannot legally impute the *facta agentis*[y] and carry out the consequences, a *forum naturale rationis sive naturae*[z] is also relevant here, to determine, for example, whether a man believes in a future life; though the tribunal of reason also has jurisdiction over outward actions, insofar as they can be known externally, and thus belong, to that extent, *ad forum humanum.* 27:573

Hence all actions, inner and outer, are subject to the *forum internum,* and the *forum externum* expresses itself, therefore, with this difference, that here another has the competence to impute the *facta agentis* according to the laws. It is called the *forum naturae* or *auctoritatis sive statutarium,*[a] depending on whether the imputation is legitimately applied by reason, or by the determination of another's will.

The *forum externum* now has an *imputatio methodica,* in that the *facta* are prepared for sentence according to certain instructions. It would be well if we had elaborated the sublime science which provides guidance on how to determine the degree of imputation, according to the disposition of the agent, *secundum analogiam mathesis forensis.*[b]

c. Now the sentence itself consists in the conclusion of an *episyllogismus imputatorius.*[c] It contains knowledge of two syllogisms, in which the law constitutes the major premise, the *factum* the minor, and the form of knowledge the conclusion. In the first inference we have: the law, the *subsumptio facti,* and the decision, whether the *factum* belongs under the law, as an observance or transgression of the same. In the second, the law,

---

[u] a wrangling lawyer
[v] tribunal or judge
[w] arbitrator of an individual case
[x] internal tribunal, or conscience
[y] his deeds to the agent
[z] natural tribunal of reason or nature
[a] of authority or statute
[b] on the analogy of a legal calculus
[c] an accusatory argument

the *factum,* and the consequences to be derived or applied from the law employed, and the determinations it contains.

§61. The *forum* is also divided into a *forum justitiae* (*stricti juris*) and a *forum aequitatis.*[d] Equity is in itself a genuine right, but has no right of coercion coupled with it, because owing to want of imputation the condition of coercion is not encountered there; it is certain, for example, that I put my servant in a position where he can defray his expenses against the services he is to render me. Now his wages are fixed, but the value of the currency is declining. The *quaestio* is: whether he can demand an increase in a fixed wage during his period of service? Equity looks to the disposition and aims of the contracting parties; strict right, however, to the content of the contract. It is thus a contradiction, to decide according to equity, and yet to be a judge. In England, to be sure, the court of chancery decides between subjects and the government, but it judges and also disposes, as it were, over the rights of the latter to the advantage of the former; for example, goods are to be levied from the countryside at a

27:574 certain time, but a mishap prevents this; if the confiscation is now suspended, and the Chancellor thus grants exemption from a governmental requirement, rather than having to decide the matter according to strict right, he is no longer solely a judge; for the latter, on the other hand, the only verdict is: *fiat justitia et pereat mundus.*[e] The judge, that is, should not determine the right accruing to the possessor with an eye to benevolence or purpose; he must determine and pass judgement, strictly according to law, on the situation before him, whether it be linked with the sustenance, welfare and fortune, or with the downfall of those obligated and other families. It is incumbent, indeed, on the state itself, that every subject be convinced that he may rely on the same secure justice; he gains confidence when he knows that the judge can take no account of ends in his verdict, and thereby bend the law. It is the business of ethics, on the other hand, to determine the bounds of equity, and there is no denying that the gibe: *Summum jus, summa injuria*[f] can find its application. For though laws must be meticulously observed, they cannot, after all, have regard to every little circumstance, and the latter may yield exceptions, which do not always find their exact resolution in the laws. The latter state only by rule the character and principle of the action on which judgement must be passed; should that judgement now be pronounced strictly according to law, it could happen, as in the case of the servant, that though no injustice is done, a person would not in fact receive what is due to him; in that case, strict justice transforms the appropriate jurisdiction into injustice, and the other party may have recourse to the *forum aequitatis.*

[d] tribunal of justice, tribunal of equity
[e] let justice be done, though the world perish
[f] the greater the justice, the greater the injury

§62. Though in itself addressed purely to inner actions, which are subject only to the judgement of the agent, the *forum conscientiae* may become, nevertheless, a *forum externum*, insofar as the agent believes in a God, and accepts the latter as his judge; it is then also given the name of *forum divinum*. In itself it cannot be competent in regard to human justice, since it can furnish no truth for the action, so that the judge finds no subject of imputation there. Yet this much is certain, that even in a man with no belief in God, a conscience can still be presumed if he possesses moral principles as such; for otherwise it would have to be supposed that he had lost all belief whatsoever, and that it would thus be possible for him to assail the right of another. An appeal to the conscience of such a man can therefore still take him aback, a testimony can still be corroborated thereby, and in courts it is indeed assumed that everyone has religion, and acknowledges a *forum divinum*. On this rests the requirement to take the oath. Yet Professor Kant is of the opinion that to let the settlement of his *juris controversus*[g] turn upon the oath of another is by no means an adequate proof of veracity for the aggrieved party, inasmuch as the oath-taker must submit to the law in this; whence this *medium probandi*[h] is wholly useless.

27:575

1. If this accessory to the truth is based on a maxim of belief, and it is therefore presupposed that the other believes in a God, such a God judges and will punish him. But if this is not assumed of everyone (and already it cannot be assumed of Quakers), then the oath is useless.

2. Since it may be presumed that God will punish him anyway, there is no need for such an imprecation.

3. It lies, of course, beyond the bounds of judicial power, to determine the consequences; it all remains reserved to the power of God.

4. The judge is not only ignorant here, to the extent of having to leave it to divine vengeance, whether the swearer be punishable, but also as to whether he is giving the swearer a pretext for relieving himself of the imputation.

5. Since in oath-taking the judge is only a man, the other cannot be bound through the oath to accept a thing as true for which he can find no proof, and of which the immediate judge can furnish him none.

§63. Now a conscience consists in the ability to impute one's own *factum* to oneself, through the law itself, and the readiness to do this is conscientiousness. He who binds himself in conscience to anything does not, indeed, strengthen the obligation, since it was already there beforehand, *objective;* but he strengthens the fulfilment of it, *subjective.* This appeal to his conscience involves the thought that he should make the entire determination of his action conform to the duty incumbent on him,

---

[g] action at law
[h] means of ascertaining the truth

and he connects the transgression or violation of his conscience with the idea of losing his entire moral worth.

27:576 Now a conscience must (a) be instructed, i.e., the agent must have knowledge of the morality of his action, so that he knows what is involved, if he is to impute his own actions correctly. He must examine the marks of truth in the *factum*, know the laws exactly, and be accurate in levelling this imputation, which has to be apposite in the required degree to the magnitude of the entire duty.

(b) The conscience must not be chimerical, i.e., it must not regard evil consequences, resulting by chance from *merita et demerita fortunae*, as imputable *facta;* for example, when a loss at cards from want of prudence is confused with a want of morality; thus a delinquent often blames himself, not for his crime, but for his lack of dexterity in committing it; as a doctor does for the death of a patient to whom he has accidentally given the wrong medicine.

(c) The conscience must not be micrological, i.e., turn trifles into an important *casus conscientiae;* though that does not allow us to set aside all accounting in the matter, but merely bids us not to carry it to excess.

(d) The conscience must not be inert or inactive, i.e., confined merely to the planning of good actions or the avoidance of bad ones.

§64. The treatment so far of the metaphysic of morals has dealt only with prolegomena to ethics, which is now to be discussed *in specie.*

In morals, the division of duties is important, but also difficult, and the more so in that this exact division by virtue of inner difference, and the ranking of these duties, is itself a duty. As the Greeks divided things,

a. The theory of morals belongs to the practical part of philosophy, and comprises ethics in contrast to physics. Thus laws of action are fundamental, in that to that extent the object of practical philosophy can already be determined in general, since it comprises every practical treatment of nature; but *in specie* it includes within itself the actions that are necessary according to laws of freedom, just as physics contains the laws, rules and precepts concerning the treatment of nature, whether they are dealt with empirically or in pure form, i.e., the laws may rest on experience, as in all experimental sciences, for example, or on universal principles known *a priori*, as in mathematics, and in one as in the other, rules may be given for dealing with the objects; for knowledge of the laws themselves would be

27:577 the theoretical part; but here the doctrines of nature and freedom are understood as practical sciences.

b. *In specie*, under practical philosophy, we in fact understand only the doctrine of morals, or that of freedom under laws. The Greek philosophers take the word 'ethic' to mean doctrine of obligation as such. The moderns divide practical philosophy into the doctrines of right and of virtue, calling the latter, *in specie*, morals, though by this the ancients, *sub voce* ethic, understand both parts, and thus were taking, *in sensu lato*, what we now distinguish, *in sensu stricte,* from the *leges justi,* although for the genus of both parts, namely for the *de legibus justi et honesti,* we have no term.

c. Moral philosophy rests, therefore, on practical rules or (to put it formally) on imperatives. But these laws are never technico-practical, since they have as their basic form no end chosen by the will, and thus never command (or necessitate) hypothetically, i.e., never serve, under the condition that we wish to reach the end, as necessary precepts for the actions thereby needed. Only imperatives of art are of this type, imperatives, that is, both of skill and also prudence. The former presuppose the merely possible will to attain a contingently chosen end; the latter take as their condition the end of happiness, universally acknowledged by everyone. The former serve to reach possible arbitrary goals; the latter, to obtain advantages which can be procured for us by the direction of all other men to this end. The former are problematic, since their employment depends merely on a man's possible will; the latter are assertoric, since, in virtue of the universally assumed will to be happy, they are regarded as given. The morally practical laws differ from both of them in this, that they invariably command categorically, i.e., are laws of obligation for actions that must absolutely take place in accordance with them; such actions, undertaken in conformity to the moral law, are thus also nothing but duties.

§65. Obligation, or the laws of it contained in moral philosophy, can now be judged:

A. By their form, i.e., by the manner in which we thereby become obligated. Yet even this properly refers to the actions under the law. Now to that extent they are either:

1. Duties of narrower obligation (*obligatio stricta sive perfecta*), i.e., those $\quad$ 27:578 dutiful actions that are immediately determined by the law, for example, the payment of a debt. Here, therefore, the dutiful action itself is subjected to the immediate law, which requires the absolute necessity of it. Hence the authority of the other is equal to it; *jus* = *obligatio stricta.* It is a perfect duty.

Obligation rests at all times on a necessitation through the law, and relates, therefore, to law-giving. This is the form of obligation; the law determines the mode and manner in which a person is obligated, either *late* or *stricte,* and thus abstracts entirely from the actions which he must consequently perform. If, by this, and by difference of obligation, we now divide morality, as theory of conduct, *in genere,* no rule of dutiful action can then itself be determined, because this belongs to the matter; we merely pay heed to the legislation as form, in order to determine whether and how the obligation as such is to be established. If, on the other hand, we divide up the theory of conduct by duties, we pay heed to the actions as matter, and to their diversity.

2. Duties of broader obligation, i.e., acts of duty in regard to which only the maxim of the action is determined by the law, but not the action itself to which we are obligated; *obligatio lata.* All these *late* obligating laws

belong to ethics, and rest on the two imperatives: promote the happiness of others, and promote your own perfection.

They may also be called neglectable, or better optional duties, since they leave it to the agent, how far it is possible to fulfil the end proposed to him by humanity, whether for his own person, or for the happiness of others.

Homo sum, nihil humani,[i] etc., i.e., bear in mind that everything which befalls other men may also befall you; cultivate the talents in your nature, your knowledge, improve your manners, etc., i.e., *officia humanitatis.*[j] In both, no actions whatever are ordered, save only these, in generic terms, and it is left to the scope of the agent, how far anyone may go in that respect.

27:579 　B. By their matter (i.e., equivalently, by relation, since the *diversa officia erga se et alios*[k] are quite general); i.e., by the matter or object of the law of obligation. This matter constitutes the dutiful actions to which the law obliges. To that extent, duties divide up into *duties towards oneself, and to other people (interna vel externa).*

a. Since, in themselves, duties rest on the freedom of the will, and are coupled at the same time with an absolute necessity, there is no conceiving how anyone, by the laws of freedom, can be necessitated to an act of duty against his will. It seems, rather, as if the agent, since he creates the duty for himself in accordance with his own freedom, is able, as a freely acting being, to release himself at any time from a mode of action that he has made into a rule, insofar as the duty relates, not to another, but to himself; and yet it is true that a man can necessitate himself to action; only in that case he must not take his own being in the same sense as when he considers himself in relation to others. To make a rule for oneself presupposes that we set our intelligible self, i.e., humanity in our own person, over against our sensible being, i.e., man in our own person, and thus contrast man as the agent with humanity as the law-giving party. Hence we get right of humanity in our own person, and towards others, and virtue as end of humanity towards oneself and others. All this turns us into obligated objects, and puts our self in a relationship vis-à-vis humanity.

ad a. Humanity is the aforementioned noumenon, and thus thought of as pure intelligence in regard to the capacity for freedom and accountability implanted in man. Man, on the other hand, is humanity in appearance, and thus subordinated to humanity as genus. As men we have a relationship to others, but rights and duties themselves are determined by humanity; hence, just as right itself, in comparison with visible actions by means of right, like the Idea of reason in comparison with the reason of man, is accompanied by restriction according to universal laws, so the same applies to the right inherent in man, since this is conferred under the conditions

---

[i] I am a man, and think nothing human alien to me
[j] duties of humanity
[k] differing duties to oneself and to others

determined by humanity, and depends on that. In this sense the rights of humanity in our own person, or rights and duties to the self, can be thought of no otherwise than as the highest, since they are directly dictated by humanity itself, whereas the rights of a man towards other men depend only indirectly on that. Thus the existence of rights towards ourselves, denied by preacher Krugot* and by Hutcheson, can be derived from nothing else but the moral principle they assume, namely promoting one's own happiness and contributing to the well-being of others; yet there can be no conceivable duty to promote one's own happiness, etc. Our own happiness, however, can have influence, in general, on the moral relationships of men only insofar as it serves as a means to promote all the ends of morality, to which even our own welfare may contribute, though it cannot at the same time obstruct a man's morality either. Thus squandering our own resources, for example, runs contrary to the duty of promoting our own happiness. Yet this principle is so subordinated to that of duty, that where duty has not been carried out to the full, it cannot be contemplated. It may contain pragmatic rules of prudence, by whose observance we may attain our ends; but is not therefore on a par with the concurrent duty, any more than duty is abolished when the outcome of happiness is not crowned by duty's fulfilment.

27:580

b. All duties to other men can only be adopted as reciprocal, i.e., there cannot be anybody obligated or entitled who would not be subjected to similar limitations in respect of his freedom, nor anyone with a duty who would not have a similar right *towards the other*. So one-sided duties can be thought of only in the relationship of man to God. The being, that is, to which man can alone have duties, must be such that the first and sole origin of man's existence is to be derived from Him; because man, as soon as he does not depend on that being as author of his own nature, makes claim to the universal laws of freedom.

N.B. This is to say that a mutual or reciprocal duty is one in which the other can be simultaneously obligated to myself; *officium erga obligantem qui reciproce mihi obligatus est et qui a me obligatur.*[1] For he who puts me under obligation does so by virtue of the law of freedom, but this ground of his right and my obligation is at the same time restricted by the lawfulness of my will, so that my freedom stands, in its legality, in relation to his own. Now all rational beings stand in such a relation to one another, even if, among *finite* beings, we also think an eon of the Arians[†] or another such being, sublime in understanding and power to the highest degree. A believer can obligate me to pay, only under the limits which bind him to the specific acceptance.

27:581

Parents, in relation to their children, stand as an instrument, merely, in regard to the creative ultimate source. In general, such originators do not

---

*[Martin Crugott (1725–90), a senior court preacher of the day. – Tr.]
†[The Gnostic concept of God as an eternal being, without beginning or end. – Tr.]
[1] duty to an obligator, who in turn is both obligated to me and obligated by me

exist among the rational beings familiar to us. It is necessary that such a being be thought of as elevated above all obligation, and thus above all laws of duty; what itself does not stand under the law can thus be only the law itself, and since the moral law is personified under the Idea of God, only He can be thought of as the highest moral law-giver of all laws.

It is therefore also certain that the division into reciprocal and one-sided duties is purely problematic, since there exists no person and no duty wherein the *officium erga obligantem nullo modo obligandum*^m might be found.

c. All *officia stricta* – or *perfecta* – are called duties of right, and all *officia lata* – or *imperfecta* – duties of virtue; but the concept associated therewith is not to be deemed equivalent to a logical explanation. For the character of both is actually posited in the essentially negative distinction, whereby the *obligatus* can or cannot be coerced by another into the act of duty. It is obvious, moreover, that since they are called coercive duties, they are self-explanatory in the manner indicated, and beyond that, this definition is drawn, not from the nature of the duties, but from the outcome of the duty in hand; it is a consequence of the duty that the authority to coerce accrues to the other party. Finally, not every *officium strictum,* or duty of right, is a coercive duty in the sense assumed; on the contrary, coercion is conceivable, without it presupposing a duty towards others; there are duties of right, or *officia stricta,* to which I may be compelled without anyone else being able to compel me. For example, it is a strict duty to humanity in my own person, that I be unable to dispose over my body as the owner of it; nor can another person compel me directly in that respect.

27:582 Equally little are duties *imperfecta* because another cannot compel me to perform them; I owe it, nonetheless, to the end of humanity that I perfect myself, even though the degree of perfection admittedly cannot be prescribed. Professor Kant therefore sets forth this division as follows:

Duties of right, both to oneself and to others, are *officia juris,* the former *interna* and the latter *externa. The externa* are of that type which he calls coercive duties, or genuine *officia juridica,* legal duties, and in regard to them the coercion from without is an authentic feature.

d. Finally, *ex diversitate relationis,* there arises the distinction between duties of right and duties of virtue = *officia justi et honesti.* In the agreement of the action with the law there lies the *justitia actionis,* and the judgement *an aliquid justum sit.*ⁿ But in the fact that, over and above this, the action is performed solely for the sake of the law, i.e., that the law alone is the action's determining ground or moving cause, motive and norm, there lies the decision whether it be *aliquid honestum,* or the *animus in praestanda obligatione* – the disposition with which the duty is performed. Thus the *justitia actionis* involves the legality of the act, but the *animus in committenda*

---

^m duty to an obligator in no way to be obligated
ⁿ whether a thing be just

actione[o] its morality; it also emerges from this that a coercive law can be confined only to the legality of the action, but is not thinkable in regard to its morality; for if the action is in conformity with the law, there is no more to be said about the disposition of the subject, or the subjective motivating ground to action, in the idea of the law that has been, or is to be, fulfilled; neither man nor a God is in a position to compel the agent to adopt the *animus legis*, since he has been granted the power to follow the law with free choice, and not with a mechanism. All that can correspond, like a copy, to the law is respect; i.e., the subject's consciousness of his relationship, as inferior, in following the law of his superior, and thus the intention to obey; but from that it still remains possible that he follows the law for subjective reasons, for the sake, e.g., of the reward, punishment, etc. to be expected.

If, on the other hand, the law is adopted as a maxim to the action, and so becomes the agent's motive, and the moving force that determines him to the act; and if the idea of virtuous duty itself becomes the ground of action, it can then be said that there arises love for the law, if the latter strictly enjoins in the true sense; he then performs the action because conviction of his duty is the ground.   27:583

Now virtue demands absolute morality of the action, and in that sense ethics is also properly called theory of virtue; and the course pursued from maxims of duty, or the exact and precise observance of one's duties, is *virtus phaenomenon* – virtue in appearance.

e. If everything is now taken together accordingly, there arises from the theory of morals (or from the *theory of duties,* as it should properly be called, since that is how the old jurists of the theory of right described it), the following system:

Officia are

Duties of right   and   Duties of virtue

and both are

interna	or	*externa*
a. Either strict or internal duties of right, i.e., the right of humanity in our own person, or		a. Either strict or external coercive duties, i.e., the rights of men in regard to one another, or
b. broad or internal duties of virtue, the end of humanity in our own person, or that end which humanity imposes on us, and which we should therefore possess.		b. Either broad or external duties of virtue, i.e., ends towards other men.

---

[o] state of mind in performing the act

Thus all duties are divided into

1. The right of humanity in our own person, and the right of men in regard to others. These comprise the strict duties of right.

2. Duties stemming from the end of humanity in our own person, namely our own perfection, and from the end of other men, namely their happiness. These comprise the broad duties of virtue. It should be noted here, *en générale*, that all duties of right, and the concepts to be formed of them, must be derived analytically from the concept of freedom, whereas all duties stemming from an end have to be demonstrated synthetically, merely, from the determination of human nature.

27:584 To explain further: *officium juridicum* is an obligation (a limiting determination of choice by the necessitating law, not an act of duty) for which an *external* legislation is *possible* – a legal obligation which, since it always involves a strict duty, is always related to the *jus; officium ethicum*, on the other hand, is an obligation for which an external legislation is not *possible*. Right is always the totality of laws for which an external legislation is *possible*, and under this condition alone is a coercion even possible as well; moreover, a dependence on moral coercion, as in ethical duties, cannot be brought into the definition of right. The right to coerce is based upon the fundamental law of freedom, to necessitate the other's choice through and according to the law of universal freedom; but now the choice of the *obligatus* can be necessitated by himself, without another's choice concurring with his own therein, according to universal freedom. No external legislation or command from without is then possible, nor is it present; and nor is any right or duty to coerce then possible, for the duty is one of ethics or virtue. To help those in distress, for example, is a strict duty, but an external coercive law on the subject is unthinkable, since the action itself does not fall under the duty. There are duties of virtue (or ethics), therefore, which are not duties of right, but conversely, all duties, even if they are duties of right, are so constituted, that apart from the external law under which they fall, there is also an inner law present, which necessitates their performance; and thus all legal obligation contains at the same time an ethical obligation. For example, it is right to pay, but if we take it as a maxim that payment is also to be made, even where no coercion is present, that we keep our word voluntarily, then this subjective principle in the action is ethical, and legality is then combined therein with morality.

Now since duties of virtue consist in outward acts for which no outer legislation is possible, albeit that, even if they are not simply coercive duties as well, we can and must be obligated to perform them, it follows *that all obligation of any kind, both juridical and ethical, is ethical in nature.*

On the other hand, where obligation is present, i.e., if a thing is ethical, we do not yet have ethical duty, since for this an action is itself required; 27:585 but ethical duties, unlike those of right, do not have to do with the action itself, but only with the end that is supposed to be coupled with it. The law that commands ethical duties tells us only to make into a duty the end to which the actions would be subordinated; it determines only the maxim of the action, not the performance of the latter itself; the end is thus obligation or form of the *late* determining law. But the action in accordance with that end is duty. That is also the reason why, in determining the general division, we cannot deem obligation equivalent to duty, or confuse the one with the other. So if we also wish to divide up duties, then they are all to be regarded either as duties to oneself, or to others, insofar as it is men who are said to be bound to actions.

(*Uti Cicero de officiis*)[p]

Both types, whether in regard to oneself, or to others, divide up into:

1. Duties of right, i.e., all those to which we can be strictly bound; these are *officia juris*, and are those described as *perfecta; officia* are divided into:

Officia interni juris, duties to myself;	*Officia externi juris*, to others, or *officia juridica*, i.e., for which an external legislation is possible.

2. Duties of virtue, in which, therefore, obligation is only broadly determined, i.e., the end is established as a maxim, are called *imperfecta*, and divide into:

Duties to the end of my person;   Duties to the end of other men.

Let it be understood, however, that both types of virtuous duty are also strictly binding, as soon as they are divided according to form, or in regard to the kind of obligation as such. For if they differ at once from the duties of right, insofar as the latter are based on a right, make external laws possible in regard to the action, and can produce a coercive right, the ethical duties nevertheless permit, in regard to the action's maxim, a legislation which cannot, however, be external, because it relates only to the disposition of the agent, but yet has to be coupled with it, as to the end, and thus differs from duties of right only in the matter of the duties (so that they are not truly legal ones). This, too, is to be noted in explaining the difference between *officia juris* and *officia juridica*.   27:586

The right of humanity in our person is *jus internum et officium juris*, but the opposite, the right of men in our person, is *jus externum* and *officium juridicum*, and so, likewise, with the *jus externum in specie*, or the *officia juridica* that are based upon rights of other men to our person, and that we possess towards other men.

The treatise to follow will and must now take its start from the duties to oneself; from there we shall pass on to the duties towards others, and only thereafter will it finally be possible to deal with the duties towards God. All duties, that is, relate:

a. In the first place, to men, whether they determine duties to oneself

---

[p] make use of Cicero's *de Officiis*

or to others. We thereby learn to know all the rights and ends of a man, both in his own person, and in relation to others, by the diversity of his actions. He occupies himself with the beings and things that experience presents to him. They are under the law. God cannot be that, and hence we must abstract from Him the Idea that He is a moral being, i.e., subject to the law of morality, but at the same time a law-giver; this is simply an Idea of reason, which has no existence. It may indeed be said that it belongs to the theory of morals, but only as the special relationship of a law-giver, to whom all men are subject; now since, in His case, owing to lack of necessitation, no duties are thinkable, this doctrine is not immanent in morality, but transcendent, and remains all the more so when, as will be shown, we cannot think properly how we should have duties towards a being to whom we have no relationship.

Ex adductis there now follow these at least problematic propositions:

a. All men are so situated, that in one and the same subject a right can be thought of only with the duty corresponding thereto. For the freedom of every man is limited under the condition of universal freedom, no less in the right to be exercised, than in the duty that is likewise incumbent on him.

b. Duties, on the other hand, are thinkable without right, e.g., the duty of well-doing; nobody can possess a right to demand this.

27:587 c. A right without duty, conversely, can be thought of only in a being having pure right, i.e. in the universal law-giver for all men, namely God. The first two pertain to immanent, the latter, however, to transcendental morality.

§66. All rights are based on the concept of freedom, and are a result of preventing damage to freedom in accordance with law; so they are all negative and strict in nature, as with *prohibitio ex propositione neminem laede.*[q] Now so far as concerns the *scientia juris,* or scientific knowledge of legal duties containing an external juridical obligation, this belongs specifically to the *jus naturae* insofar as it relates to the rights of men towards each other; whereas the *jus* comprising rights and duties within my own person belongs only to morality.

The division *inter statum naturalem et civilem,* and the *jus privatum et publicum* founded thereon, belongs, therefore, to the *jus naturae.* As to this, we have only the following to say:

§67. All *officia,* whether of strict or broad obligation, are – as said – either *interna vel externa as to their form,* depending on whether an external legislation is or is not possible for them. The *interna juris stricti* are all, as to form, duties to oneself, which are strict because, even though no external legislation is possible, there is nevertheless an inner one (*inde* self-coercion), since they are derived from the concept of freedom

---

[q] prohibition derived from the principle of harming nobody

through the law of non-contradiction, and thus analytically; and are there-fore such that they carry with them a necessity which also determines the act of duty itself. Included here, therefore, as to matter, are all *officia juris interni stricta*, e.g., the duties not to mutilate, sell or kill oneself.

This, then, is the right of humanity in our own person.

All outer legal duties (*officia externa*), on the other hand, are juridical duties (*officia juridica*) as to form, and include, as to matter, all dutiful actions *juris externi*. Now these, as said, are one and all prohibitive and negative, and all have to do with mine and thine, *vel suum alicujus;* from which it then follows that to acquire the *suum alterius* can in no way be the topic of *jus*, at least *in statu naturali;* for its law can aim only at preserving one's own, by the use of a law-abiding choice. Hence we get a division of all legal duties and rights into:

1. *Jus connatum*, in contrast to *jus acquisitum.*[r] Both rest on the supreme   27:588
principle of all external duties of right:

Act so that your freedom may be compatible with the freedom of everyone, by universal laws;

which naturally presupposes such duties as those wherein an external legis-lation is possible, and thus refers to a relationship which men exercise towards each other by means of the legitimate use of their freedom. This use of their freedom under the condition of the above principle is right as such; and coercion arises only when an injury to this freedom results, to one on the part of the other. The term *innate right* can therefore refer to nothing else but the use of my choice, or the freedom to resist the other's choice, insofar as the maxim of my action is compatible with the freedom of others according to a universal law. It is to this, too, that all supposedly individual *jura connata*, so called, are directed – freedom, equality, honour.

Thus everyone is entitled to curb the choice of another, insofar as the latter's action, by universal laws, would contradict the freedom of every-one else. And everyone is to that extent required to subordinate himself to the general freedom. Hence it is assumed of nobody, without proof, that he has violated another's freedom: i.e., *quilibet praesumitur bonus*, etc. Everyone is taken to be good.

As to the object of innate right, viz. mine and thine, it can consist in nothing more than the possession of one's own person, in the totality of all those rights that constitute a part of me, and thus cannot be separated from me without violating the laws that comport with the freedom of everyone according to universal laws. So the *jus acquisitum* can also be no more than the use of my freedom to hold on to what is mine. But this happens in virtue of my innate freedom to curb the unlawful freedom of another. Thus at least *in statu naturali*, there is no acquisition or *actus*

[r] right of action/right of property

juridicus – an act, that is, whereby something becomes mine that was not mine. But nothing can become mine to which I was not already entitled under the condition of lawful freedom, the universal freedom to resist the other party's choice to strive against me; and the latter would have no obligation to submit to this use of my own choice. No more, on this principle, can a right against us accrue to the other *in statu naturali.* So this division is no less unfounded than the subdivision of the *jus acquisitum* according to source. It is held, that is, that the right would be acquired *vel facto justo suo, vel facto injusto alterius.*[s] But the former, *ex adductis*, is already unthinkable, and the latter involves nothing more than the preservation of what is mine, by compensation as the means.

27:589

Now ethics differs in this respect from *jus*, inasmuch as it rests on a *principium affirmativum,* namely:

Give to the other from what is yours.

This comes about because of the end which underlies the maxim of virtuous duty. Since this is supposed to serve the end of other people, it becomes clear, in the light of that, what the rule wishes to say: We should use other people, not as a means merely, but as an end. This imposes no limitation on freedom, however, or on the right arising therefrom, but belongs only to the doctrine of virtue.

Men under the law have also been conceived in a different state, and the *status naturalis* has been distinguished from the *status civilis*, in that entry into the latter is attributed to a voluntary *pactum.* It is, however, an error here to suppose a different state, since in regard to their rights, the situation remains the same in both *status naturalis* and *status civilis;* right is merely considered, to that extent, in a different respect. In itself, the *status naturalis* does not exist at all, and never has; it is a mere Idea of reason, containing judgement of the private relationship of men to one another; how, that is, the freedom of one is determined against that of another, according to the laws of universal freedom. Such an examination of rights occurs without regard for any difference in this *status.*

The basis of the distinction really lies only in this, that in order to be able to make an assured use of his freedom, an irresistible force is needed, which compels one against the other, so that he may exercise his freedom by universal lawfulness. Now it is left to the judgement of every individual man, what he will acknowledge to be right or wrong, and he is therefore able to infringe even the freedom of another without hindrance. This state of injury would be everlasting, so long as each would be sole law-giver and judge. It is this that we call the *status naturalis*, a state, however, which runs totally counter to innate freedom. It is therefore necessary, as soon as men come close to exercising their reciprocal freedom, that they leave the *status naturalis*, to come under a necessary law, a *status civilis;* there is need, that is

27:590

[s] either by one's own just act or by the wrong-doing of another

to say, for a universal legislation that establishes right and wrong for every-one, a universal power that protects everyone in his right, and a judicial authority that restores the injured right, or dispenses so-called *justitia distributiva* (*suum cuique tribuit*). It is this which, of all natural right theorists, Hobbes alone takes to be the supreme principle of the *status civilis: exeundum esse ex statu naturali.*[']

So the difference consists in the private or public (*singulus vel communis*) determination of the lawfulness of the action, and assurance of what the proper outcome may be.

Status naturalis is thus the private right of anyone; *status civilis* the public right of anyone who has entered into that status with others.

The collective rights and obligations of private right also become right of humanity *in statu naturali*, just as the same collectivity, considered under the public laws of men, is called *jus publicum in statu civili*; so, *status naturalis – jus privatim, status civilis – jus publicum.*

In statu civili, therefore, there is always the thought of a multitude of men, who stand under a public law and authority, whereby the determina-tion of their actions is guided and restricted, as it no longer is by their private judgement. This relationship under public laws provides them with public rights against each other, since these are openly and definitely secured. Now just as private persons stand to one another, so entire peoples also stand to each other, and hence arises the difference between

a. *jus privatim gentis*, and

b. *jus publicum* or *jus gentium*.

The first is a *jus publicum internum gentis*, i.e., where a multitude of men, considered as a public entity, submits to a public system of law; now considered in relation to every other people, this people stands *in relatione privati contra privatum*,[''] and the *jus* is *privatum*, in the sense that the inhabitants of any state, so long as they judge self-lovingly and for them-selves the rectitude of their actions against some other state, are always exposed to a condition of violence, so long as wars always remain neces-sary, since there is want of any judicial determination of their power and rights over each other. So if a public right of peoples against peoples, or a *jus gentium*, is to arise, it is necessary for them to exit from this condition, enter into a general league of nations, establish a public legislation, define a public authority to apportion national prerogatives, and thereby make possible a universal peace. Till now, such a *jus gentium* has been simply an Idea, that is not in fact carried out; this league is called *foedus amphic-tionum*, since the union of the Greek states at the outset of their constitu-tion, doubtless in its representation of the Amphictyony at Delphi, can be taken for a similar development.

27:591

['] we must escape from the state of nature

[''] in the relation of one private person to another

To be sure, the present relationship of peoples to one another, which (strangely enough!) they also think it absolutely necessary to maintain, cannot be called a condition of violence, or as Hobbes puts it, a *bellum omnium contra omnes*.*^v* For this, though without historical evidence, would be a *factum* which cannot be required to justify the principle that peoples must forsake this condition. On the other hand, constant hostility over the ever-possible violation of their rights is also at all times possible, and so here we have a condition of possible enmity and possible infringement of legitimate freedom (*conditio hominum per quam meliorum jurium capaces sunt*).*^w* It should be called only a *status belli omnium contra omnes*, a condition of injustice; a legal condition (for every condition must be legal) in which the determining and deciding of what is to be law can occur no otherwise than by violence; so that even in their constitutions, all peoples are prepared for this. It is therefore nothing more than the *status naturalis*, in Idea.

Brennus, when as prince of the Gauls, he overran the Romans in war, justified his conduct to them by asserting that it was:

The right of the stronger against the weaker, which is implanted in everyone, from Gods to unreasoning creatures.

This was the sentiment of a *homo brutus*, who showed no respect for the law-governed freedom of men in their unity, but described quite correctly the *status naturalis* of nations one to another. In this condition, it cannot even be said that one people may do wrong to another. For the possibility of violating their legitimate freedom is so acutely and continuously present on both sides, that the state of peace seems merely to be an armistice. So long as they persist in the *status naturalis*, peoples do certainly rob one another of the basic law for assuring their prerogatives, and cannot demand that they be respected on one side, since those on the other have equally no security against violations of some kind. It is true in itself that he who injures the freedom of another people, by taking away their land, for example, is doing wrong, but from this it does not follow that he is doing wrong to them. For since the yardstick for judging right and wrong is left merely to the choice of one such people, nobody has an exclusive right.

Wrong is done, for example, by one who revolts against the constitution of his country, and plots to overthrow it; he does indeed abolish the *status civilis*, and plunges himself and others into the *status naturalis*, in which nobody can expect any public assurance of his rights; and he therefore breaches the universal basic law of acknowledged justice. This the people of Brabant did to their emperor; yet they did him no wrong on that score, because he had infringed the *joyeuse entrée*.

27:592

---

^v war of all against all
^w a condition of men whereby they are capable of better laws

Between peoples *in statu naturali,* there can be no deciding at all as to what is right, since public justice is lacking.

§68. The first section of duties of right (in contrast to those of broad obligation) has to do with:

Duties to oneself, or inner duties of right. They are called right of humanity in our own person; *jus humanae naturae in nostra persona.*

N.B. We might call it *humanitas nostrae naturae,* in that the term really designates humanity in our person, since we call *humaniora* those *artes ingenuas et liberales*[x] whose cultivation extends beyond the merely sensuous, so that to that extent the humanity in our own person is nurtured. But this term has already become ambiguous, since we also mean by it *humaneness,* i.e., the goodwill towards others of making them into an end of our action, and thus not merely legitimacy of action, but also the maxim of contributing something from our own store to that of the other, e.g. remission of the other's debt.

Analysis of right in one's own person. Just as to every right there must correspond a duty, at least (if not a coercive, yet) an inner duty, so humanity also has a right against me as a man, and thus an *obligatus* confronts an *obligatum* here. This requires a double nature to explain it. We conceive of man first of all as an ideal, as he ought to be and can be, merely according to reason, and call this Idea *homo noumenon;* this being is thought of in relation to another, as though the latter were restrained by him; this is man in the state of sensibility, who is called *homo phenomenon.* The latter is the person, and the former merely a personified Idea; there, man is simply under the moral law, but here he is a phenomenon, affected by the feelings of pleasure and pain, and must be coerced by the noumenon into the performance of duty. So we can here draw an analogy, from the way that one man stands in relation to another.

27:593

§69. The objects of the right of man in his own person can be defined like the three categories of relation (in metaphysics):

I. In regard to his substance, or in respect of the right to dispose over his body as a body.

Humanity in his own person (*homo noumenon*) can so far restrict the right to make use of his body, that all use of it as a thing is forbidden to him. He is indeed the *proprietarius* of it, i.e., he governs and rules over it, but as over a person, i.e., insofar as he would dispose over it as a thing, the phenomenon appears restrained by the noumenon. He is therefore not the *dominus* of his body, since he may not treat it as *res sua,* or as the *dominatio servi*[y] might do.

He may therefore mutilate neither himself nor others, and may make no eunuchs – the error of Origen, the fanatical church father, who muti-

---

[x] we call more humane those noble and liberal arts
[y] lordship of a slave

lated himself to subdue his lusts. He cannot dispose over himself as Murcus, i.e. cut off his thumbs, as the ancients did, to make himself incapable of drawing the bow-string in battle, and become a poltroon *per truncationem pollicis.*

27:594

(*inde* cuckoldry, from the decapitation of cocks and grafting of the implanted spurs.* Emperor Charles IV. Cuckold's society in Maesius: *History of Curiosities*). Or if someone were to sell his sound teeth as a replacement for the decayed dentition of somebody else. Thus suicide violates the law of the noumenon, and respect for the latter.

II. In regard to causality, or the personal capacity and power of a man to bring about effects. *He cannot, to that extent, dispose unreservedly over his freedom,* i.e., he can indeed make a *definite* use of his powers for others, and he can authorize the other to demand them from him in a purposive way, e.g. the manual worker; but he is forbidden by the right of humanity to make every use whatever of his powers, and to grant the other an unlimited disposition over them.

Freedom consists only in this, that the agent utilizes his powers at his own choice, in accordance with a principle of reason; now anyone who ceded himself, with all his powers, to the disposition of another, and thus voluntarily enslaved himself, would alienate this freedom; he would treat his person as a thing, and this he cannot do.

III. In regard to the *commercium* with others, or the relationship of men to one another in society, the agent is prohibited from letting himself be robbed of his honour, or robbing himself of it. Such a debasement does not permit the respect that he must have for humanity. He must not deprive himself of his honour, either after his death, or still more so, during his lifetime. Hence not even a son would be entitled to let himself be punished in place of his culpable father, and thus admit to a crime committed by the latter, inasmuch as he would thereby become dishonourable.

The saying, Avoid the semblance, is meant, indeed, to indicate just this, namely respect for the law of honour, even though no case of a breach of honour is involved.

§70. Now the opposite of inner right is outer right, and insofar as the latter is based on coercive or juridical duties, it belongs, indeed, not to ethics but to *jus;* yet since all laws of right must also be observed out of a duty to virtue, knowledge of the *jus externum* must likewise be a preparation for ethics – whence this excursus into outer right. The latter, now, is all right in things outside me, and is either hereditary or acquired/acquirable. In general, both are negative, and based on the principle that nobody can diminish the hereditary or acquired right of another; if there

27:595

*[Kant's etymologies are dubious, but he is evidently explaining *Hahnrey* from the ancient practice of grafting spurs on the comb of a fighting cock – which may have some analogy with the traditional horns of the cuckold – Tr.]

is a violation, for example, of body, causality or honour, it affects what is mine in my person, and since this cannot be acquired, involves a relation to inborn rights; to abuse someone is merely to rob him of respect, and thus negative.

Acquisition refers, therefore, to things outside my person. It takes three forms:

I. Acquisition of the substance of things. It follows automatically that, as to substance, no subject endowed with freedom, i.e., no man, can be acquired or become mine, because nobody can dispose at his choice over his own substance, or that of others; the objects, rather, must be such that we have no obligation to them. We can then acquire them arbitrarily – in *occupatio* or *originaria acquisitio*, as contrasted with a derivative acquisition, i.e., one which can only be derived from the consent of another party. Now since every acquisition involves an authority to exclude the other from possession, though it does not amount to physical custody of the thing (for in that case every incursion upon it would properly be an injury to the person), Professor Kant requires that all occupation of property be preceded by acquisition of the ground on which it stands, i.e., the ground-right, whether it be *originaria* or *derivativa*, e.g., by the common consent of all. For so long as the ground has not been acquired, no reason can be given why any other person should not be entitled to thwart my occupation, or usurp it himself; anyone, for example, may push away cast-up driftwood, so long as I have not captured it. This rests on the *principium* that whoever possesses the substance of a thing also owns all the *accidentia ejusdem rei,*[z] i.e., *accessiones* thereto, and acquisition therefore takes place *per accessionem*. This is *acquisitio solo facto*, i.e., without any *actus juridicus, ex jure rei mere;*[a] for example, I have the right to sell, once I have become owner of the wood.

From this we distinguish all acquisitions that require an *actus juridicus*.

II. Through acquiring the other's causality. This happens if we acquire the *praestatio alterius*, i.e., the authority to coerce him to a *factum* according to law. This acquisition relates to the person of the other, and is therefore based on a determination of the will; now the latter, if it is founded on a ground of right, and directed to a *factum*, is called a *pactum*. It requires a reciprocal determination concerning a *praestatio,*[b] i.e., it is *factum bilaterale* – the consent of the other to the *praestatio*, and his willing in regard to the *factum praestandum*. The right to this (in a *pactum* to be concluded) is reciprocal, but not always is this so of the *factum* or *praestatio alterius* – which may thus be *unilaterale* or *bilaterale*.

Suum alicujus pactitium is thus the thing to be performed under the

27:596

---

[z] accidents of that same thing
[a] simple acquisition without title, by the mere fact of the matter
[b] performance/thing to be performed

pactum, which need not, indeed, be in my possession, but in regard to which I nevertheless have authority to coerce the other *ad praestationem rei.*

III. Through *commercium* with others. Here there never arises a *dominium* over an object that is a *praestandum,* but merely an exclusive right to the use of the thing, or a property-right; the right, that is, refers to all permitted forces of the other that he is to exert; for example, marital and family relations, *societas herilis,* master and servants. In conceiving of *possession* of the object of the right, we must abstract entirely from the physical custody of a thing, *qua objectum juris.*

All concepts of right are intellectual; but in order to apply them, to present them as phenomenon, they always have need of physical actions, though these do not necessarily pertain to possession, and the latter is therefore intellectual, merely, or the Idea of disposing over the thing by means of the right. It is merely thought, therefore, and does not require physical custody of the object of the right; so *mine,* likewise, is only that, the possession of which can be thought by me. An apple that is in my hands is to that extent not mine; if somebody wanted to snatch it from me, he would be violating, not mine, or my property, but my person, my inner right, by virtue of which I could protest his action. *Mine,* my property and possessions, are therefore dependent on objects that are not my person. An interference with such things as are not my person would nevertheless be an injury; but this it cannot be unless, in regard to ourselves, there is a thinkable relation to the thing, which gives us a right to protest, and this occurs by virtue of the right to possess that thing. This right is inseparable from the thing, and hence we call a possession that thing which we do not 27:597 actually have in our custody. From this it follows that something can become my property *per possessionem mere juridicam,* without any bodily transference; for example, *in pacto consensuali,* the ownership of a thing purchased already passes to the buyer, before it has been handed over. The causality of the other, to deliver the article bought, is governed by the pact, and I thus have the right to coerce him *ad praestandam rem;* this article is *objectum pacti,* and hence he can no longer dispose over it, and I thus already possess it, albeit only in an intellectual sense. The possession of a person is to be similarly understood; the father, for example, possesses his children, the husband his wife, the master his servants, *inde vindicatio uxoris, filii, servi,* the exclusive right to lay claim to their powers.

Quoad praestationem facti, the *thing* is not yet mine until the *factum* is accomplished, e.g., *in pacto reali.*

In acquisition, moreover, the *modi acquirendi* come to light, as follows:

I. In respect of this, that they are subsumed under a possible external legislation, i.e., that we presuppose a *status civilis,* and consider the mode of acquisition in Idea.

a. By long custom. This is a putative ownership, that has arisen from long-continued possession; hence, insofar as it is held to justify an external right to the person of another, it rests on no legal grounds that it has to acknowledge from the matter itself. But since the security of ownership requires that a man be protected in a possession whose legality or lack of it cannot be demonstrated, the appeal to a possession *in statu civili* must to that extent be assumed as necessary, in order to recognize a person as the owner. *In statu naturali* there can be no thought of any such determination, since arbitrary legislation cannot be assumed there. So inasmuch as long custom produces a *presumptio juris et de jure*, it belongs *ad jus civile*.

b. By inheritance. *Testamenta* do not exist under *jus naturae*. The *testamenti factio*[c] contains a promise of ownership to one who does not accept it. The ownership ceases at death; thereafter the heir wishes to take over a property that can no longer be transferred to him, and without acceptance no right – *ad praestandum* – can enter here; hence the *addictio hereditatis*[d] can be thought of only *in statu civili*. Here, in fact, the state steps in to replace the *testator*, and may be assumed to be the depository of the will of the *defunctus*, and to undertake to hand over the inheritance to the heir, and to fulfil the *testator*'s promise, as soon as the heir accepts it.

27:598

c. By vindication, i.e., a re-acquisition of that which *in statu naturali* would have been lost, but by the concept of an external administration of justice is regarded as if it had remained our own.

Professor Kant assumes that the owner has not ceased to be such, and concludes from this, indeed, that the subsequent possessor must restore the article without substitution. He likewise maintains, *in contrario commendati*,[e] that if nothing has been agreed *de periculo rei*,[f] no ground is present in the thing itself, whereby the *commendatorius* should not have to bear the *casus fortuitus*.[g] Only the use of the thing was the *objectum pacti*, and a special contract would have been needed concerning the takeover of safety and danger, which is quite different from that. In that case the *commendans* could ask for the thing back *illaesa*, i.e., *in eodem statu*;[h] the onus of safety lay upon the *commendatorius*, and he would have to free himself expressly from that; if he has made no stipulation on the matter, he must take the danger of the thing upon himself.

In statu civili, however, where nobody is sure who is liable for possible injury, because the matter is not provided for, and the *pactum*, in short, is *incertum* here, and where it would be too difficult for the judge to settle this *in quovis casu*, the matter has been decided in advance, and in such a way that no further conflict about avoidance of the law is possible:

[c] making of a will
[d] award of the inheritance
[e] as against the person entrusted
[f] as to the danger of the thing
[g] chances of the matter
[h] undamaged, in the same condition

In this way has arisen the rule of law: *casum sentit dominus,*[i] which is merely supposed to decide, in this case as in the previous one, who should bear the damages. It is meant to make the judge's decision easier for him, just as there are many such laws, that cannot be evolved *ex natura rei.*

II. There is indeed also an accepted *modus acquirendi* in regard to legal determinations, where acquisition is made, not immediately, but through representatives of the acquirer, e.g., *a mandatorio.*[j] Likewise, the *modi corroborandi possessionem,* e.g., through an oath, are mistakenly included among the means of acquisition.

III. In regard to legal authority, a distinction is drawn between *strict right,* or the entitlement to coerce that is founded on a duty defined in the laws; *fairness,* i.e., where a juridical law is wanting, but a maxim of action or duty of virtue underlies the situation; and a *right in need.* That which we expect from the other's fairness, we expect from his obligation, not his beneficence. If, on the other hand, we expect something from his kindness, we assume we shall be obligated by our benefactor to a duty in return, or to gratitude; the action from fairness, however, is merely a fulfilment of the other's duty, and he who has a right to it has received settlement in full from him. Fairness is thus a coercive or strict right, but with this difference, that the laws one may appeal to do not define the right demanded; we are compelled, rather, to leave it to the judgement of the *obligatus* to derive the act of fairness from them, and thus make him his own judge. A so-called *factum aequitatis* cannot exist, therefore, since it pertains only to a duty of virtue.

There can be no such thing as a right in need. It is assumed that here the *casus necessitatis* possesses a *status extraordinarius,* such that it is coupled with the danger of innocently losing one's life, and that to preserve this, an otherwise impermissible action is allowed; if this were correct, then (a) every act of violence would be allowed, in that it is only one life against another to take bread, for example, from someone to appease our own hunger, or to save one's life by robbing the other of the means by which he is trying to preserve his own. (b) The amount of danger is arbitrarily defined. The amount of need would correspond merely to the amount of loss to be feared of that to which we have the greatest inclination, which here, admittedly, would be the preservation of life. But inclination cannot become the ground of a right and a law, and how far is this inclination to go? Suppose that someone valued his honour more than his life; it would thus be capable of an arbitrary determination. So inclination and the need to satisfy it cannot furnish a right; two men, for example, are trying to get hold of a plank, to save their lives from shipwreck; so long as neither has possession of it, it amounts, in effect, to the right of the stronger, but nor is there yet any

[i] the owner takes the blame, or loss
[j] under commission

question here of a collision of rights; once the plank has been comman-
deered, however, the other cannot throw his rival off it *in statu naturali*. Yet
in statu civili we have to suppose that an action which was otherwise not
allowed becomes permissible *per casum necessitatis*, and that the agent cannot be punished, because there can be no law that might enjoin omission of
the action *cum effectu;* for to punish with death a man who can save his own
life no otherwise than by the loss of the other's life, is merely to leave open
to him the choice between two kinds of death; either he chooses death in
sparing the other's life, and here it is certain; or he takes the other's life in
preserving his own, and subjects himself to the rigour of the law; he will do
the latter, since perhaps he can escape the consequences by flight.

27:600

We have here a case, therefore, where a natural right cannot be applied
in statu civili.

§71. So much for the duties of right; they may be viewed as inner or
outer, insofar as they appear as obligatory duties (*officia debiti*), i.e., insofar
as the dutiful actions are determined by law, and we are brought to
perform them, either by others, through coercion, or by ourselves,
through inner necessitation. To that extent, both as to inner and outer
obligation, they stand in contrast to:

Duties of love (*officia meriti*), meritorious duties. These are determined, not directly, through the law, but merely through the end associated therewith, and we are only obligated to them by that. Moreover, they
always go beyond what is merely due from us, i.e., precisely because they
are supposed to be merits, they contain in themselves more moral goodness than is determined as necessary by the law; they demand, therefore,
that apart from following the law in form, we also make ends of our
actions into the maxims thereof; for by this they become meritorious. Now
no legislator can make the coupling of these ends with our actions into a
rule of specific actions; on the contrary, the agent must draw it from
himself, as to how far he can couple and fulfil these ends. This alone is
meritorious, that he follow what was merely made available to his choice.
Hence even the *principia* of ethics are not to be derived from the nature of
a man's person, but must be evolved synthetically, because the *officia meriti*
can at all times be appended, merely, to the *officia debiti;* in relation to the
latter they are thus at all times ampliative, e.g., cultivation of talents,
promotion of the welfare of others. Such things can be a duty only if they
can coexist with the observance of strict duties, and the degrees thereof
are still undetermined. It also follows from this, in regard to the treatment
of ethics, that the *officia meriti* are always explicable only in relation to the
officia debiti, whether they concern duties to oneself or to others. Hence

27:601

§72. The first topic of all is the analysis of *officia debiti to oneself,* that
can be regarded as duties owing.

Now here we must prefix the identical principle:

Man belongs to himself – *homo est sui juris.*

347

This is based on the right of humanity in our own person, and so runs: he belongs to his own humanity as an intellectual being. From this follows the first right and duty of man in his own person

> Man can never treat himself as a thing.

This is an indispensable duty; thus those moralists are mistaken, who adhere to the axiom,

> *Homo est mancipium sui.*[k]

This would mean that a man can dispose over himself, as over a thing situated outside him; but the *jus disponendi de re sua*[l] never holds in regard to the person – my own person – but only over things outside us; hence the correct principle, rather, is this:

> *Homo non est dominus sui ipsius, sed tantum proprietate gaudet.*[m]

It is thus a duty in regard to his substance

a. Neither totally nor partially to damage or destroy it, e.g., by suicide, nor to incapacitate himself for the natural determinations of his substance, or of any member of it in particular.

N.B. The duties of humanity in his person, insofar as they flow strictly, unconditionally and negatively from the concept of freedom, rest on three types.

1. A man cannot dispose over his own substance, for he would then himself be master over his very personality, his *inner freedom,* or humanity in his own person. These, however, do not belong to him; he belongs to them, and as phenomenon is obligated to the noumenon. He is therefore not *dominus* over his personality, considered as an *objectum reale.*

2. He cannot dispose over the causality of humanity, i.e., of freedom, insofar as this is *outer freedom,* in opposition to the inner freedom of 1. He cannot therefore rob himself of his freedom, which would happen if he were willing to hand over the totality of his forces and powers for the arbitrary, absolute, unpermitted use of another. These forces belong to humanity in his person, and not to him, and he can treat them only in a permitted way, therefore, and not so arbitrarily as a thing.

27:602

3. He must preserve his honour, i.e., the *justum aestimum sui ipsius vel humanitatis in sui ipsius persona,*[n] for humanity is an inviolably holy thing.

b. Nor to hand over his substance to others as an object of enjoyment, i.e., make himself into a thing which he gives others permission to treat as something to be enjoyed. This seems, indeed, to run counter to the congress of the sexes, where one party really concedes to the other the enjoyment of his person, albeit this, too, is only permitted under other conditions.

---

[k] a man is his own possession
[l] right to dispose over one's own
[m] a man is not master over himself, but enjoys a sort of proprietorship
[n] just esteem of himself, or of humanity in his own person

In virtue of his causality, or force acting through freedom, *he cannot*, either, make himself the physical property of others, i.e., give up his freedom and personality so entirely that the other can treat him as a thing.

In virtue of his *commercium* with others, *he must* retain the respect of others for himself, i.e., his honour, i.e., he must in no way give ground through his behaviour for any damage to his good name (*bonae ex aestimatione*); for example, under suspicion for a crime, he *must* exculpate himself.

These duties must now be classified in more detail.

§73. A man cannot dispose over himself as over a thing, e.g., let himself be accounted a liar, let a tooth of his be pulled out, or his hair be shorn, for money.

Since, in morality, the imputation of our action is determined by the principle of reason, we can, in fact, always set the latter in relation to the sensory being, or man as phenomenon, and assume accordingly that the sensory being belongs to the rational one. In respect of its power, the sensory being is so far dependent on the *noumenon*, as intellectual being, that it is subordinated thereto, and the substance of the sensory being is merely entrusted to it thereby.

To destroy oneself, therefore, through an act voluntarily undertaken by the sensory being, can never be permitted, so that a suicide (*autocheiria*) can never, under any circumstances, be regarded as allowable. 27:603

Suppose, if you will, such cases as that of a slave, for example, who should lose his life in consequence of an attempted but abortive bid for freedom; or that one bitten by a mad dog should feel quite plainly the effects of madness; can either of them take his own life? The first considers a life of slavery to be no such life as is suited to humanity; the second foresees his own death, and the possibility, likewise, of harming others through his urge to bite. Nevertheless, they both frustrate all attempts whereby they might be freed from their unhappy condition and are preserved from harm, e.g., by having themselves tied up at the appropriate time; quite recently a remedy for the mad dog's bite has been found, in administering oil to the victim internally, and trying to anoint him completely on the outside. It is worth noting, however, that Greek philosophers of the Stoic sect considered it a privilege of the sage, when life became intolerable, to go out from thence, as one goes out of a smoky room.

This principle prevailed, indeed, among all men of education (in the Epicurean sect). To be sure, the Roman state forbade suicide, and laid upon it the *privatio testamenti factionis;*[o] yet in special cases permission for it was granted, e.g., by Augustus, to a military veteran.

§74. Duties to oneself relate, not to the man as a physical subject, but

[o] denial of testamentary rights

always to the right of humanity in his person, or the right that it has over him and his person. Since duty can only tell us what is right, or rather since both must be derived from obligation, the duty to oneself will also depend on the right of humanity itself. Moreover, just as each and every duty is either perfect, and a duty of right, or else a duty of love, so the duties to oneself are also of this double nature, depending, that is, on whether they refer to the right of humanity in a person, or to the end of humanity in him.

Now it is certainly also (a) an error, when some maintain that there is no duty at all to oneself, since it is only incumbent on a man to keep his own welfare in view, and to promote his own happiness. This, however, is 27:604 simply the aim that everyone seeks to realize, which cannot be commanded at all; and the maxims that pertain to it are practical or pragmatic rules, rules of prudence; a different thing entirely from the commands of duty, whether they relate to duties of right or those of love; though admittedly solipsism, or practical egoism, conceives the latter as love for oneself and one's person, not as love for the right of humanity.

(b) Others, though equally from misunderstanding, are rather more gentle, and claim that we have to confine the duties of self-love as much as possible, so as to express the more strongly our duty towards others.

In short, assuming there are duties to oneself, *the duties of right in that regard are the highest duties of all.* They relate to the corresponding right of humanity in our own person, and are therefore perfect duties, and every act of duty is indispensably required by the right of humanity, and is a duty in and for itself. Any transgression is thus a violation of the right of humanity in our own person; we thereby make ourselves unworthy of the possession of our person that is entrusted to us, and become worthless, since the preservation of our own worth consists solely in observing the rights of our humanity. We lose all inner worth, and can *at most* be regarded as an instrument for others, whose chattel we have become. The individual rights of humanity, or strict duties to oneself (as distinct from a man's duties of humanity to himself as a man) have hitherto not yet been systematically worked out, but merely collected. The principle from which they have to be derived is lacking, and that accounts for the want of completeness with which the subdivisions should have been recognized and always brought into subordination. Yet they are indicated in a fragmentary way, particularly in establishing the fact that they are the highest duties of all:

a. Lying, in the ethical sense at any rate, is to be viewed as the transgression of a duty to oneself, since it injures the respect for one's own person. The jurist recognizes and applies this only insofar as it involves a violation of the duties towards others (*officii juridicorum*), and understands thereby a 27:605 *falsiloquium dolosum in praejudicium alterius;*[p] he is therefore looking to the

[p] deceitful falsehood to the prejudice of another

consequences and relation to others. But this does not make it into a self-regarding duty, and yet, without any reference to the consequences, it has to be a transgression of the right of humanity. In the ethical sense it comprises every intentional untruth, or every intentionally false statement of my disposition, and is blameworthy in and for itself, regardless of whether any harm may have arisen for others, or not. A man who lies demeans himself in the eyes of others, in his testimony and judgement he loses all credibility; for society, he is to be regarded in all his tales as a mute, since we never know how far he can be trusted. There is no connection here with whether his lie may be harmful to those who trust him; it is also possible that it might be useful; enough that the liar neglects the duty of respect for himself, and thereby violates a higher duty than that which he owes to others; for the harm can again be made good to others through further duties.

b. Retraction, insofar as it is not merely an acknowledgement of error, implies a declaration that one has deliberately assumed something that is false to be true, or has held it to be so; in opinions ventured, for example, on government or religion, as with Helvétius' retraction of his work *De l'esprit;* such a one confesses himself, to that extent, as a liar, and lowers his reputation, since he violates respect for himself.

c. To incur debts likewise involves a lowering in the value of one's own person, in that the debtor gives authority to the creditor to treat him arbitrarily (by extending the scope of his duty), and this rightly so; to heap bitter reproaches on him, and even to give evidence of his contempt. The debtor is put into the position, that with every call he will be expected to bring something.

d. By begging, a man displays the highest degree of contempt for himself, and so long as people still have some feeling, it tends also to be the last step that they take. It is a man's obligation to exert himself to the utmost to remain a free and independent being in relation to others; but as a beggar he depends upon the whims of others, and sacrifices his self-sufficiency.

e. Despondency. Mistrust of one's own powers is always unfounded; 27:606 man has a capacity to keep himself independent of everything. This he must retain in the greatest of enterprises. He must be able to learn to bear all the troubles in the world. He has self-possession, and his existence does not, therefore, depend on others; so he must locate it in his own person, and not in things outside him. The despairing man is therefore wholly forgetful that he is subject to a right of humanity.

f. By a mean parsimony we not only violate a duty to others, but also to ourselves. The miser merely collects resources, but eschews every method of employing them. In regard to the state, therefore, he withdraws from industry as much as he collects without effort from usury or the diligence of others. Adam Smith, indeed, in his *Wealth of Nations,* distinguishes the miser from the spendthrift, in that the former at least allows the hope that by means of his wealth he may yet show himself active on behalf of the state, in that he can apply it to useful public causes; though experience tells against this. But the miser also violates a duty to himself. He possesses money, and thus a means of attaining all ends, but does not attempt thereby to become more perfect, since he renounces every use of it. He therefore contradicts himself in determining his own action, behaves absurdly, and is the greatest of fools. He possesses money *in potentia* only, but not *in actu.* Imagination, for him, replaces enjoyment. His mean-minded fancies betray the want of duty in his conduct. He wishes, and yearns for the fulfilment of his wishes. In this respect he differs from a thrifty man in the forgoing of superfluous wants; the latter may eat and drink less than his resources permit, but save up for necessities. The miser cannot do that.

g. Another who demeans his worth is the sponger (of whom the parasite constituted a special profession among the Romans); for he obtrudes himself on others, and sacrifices his personality to the fulfilment of his urge.

h. To let oneself be insulted without reprisal is already a diminution of one's own worth. The man who lets himself be trampled underfoot, shows himself to be a worm, a bee without a sting. He displays a want of forcefulness, whereas his duty is to stand opposed to all attacks on his personality. If he wishes others to have respect for his person, he must likewise hold fast to it, and show that he respects himself. He must at least bring the offending party to the point of an apology, so that he may be forgiven.

27:607

i. Even external religion presents us with something that contradicts the duties to oneself, for example, idolatry, the bowing-down to images. The image, after all, is man-made; it is not in such outward behaviour that God decrees the reverence due to him, but rather in the upright determination to perform one's duties, and so likewise in respect for oneself.

§75. On the system of Baumgarten. The latter deals with duties to oneself in the section where he first discusses such duties in general, and then treats of them specially, *quoad animam* and *quoad corpus.* Professor Kant, however, rejects this arrangement; all duties, including those to oneself, are addressed to the person, a being, that is, who has freedom in the use of his powers. The body is merely a part of that which must be determined through duty; the soul a still dubious idea, insofar as the principle of thought is supposed to be something distinct from the body. But in regard to the one, as to the other, every duty is one and the same.

Moreover, it creates difficulty in morals, to designate the *oppositum* of duties of right as duties of love, for this word has acquired a double meaning that must be wholly separated from duty. We mean by it a *habitus,* either (a) of satisfying one's own inclinations, and this is self-love, *philautia;* or (b) of promoting the ends of others in one's own person; the latter alone is the correct meaning, since we only fulfil the duty of love, i.e., love others, when we show ourselves active in promoting their ends.

Now since all duties of love have to do with promoting the ends, either

a. of man in his own person, or
b. of other men,

it is quite certain that duties of right to oneself are distinguished from duties of love, and that the latter are called duties of virtue when their aim is to promote moral goodness in other men, and thereby to extend the underlying duty of right. Moreover, we have regard, as Kant will also do, to both types of duty in determining the particular kinds thereof. For the rest, Baumgarten derives all duties to oneself from the three capacities of the soul: (a) the faculty of knowledge; (b) the feeling of pleasure and pain; and (c) the faculty of desire.

§76. The first duty discussed, §150–§167, is the *nosce teipsum,*[q] in which our author includes the examining of our moral condition and assessment of our moral worth.

Exploratio et judicatio sui ipsius.[r]

Professor Kant observes that for fulfilment of all moral duties, it is first of all necessary to know oneself. For, just as in the metaphysical sense, self-knowledge is presupposed in apperception of the determinations present in us, and consciousness of everything that goes on in us, so it is also presupposed in the moral sense, and consists in examination of our past state, or comparison of our actions with their dutifulness, insofar as we *fulfil* or *transgress* the same.

Transgression he takes to be every delinquency in fulfilling the moral laws of reason, and distinguishes this from vice, by which he means a readiness to such transgression; and applies both to *sin,* as transgression of a duty considered as a divine command.

We would have to direct our method here to investigating our moral condition over a period of time, and not just as it now is. In so doing we would need to have laws in view, and judge our actions honestly in accordance with them, and be actively endeavouring to amend our faults. If we merely take our present condition as the standard, we fail to discover which resolutions have been left uncompleted; we make new decisions to behave well, and fail to execute them, because there is still a lack of persistence in the fixed determination to mend our ways, which the conviction of often having made the resolution in vain does much to alleviate. Here we must not render our condition either better or worse by fabrication; in either case, the judgement about moral worth as such then comes out wrong.

[q] know thyself
[r] examination and judgement of oneself

That otherwise great man Haller evinces, through his moral journal, a very great weakness. Right up to his death he finds himself full of faults, and is forever reproaching himself over his want of improvement; it consisted, with him, in a mere persuasion of the possibility of being able to better himself by sheer resolve; he was not honest in his orthodoxy or with himself. A man can tell himself lies about the good and bad in his actions, and really imagine a situation that he is not in at all.

27:609

Hence a just self-assessment, the *justum sui aestimium*, is of great value. It consists in a judgement of our moral worth, i.e., in a testing of our action by its agreement with, or deviation from, what is said by the moral law, and by the extent to which it is undertaken, not merely in accordance with, but for the sake of the law alone, without interest or other ends; and it takes on a dual aspect, namely

a. with respect to the worth of humanity in our own person, i.e., that worth which can be laid upon the actions by the intelligible man, according to the whole determination of his existence. The attainment of a total agreement, or the entire worth of humanity, is a thing that man is far removed from; it is a state of holiness, but for that reason, too, its violation is the supreme breach of duty.

b. with respect to the worth of man in his person, or his self-esteem as a man. A man compares himself to that extent with humanity, in regard to his inclinations and drives, and in this quality he actually seeks virtue, or the persistent, steadfast endeavour, by overcoming of his inclination, to bring about agreement, in his action, with the law of humanity. Humanity itself, if we wished to personify it, actually lacks any inclination to evil, but the more a man compares himself therewith, the more he finds out how far away he is from this.

Hence meekness, the *humilitas animi,* by which indeed nowadays we understand only a concept that pertains simply to the Christian religion, as inadequacy of our behaviour to the divine law, but which the Stoic philosophy posits in the sublimity of disposition under the law. It is a poorly understood humility, if we think the less of ourselves in comparison with others. In general, we cannot compare ourselves with beings of the same kind; every man must have cause to believe that in regard to moral worth he can vie with every other man. For otherwise there comes of it self-belittlement in a higher degree, namely the *abjectio animi.*[s] The opposite would be arrogance, insofar as a man seeks, in the comparison with other men, to garner perfections from himself in his own opinion, since he thinks himself the better. This may or may not be true, but it remains only relative.

27:610

The one and only comparison allowable here is the relation of his conduct to the moral law, which in respect of its definition is identical with

[s] habit of self-abasement

humanity and the Idea thereof; it is rendered practical, if we conceive thereunder a person adequate to the Idea, or an ideal, just as Christ, for example, is presented to us as an ideal.

Now in such a comparison we find:

1. on the one hand, the insignificance of our moral worth in consciousness of its inadequacy to the law;

2. on the other, since this comparison has to do with no special duties, but only with the general dutifulness that we must observe in all our moral conduct; and since an anxious despair at discovering our deficiencies would merely produce despondency, while a special duty of virtue is not at issue here; though we must nevertheless determine ourselves as to our conduct, in order not to wax fanatical about it; there is therefore a need alike for firm determination in our principles and tenacious pursuit of them, and an outcome of this testing in the recognition of our absolute weakness in relation to the moral law. These two things found expression in the *humilitas animi* of the Stoic, and constituted the sublimity of mind whereby, conscious of his inner strength, he took his humanity calmly, and determined himself in dutiful obedience to the law, in that he unceasingly endeavoured in his actions to approximate to its holiness. This, however, is merely the concept of the Stoic *humilitas*, which in itself is a true concept in that respect; and when so construed that the comparison is to be founded upon divine laws, it has arisen solely in the Christian religion.

The *humilitas animi* of the Stoics consists, briefly, in a lessening of our estimate of our own moral worth, when we compare ourselves with the moral law. Two defective dispositions are to be set apart from it, namely pusillanimity or despondency, the decision arising from doubt as to man's capacity for ever attaining to the moral law, whereby we give up all effort to approach it, and declare ourselves incapable of improving or elevating our worth; secondly, arrogance or self-conceit, the tendency to ascribe to ourselves, without proof, a worth, or a higher worth, that we do not possess. The sure warning against this is when examination reveals the lessening of our worth against the law of humanity, in that consciousness of our remoteness from the holiness of the law (taken, that is, in all its irreproachable purity) persuades us of what our worth actually amounts to; that since we cannot possibly attain to the law, we really can never do anything of merit, and so cannot arrogate anything to ourselves. For were there to be merit in our moral action, there would have to be more than *rectitudo completa* present therein; but this already consists necessarily in the quality, that the action should have arisen from a purely moral intent, or that only the moral law, and not inclination of any kind, should have been the motive for it. It remains, therefore, a more useful endeavour to seek out the motive of actions, than to esteem them more highly in regard to our moral worth, out of the self-conceit (whose ground, indeed, they contain).

27:611

§77. In §107 our author assumes the possibility of an *excessus et defectus* of morality (deficiency and surplus in duties of virtue), holds both to be *peccata,* and locates the guideline of moral conduct in the avoidance of both errors, or in *mediocritas: medium tenuere beati.*[t]

Aristotle, in his day, located virtue in the mean between two extremes: courage, for example, between cowardice and recklessness; thrift between miserliness and extravagance; but the rule, that we should do the good neither too much nor too little, loses all logical correctness and use in morals. For (1) it leaves the resolution of the task quite indeterminate, and solves it only by a tautology: the too much and too little of moral goodness stands related to the conformity of our actions to moral law; and both would represent a want of conformity; but the possibility of attaining the middle path has remained unproven. Less good than needed, like more good than needed, is equivalent to not-good; and not-good, of course, is not equal to good. It is impossible to perform more than our duty, and so in duty one cannot do too much. Too little = that we may in our duty do as little as possible, and then it is not yet wickedness, after all, and cannot become so either, so that here there is no talk of two extremes and a middle road. Thus we say, for example, that passions should be confined, and specify this by stating that we should create for ourselves a clear conviction of our acts of duty, should not be over-hasty in our decisions, etc.

27:612

But this merely tells us: try to act without passion, and then you will avoid it. A tautology, therefore. Passions, as such, are in general reprehensible; for since they run counter to that *imperium in semetipsum*[u] which is presupposed by the fulfilment of duty, they are also contrary to duty itself, whence the whole task, and its principle, are false.

(2) *In eodem genere* of the determining of duty, there can certainly be degrees, which have to do with the quality of dutiful acts, but must be the genus of the duty itself. If, however, the qualities of the dutiful acts related are in opposition, neither degrees nor a middle road can be thought of, since in that case a transition occurs into a quite different genus (*metabasis in aliud genus*), and *in diverso genere* no *excessus vel defectus* in the fulfilment of duty is conceivable, since these opposites are in *contradictorio opposita.* Take honesty, for example; how is it thinkable that one might do too much or too little in this? and still less, how it might become a *vitium* (*peccatum,* the author calls it)? Honesty is assuredly accompanied by the concurrence of my disposition with that which should be done from duty, and is thus the ultimate that we can attain to; not to be honest, as a mere *oppositum,* is not yet vice; an *aliud genus,* e.g., the maxim to do harm, must first be assumed, before we can think of a *vitium;* but then we are thinking, not a mere lack, but a positive *in alio genere.*

---

[t] moderation: to pursue a happy medium
[u] self-command

Good husbandry: this is a definition of the duty itself, and the highest form of it, so it cannot be altered; but thriftiness is a quality thereof *in eodem genere,* and may thus have degrees; it rests merely on the rules of prudence for employing our means purposefully, albeit under the principle that the action, on any given occasion, be in conformity with the law. 27:613 This may not only have degrees, but also excess; a person who is now too thrifty is like one who is not thrifty at all, even though he saves to support the poor; for in that he deprives himself too much of the needs for body and soul, he is acting contrary to the duty of humanity. Yet this *excessus* can no more become a vice than the deficiency can. It is taken, of course, *sub eodem genere virtutis,*[v] and stands not, in and by itself, in the series of virtues and moral properties, since it merely comprises the rules of prudence in applying duty. If, therefore, excessive thriftiness is to become a vice, the genus of the virtue must first of all pass over into a species of another kind, i.e., we would here have to append the maxim of attaching value to the very means of livelihood, and using the latter as an end in itself; the agent is then renouncing the end that he might reach, through his income, for himself and others; he thereby abolishes the possibility of promoting his own and others' welfare, and so violates humanity in his own person.

It would thus be morally indifferent, how far he would want to go in economizing; performed as a duty of virtue, it would always imply nobility of soul. It could never become vice in that respect, since it would continue to belong *sub eodem genere* to virtue, and thus can never be the basis for a gradation from that which may be morally approved to that which must be termed a vice; it must, on the contrary, be a transition to a wholly different genus that constitutes the basis; lying, for example, can never pass over into virtue, or truth into vice, however large or small the degree of one or the other may be, so long as the one, like the other, remains under one and the same principle; so to that extent, neither *excessus* nor deficiency is conceivable.

We might, indeed, in boldness, for example, as opposed to timidity, suppose our duty to lie in a *mediocritas;* this is courage proper; but the first two are neither *excessus* nor *defectus* of the third, since in and for themselves they do not pertain to the duty of *courage,* but are both qualities of temperament, which mingle with this duty as constituents alien to it, i.e., they do not themselves reside in the essential nature of that duty.

§78. The doctrine of conscience is of the greatest importance in morals. *Conscientia,* taken generally, is the consciousness of our self, like *apperceptio; in specie* it involves consciousness of my will, my disposition to do right, or that the action be right, and thus equals a consciousness of 27:614 what duty is, for itself. Anyone, therefore, who in a theoretical concept is

---

[v] under the same genus of virtue

not aware of all the representations on which it is founded, is certainly deficient in knowledge, but conscience is not lacking in him.

Defective consciousness of our duty is not yet a want of conscience, just as consciousness of duty by itself does not yet constitute conscientiousness; the division *inter conscientiam erroneam et rectam*[w] is therefore all the more false when it is a matter here of a conscientious judgement, or the reverse. When the consciousness of what constitutes our duty is coupled with the judgement that a thing is right or wrong, though in itself it was impermissible or right, such an understanding merely judges erroneously; it is different, however, and does concern conscience, when to this is coupled the agent's awareness of the wrongness of the reasons, and that his judgement is founded on them, and he nevertheless regards a thing as right, which he knowingly holds to be wrong; if he has previously concluded that his judgement is false, and yet decided in favour of this opposite, he has acted without conscience. From this it also follows, on the other side, that nobody, for example, can be punished for religious dissidence, and that all religious persecution is impermissible. For this is a matter of reason on which judgement can be in error. The opponent wishing to punish the dissenter must necessarily have attained beforehand to a complete certainty, that the other's judgement runs counter to the possible consciousness and truth of his reasons; but this cannot possibly be the case here, since his contrary judgement, like the laws of positive religion, can furnish no adequate grounds for deciding the matter.

The judgement of conscience is addressed to a *factum*, the judgement of understanding to a general proposition. A *factum* can be based only on the conformity of circumstances to the fact, and on the truth of the same. The consciousness of its truth calls for examination of the truth of the circumstances, and is founded, therefore, on subjective certainty after suitably conducted tests. From the nature of the case, it is a strict duty to ensure that no object is present in the *factum*, and known to us, that has not been examined and taken into account. Now this assurance, up to complete certainty, that in order to accept a thing we have previously examined everything, and that the *factum* can accordingly be no otherwise, is the object of conscience, and thus a *factum* on which judgement is now based by the understanding.

27:615

Nobody can take a thing to be right or wrong, even when probability is present, so long as he cannot dismiss the possibility of the opposite, that his assumption is *in facto* incorrect, and thus that what he determines to be right is actually not permitted. Nobody can take a chance on this danger, without acting in a conscienceless way.

Si dubitas, ne quid feceris, says Pliny, *non facias.*[x] It is doubtful, for

[w] between an errant and a sound conscience
[x] if in doubt whether to do something, don't do it

358

example, whether a testator has paid a debt. The heir can in conscience neither pay nor reject the demand. Now we can all tell whether someone has properly examined the *veritas facti*, and arrived at total certainty about it; conscientiousness consists in the *habitus* or principle of being totally certain that a thing could not have occurred otherwise, and lack of conscientiousness in the fact that we have taken something to be certain without proper examination, and hazard the assumption that it is right or wrong, with the risk that it might also be wrong or right, and thus the opposite.

It shows a want of conscience, therefore, that by interpreting the scriptural passage: Invite them to come in* (which it renders in a coercive sense, *compellite intrare*) the Roman church should justify the coercive principle, that everyone must believe in accordance only with the *principia* of the catholic religion; that it should threaten anyone who introduces opposite opinions with burning at the stake; and that Torquemada the inquisitor should have held himself entitled, therefore, to dress such a person in the *Sanbenito* (St. Benedict, the sulphur-coloured shirt and sulphur-painted cap); because here there is a lack of certainty as to the *factum*.

It also follows very clearly from this, that the judgement founded on examination of the *factum* does not, by itself, constitute conscience, and that indeed this judgement may be an error, whereas conscience can never be that, whence the division *inter conscientiam erroneam et rectam* is totally false and unthinkable.

Baumgarten locates conscience merely in the *subsumptio factorum nostrorum sub lege.*[y] This amounts, therefore, to equating it with the soul's faculty of judgement, whereby the *facta judicantis*[z] would be subjected to the rules of the understanding. From this the rectitude or otherwise of the action would emerge, but not whether the agent is behaving conscientiously. The duty of conscience presupposes, rather, that an action be legitimate or right; in this conception, conscience is regarded as a *potestas judiciaria,*[a] just as it is also called *potestas legislatoria* and *executoria,* since it really is based on determining rectitude as such, on judging the *factum* by the laws of duty, and on establishing the *effectus a lege determinatorum et applicatorum,*[b] and deliberately adopts conscience as a valid imputation of our actions. All this, however, belongs to practical reason; but to that extent we may also suppose a *potestas exploratoria,* inasmuch as reason examines whether the *factum* is really present as such, and how it must be constituted, in order to bring it under the laws of duty. This we might call the *examining conscience,* in contrast to the *judging* one.

27:616

---

*[Luke 14:23–Tr.]
[y] subsumption of our doings under the law
[z] matters to be judged
[a] judiciary power
[b] effect of what is determined and applied by law

The examining conscience is occupied simply with looking into the *factum,* and this includes:

1. Consciousness of the fact that the subject has decided on, inaugurated, or is actually engaged in, self-examination. This is a criterion by no means compatible with the idea of an error.

2. Consciousness of the certainty of the *factum.* Here error is possible insofar as we wish to attain complete objective certainty, but the want of it would merely be an error of the understanding. Conscience involves only subjective certainty, i.e., the subject is unaware of other possible circumstances that might cause his certainty to waver.

3. Consciousness must be accompanied with an attitude of sincerity, i.e., that the subject be aware of having entered upon his examination with an eye to probability; this examination always has to do, of course, with the merely external circumstances in the action; it calls for a customary rigour, in order not to view a *factum* as other than it really is; man is only too readily inclined to persuade himself of something, and conjure up more than the truth. There are tendencies, indeed, in the souls of many, to make no rigorous judgement of themselves – an urge to dispense with conscience. If this lack of conscientiousness is already, in fact, present, we never get that person to deal honestly with himself. We find in such people 27:617 that they are averse to any close investigation of their actions, and shy away from it, endeavouring, on the contrary, to discover subjective grounds on which to find a thing right or wrong.

On the other hand a man, in the utmost exertion of his dutifulness, can only get so far as to be conscientious, and should he still be able to err in this, one would deprive him of the greatest treasure of which he is capable. But in order to attain to this, a repeated *awakening* of conscience is needed, i.e., the frequent evocation of the consciousness of his deeds.

§79. Professor Kant completely rejects Baumgarten's assumption, in §180, of a *conscientia naturalis.* For firstly, we cannot contrast to it the *oppositum* of the *differentia specifica,* viz. a *conscientia artificialis,* and the author's definition is false for this reason, that conscience or conscientiousness does not depend on knowledge of the laws of duty, but rather presupposes them. Both kinds of dutiful laws, whether they be *leges naturales vel statutariae,*ᶜ must be equally holy to the subject. From the *leges mere statutariae* he can allow himself no remission whatever. If it is argued, for example, in the case of contraventions, that only the public treasury stood to benefit, that it is sheer oppression, and that the offence does no harm, then the argument is always false, as soon as it has to accept the necessity of laws as such, and grants the law in question advantages on the other side, at least, since the government certainly has need of it. In general, it is a duty to compare every action with the law of duty under which it may

ᶜ natural or statutory laws

stand, and thus to be aware of having done everything to get to know the law, and carefully examined the action in relation to the latter.

§80. Of section §181, Professor Kant says that we cannot properly conceive the possibility of a *conscientia concomitans*, if it is to operate during the action. For the latter, as consequence, always presupposes already an approbation on the part of conscience, and we are merely postulating in our actions two stages that follow directly on each other, and therefore call them *concomitantes*. Cultivation of the *conscientia antecedens*[d] is thus the primary need; for the examination of past actions, or *conscientia consequens*, is the judging conscience. A deliberate failure to examine that which is capable of imputation in an action, is want of conscience. *In antecedenti* it is present in full, and *in consequenti*, partially so.

27:618

The *potestas judiciaria* before the judging conscience includes also the twinge of remorse: *morsus conscientiae*, i.e. a *letus conscientiae*[e] that imputes a *factum praeteritum*[f] in demerit. Here, as with the *conscientia latrans*, or nagging conscience (where the degree of reproach is different), the right way to silence it is not self-anguish, but a bettering of the action's consequences (so far as this may be), or an endeavour to hold off the worst consequences, and an effort to make them good.

§81. Professor Kant rejects the division into a broad and a narrow conscience.

Since conscience involves an examination of our moral conduct that cannot, in duty, be omitted, it is impossible to suppose that anyone might leave anything out here, or could push exactitude too far. It is a strict duty, and only broad duties have degrees in regard to acts of duty, e.g., good-heartedness. The concern lest all the care employed by the agent in his examination might still not have been sufficient, can at least not be accounted to him as a fault that he would need to avoid (§183).

§82. There is also the notion of a *forum conscientiae*, involving the assumption of an accuser, who seeks to arouse the conscience; a defender, who tries as an advocate to assuage it; and a judge, who assesses the action by the laws of duty and establishes the consequences. It is clear that, insofar as consideration is given here, in and for itself, to the laws of duty that must serve as foundation, the latter do not belong before this forum, but before that of the understanding; on the other hand, the subsumption of a *factum* of which conscience has become aware that it is one for which it might be held accountable, does belong here, as does the judging conscience (*potestas judicatoria*), in that the latter establishes and executes the *effectus a lege determinati*.

Thus understanding, judgement and reason are operative in the pro-

---

[d] conscience before and after the act
[e] pang of conscience
[f] a past deed

cess: conscience here reinforces awareness that the subject is in a situation that is governed by the laws of duty.

The defending or consoling conscience may work very much to our disadvantage. It is a fact of experience, that merely subjective grounds of consolation not only leave the consequences of action unamended, but are very dangerous to our progress in morality; hence the objectionable nature of consolations drawn from religion, which refer our liability to punishment to the name of another, or merely to the pity of God. Even in the hour of death, that is not a conscientious course.

27:619

It is our duty to arouse our conscience honestly, to prevent, eradicate and amend the evil consequences that we see to arise from our actions. It is beneficial for a man to accept the reproaches of conscience, and to show himself better and more active against his failings, than to leave their consequences unredeemed. Nor can we expect, from the indulgence of others towards ourself, that despair will not arise here, or that we shall not endure the pangs of conscience. Thus even in death we must be meticulous in preventing evil consequences of our actions from arising after our demise, and so must not disdain even the seeking for forgiveness. In this regard the Persians had a pictorial image (the pure idea of it is also in the Bible), in the shape of the Pulcerra (bridge of Serat), whereby the soul was conceived as wishing to pass into the next world over a bridge; yet it would be repulsed so long as it had not made a reckoning with its evil deeds here on earth.

§83. Professor Kant finds fault with *conscientia certa* (§189), insofar as this is taken to mean the objective certainty of the rectitude of the action. It is the business of the understanding to examine whether an action be right or wrong; conscience presupposes this, and is subject only to the duty of providing an awareness of having undertaken the examination with great thoroughness.

§84. The *casus conscientiae* is in morals what the *punctum juris* is in law. It is always concerned with an uncertainty as to what, in certain cases, would by moral standards be right or wrong. It would certainly be desirable to establish a system of casuistics in morals – a procedure in order to determine in every kind of situation what would be rightful or otherwise, depending on differences in the action. Such *casus dubii* cultivate a man's understanding, and also his morality. But cases of conscience commonly have to do, not with duties themselves, that we seek to determine, but with *adiaphora*, that are made analogous to duty; at least what are merely duties in the broad sense are made into strict

27:620

duties, e.g. refraining from all work on Sundays, fast-days etc. In such usages we fabricate a morality. According to the critic of actions, such a casuistic is sophistry, a procedure of deceiving or quibbling with conscience by sophistry, insofar as we endeavour to lead it astray; e.g., when we invent good intentions in actions that involve a transgression of duty, or also turn into cases of conscience what can only be called introductory means thereto.

§85. Professor Kant holds the preoccupation of conscience to be always practical, since it has to do with persuading us as to whether a duty has been fulfilled or transgressed.

§86. Our author has not adequately distinguished *philautia* from two other competing concepts. There are people who see themselves as objects of general love in relation to others, and also behave to others in such a way as to demand general love and respect from them. *Philautia* therefore rests on having a good opinion of ourselves; only with this difference, that in so doing we either regard ourselves as a subject worthy of love, and this is *philautia*, or as one worthy of respect, and this is arrogance. *Philautia* is divided into:

a. The *love of well-wishing towards oneself*; considered exclusively in relation to oneself, and thus without any regard for the duty of love towards others, this is solipsism or egotism – the *amor acquiescentae in semet ipso*[g] §191, §195.

N.B. Love, generally speaking, is opposite to the will's determination to strict duty, and consists in the inclination or will to promote the ends of others. Just as the duty of love, as opposed to the duty of right, is at all times directed to agreement with the ends of others, and thus to promoting the same.

Now this love, when self-directed, is *vel amor benevolentiae*, which considered in an exclusive sense, is solipsism or egotism – of which more anon – *vel amor complacentiae erga se ipsum*, self-satisfaction, for which see b.

As such, there is in all men without restriction a love of well-wishing towards themselves, and it only becomes a fault, therefore, when it excludes others from our love or inclination towards them. Now the rule: *Be not selfish*, or the duty in regard to solipsism, is twofold, in that it concerns both love for others and the end of the action as such; hence it splits into two rules: 27:621

1. Do not act selfishly, i.e., do not act merely for your own sake, but also for the benefit of others; love others, too, in *that* respect, therefore, and do not exclude them from your self-love.

2. Act unselfishly, i.e., act not from the principle of utility, merely, but also from that of duty. In the latter regard, the duty to oneself, respect for the right of humanity, is the motive of action and the condition under which self-satisfaction becomes rational; whereas this is set aside when self-love is restricted merely to the utility of the action. This follows from the nature of a duty that must be determined, not from utility as an end, but from the condition of action as such; otherwise it would become a rule of prudence.

---

[g] loving self-approval

b. *The love of well-liking towards oneself.* This, too, is *philautia,* if it is exclusively entertained towards oneself, but also becomes unreasonable. For anyone who has liking only for himself puts himself in danger of being incapable of examining or amending his faults, and of imputing to himself, in relation to others, a certain moral worth, which he first has to acquire. This cannot be assumed, unrestrictedly and without limits, in everyone; for it cannot be extorted from a man that he should be pleasing to himself, when he examines himself according to the requisite conditions. In comparison with others, this love of well-liking towards oneself is differentiated and transformed into *self-estimation of oneself.* If it rests on a prior close examination of oneself, it not only differs from self-love, namely well-wishing, but is also self-justifying in its own right; but if it rests, without examination, on a judgement of oneself, whereby the agent makes himself an object of the respect that we require from others, and enhances his worth, without justification, over that of other people, then it is arrogance, and a fault.

This type of self-love may occur without any selfishness, insofar as we harbour a high degree of well-wishing towards others. It is true, however, that owing to it there commonly arises the source of self-complacency in its defective form, in that by unselfishly promoting the welfare of others we engender a self-satisfaction in ourselves, and respect ourselves self-lovingly, without assessment of our true moral worth. If this self-satisfaction is to be true self-esteem, we have to distinguish between the performance of obligatory and meritorious acts of duty. Obligatory duties towards others are indeed a mere settlement with them, without our being able to demand anything from them on that account. From this arises merely the minimum of self-esteem for our own worth, in contrast to the direct omission of duty. But if, on the other hand, meritorious duties are performed towards others, i.e., acts of duty whereby, apart from fulfilment of our own obligation, we oblige ourselves to other things as well, and thus do more than it behoves us to do, a justified satisfaction with self is thereby engendered, which entitles and obliges us to impute a moral worth to ourselves; we thereby add a supplement to morality, which we are obliged to respect, since we would otherwise denigrate ourselves, as monks do. We can thus acquire merit in relation to others, as to God, only because we are no more able to bind ourselves to such services than the law itself. The case would arise, for example, in remission of a debt, or in the rescuing of an unfortunate from distress. See continuation in §88.

§87. Professor Kant takes the opposite view from that of Baumgarten in *assumptum* §193, where the latter explains probabilism in morality as a judgement that is founded on an improbability. Professor Kant locates the nature of it precisely in this, that in our judgement concerning a matter of conscience we follow merely the probability that a thing may be permitted, coupled with the possible danger that it may also not be permitted.

27:622

The Jesuits have a twofold probabilism:

1. Philosophical, whereby one may do something bad for the sake of a moral good, i.e., with morally good intentions.
2. Under *reservatio mentalis*,[h] which rests on an equivocation and sophistication of ambiguity, so as to deceive the understanding through a mistaken usage, e.g. in an oath.

§88. The improper love of well-liking towards oneself is thus the cause of much harm, if we do not take as our principle the strict performance of our duties, but assume instead that the laws of duty, whether they relate to the laws of actions themselves, or to their maxims, may be thought of merely as *lata officia*,[i] and thus only require to be fulfilled in that way as well. It is natural, in that case, that our judgement of our actions, and of ourselves, should become indulgent, and that we should grant ourselves approval in the fulfilment of our duties, albeit that they are impurely and imperfectly performed. Strict duties are incompatible with love, unless we have actually postulated an *ethica laxa*, in opposition to an *ethica rigorosa*, and have totally rejected *rigorismus moralis*, i.e., the moral conduct which makes it a principle, in the fulfilment of all duties, to regard them as inescapable and unconditional commands, and to execute them without regard to any end or use, merely with an eye to the principle of duty itself. One may therefore ask whether it is detrimental and blameworthy to couple man's moral worth directly with his inclinations in the determining of his dutiful behaviour, as Schiller does, for example, in his *Thalia*, when he advocates *worth with comeliness,* and maintains that it would be a repulsive, crude, Carthusian morality, to wish to establish the basis of one's actions merely upon strict respect for the law.

27:623

This much is certain, that all acts of duty are based upon a necessitation by the moral law, which, insofar as it counteracts the impulse to transgression, compels the latter to comply with the law. Comeliness, on the other hand, would determine duties in accordance with our inclinations, but to act in accordance with the latter, there is no need for any commanding law, to keep them in thrall to the rule of duty; inclinations are in conflict, therefore, with the laws of duty, and so no comeliness is conceivable in the observance of such laws.

The worth of the law, on the other hand, can certainly be conceived in the subjective presentation thereof, and Schiller is right to this extent, that such worth lies in the intellectual nature of the determination to duty. But the moral law also engenders worth through the very compulsion that fetters us in obedience thereto. If this compulsion were pathological or physical, it would arouse fear and a simultaneous aversion, but it is *moral*

[h] mental reservation
[i] imperfect duties

coercion, i.e., our determination to obey duty arises from free will, *ex spontanea determinatione mentis,*[j] and this commands respect, not servile subordination; we feel ourselves to be such that we can determine our duty, contrary to inclination, in accordance with duty's law. It is on this that the compulsion rests, though it involves only a voluntary feeling of respect. So there can be no thought of severity, but only of the worth of the law.

27:624

Now this respect for duty is the motive of our dutiful actions, or their subjective principle; this is determined, and alone is able to determine a rigorist morality. Were there also to be a need of inclination for the goodness of actions, from other motivating grounds than that of the principle of duty alone, then morality would be subject to conditions that run wholly counter to the principle of duty; for example, good intentions, the advantages of actions, or agreeable feelings. It is certain, therefore, that virtue is stripped of all graces, and founded solely on the respect due to the law, so that an *ethica laxa* must be utterly repudiated.

Philautia, or complacent self-love, takes its origin solely from the latter. It is contentment with oneself, from a disproportionate self-esteem. We imagine to ourselves a conformity with the law, and assume, in judging the action, an indulgent relaxation of the strictness of the law in our own regard, excuse the lack of congruity by our own innate weakness, maintain that our kind heart and good will have alone executed the law itself, and deceive ourselves, in following duty, as to the demands of the law and our own disposition, and in this way disencumber ourselves, undeservedly, from the strictness of the law, which in fact we have not obeyed. There is indeed an underlying respect for the law in this case, and between this and contempt for the law there is a great difference; but since only strict observance of the law, and that solely for the law's sake, can furnish true contentment, there is here only a lesser ground present, than if the law had been transgressed, for a lack of self-contentment. But now it is impossible for man to perform a pure act of duty, merely from the idea thereof, since the natural inclination to deviate from the law prevents us, and the observance rests upon many collateral grounds of motivation that cannot always even be fathomed; hence a complacent self-love, that actually claims to be well merited, is unthinkable in the principle of morality, and, considered as an inclination, is not permitted.

How would a man ascertain whether his joy at the rescue of an unfortunate family stems from sympathetic, pathological fellow-feeling, or from pleasure at the fulfilment of his duty, or whether, in his action, the love of honour or advantage did not obscurely play a part? *Philautia,* in that case, is just the same as moral egoism, when the latter not only rests on the arrogance of granting preference to the agent, and his own worth, in

27:625

---

[j] from a spontaneous determination of the mind

relation to others, but is accompanied by the persuasion or preconceived opinion of the benignity of his own will; such that, regardless of his having taken no pains to assure himself of the true state of purity of his moral disposition, he yet flatters himself with the conviction that he is just able to act morally well.

§89. To the author's definition, in §200, concerning self-mastery, Professor Kant here rejoins only that this should be called, not *dominium sui ipsius*, but *imperium sui ipsius*,[k] since *dominium* can be compared only *quoad res*, whereas a man indeed belongs to himself, has his own personality, and can determine his own condition according to his own choice (law-abiding as it may be); but this implies merely *proprietarium*, not *dominium*, since otherwise he would have the right to destroy or mutilate himself, etc., although this runs counter to his inner duty.

Imperium, on the other hand, or the duty of self-mastery, follows from the concept of duty; duty is the *ground* of the determination of free choice according to pure reason. This ground is unconditioned and necessary, and hence the formula of duty is always an imperative, whereby the nature of the mastery is indicated. Whence *imperium*, and one that is exerted, *in casu*, over oneself.

§90. From §201 on, Baumgarten treats of the *officia erga animam*.[l] Professor Kant censures his plan for the following reasons:

1. Morality does not presuppose the certainty of a soul. The knowledge of such a soul, of its various powers, and of the way to extend them by cultivation, belongs to psychology, though in and for itself the duty of man to develop his powers *quoad maxime* is at once assigned to morality.

2. In morals it must be left undecided whether man has a soul – this is a matter for adepts in psychological investigation; morality calls only for common understanding, and for laws that are recognized by reason, without necessarily presupposing education. In morals, therefore, we may only assume that we are able to think ourselves an object of inner sense, whereby we become capable of obtaining consciousness of ourselves and our states, and this we may presuppose – *qua* soul – in morality. Such a soul has powers whose cultivation is necessary for the ends of humanity. In regard to our own person, humanity is an ideal, to which we owe the duty of perfecting ourselves, so that we may fulfil the duties that it imposes on us. Now cultivation itself is applied to an inner capacity of the soul, by whose essential nature man attributes a free person to himself, and which is thus the personality of man, as a being endowed with freedom. So all duties that are incumbent on him in regard to his own person take account of him as noumenon, or as a being that acts in freedom; and to that extent we may say that man has a soul.

27:626

[k] self-mastery/self-command
[l] duties to the soul

§91. All duties that are now incumbent on him in regard to his soul can be reduced to three general determinations:

a. *To possess oneself,* i.e. to determine all actions by way of a free choice. This is what is called *animi sui compos,* or having a settled disposition. For man has a capacity to employ himself in a purposive way. But he attains this only by subjecting all his powers and capacities solely to his free choice, and employing them accordingly: the opposite is every state that is accompanied by actions which come about involuntarily, or through the necessity of natural impulses. He can, however, countermand this natural necessity, and it is thus within his power, whenever actions are involuntarily undertaken on his part, to determine nevertheless, whether he will make use of them or not, whether he wishes to pay attention to them or abstract from them, and whether, by the former, he is minded to strengthen them and extend their consequences, or to distance and destroy their effects. If he cannot exert such control over himself, he is in the position of an enthusiast, who is involuntarily given over to his ideas, and acts without reflection or freedom, for example, a hypochondriac. The latter has to rid himself of the condition of not feeling well, just as everyone has the power to drive away from himself the condition of idleness. To that extent we may say that man has a *dominium* over himself, meaning by this a *dominium facultatum,*[m] when he has free authority in respect of these powers to employ them purposively according to his own choice; they are then to be regarded as *incorporales*[n] of himself.

27:627   b. *The duty to govern oneself.* This involves cultivation of the mental powers to those ends with which they are collectively compatible, and constitutes, therefore, the essential in the soul's capacity or readiness to enlarge the *facultates animi* for all moral ends, and to direct them thereunto. Man has a multitude of natural tendencies . . . [Text breaks off.]

[§92. I.] The impermissibility of suicide must therefore be presupposed, in order to infer to a divine prohibition of it. The ground thereof is thus a law of reason, from which the immorality of this action proceeds. Nor can it be any more permissible, to take one's own life under conditions. For were this duty conditioned, the condition would have to lie in the agent himself, and could not be compatible with his existence. From a moral standpoint there is no such condition. It would have to be a duty in the broad sense, and this would consist in a man's love and well-wishing for his own person, for the sake of certain ends. Hence it would be impossible to furnish any standard, for how far I may go in the preservation of my life; other people would have no right to compel me to preserve my life, indeed I myself would not be unconditionally subject to this duty.

[m] command of one's faculties
[n] non-physical properties

But in that case it would never be sufficiently determined, whether and when I might shorten my life. But now suicide is contrary to the concept of the right of humanity in my own person; and humanity is in itself an inviolable holiness, wherein my *personhood*, or the right of humanity in my person, is no less inviolably contained. It demands the duty of morality, and it is only man who demands happiness, which must be unconditionally subordinated to morality.

Personhood, or humanity in my person, is conceived as an intelligible substance, the seat of all concepts, that which distinguishes man in his freedom from all objects under whose jurisdiction he stands in his visible nature. It is thought of, therefore, as a subject that is destined to give moral laws to man, and to determine him: as occupant of the body, to whose jurisdiction the control of all man's powers is subordinated. There is thus lodged in man an unlimited capacity that can be determined to operate in his nature through himself alone, and not through anything else in nature. This is freedom, and through it we may recognize the duty of self-preservation, which cannot, therefore, be plainly demonstrated. The feeling that is based on this duty finds expression whenever our life is neglected; in a guilty manner, we always become an object of contempt and aversion in the eyes of others – for example, a bankrupt, who brings misfortune on himself and his family through risky enterprises, and then takes his life. If he abandons them, instead of this, or shows himself wholly unconcerned and without feeling about the consequences of his behaviour, such aversion increases.

27:628

And so it is, too, with every subject who has taken his own life; it remains an unpardonable reproach.

So neither the greatest advantages, nor the highest degree of well-being, nor the most excruciating pains and even irremediable bodily sufferings can give a man the authority to take his own life, to escape from anguish and enter earlier upon a hoped-for higher happiness. The preservation of his life is a strict duty, resting upon respect for the personhood accorded to him as a rational being, and of which, as a sensuous being, he may not divest himself.

In the Stoic's principle concerning suicide there lay much sublimity of soul: that we may depart from life as we leave a smoky room. The primary criterion of the ideal they had fashioned of a *sage* consisted in this, that he alone is free, i.e., that he can be coerced neither by himself (through inclination, feeling or passions), nor by others (i.e., through physical evil); that he robs himself of freedom only by transgression of his duty, in that he abolishes the conformity of his freedom with that of everyone else, and thus acts contrary to the concept of freedom, or that of right, duty and the juridical laws; and only then is a slave and really suffers. They thus assumed it possible that even personal slavery, or the harshest bodily suffering, can be compatible with a man's freedom, in that he is not being coerced, through inclinations, by himself, but is oppressed only by contingent evils. Presuming, therefore, that a person has fulfilled all his duties in this world, and only when his situation can no longer have any value for him, they permitted suicide. For in such a situation, no duty any longer, but only inclination to life, could fetter him into preserving it; yet this inclination would compel him to act contrary to his freedom, and thus turn the sage into a coward.

27:629

This principle embodied a lofty habit of thought. For the sublimity of humanity in its perfection, it is necessary to assume, at all events, that a man has something that he must value more highly than his physical life. He must therefore give up that life, if he can preserve it only under the condition of doing something shameful, of having to forfeit true honour and virtue; in this connection he must put a lower value on pain and death; for if he treasures a life that makes him unworthy of humanity more highly than a painful death, and thereby forgoes the latter, he is of mean quality. He is already morally dead, if he lives only for crime and can preserve his life only by the practice thereof. But how does the conclusion follow from this, that he is entitled, under such circumstances, to take his own life? No undeserved distress can compel him to the transgression of his duty, and if it is deserved, his offence is still an offence, and he cannot put it right by suicide. There is no physical evil that would match up to such a violation.

§93. It remains, on the other hand, contemptible and contrary to duty, to promote the maintenance of life at the price of one's morality, and to treasure *living* as a boon, even were its maintenance to be coupled directly with crime, and the death that we have to endure with the moral worth of man. For example, if someone were to be promised death, or the enjoyment of a happy life at the price of a shameful treason or other criminal act.

In many situations the case seems to be plausible, and also an – albeit incomplete – reason for the same, that one should think less of preserving one's life than performing a duty; or there are also reasons and causes, why death, though one has to preserve one's life, is nevertheless welcome, just so long as we are not the agent of it. (The latter is doubtless the key to the Stoic principle.) It is permitted to venture one's life against the danger of losing it; yet it can never be allowable for me deliberately to yield up my life, or to kill myself in fulfilment of a duty to others; for example, when Curtius* plunges into the chasm, in order to preserve the Roman people, he is acting contrary to duty; but when a soldier pits himself against the foeman's steel, he is merely risking his life; the seaman likewise, the fisherman and other people with dangerous occupations risk their lives,

27:630

---

*[Marcus (or Mettius) Curtius, who in 362 B.C. leapt fully armed into a fissure that had opened in the Roman Forum (Livy, 1.12, vii.6). – Tr.]

and if they did not, one might indeed take it that they were expending less effort than they might, to sustain themselves, or to maintain a limited use of their freedom.

INCOLUMITAS (CARING FOR ONESELF)

II. It is likewise a duty to oneself, to renounce all disposition over any substantial portion of one's body, and similarly

III. To make no misuse of one's body.

So nobody may therefore voluntarily mutilate himself in the important parts of his body, and still less so for the sake of gain, without lowering himself. For example, accepting money to have a tooth pulled, for another's use. The cutting of hair would doubtless be different, for since it grows back again, it is no essential part of the body, yet if it were done for money, there would still be something base about it.

In misuse of the body, it is primarily a matter of not deliberately exposing it to injury, since *incuria corporis*ᵒ can yield no strict determination of duty; for example, in regard to immoderacy in one's way of life, behaviour that we know to be damaging is certainly contrary to duty, but if due merely to inattention, it is no more a breach of duty, than excessive anxiety to spare one's body can be called an observance of the same.

Hence the latter case is described as *vita avaritiae*, and the former as *vita prodigalitas*.ᵖ To be weary of life is a thing that no man can really claim of himself. For so long as he *can* live, he has not yet lived enough. Only on his deathbed can he say that he has lived enough, and that only in the sense that he has fulfilled all duties as exactly as was possible for him, and to that extent has done enough in the way of goodness; not, however, that he is renouncing any enjoyment of life, for though the recollection of such things may be coupled with the pain of no longer being able to enjoy any more of them, the former still have an enduring worth. A man calms himself for the future with such an idea, and this shows how estimable the moral feeling is.

§94. The second duty towards the body concerns health, whose opposite is sickness. The middle state between the two is ailment of body, insofar as we feel an impediment to health. The man who feels strong is not always healthy; he is merely too dull to sense the condition of ailing until such time as he is steeped in sickness. The ailing man is weaker by nature, and seems to possess more refined feelings. *Diet*, now, consists in the dutiful attention to preserving the body's health by natural means. Just as the theologian extracts the generally comprehensible, and thus also what is generally useful, from the totality of all theological learning, and the jurist endeavours to reduce the multitude of indefinite and constantly

27:631

ᵒ physical self-neglect
ᵖ a sparing or wasteful way of life

self-restricting laws to *principia,* and everything in the sciences is unified, so as gradually to approach philosophy, and thereby, with less and more concentrated learning, to approach still nearer to the goal, so we also take trouble to strike out a natural path, in order to be able to keep healthy without recourse to art.

Now it absolutely cannot be determined by any rule, how much a man needs, and of what nature, to keep his body in good health and maintain dexterity, i.e., that degree of life whereby he remains in a position to make an appropriate use of all his powers. So how much a man employs for nourishment, to manage the appetite that determines the body's needs, is no more reducible to a regimen than it can be necessary for bodily agility, i.e., cultivation of the same with respect to one's organization, so as to be able to use it with ease for all possible purposes, that everyone should pursue *gymnastica, athletica* or *histrionica.* The whole duty of caring for oneself reduces to the two objects: *victus et amictus.*[q] The former relates to enjoyment and nourishment of body, the latter to care for its exterior. Hence the inclinations, (a) as urge to enjoyment, and (b) as urge to care outwardly for the body, insofar as it rests upon a mania, or the judgement and opinion of others.

§95. That man is not healthy, who does not feel his body; for since even to every thought there corresponds a bodily sensation, and the one certainly causes the other, the condition of insensitivity is also that of a dulled body. From this it follows, in regard to enjoyment, that in order to avoid intemperance one must conserve feeling for every barrier to a greater excess. The stifling of such feeling represents a blunting of nature's own effectiveness.

In itself, therefore, the maxim that one must eat in order to live is just as false as its negative, that one must not live in order to eat; for the former, were it to have no bounds, would deprive the body of its powers for moral activity just as much as excess of enjoyment would. Just as a man must preserve moral worth in what he does (moral diet), so he can only have physical worth in that he tries, both in quality and quantity of enjoyment, to preserve bodily well-being, and does not endeavour thereby to injure morality, i.e., make himself morally incapable of acting.

Just as the mathematician uses the diameter, the *maxima chordarum,* as the measure of all circles, so likewise in morals we postulate a minimum of humanity and a maximum of brutishness, and distinguish the vices as follows:

a. Physical vices, having to do with enjoyment, namely *ebrietas* and *voracitas.*[r] By each of these a man lapses out of humanity, and becomes equal to the brute; he thus degrades himself below humanity.

27:632

[q] sustenance and clothing
[r] drunkenness and gluttony

b. Devilish vices. Here a man oversteps moral viciousness, or the natural tendency of man towards evil, and thus his tendency to vice is greater than human nature allows, and he seems to have adopted the *principium* of evil itself. Among such vices are ingratitude, envy and *Schadenfreude* (*ingratitudo qualificata*).[s] This represents the maximum of brutishness (not as an ideal, owing to the lack of a model to be imitated, but merely as a measure of the determinable).

c. Unnatural vices (*crimina carnis contra naturam*). These pertain to bestiality, and degrade a man even below the beasts, so that he actually behaves contrary to the natural laws of the brute creation.

§96. Now in satisfying enjoyment we may overdo things both *ratione quantitatis* and *ratione qualitatis;* the former is *luxuries,* and the latter *luxus.*[t]

a. *Luxuries* divides into

1. The propensity for intoxicating liquors. Intoxication in and for itself does not aim at immediate sensory enjoyment, but the inclination to it rests on the livelier play of imagination, enlarged by a sharpened fancy. This is *temulentia,*[u] and thus markedly different from *ebrietas.* Of Cato's virtue, Seneca says: *Virtus ejus incaluit mero.*[v] It awakens much activity, and is to that extent acceptable for morality; indeed owing to the advantages that *temulentia* exhibits in regard to social life, promotion of the tendency thereto seems impossible to quarrel with. The power of representation becomes more vivid and effective, communication is enhanced, we enjoy the social pleasures for ourselves and for others with greater satisfaction, we forget and overlook the weaknesses of others, we become more open-hearted, i.e., we do not mind revealing the truth purely and frankly, when otherwise people in a state of sobriety, out of a naturally grudging temper, are too secretive in their views of one another to be capable of communicating with candour (a reason why we look so much for a friend in whom we are able to confide). Finally, experience teaches that people who are otherwise strict and hard-hearted become, through intoxication, good-humoured, communicative and benign, as has been noted of King Frederick William the First. Things are very different with the consequences of the inclination to drunkenness or *ebrietas.* The propensity to this condition makes a man incapable of conducting his affairs. It is an excess in use, whereby physical powers are attended with derangement, the feelings are muffled and, as it were, lamed; so the victim feels no pain, and hence no pressing cares; his fancy paints him only pleasing pictures, and arouses retroactively a constant craving for drink.

27:633

[s] ingratitude with malice
[t] excess and over-refinement
[u] conviviality
[v] his virtue was kindled by wine

Yet it is most shameful of all for a man to get drunk by himself; he cannot, in fact, drink so much as he can in company, and weakens himself with agreeable reveries. Wine differs from brandy and opium in this, that the latter two make a man self-enclosed and self-preoccupied, over-clever and silent, which also stems from shame at himself and selfishness in regard to others, and blunts him far more than the animating spirit of wine.

2. The propensity for eating, or voracity. This appears to be more brutish, since it is already attended with a shameful insensitivity of the body towards the feeling of surfeit. It oppresses the spirit, and is therefore still more dangerous than the inclination towards drink.

It is similar to

27:634   3. The inclination to daintiness, which rests upon excessiveness in *luxus*, when in fact we become fastidious over the choice of enjoyments, and take so much pleasure in superfluities that we become sick or impoverished as a result.

Daintiness or *gulositas*, as a fault, is due to this, that the stimulations of the palate are carried further than need or well-being demand, and that morality is infringed thereby. In modern times, the use of tobacco is a case in point.

Yet in itself, to find pleasure in taste, insofar as the latter pertains to enjoyment, is permissible, and it is even the mark of a good host to discern and be a good judge of that which will be agreeable to the majority of his guests.

This is *sapor non publicus*,[w] and the Romans call the opposite *homo sine sensu sapore*,[x] just as they themselves related *sapor* to intellectual taste. The cultivation of such endeavours enlivens and constitutes social well-being.

§97. The *ede, bibe, lude*,[y] the revelry of Sardanapalus, therefore came to no more than this, to tickle the palate with daintiness, to encourage the play of fancy by intoxication, and to idle about.

No less erroneous is the *mortificatio carnis*, or *mors philosophica*, the mortification of the flesh, which consisted in deliberately divesting oneself of all bodily needs, to the point at which the body retains no influence upon the soul, so that one may share in the direct influence of the community of spirits. (Demonology was the basis for the rise of this doctrine.) People tried, by asceticism, to attain this independence of the soul from the body, for it contained the totality of those doctrines whereby the body was trained (*telestica exempla*).[z] It was supposed to be a liberation from sensual desires, so as to avoid any departure from dutiful conduct. It did

[w] uncommon taste
[x] a man with no sense of taste
[y] eat, drink and be merry
[z] guiding pattern

not occur to anyone, that weakening of the body increases the stimulus, and that the body thus retains its rights. This doctrine stems from the system of Plato, who certainly overstepped the bounds of philosophical critique by assuming Ideas incapable of demonstration, though it was his followers (the eclectics) who gave out and disseminated them as his teaching. Plato, in fact, supposed that the soul was lodged in the body as if in an *ergastulum* (prison) into which it had been thrust for punishment; that owing to the fetters of the body it was incapable of acting freely, by pure system and holiness, in that it was dependent on the body; that to that 27:635 extent the soul was morally dead, so long as, and inasmuch as, it was fettered by the body; and that such durance ceases only with death, which thus effects its liberation, and allows it to become capable of a pure enjoyment of life. The neo-Platonists, in their fanaticism, took many principles from the Egyptian theology, made out that such had already been the teaching of the old philosophers – Plato in particular, and clothed these principles in ancient philosophy; and hence, too, the methods aimed at liberating the soul from all requirements of the body engendered the practice of pure monastic virtue.

§98. As to what specially concerns duties to the *amictus*, or outward form of the body, they are largely subject to contingent circumstances, though it may nevertheless by taken as an essential duty, that it redounds to the completion of our moral perfection to bring our inner morality into conformity with our outward appearance. The foundation of this is an extension of our heed for the influence we have upon others. For in that a man appears at his best in the eyes of others, to make himself worthy of respect, he is in a position, as it were, to present his inwardly virtuous disposition in appearance, and make it outwardly noticeable; he thereby promotes the dissemination of virtue, to which we are obligated in any case; he acquires for himself, and for moral perfection itself, an influence upon others that resides in the feeling of taste. As we see, respect for the outer demeanour creates a good impression, we associate this with inner perfection of mind, and feel compelled to reward such conformity with approval; even the man's moral perfections may thereby exert a wider influence upon others. Omission of this duty would indeed degenerate into making him contemptible in the eyes of others, inasmuch as the neglect of outward appearances could argue that he sets little store by punctiliousness in the maintenance of his own worth. This pertains to the duty of loving honour, insofar, that is, as the latter remains genuine; for to that extent it is the principle of not lessening one's worth in the opinion of others, and differs in that regard from vanity; as an ambition, it also differs from humility, in that the latter consists in confining self-esteem to its legitimate bounds, whereas the former goes so far towards an enlargement of respect for ourselves, that we are obligated not to demean the 27:636 worth of our own person in the judgement of others.

Now the outward demeanour particularly includes all means of beautifying the body's external form by appendages, insofar as they are thereby in accordance with the laws of taste, i.e., the laws of sensibility. Taste makes a good impression on others, and our morality thereby obtains a vehicle for gently exerting its influence on them. Now cleanliness here takes precedence over elegance of any kind. For the former is adapted to taste only inasmuch as we thereby prevent ourselves from becoming contemptible to others; but this is the most essential thing for which we are required to care.

§99. *Otium.*[a] We may take it that a man who has empty time will endeavour, with all his powers, so to fill up the course of the day, that its length will become as little noticeable to him as possible; if he is unable to do this, he will sooner devote himself to acts of wickedness than do nothing at all. Hence *tempus farcire* – the shortening of time – is one of men's natural impulses; it is striking, that the less a man has done in the course of his life, the shorter it seems to him to be, whereas the more he has laboured, the longer his lifetime appears to have lasted. It seems to depend on the dearth or abundance of objects for recollection, just as we have a similar feeling on completing a journey in a barren region, or one more fertile and rich in things to see; hence the length of the miles, when they are measured out by feeling. The *factis extendere vitam*[b] seems, therefore, already to be a duty by instinct.

Now the state of being occupied may concern itself either with working to a specific end, and this is *negotium,* or with trying, in the absence of any immediate purpose, to find pleasure in the endeavour itself, in that we set our forces in motion for agreeable play. The latter is leisure, or *occupatio in otio,* and this therefore stems either from our seeking the enjoyment of a pleasure, or from our being in a state of mind sated by all enjoyments. The latter is emptiness, which nature abhors like the *horror vacui* in physics. If, on the other hand, the specific end that we are concerned with is attainable only with hardship, the occupation as such being disagreeable, and only the end itself giving pleasure, then we call it *labor.* Now rest after *work,* or recreation, is always agreeable in itself; we approve it, in that after bending our efforts we are content with ourselves, and have earned a state of rest. At the opposite pole, however, stands the *homo male feriatus,*[c] who has an aversion for ever undertaking burdensome toil, and thus at all times neglects his work. Diligence (or *laboriositas*) rests on the inclination to occupy all one's forces; it is thus an impulse to work, and so does not include, say, the ease of working that is attained by practice, or has become natural owing to one's constitution. If this inclination is capable of

27:637

---

[a] leisure
[b] prolongation of life by activity
[c] culpably idle man

carrying out burdensome toil for specific ends, then it evinces a staunch temper, with courage (*animus serenus*). If the impulse to work is persistent and enduring, the diligence is *solertia.*[d]

The opposites of these are *socordia*, laziness, a blunting of energies; lassitude, *desidia*, an inclination to toil, coupled with insufficient exertion; and indolence, *inertia*, an inner resistance of the soul to being able to set oneself to work. This cannot always be overcome; it may be innate, in that the vital forces may not be present in such degree as to permit the needed expenditure of them; it is therefore not possible for such a person to undertake persistent labour, though the motive to work is present. If even the latter is lacking, then it is aggravated laziness, which does not even have the good will to bestir itself.

The regular division of times for work and recreation pertains to order, and this determining of occupation in regard to periods is the *pensum*[e] of work, rest and recreation, sustenance, sleep and society.

§100. In the sexual inclination, it is essential that one subject is presented to the other as object of enjoyment, and that we do not take this to mean a service of one sex towards the other, whichever it may be. The concurrent duty may be called that of chastity, in regard to the genuineness and purity of which, we have to distinguish genuine motives from spurious ones. For if they are spurious, and especially if carried too far, the result is purism in regard to the judgement of chastity, and likewise the vice of impurity in regard to behaviour that runs counter to the moral relationships of the two sexes. Now since nobody, as such, has the *facultas disponendi de substantia sui corporis tanquam de re sua,*[f] whereas anyone making themselves into an object of the other's lust is after all treating the substance of their body as a thing to be enjoyed, it seems as though all sexual inclination would run counter to morality. For the case is quite different from the permitted use of one's powers that is granted to the other, or any *praestatio operarum;*[g] when a wife concedes the substance of her body to lust, she deteriorates through using up her forces in pregnancy; she subjects herself to the danger of dying in childbirth; – and yet the sexual impulse is not only a human inclination, but can also, under the name of love, be a duty. 27:638

In the first place, sensual congress of the sexes is a phenomenon in man that is entirely similar in function to that of animals; this bodily act of physical nature also engenders shame and turns it into an obscene act, i.e., one that in public presentation would awaken repugnance, accompanied by the notion of *impudicitia.*[h] Now if the act of intercourse were permissi-

---

[d] industriousness
[e] remuneration
[f] right to dispose over the substance of one's body, as over a thing that is owned
[g] evidence of performance
[h] lewdness

ble, in and for itself, there would be no explaining the shame; and it rests on nothing else but this, that in presenting ourselves to the other as an object of enjoyment we feel that we are demeaning humanity in our own person and making ourselves similar to the beasts.

It also follows from this that nobody can make themselves into an object of the other's enjoyment if it is injurious to their personality, and that a strictly incumbent obligation to consummate a promise of carnal intercourse cannot be admitted. A *pactum concubinatus* is *turpe*,[i] null and void, and the concubine can therefore breach it at any time.

So if the sexual inclination is to be recognized on the side permitted by morality, it must be able to co-exist with the freedom sanctified by humanity. Now since one party is conceding possession of their substance to the other, each of them can only remain free if, in the bond of common sexual possession one of another, and in precisely the degree to which each possesses the other, the one who allows the other to have *dominium* over them at the same time subjects that other to their own possession, so that they each recoup themselves. The two of them mutually acquire each other; each becomes *dominus* of the other and in that case remains also self-possessing, and is free. This is the institution of *matrimonium*, and consists, therefore, in a *jus mutuum perpetuum ad commercium sexuale*,[j] i.e.,

27:639 for a continuing enjoyment of the *membra sexualia et facultates*;[k] here, both parties reciprocally acquire their whole *conditio vitae*,[l] and each is *in dominio alterius dominus ejus.*[m] Both entirely possess each other, for since they each make over, as it were, their *membra sexualia* to the other, and the ownership thereof accrues to the latter, neither is subjected to an arbitrary use of their substance on the other's part, since only so much is allowed as can be required of the other. Now in this, that they both fully acquire each other, and one becomes the other's property, there is constituted the *union* of the two conjoined sexes, in respect of all their relationships. Yet each, for all that, is self-possessing, although given over to the other as a thing, since each retains freedom to dispose over the other's property as *their own*. If, instead of this, the conjunction were to be founded on a voluntary concession of the one party's sexual member to the other, that one would be in the position of letting himself or herself be treated by the other as *objectum reale*,[n] without taking account of their personhood; this would be a beast-like condition, a conjunction aimed merely at a satisfying of the natural impulse. Now since this runs counter to all morality, no other

[i] a concubine's agreement is shameful
[j] an enduring mutual right to sexual intercourse
[k] sexual organs and functions
[l] condition of life
[m] in the other's power, the other's master
[n] physical object

assumption can be made, therefore, but that modesty is not a mere natural instinct, but in truth an idea founded upon morality; even rude peoples possess it, and we find but few, and those in the rawest state of nature, who have paid no regard to it, or could do so.

Now from this it also follows that the end envisaged in sexual intercourse – *ad propagandam et procreandam subolem*[o] – is not confined to that. For though nature, in implanting the sexual impulse in man, has assuredly had this end in view, it does not follow from that, that man is also required to direct his attention solely to this purpose. For to pursue it exclusively can occur no otherwise than by attending not at all to the worth of our humanity; the impulse would be satisfied just like the appetite in eating; this makes it a natural urge on a par with every other inclination that nature has ordained in the bodily mechanism. It would follow from this that persons who by reason of age or infirmity did not possess this impulse, or could not fulfil it, would have to separate, or would not be able to conjoin. The *consortium conjugale*[p] would become merely transitory, and not be perpetual; in marriage one would never have a right to possession of the other as an exclusive property, but only a temporary use of the other's substance, without being able to demand it with freedom. This would all represent a debasement of our personhood, although that must absolutely never be infringed. This bond must therefore absolutely rest upon the conformity of the natural impulse with the moral law, and only with its sanction, or in conserving our personhood, can the sexes possess one another for mutual use of their substance, in that they acquire each other as common property. Marriage is for this reason also a *pactum commercii perpetui,*[q] that only therein does the property of the one remain that of the other, so that it lasts enduringly and is not transitory; for otherwise it would not be an acquisition, but a temporary use, of the members of the other. 27:640

Now from this it follows:

1. That among married people, nothing can belong to the one that does not also, *aequo jure,*[r] belong to the other. They can indeed abandon this, *per pactum,* insofar as it has no influence on the conjugal relation, but so long as that has not been done, the above consequence must be accounted to the nature of this union.

2. A voluntary separation cannot take place, since the union cannot be a temporary one. Separation can rightfully occur only (a) *in adulterio,* since one party thereby seeks to withdraw from the primal duty; (b) from circumstances that make it a physical impossibility to form a union of the person

---

[o] for the propagating and procreating of a child
[p] conjugal partnership
[q] pact of enduring marital union
[r] by equal right

together, e.g. impotence, the bodily infirmity of a hidden recalcitrance, since this runs contrary to the reciprocity of the right. But, to be sure, such an obstacle must have been present on entry into the marriage; for by subsequently occurring maladies, an acquired right cannot be lost.

3. There can never be polygamy; neither polygyny, as with many Eastern peoples, nor polyandry, as in Tibet and among the Cairenes on Thalabar (noble families), for each husband or wife would acquire only a part of the other, though giving themselves completely; the condition of personal freedom would therefore lapse. . . . [Text breaks off.]

4. Still less can concubinage be permitted. This union is only transitory, and its purpose is merely that one party allows their person to the other for enjoyment, without acquiring the person of the other.

27:641

5. Nor can it be denied that a morganatic marriage does not fully accord with the right of humanity. For the wife is not put in possession of all the husband's rights, and so does not have total possession of him, though he has absolute disposition over her.

6. *Fornicatio* (*fornices in lupanariis*[s] of husbands) involves, of course, a service similar to a *praestatio operarum*. The woman offers up her body for the other's enjoyment, in exchange for money, and so treats it, contrary to humanity, as a thing. Of somewhat more refined character, in this relationship, were the courtesans of old; and the ladies of Venice still practise it today. Without pecuniary motive, they permit themselves to associate with various lovers, among whom they favour one, albeit with the freedom never to be tied to him, but rather to change, while continuing at the same time to consort with several others. Dínand de St Claude was famous for this. It is a striking fact, that the clergy at the Tridentine Council should have permitted themselves to behave thus; *erant* – so we are told – *tridentini ducentae meretrices honestae, quas Cartejanae vocant.*[t] In general, a *vaga libido*[u] with unfettered inclination to choose any object for the satisfaction of its lust, cannot be allowed to either party.

7. Now if, in the congress of the sexes, it is not merely a matter of satisfying an impulse of nature, the personhood of the one we conjoin with must also be conserved; we are required, therefore, to uphold our right of humanity, by sacrificing all inclinations that run counter to it; though we have a right to exclusive possession, the lawful union of the two sexes is attended with many restrictions; thus a contravention against the end of nature is not only a demeaning of humanity in our person – we also make ourselves an object of the greatest abhorrence, whether our lust be vented upon ourselves, or upon an object of the same sex. Pederasty was origi-

---

[s] consorting with prostitutes
[t] at the Council of Trent there were two hundred honest whores, whom they called courtesans
[u] promiscuous desire

nally a praiseworthy thing, for one picked out a promising youth to rear and educate, as was the case with Socrates and Xenophon; but it came in the end to be an impermissible association. All these *crimina carnis contra naturam* involve a bestial element, i.e., they demean man below the beasts, among whom there is indeed no communality, but nevertheless a mating of opposite sexes, and likewise among the same animals. If these crimes are compared with suicide, feeling already tells us that the suicide is not contemptible in the same degree. 27:642

The crude suicide is an object of general hatred, since everyone must think of such a person as dangerous to them and to their own life, and is bound, therefore to hate him, since fear engenders hatred. The subtle suicide, i.e., one who shortens his life by intemperance and robs himself of his powers, is an object of contempt, and thus also of hatred. The person of unnatural lusts is similar to him; but since he brings humanity itself, in his person, into undeserved contempt, he becomes an object of abhorrence, in that in his case nothing remains that could be thought to contribute to the defence of humanity, whereas in the suicide there may still be features that could betray a worth of the soul, e.g. the conservation of his honour, or excess of remorse over his transgressions of duty.

8. It is evident, *ex adductis*, in what manner the person of one individual may belong to, and be in the *possession of, another*. Three such ties are possible:

1. Between husband and wife, reciprocally; for if it is just assumed that *quoad servitia*^{v} the wife belongs to the husband, this is due merely to her lesser ability to provide for herself
2. Between father and son
3. Between master and servants

The *suum paternale et domesticum*^{w} must also be coupled to the personhood of these individuals, so that the use of all their powers does not include arbitrary treatment, and the *servitium juris in re,*^{x} so far as it includes possession, is expressed only *contra tertium,*^{y} i.e., *contra quemlibet ejus possessorem;*^{z} and rests on the exclusive right to ownership. In regard to the person in question, the owner has no *jus in re*, but only *contra tertium*, and it is thus merely analogical. He can reclaim wife, child or servant from any third party.

§101. The third class of duties to ourselves brings into consideration our outer condition, or truly our condition in general. By this we mean the

---

^{v} as to servitude
^{w} possession of children and servants
^{x} owner's right to service
^{y} against a third party
^{z} against any possessor thereof

coupling of a person's contingent determinations with his necessary ones (*variabilia cum fixis*).[a] Now the moral laws yield in part absolutely necessary, and in part contingent determinations; the first, and thus the necessary determinations of the moral condition include, for example, all duties of right, and the duty in regard to the substance of our body; the second, and thus the contingent elements in our moral condition, include, for example, beneficence and the cultivation of our powers on behalf of others. Now this condition may be viewed from both a moral and also a physical standpoint, and there is a corresponding difference in *contentment.*

27:643

For this takes two forms, yet in such a way that both aspects fall within the scope of the concept.

There is in fact a self-regarding duty to seek a condition with which one can and may be content, i.e., which is based upon such means as are ordained and permitted by the dutiful nature of our conduct, and also offer the possibility of fulfilment. This contentment with our lot, conceived as a result of the conditions employed, has as its opposite discontent, which is always founded on the nature of our actions, which do not allow us to be contented with our lot; we have thus transgressed our duties, and by its very expression our discontent is a breach of the duty to oneself. Contentment is thus of two kinds, namely, (1) with oneself and (2) with one's lot. By this we mean

a. Happiness, insofar as contentment is taken in a pathological sense; it consists in that state, depending on laws and objects of nature, with which we are content, insofar as it accords with nature's laws. It is based on the feeling of pleasure and pain, and the objects of happiness may present themselves in appearance both outwardly and inwardly as well; for example, all *merita fortunae:* congenial temper, readiness of comprehension, talents and merits of a person. This yields, therefore, the negation of moral contentment, in that the reason for it never originates in our freedom or in ourself.

b. Contentment in the moral sense, however, always has reference to a state founded on consciousness of the law-abiding use of our freedom, and thus on the conformity of our own actions with the moral law. It relates, therefore, to the agent and the actions he has decided upon as a free being, and is truly a contentment with himself, since it can only be effected through a state of affairs in accordance with the moral law.

27:644

We use the word *blessedness (Glückseligkeit)* to express a state of contentment in the conjunction of happiness (*Glück*) and bliss (*Seligkeit*); but if the enjoyment of the two is coupled therewith, it leads to a misunderstanding.

Bliss, *beatitudo,* is quite different from that. But normally it is taken to mean that condition whose contentment is independent of all natural causes, or happiness, and arises solely from the lawfulness of our actions,

[a] variables and fixities

or from ourselves, as purely free beings. But a state whose comfort has its source merely in things of nature, or in good fortune, and of which I am not the author through my freedom, would not be called "blessed" ("*selig*"), and would have to be called "fortunate" ("*sälig*"), in that here the word *Saal* is at the bottom of it – as with every state of things – just as it has this meaning in the words *Schicksaal* (fortune) and *Trübsaal* (misfortune).

§102. Conditions of our contentment in general are called *needs;* but that need whose non-fulfilment must make us discontented with our whole existence is called a necessity; in the physical sense, for example, hunger, when we want for food. In the moral sense, the outcome is *misery,* just as, in the physical sense, it is ill-fortune. Both are based on the fact that no substitute means are available, to remedy the means to contentment that are wanting, and to make the want superfluous.

Misery, then, is that condition in which a man must deem himself unworthy of his own contentment, because he has made himself unworthy of his existence; and ill-fortune, on the other hand, is that condition in which there is a want of those natural things that a man deems necessary for his contentment. Misery is thus coupled at the same time with such depression of spirits, that it no longer permits any consciousness of the superiority of one's strength of mind; it is founded on condign causes of one's discontent, for example, a man who has deliberately occasioned an irreparable injury to another, and now frets at being unable to make it good. A virtuous man may therefore certainly be unlucky, i.e., have to endure all the pains of the body, and experience every mishap in his outer circumstances. Yet the sublimity of his self-feeling keeps him upright, and   27:645
miserable he can never be.

§103. Insofar as contentment depends on things of nature, this condition calls, in a pathological sense, for two requisites:

a. A positive factor, namely, the *agreeableness* of the state, *jucunditas vitae,*[b] i.e. an enhancement of well-being
b. A negative factor, namely, *comfort, commoditas vitae,*[c] a state that puts us in a position to prevent any diminution of our contentment

We might call them both *commoda vitae,* but in fact only the positive quality, of the agreeableness of life, is understood thereby.

Now a receptivity of mind, both for agreeableness and convenience, and also for their opposite, the pain and trouble of life, is called sensitivity. This is based on an acuity of the *judicium discretum,*[d] to recognize what pertains to the agreeable or disagreeable, in regard both to myself and others, and what is able to arouse either pain and trouble, or pleasure. It is

[b] enjoyment of life
[c] amenity of life
[d] discerning judgement

at all events a duty to be cultivated, since for want of such cultivation it may happen even to people of understanding and kindheartedness that they state truths with a harshness that they do not feel, and behave in a wounding fashion, though it does not occur to them that they are thereby occasioning bitter pain to the other party.

Pampering is sensitivity to the agreeableness of life – while *flabbiness* includes all sensitivity to what is disagreeable therein.

Manliness, animus masculus, is the ability to endure evil, and likewise the hardship of life, without discontent. That includes both labours that are intrinsically disagreeable, since they are coupled with the feeling of aversion, and also those evils and pains that nevertheless are a burden only because their outcome yields pleasure. This ability is the effect of an existing stock of inner contentment, which bestirs the manly powers. The direct opposite is flabbiness, *animus effeminatus,* the inability to endure evils. Between them, in the middle, we would have to put *patience,* the ability to get used to suffering hardships. It seems to be more of a female virtue, to determine oneself to get used to evils, since here no powers are employed to resist them; we succumb to them, rather, and expose ourselves to them at length, in order, by growing accustomed, to make ourselves indifferent to bearing them. Indeed even in regard to *luxus,* or the propensity, coupled with taste, towards enjoyment of the superfluities of life, there is a difference between manly and womanly *luxus;* cultivation of the former is associated with strengthening of the body, for example, the horse-racing and hunting of the English; but in cultivating the latter, there is no such connection.

27:646

§104. It has been supposed of Epicurus, that he makes *voluptas* the source of all duties. This would in itself have been false, in that it can certainly furnish a condition to our moral conduct, but cannot yield the principle; moreover, his adopted principle of the state of contentment consisted, in fact, only in the essential duty of keeping *a constantly cheerful heart.*

N.B. It was only later that *voluptas* came to be interpreted as voluptuousness.

Now that this cannot actually be a duty, but only an end, is already clear from the fact that contentment as such cannot be commanded by any law. The actions that may lead us to contentment can indeed stand under laws, yet such precepts can still only be doctrines or counsels of prudence, not absolute laws. Nor did Epicurus really deduce morality from his principle. He understood by it, not merely contentment with our natural endowments and conditions, but also with the state that arises in the moral sense from our conduct; yet he insisted, as we interpret the principle, on the fact that morality in conduct was made basic, even to the state of physical happiness. He thus taught virtue, indeed, but defined its basic principle so ambiguously, that the Stoics were bound to find it different from their own principle, and to attack it. They explained matters as though Epicurus had founded contentment on the conformity of our physical with our moral state, and themselves claimed that self-contentment rests merely on virtue or morally good behaviour, and the endeavour to be worthy of happiness. At bottom, it was only a misunderstanding lying between the two that produced the difference. The highest good has two elements: morality and happiness. The possession of the highest good, and of the conditions under which we can participate in it (though in fact we can do so *partialiter* only, and to an approximation), consists in the two necessary requirements; to be conscious of being adequate to the moral law, or to be worthy of happiness; and at the same time to be sure of having the prospect of being able to participate in happiness.

27:647

Now if we bear in mind that Epicurus promised to give the disciples who wanted to visit him, in his *hortus epicuraeus*ᵉ at Athens, nothing else but pure water and a share of his *polenta,* we can certainly see that he limited the needs of nature to the smallest and most easily satisfiable necessities, and coupled with that an awakened heart.

Polenta is a paste, kneaded into form in those days from barley, and nowadays in Italy from maize-meal and some butter (Frederick II ate it seasoned with Parmesan cheese and hot condiments).

Aristippus, of the Cyrenaic school, subsequently assumed that our knowledge has no reality in objects, but that just as all duty arises from the feeling of pleasure and pain, so such knowledge arises as the absolute result of all duty, in that we have obtained concepts of the latter only by observation of the relationships of things (which is certainly a defensible view); to that extent he altered the system of Epicurus, in that he reduced everything to pleasant and unpleasant feelings, though for him they included correct knowledge of the moral laws, insofar as the latter are thereby made naturally accessible; he therefore seasoned all social intercourse very agreeably by comparing the relationships of things, in that he sought by this method to arouse dutiful feeling among those in whom he could not presuppose a complete involvement with the laws of morality. He and his system were therefore much discussed.*

Now contentment with our moral state deserves just as much consideration as contentment with our physical state. The contentment of our heart is intellectual, when it springs from our conduct itself, and the consciousness thereof, and thus from inner sources. A striving towards it establishes firmness of mind, teaches us to tolerate all the ills of life, and is free from any inward reproach. But man is also a natural creature, and to that extent is subject to conditions of nature, which absolutely demand satisfaction. He can forgo nothing that his necessity demands. It is a duty,

27:648

*[Reading *herumgekommen* for *herumgenommen* – Tr.]
ᵉ garden of Epicurus

that his needs be appropriate to this necessity he has, i.e., that he does not let anything become a need, which nature does not necessarily require to be such; all other things are amenities of life; to let the natural inclination to all objects of that kind grow in that fashion, and again to let the particular objects, that we are inclined to, mount up, brings about a need that we see ourselves compelled to satisfy, insofar, that is, as the want of these objects has become an evil for us. But now the satisfying of the inclination merely removes an evil, and pacifies us on the matter; it no more confines this inclination, however, than it provides us with mastery over all inclinations, and so produces no change in our overall state; by allowing our needs to germinate and grow, and by granting them influence upon us, we can never, therefore, attain to happiness. Achievement of this end thus absolutely entails the duty of making ourselves as independent as possible of external things, and of contenting ourselves in this condition, and of not accumulating needs that nature does not insist upon as necessary. For the objects of inclination are invariably things of nature; our own personhood is free from all needs, but the natural man is subordinated to them. This duty is therefore addressed, not directly to our morality, but to our happiness as a means of attaining to contentment with our state, this being the essential component of happiness. This is a duty to our own person, since it pertains to being worthy of a state of happiness; yet it differs from being contented with oneself, since the latter consists in consciousness that our actions conform to the moral law; here, however, we are talking of contentment with our state in regard to natural needs, and it was in that connection that independence of all non-necessary needs of nature was expressed in the principle of Epicurus: a constantly cheerful heart, *voluptas* – contentment under all circumstances whatsoever; though this arises, not from satisfying the inclinations to contingent things of nature, but from the man himself, in virtue of the law-abiding character of his action.

27:649 Epicurus did in fact enjoin independence of all natural things, and told us: Act so that you can be content with your own person. Be resigned in all circumstances, learn to endure evils that cannot be averted, cherish all the joys and pleasures of life in such a way that they can be dispensable to you.

In his principle, therefore, Epicurus is not subject to the censure visited upon him by the Stoics. He demanded, as they did, that the amenities of life should be dispensable, in the scale of need; he demanded conduct, on man's part, that could coexist with the worthiness of humanity in his person; he demanded, therefore, a cheerfulness that arose from and was founded on contentment with oneself. He demanded intellectual desire, i.e., desire that was confined to the lawfulness of reason. All these things were likewise wanted by the Stoics.

Any man has and must have it in his power, to provide himself with self-contentment; for it rests, of course, on consciousness of the conformity of our actions with the moral law. This quality of our actions is a requisite, however, so it is an absolute duty for us to give it to them; but it could not be a duty if it were impossible to attain contentment. The possibility of contentment in regard to natural needs is not so securely grounded. If our state is especially independent in regard to external circumstances, one can, indeed, go very far in that direction, and employ very few needs to give oneself a sustenance that is coupled with freedom of mind and total good cheer; but all that can be laid down as a rule is: Try to maintain your state so that you dispense with as much as is needed to establish your contentment on the fewest conditions possible.

Happiness must absolutely be founded on contentment with oneself, for by this we become worthy of it, give the worth of our person its due place, and fulfil the moral law; but in order to be happy, we need to be contented with our whole condition, based on the principle of maximum dispensability, and thus in respect of our natural needs. There is no inconsistency in a person being able to feel himself happy from a physical viewpoint, and thus *in sensu speciali*, without his allowing the laws of morality to influence his actions in the least. The man of means, whose ventures all succeed, is merely pursuing contentment in his fortunes, without giving ear to the summons of morality. He cannot, indeed, be   27:650
content with himself, but nor does he give any thought to that; the acquisition and gratification of his outer needs are quite sufficient to content him. It cannot be assumed, therefore, that happiness pertains to moral contentment; if we do assume it, we are already at the same time presupposing the happy man to be virtuous.

The principle of Diogenes, like that of his successors, was defective in being a quite one-sided caricature.

Diogenes took virtue and honesty to be the basis of happiness, but in regard to the impulse towards happiness, or to the satisfying of inclinations by things of nature, he overdid the duty of doing without, to the point of subordinating thereto everything that can be easily acquired under all circumstances, for example convenience of habitation, nourishment of the body, etc. He thereby gave a caricatured rendering of the character of an unassuming man; of which it cannot indeed be denied that it betrayed a strength of mind all the greater, when it set out to endure the discomforts of life, without seeing them replaced by comforts. Cicero says that his notions of virtue and contentment were made too subtle and carried too high, since according to them, as is necessary, indeed, and as Epicurus himself demanded, the sacrifice of life's amenities would produce no pleasure.

His successors, on the other hand, lost sight of the morality, and pursued an ethic that was coupled only with a new enjoyment of pleasure; they heaped up their needs, but also drew upon themselves a misery that was all the greater, the greater the want of morality. Now how far, on these principles, it can be a duty to promote one's own happiness, is self-evident. No duty can be directly ordained to this end, since *in sensu speciali,* in regard to natural needs, it rests merely on the agent's inclination, and the degree of it, as to how far he wishes to be happy. Still less can there be a general principle for all duties; at most there can be only a special duty, and this can thereby effect happiness only in an indirect fashion, viz.

> 1. Seek to attain a state with which you can be content, and to avoid those that would make you discontented:

27:651   This duty rests on the fact that discontent with our condition becomes a temptation to much that is morally bad. A spendthrift, for example, feels the pinch of his situation with displeasure, he may be induced to satisfy his desires in a low fashion, he gets into debt, becomes a swindler, etc. So in that he has to endure evil, he finds his way into crime.

> 2. Seek independence from all things of nature, as needs, and likewise from other people.

To attain this duty, contentment with one's condition must already be present, and with it the maximum degree of doing without. For the more we depend on other people and things, and the less freedom we have to act according to our own principle, the more we restrict the worth of our humanity.

§105. The principle of all imperfect duties is:

To oneself: Promote your own perfection; and

To others: Promote the happiness of *other* people.

It is no more possible to invert this principle, than it is possible to leave anyone the choice whether he will make perfection or happiness, to himself or others, into the end and maxim of his actions.

Of other people we can only assume that they desire to be happy; even if this is coupled with achieving pure perfection, we must first be certain that they deem this perfection to be needed for their happiness. Moreover, it cannot amount to a fancy here, on which the other has to, or is going to, found his happiness; I must be able, rather, to judge whether the other concurs with me about it, in order to count a thing towards individual happiness. In regard to ourselves, the maxim of duty can be directed only towards rendering perfect, since to further the happiness of others is an end, the means to which I can furnish no otherwise than through my own perfection, in order to act in accordance with this moral aim. For perfection as such, and taken as *genus in abstracto,* is completeness, suitability of a thing to all kinds of ends, or formal perfection in relation to every material perfection that one can enumerate singly in regard to all the capacities of mind or body. *In specie,* here, in the moral sense, perfection is the conformity of all our powers with the end of humanity, i.e., happiness;

and if our actions are directed to seeking our own perfection for the   27:652
happiness of others, they conform to the end of humanity; indeed, if the
law of morality thereby comes to fulfilment, we reach the final end of all
things, the highest good, which man can attain to only by making himself
fit for that purpose. To what degree he wishes to cultivate himself here,
and what perfections he endeavours to attain, is still left to his free choice.
Now in order to bring this about, he has to observe both duties to himself
and to others, which are called *officia amoris.*[f]

Under the duty of love towards oneself, we cannot understand, as is
commonly supposed, the duty of well-wishing, or self-love (*philautia* in
relation to others), but rather the duty so to act, that one may cherish, in
virtue of one's actions, a moral satisfaction towards oneself. It is then that
we fulfil the duty of love towards ourselves.

§106. In order to obtain the power of being able to approach self-
sufficiency, i.e., of being able to do without, we require:

1. Never to seize upon the amenities of life with such inclination that
they can become needful to us. For in that case they are a burden, and
restrict our freedom in the fulfilment of duty; they seduce us, indeed, into
actions which conflict with duty, notwithstanding that in this respect we
are at all times capable of keeping them dispensable to us, in order that we
may act in conformity with duty. All inclinations to *luxus* are included
here, insofar as their gratification is coupled with taste. In regard to his
capacity and health, a person can here get into a bad way, he can let
himself be so carried away, that in the end he becomes unable to do
without, so that his body and his affairs suffer. Thus in Athens, at the time
of Pericles, many families became impoverished owing to their excessive
tendency to *luxus.*

This by no means refers to a free enjoyment of agreeable feelings of
taste, namely pleasures, and its possession must not rest on need, but
merely have as its basis the end of good cheer, and to that extent the
culture of our soul.

2. In doing without, always to retain a cheerful heart. It is therefore
self-evident that we cannot deprive ourselves of natural necessities, since
they are absolutely required for our own conservation. To be able to rid
oneself of all needs, one would have to be a higher being, having as its   27:653
only need the pure determination of duty, and fulfilment of the same; but
men, in respect of their physical nature, are not capable of total self-
sufficiency; dispensing with the dispensable is alone possible for man, and
every such dispensation provides new pleasure; we feel ourselves freed of
a burden, feel that even without this enjoyment of amenity we can nevertheless be content and satisfied, and are happy, therefore, by the shorter
route. All that is involved here is a free endeavour to be able to control

[f] duties of love

oneself; all disagreeable and merely physical coercion, on the other hand, having visible ill effects, is here to be rejected, since after gaining the battle, a cheerful heart must be the reward for fulfilment of duty. It all comes down to this, that in regard to everything to which a man is receptive through the senses, he should seek to confine himself to the bounds of a free dutifulness of behaviour. Hence

3. The duty of being able to do without can be confined only to those bounds, beyond which the satisfaction of inclination would be a hindrance to virtue and fulfilment of duty. In this consists *autarchia*, i.e., the capacity to master oneself, to possess oneself, to be sufficient to oneself. To arrive at it we need courage, *fortitudo animi.* By this we generally understand trust in oneself, to be able to overcome all hindrances and inconveniences of life, insofar as they run counter to the end of what is to our benefit. But since this may include bad ends as well as good, we understand by it, in the *moral sense,* a firm self-confidence in being able to conquer every one of the hindrances in that which is a duty for us, and to which they would do injury. Cicero and Aristotle made this into a special duty, but this it is not, since it lacks a specific object. It is a strength of mind which in general operates concurrently with respect to our dutiful behaviour, and is not, like a virtue, acquired through the use of our freedom. It is often the case, to be sure, that nature has faults in its physical organization, which it sets in opposition to the fulfilment of duty, and if a man endeavours, by means of principles, to overcome these natural hindrances, which are responsible for his lack of natural courage, we might well call this a moral strength; but it is not actually courage. The latter is physically inbuilt, and belongs, like all talents, to a man's natural endowments. A naturally diffident man will never acquire courage, though by exerting his powers of resistance he may habituate himself to overcoming dangers. Now concerning this courage in the moral sense, it is an absolute duty for everyone to maintain that firm resolve over himself, whereby he makes himself able to oppose all hindrances of every kind, insofar as they might be damaging to his duty.

In this he merely acts according to duty, and can never go too far in that respect, as Aristotle supposes, in consequence of his intrinsically quite erroneous principle of duty, that *Virtus consistit in medio.*[g] If this were correct, that in fulfilment of duty we must choose the middle path, then it would have to be possible to determine the bounds of this, and of the *excessus* and *defectus* as the two extremes. But Aristotle and his adherents are alike unable to do this.

According to him, courage would have to be situated in the middle, between (a) boldness, foolhardiness, as the *excessus,* and (b) faintheartedness, cowardice, as the *defectus,* and would indicate a proper confidence in

27:654

[g] virtue consists in a mean

one's power of being able to overcome hindrances to certain ends. These ends might be good, but also bad; in the fulfilment of duty, ends do not come into it at all; so this can only be called courage in the physical sense; but in matters of morality we have to assume that every fulfilment of duty, however onerous it may be, is possible to the agent, since it is absolutely enjoined upon him. Now according to the determination freely available to him, he can choose only two courses: either to act in accordance with, or contrary to, duty. In the first case, he of course does no more than the law requires of him, and an excess is simply not thinkable; in the second, he succumbs to the idea of how difficult it is to fulfil one's duty; he acts contrary to duty, in that he absolves himself therefrom. In general, faults in our performance of duty can differ, not in degree, but only in quality, in order to be in opposition; two crimes *ejusdem generis in opposito*[h] are not thinkable. In that regard, so far as the action depends on physical or natural determination, it is possible to suppose degrees, which may become for us the basis of an amenity or lack thereof, i.e. advantageous or the reverse; but then the question is not about virtue and the extremes.   27:655

Now this is the source of what we call *indoles strenua-languida, mascula-effeminata, delicata. Indoles strenua,* a *sturdy* frame of mind, whether in the physical or the moral sense, is the courage to pursue one's good ends under all hindrances. *Indoles languida,* on the other hand, is want of strength in the motivation to resist great obstacles. *Indoles mascula* is the frame of mind of one who, in pursuing good principles, is not afraid of hardship. But if he lets himself be deterred thereby from attaining good ends, that is a womanish, effeminate cast of mind.

It is now very easy to see what the duty of *toughening oneself,* i.e., to take on difficulties, consists in, and what is required for that. It is absolutely needful that, in order to attain the *abstine et sustine,*[i] we make it a law from youth onwards, to carry out our actions by strictly followed rules: allow ourselves to be deterred by no hindrance from our good, well-chosen ends, whether they involve pragmatic actions, or moral acts that are unconditionally necessary; learn, in so doing, to sacrifice the comforts of life, and to endure its inconveniences; and yet retain throughout a spirit of cheerfulness. It is therefore necessary for a man to examine, subsequently, the education given to him, and investigate his deficiencies, as to how far he may be well enough trained to be fit for every end of life that is needful to him, and also be able to act in accordance with the law. For the very acquisition of a virtue rests upon overcoming the difficulties that militate against it, since so long as the latter make it hard to fulfil his duty, no virtue of dutiful action is yet thinkable; the more sacrifice he makes, and the harder it is to overcome the obstacles, the greater grows that courage

[h] of the same kind, although opposite
[i] forgo and endure

which we call *animus strenuus,* to venture on new attempts, and the greater, too, grows the pure pleasure at his conduct, and only through conquest of the difficulties does it become possible for him to act from duty in conformity with the law. It is certain that at first the following of the law will occasion us pain and inconvenience; but once we are inclined to it, the

27:656 problem disappears. Hence we may assuredly take it, that so long as anyone bows to the law only with grief and lamentation, and it costs him trouble to fulfil it, he is still nurturing a hatred for that law, as the slave does for his master.

Man must at least get to the point of acquiring respect for the moral law, even though loving it is a degree of inclination that is unattainable, owing to human desires, and seems, like the state of pure *blessedness,* where the will only chooses the law, and knows no needs, to belong solely to the almighty. In testing everything that pertains to his moral conduct, a man must curtail all his rooted inclinations by laying down purposive principles for himself, whereby he sets himself against them in the performance of his duties. Once he has become conscious, in doing so, of the maxims of his actions, the conformity of the action with duty occasions in him cheerfulness of mind; if he knows himself with inner approval of his conduct, and is capable of persisting therein, he achieves a state, of which he is himself the author, that grants him self-contentment; he knows his inner worth, and this is at least an *analogon* of blessedness. The foundation of this practice lies, therefore, in the negative and positive discipline of the body, by cultivation of his mental powers, enlargement of his knowledge, removal of his errors, limitation and refinement of his capacities for desire; a resistance that, by toughening of the body, he puts up to all contrary inclinations, and to flabbiness. Locke gives a number of practical rules on this subject, and rightly thinks that such toughening will itself be advantageous to the body.

What is simultaneously needed is, that in the account a man must give of his actions to his intellectual nature, he try to retain its approval, and endeavour, indeed, to accord it unlimited authority over his sensual nature, and follow its guidance in all his behaviour. All the good resolutions that the will recognizes, according to the laws of the understanding, may be regarded as promises that we offer to our intellectual nature, and *keeping one's word* is an essential duty that we owe to humanity in our own person, in virtue of the respect due to it. Hence every postponement of

27:657 execution, in those actions that contribute directly to our dutiful behaviour, or the fulfilment of duty, is a neglect of the promise given, and dreadful is the condition of a man who, in making such resolutions, tells himself at that very moment that he is actually doubtful of fulfilling them.

§107. Occupation includes within it both business or work, and pastime. In the latter case the occupation is agreeable, in and for itself; in the former, business is in and for itself disagreeable, but the end associated therewith makes it agreeable. The *oppositum* is recreation after work, which restores our energies partly through suspension of toil, and partly produces the same effect owing to difference in the mental powers when we vary the work we are employed on, for example, philosophy, history or poetry. Thus Wieland would busy himself on three kinds of work at the same time. This is the best form of recreation, in that by alternation the mental powers are exerted and practised in a variety of ways. Now by cultivation of our abilities we become assured of our duties, and able to recognize and carry them out: it is a self-regarding duty for us, both to be busy and also to engage in that recreation which itself keeps us occupied. Now such occupation requires a specific end, and in order to acquire this inclination to be occupied, which in man must always be directed towards work, we have to set up specific goals, depending on whether the decision to occupy oneself purposefully itself involves work or an aim. If the ground of occupation were merely the immediate enjoyment thereof, and nothing else, it would depend simply on sensory inclination, and would then interfere with a man's activity. If the latter is to be maintained and cultivated, he must attach absolutely determinate ends to his work; otherwise he gets the habit of an undetermined will, which is content merely with unfulfilled resolves, and thereby becomes inactive and engenders many failings.

The acquired impulse to work is industriousness; the *oppositum* is laziness, insofar as we have the urge to find satisfaction merely in ridding ourselves of work. This brings a man into low esteem, since it is contrary to both the right and the end of humanity in our own person. It has the right to coerce us into following its laws, and defines the cultivation of our powers as a requirement for our vocation; a lazy man tramples both underfoot, and his punishment is therefore self-contempt.   27:658

Laziness is distinct (1) from indolence, which consists in the urge to be occupied only with passing the time, or insofar as the occupation is immediate enjoyment without activity. (2) from busyness or *polypragmosyne*, bustling about, which consists in the diversity of occupations that a man takes on all at once. This is a species of laziness – the man does not have powers enough to undertake with thoroughness a multitude of differently ordered occupations; he therefore scamps and neglects every one of his tasks. A particular variety of this is *polypragmosyne successiva*[j] which is coupled with a prevailing *animus desultorius*,[k] and in which the agent alternates from moment to moment in the nature of his occupation. The inclination to change rests on a weakness in the power of exerting oneself, and a lack of the concerted planning whereby every task must be carried out.

---

[j] fidgetiness
[k] fickleness

To this class belong the busy idlers, who do indeed have an urge for business, whose satisfaction is agreeable to them in any way that presents itself, but to which they couple no definite end or intention; they are especially officious, indeed, and readily undertake matters for others, without being qualified to do so. Now from this it appears that a lazy man can be very busy; he shuns the pursuit of purposive concerns, but busies himself to no purpose.

(3) from languor (*desidia*), which rests on the want of a degree of effort in the powers, sufficient for purposeful endeavour. In industry, we distinguish, as to the end, *labor de pane lucrando*[l] from work in the moral sense.

A *non nisi de pane lucrando laborans*[m] makes it his goal merely to satisfy his sensory needs, and acts *secundum indolem servilem;*[n] he works in a merely pragmatic way. But the end of humanity in our person calls for a higher purpose; only work in the moral sense must become an end for us; we must execute it with an *indoles ingenua,*[o] so as thereby to promote the *dominus in nosmet ipsos.*[p]

§108. Among all means of acquisition, none has a value so predominant as money, since it is taken as a sign for everything open to acquisition. The reason for it lies, and its high value resides, in this, that its whole use consists essentially in mere alienation; that taken for itself, as money, it has no specific use or utility, but can be set in relation to all things alienable, and employed in every transaction, as a means thereto. Now a man's inclination to use others for his purpose finds in money a highly convenient means to that end; hence the great attraction that it has for men, whence *avarice,* i.e., the desire for acquisition, and particularly by way of the medium which has such universal influence.

27:659

Miserliness, however, differs from this, insofar as it properly includes stinginess and parsimony. It can just as well relate to money, as to all other things employable by use, e.g., consumables of every kind, and consists in the desire to possess the means, without regard for the end that can be attained thereby.

It is an excess of thriftiness so great, that along with the strong desire to obtain the means of acquisition, it renounces the use thereof, to the point where the miser deprives himself of necessary requirements, and finds his satisfaction in possessing the means without using them. The inclination turns to miserliness, in that means of this type are such that they are employed through using them, e.g., money and food. The miser therefore sees himself instantly robbed of these things by the use or enjoyment of

---

[l] breadwinning
[m] one who works only to make a living
[n] in a servile fashion
[o] upstanding attitude
[p] command of ourselves

them for any purpose; but the possession of them remains necessary to him, and he thus finds sufficient pleasure in contemplating, through possession, the prospect of their possible employment for all conceivable ends, and the freedom to utilize them, and entertains this pleasure in his imagination. Now the want of morality here does not properly lie in the failure to employ these means for any purpose – that he deprives himself of all amusements, and shares nothing thereof with others, for their pleasure or use or necessity; it lies, rather, in the principle he has adopted, of retaining in his possession the means for using, while renouncing any such use. He becomes a mere custodian of his money or other property, without attaching the smallest use or purpose thereto. He becomes, therefore, an instrument, a mere means to no end, like a watchdog, and this is a maxim to him. Now since a man, in and for himself, is supposed to be an end for his humanity, the miser assuredly violates humanity in his own person, in that he puts out of sight the end prescribed to him, and looks upon the means given for that purpose as though he were himself a means in that regard.   27:660

The *contrarie oppositum* is extravagance, which consists in use of the means, insofar as the agent thereby deprives himself of the means to his necessitous requirements. Now it is a duty to be in possession of those means which are needed for the fulfilment of morally good ends, since only thereby do we put ourselves in a position of being able to fulfil them; so extravagance, no less than parsimony, is an action contrary to the duty to oneself. That a person makes a counter-purposive use of his means, continues to lie beyond the bounds of extravagance, so long as he still retains enough for his necessary requirements.

Now Aristotle takes thriftiness to be a mean between parsimony and extravagance; however, the parsimonious man is no less thrifty than the extravagant one, since thrift consists only in the inclination to retain possession of means, even though a purposive use of them is not in fact coupled with this. Now whether the use be excessive or entirely set aside, the inclination is the same. In general, if there is here to be a *contradictorie oppositum*, i.e., *in diverso genere*, no principle can be discovered in the *mediocritas* of two opposing vices, since each of them stands under its own species-concept. Moreover, we must always distinguish between the right of humanity in our person, the end of humanity therein, and the end of men. Now that which may be right and wrong is impossible to discover by comparison of two vices in contradictory opposition, which are thus in conflict. What right or wrong may be must therefore be established *in eodem genere*, and only then can it be stated, in regard to the end, whether in fulfilment of it there has been too much or too little; the two, however, are but *contrarie opposita*, and these allow of a *medium*. Thus the dutiful principle between parsimony and extravagance would lie in good husbandry, which yielded the *extrema*, allows too much or too little of goodness, and has bad husbandry as its opposite; good husbandry and bad, that is, allow of no *medium;* they determine merely, as *a* or non-*a,* that which is absolutely permitted or not permitted, so that if parsimony were the vice, good husbandry would be the *contradictorie oppositum* in determining duty, or that which would be right or wrong. Extravagance would in this respect

27:661   be more than mere want of good husbandry, not non-*a,* merely, but actually minus *a;* for here, not only is no use made of the means at all, but the agent actually robs himself as well of the means to all possible ends. A fault *in excessu.* So in relation to the agent himself, as regards the right of humanity towards himself, it would be bad husbandry, were he to deprive himself of means, in order merely to employ it all on benefactions and acts of kindness; or let himself suffer distress and practise the worst of husbandry at home, from parsimony; and likewise to others, in relation to the right of humanity in his person, were he to employ nothing of his resources for their benefit. In all these cases, the test now relates solely to that which is right, and there we have no opposition between parsimony and extravagance, since both are forms of bad husbandry.

Yet they may be opposed, as *a* to minus *a,* and there the *medium* would equal o; when we take account, that is, not merely of the permissible, but also of the purposiveness of the action, or of that which is present there *lati officii;* to that extent we may do too much or too little for the end of humanity in our own person, or for the end of man. Though an action may be righteous by quality of duty, it can go over in quantity, and in respect of its end, to one of the two extremes. In deciding what is right or wrong, the choice as such is guided only by the laws of reason, and thus determined *formaliter;* here an overplus of good is equivalent to not good, just as is a deficiency; there can be no *medium* whatever, but only a *contradictorie oppositum,* such as always occurs in the formal aspect of duty. But if our choice is directed to a certain object, then the dutifulness of the action points to a specific end, so that the judgement has to do with something material or purposive; now here there occurs a *contrarie oppositum,* as to possibility, for everything rests here on empirical principles, whose application may here have in view a defective end, or more of an end than duty demands; it then becomes excessive, either inside or outside of the end (of humanity). Since the two extremes of parsimony or extravagance cannot be used for the purpose, it thus remains to be deter-

27:662   mined what is right only by comparing them – that we should likewise know and enquire beforehand what is right in all *contrarie opposita,* and thus *in casu,* what good husbandry consists in; and only when we know this are we able to determine what is purposive or counter-purposive, i.e., is too much or too little; just as we cannot determine the crooked angle, in excess and deficiency, until we know what a straight angle is. That when it comes to determining duty, in and for itself, no *mediocritas* can be made into the principle, is also evident from the two extremes adopted by

Baumgarten and others, of apathy, or the renunciation of all feelings, and empathy, the passionate abandonment of the soul to all of them, where mediopathy is taken to be the norm; for this can be nothing else but self-possession, self-mastery, a governance of inclination, and command over it, that is ordered according to the laws of reason; but this allows of no plus or minus, since we must absolutely never permit feelings to have influence over us; nor is it here a matter, either, of dutifulness with respect to an end to be determined.

§109. Inner and outer enjoyments may contribute to providing us with a nourishment for the soul, which gives it a pleasing dress, gains a man an easy deportment in his bent for moral actions, and awakens in him a satisfaction in performing his duty; the cultivation of polite sciences, for example, agreeable company, and all enjoyments, represents a voluntary accession to our well-being, and thus enlarges the latter, without being a requirement. Now since moderation is a duty, the increase of well-being can never be a duty, because it would, in fact, be contrary to the duty to oneself, to nourish an inclination for enjoyments, whether they be restorations of our spirits through pleasures of the soul, or through outer occasions, in that they then become a need, and might become injurious to our self-contentment; only inasmuch as they are innocent in themselves, i.e., not contrary to morality, and present themselves spontaneously, may we adopt them, but never go in pursuit of them. (The *oppositum* would consist of voluptuous enjoyments, which lead a man astray, into giving sensory feeling predominance over reason.)

Yet here, too, we must distinguish the *ethica morosa*[q] (*rigoristica*), like the *ethica blandiens*, from the *ethica rigida*. The latter demands that all duties determine strictly (*stricte*) and absolutely, yet not with the stifling of all sensory inclinations, insofar as they may give us pleasure with the approval of our intellectual nature. The *ethica morosa*, on the other hand, demands, in addition, that a man repress all the joys of life, crucify himself and his flesh, renounce himself, and thus must be his own self-torturer. The *ethica blandiens*, by contrast, calls for fulfilment of duty with an indulgence whereby it accords to the agent every convenience in doing so, requiring no sacrifice of what is pleasing to his inclination, no endurance of the hardships of life. It is very easily seen that both of them transgress against the true discipline of man. The former can hardly think of him as a taskmaster, who must constantly punish and demean himself, even, as a criminal, without turning him into a fanatic, who must actually regard himself in a supersensible light, since he sacrifices all wished-for enjoyment of happiness. What is called for, rather, is merely a constant vigilance over the sensual man in regard to all his inclinations, so that in good or ill fortune he knows how to determine himself on principle in all moral

27:663

---

[q] killjoy ethic

situations, and in sacrificing what would injure his morality is able, with some force and vigour, to create in himself the feeling of moral perfection.

It is proper, moreover, that it be a duty of avoidance, to ensure that our enjoyments should give no offence to others. This we call *scandalum*, whose nature consists in this, that our behaviour may be a ground and occasion for bringing the law of duty into contempt even among others, and for just that reason (*transgressio legis contemptum legis creans*);[r] albeit that a law of duty must itself be violated, by adultery, for example; not, though, by illegitimate childbirth, innocent dancing, or a clergyman's card-playing. In these there is no transgression of a moral law, and hence there can be no thought, either, of any contempt for lawfulness in our behaviour; for in *transgressio legis* alone there is no more *scandalum* than there is any resultant obstacle to the promotion of morality. A thief, so long as he is punished for his crime, arouses no *scandalum*, since the law thereby receives a quittance, in that it is upheld, and the breach of duty in the action recognized; but the swindler, whose act goes unpunished, either because the law has failed, in any positive sense, to declare it punishable, or because the judge, in view of the authority of the offender's position, or for other subjective reasons, lets him go unpunished, has the effect of bringing into contempt the law of morality, as propounded either by the legislator of positive law, or the judge; since others then also lose sight of the reason for respecting the law, and allow themselves to be misled into doing the same thing. For example, marriage with an adulterer always remains an act which, even though it should do no hindrance to the positive law, still runs counter to the law of duty that is fundamental in marriage; and were it then declared permissible in a country, such a law would itself bring lawfulness into contempt. And finally, among children, among persons, that is, who in their upbringing take the conduct of others as their rule, a thing may be a scandal, which would not be so among adults. Children take their elders as a model for their action, since imitation is encouraged, in their case, as the primary ground of education. To disdain the natural abhorrence (given by the obscure voice of reason) is to have even less respect for a law; to increase their inclination to satisfy their wishes, and lessen their aversion for transgression of the law, is the result of a bad example, and a temptation to similar transgression; so elders, in the presence of children, must neither swear, lie nor defame, nor give approval to others doing so, nor themselves engage in those actions, such as natural evacuations or satisfactions of the sexual instinct, which are contrary to natural modesty.

§110. The love of honour, *philotimia*, which is very different from the desire for it, is not considered here insofar as it belongs to the duty towards others, but rather as it pertains to the right of humanity in regard

27:664

[r] breach of law that creates contempt for law

to our own person. Thus in regard to others, a skinflint may be an honourable man, since he does not encroach upon their rights, as does the avaricious man, who to satisfy his aims is capable of undertaking injustices towards others. Now the love of honour is the highest duty of humanity to oneself, so little capable of abridgement, that it has to go further than love of life. It is founded upon *true honour,* in contrast to vanity, or all that false honour which does not constitute a person's worth, e.g., fine clothing, to find favour in the eyes of others, or arts and means for snatching their praises. To this end our morality is no contributing cause.

True honour is, (a) in the negative sense, that which nobody but the agent alone can give to or take from himself, i.e., which rests on the worth that is conferred only by morally good conduct. So insofar as anyone 27:665
deserves to be recognized as worthy of humanity, to that extent he possesses true honour. If he everywhere acts in accordance with duty, even the greatest scoundrel must pay him respect, and even the tyrant cannot rob him of the idea of self-respect, and the worth arising from his merit. A lover of honour finds in himself no need to be known (no *appetitio innotescendi*);[s] he does not require to be highly esteemed by others, yet his moral conduct is such, that if it were to be known, he would be acknowledged as one who is worthy of the *bona aestimatio*[t] of others. This concept is negative, because to that extent the agent merely refrains from acting contrary to his humanity and its worth; for without this condition, even under circumstances to be admired by everyone else, the concept of an honour-loving man would come to nothing; a son, for example, cannot take upon himself the crime of his father, which has brought disgrace upon him, as if he had committed it himself, and even were he able to save his father from death; he would be demeaning the humanity in his person.

(b) The positive concept of true honour consists in this, that it essentially takes on actions that involve a merit – more than what is required; so if a man merely does what is required of him, he has simply averted dishonour (see a, above); he has not exposed himself to contempt and reproof. But if he has done those things that contain more good than obligation required of him, then merit can arise for him, and this may bring him true honour. Now it is indeed impossible that in the sight of God, as the law of the highest morality, we can do more than is incumbent, since in regard to Him, everything is required; but in relation to other men, we can certainly have merits, if we measure our actions against our coercive duties, e.g., beneficence towards the poor. *Merita fortunae,* on the other hand, e.g., talents, understanding or motherwit, can no more be a merit than inherited money can; they cannot be accounted to honour or the values thereof; they are merely means to an end, and only those

[s] craving for celebrity
[t] good opinion

actions that are conjoined with good ends can extort our respect. These things are but means thereto, whose conjunction, particularly the mental capacities, we gladly admire in an agent, but can by no means be moved to honour him on that account.

27:666 §111. The desire for honour, on the other hand (*ambitio*), is an endeavour to possess worth in the opinion of others; it can indeed be the case, even with the lover of honour, that he is attentive to the approval of others in regard to his moral conduct, and to whether he has praise or blame from them; the reason being that he is uncertain whether his endeavour to act well, morally, can also be defended on social principles; it is thus mere reassurance that he seeks, and the approval he gains becomes for him a motive to seek true honour along the path he has entered into. He sets out from self-esteem. The desirer of honour, however, does not set out from principles and the steady pursuit of them, but from pragmatic means of making the actions he thereby engages in glitter to the eye, and extort the approval of others, although on scrutiny they lose their moral worth.

He thus feels a need to be known by others in what he does, and to be seen by them as an estimable man. Now if he couples with his action no inner moral worth, he not only behaves clean contrary to the principle of a true love of honour, and the laws of virtuous duty, but also like a fool, in that his chosen means for glittering in the eyes of others may draw their contempt upon him instead; or if he at least chooses such means in order to enhance his scanty moral worth, he behaves like a simpleton, in that he chooses false means, whereby he misses his mark.

1. Because nobody else is under any obligation to trouble himself about my honour, or to recognize and give it to me; he must merely not take it from me, and cannot in fact do so. The aim of the honour-seeker is therefore mere arrogance, to which he has no right.

2. The other's receptivity delights him, and makes him frugal in himself displaying outwardly the smallest degree of respect. For the honour-seeker cannot demand it otherwise, save under the condition that the other abase himself to precisely the degree that he acknowledges a superiority in the first.

3. This is especially so in that love of honour which is pride (*superbia*), or downright conceit, depending on whether the agent gives more or less blatant expression to his claim that he be honoured by others. He demands that, in comparison with him, the other should perceive his distance and think humbly of himself.

27:667 4. Now the honour-seeker thereby obviously makes himself dependent on the other's choice. For since he seeks honour not in his own inner worth, and it simply depends on the other's will as to how much respect he wishes to display, the honour-seeker must either see himself respected merely according to the other's opinion, or often, to his chagrin, treated with disdain.

5. Such arrogance always betrays little understanding, for it is the act of a fool not to strive for the possession of true worth by self-mastery and the trustworthy performance of duty on principle but, rather, to seek honour in casual outer circumstances, paying no respect to one's humanity, and thus demeaning himself.

The lover of honour, on the other hand, strives for unpretentiousness, i.e., not just (1) for modesty, or restraint in regard to others, but (2) for willingness to forgo any external acknowledgement of his inner worth. For every claim to honour that we can and wish to expect from judgement is always in itself a pretension, since nobody else is called upon to declare respect for me or acknowledge my merits; it is thus an unfounded claim, to which I cannot obligate him. Hence we must wholly abjure the desire to see ourselves outwardly honoured by others. But this unpretentiousness should have no bearing on that self-esteem which underlies true honour; for the opposite to love of honour is produced by self-abasement, i.e. the disposition whereby we renounce the respect that others may have for us (an *animus abjectus*). By this deliberate forfeiture, we voluntarily make ourselves an object of contempt in the eyes of others, and since we are simply violating a self-regarding duty, we dispose over ourselves to the shame of humanity, and are acting contrary to the right thereof. What matters here is not any situation that we find ourselves in, but the arbitrary treatment of those personal assets which determine our worth; it is coupled with impudence if displayed by overt actions or otherwise without concealment, and with insolence if we express disdain for the judgement of others upon us.

§112. Now *honestas morum* is that dutiful conduct which rests upon preparedness for those actions that are worthy of honour. Respectability we cannot call it, for it involves less, namely the expression, merely, of a disposition appropriate to such honour-worthy actions. It therefore has a dutiful demeanour as its basis; but the fulfilment of all our strict duties as such, or the dutifulness of our actions as such, already demands strict rectitude, and does not express what the decorum of the action wishes to say. It therefore contains, not only (a) the negative concept, of abhorring all actions that could make me an object of contempt, but, *specifice,* (b) the positive concept, or the endeavour to make myself *worthy of honour,* i.e., strive for that worth which, if our actions are known, assures approval, and thus makes us of honourable repute. To effect this, the dutifulness of the action must be supplemented by moral goodness, viz., that the idea of duty should have been the motive to the action, and that we should thus have acted from duty and no other motive. To attune our moral disposition to this, and order our conduct thereby, is a duty, and one whose fulfilment lies in the *honeste vive;* it is that which does us honour. Towards men we realize more morality than is incumbent on us, and in this, therefore, lies at the same time the merit of our actions. This *honestas* can

27:668

be attained by practice, no less in conduct towards our own humanity than in serving the ends of other men; for example, when the manual worker cultivates his talent beyond the call of duty, so as thereby to become more useful to others, and is guided by the dutiful conviction that he is bound to cultivate his talents to the best of his ability.

§113. To get a proper grasp of the concept of philanthropy – love of mankind – we have to distinguish love due to feeling or inclination for objects from practical love, or love from duty; or, what comes to the same, pathological love, i.e., due to inclination, from that whose determining ground is moral.

In §302, our author demands a *Pamphilian*, whereby we are to love all objects of nature in proportion to their known perfection. This is based on the pleasure we take in the purposiveness of every natural object. It is love from feeling; for if it were practical there would have to be an obligation incumbent on us, to preserve, foster and amplify the truly good in all natural objects so far as possible; and yet this we cannot assume, though it is intrinsically correct that this love of natural creatures, and the knowledge of them, can contribute to our self-perfection and morally practical activity. We are obliged, that is, so to adjust this inclination of ours, that we confine our demand upon these objects to a sufficient ground of satisfaction, because we thereby create for ourselves the condition of self-contentment with our conduct, and the corresponding satisfaction with the objects in question. This moral satisfaction has the beneficial effect, that it enlarges both our receptivity to all perfections of the kingdom of nature, and our moral disposition. We are in a position to love the objects of nature, although we love our own condition, and merely transfer it to the occasion thereof, as though the latter itself were to have been beneficial towards us. This duty is naturally an imperfect one.

The love of humanity in particular, as that to which we are bound by obligation to the universal rule, and which constitutes practical love, seems, when considered as a *debitum*, to be in contradiction to the law that enjoins us, since the latter is fulfilled only out of respect for it, and not out of love. Moreover, it seems to be a meritorious thing, when we love people, and we only enlarge such a disposition by that which relates to the good as such. In itself, too, the duty that refers to love towards other people is merely an *officium meriti*,[u] never a *debitum;* for it rests on the fact that we have a demand and a will to contribute to their happiness; now nobody has a claimant's right to demand that I promote his well-being – indeed, since here something material is involved, namely to work for the man's end, it already emerges from that, that the love of man belongs merely *ad officia lata vel imperfecta*,[v] in which, therefore, the act of love

27:669

[u] a praiseworthy duty, not a requirement
[v] to broad or imperfect duties

cannot be strictly enjoined. Now from this it follows that, since the *officia debiti* contain the necessary condition, that only fulfilment thereof first affords freedom to fulfil other duties and enlarge one's dutifulness, nothing can be or is done from love, in all those cases where the agent is limited by the other's strict right, and that therefore, *in casu collisionis, officia meriti* must always give way to *officia debiti.*

1. Already, in and for itself, no duty, and hence not the duty of love   27:670
either, can be founded on inclination; for example, inclination towards nature's products, the perfection of structure in a spider or an insect, can bring it about that through knowing the object we love it – not, however, from duty, but by virtue of the attraction of natural impulses, *per stimulos.* This is the basis of love in all those cases where, in exercising the act of love, we have our own welfare in view; although inclination itself, without personal interest, may also envisage, when acting, the end of making another's state agreeable.

We call this love from inclination kindness (*favor*), when it has the intention of laying upon the other an obligation towards us, and is thus coupled with an interest.

In both cases, the other has no right to demand this action of us, and he must consider it, rather, as a beneficent action whereby he becomes obliged to us. This is the basis of sexual love, and the inclination to reciprocal conjunction with others, insofar as a physical, pathological satisfaction is thereby accommodated.

Of the love for our posterity, or between parents and children, the assumption is that it is directed more downwards than upwards (§305). Both parties are coupled together in this way by procreation. Among parents, the innate inclination towards their children arises from a natural instinct, love, which in itself, however, does not include duty; for the child, no ground for love can grow out of the fact that the parents are the cause of his physical existence; this is not a boon that engenders gratitude. As *causa vitae*[w] the parents are bound by a coercive duty to nourish their children; a *mere debitum,* therefore, whereby they do nothing meritorious towards the child, and hence the children cannot be thereby obligated to anything towards them either, since in that respect there is mere execution of the right which humanity itself demanded of the parents as a duty. But the rearing of children up to the point of self-sufficiency, i.e., an education so ordered that the children thereby obtain contentment with their lot, and pleasure in their existence, is an *opus supererogationis*[x] on the parent's part, a thing superadded, a kindness which involves something meritorious, and this it is which must bring the children, by reason, to the conception of filial gratitude, and awaken in them the determination to   27:671

---

[w] cause of life
[x] work of supererogation

love their parents; yet it can never be claimed that they are obligated, as a perfect duty, to render love.

Now since love, in and for itself, belongs to the moral duties, in that the promotion of happiness depends on it, whereas an inclination thereto cannot be extorted by the law, it follows that

2. in a *moral* respect, the only love thinkable is one that is founded on principles, and this will be the duty to which morality binds us.

This rests on the product of the principles that we have acquired; it is this, and the acquisition of such principles, that alone can be commanded, not that pathological love which has its determining ground merely in the operation of natural urges.

Love from inclination can indeed make a start for people, e.g. the love of the male and female sexes normally begins from pathological love, and hence, too, the wife convinced of the physical love of her husband esteems him more highly, and thinks herself more secure in possession of him, than if she could only expect a dutiful love on his part; but this love from inclination must not determine him; his respect, rather, must be based on a principle of duty. This does not fade away, should the instinctual attractions, such as beauty or talent, disappear.

§114. In the outward expression of this love of persons, our author, §309, takes *humanitas* as his foundation, i.e., the cultivation of *humanity* as such, as the first duty of man towards himself. It consists in the totality of all the properties of man, considered as an intelligent being, and whereby he is set in contrast to the *homo brutus* in his animality.

Were we to understand by this a mere pity or sharing in the well-being of others, and to that extent love for them, supposing this concept to be applied to the fulfilment of duty, then this would be mere humaneness, and would say too little, since such a feeling is not only characteristic of man, but also of animals as well; e.g., when one is in danger, the others display uneasiness and an impulse to protect – the *oppositum* would be downright cruelty, i.e., satisfaction at the sufferings of other men; but here we have to build upon the characteristic feature peculiar to the human race, namely the inclination of men to impart their feelings and sensations to one another, as they do their information; and this is the inclination which determines the practical in human nature, and demands unceasing cultivation for that purpose.

27:672

§115. I. The contradictory opposite of philanthropy is the *animus frigidus*, or callousness, which consists in indifference towards the state of other people – a person who is devoid of love for others. This indifference rests on *solipsismus*, or a care for one's own welfare that is guided solely by partiality for oneself.

II. The diametrical opposite is hatred for men, misanthropy (because the latter is not merely negative, as in I, but positively and materially opposed). This makes a person an *enemy of mankind*, a *hater of men*, i.e., one who has the purpose and will to destroy the welfare of others and do them a mischief; or a *fugitive from mankind*, a recluse, who distances himself from all men, because he regards them as his enemies, and apprehends harm from everyone. Included here are those who from an exaggerated principle of virtue remove themselves from social life, because their days are embittered by many undeserved sufferings. We may call the enemy of mankind the positive, and the recluse the negative misanthrope, and oppose to the former the *animus pacificus*, i.e., the peace-loving disposition, because such a person not only shuns all enmity with others, but even any conflict with them.

We may aptly call the negative misanthrope *anthropophobus*, i.e., one who withdraws himself from everyone, because he is unable to love them. It is impossible for him to find anything pleasing in other people, because he has made it a principle that in his regard everyone is oblivious to all the respect due to himself; he wishes them well, indeed, *per se*, but cannot prevail upon himself to contribute thereto. He has experienced nothing but ingratitude for services rendered, disloyalty, misuse of integrity, love spurned, etc., and therefore sees all men as false, and so on. Anthropophobia thus has its ground in *displicentia*,[y] and hence in the total contrariness of his disposition; enmity to men, however, is grounded in *malevolentia*, which wishes the evil that others may endure.

§116. The love for others can be considered in its generality, and to that extent it rests on this, that our ends coincide with those of others in such a way that they are able to co-exist together according to the universal rule of duty.

27:673

In this respect there is a general love for every other person as such, for certain kinds of persons, and for the entire human race. Patriotism, the love of the fatherland, also belongs here, as does cosmopolitanism: in both, the determination to love of others rests upon common descent, though the former is local, and is properly love of the fatherland when it is directed towards a united national community that we regard as the root-stock, and ourselves as a member thereof; otherwise it is directed to our common world ancestry. Finally, there is also love for a particular group, or common obligation under a particular rule, to which there arises by custom a distinctive adherence; included here is the love for societies, for orders of freemasonry, for the station one belongs to, and for sects, such as the Herrenhuter. If we take the latter association, it is obviously detrimental to the propensity for a general love of mankind; to the member thus associated, the class of men with whom he stands in no connection seems to become indifferent; he behaves as though he had separated himself from the generality of mankind, loses his allegiance thereto, and bends his moral endeavours solely in accordance with that shibboleth to

[y] ill-humour

which he has subjected himself; the friend to all humanity, on the other hand, seems equally open to censure, since he cannot fail to dissipate his inclination through its excessive generality, and quite loses any adherence to individual persons, so that only love of country seems to figure as the end in view, though there is no denying that the great value of human love rests in the general love of humanity as such.

N.B. ad §116. Just as the cosmopolite views the nature round about him in a practical light, for the exercise of his well-wishing towards it, so the otherwise distinct *cosmotheoros*[z] busies himself with nature only in regard to that knowledge thereof in a theoretical sense, which needs to be increased. This by no means coincides in a moral sense with dutiful global and local patriotism. Both are proper to the cosmopolite, who in fealty to his country must have an inclination to promote the well-being of the entire world. An error that the Greeks displayed, in that they evinced no goodwill towards *extranei*,[a] but included them all, rather, *sub voce hostes* = *barbari*;[b] a prime cause contributing to the downfall of their state, in that this want of inclination and tendency to oppose the interest of foreign states brought enmity and jealousy upon them. Separatists and sectarians of every kind, clubbists, lodge-brothers, Herrenhuters and Pietists, are likewise destroyers of general goodwill and philanthropy; in brief, a society may be aiming at a narrower bond, in regard to morals, politics or religion – its members' adherence to their sect, and the *esprit de corps* founded on this, make for an indifferentism towards the human race, which inhibits the dissemination of general human goodwill and prevents any communal participation for everyone. *Esprit de corps* leads the disposition away from objective moral principles, and reduces it merely to this subjective relationship as a foundation for one's actions; there comes to be prejudice in its favour, and contempt for whatever is *profanum*. On this the fame, pride and seeming courage of the martyrs was founded – nor can it ever be otherwise among the Jews that all estimation for other men, who are not Jews, is totally lost, and goodwill is reduced merely to love of their own tribe, under which they are wont to cherish one another according to the *principia* adopted, and receive the more credit, the more the agent approaches to a maximum of expediency, deals falsely, is lucky in turning a profit, or possesses cleverness, cunning and craft.

§117. Nothing seems to be harder than to give honest expression to our sympathy at the honour of other people, and then impart it to others, insofar, that is, as it rests on the approving judgement of others at those of our actions that deserve honour. If the object of the inclination in which we see desert is different, then honesty of judgement prevails; but among

27:674

---

[z] student of the world

[a] outsiders

[b] under the name of enemies, or barbarians

those who locate their point of honour in the same object, e.g., among scholars in the same field, the relationship is such that there is always the danger that the other is a rival, and will be preferred in comparison with oneself; but now if two or more are making the same claim to such preference, the view to be taken on the matter is subject to great contention, and so, for that very reason, would be much weakened if they all should have an equal share in it; and hence the jealous propensity to grant it to nobody, since none ought to possess it *privative.*

27:675

§118. The idea of friendship has, since ancient times, been partly championed with enthusiasm, and partly lamented on the ground that it is so seldom to be met with in appearance. Something was felt to lie in man, as the end of human nature, but to lie very deep, so that it was always considered an ideal, merely, and taken to be unattainable; and yet the attainment of the idea was found to be so very needful for the elevation of human life, and a moral reality to be developed therein for man's end, that nobody was able to develop. The development is at all events difficult, since this idea presents itself, so to say, as a supersensible and mysterious thing.

Now to grasp the concept of friendship, attention must be given to the following components:

1. Well-wishing love to others. The love of well-liking (*complacentia*) and that of well-wishing, to oneself (*benevolentia*), are not always united one with another, though they should be. Man, that is to say, always wishes well towards himself, i.e., has at all times the intention of promoting his happiness; but he is not always pleased with himself, i.e., cannot credit himself with having acquired a moral worth of his own; on comparing his actions with the moral law he finds, rather, so great a deviation that he is in every way displeased with himself. There was, indeed, a fanatical opinion of the Jansenists, which at the end of last century infected even that otherwise great mind, Pascal (whose writings still deserve every respect); he depicted human nature with tendencies so dire that the purely moral feeling would thereby be unattainable, and man, quite regardless of all his efforts, would be bound to remain a creature of iniquity. This exaggerated view remains, nonetheless, a prospect, since to achieve self-contentment a man simply must acquire self-confidence, on one point or another, at least, that he will be able to approve his own moral conduct.

The love of well-wishing towards others does not differ from that towards oneself, but is *toto coelo* distinct from well-liking towards them. For well-wishing to others is the universal duty of love, which we owe to every man, since we must absolutely make it our maxim to promote goodness in others. The expression: *I am his friend; he is my friend* therefore means nothing else but, I cherish the inclination of well-wishing towards him from maxims = I love him from duty. But well-liking for another can never be wrung from us, by inclination, without an occasion;

27:676

so it can never be commanded as a duty. This liking is based on the esteem the other has acquired through his characteristics, and the acknowledgement of his worth; whereas we still have to wish him well, even though he presents himself to us as extremely faulty, since we have to promote his improvement.

Well-wishing towards others is, however, more closely and strictly coupled with the idea of friendship, if the criterion of reciprocal well-wishing is attached to it; for *in sensu lato,* the expression *to have true friendship for another* is not necessarily associated with the idea that this other is also grateful in return, and harbours the same well-wishing towards ourself. There can therefore be *amor unilateralis;* but strictly such well-wishing changes into friendship (*amicitia*) through a reciprocal love, or *amor bilateralis.*

N.B. This expression is also equivalent to: being everyone's friend; it does no more than formulate the duty to harbour well-wishing love for the happiness of others, and is quite different from the term: to *make friends* with everyone. This involves the idea of friendship itself, is based on a reciprocal trust that the other also views my best interests as his own and is a bilateral bond; whereas the former relation involves only a unilateral bond, and it is self-evident that for this purpose there can be no obligation incumbent on us to enter into that relation with everyone.

2. That those who love are equals; well-wishing, love and friendship differ from *favour,* in this respect. The ability, that is, to promote the other's well-being, and do him good, must be the same in both, whether it be a question of their powers, or of wealth and influence. The relationship of unlike persons produces only favour, since the activity of repaying the other for the love displayed is too weak; so *inter superiores et inferiores* no friendship occurs. To be sure, we often, from politeness, call that well-doing favour as well, which might equally be called friendship, since the other, *in substituto,* could at least afford his benefactor a similar contentment.

27:677   3. The communal possession of one person by the other, or reciprocal possession, i.e., union of their person as to moral disposition. It is somewhat the same as in marriage. This reciprocal possession is founded, however, on moral principles and a mutual love derived from that, and is thus an intellectual or moral possession. It cannot therefore be sought in the likeness or affinity of inclinations, which frequently have physical or sensory need as their basis, e.g., pleasure in playing together, whether it be chess, cards, music or other pastimes.

The essential thing here is the idea that each has of the other, that one belongs to the other, and that they possess each other in respect of their whole moral disposition, and each mutually shares in every situation of the other, as if it were encountered by himself; and this, indeed, by laws of moral freedom, though no communality of resources or of enjoyment of happiness is understood thereby.

Professor Kant explains the saying of Chremes, in Terence: *homo sum, nihil humani* etc. to mean that I am a man, and everything that involves other men is also of interest to myself; I cannot limit my well-wishing to myself only, and must show it to be active in regard to every other.

4. The reciprocal enjoyment of their humanity, i.e., that in the mutual relation in regard to capacity, and the satisfaction of the power and need so typical of man, they stand together, to communicate not only their feelings and sensations to one another, but also their thoughts. Of these two kinds of communication, the mutual disclosure of thoughts is the best, and is truly the ground for the communication of feeling. For feelings can be disclosed no otherwise, than by the imparting of thoughts; thus we must have an idea of the feeling in advance, and must hence have employed reason, in order to have known it accurately before we share it, so that the feeling thereafter may be correct and not instinctual; without thoughts, therefore, we would have no feelings, at least none of a moral kind; the other would be able to evince, not moral, but only instinctual fellow-feeling (sympathy). This mutual enjoyment, which arises in that a man shares his thoughts with the other, and the other, conversely, with him, is the foundation of openheartedness, *animus apertus sinceritas aperta.*[c] So this is not merely based on expressing one's humanity, i.e., our sensory 27:678 fellow-feeling, our receptivity to the joys and sorrows of the other; for this would be a kind of sharing that had its ground in kindliness. By the constitution of human nature, openheartedness absolutely requires certain limits, whose transgression, through kindliness, even on the part of a friend, could become dangerous.

Not that there is any question here of a limitation of *honesty*. For this is an absolute duty, and one purely lodged in human nature. But the latter seems to have a blemish in this respect, that man seems to have acquired, not a propensity merely, but a well-considered inclination, to hide from his fellow-man in sharing his inner state. This is based on a rule of prudence, that experience gives us, to make a detrimental use of the other's faults and weaknesses, no less than his perfections, so that his superiority over us is prevented, and so that by hiding our imperfections from him we are assured the respect that we wish to hold on to. So we must always take care lest the other conceal from us his weaknesses, his faults and his purposes; whence mutual distrust and reserve. The purpose of nature would appear to be promoted by this, that providence has implanted in mankind an impulse to mutual emulation among themselves in order thereby to compel them to be active in enlarging and cultivating their powers. This easily leads, however, to disparagement in the course of emulation, and thus arises rivalry, or a relation of men to one another that awakens envy of the other's merits, and shuns every danger that

[c] a candid and sincere disposition

might occasion weakness, vis-à-vis the other, want of equal perfection, or even the latter's superiority; we actually hate his very virtues, and feel an inner joy at viewing him with less respect; we notice the other's failings more shrewdly than his merits, in order to put him down. In short, this result of emulation is really a side of human nature that has become malignant, notwithstanding that the purpose of emulation really lay in inciting men to constant cultivation of greater perfection in themselves, by comparison with others. This envy of the other's merits is the basis for mistrust and reserve, and the greatest obstacle to friendship; among men, indeed, it can lead to the worst consequences, and even to immorality; in the rooted tendency there is already an *analogon* of vice, and in any event the suspicion aroused by emulation ensures that the other never discloses himself completely; the evil is that we virtually never regard the other as a friend, but rather as an opponent, who will exploit our weaknesses, but cleverly conceal his own. Hence the accepted rule: Deal with your friend as though he may well in the end become your enemy, can be explained as follows: Trust him with caution only, and disclose to him nothing which he might be able to misuse, to the detriment of your respect. And this, too, is all the more correct, in that an openheartedness which, in discovering our inner self, pays no regard whatever to the disposition, principles and inclinations of the other, but unabashedly lays out everything, whether it does honour to our humanity or not, is really ill-advised, and can itself be detrimental even among friends, owing to the mutual respect that absolutely has to be obtained.

27:679

From this it follows that in itself it can never be made a duty, that men should be openhearted one with another; for here we cannot take up anything unconditioned as a standard, nor is it possible, either, to determine how far caution may be needed. Yet it is true, nonetheless, that in the mutual humanity among friends, openheartedness must serve as the basis, whereby alone the so needful sharing of feelings and thoughts, the necessary enlargement of our various perfections, and the closer bonding with the friend is accomplished; whereas sympathy in feelings and honesty in communication merely prevent the evil which inclination and disposition might otherwise occasion, and are thus a negative good.

Among friends, indeed, there should be none of that antagonism which so greatly limits men in their mutual satisfaction of a naturally implanted need to communicate; for otherwise what is highest in friendship goes for nothing, since the caution that each must exercise in the disclosure of his mind weighs heavily on his heart, and it must be disagreeable to him to feel himself confined in this respect; yet experience teaches, how seldom human nature renounces its ways in that regard. In every man, even in the noblest understanding, there is imprinted a love of honour, and this is the source and principle that finds expression in emulation; so without even thinking of ambition, egotism or selfishness, there nevertheless arises in

27:680

410

all – even in well-meaning people – a drive constantly to perfect oneself in comparison with others; an unconcealed communication of all one's means, ends and endeavours, from the innermost soul, will therefore seldom occur. The natural antagonism of our dispositions does not permit it, and for this reason, and insofar as we demand friendship in its ideal form, Aristotle is correct in saying: My friends, there is no friend.

Among men in general, it would be a noble maxim to follow, that we so act towards our enemy, as if he might one day become our friend. In this would lie a course of conduct appropriate to the use of reason, and conformable to the laws of morality; the other remains to us entirely deserving of respect, and if we actually gain him as our friend, we do a service to mankind, or to humanity, and certainly in bettering the other; and ourselves have a pleasure that must render us self-contented.

5. The love for mutual well-liking. But the latter lies solely in the intellectual disposition of the friends, engendered from the material of reciprocal esteem, and on this rests the intellectual need for friendship.

These components of friendship, taken together from 1 to 5, give us the concept of it, as follows:

a complete love of well-wishing and also of well-liking among equals, in regard to their moral disposition and inclinations.

This, though, is a concept that directly relates to an ideal of friendship, which men envisaged as a need still earlier than the concept itself; the latter was thought out and formed accordingly, and men certainly strive to attain to that ideal, though they are capable only of approaching it. They assuredly see friendship as a need, but since nothing in experience corresponds to the idea of it, the thing was to be considered as intellectual, merely, as a concept whose perfection is never attained by men. They find, indeed, a union of men in experience, that is founded on the satisfaction of sensual needs, and call it friendship, or a mutual love of like persons, based on those needs. We thus find Theseus and Perithöos, or Orestes and Pylades, depicted as such children of nature, who supported one another at peril of their lives. So likewise, among the Canadian and other North American savages, protective alliances against enemies are sworn to the utmost degree of personal courage and loyalty, having unquenchable vengeance as their consequence. We find something similar among the Morlacks, a mountain people in Dalmatia, to whom the Venetians, their overlords, were unable to give adequate protection against the Turks, their enemies – unions that individual persons even consummated by copulation at the altar; yet it is easy to see that here it is only the need for self-preservation, the protection so sorely needed against hostile threats, which constitutes the bond that chains them thus, and that in this there is no satisfaction of any need pertaining solely to the understanding and its culture, though that is the essential element where friendship in the moral sense is concerned.

27:681

No more can we define friendship in the moral sense by that wherein the ideal of it is depicted in an aesthetic guise. The latter rests, not on maxims and principles suitable for action, but on the aim of awakening a lively feeling of this ideal. The intellectual need of friendship is the intimate communion of feelings and thoughts. It is the need to further their humanity which friends are seeking, and insofar as they participate in the enjoyment, they consider themselves to that extent as alike.

N.B. Thus even similar situations of human life, a contingent likeness of circumstances, can produce an inclination to bonding among persons, and actually institute friendship; compatriots, for instance, find themselves in a strange place, together in a foreign land, where they are isolated among strangers. Man has a natural tendency to approach anyone to whom he can unburden himself, and make a union with him, and among men it all comes down to the fact that the two of them approximate to one and the same principle in their mode of thought, or maxims of action; every convergence gives a motive for uniting, whereas the discovered incompatibility of their principles equally distances and destroys any instituting of friendship; for even though they may be able to support one another in respect of their *commercium vitae*, their acquaintance is still subject to everlasting checks, and the physical enjoyment in such acquaintance does not occur. *In casu dato* especially, however, the compatriots find quite different principles, which they have either never adopted, or are utterly opposed to; thus the impulse to communicate automatically guides them to those fellow-men in whom they can presume a similar outlook, governed by the principles of their native land; and thus there often arises a very close association.

It already lies in human nature, to love something *outside oneself,* and especially another human being. It would be an unnatural coldness in a man, to feel no interest whatever in things outside him; we are given, at the least, to showing attachment for animals or inanimate objects, and thereby to the satisfaction of this need. It is not at all necessary that there be a return of love; for the desire to be loved by others betrays vanity or egotism. So when friendship demands a reciprocal love, in that it is based on unity of the moral disposition, this is not a natural inclination, but rather an intellectual unification of the feelings and thoughts of the parties, and the well-being that springs from this constitutes reciprocal love. Hence, too, the inequality in rank, means, or other aspects of worldly fortune has nothing in common with friendship. This reciprocal love must absolutely be coupled, among friends, with mutual respect for humanity in the person of the friend, and it is this we call delicacy, and to which we must apply the saying, that friends must not demean one another. In friendship we are obligated to preserve respect for our own person, or our own self-esteem, and cannot permit the other to come too close to it; and we are likewise obligated to ward off everything that might take away respect for the humanity of the other. This mutual respect for humanity in the person of the other must at least be exercised negatively, albeit that the positive endeavour to increase and fortify respect is not thereby ruled out. Now in this lies the mutual restriction of reciprocal love among friends, and it is this which makes the nature of friendship, namely the moral union of their feelings and thoughts, into the satisfaction of a purely intellectual need.

In friendship, we might say, the unity of the persons, or the reciprocal possession of one another by two persons, whereby they feel and think in common, is still more perfectly present, and with more equality, than in marriage; for here there is no denying that owing to her weakness the wife needs the protection of the husband, and is subject to his deciding influence in the directing of her actions, which are nonetheless the product of her thoughts and feelings, so that in this case the relationship is one of *superior erga inferiorem.* The wife's respect for the personhood of the husband is therefore even greater than his for hers. But owing to this very inequality, we also see that natural antagonism shows its power, and disturbs the unity of disposition. Among friends, such resistance to the other's arrogance can really not take place, since each is obligated to preserve the other's respect, and unite only with his disposition. From this, therefore, it emerges that only a reciprocal love based on respect can secure a lasting friendship, in that only to that extent is the disturbing antagonism restrained. 27:683

The sweet delight in the enjoyment of friendship is afforded only by the harmony of judgement, i.e., that the feelings and thoughts of the parties are derived from the same *principia.* For the possession of a friend affords pleasure only in that the need to communicate our feelings and thoughts can be satisfied quite unconditionally and unrestrictedly, without reserve or any seeking for advantage, and thus without interest. Only that pure interest which is the end of this inclination converted to a need, namely to perfect our acquirements by communicating, rectifying and determining them through the judgement of others, is the one pure goal that must lead us to friendship. This is all the more beneficial, in that we cannot rectify circumscribed ideas and thoughts in any other way than by sharing them, and should this not occur, we are never secured against errors; nor is it established by any certain means, under what rules we should proceed in judging and testing our opinions, or are able, *a posteriori* at least, to make any certain test of their correctness through the communication of judgements; experience therefore teaches, moreover, that though men may be as benevolent to one another as is possible, they still do not long remain friends if they differ from each other in their *principia,* or in the operative force of their faculty of judgement. For naturally, since each idea that is subject to the *principium* has a different outcome in either case, because they proceed from a different *principium,* though the ideas 27:684

stand connected to one another, and since friends must reject everything which, were it only by producing unpleasant situations, would tend to give a check to their respect, it is evident that there will be very many topics on which they will not be able to communicate their thoughts and feelings, and which will therefore have to be avoided; the reciprocal sharing and disclosure of their thoughts is thus restricted, though that essentially disturbs the friendship.

Friends do indeed undertake to support one another in their needs with all their powers and means; and it is in itself reassuring to be able to count on such assistance, on the resources, pledges and favourable influence in case of need; yet it is prudent, and a sign of much greater and purer friendship, to abstain from those needs which make it necessary to call upon our friend for help. For to demand such support in the way of funds, or the attainment of specific ends, really lies beyond the essential limits of friendship; it can become burdensome to the other, to meet my needs, and may be accompanied by a sacrifice of resources or by unwelcome conditions; our intercourse is tempered by the fear that such services may be called for more frequently; that engenders reserve, and the supported party loses in the freedom of his judgement, the purity of his maxims; he becomes in a certain respect dependent in his conduct, and must acknowledge the superior powers of the other to whom he is beholden, and forfeits his self-possession. So if one wants to establish a perfect friendship, other rules of prudence are also required:

1. Not to burden our friend with our requirements. This lies quite beyond the bounds of friendship. It is far better to bear evils willingly than to demand relief from them. We must never let him fear that we may request something from him, on grounds of friendship; on the contrary, he must be quite convinced that he will never be called upon to benefit us.

2. Intimacy in the mutual disclosure of thoughts calls for *caution*, i.e., that we open our mind to the other only so far that we do not run the risk of thereby forfeiting his respect, by the standards of his judgement and the degree of his practical prudence. 27:685

3. In the colloquy and enjoyment of friendship, every degree of modesty, or likewise of delicacy, is needed, in regard to the other's personal self-esteem. To uncover his weaknesses, censure his errors, pretend to great insight about him, or in any way evince superiority over him, must injure his self-love, and in every case thereof such conduct is contrary to the duty of friendship. Thus a friend has no duty to reprove the other's moral faults, and point them out to him; it is almost impossible to do so without assailing his self-respect; the other takes offence because, though he has often been well aware of his fault already, he still fancied it to have gone unnoticed. Now the friend has no call to wound the other's self-respect. If such censure can be effected without loss of respect, it does not

clash with the impulse to friendship, but much caution is needed for this, and it always remains a gamble. So that, too, is a duty.

4. To keep sufficiently at a distance from our friend, that the respect which in all circumstances we owe to his personhood is in no way infringed thereby. This happens primarily by incautiously obtruding our goodwill, by rash communication, and by unrestrained love. Too deep an intimacy detracts from worth. There may well be people who live quite intimately together, though they behave with unthinking frivolity and rudeness. They may exchange coarse rebukes and at once return to amity. We say of them: Rogues fall out and rogues fall in.

5. It is prudent to engage in a reciprocal development of our principles, and above all to track down those on which we have a need to decide with our friend whether there may be any misunderstandings that hinder agreement; to clear up errors and come together as much as possible, e.g., in religious opinions. We see clearly from this that it is almost impossible to have many friends, and that this expression means nothing more than to have goodwill towards many people. A complete friendship also calls for an unrestricted enjoyment of similar disposition, an unconcealed sharing and participation in one another; but is it possible that anyone can wholly 27:686 devote himself in this fashion to many people at once? There is also the difficulty of uniting all the *requisita* in one subject, to make a friend. One must be capable of being able to have a friend, and to be a friend to the other. There are people of a temperament so cold and self-willed that they are simply not receptive to friendship, or they lack a similar education, so as to communicate in the same way, etc.

§119. The concepts of enmity, hatred, wrath, vengeance, etc., are also worth further development. It is a self-regarding duty to hate nobody, which is embodied in the rule:

To be nobody's enemy – the *oppositum* of being everybody's friend. In no way is this connected with any departure from the right and the duty *to prevent offences to oneself.*

The difference lies in this: to resist the offender, i.e., compel him to desist from the offence, and visit evil upon him that is appropriate to the context and suitable to the purpose, is a right of the person offended, since he may not let himself be subjected to offence. But anyone who seeks to avert unjustly perpetrated evil from himself treats and considers the other merely as a machine that may be injurious to himself, and to which he assigns limits under which it cannot do him any harm. *So little, therefore, is a hatred of the offender's person connected with this,* that it is, on the contrary, quite possible to make the resistance without hatred, although this is difficult for human nature; thus even in such resistance there is no enmity to the offender. For hatred expresses not just the indignation we feel at the other's action, but properly includes joy at the evil meted out to him, and if this joy is simultaneously coupled with the fact that we are *auctores* of that evil, and are making him suffer, then only is the concept of enmity satisfied.

N.B. The *status hostilitatis*[d] therefore by no means necessarily includes any enmity, but merely serves the purpose of protecting ourselves, by coercive means, in the possession of reciprocal rights. Hostilities between territorial rulers, who settle matters by force of arms, and are called *hostes*, are therefore not cases of enmity (*inimicitia*).

27:687   The *pacificus* is a peacemaker who seeks to prevent all hostilities, as distinct from a peacelover, who does not indeed engage in hostilities himself, but also does not show himself to be active in preventing them.

The hater or enemy is thus the *oppositum* of those who wish other men well. But thereby a self-regarding duty is violated. For since everyone must wish for the well-being of others, the man who hates seems clearly to be in conflict with his own principles; he sees himself in a state where he can censure himself, and must even reject himself; he feels himself to be acting contrary to the end of humanity in his own person, if he is able to feel a positive joy at the sufferings of another, and still more so if he has himself caused this evil in the first place. *He is an object worthy of hatred*, just as the injured party, who is unable to bear his sufferings, can still remain a lovable one.

To the concept of enmity there pertains also the idea of the scandalmonger (*susurrator*), i.e., he who seeks to disclose to another what he knows as an action of someone that injures the honour or right of that other, with a view to arousing an enmity between him and the agent. So this presupposes a propensity for hatred and enmity to the other on the part of the scandalmonger himself. There is a difference, however, between this and the so-called tale-bearers or go-betweens, who, whether from mere candour, or because they are wont to act without principles, simply discover or disclose to the other, for that reason, a thing that may rouse his sensibilities or give occasion for ill-will, though without any deliberate inclination to stir up enmity – simply in order to tell him something interesting or obliging, and curry favour with him; the basis for this lies in want of discretion.

Hatred, however, is essentially different from *anger*. The latter is a form of the feeling of indignation; hate, however, is a passion that points to *malevolentia* in regard to the other, just as anger tends merely to *displicitia*.[e] Anger, to be sure, is also contrary to the duty of apathy, whereby we must not abandon ourselves to any emotion; albeit that as a psychological phenomenon the greatest anger may very well consort with the utmost love towards the other, and even presupposes love for

[d] belligerent attitude
[e] displeasure

him. Thus it is from real love that parents are angry at their children
for bad behaviour, or a man is angry at the conduct of a friend who, in   27:688
his opinion, is wantonly turning away a benefit, or a patriot is angry
when he considers acts of government to be detrimental to his country;
this could not occur if he did not presuppose that the opposite conduct
would be beneficial to the other, and thus was concerned for the latter's
welfare. Hence, too, we cannot be angry and at the same time hold the
other in contempt; for just as anger involves an emotion that presupposes a great exertion of effort to resist the impression of a felt offence,
so contempt incorporates a conviction of the object's unworthiness for
employment of such a resistance on its behalf, and is therefore coupled
with calmness.

Now from this there automatically develops the concept of *vengeance;* it
is permissible to obtain satisfaction (*mitigatio*) for oneself. But this involves
a *reparatio damni,*^f and thus consists in the *extensio damni reparandi;*^g but
this *mitigatio* is wholly distinct from *vindicta,*^h i.e. the revenge forbidden in
regard to the evil done to the other. So it is also clear that it is never
defensible that we should have to endure injustice, so long as we are able
to oppose it (*mitis injuriarum patientia*).ⁱ This endurance of the evil done
by the *laesio* of the other conflicts with the duty to oneself. Here, indeed,
we are referring to *laesio dolosa;*^j in this case there is an injury to humanity
in our own person; it would be affronted, and the respect owed to it would
be lost sight of, if we were willing to let the rights of our humanity be
toyed with. We must therefore possess a desire for justice, in order to
demand satisfaction from the other for injury deliberately inflicted. This
reparatio damni occurs either through compensation or apology, depending on whether it relates to resources or honour. If we want neither of
these, the other must be got to the point of acknowledging his injustice,
and expecting it from us as a favour, that we remit the satisfaction that he
owes us.

N.B. The desire for revenge is permitted, and a duty, insofar as it
coincides with the grounds from which it arises, namely respect for the
right of other people, and the duty to love justice which springs from that.
For we are obligated to honour the rights of men, since all fulfilment of
duty rests, as on a necessary condition, upon this respect for the rights of   27:689
humanity as such. So to injure these rights in the person of others, or let
them be injured in our own person, is in both cases a thing not permitted,
and intrinsically contrary to duty. We are authorized and obligated to

---

^f amends for harm or damage
^g extent of damage to be repaired
^h retribution
ⁱ meek acceptance of wrongs
^j injurious offence

ultio.[k] This originally meant punishment for injustice suffered, but in the moral sense it means that legitimate resistance which we exercise towards others when our rights are injured, in order to obtain restitution. This demand for recompense (*reparatio damni*) has to do, either with *restitutio damni*, i.e., the immediate restoration of our rights, or, in all cases where this cannot be accomplished, satisfaction, i.e., the obtaining of payment or requital through an equivalent. If neither is possible, then by the common rule we doubtless have: *Qui non habet in ore . . . ,*[l] though *in statu civili* this satisfaction is the immediate duty of the judge, and not that of the injured party. From this is derived the *jus talionis*, which thereby differs from *ultio*. *In statu civili* we can obtain this repayment only mediately, through the judge, and to take it for ourselves would be revenge. Revenge, however, is always an immediate pleasure at the suffering of the offender, and is all the more contrary to any duty of virtue, as it is contrary to humanity; it can be conceived and realized, indeed, only under presupposition of a degree of hatred of men. Even should it also be *not unjust*, or *be just in regard to the offender*, to again injure him directly (*justum*), it still remains in itself *injustice, minus rectum,*[m] in regard to universal human duty.

There is a difference between enduring injuries inflicted and remission of the compensation or payment, which is called *injuriam condonare*, or *forgiveness*. This is a duty of virtue, insofar as it can occur without permitting any affront to humanity in our person, and the love of justice is content with more lenient means of punishment than the offender deserved. Conciliation is likewise a duty to be embraced, since the renunciation of all vengeance operates against the jolt to duty arising from vengeance itself, and restores goodwill and love towards the other party. But pardon or forgiveness implies no forgetting of a breach of duty against us, insofar as the transgression was a deliberate one. It is a rule of prudence to behave so cautiously towards anyone who has once deliberately injured us, that he can have no occasion to breach his duty a second time; this would be our own fault, and we should deserve reproach for it. Thus even a man who acts without delicacy, and actually with coarseness, albeit not with malice, will never be able to possess our total confidence; morality requires us only to abide by the amnesty, i.e., to consign his offence to oblivion, in regard to saying anything about it, and to display towards him the appearance of no longer recalling it; but actually to have no such recollection would be superhuman virtue; though in case of mere oversight or negligence on his part, this too is a duty.

27:690

---

[k] vengeance

[l] [The rest was unreadable to the German editors, though the last word is said to be 'corpore'. This suggests the old legal maxim *Qui non habet in aere, luat in corpore:* Who cannot pay in cash must suffer in person – which seems to be what Kant said.–Tr.]

[m] less than right

§120. Any *laesio* actually presupposes the violation of another's coercive right, and transgression of the coercive duty towards him, so that the concept of *laesio* belongs, materially, to *jus*. For where there are coercive rights and duties, an external right must be possible, to accompany this coercion, whether we consider ourselves to be really under a *status civilis* and valid external laws, or merely envisage such a possibility. Even where the relation of our choice to duty is determined as such, and we abstract entirely from the exercise of a possible outer right of coercion, there still remains the formal element of our dutiful obligation, which furnishes *a priori* the norm for our actions. It is the determination of our disposition to act in accordance with duty, regardless of whether we are constrained by the presence of an external law, simply because we recognize it as a duty from our own conviction, and make this the motive for our behaviour – it is this which belongs to ethics, and which enables something to be a duty, without it having to be a legal duty, or without there having to be an external compulsion thereto present in the *status civilis*. For example, by a contract made with another, I have made a profit, while he has chanced to have losses; the making good of this loss is never a coercive duty, but only a mere duty of virtue. So to that extent transgressions also belong to ethics only inasmuch as the legal duties themselves must be practised, as to form, from virtuous duty. Only wrongly does our author maintain, §316, that there can be a *suum ethicum.*[n] For where there is no coercive duty, any injury to the other's coercive right is likewise unthinkable, though we can certainly conceive the duty of giving to the other from our own store; but this, of course, was not yet *his*.

Laesio has damage as its consequence, i.e., *malum ex laesione proveniens.*[o] If we abstract here from restitution as a coercive duty, there is still a *damnum in consequentiam veniens,*[p] e.g. by dismissal from service *cum jure*[q] 27:691 the other suffers damage through unemployment; to make good the damage is an ethical duty.

§121. In human nature there is a *corruptio*, i.e., all men are susceptible to a *transgressio legis culposa.*[r] This arises from their *depravity*, a weakness of our sensory nature, and thus is a sin of weakness; but *criminal wickedness*, or the malignity of human nature as such, is acquired, i.e., a deliberate or consciously undertaken transgression of our duties, and this especially according to a maxim we have adopted.

N.B. As a genus, depravity is the opposite of *rectitudo actionum*, and has

[n] moral entitlement
[o] harm arising from an offence
[p] loss occurring in consequence
[q] as the law allows
[r] culpable breach of law

as its species malignity and malevolence, which involve a wickedness in the way of thinking about others.

Now in regard to these deliberate transgressions of duty we encounter three maxima, which figure as *monstra* of inhumanity:

Envy, ingratitude and *Schadenfreude*.

Especially in objects that we need to think of under concepts, as already with things in their kind, we have the inclination to picture a maximum, whereby we judge and deal with the things themselves, in that even though we cannot reach this maximum, we at least try to approach it. And so too, in his moral behaviour, does man range in thought from the lowest abasement to the highest elevation that he is capable of approaching, i.e., down to the beast, and up to the angel. Vices, though, like virtues, remain always human, and the maximum of evil, and of good, in devil and angel, is merely an unattainable ideal; a notion of the uttermost degree thinkable, that was already to hand before it took on symbolic form under the image of devil and angel. We are also indebted to it for the picture of heaven and hell, in that we have supposed a state containing nothing but evil and involving a total loss of consolation and the utmost pain, and likewise a state of the utmost blessedness.

Thus the bestial vices also demean man the most, in that partly they make him equal to the beast, e.g. drunkenness and gluttony, so that he becomes incapable of using his reason; and partly they bring him even lower than the beast, e.g., the *crimina carnis contra naturam*, which are called unmentionable vices, because they so demean humanity that even to name them already produces horror, and we are ashamed that a man can stoop to them.

27:692

So man also raises himself to the highest peak of iniquity by practising the devilish vices. They surpass *in opposito* the level of human viciousness, just as do the angelic virtues, and we are acquainted with both only under the Idea of heaven and hell. Human vices lie midway between them, and in appearance, just as the earth is midway between heaven and hell.

All three of the aforementioned maxims of viciousness take the ground of their origin from a property of human nature native to man, which not only makes us intrinsically guiltless, but also determines us to an admirable purpose: namely the instinct of antagonism or rivalry, i.e., the inclination to work against the perfections of others, or to surpass them by ever-increasingly promoting our own cultivation, in agreement with the laws of morality. This is shown in appearance by the fact that we constantly compare ourselves with other men, and feel a chagrin on discovering their good points, whether it be their dutiful conduct, their honour or their well-being. This is the source of *jealousy*, and it is not accompanied by any malevolence, but rather presupposes a misliking, merely, of the other's merits.

N.B. Such vices are contrary to humanity; for just as the latter involves a participation in the person and state of the other, and is evinced in well-wishing, so these three vices involve a lack of participation, such that they evince an aversion, a dislike for the worth of the person, and for the other's merits and happiness, a contentment with his misfortune. Hence they also, and *Schadenfreude* especially, are directly opposed to moral sympathy, and indicate *inhumanity*. Each of these three inhuman vices is called aggravated, if it is coupled, not merely with aversion for the other's merits and condition, or joy at his misfortune, but also with a desire to damage him in his merits and to contribute actively thereto as author.   27:693

.There awakens in us a discontent with our own condition, by comparing it with others, and hence arises emulation or jealousy (*zelotypia*), because we have perceived an inequality with the other's well-being, or an equality with our own, which could only have been prevented by ourselves. The result of it is an immediate endeavour to pull level with, or get ahead of the other, accompanied, therefore, with activity designed to enlarge or extend our natural endowments. But the effect is totally different if it arouses envy (*invidia*) in us. This consists in hatred of the other, simply because he is (*comparative*) fortunate, or has advantages over us. Envy has its immediate ground in emulation; although here, as with ingratitude and *Schadenfreude*, it is hard to impute to human nature such a tendency to these vices and their maxims; for ingratitude consists likewise in hatred towards a benefactor, simply because we are obliged to him for his well-doing; one would have supposed that, out of gratitude, the man would still not deny the other the sweet pleasure that is owed to him on that account; and *Schadenfreude* contains hatred of the other as such, because he is not unfortunate. It seems to be impossible to human nature to maintain oneself at least *in statu indifferentiae*⁵ in regard to one's fellow-man, i.e., to feel neither pleasure nor pain at his weal or woe.

1. Now so far as concerns envy, in particular, the *invidia qualificata*ᵗ aims at weakening the other in the possession of his merits. Now since, in order to get equal with him, no exertion of our own is needed, to enlarge our own personality or the extent of our own well-being, but merely the destruction of the other's well-being, to make him less fortunate than ourselves, we find, even in appearance, that envy is more often at work than jealousy. Even the method of rearing children engenders envy of the other's merits. Children are accustomed by their mentors to compare their actions with those of others to whom they might feel themselves equal; they look to others as their models; to reach that costs trouble, and   27:694 that arouses pain, and this is naturally a temptation to envy, since if the object clothed with merits were not there, the child would itself pass for a model who would not be loaded with faults. There is the further point,

⁵ in a state of indifference
ᵗ aggravated or malignant envy

that if the child now attains to its model, it may still have remained at a low level, since the model was too, though not to such a degree; for comparison with others still yields only an *abstractum,* and thus rests on subjective grounds, though the only thing worthy of love and respect is that which agrees with duty and honour; whence it is also a duty to establish duty and love of honour by exhibiting the relation of human capacity to the idea of holiness, of duty itself and its laws, and to awaken in the child an inclination to attain this. With envy for others' merits there is associated, to nourish it, the weakness of those others that he envies, in that they despise the envier, or anyone who is happy to a lesser degree; the antagonism goes along with an enhanced wish that the other, to persuade himself of his unhappy condition, may himself be plunged into it. This is even the case in regard to a person who is ill (though not dangerously so); the healthy man presents him with plain reasons for attributing his illness to the patient himself, and never takes the latter's sufferings so much to heart as the victim does. (The patient feels this debasement of his condition, and wishes that the other might experience it, so as to be able to realize the pain.)

Thus envy extends, not only to all the praiseworthy features necessary to man, but also to talents and fortunate circumstances of every kind.

If the other's advantages arouse merely distress in a man, because on comparing his worth with the moral standing of the other he feels himself degraded, this is merely *misliking* or *invidia in genere.*" He feels merely his own unworthiness by the comparison made, and is discontented because the other possesses advantages. But such envy becomes *invidia qualificata,* i.e., *livor,*" when within him there is simultaneously awakened the desire to lessen those advantages, and to injure the other on that account.

2. Ingratitude *in genere* (*ingratitudo*) is likewise a displeasure or discontent at the obligation which the other has laid on us, through the kindness he has shown towards us. And it becomes *qualificata* if from this there arises a hatred for the well-doer, and a passion for doing him harm and evil, just because he has conferred benefits upon us.

3. Again *Schadenfreude* (*vulgaris*) is malevolence or joy at another's misfortune, which seems, therefore, to be founded on envy, or discontent at his happiness. It is *qualificata* if it is coupled with a desire to render the state of the other unhappy. It differs, therefore, from envy of the same type, in that it seeks to lower, not the worth of a person, but his state of happiness. Now all three vices are quite manifestly opposed to the duty of apathy; yet from another viewpoint they take their rise from an inborn human tendency to set oneself against the other's superiority. This inclination prompts the activity of making oneself equal to the

27:695

" envy without ill-will

" malicious envy, or spite

other in every respect; nature has implanted this emulation in us, and it therefore must absolutely be cultivated; and it serves merely to extend our animal nature and make it adequate to humanity, or the intellectual being within us, and to its laws. On the approval and assenting judgement of this intellectual man, the worth of the sensory man depends; the latter will retain this approval if he has been able, by sensory cultivation, to further acquaint himself with the laws of the intellectual man, and to pay attention to them in his actions, and test his own worth accordingly. But this is where the error lies. That method would establish true love of honour in us. But in judging himself and his inner worth, man founds and measures it instead on a merely comparative estimate of his person and condition against the worth and condition of other men. Hence arises the love of honour in a bad sense; if he finds himself lowered by comparison with the other, that arouses in him dislike of the other's person, and instead of actively exerting himself to become equal in value with the other, he succumbs to resentment at the latter's worth and merit, or tries to diminish him.

The fact that the other has done more for us than he was required to do, arouses ingratitude; for all his *merita* in regard to our person, or fortunes, bring it about that we are thereby obliged to him on that account; but in that he has had an influence on our well-being, he has an advantage over us, whereby he is elevated above our worth, and we, on the contrary, have become *inferiores* in his regard; for assuming that the estimation of our self rests on a comparative judgement with the other's worth, this degradation displeases us; we are tortured by the obligation he has laid upon us, and so envy hinders our participation and interest in his welfare. It is the same whether the source of the advantage rests on *merita fortunae* or services rendered. Love for the benefactor, on the other hand, or knowledge of our duty to him, through active participation in his well-being, and by acknowledging the obligation he has laid upon us through his well-doing, i.e., by his useful and serviceable action, would be gratitude. It seems, however, to conflict with the instinct for jealousy of everything wherein the other does us a service; it seems to be contrary to our self-esteem, since it can almost never appear without the benefactor's worth being coupled with a demeaning of the value of the other party. Even among friends, acts of friendship are certainly duties to which they are obligated, since their interest in mutual support is common and simultaneous; yet it still needs delicacy to avoid all acts that would engender, not the duty of friendship, but well-doing or service towards the other. And thereby, too, friendship in its personal unity is restricted. Here, also, benefits create an obligation from which the other wishes to be spared, and cannot unburden himself. For even reciprocation of the greatest benefit does not settle the score in this respect, that the other's benefit came first. The friend feels, therefore, the other's superiority, and the

27:696

lowering of his own value. In duties of friendship this is not the case, since it is compensated on the spot by the other's claim.

It is therefore contrary to the true love of honour to accept benefits, since the worth of humanity in our own person is thereby diminished, and we let ourselves be put by the other into a state of dependency, which hampers us in making free use of our friend's company, and in unrestricted participation with him. More pressing, therefore, is the duty to frugality, which is embodied in the rule: Shun poverty, and seek your own welfare, else you will become a beggar. So if kindness is shown, furthermore, in the unconcealed form of a benefit, this arrogance in doing the other a service is often a source of ingratitude, in that the other must feel all the more vividly the debasement he has brought upon himself by acceptance of the benefit. The only way left, therefore, to confer a benefit without injuring the sense of honour, is to so wrap it up that it would seem a duty of friendship if the other were to accept it, so that only a duty is being met. It is easy to see, therefore, how reprehensible it is to thrust benefits on the other, and how easily it is possible, indeed, to make enemies by beneficence. For the recipient has only to possess the inverted pride of wanting to show at once that he has no need of the kindness the other has shown him, and he then certainly hates his benefactor all the more, when oppressed by the state of debasement he has endured, and despises what he has received; if ill-natured, indeed, he may seek to injure him.

We see from this the natural urge of men against each other, to raise themselves to equality in their worth, and that in order to attain this they make it their aim to forestall and surpass the other, because by counter-effort the equality with others is thereupon brought to pass. In this there is very often a cause for open war. Since the man given to *Schadenfreude* does not remain a mere spectator of the other's sufferings, but at least participates in them through the glee that he feels at the spectacle, this vice, as an evil inclination, already seems to be the farthest removed from humanity; it is not in a negative relation to the other's sufferings; it also seems to rest upon the antagonism in human nature that – to put it at its mildest – we take it not unkindly when the other meets with misfortune; we are then persuaded that in a similar case he will be forbearing towards ourselves. Rochefoucauld says, that in the sufferings of our best friends there is something that does not wholly displease us. The misfortune that has befallen him can also befall us; in this case we are persuaded in advance that he will not set a lower value on our worth, and we have a similar opportunity to establish our own worth in regard to his; this presupposes that we can do nothing active to relieve his sufferings; for were this the case, we would have helped him, because we do not wish for his misfortune, like the exponent of *Schadenfreude qualificata;* but then we should also have obtained an advantage over him. So here, too, there is a natural instinct in man to be jealous

27:697

27:698

424

over all the mental and physical powers of the other, since he can thereby acquire *merita* over us. *Schadenfreude qualificata*, on the other hand, must be acquired and unnatural, since there the agent wills the other's evil, and can become an author thereof, in order to bring it about.

§122. Now just as the *crimina carnis contra naturam* bring humanity directly into contempt, so envy, ingratitude and *Schadenfreude* give occasion for the same thing, at least through the denatured character of the inclination. We say of begrudgement that a man can endure no one happy *above him*, but of envy that he can endure no one happy *beside him*. The former is a human vice, but the latter a devilish one, since in that case the agent must have an immediate satisfaction in the practice of such a vice, and be acting like the devil, or the principle of a thoroughly evil being. *Schadenfreude*, the opposite of *pity*, is not always rooted in wickedness, for in that sense it always has reference to diminishing the other's happiness, to the adding of an equally irreparable injury; but it often has its source in mere *mischief*, glee at the other's mishap, which is frequently coupled with an intrinsically inconsiderable access of happiness, though it evinces an act which includes joy at the other's inconvenience, embarrassment, or the disturbance of his state of tranquillity as such. Such would be a man, for example, who drinks the other out of wine, as opposed to one who lets the wine-cask run out from malice – glee at the other's antics when he falls, the mischievous frightening of others to enjoy their alarm. In short, even though the aim is merely *laughter*, there is in all these cases an ethically objectionable *Schadenfreude*, since we can only laugh ourselves if the other's circumstances permit and enable him to laugh with us, but never when his condition is repugnant to him.

§123. So the stronger the instinct is operative in man, to assume his worth always by comparison, the more we need to take care that we never preclude the law from estimating our action, that we compare ourselves with our dutiful circumstances, and examine closely how far we may approximate to them, and never, therefore, consider ourselves less happy than others, but compare ourselves, rather, with those less happy than we are.

§124. The opposite of the aforementioned devilish vices are called angelic virtues, which in themselves are not implanted by nature, but have to be acquired, and consist, 27:699

1. In rejoicing at the merits of the other, who thereby lowers us in our own worth. This moral joy rests on knowledge and willing of the good, with complete disinterestedness, and thus even regardless of the fact that our own worth is thereby devalued.

2. In well-doing, even when aware that we shall be rewarded with ingratitude.

3. In not letting ourselves be deterred from *goodwill towards them*, by the insolence or hostility of others towards us, even when they wish our

misfortune; i.e., in loving our enemies. It is only goodwill that can occur, for well-liking our enemies can never give us, since they are ill-disposed and forget their duty; we can, however, see it as a misfortune that they hate us, since this hatred disturbs the other's peace of mind, and thus punishes him for the most part by troubling him, so that he feels the injury that he undeservedly inflicts upon us.

§125. In all signs of well-wishing, it is a matter of removing inconveniences or providing amenities for the other, so a friendly manner and politeness are also natural. But if the intention of beneficence is in doubt there, the expressions are affected, as with compliments, for example. . . . [*Text breaks off.*]

§126. Uprightness, and that in its greatest purity, i.e., integrity, *candor et sinceritas,* are natural obligations of man, and so everyone must frame only such utterances as can coexist and agree with the greatest consciousness of truth and the total absence of any consciousness of the opposite. Openheartedness, on the other hand, is subject, even among friends, to those limits beyond which it might bring our worth into contempt, or could engender misuse; thus the effect of openheartedness can also be that we are despised, that the other simulates to his own profit and gains advantages over us. Hence *concealment,* reservation, is a precaution that is approved of in ethics, though admittedly it is expressed (a) *dissimulando,* i.e., negatively, when we do not disclose, or allow it to be seen, what we are thinking; (b) *simulando,* when by fabricating the opposite we try to occasion an error on the other's part. The former deceives (*fallit*), but the latter endeavours to become the *auctor erroris in alio.*[w] We may knowingly deceive the other in a permissible way, if we try by our action or utterance to promote the truth, or avert an evil; e.g. a pretended journey, to uncover and thwart a crime.

Simulation can only be impermissible, though, when a person gives signs indicative of thoughts that he does not have, and thus becomes *auctor erroris* in the other, at least to sniff out what the latter was thinking about it. Should the other in turn try to protect himself from this by simulation, i.e., by reserving his own thoughts, he is acting merely on a rule of prudence, whose neglect might bring him disadvantage; and this is not impermissible.

He alone is a *betrayer,* who deceives *dolose (dolose fallens).*[x]

Hence an untruth differs from a lie in this, that both, indeed, contain a *falsiloquium,*[y] i.e., a declaration whereby the other is deceived, but the latter is uttered with an associated intention to injure the other by the untruth. Hence, too, a lie is subject to judicial reprimand, at least as an

27:700

---

[w] cause of error in another
[x] in a harmfully deceptive way
[y] false statement

offence, but not as an untruth. *In ethics,* though, every *falsiloquium,* every knowing deception, is impermissible, even though it be not immediately coupled with an injury, and would not be imputable *coram foro juridico.*[z]

N.B. Hence the telling of tall stories, or braggings in company, demean us, and can only pass as a jest if the judgement of others about the content of their truth cannot be in doubt.

There is always a violation in this of humanity in our own person, as well as in regard to others; we carry on a traffic with words, but not with thoughts, and so no communication can be thought of here, that would have reality. If it is a lie, however, then there is a worse degree of baseness in it than in force. For deception evinces a cowardice that is not found in violence. Hence a *falsarius* (perjurer) by his deceit, removes all credit and worth from the *instrumentum* of public trust, and commits a greater crime than any wrought by open force.

27:701

In *sensu juridico,* the *mendacium* is a *falsiloquium dolosum in praejudicium alterius,*[a] but *in sensu ethico* it is already any deliberate untruth. To utter one cannot be called in any wise permissible. It violates the human duty towards others, as it does the humanity in our own person, which is thereby depreciated. Uprightness alone can earn us the confidence of others. If there is deception here, the credulous one, who takes the story to be true, and makes use of it to his injury, in that he accords belief to an untruth, runs the risk of himself in the end being despised, if he is often taken in in that fashion; the liar ceases to be a man to whose communication we attach any value. The lie finds a seeming defence in the case of those told in jest, out of politeness, or under necessity, in that here the presumption holds, that the other does not want to hear the truth, or that it serves in some way to prevent harm. If, when others are flattering, for example, and one who also insists (or even hints) that I say likewise, does not want to hear the truth, this would be a lack of courtesy, and if I am unwilling to do it, or even lay upon myself an overstepping of the truth, there is but one way out – by an unexpected turn of the conversation to divert the others in a direction where it remains doubtful what my true or ostensible judgement will be. Not every one is in a mood for this, and not on every occasion; yet silence is also not possible, and so it often happens that men palm off untruths on one another, and simulate and dissimulate each to each. Although no immediate harm may come of it, it never redounds to our credit. Men also lie in this way, to prevent harm; but here, too, we perceive the regrettable weakness of human nature, which sets bounds to the sublimity of an unconstrained openness of heart.

There may, in general, be no unpleasantness in social situations that could rightfully seduce us into wrongdoing; yet, given the weakness of

[z] before a court of law
[a] a lie is a harmful falsehood damaging to another

human nature, it is true nonetheless that the strict laws of duty must here endure many a jolt. A moral casuistic would be very useful, and it would be an undertaking much to the sharpening of our judgement, if the limits were defined, as to how far we may be authorized to conceal the truth without detriment to morality.

27:702   Along with lying we may include: (a) *aequivocatio moralis,* i.e. moral ambiguity, insofar as it is deliberately employed to deceive the other; for example, a Mennonite swore an oath that he had handed over the money he owed to his creditor, and in a literal sense he could swear this, for he had hidden that very sum in a walking-stick and asked his adversary to hold it. (b) *reservatio mentalis,* which expresses a kind of ambiguity, whereby we take only with a mental restriction, what we say in words without any restriction whatever. A Mennonite was expecting another to ask him for a loan; instead of refusing it to him, he counted out the money under a cup and stipulated to the borrower that he could not give him money, but that if he would pledge this cup, then etc; this meant lifting it from its position, but also a pawnbroker's loan; or when Menno, the founder of the sect, was due to be arrested, and escaped by mailcoach, the arrest-warrant arrived first, at one of the stages, and the postmaster asked each of the passengers if Menno was on the coach. Instead of lying, that he was *not* on board, he asked his companion if it was being asked whether Menno *was* on board; but since the latter did not know Menno, he remained undetected.

The first example is surely, beyond dispute, a case of equivocation.

We may also include here:

(c) *peccatum philosophicum,* [b] i.e., contemplation of an intrinsically punishable undertaking, which is held, however, to be good and useful. Utility, indeed, can furnish no moral justification for any action, but it also cannot be impermissible to pursue truth; thinking as such, without punishable action being deliberately coupled with it, can also not be impermissible, and so this sin does not belong here.

§127. There is a difference between lying and breach of trust, or *mala fides in pactis servandis.* [c] He who makes a promise allows the other to acquire *res vel praestatio facti* [d] over him, whose truth the promiser knew as such. But he acts unfaithfully if, because he regrets this promise, he fails to carry it out. The liar acts contrary to the duty of humanity in his person, and mediately against the duty to others; the contract-breaker acts contrary to the duty towards others, and mediately against himself. So *pacta sunt servanda* [e] (*cum stricto jure*), that is, they are holy and inviolable in

---

[b] letting the end justify the means
[c] bad faith in keeping a bargain
[d] a thing or the doing of something
[e] promises must be kept

themselves; they are the sole possible ground whereby men reciprocally   27:703
promote their common end among themselves, and are able to unite for
communal purposes. So nobody by himself may deviate even in the smallest degree of fulfilment from his duty; nor can the *jus talionis* ever hold
good, viz., that he who is betrayed by the other's faithlessness should be
authorized, for his part, to betray in return. He is always acting contrary to
the supreme law of humanity. Nay, even if the other thereby acts with the
utmost injustice towards me, in not fulfilling his promise, it is not allowed
for me, in any other matter, to repay him in the same coin. For example,
when Graf Schmettau, at the capitulation of Dresden, found that
nonengagement of the besieged troops by the Austrians was not observed,
the question arises, whether he could have done likewise if the situation
had been reversed? Joseph II violated the *Joyeuse entrée* of the Dutch; were
they therefore entitled to renounce their duty as subjects? Neither of the
two. By repayment of an injustice the act does not in itself become just,
and by the law of morality an action remains unjust, even though the other
has no call to complain of injustice.

§128. The judgement of others, i.e. comparison of one's worth with
that of others, is not only permitted to everyone, but even a duty, since we
cannot judge ourselves in any other way, save by putting ourselves into
comparison with other people; and a *tertium comparationis*[f] is called for, in
order to pass a correct judgement. Personal self-assessment, or the determination of one's own moral worth, the *justum sui ipsius aestimium*,[g] rests
on a comparison of one's action with the law, and to that extent the
humilitas comparationis,[h] i.e., the maxim of determining one's worth by
comparison with others, and of requiring in the process to accord oneself
a lesser value, but a higher one to others, is quite contrary to duty, and a
monkish virtue, that makes a man a cringing creature, who does not dare
to raise his worth by cultivation, so as to obtain the advantages of others,
because he obstinately mistrusts his own powers and talents, and reso-
lutely depreciates his own worth. This is not that *humilitas absoluta* which
on comparison with the law makes us sink back in face of its holiness and
purity, and which consideration of the teaching of the Christian religion is
meant to evoke in us, though not demanding it in advance. Comparison
with others in determining our own worth can thus be aimed only at self-   27:704
instruction concerning our value; for self-knowledge, *anthropognosia
moralis*, or the moral knowledge of men, is likewise of service: the study of
men and their actions, in order to get to know them. It is a duty here, to
seek out the good that we can discern in their actions, for the use of it
really consists in this, that now their actions become motives to prod us

---

[f] third term of comparison
[g] just estimate of oneself
[h] humble mode of comparison

into the practice of virtue, in that we thereby become assured that in comparison with the law, and the fulfilment of it achieved by others, our practical virtue is still weak, or in some degree may surpass others. A common error here is that in so doing we compare ourselves more with the faults of other people than with their good points – from self-seeking; the faults of others must certainly be judged and examined, in order not to take what is a failing for something good; but they must have no influence on the determination of our worth.

§129. The judgement or adjudication of others (*judicatio*) differs greatly from the execration or condemnation (*dijudicatio*) of their faults. The latter consists in judgement with decisive legal power, by determination of the consequences. Such decision in regard to the moral disposition of the agent is impossible. Here it is a matter, not of external actions, which are the object of judicial sentence *in foro externo sive juridico,*[i] but of knowing the agent's motives; but now outwardly we do not know what sort of sensory impulses (*stimuli*) concurred in this, or how far temperament contributed, or what sort of product a man is capable of achieving in his action, through his education or mental powers. It is even less possible to learn this in others, than it is hard, in our own case, to discover the motives that underlie our actions. Hence it is impossible to judge oneself or others internally, either through a judge set up by the public law, or *in statu privato;*[j] it belongs only *ad forum divinum,*[k] but also creates for us the beneficial duty of taking a very mild view of the specifically illegal acts of other men, and judging them with leniency. It is a question whether the principle of transmigration of souls, to which Plato gave rise by depicting the body as *ergastulum*[l] of the soul, did not also have regard to a person's still outstanding *demerita.*

27:705 §130. The censure of others is in itself permitted, but it can rest as such only on the limits within which I can promote their happiness. This is an imperfect duty, since it is incumbent on me only in regard to the end of humanity. It presupposes that I seek to attain the end of humanity, which I must have both in my own person, and in respect of others, i.e., that I make myself fit, by my own acquired perfection, for all possible ends; then alone can I also promote the perfection of others, insofar as their end lies in agreement with my own capacity, and they are able and willing to make use of it. The beginning must therefore come from the cultivation of my own capacity, in that it is only through my own moral perfection that I put myself in possession of the means to all possible ends, and can thereby make it possible to employ them. If there now arises

[i] before an external or legal tribunal
[j] in private
[k] to the tribunal of God
[l] prison-house

thereby an agreement of our whole condition with the sum of all possible ends, the result is happiness, and this is my own, if I am put into the state of utilizing all acquired means, and also of possessing the latter, so that I can apply them to all ends. Only so, therefore, can our own perfection be applied to the happiness of others, and the agent himself become happy in consequence. These two duties, however, have their foundation in the duty of morality. On this presupposition, therefore, there also depends the question, as to how far censure, or its opposite, flattery, are permitted?

To be a flatterer presupposes that we harbour a decided preference in the other's favour, though it also exposes us to the danger of being despised by the other; so this always runs counter to the duty towards oneself.

Equally little is the fault-finder entitled to reprove with bitterness, i.e., to pass judgement on the other's action by casting aspersions on his person; ridicule and *reductio ad absurdum* therefore obviously damage the possibility of communication in human relations, and a *spiritus causticus*[^m] is thus objectionable, since it at once combines with its judgement the inclination to make mock of the other's action.

§131. The duty of tolerance is only a figurative thing. Intolerance rests upon quarrelsomeness, and the associated hatred of the other, merely because he thinks differently (for the diversity of moral actions is not at issue here). This is a wholly unnatural thing, since nobody can have the right to demand of another that he be of the same opinion as himself; hence all tolerance is likewise something contradictory to the worth of humanity; the tolerant man is he who does not wish to hinder what he would otherwise certainly have a right to hinder; but this never involves giving another permission to think, so the latter is mere arrogance. Our duty, rather, is to acquire an inclination to adopt a friendly attitude towards, and even to love, those who differ entirely from us in their principles of thinking. Hence, too, the endeavour to maintain peace, or the *studium irenicum*, cannot be founded on a *pactum*, for this would not last long.

27:706

§132. The duties of giving *alms to the poor*, and of *assisting those in distress*, are different in this respect, that the former, from the poor man's viewpoint, is aid that he begs for, and which is founded on a need that calls for continuous help; whereas the latter presupposes a temporary condition, or particular situation, which puts a person in need of help, in order to rescue himself from this plight. A poor man who begs is constantly depreciating his personhood and abasing himself; he makes his existence dependent on other people, and accustoms others, by the sight of him, to the means whereby we neglect our own worth. The state must therefore restrict open begging as much as possible, rather than encour-

[^m]: a sarcastic outlook

age it; it is permissible only to activate the natural feeling towards love of mankind.

§133. To make the estimable nature of virtue beloved, by constant cultivation of our manners, is a duty, and on this rests decorum, the outward appearance of propriety in our actions, or the seemliness of our behaviour towards others. This is virtue considered according to the rules of taste, beauty coupled with respect for the holiness of the duty to virtue. In seemliness, virtue presents itself as *virtus phenomenon*, i.e. man's conduct in appearance must indeed be suitable to, and based on, the laws of virtuous duty, but at the same time must also not contravene the laws of seemliness; so here it is not yet required that the laws of taste be observed, or that virtue be coupled with civility, but only that the negative aspect of decorum be avoided. This negative aspect, however, is scandal, since it straightway brings the laws of seemliness into contempt. The opposite of negligence would be purism in regard to taste, which – just as in regard to duty it runs to punctiliousness – here likewise betrays a pedantry which, to find departures from the rule, deems trifles (*micrologia*) to be important breaches of duty. Seemliness, moreover, must not rest on mere seeming (*speciosa*); this is a self-deception which creeps in all the more easily, in that others judge the moral disposition only by the outward marks of the action, or by the form of virtue, so that it then comes down so very much to an exact observance of outward deportment in our dealings with men.

27:707

It is all the more a matter of observing decorum, and the acquisition thereof, in that the principles of taste are so closely related to those of virtue that they intertwine, so to speak, and hence that so long as crudity is present in a subject, neither taste nor virtue will be found there. Judgements of taste, for example, must be just as devoid of all interest as a judgement based on moral principles; nor can there be any rules as to where the bounds of respect for decorum terminate, and the limits of purism begin; here it all depends on cultivation in manners to determine the degree of our duty; thus we walk in shadow, for example, when there is talk in company about sexual love. Decorum must be founded on duty, and the latter may be subject to decorum, as an essential component of duty; as Schiller says, we must couple virtue with graciousness. Duty can never guarantee the latter, since it contains in part an imperative of law, and in part can give worth, of necessity, only to the disposition required for its fulfilment; that whereby we can lend to virtue a vesture of graciousness is the outer appearance of the disposition; we thereby endeavour not to act in contravention of the laws of seemliness; so those on the other side are sinners against the graciousness of virtue, who seize only upon the positive aspect of decorum, and prefer a mere outward veneer of seemliness to the true disposition towards virtue, and to some extent practise an affectation of the latter. Decorum may be preferred to the *utilis*, but never to the *honestus*, to the useful, that is, but never to strict duty. Just as

customs are distinct from virtue, in that they are actions in conformity   27:708
with general usage, so in our outward conduct we must avoid that *false
shame*, which from weakness contracts the bounds of seemliness, and
must equally be neither flatterers, nor hypocrites (given to anxiousness
and sighing, of an affected kind), nor faultfinders, nor eccentrics. It comes
down to a certain politeness, a certain address in our behaviour (what the
French call an *élégant de la coeur*).

§134. The concepts of pride and arrogance (*ambitio – superbia*) are very
different. Every man is called upon to concede nothing to another, insofar
as the latter seeks to arrogate to himself a precedence over us; this is
legitimate pride, which is unwilling to yield anything to the other's pre-
sumptuousness, because we would thereby render ourselves inferior. It
remains an arrogance on the other's part, if he demands more respect
from his fellow-man than the latter is prepared to grant him, and here
such refusal is proper pride; but if it takes the form of being jealous of the
other's achievements, then it is pedantry, coarse pride, e.g. to despise the
man of rank because of his gentility.

Arrogance, on the other hand, is founded on the demand a person
makes, that others should hold themselves in low esteem, in comparison
with himself; this, therefore, is associated with a demeaning of the other's
personhood, and is thus more mischievous than pride, which is addressed
only to preserving parity of respect for oneself. The fault always lies in
this, that the agent makes his self-estimate on a comparison, not with the
law, but with his fellow-man. It should be noted, of course, that here we
are talking only of the outward marks of respect, not of any inner respect,
and thus of reverence for the man.

Arrogance is thus a form of folly, since by the principle on which the
agent acts, it follows directly that he is working against his own aim;
indeed, since this propensity to demean the other contains, at the same
time, a possibility that the latter may commit an act of meanness towards
oneself, it is insulting to his morality, and hence the arrogant man is hated.
It is thus different again from *vanity*, since the latter involves a pursuit of
honour that is sought in things that have no intrinsic worth. This is
stupidity, and a person of that kind is therefore laughed at.

If someone betrays his arrogance or vanity by his outer demeanour,   27:709
there arises the *fastus*[n] that we call being puffed up. The physiognomy
here is based on the psychological rule, that thoughts and emotions operate directly upon the countenance, and the latter in turn upon the former;
which goes so far, that in imitating a facial expression, or a character, the
state of mind also arises in the soul.

Uncouthness is a kind of behaviour whereby a man opposes himself to
another, with the aim of circumventing his airs of arrogance. He wishes

[n] form of pride

thereby to destroy all civic inequality, because he demands civic equality. In this he acts no less absurdly than a scoffer who wishes to be Democritus, by turning everything to ridicule. Everyone, for that matter, will sooner see himself hated, at worst, rather than viewed with contempt. Hatred presupposes that we refuse to acknowledge the other's character, because on comparing ourselves with him we have found his personality repugnant; but contempt is based on a judgement that denies to the other any legitimate moral worth. A person deserves contempt when in himself he is worth nothing, i.e., when he has no moral worth in any respect. The despiser thus impugns the other's humanity directly, whereas the hater, merely from passion, takes an adverse view of the other's cultivation, in comparison with his own.

§135.* Now among the objects to which we have duties there are also reckoned those entities that are intrinsically world-beings, but not men (whence God is not among them, since He constitutes no part of the world). These beings are *vel animata, vel inanimata,* living or lifeless.

1. Towards lifeless beings, or corporeal things in general, it is a duty only to have no *animus destructionum,* i.e., no inclination to destroy without need the useable objects of nature. As pictured by the poets, the things of all lifeless nature are presented as alive, e.g., the dryads. Contemplation of their organization and ordering, one to another, unquestionably cultivates the understanding, and since the need to love other things outside us must not be self-serving, it cannot be more disinterestedly satisfied, from a moral point of view, than when this inclination is directed upon lifeless objects; would not the opposite, then, be delight in destroying things of nature or craft-products, whose use must be serviceable and necessary to us, and thus morally worthy of love?

27:710

2. Towards living beings that are not human. These are either (a) beneath humanity by their nature, or by their animality. Such beings are *bruta* (for in regard to morality no relationship can here be contemplated, since they lack understanding). Towards *bruta* we have no immediate duty; among men, indeed, no less than animals, if we consider the animosity of the one to those of the other species, the inclination and physical instinct might well prevail, to destroy one another for the satisfaction of their needs. Yet it cannot be denied that a hard-heartedness towards animals is not in accordance with the law of reason, and is at least an unsuitable use of means. Any action whereby we may torment animals, or let them suffer distress, or otherwise treat them without love, is demeaning to ourselves. It is inhuman, and contains an analogy of violation of the duty to ourselves, since we would not, after all, treat ourselves with cruelty; we stifle the instinct of humaneness within us and make ourselves devoid of feeling; it is thus an indirect violation of humanity in our own

*[There is no §136; §137 follows. – Tr.]

person. In Athens it was punishable to let an aged work-horse starve. In England, likewise, all cruelty to animals is forbidden under punishment; it is recognized, therefore, that in this there is something improper, which at least can render us immoral.

(b) beneath humanity, not by their nature, indeed, but in respect of morality. These are the *spiritus cacodämones,*° or such living beings beyond the pale as have reason, but are not confined within the space of the body. Hence they are by nature properly unconfined, and above humanity, and can have influence upon all beings confined to the body. These evil beings are called spirits, *sub voce* devils.

(c) beings that surpass humanity, not only by their nature, but also by their morality, i.e. the *spiritus agathodämones,*ᵖ which differ from the foregoing only in this, that they are also superior to man in their morality, by virtue of their greater understanding. They are called angels, and set in contrast to men, who as animal and corporeal creatures are thus restricted in regard to their activity, duration and effect.

There are, indeed, assumed to be duties towards these Ideas under (b)   27:711
and (c), or to spirits in theurgy; but to angels and devils there can be no duties, since they are unthinkable. For were this not so, it would have to be possible for the human understanding to gain knowledge of these spirits, their nature, existence and constitution; but even as mere Ideas of reason they are incomprehensible, since other concepts and moral data known to us cannot be used as a foundation, from which we might infer to them; still less does there correspond the object of any experience that we might either have undergone directly, or that others might have had, and that we could then have obtained from them indirectly. It is visionaries alone who have an apparition of spirits unknown to us, who conceive of them as objects of the outer senses, who discover rules whereby to judge them, and who imagine duties accordingly, which they carry to perfection; for others, who do not possess the special sense of spiritual intuition, all knowledge of this kind is impossible. The doctrine of these duties towards spirits rests on the theurgy of the ancient Chaldeans, Egyptians and Greeks, which for centuries constituted a practical morality, and contained the totality of duties towards good spirits, in order to become skilled in finding favour with them, and practising communion with them by purifying the soul of sensuous inclinations and feelings, and obtaining influence, and discovering their will, and thus indirectly the will of God.

The belief of Pythagoras and Plato, that the soul is shut up, as in an *ergastulum,* within the body, laid the foundation for theurgy, in that their disciples after Plato's time, the neo-Platonists Jamblichus, Plotinus *et al.,* did much to spread the doctrine of the influence of spirits on men, and

° evil spirits
ᵖ good spirits

the means of obtaining purification of the flesh from all bodily hindrances, and in general busied themselves greatly with theurgy; they gave out that their ideas of philosophy had already been taught by all the old philosophers, that they had unified them in their principles, and thus became eclectics – magic, or the art of performing wonders (*ars thaumatologia*), was the outcome of theurgy. Wonders are supernatural things, and may be divided into *miracula rigorosa*,[q] i.e. wonders of which no being in nature can be the cause, and *miracula comparativa*, wonders whose cause is admittedly no being distinct from the world, but whose laws of operation are utterly unknown to us. Now wonders are a thing revolting to reason; for to explain an effect from something as cause, notwithstanding that we are unable to know the cause, is to assume an uncaused effect; for it is contradictory that anything should be an effect, even though I do not know the cause of it; it is simply inferred on the analogy of physical effects, even though there is no basic law whatever that obliges us to adopt any similar procedure in the case of wonders; for men are acquainted only with nature's forces, and their effects, too, are limited merely to what nature is capable of. How can that which occurs supernaturally be seen, judged and known by beings of nature?

27:712

Here also is the terrain of necromancy, the special art of prophesying through inspiration of the signs presented by the souls of the dead. It is a branch of *mantica*, or the art of prophesying from given signs in general, which even the Greeks assumed to be possible in regard to things both present and future. They had their prophets, and each of them his *mantis*, a crazed person, whose signs and unintelligible speech they reduced to inspired utterances, and then explained them.

§137. The duties of men toward a certain state, whether, like learning, it relates to meritorious duty, or like the state of perfecting oneself, or of health, or of honour, it has to do with strict duties towards oneself; and likewise the duties towards others in respect of a certain state, which Baumgarten discusses in *Pars II specialis*, are not further explained by Professor Kant, who recommends, rather, that the author should be read on that subject.

DUTIES TO GOD

§138. In order to entertain the concept of religion and theology, it is necessary to assume that a God exists. The theoretical knowledge of Godhood is theology, but the practical knowledge of God is religion. Albeit practical knowledge, or morality, makes reference to theology, or theory. In a brief conspectus of their theology, the ancients pictured the supreme being as (1) a freely acting world-cause, lying outside nature; (2)

[q] strict and relative miracles

a world-cause with free will; and (3) the highest good, or the world-ruler and originator of human laws. Theology, however, was not religion, since it was directed merely to investigating the divine nature, whereas religion took account of human morality.

27:713

Religion is the totality of all human duties as divine commands, and thus it cannot be a totality of man's duties towards God.

It is presupposed, therefore (1) that our laws of duty are thought of as given by a being whose influence has contributed, as it were, in the knowledge of our reason, to provide an output of laws, as they would have to have been framed for the reciprocal fulfilment of our duties. But in no way is the necessity of God's existence taken in an absolute sense; it is hypothetical, merely, and it is certainly not to be supposed that duties should have been prescribed to us as laws given by God.

(2) that we can have no duties towards God. Duties are merely actions that arise out of obligation; actions are effects. Now it is impossible for us to suppose duties present, where we can produce no effect; all duties are reciprocal, and by nature determine the will to a moral conformity of the action with the obligation. God is the law itself, and so cannot have need of morally coercive means in order to move His will; nor can we act upon His will, for it is unalterably certain; or move Him towards us. Action and reaction, and thus the sources of dutiful action, are here at an end; here there is mere obedience in following His duties as His commands, if we give the law a personal form. Hence only human duties are thinkable, to oneself and to others, though the duties themselves are conceived under the image of divine commands.

(3) The objective idea of religion (whose counterpart is reverence for the law, or for Godhood, as subjective religion) lies in that very concept which consists in consciousness of man's obligation to God, and his disposition to act in accordance with the knowledge of his duty. Thus a man has religion if he is aware of his duties, and has the disposition to order his actions accordingly, out of inclination towards these duties. He has no religion, if he either has no awareness of his duties, or no disposition to perform them for the sake of the law, as a command of the supreme being.

(4) Religion is based on reason, is thus possible to everyone, and so requires no theology; on the contrary, it must be founded on the minimum of theological knowledge that can be demanded of men; i.e., so little is there need of great theological or philosophical knowledge for the purpose, that on the contrary, the greatest comprehensibility and easiness must be coupled with the presentation, if it is to penetrate, especially, into the untrained mind. A learned preacher is therefore full of theory, but unsuited to the task, since practical conviction must depend, indeed, on a specially tested correctness of the principles, but also on clarity of presentation. This is harder to achieve than learned theology.

27:714

437

§139. To achieve knowledge of God's commands, it is first of all a question of how we arrive at this knowledge, whether by reason or experience, and so whether we must know beforehand that something is our duty, before it can be viewed as a command of God, or whether we must have experienced God's command in order to know it as our duty, in virtue of our obedience to Him as our superior, and so be led into fulfilling it. On these differing constructions of God's command there rests the narrower distinction between:

a. The religion of reason, which is called natural religion; *rationalis*, because it abstracts from all experience; and

b. revealed religion, or such as properly requires a revelation, or needs to be revealed (*revelanda*); one that rests on empirical principles, whether they be imparted *oraliter,*[r] or presented by way of *indicia naturae.*[s]

Now it can be taken as proved, that all men presuppose the concept of God in their religion, and it is no less generally true that commands, if they are to bind us to duties, are regarded as commands of God. But every true command is morally possible, and so long as there has been no reason to suppose that God has ordered the opposite of it, we are obliged to obey it; but to recognize the given opposite is not possible to us otherwise than by morality or concepts of reason; so that which is presented as a divine command can only be known to us as a duty, and thus a thing can only be God's command, if and insofar as it is a duty for us. It will therefore be more readily possible and needful to know that something is a duty, than to be aware that it is a divine command, and these are the duties of natural religion; whereas duties that are only known to be such because they have first become known to us as divine commands, are called duties of revealed religion.

§140. Religion is thus founded on morality. Now in the latter, the dutifulness of our moral actions appears as *virtue,* i.e., under the disposition to perform all the duties we have, to ourselves or any other world-beings, on account of the obligatory character of the action, disclosed through reason; and this is *virtus.* But in religion our dutiful acts appear under the disposition to fulfil them with observance and regard to divine commands; and this is *pietas.* The Romans did not attach this meaning to the word *pietas;* they understood by it a love, coupled with reverence, that is always felt for superiors, e.g., *erga parentes.*[t] So the term is not suitable here. Godliness is even less suitable, since it means everything that is partly innocuous, and partly useful; godfearingness, *timor dei,* would at first sight be a more apposite term; but one would have to construe *timor dei = reverentia* as awe or supreme respect for the will of the law-giver, as

27:715

[r] by word of mouth
[s] signs in nature
[t] towards parents

438

ground of duty; and *pietas* would then express the disposition to perform virtuous actions in a godfearing frame of mind, representing the highest stage and a pendant to duty, since human duties are here construed as commands of God. The same thing holds also of *peccata*, compared with moral breaches of duty, or vices, *vitia, transgressiones legum moralium*,[u] in that even *peccata* are regarded as breaches of divine commands.

§141. A knowledge of God and His divine nature is attainable by man no otherwise than through acquaintance with the nature of things in the world; that is *natura naturans*, or *natura naturata*,[v] as they call it. It is possible thereby, and without recourse to any knowledge of our duties, to frame a concept of God as the supreme cause of things in nature, and also to discern their purposive connection. But by this we are not yet in a position to conceive of God as a moral being, or to come to know our duties as divine commands. But if we are to come upon the existence of a religion, the latter presupposes, after all, the assumption of a supreme moral being, who, apart from being the creator of the world, would also have to be regarded as a world-ruler and lord over all beings. It emerges on closer examination that morality, to complete itself in its purpose, leads us directly to the assumption of a rational world-ruler. For on considering things in the world:

1. the contingency of things, the mutability of world-beings, and the fact that all things nevertheless together constitute a whole, intimate to us that they all are grounded, as to their origin, in a supreme cause. Reason elicits from us the need to ascend up to a deity as first cause of the world. So in this respect God is *ens summum, ens entium*.[w] It is thus that deism postulates the existence of God, and combines with it the idea of the physical necessity of a supreme universal world-cause, while abstracting from all knowledge of its nature, properties and constitution. (The opposite of this is dogmatic atheism. For sceptical atheism might well agree with the deists to this extent, that both abstract from any knowledge of God, and thus merely suppose the existence of a possible supreme cause of the world, who is unknown.)

2. But if, amid the contingency of things, we simultaneously have regard to the fact that we perceive in them purposiveness, or their combination towards an end, this compels us to suppose a being who is not only *ens summum*, but also acts according to a universal purpose, and thus has *summa intelligentia:* a supremely wise being. To this we are led by physicoteleology, *in specie* natural theology. The origin, growth, perishing and reproduction of plants, for example, the nourishment they give to animals, and that animals give to men, in short, the way things in nature combine

27:716

[u] breaches of the moral law
[v] nature as process, or as product
[w] supreme being, being of beings

towards an end, presupposes the conception of a supremely wise being, whose purposive arrangements we perceive herein. It teaches us that in nature everything leads to an end, whether it be its own end, or the means to a higher one; yet this purposive action and coordination of all parts toward a total world-structure indicates no more than the utmost natural art, a wisdom in the arrangement that is beyond our comprehension. But since, in being determined by free will, rather than instinct, we are not under absolute coercion, and do not even possess thereby a directly known law that would compel us to act accordingly, as the arrangement of nature is brought about by nature's cause, there is therefore no knowing thereby, how God may be able to rank, for free beings, as the legislator of

27:717 their actions. Moreover, the quality of a supremely wise being does not yet necessarily entail the quality of a moral being. For in that case, for example, mere instincts would be operative: men would devour animals, and animals men; every creature would know, and have feeling, only for its physical needs. God, in virtue of His maximal understanding, would thus possess the highest possible theory, and would have applied it, in virtue of his artistic skill, in the pragmatically best manner. But artistic skill does not necessarily have to be combined with morality, in that His product will have arisen merely from speculative reason, and not from that practical reason which must nevertheless be operative in a moral being.

3. In the combination of all ends it is, however, possible to find the sum thereof, to which they serve as means, and this is the highest good of the world, the *summum bonum*, or morality coupled with happiness to the maximum possible degree. Man himself, in virtue of his practical, free-acting reason, is never, indeed, a means to this highest end, but is his own end, in that by morality he makes himself worthy to become happy in due proportion; but this very worthiness is the end that practical reason prescribes to him, and thus the condition of that end that lies within himself. Only if he follows the prescriptions of the morally legislative reason that operates within him, is it possible for him to act purposively, or to become happy, by following his duty and promoting morality. But now because this happiness cannot be attained by his disposition and moral activity alone, since he does not have it in his power to become happy thereby in due proportion, though he has to assume that the laws of morality lead, by their fulfilment, to the highest end, he must therefore suppose a supreme being, having the sum of all ends in His power, and thus possessing the highest reason and living will, whereby He wills a man's happiness in due proportion. This, then, is the supposition of theism, and of theology, to which we are brought solely through morality, and not through physico-teleology.

The ancients assumed of their gods the idea that they were powerful beings, but did not endow them with morality. They took it that men were in the physical power of the gods, and under their dominion; they thereby procured for themselves the reverence due to them, in that they had a

hold over man, who would otherwise rise up against them, treat them with   27:718
unconcern, and no longer serve them. *Sunt superis sua jura,*[x] says Lucan;
the power of the gods cannot be compared with the prerogatives that men
exercise over one another.

The proof of the fact that we must conceive of God as a moral being, in
whom the highest good is united, is not, as such, to be elicited by any
theory, but lies merely in the moral need we have of such a being, that
through the worthiness attained owing to the fulfilment of duty we may
expect from Him also a condign happiness, and so labour thereby towards
the supreme end of God; hence, too, it comes about that we ascribe to the
divine being those moral attributes, whereby His nature is enabled to
promote the supreme end. He is almighty, eternal, immutable and assuredly all-benevolent as well, in virtue of His universal goodwill towards the
human race. This ethico-theological principle has admittedly also been
proposed by Professor Kant in his *Essay on the Only Possible Proof for the
Existence of God;* but he explains that his aim was not to offer such a proof,
but merely to draw from the principle that belief in a deity which our
practical reason must endorse.

Theology, indeed, must be basic to religion, albeit that our need does
not demand any theoretical development of the knowledge of God, or of
His attributes – this being the province of speculative theology – but only
an awareness of what the attributes of the divine nature are worth to us in
a morally practical respect.

The word *religio* cannot be straightforwardly translated in German,
although we substitute the word *Glaube,* belief.

The ancients understood by *religio* what the concept of scrupulosity
seeks to express, so it did not refer to any fully defined object – our
obligation to duty, under the condition of divine prescriptions to be fulfilled. There are, indeed, peoples who neither believe in, know or assume
a god, and so objectively have no belief in anything definite. Such
scrupulosity denoted only that consciousness of the obligation to rectitude
in all avowals, punctiliousness in the fulfilment of this rectitude, in an   27:719
observance of duties, whatever their nature, permitting no violation of
them, even in the slightest degree; yet subjectively the belief may therefore be mistaken, as a subjective conviction of the truth of one's obligation
to duty, and the disposition to act which arises from that.

§142. Religion calls for no speculative requirement, to investigate the
divine nature. It is merely a matter of the divine determinations of His
will. For God has practical influence, in that He is thereby presented as
the supreme legislator. It is theological concerns, however, that have
brought it about that the *principia* of positive religion have been so
variously laid down, in that speculative concepts of that kind have been

---

[x] their laws reign over us

intermingled with the principles of practical religion. Hence deism, atheism, polytheism and monotheism. The Jews, like the Mahomedans, despised the maxims of all other religions, since it was they who were uniquely in the possession of a deity, who alone could rank as God, and for whose sake they believed themselves obligated to hate all other deities.

Spinozism/pantheism. The latter takes the totality of things to be God, as *partes constitutae*[y] in space, wherein things would be modified under shapes, as bodies; Spinozism, however, held that this totality of things is underlain by a unity in God, and that things would be accidents emanating from the unity of substance and the workings of deity. Socinianism/ fatalism, whereby it was assumed either that God has no foreknowledge of human freewill, or that there is no freedom, but only natural necessity. Manichaeism supposed good and evil to exist in the form of divinities. Dippelianism, which denied the *justitia punitiva in deo*,[z] because God cannot be subjected to offence, notwithstanding the breach of human law, and because resistance evinced from the standpoint of rectitude might well be essentially different from giving offence.

Epicureanism: the principle that there is no special foreknowledge, but only a general providence. Its opposite is *praedestinatio*.

It is easy to see that for man there is no way left, but that of fashioning his own God on the basis of morality.

27:720   §143. Love towards God is the foundation of all inner religion.

The maxim of gladly following a law is love for the law itself, which presupposes a liberation from the inclinations that hinder us from following it; and hence we do that very unwillingly, so long as such contrary impulses are still to be found in us, representing an obstacle to be overcome.

To have respect for the law, as a command of reason, already lies in the nature of the case, and in the concept of a law whose observance is incumbent on me; but at the same time it is typical of human nature, that the conception of the law is coupled with an impulse to violate it, and hence there lie in man's nature those impulses that constantly hinder us from following a law with gladness. Thus to acquire a love for the law, and respect for it, and likewise a transplanted moral love and respect for the possessor thereof, is the highest stage of morality.

If we are to think, morally, that we love God, then it is necessary for us to presuppose His love for us, and His will for our well-being, or His loving-kindness. For no return of love can be elicited there, if the command to that effect does not itself arise from moral love. This is also, however, explicable, if we were able to view religion, objectively considered, as the divine legislation of our duties, and to reduce the whole of

[y] constituted parts
[z] God's punitive justice

religion to that; from which it again follows that religion is rooted in the love of God. Now every *potestas legislatoria*[a] presupposes that the law-giver be well disposed towards his subjects, and hence that in virtue of this he intends their well-being; for only through such an intention is he in a position to bind us.

That moral laws are absolutely binding on us seems in no way to involve the will of another, who means us well in imposing them; yet if we conceive of moral laws as commands, the law-giving of the other can be founded only on his loving-kindness, i.e., on the intention of thereby benefitting us, and hence insofar as we look upon God as a kindly, law-giving being, there arises therefrom His kindly will, as the basis of the force that binds us to follow His laws for the sake of our own welfare; and in religion this idea comes to be coupled with the law itself, which does not presuppose this kindliness on the part of a legislator. God's love for us (also expressed by the words: *God is love*) is thus the divine benevolence and kindness toward us, which constitutes the foundation of the *potestas legislatoria divina.* Now to return that love is the corresponding duty of all His subjects, and constitutes the prime source of any disposition to religion. But this love of God can be known only through our reason, and only so can our relationship to God be determined. There can be no sensuous feeling of love without a concurrent pathological effect; to love practically, means merely to perform one's actions from duty; so in love of the law there is no command, and the so-called categorical: *Love God* tells us no more than to base our observance of laws, not merely on obedience, which produces the coercion and necessitation of the law, but on an inclination in conformity with what the law prescribes.

27:721

If we assume, then, that God is the foundation of our whole morality, and the animating moral being in relation to us, His creatures, then within this there lies a triple division of the ideal notion involved:

a. God, as holy law-giver, is an object of respect.
b. God, as kindly sustainer and ruler, is an object of love.
c. God, as righteous judge, is an object of godly fear.

Of all these three powers in the divine constitution, it is hardest to frame to oneself a correct and efficacious conception of the love of God; it is much easier to think of Him as law-giver and judge of the world; but to think, subjectively, of God as a being who, with His all-sufficing power, is benevolent to all creatures and confers benefits upon them, is difficult because it is always a merit to be mindful of the source of benefaction; now though God may do, and have the power to do, as much good as He pleases, the objection is still promptly levelled, that in virtue of His om-

[a] legislative authority

nipotence it costs Him no sacrifice, that in His case there are no obstacles for Him to overcome, as there are with men, and that He therefore does not act meritoriously; we cannot calculate the magnitude of God's power, and so nor can we reckon, either, the degree of benevolence shown to us. Hence it is also quite false to give sensuous form to this Idea, and confer on it a self-subsistent reality. The love of God is reduced to the rational Idea of His commands, and our love in return to the Idea of our duty; from the notion of the sum of all our duties, we ascend to the source of 27:722 laws, and persuade ourselves that He has given them to us out of His goodness; we revere the holiness of His nature, and obey His commands from inclination; and this is God's love, and our love in return, as the highest stage of morality.

Now from the love for God, the second commandment, to love thy neighbour as thyself, is known by inference. God loves all men, i.e., He makes their welfare His end; now in that we make this end of His into our own, we love all men, and since this consists in observing all our duties, and thus primarily the duties to oneself, we love ourselves for the sake of other men, or others as ourself; the self-regarding duties are thus indirectly included here, and the source of all love is the commandments given to us out of God's goodness, which = our duties.

Reverence for God, awe or *pietas* becomes veneration of Him when the respect for His commands is combined with love for Him; and hence arises worship of God, *adoratio,* once the inner veneration of God rests upon a continuous state of mind within us. The opposite to this is idolatry, i.e., the veneration or adoration of an object that is either not conceived to be God, or, insofar as the venerated being is indeed so regarded, is still not coupled with the Idea of a morally living being who requires inner veneration for His laws, but sets store, rather, by outward signs in religion; God being regarded, for example, as an almighty being whose commands to do him honour are concerned with *praestanda physica opera operata,*[b] e.g., sacrifice and other ceremonial rites; these would thereupon take the place of moral laws, and God would be thought of as a political law-giver, without, however, basing that on the morally living being, in whom the *summum bonum* is essentially apprehended; so it would not amount to a religion coupled with the betterment of our moral principles, and our corresponding disposition to fulfil them.

§144. There is a false notion of *God's nature* to be found in the received idea of *imitating God (imitatio, assimilatio dei)*, and in the supposition that man may take on the *likeness of God.*

For what is proper to God as supreme law-giver, is no more appropriate to man as *subditum,*[c] than it is proper to the plant to become similar to

[b] physical performances to be carried out
[c] an underling

the sun, because the latter is the principle of its fertility. God's nature as   27:723
the law itself is incomprehensible to us; all that corresponds to it is
obedience to His law, i.e., the rectitude of our actions in accordance with
His will and His commandments; there can be no thought of any possible
resemblance that might exist between man and God. It is equally incorrect to suppose that God fashioned man from out of Himself; that man is
now indeed corrupt, but that he may yet be restored, and then become
equal to God or turn into a likeness of Him. It is possible to find a
similarity only in the analogy that man possesses in virtue of his reason;
nor has he ever lost this portion, he has only to cultivate it; so there is no
need for any restoration or transformation of man's nature; and he does
not thereby become any likeness of God; he cannot attain to that, and so
all imitation of God is an affectation, a mere sham, which debases the
worth of the Idea of God and is insulting to His majesty.

§145. The first principles of the ethical grounds that determine our
moral conduct lie apodeictically in ourselves, and on these is founded the
concept that we have to frame of God, a concept that hence must also be
in accordance with the moral *principia.* The source of belief in a God is
therefore not theoretical knowledge. The ancients, who wished to discover the divine nature and its properties from theory, found themselves
obliged, therefore, to assume that God has still reserved to Himself certain special perfections, of which men would have no knowledge, in order
to have dominion over the world, and to guide its destinies. As a being of
nature, one may think of God as the mightiest, and it must indeed be
assumed, by the theoretical concept of God, that He is almighty; experience, however, knows of no such object, nor can reason frame any concept
thereof. So only a belief in God is possible, and this must be founded on
morality.

Now a man can make, or profess to, an oral confession of his faith =
opinion, without being honestly convinced, insofar, that is, as the antitheti-
cal doubt about it would not be to his advantage; this is the basis of the
credo, which the external church authority can require of him. But the
sincere or *inner conviction* that we mean by *faith,* i.e., that of the opinion we
grant approval to on closer examination, is then quite different; the conviction that dwells in a man after plumbing the depths of his inner state, and
the confession that he honestly makes only to God, is necessary for moral   27:724
faith. This faith is not theoretical, either empirically or rationally, i.e., the
ground of his knowledge of God is drawn neither from experience alone,
nor from reason alone, and is equally little dependent solely on a mere
insight as to the nature of an actual deity; it is based, rather, on grounds
which are the source of the moral actions of men, and is thus practical. If
an honest moral conviction determines a man, as ground, to his ethical
conduct, the assumed existence of God becomes the motive of his moral
action; he assumes as a practical hypothesis, that if it is true that the

grounds of morality and its laws lead only to the highest end, a supreme being must actually exist, whereby the highest good is possible, in that otherwise the highest end of his moral actions would not be possible. The concept of God therefore presupposes morality, in that God is only conceived as law-giver of morals, as the supreme moral being, as the *ens summum originarium, bonum,*[d] as *natura naturans,* or as the supreme being of nature, so that the concept framed of God shall also be in accordance with the moral faith of the individual man.

Hence it is also quite understandable that every man must himself frame his concept of God accordingly. And it is likewise also necessary in one's practical faith to see in God all those attributes that are needed for realization of the highest end. For by this the conviction grows, that if the moral grounds of determination in my conduct are in accordance with the highest end, I may then expect that the latter will be assured; and this is *fides constans,* or practical steady faith.

§146. True and worthy veneration of God (inner veneration) includes (1) fear of God as a law-giver, i.e., respect for our duty as a divine command; God is seen as a being of the highest *auctoritas,* having all things for furtherance of the final end in His power. This fear must be a binding tribute of honour, not servitude; for in the latter case, dread of evil as punishment would compel us to obey, and all such deviant sensuous motives involve superstition. Equally little should it be pathological, or founded upon interest concerning the harm to be feared in regard to our interest.

27:725

(2) love of God, i.e., the willing fulfilment of His commands from a high regard for His laws. This entails that the observance of God's laws be taken up into our disposition, and that the motive of action lie solely in the veneration due to them.

In this sense it is said that God's yoke is easy; not that it should not be difficult to observe the laws as such, and without inclination; but when once we have acquired a *habitus* in virtue, we love it in that we think well of our good conduct, we recognize its inner worth without coercion or judicial authority, and this awakens an attachment to the law, so that no outer ceremonial exhortations are needed in order to adhere to it. As such there already lies in the nature of the law itself a reverence for it, or estimation thereof, even without its being commanded; but when this is appended in thought, it brings about a veneration for God that is coupled with an agreeable temper of the disposition, and this is the veneration of God with a joyous heart, the cheerful submission to the law which is quite different from that observance of it wherein the law's authority merely brings about a palpable sense of constraint, in which we hate the law as such, but fulfil it with reluctance, or with a downcast heart. Here, by

[d] supremely good creator

446

contrast, virtue is practised with a good grace, with *alacritas pietatis.*[e] It is self-evident, moreover, that such love of God can never be pathological; for in a moral veneration of God, sensibility can never serve as the motive or determining ground for action; and since we thereby expect fulfilment of the highest end, a pathological love would betray an equality or felt unity of the lover with God, in regard to this end, instead of which we in fact are only capable of appreciating the worthiness of God's command, not of collaborating in the production of the highest end; so here an intellectual love is alone to be understood.

(3) respect for God, i.e., a glorification of Him in our person, in that we depict ourselves, in our person, as an example of the highest end, and act accordingly. Since the highest good is the highest end, of which God is the sole creator, we present ourselves, according to the divine will, as an object of the supreme final end, when we act in accordance with His will, and thus make ourselves worthy of this end.

27:726

Man thereby becomes an individual testimony to God, a work that praises its master. The creation of a free being is, indeed, incomprehensible to us; yet the man who through the highest degree of morality also becomes worthy of happiness, and can thus regard himself as subject of a being commensurate with the highest good, remains always an admirable subject, and God, as his creator, still deserves veneration and respect. Totally opposed, in part, to the intellectual love of God, is that fanatical love which consists in the illusion or fancy of a sensuous feeling of divine influence; for if veneration for God is to depend on the worth of the morality of laws, it is easy to see that here there must be banishment of all sensuous feeling evocative of love, to which this illusion is directed; and in part also, the glorification of God through morality is opposed to that arrogance which consists in an apotheosis of humanity in our own person, by virtue of which we imagine a fellowship with God, a social intercourse with Him. This is enthusiasm; for the man, of course, is telling his thoughts to himself, and in intercourse of that kind, all communication and equality are lacking.

Nor is the moral veneration for God to be confused with that whereby a man dedicates God to himself like a gift, in that he freely gives himself powers such as those used in the old anathema (*deo sacratum dominium,*[f] which differs from anathema, as a means devoted to removing guilt due to God's curse).

There are therefore the following errors in divine veneration:

a. Servile fear, which arises from superstition.
b. Fanatical love, i.e., the illusion or fanciful belief in a supernatural feeling of divine influence.

[e] the eagerness of piety
[f] power dedicated to God

c. Arrogance (an apotheosis of humanity in our own person) or the claim to an immediate intercourse, fellowship and social connection with God.

In short, no sensibility may be the motive or determining ground in the morality of divine veneration; moreover, all sensuous feeling of love towards God is enthusiasm, and contrary to morality, since it does not arise out of respect for the moral law, and in fact is adverse to the latter's worth. The love of God cannot be conceived in a pathological sense, since the unity of the end of love for God cannot be produced by feeling, from a similarity thereof. It is merely intellectual, and rests on an appreciation for the worthiness of God's command.

27:727

(4) *Fiducia*, i.e., the moral trusting to God, that whatever is wanting to our final end, insofar as it is not attainable through our own powers, will be made up by Him, for instance, that where morality is strong He will compensate, *pro futuro*,*g* for the want of happiness.

Hence arises *thanksgiving*, i.e., acknowledging to the supreme being that He has lent us the talents to be receptive to morality.

Fiducia carnalis[h] is the opposite of *fiducia moralis;* a sufficing trust in ourselves, or other people, that we may come to participate in the end, without the help of God; – any sort of trust in nature.

Tentatio Dei,[i] a simulated trust in God, whereby we hope to move the divine will to our own purposes; hence the attempt to use God, as we wish, for a means in the fulfilment of our end, without calling upon our own prudence and support. Plainly, the intention here is simply to divert God's wisdom from its end, whereas the petitioner was in fact obligated to align his actions to God's purpose, and then resign himself to the divine decree. All trust creates an obligation, indeed, but with God we cannot thereby instill a motivating ground that requires Him to fulfil our wishes.

(5) *Prayer* contains a wishing or yearning for that of which we are conscious, that it is not wholly in our power. Man has a propensity for quite empty wishes, i.e., those whose fulfilment is either quite impossible in itself, or at least would be unattainable by his own powers; by putting his trust in God, he therefore awaits with longing the fulfilment of his request. There is thus a praying in faith, i.e., a declaration of one's wish, with trust in its fulfilment. In prayer we need to consider more closely:

a. The wish itself. Every wish is impermissible, insofar as there is a lack of any rational ground for anticipating its fulfilment in accordance with the divine wisdom; so the only allowable wish is the *moral* one, i.e., that the petitioner's actions to the desired end be so constituted, that his own conscience may grant him approval, and that, insofar as he may think

27:728

g in time to come
[h] trust in the flesh
[i] trying to influence God

448

himself incapable of achieving it by his own powers, he may hope that God's assistance will be vouchsafed to him. This wish is good in itself, and conformable to morality. But if the object whose fulfilment we await from God, and of which we disclose our hopes to Him, is unattainable for us, or such that there is no reason to expect it from the highest wisdom, then the prayer is unreasonable; hence every *pathological* wish is ruled out, i.e., the request for fulfilment of any physical or sensuous need, with the desire of seeing it effected by God's help, e.g., health, wealth, honour, etc. There is no reason to suppose it an aim of the highest wisdom to satisfy such a wish. God's ends are inscrutable, and we cannot expect to know whether we shall recognize them as good and suitable for ourselves. A prayer for the relief of physical need is never coupled with trust in its assured fulfilment, since it can never be presupposed that the wish will coincide with the divine wisdom, so that we merely make trial of God, e.g., in praying for our daily bread. In itself, though, that is a physically necessary wish, and we have a duty to live. It is to be expected that God will sustain our wish to live, and hence it is not so utterly without reason that we hope for God's goodness, since the wish contains only what is necessary within itself.

A moral wish is one that can be granted. It is well-pleasing to God, since we only wish to see Him amplify what proceeds from our moral disposition, and thus are using the wish only to arouse that moral disposition anew, in full confidence that it is appropriate to God's wisdom to grant it.

b. The declaration of the wish. In itself, the *making of requests to God* is quite useless, since He already sees the inmost dispositions of the heart, and thus the inner determination to the wish is by itself sufficient. The latter, that is, has to do with the spirit of the wish as such, which is distinct from the letter of the prayer. The declaration of the wish to God – the prayer of thanks, praise or petition – is simply the formula which enables a man to make his wish comprehensible to himself, just as we make ourselves intelligible, to ourselves or to others, by means of words; it is not possible for a man to understand himself clearly, if he has not first drawn up the idea from his soul, as if from within. The only thing needed is that in this moral disposition uplifted to God, he should keep in view the spirit   27:729 of the action he is seeking to carry out. By the prayer, he merely makes his moral wish more easy for himself to grasp, merely renders his moral request more active, and awaits from God the strengthening of his powers, but not the fulfilment of his aim, as a substitute for his own efforts. For the particular concern of

c. The aim and purpose of the declaration, is the hope that he will move God to fulfil his wish; but we are only entitled to expect that God will promote our moral welfare, not that He will take charge of it; so our own activity is absolutely necessary as well. Hence the declaration itself can also do nothing more than to reinforce the spirit of the prayer by words (orally or in writing), and *preces orales* must be founded upon *preces mentales.*[j]

OUTER RELIGION *SIVE CULTUS EXTERNUS*

§147. It is properly the latter which may be understood by the term external religion; for a purely outward religion cannot exist, since religion as such depends on the inner moral disposition to carry out our duties as divine commands, and this cannot, in fact, be transformed into expression by means of symbols. Outer religion, however, is the use of external symbols as *signa* of religion, and so if it is not based on inner religion, it is nothing but superstition; it is thereby reduced to sensuous representation, and does not fulfil its purpose, namely, to strengthen, promote and reinforce the inner disposition. So kneeling, *sacrificia*, use of sacraments and outward prayer are in themselves not religion, but merely *signa religionis*. Outer religion is the condition of it viewed in conjunction with a public society, and thus, as it were, under the image of a divine polity, a *status sub imperio divino*[k] in which men, so to speak, have cemented their ties according to ethical laws, namely the *church*. It entails *status publicus* under a supreme moral law-giver, i.e., a theocracy.

The condition is inner and moral, not civic. All men consider themselves as a people of God, united for the practice and promotion of virtue and the ethical laws. It is an invisible Idea, carried out in a visible form. The *imperium divinum* form of a church consists in the fact that all its members are *subditi* of the divine sovereignty, bound together on *principia* of equality, unity and freedom; a moral monarchy. Their unity is the common end of promoting a unified moral disposition, and showing themselves therein as a whole; their laws are those of morality or freedom, and thus they are equal among themselves, and any aristocracy, of bishops, for example, is objectionable. Their outward formalities are symbols that prompt the bringing into view and reinforcement of the moral Idea; in itself no outer religion is possible in theory, since all such knowledge is transcendent, but for the training of a practical disposition it provides an immanent means.

27:730

The service of God is very different from a veneration of Him *per opera operata.*[l] The actions of the former have as their purpose the promotion and maintenance of the moral condition of the church's members; those of the latter are *substituta* for the moral disposition, and are practised in outer actions with the object of thereby becoming pleasing to God, i.e., of

---

[j] oral and silent prayers
[k] status under divine rule
[l] by the doing of good works

usurping the place of the law that needs fulfilment. For example, pilgrimages and mortifications; the belief is, that in these actions there lies such a magical power, that in place of active moral virtue they nevertheless engender a disposition of duteousness pleasing to God, and such that He gives it His favourable assent. It is, however, mere fetishism and superstition, and is just the same as when the Indians on the coast of Guinea suppose of mussel shells, the conches, that they possess a magical power of bringing men every kind of misfortune. Veneration and use of such magical practices, in place of a moral disposition, with the intention of thereby furthering the latter to equally good effect, are nothing but *opera operata*. It is only under the presumption of *opera operata* that *opera supererogationis* or works of superadded merit can occur. They presuppose that *opera operata* fulfil the purpose of substituting for the duty of religion, and thus arises the possibility of doing more than is required, and this superfluity becomes a work of merit for us, and God our debtor; for example, the six-month fasting of the Russians, and the nine-month fasting of the Georgians. The outcome of this is an active banking system, whereby sins are indemnified with God, and past ones wholly paid off, in that God must deduct them till we get into credit.

§148. In regard to outer religion, the universal church is distinct from   27:731
any of the particular sects. The universal, insofar as it is united under a common law-giver, is the Catholic church; this universality of the church is denied by the Protestants, because they cannot unite over the use of the form of outer symbols, and differ again in this respect by reason of differences in country and rulership. The *sectae* are private societies and come together for secret assemblies, which therefore do not belong to the public church. The question whether we have special *praestanda*^m towards God, that are not at the same time duties, is in any case to be answered in the negative. All our dutiful actions are at the same time divine commands, even though in this world they are directed to ourselves and to our fellow-men. As duties, they are actions to which we are obligated, and thus effects that are confined to the world, although the obligation to perform these actions lies outside the world. Reverence towards God is merely the practical consciousness of obligation arising from the divine command. Piety is the acknowledgement of God's will as the *complerens*ⁿ of all commandments to duty. The *Cultus externus dei*, i.e., church-going, is therefore only a means of strengthening the disposition to religion by the performance of actions pertaining to the service; for man as such, in the moral sense, is constantly in the service of God, since he must always be obeying the divine commands, as the spirit of religion. All outward symbolic practice of religion, the maxims of faith, even belief in miracles

^m things to be done
ⁿ necessary adjunct

and mysteries, where historical faith takes the place of knowledge, serve merely to broaden and strengthen the inner side of religion, and to bring it among men.

In practising religion we do not, however, find ourselves in a state of devotion, i.e., in a mood directed to the immediate contemplation of God, and withdrawn from all sensible objects; we would then never have the letter of the law before our eyes, which, without being God, is not possible. Even to be able to align oneself briefly in that direction calls for a great deal of cultivation. A bigot is then one who practises the state of devotion as an *opus operatum*, a hypocrite, and this is not adoration of God, since he lacks the disposition to obey God's commands from respect and love. To let one's light shine before men is a duty insofar as outer actions have the aim of creating a good example for other men, but not in order to provide an *ostentatio pietatis.*[o] The latter, however, is not to be confused with that *pudor pietatis*[p] which consists in a bashfulness about avoiding in one's actions any suspicion of bigotry, since others are much inclined to attribute our actions of devotion to hypocrisy, and nobody likes to be accused of such a thing.

27:732

[o] display of piety
[p] modesty in regard to piety

452

Select Bibliography

In this bibliography we list only items that have been consulted in preparing the present volume. A good bibliography of Kant's works on ethics and of books and articles about his ethical theory is given in Paul Guyer, ed., *The Cambridge Companion to Kant,* Cambridge: Cambridge University Press, 1992.

ADICKES, ERICH. *Untersuchungen zu Kants Physischer Geographie.* Tübingen: Mohr, 1911. Useful information about Kant's lectures generally.

ARNOLDT, EMIL. "Möglichst vollständiges Verzeichnis aller von Kant gehaltenen oder auch nur angekündigten Kollegia," in *Gesammelte Schriften,* ed. Otto Schöndörffer. B. V, Berlin, 1909, pp. 173–344. The most thorough investigation and record of Kant's teaching, year by year.

BECK, LEWIS WHITE. *Early German Philosophy.* Cambridge, Mass.: Harvard University Press, 1969, pp. 382–92. Standard account of its subject, providing an excellent overview of the German background of Kant's thought and a survey of Kant's main works.

BEISER, FREDERICK C. *The Fate of Reason.* Cambridge, Mass.: Harvard University Press, 1987. Very readable study of the developments in Kantian philosophy that led to Fichte.

BRANDT, REINHARD, AND WERNER STARK, EDS. *Neue Autographen und Dokumente zu Kants Leben, Schriften und Vorlesungen (Kant-Forschungen I).* Hamburg: Felix Meiner Verlag, 1987. Contains several studies (listed here separately) useful for assessing the student notes on Kant's lectures.

HENRICH, DIETER. "Hutcheson und Kant," in *Kantstudien,* Vol. 49, 1957–8.

"Über Kant's früheste Ethik," in *Kantstudien,* Vol. 54, 1963. Two pioneering studies of the development of Kant's ethics.

KÜENBURG, MAX, S.J. "Ethische Grundfragen in der jüngst veröffentlichten Ethikvorlesung Kants," in *Philosophie und Grenzwissenschaften,* Vol. I, No. 4. Innsbruck: Rauch, 1925. The first study of Kant's ethics lectures, published just after Menzer's edition of student notes.

LUDWIG, BERND. *Kants Rechtslehre.* Hamburg: Meiner, 1988 (*Kant-Forschungen,* Vol. 2). An edition with a valuable introduction and important textual notes.

MENZER, PAUL. *Der Entwicklungsgang der Kantischen Ethik bis zum Erscheinen der Grundlegung der Metaphysik der Sitten.* Berlin, 1897.

"Der Entwicklungsgang der Kantischen Ethik in den Jahren 1760 bis 1785," in *Kantstudien,* Vol. 2, 1898, pp. 290–322, Vol. 3, 1899, pp. 41–104. Though now outdated, these studies by Menzer were major pioneering investigations of the development of Kant's ethics.

PINDER, TILLMAN. "Zu Kants Logik-Vorlesungen um 1780," in Brandt and Stark, 1987, pp. 79–114. Concerns Kant's logic lectures but sheds some light on the ethics lectures.

SCHILPP, PAUL ARTHUR. *Kant's Pre-Critical Ethics.* Evanston, Ill.: Northwestern University Press, 1938. The first book on its subject in English; useful for translations but otherwise seriously out of date.

SCHMUCKER, JOSEF. *Die Ursprünge der Ethik Kants.* Meisenheim: Verlag Anton Hain KG, 1961. Still the finest and fullest study of the early development of Kant's ethics.

STARK, WERNER. "Kant als akademischer Lehrer," *Wolffenbüttler Studien zur Aufklärung,* Vol. 16. A helpful essay on Kant as teacher.

Nachforschungen zu Briefen und Handschriften Immanuel Kants. Berlin: Akademie Verlag, 1993.

"Neue Kant-Logiken: Zu gedruckten und ungedruckten Kollegheften nach Kants Vorlesungen über Logik," in Brandt and Stark, 1987, pp. 123–64.

"quaestiones in terminis: Überlegungen und Fakten zum Nachschreibewesen im universitären Lehrbetrieb des 18. Jahrhunderts," in *Textkonstitution bei mündlicher und bei schriftlicher Überlieferung,* ed. Martin Stern. Tübingen: Max Niemeyer Verlag, 1992, pp. 90–9. This and the preceding essay contain technical discussion of the texts of student notes of Kant's lectures.

VORLÄNDER, KARL. *Immanuel Kant: der Mann und das Werk* (1924). Hamburg: Felix Meiner Verlag, 1977. An old but rich and full biography.

WARD, KEITH. *The Development of Kant's View of Ethics.* Oxford: Basil Blackwell, 1972. Uses only material available in English.

ZELAZNY, MIROSLAW, AND WERNER STARK. "Über Mrongovius," in Brandt and Stark, 1987, pp. 279–92. Discusses the owner of two of the student ethics notebooks.

454

Explanations of names

We provide here brief accounts of people, places, and events mentioned by Kant in his lectures, and of some doctrines to which he refers. Where we are unable to explain a name, we make no entry. We do not offer accounts of Kantian philosophical terminology. We have drawn on a number of sources for what follows, including the material provided by the editor of the German edition of these student notes, Gerhard Lehmann.

ALCIBIADES (c. 450–404 B.C.): Athenian aristocrat and politician. Educated by his guardian Pericles, he became a follower and friend of Socrates'. After he was condemned to death for wrongdoing in Athens, he fought for Sparta against Athenian rule but later returned to lead unsuccessful Athenian naval expeditions. A man of great beauty and magnetism, he was known as a brilliant politician and military leader but was distrusted for his unscrupulous ambition and dissolute character. He was eventually assassinated. He figures in Plato's "Symposium" and in the spurious Platonic dialogue "Alcibiades."

ANAXAGORAS (mid-5th century B.C.): Philosopher-scientist. One of the earliest philosophers to settle in Athens, he was brought to trial on charges of impiety and treachery but escaped with the aid of friends. Few fragments of his writings survive.

ANTISTHENES (c. 445–360 B.C.): Athenian philosopher, a pupil and friend of Socrates. He is considered the founder of the Cynic school (see below). Only fragments of his writings survive.

ARIANISM: See Arius.

ARISTIDES, known as "the Just" (died c. 468 B.C.): Athenian statesman famous for his rectitude, patriotism, and moderation. Ostracized in 482, he returned from exile in 480 to lead Athens again in war. During the Peloponnesian War he was entrusted with the task of fixing the tribute to be paid by each member of the Delian League.

ARISTIPPUS (4th century B.C.): Philosopher of Cyrene, follower of Socrates and founder of the Cyrenaic school of philosophy (see below). Because of his hedonistic teachings he often figures in others' writings as a stereotypical pleasure seeker. His works were lost.

ARISTOTLE (384–322 B.C.): Greek philosopher who studied with Plato in Athens. He was later invited by Phillip II, king of Macedon, to be tutor to his son Alexander (the Great); he then returned to Athens. His students and followers constituted the Peripatetic school. Aristotle wrote about every branch of knowledge then known, covering logic, physics and its presuppositions, biology, psychology, ethics, politics, rhetoric, and poetics.

Aristotle explains virtue as conduct arising from states of character that are a mean or balance between two bad extremes, as courage is intermediate between rashness and cowardice. His main work of moral philosophy, the *Nicomachean Ethics*, continued to serve as a university textbook well into the eighteenth century. Some of Kant's predecessors at Königsberg taught from it, but Kant did not.

ARIUS (c. 250 – c. 336): The most important of the early Christian heretics, he propagated the view that Christ, God's Son, is not of one substance with God but is a created substance subordinate to the Father. Arianism was declared heretical at the Council of Nicaea in 325.

ATHEISM: The belief that there is no God. Avowed atheism was rare in the seventeenth century, and not common even in Kant's lifetime. It was widely held that atheism necessarily led to immorality. Some of the French *philosophes*, such as Holbach, openly espoused atheism; others, such as Voltaire, abhorred it.

ATTICUS, *Titus Pomponius* (110–32 B.C.): Friend of Cicero's, whose correspondence with him is preserved in the *Letters to Atticus*. A landowner, man of letters, and philosophical Epicurean, he remained neutral among the Roman political parties. He gave sympathy and advice to Cicero in both personal and political affairs. Suffering from an incurable illness, he ended his life by suicide.

AUGUSTINE, *Bishop of Hippo* (354–430): Saint, philosopher, and theologian, born in North Africa. He came to Rome in 383, became professor of rhetoric at Milan in 384, and after coming under the influence of St. Ambrose was baptized in 386. His Neoplatonism greatly influenced later Christian thought through writings such as *The City of God* and the autobiographical *Confessions*.

AUTHOR: When Kant uses this word without explanation, he refers to the author of his textbook, i.e., Baumgarten.

BALMERINO, *Arthur Elphinstone, Lord* (1688–1746): Scottish Jacobite beheaded on Tower Hill in London for his participation in the 1745 rebellion.

BASEDOW, *Johann Bernhard* (1723–1790): German Enlightenment writer whose polemical essays were attempts to expose superstition and defend philosophy. He was an important educational reformer, insisting on physical education for children and on the teaching of German, and emphasizing the need to establish links between academic studies and the world beyond school. *Elementarwerk* (1774) is his fundamental treatise on education.

BAUMGARTEN, *Alexander Gottlieb* (1714–1762): German philosopher and disciple of Wolff. In his *Aesthetica* (1750–8) he initiated the treatment of aesthetics (the theory of the beautiful) as an independent science. He there identified feeling as the ultimate basis for judgment concerning questions of beauty. From 1740 until his death he taught at Frankfurt-an-der-Oder. See Section V of the Introduction to the present volume for a brief discussion of his views.

BAYLE, *Pierre* (1647–1706): A controversialist and historian, he wrote a great *Historical and Critical Dictionary* (1697) in which he attacked many widely accepted beliefs. In other works he argued that a community of atheists would not need to be any more immoral than many Christian communities are, and that the Scriptures must be interpreted so as never to require anything morally iniquitous, such as torture or burning at the stake. Only argument should be used to convert unbelievers to the truth. He made widely known for the first time the proposition that we should test claims about God's commands by the moral principles we already know, rather than take God's commands as tests of moral truth.

BEDOUINS: Arabic-speaking nomadic peoples of the Middle Eastern deserts, particularly in Arabia, Iraq, Syria, and Jordan. They herd camels, goats, and cattle and have a tribal, patriarchal social structure.

BÉLISAIRE: A historical romance by Marmontel consisting of conversations between the aged Roman general Belisarius and the emperor Justinian and his son. Its outspoken political and social views, particularly in a chapter advocating freedom of opinion and religious toleration, caused the book to be condemned by the Sorbonne. The preacher J. P. Hofstede wrote a version of the novel that was published in German translation in 1769. Marmontel, followed by Hofstede, attacks the moral character of Socrates.

BENEDICT, *Saint* (c. 480 – c. 550): Patriarch of Western Christian monasticism. He founded a number of religious communities, including one at Monte Cassino, for which he composed a set of directives for the reform of monasticism. The Rule of St. Benedict (c. 540) was widely accepted as a model for the spiritual and administrative life of a monastery.

BRABANT: The revolt of the people of this province of Flanders led to Philip II's loss of the Netherlands.

BRENNUS: Leader of the Gauls who invaded Italy and captured most of Rome in 390 B.C., allegedly slaughtering the unresisting Roman priests and aged patricians. According to legend, Rome bought its freedom with gold after a six-month siege. Brennus and his army were destroyed before they could flee.

BRUTUS, *Marcus Junius* (85–42 B.C.): Praetor under Julius Caesar's dictatorship and a favorite literary adversary of Cicero, he was persuaded by his fellow praetor Cassius to lead the conspirators who assassinated Caesar in 44 B.C. in order to restore the liberty of the Republic. He committed suicide after being defeated by Octavian and Mark Antony at the Battle of Philippi in Macedonia.

BULENGER, *J. C.* (1558–1628): Jesuit priest, author of *Opusculorum systema*, London, 1621.

CAESAR, *Gaius Julius* (102–44 B.C.): Roman general and dictator, assassinated by conspirators led by Brutus and Cassius. He achieved wide conquests in Europe and Africa, brought about major reforms in Rome, and was enormously popular among the army and the Roman people. But the virtually monarchical power he held, and his evident intention of ending republican government by keeping supreme power within his own family, led to his death.

CALAS, *Jean* (1698–1762): A Protestant merchant of Toulouse who was executed on a false charge of murdering a son who wished to convert to Catholicism. (The son, in fact, had committed suicide.) His interrogation, trial, and execution were carried out with notorious brutality, and his case was subsequently championed by Voltaire. In 1765 the verdict was reversed and Calas's innocence established, inspiring widespread public rejoicing in France and abroad.

CARTHUSIAN: Member of a contemplative monastic order founded in 1084 by St. Bruno. The order was characterized by strict austerity and self-denial.

CARTOUCHE, *Louis Dominique Bouguinon* (1693–1721): Leader of a famous band of robbers, who was finally caught and broken on the wheel. His skill and audacity made him a legendary figure, and he appears in several plays of the period.

CASUISTRY: The application to different cases of accepted moral rules or principles. Books of casuistry were first written to help Roman Catholic priests handle unusual problems brought to them in the confessional. Critics of casuistry, of whom the Catholic Pascal was the most brilliant, thought that it led to evasion of moral requirements and that it damaged the spirit that should lead one to do as one ought. After the Reformation some Protestant casuistry was written, but by Kant's time it was generally identified as a Catholic enterprise.

CATO, *Uticensis, Marcus Porcius* (95–46 B.C.): Roman aristocrat, politician, and Stoic, famous for his stern traditional morality. He was regarded as a champion of the Republic and freedom. An opponent of Caesar and follower of Pompey after the outbreak of civil war, he committed suicide after the defeat of the Pompeians at Thapsus.

CHALDEANS: Ancient Semitic people who ruled in Babylonia. Their contribution to philosophy is discussed in the history of philosophy by Jacob Brucker, *Historia critica philosophiae* (1742–4), a work Kant used.

CHARDIN, *Jean* (1643–1713): Author of travel books on Persia and India. His *Voyage en Perse et aux Indes Orientales* (1711) fostered wide public interest in the East.

CHARLEMAGNE (Charles I) (742–814): King of the Franks, he was crowned emperor of the West in 800. He established his empire through continuous warfare but promoted order, justice, and learning in his realm.

CHARLES IV, *Emperor* (1294–1328): King of France (1322–28), he was known as Charles the Good.

CHREMES: See Terence below.

CICERO, *Marcus Tullius* (106–43 B.C.): Roman orator, statesman, philosopher, and writer of letters, renowned for his patriotic devotion to the restoration of the liberty of the former Roman Republic. His philosophical works on morality and the good life, on religion, and on education were among the first Latin presentations of the arguments of the Greeks. In the *De Officiis*, Cicero reviews all the duties (*officii*) an upperclass Roman gentleman would be expected to carry out. In *De Finibus* he discusses the ends, or goals, of life as the different schools of antiquity understood them; and in the *Tusculanae Disputationes*, he discusses moral psychology. In these and his other works he was forced to create new terms in order to translate Greek technical philosophy. He thereby created a large part of the Latin philosophical vocabulary. His works preserve many fragments from authors whose writings are otherwise lost, and give full if often somewhat superficial accounts of the important schools of thought of antiquity. Cicero was eclectic philosophically, but inclined to Stoic views in ethics. All of Kant's students would have been compelled to study at least a little Cicero before attending university.

CRUSIUS, *Christian August* (1715–1775): German philosopher and theologian. The most prominent German critic of Christian Wolff, he reasserted the view that morality depends ultimately on God's unconstrained will. To Christian Wolff's intellectualism he opposed a Lutheran emphasis on the value of personal religious experience and feeling. Rejecting Wolff's claim that human autonomy and fulfillment arise from the increase of knowledge, Crusius stressed the importance of obedience to God's laws, which are available to all persons through conscientious feeling. He held that we are morally obligated by laws that bind us just because they present God's commands. Our will has an innate grasp of these commands, and its freedom gives us the ability to obey or disobey regardless of our desires and our concern for our happiness. His *Anweisung, vernünftig zu leben* (Guide to living reasonably) (1744) influenced Kant's ethics.

CUMBERLAND, *Richard* (1631–1718): English philosopher, cleric, and antiquarian. His only philosophical work is *De legibus naturae* (A treatise of the laws of nature) (1672), in which he argues against Hobbes from a Christian point of view. He draws on the best science of his day to defend the central Christian idea that love is the core of morality. God's one and only basic law expresses his love of us and commands us to promote the happiness of all rational beings. Ideally, we should do so out of love. Cumberland is generally said to have taken the first philosophical steps in the direction of what is now called utilitarianism.

CURTIUS, *Marcus*: Legendary Roman hero who in obedience to an oracle saved his country by leaping, armed and on horseback, into a chasm that suddenly opened in the Forum.

CYNIC: Any Greek philosopher following the principles of Antisthenes and Diogenes. These philosophers developed no elaborate system or school, but held a range of beliefs clustered around the central tenet that self-sufficiency could bring contentment no matter what fortune brought. The figure of the cynic philosopher wandering through Greece with his stick and knapsack and disregarding all the conventions was a frequent object of literary mockery. Kant sometimes treats Jean-Jacques Rousseau as a modern representative of Cynicism, contrasting his outlook with Stoicism and Epicureanism. See Diogenes below.

CYRENAIC SCHOOL: School of philosophy founded at Cyrene by Aristippus. It taught that the good life consists in present enjoyment. Welcoming all pleasures, the Cyrenaics were more extreme hedonists than the Epicureans, who more cautiously urged pursuit of only those few mild pleasures that will not be followed by painful aftereffects.

DALMATIA: Roman province on the east coast of the Adriatic Sea (part of the territory of Illyria).

DAMIEN, *Robert-François* (1714–1757): A fanatic who attempted to kill Louis XV of France. He was tortured and executed in public for his crime.

DESCARTES, *René* (1596–1650): Philosopher, scientist, and mathematician, one of the greatest influences on the development of modern thought. He wrote on mathematics, optics, natural philosophy, metaphysics, epistemology, and psychology. Although he wrote no formal treatise on ethics, his views on moral philosophy were available in his published correspondence, which was widely read.

DIOGENES *the Cynic* (c. 412–325 B.C.): The first cynic philosopher. His rejection of social conventions and his fanatic espousal of the "natural life" stemmed from his view of happiness as consisting in the satisfaction of basic natural needs. Self-sufficiency can be achieved, he taught, through strict self-discipline, the renunciation of all possessions and personal relationships, and abandonment of the conventional sense of shame (hence the nickname "Dog," or *cynic* in Greek). Diogenes' views were spread by his disciple Crates.

ELEUTHERIOLOGY: See Ulrich below.

ENTHUSIASM: The religious conviction that one is directly inspired by God. The charge of enthusiasm was often brought against members of especially pious sects, both Protestant and Catholic. Enthusiasts were thought dangerous because their alleged personal revelations about the proper direction of politics could make them a threat to civil peace.

EPICTETUS (c. 50–120): Stoic philosopher, born a slave and later freed. He emphasized the importance of achieving independence of the external goods of life through endurance and abstention. His teachings survive in a manual known as the *Encheiridion* and in four books of essays by his disciple Arrian. For Stoic doctrine, see Stoicism below.

EPICURUS (341–270 B.C.): Athenian philosopher, founder of the Epicurean school, who taught atomism and hedonism. By giving scientific explanations of the world in terms of the motion of atoms in empty space, he hoped to free men from superstition and the needless worries it causes. The life of virtue, he taught, is valuable because virtue is the means to happiness. Happiness is the enjoyment of pleasure; but he did not urge us to pursue carnal or other extreme delights. We are, rather, to avoid pain, to limit desire, and to attain tranquility of mind through a proper understanding of, and withdrawal from, the world. He also taught that because after death we do not exist at all, the period after death is no more to be feared than the period before birth. Most of his works were lost, but his views were transmitted by the "Life" in Diogenes Laertius and by Lucretius's great poem *De rerum natura*. Epicureanism was often thought of as the "pig's philosophy," but Kant realized that it recommended only an austere kind of pleasant life, and he praised it for recognizing, as Stoicism did not, that satisfaction of our unavoidable desires is an essential part of the human good.

FLAGELLANTS: Whipping, or flagellating, oneself was considered by some an acceptable religious penance. In the Middle Ages, there were sects that practiced self-flagellation in public.

FORUMS, *inner, outer, and divine:* Terms for distinguishing among judgments of conscience (the inner forum), of courts of law (the outer forum), and of God (the divine forum).

FREDERICK II, *"the Great"* (1712–1786): King of Prussia (1740–86). Considered the model of enlightened despotism, he was associated with the French *philosophes*, especially Voltaire. He was responsible for the reorganization of the administrative and legal system of Prussia and the modernization of its economy. Under his patronage the Berlin Academy became one of the leading European centers of learning. Frederick used French for all his work, as did most of the members of his Academy. He found time and energy to be a substantial supporter of the arts and an accomplished flutist, while pursuing a brilliant and largely successful aggressive foreign policy.

FREDERICK WILLIAM I (1688–1740): King of Prussia (1713–140). He was the subject of many anecdotes concerning his military eccentricities and his Tabaks-Kollegium, a favorite form of evening entertainment in which he and his friends drank, smoked, and indulged in much crude talk and joking. On being told that Christian Wolff taught views that entailed atheism, he expelled Wolff from his domain; Wolff returned only after the king's death.

GELLERT, *Christian Furchtegott* (1715–1769): Prolific German writer of fables, comedies, and verse. In addition to writing sentimental poetry on

God and morality, Gellert published the lectures on moral philosophy he gave for many years as a university teacher. In them he popularized Crusius's views (see Crusius above).

HALLER, *Albrecht von* (1708–1777): Swiss physiologist and writer, regarded as a foremost medical authority in eighteenth-century Germany. Practicing medicine in Bern, he wrote important and widely known works on physiology, as well as poetry and novels. His journal was published in 1787. Kant admired and quoted his poetry.

HELVÉTIUS, *Claude-Adrien* (1715–1781): French materialist philosopher. His argument in *De l'esprit* (On the mind) (1758) that humans are completely determined by their education and environment caused a scandal, and he was nearly imprisoned for it. His *De l'homme* (On man) was published posthumously in 1773. In both works he argued that earthly happiness is the human good and that only the faulty organization of society prevents people from enjoying life much more than they do. Education, he thought, could make us find our own happiness, which we necessarily aim at, in the happiness of our whole society, which morality teaches us to pursue.

HERCULES: Mythical Greek hero famed for his strength and courage, sometimes serving as an ideal of human conduct. He is often pictured carrying a lion skin and a club. A widely circulated tale has him confronted at a crossroads and required to choose between a life of pleasure and a life of virtue. Of course, he chose the latter.

HERDER, *Johann Gottfried von* (1744–1803): German philosopher and literary critic. After studying theology at Königsberg (where he attended Kant's lectures), he wrote treatises on German literature, the origin of languages, and the historical evolution of human cultures. Although he continued to admire Kant the man, he broke away from Kant's doctrines, eventually abandoning the belief in universal standards of reason. He was one of the first to stress the importance of understanding the unique features of different cultures. Kant and he engaged in some published polemics about each other's views.

HOBBES, *Thomas* (1588–1679): English philosopher, political theorist, scientist, and mathematician. He was held to be both an atheist and a believer in the doctrine that all the voluntary actions of humans are selfish. He held that soul as well as body is nothing but matter in motion; and he tried to derive laws of psychology, morality, and politics by building on the laws of physics as he understood them. Outside society, he held, good and evil can only be defined in terms of individual desires and aversions. The state of nature is a condition of war of each against each. The laws of morality are simply the doctrines that teach us how to attain peace. They require us to submit absolutely to a ruler whose wishes will thereupon become the common standard of good and evil. Hobbes was one of the critics of Descartes's *Meditations* and a translator of Thucydides. His works include *De cive* (1642), *Leviathan* (1651), *De corpore* (1655), and *De homine* (1658).

HOFSTEDE, J. P. (1716–1803): Preacher resident in Amsterdam. He wrote *De Belizarius van Marmontel beoordeld,* a criticism of Marmontel's novel *Bélisaire,* and translated the novel into German.

HOGARTH, *William* (1697–1764): English painter, engraver, and aesthetician known for his satiric, moralistic depictions of the dissoluteness of eighteenth-century English society.

HOTTENTOTS: A people of southern Africa subjugated by the Dutch during the eighteenth century. Kant was deeply interested in what we call anthropology and regularly taught about non-European peoples. He is considered one of the founders of the discipline, although he himself never traveled and relied entirely on reports published by those who did.

HUFELAND, *Christoph Wilhelm Friedrich* (1762–1836): Prominent physician and professor of medicine at Jena and Berlin. He wrote medical works for the lay public on health and child rearing.

HUME, *David* (1711–1776): Scottish philosopher, historian, and essayist. His views on epistemology, psychology, and ethics were first published in *A Treatise of Human Nature* (1739–40) and then rewritten in *An Enquiry concerning Human Understanding* (1748) and *An Enquiry concerning the Principles of Morals* (1751). His other major works include the *Essays Moral and Political (1741–42),* the posthumously published *Dialogues concerning Natural Religion,* and a multivolume *History of England.* Hume's general philosophical aim was to explain all of human experience by appeal solely to natural events and thought processes occurring in relationships discoverable through scientific study. Widely viewed as simply an antireligious skeptic, he used his naturalistic accounts of human belief to undercut theistic, supernatural, and metaphysical theories. In ethics he argued that reason can show us at most the means to ends given by desire; and he took moral beliefs to come not from reason but from feelings of approval, given us by a moral sense. We approve, he thought, what we believe to be useful or immediately agreeable, to ourselves or others. He dismissed all alleged virtues that do not contribute to the enjoyment of life, and thought that as people learned more about the deeper causes of approval, they would cease to think of "celibacy, fasting, penance, mortification, self-denial, humility, silences, solitude, and the whole train of monkish virtues" as being real virtues. Kant knew some of Hume's work in German translation.

HUTCHESON, *Francis* (1694–1746): Scottish philosopher and Presbyterian minister. In his *Inquiry into the Original of Our Ideas of Beauty and Virtue* (1725), he argued that morality results from the special feeling with which we respond to benevolence. He considered Hobbes and his followers mistaken in thinking we have only self-interested desires. We have benevolent motives as well; and when we notice these at work, we approve of them. There must be a moral sense that gives us the basic feeling of approval, since it is simple, undefinable, and unique. Hutcheson's acute arguments against Hobbesian psychology, and his support of the emotional nature of our basic moral concept and of a morality of benevolence, were widely influential. Kant owned German translations of Hutcheson's important early writings.

JAMBLICHUS or *Iamblichus* (c. 250 – c. 330): A major Neoplatonist philosopher of the Syrian school. He distinguished between the transcendental and the creative aspects of the One Being of Plotinus's theory (see Plotinus below), held that there is mediation between the spiritual and physical worlds, and incorporated details from Greek and Oriental pagan mythologies into his system.

JOB: The central figure in the Book of Job in the Bible. Job is an upright man who is devastated by endless troubles. When he questions God's justice, he is comforted by friends who assure him that he must indeed be wicked to deserve such treatment. But what he learns is that God is beyond our understanding. He is frequently discussed by those considering the problem raised by the apparent existence of evil in our lives. If there is an all-powerful and benevolent God, why does he permit innocent beings to suffer? Leibniz wrote a major treatise, the *Theodicy*, to answer the question, and Kant wrote an essay arguing that no theoretical solution to the problem can be given.

JOSEPH II (1741–1790): Holy Roman emperor and ruler of Austria (1780–90). A determined reformer, he reorganized the governmental and legal system, mitigated the severity of the penal code, encouraged education, attacked clerical privilege, and abolished serfdom. His expansionist schemes made him feared abroad, but he was forced to abandon many of his reforms after rebellions in his territories.

JOYEUSE ENTRÉE: Charter of liberties presented in 1356 to the duchy of Brabant in Flanders by its rulers. It confirmed that Brabant's liberties were to be protected, including its territorial integrity, its government's right to be consulted on vital matters, and the exclusive right of its citizens to hold public office. This became the model for other charters protecting the liberties of the other Low Countries provinces.

JULIE, or *La Nouvelle Héloïse* (1761): Romance by Jean-Jacques Rousseau (see Rousseau below), told in the form of letters between the virtuous Julie and her tutor St. Preux, who remains devoted to her after her marriage to another. In this drama of sentimental love and dutiful conjugal fidelity, Rousseau attempts to portray human nature in its innate purity, uncorrupted by the influence of civilization. The novel was enormously successful and exerted great popular and literary influence through its depiction of feeling and virtue.

JUPITER: Italian sky god, also considered god of the Roman state and god of protection in battle. He was worshiped under several aspects by various Roman and Etruscan cults.

KLEIN, *E. F.* (1744–1810): Berlin jurist to whose work on freedom and property Kant may be referring.

LA METTRIE, *Julien Offroy de* (1709–1751): French physician and materialist philosopher. His *Histoire naturelle de l'âme* (1745) aroused much public hostility for its apparent subversion of religious belief, and he was forced to flee France after publishing his materialist views in *L'Homme machine* (1748).

LA ROCHEFOUCAULD, *François duc de* (1613–1680): French writer. His *Maximes* (1665) is a collection of several hundred brief comments and apothegms, analyzing the motives of human conduct in terms of self-love or interest disguised under the appearance of virtue. Only by deceiving themselves and others, he held, can people deny that egoism dominates their lives and sentiments. His brilliantly stated views express a Christian pessimism about the effects of original sin. He had a considerable influence on later moralists.

LAW, *John* (1671–1729): Scottish financier and speculator who wrote a treatise advocating the issue of paper money. In 1716 he founded the first French bank, which gained control of Louisiana, and launched a disastrous speculative scheme in France for investment in Mississippi. He fled France after the collapse of the scheme in 1720.

LEIBNIZ, *Gottfried Wilhelm* (1646–1716): German philosopher and mathematician. A political attaché, he traveled widely in Europe, associated with the prominent intellectual figures of his day, and became the first president of the Berlin Academy of Science in 1700. He argued that the only way to explain the apparent connections between mind and body is by holding that there is a divinely ordered, preestablished harmony between what occurs in the mind and what the body does. The world, in his view, is made up of monadic, or indivisible, spirits of varying degrees of complexity. Against those holding that God's will is the origin of the world, he argued that God always acts for a sufficient reason. If God can do several different things, he always does the best. One consequence of this is the famous thesis that this is the best of all possible worlds, lampooned in Voltaire's satire *Candide* (1759). Kant probably had read Leibniz's *Theodicy* (1710) and *Monadology* (1714).

LICHTENBERG, *Georg Christoph* (1742–1799): German writer and physicist, professor of physics at the University of Göttingen and member of the British Royal Society. A frequent visitor to, and admirer of, England, he wrote humorous essays satirizing German irrationality and provincialism. He is best known for his profound and often very witty aphorisms.

LIVIA (58 B.C. – 29 A.D.): Wife of Tiberius Claudius Nero and later of Emperor Augustus, she was known for her intelligence, dignity, tact, and beauty. She gave valued counsel to Augustus and was revered by the Roman people. Later in life she adopted the name Julia Augusta.

LOCKE, *John* (1632–1704): English philosopher and political theorist.

While serving as a physician to Lord Ashley, he was tutor to his employer's grandson the young Shaftesbury. Locke's *Essay concerning Human Understanding* was written during his exile in Holland and appeared in 1690 along with his *Two Treatises on Civil Government*. His views on morality appear primarily in his epistemological discussions. Moral ideas, he argues, are like all other ideas in being derived from experience. He defined good and evil in terms of causes of pleasure and pain. Morality requires obedience to God's laws. Although Locke claimed that there might be a demonstrative science of moral laws, he never produced one.

LOVAT, *Simon Fraser, Lord* (1676–1747): Scottish Jacobite noted for his violent feuds and changes of allegiance. After the Jacobite defeat at Culloden, he was captured, condemned by the House of Lords, and executed on Tower Hill in London.

LUCAN (*Marcus Annaeus Lucanus*) (39–65): Roman poet. His poem *Pharsalia*, dealing with the civil war between Caesar and Pompey, was much admired by Enlightenment writers such as Marmontel and Voltaire for its brave outspokenness against tyranny and for its portrayal of the ideal Stoic statesman. Lucan committed suicide when condemned to death for conspiracy against Emperor Nero.

LUCRETIA: Legendary Roman model of feminine virtue. Wife of Lucius Tarquinius Collatinus, she was raped by Sextus, the son of Tarquinius Superbus. Her confession to her husband of her dishonor, and her subsequent suicide, led to the expulsion of the Tarquins from Rome.

LUCRETIUS (c. 98–55 B.C.): Roman poet, author of the philosophical poem *De rerum natura* (On nature). This exposition of the atomistic and ethical theory of Epicurus aims to free humans of their sense of guilt and the fear of death by dismissing superstition and explaining the material nature of the world and the mortality of the soul.

LUTHER, *Martin* (1483–1546): Founder of the German Reformation. Trained as an Augustinian priest, in 1511 he became professor of theology at Wittenberg University, where his teaching began to diverge from traditional Catholic doctrine. He taught that faith justifies without works, and hence that the mediational function of the Church and the priesthood were unnecessary for individuals to achieve salvation. In 1517 he posted ninety-five radical theses about religion on a church door in Wittenberg. Thereafter his ideas spread throughout Germany, bringing about a revival of popular religious enthusiasm and abandonment of many traditional Catholic practices and doctrines. Luther also was the first to translate the Bible into the German vernacular. Lutheranism developed as a Protestant denomination taking as its principal tenets the views that justification is through faith alone and that scripture provides the sole rule of faith. It holds that human bondage to sin is redeemable only through faith in Christ, and places a strong emphasis on the all-pervading action of God.

Luther held the "voluntaristic" view that right acts are right because God commands them. God's absolute will or absolute decree is unconstrained by any norm independent of him, but once he has willed a specific law, he himself abides by it. This doctrine was taught by leaders of the Pietistic revival of Lutheranism, the religion in which Kant was raised.

MANDEVILLE, *Bernard* (1670–1733): A Dutch physician living in London whose treatise *The Fable of the Bees; or, Private Vices, Public Benefits* (1714) brought him great notoriety. In it he presents human society as flourishing through greed; it is not benevolence, as the moralists think, but the unintended economic consequences of selfish vices and private desires, he argues, that produce public benefit.

MANICHAEISM: Religious doctrine originated by the Persian Mani in the third century, teaching that there are two eternal deities, one good and one evil, locked perpetually in battle.

MARMONTEL, *Jean-François* (1723–1799): French man of letters. A friend and disciple of Voltaire's, he wrote tragedies, comedies, historical tales (including *Bélisaire*), and literary articles in the *Encyclopédie*.

MENNONITES: Followers of Menno Simons (1496–1561), a Roman Catholic priest who joined the Anabaptists in 1536 and organized communities in Holland. Their views stress believers' baptism, a church organization with emphasis on the responsibilities and rights of local congregations, and nonresistance. A large and influential community in Holland in the seventeenth and eighteenth centuries, they are now spread throughout Europe and North America.

MOMUS: Stock literary character – the fault finder who mocks his fellow gods. He is associated with folly and harsh satire, and is often depicted as taking off his mask to reveal the reality underneath appearances.

MONTAIGNE, *Michel de* (1533–1592): French noble, known for his *Essays*, first published in 1580 and continually revised until his death. After serving in various political offices and as mayor of Bordeaux, Montaigne retired to private life and composed essays on a great variety of topics. In them he explores his reactions to conventional norms and manners, and to traditional wisdom about how to live. He comes to skeptical conclusions about almost all claims on these subjects, including morality. People in different parts of the world live by very different moralities; Montaigne can discover no proof that one rather than another is true. In the end he finds that he can accept only the demands that his own nature places on him. Kant admired the *Essays*.

MOSAIC TEN TABLES: Presumably the ten commandments, usually referred to as the two tables of the law.

NATURAL RELIGION: Religion resting not on revelation but on rational inference from evidence available in experience or from a priori truths knowable by all human beings. Revealed religion includes truths that reason alone could not attain, such as the doctrine of original sin and the need for a redeemer. Orthodox Christians have held, accordingly, that natural religion is profoundly inadequate.

NEWTON, *Isaac* (1642–1727): English scientist and mathematician. His theory of the laws of gravitation, expressed in terms of the differential calculus, published in his *Principia* (1687), became the great model of science for the eighteenth century. He was a professor of mathematics at Cambridge University, held a seat in Parliament, and was president of the Royal Society from 1703 until his death. He held that his scientific view of the world supported religious belief.

NIEHBUHR, *Carsten*: Author of a work on Arabia (1772).

NOVAYA ZEMLYA: Two islands in the Arctic Ocean belonging to Russia.

NUMA: See Romulus and King Numa below.

ORESTES: In Greek myth, the son of Agamemnon and Clytemnestra. Brother of Electra and Iphigenia, whose sacrifice by her father caused Clytemnestra to murder Agamemnon in revenge, Orestes avenges his father's death by murdering his mother and her lover, Aegisthus. He then flees from the Furies, is defended by Athena, and is allowed to return to Athens. This saga of the House of Atreus is told by Aeschylus in the plays that constitute the *Oresteia* trilogy.

PAMPHILIAN: A medieval erotic poem written in Latin, the title of which comes from the Greek term *pamphilos*, lover of all.

PANTHEISM: The doctrine that God is in everything and that all things are part of God. Spinoza was taken to be a pantheist, and his pantheism was held to be equivalent to atheism.

PAUL, *Saint*: Known as the Apostle of the Gentiles, he was born of Jewish parents in Tarsus, became a rabbi in the Pharisee sect, and then while traveling to Damascus to engage in persecution of Christians he was converted by a vision of Christ. After extensive travels and preaching in Asia Minor, he was executed in Rome under Nero's orders. His New Testament works include the epistles to the Galatians, Romans, and Corinthians (I and II); there is scholarly dispute concerning his authorship of other epistles attributed to him. Kant refers to a passage in Romans 2:14–15: "For when the Gentiles, which have not the law, do by nature the things contained in the law, these, having not the law, are a law unto themselves: Which shew the work of the law written in their hearts, their conscience also bearing witness, and their thoughts the meanwhile accusing or else excusing one another."

PERITHÖOS: In classical mythology, son of Ixion, king of the Lapiths. At the feast for his wedding to Hippodamia, their guests the Centaurs tried to carry off the bride and the other women. The event is depicted in Greek friezes on the Parthenon and the temple of Zeus at Olympia.

PIETISM: A form of Lutheranism (see Luther above) that stresses individual spiritual development and emotional commitment to the truths of

Christianity rather than purely rational attachment to doctrine. Divine grace, and moral virtue springing from love of God and man, mattered more to pietists than observance of any external forms of worship. Kant's family was pietistic.

PLATO (c. 429–347 B.C.): The first Greek philosopher of whose written work a great deal survives. Through his writings, more than through those of any other Greek, we learn about Socrates' life and thought; and his *Republic* was the first systematic study of moral and political thought. Kant has little to say about Plato.

PLINY *the Elder* (23–79): Roman warrior, statesman, and scholar. He wrote on history, rhetoric, and equestrianism, but only his *Natural History* survives.

PLINY *the Younger* (c. 61 – c. 112): Roman administrator and author of nine books of literary letters describing the high society of contemporary Rome.

PLOTINUS (205–270): Greek philosopher and founder of Neoplatonism. In his *Enneads*, philosophical essays collected by his pupil Porphyry, he depicts the universe as a chain of being in which reality emanates from higher to lower levels. At the top of the hierarchy is supreme goodness (identified with the Platonic Idea of the Good), which is the one wholly real Being. This Being overflows in love, thus creating the rest of the world; but the amount of reality diminishes at each descending level. Through self-purification and love, Plotinus holds, humans can achieve transcendent unity with the One.

PULSERRO: According to Islam this is the bridge to Paradise, narrow as the edge of a sword, which only the virtuous can cross. Kant uses an old form of the name; it is properly called Al-Serat.

PYLADES: In Greek myth, Orestes' friend who accompanied him in his travels and helped in his revenge slaying of Clytemnestra and Aegisthus. He later killed Achilles' son Neoptolemus at Delphi and married Orestes' sister Electra.

PYTHAGORAS (6th century B.C.): Early Greek astronomer, magician, and religious leader. It is uncertain what he wrote, but he attracted many followers who accepted his mode of life and his doctrines, which include the transmigration of souls, reincarnation, and the view that the rational soul can eventually free itself of the prison of the body through following a regimen of austerity. He is also linked to discoveries in astronomy, music, and the theory of numbers and proportions.

ROMULUS AND KING NUMA: In legendary Roman history, Romulus and Remus were twin sons of the god Mars and the mortal Ilia. Romulus founded Rome and was proclaimed divine after being enveloped in a cloud during a thunderstorm. Numa Pompilius succeeded Romulus to become the second king of Rome and had a long and peaceful reign.

ROUSSEAU, *Jean-Jacques* (1712–1778): Swiss philosopher, novelist, and man of letters. He was a central figure in French intellectual life during the

Enlightenment. After beginning as a contributor to Diderot's *Encylopédie*, he turned into an outspoken critic of many of the *philosophes* and their ideas. His *Discours sur les sciences et les arts* (1750) attacked the idea that increased cultivation of the mind is always beneficial and championed the natural goodness of humankind; his *Discours sur l'origine de l'inégalité* (1755) contrasted the virtue and liberty of primitive man with the decadent corruption of contemporary society; *La Nouvelle Héloïse* (1761) and *Emile* (1762) dealt with virtue and the cultivation of sentiment; and he developed a radical theory of political freedom and government in his *Du contrat social* (1761). Kant was profoundly influenced by his work.

ST. PIERRE, *Abbé de* (Charles-Irénée Saint-Pierre) (1658–1743): French economist and political thinker. He designed many projects of political and economic reform and was an outspoken critic of the administration of Louis XIV. Though respected by Montesquieu, he was often ridiculed by contemporaries who thought his plan for a world organization to ensure perpetual peace was absurd.

SAN BENITO: The costume, named after St. Benedict, worn by those about to be burned to death by the Inquisition for holding heretical religious beliefs.

SARDANAPALUS (669–640 B.C.): King of Assyria. He was a noted patron of art and letters, and his reign marked the height of Assyrian flourishing.

SCHILLER, *Johann Christoph Friedrich* (1759–1805): German poet, dramatist, and historian, one of the greatest German Romantic playwrights, and a chief figure of the *Sturm und Drang* period. His plays deal with themes of personal and political freedom and responsibility and are often critical of political despotism. *Die Thalia* was a periodical Schiller published from 1785 to 1793, chiefly as a vehicle for his own plays, fictions, and philosophical works. In poems and essays, he criticized some of Kant's moral views.

SCHMETTAU, *Karl Christian Graf von* (1696–1759): Prussian field marshal who defended Dresden against the Austrians in 1759.

SENECA, *Lucius Annaeus* (c. 4 B.C. – 65 A.D.): Roman orator, Stoic philosopher, and tragedian. Tutor and then adviser to Emperor Nero, he later was accused of being involved in a conspiracy and was forced to commit suicide. His dialogues, treatises, letters, and verse tragedies are all efforts to teach how to give reason control of the passions and thus to achieve a Stoic indifference to fortune.

SHAFTESBURY, *Anthony Ashley Cooper, Third Earl of* (1671–1713): English politician and writer. In his philosophical views he was a deist opposed to religious enthusiasm, and a sentimental moralist opposed to the pessimistic, hedonistic views of human nature held by Hobbes and Locke. His *Inquiry concerning Virtue, or Merit* (1699) argues that humans have an innate "moral sense," which distinguishes right from wrong by discerning the beauty or ugliness of sentiments and affections. As the individual's own good is included in the welfare of society, there is no conflict between them. True virtue, however, consists in a proper harmony or balance of all our desires, with disinterested affection for the good of others having a substantial predominance. His views influenced later moralists of the eighteenth century.

SMITH, *Adam* (1723–1790): Scottish moral philosopher and political economist. Although he was influenced by Hutcheson and Hume (see above), his *Theory of the Moral Sentiments* (1759) argues that moral approval and disapproval do not arise from a special sense. Our power of sympathy enables us to feel what others feel; and when we find that we would feel just what they do, were we in their situation, we approve of their feelings, and of actions springing from them. Kant admired this work, which was published in a German translation in 1770. In *An Inquiry into the Nature and Causes of the Wealth of Nations* (1776), Smith works out a theory of economic conduct in which he argues that the competitive pursuit of individual self-interest is capable of bringing about a harmonious and prosperous public order.

SOCRATES (469–399 B.C.): Athenian philosopher. Although there is no record that he wrote anything, we know about him through Xenophon's *Socratic Memorabilia* and Plato's dialogues, the earlier ones of which are considered to present Socrates' methods and ideas in their purest form. Xenophon claims that Socrates was the first philosopher to turn away from speculation about the nature and origins of the universe and take up moral and political concerns instead.

SPALDING, *Johann Joachim* (1714–1804): Liberal Lutheran pastor and ecclesiastical statesman. He had a distinguished career in Berlin and was then confessor to the queen of Prussia. A leading exponent of Neology (a rationalist Lutheran doctrine), he held that revelation revealed only what experience would find reasonable; hence there was no essential need for revelation. He published sermons as well as a German translation of Shaftesbury.

SPINOZA, *Baruch* (1632–1677): Dutch philosopher of Portuguese Jewish descent. In his *Tractatus theologico-politicus* (1670) and his posthumously published *Ethics*, he expounds a rationalist metaphysical system providing a comprehensive explanation of the place of humankind in the universe. His doctrine identifies God and Nature as one substance of whose infinite attributes only thought and extension are comprehensible to us. Because he held that God and Nature are one, he was taken, in the eighteenth century, to be an atheist and a materialist. In his moral theory he teaches that happiness consists in making progress toward becoming like God, and that there is no conflict between attaining happiness for oneself and helping others to attain it.

STOICISM: A comprehensive philosophical doctrine developed in Hellenistic times and transmitted by Cicero and Seneca, who admired it, and by Plutarch, who did not. Founded by Zeno (334–262 B.C), whose writings do not survive, its basic doctrine is that the universe is governed by a divinity who steers all things for the good. Hence nothing ill can happen to anyone. We mistakenly fear various events, but if we knew the full truth, we would simply accept whatever happens. Virtue is the highest good. It consists in the state of mind that results from complete knowledge of all things and their necessity; satisfaction of desire and enjoyment of pleasure are not needed for a completely good life. The Stoic sage who attains virtue will live the life of a dutiful citizen, marry and beget children, and participate in affairs of state; but he will never be disturbed by feelings about what he does or those with whom he lives. Kant knew about Stoicism from Cicero and Seneca. He refers to it frequently with admiration, although he does not discuss it at any great length. The Stoics, he thought, were the first to see clearly that virtue is not simply a means to happiness, and that one must be virtuous before one is entitled to be happy; but they were mistaken in thinking that virtue alone could suffice as the whole human good.

TALAPOINS OF PEGU: Buddhist monks of Pegu, an important religious center in Burma, which was destroyed by the Chinese in 1535.

TARTAR: Name applied to nomadic tribes inhabiting the steppes of central Asia. They invaded Europe in the early thirteenth century.

TERENCE (c. 190–159 B.C.): Roman writer of comedies. His plays were much admired by Cicero and Horace and continued to be read in the Middle Ages and after. In *Heautontimorumenos* (The Self-Tormentor), the character Chremes speaks the well-known line: "I am a man; I count nothing human foreign to me."

THALIA: See Schiller above.

THESEUS: Legendary hero of Attica. Son of Aegeus, king of Athens, he lifted a rock to find his father's sword and sandals. He volunteered to be one of the youths sent as Athens's tribute to King Minos of Crete. Once there, he slew the Minotaur in the Labyrinth and escaped with the aid of the thread given him by Minos's daughter Ariadne. On his return he became king of Athens.

TORQUEMADA, *Tomas de* (1420–1498): Spanish Grand Inquisitor. A Dominican prior and confessor to Ferdinand and Isabella of Spain, he was appointed Grand Inquisitor in 1483 and told to rid the country of Jews and Mohammedans who pretended to be Christians. His notorious methods included torture in judicial procedures and the burning alive of heretics.

TRIDENTINE COUNCIL, *or* COUNCIL OF TRENT: A series of ecclesiastical conferences held between 1545 and 1563, inspired by the spread of Protestantism and the urgent need for moral and political reform within the Roman Catholic Church. Convoked in Trent by Paul III, its decrees were confirmed and summarized in 1563 by Pius IV in his "Profession of the Tridentine Faith," also known as the Creed of Pius IV. The council sought a solid basis for the renewal of Church discipline and religious life, formulated a clear doctrinal system, and enhanced the religious strength of the Church in its struggle against the Reformation.

ULPIAN (Domitius Ulpianus) (d. 228): Roman jurist who summarized earlier legal writings in his nearly 280 books, none of which survives. Much of Justinian's later codification of law in the *Digest* is taken from Ulpian's works. In I.I.19, Ulpian is quoted as saying, "Justice is a constant, unfailing disposition to give everyone his legal due. The principles of law are these: Live uprightly; injure no man; give every man his due" (*The Digest of Justinian*, trans. Charles Henry Monro, Cambridge: Cambridge University Press, 1904, vol. I, p. 5). Kant quotes these at 27:280, and 27:527 and discusses them there and elsewhere.

ULRICH, *Johann August Heinrich* (1746–183?): Author of *Eleutheriologie oder über Freiheit und Notwendigkeit* (Eleutheriology; or On freedom and necessity) (1788).

VOLTAIRE (François-Marie Arouet) (1694–1778): French poet, novelist, historian, moralist, dramatist, and critic. A freethinking deist and relentless critic of the despotic cruelty and traditionalism of the ancien régime, he was also a lifelong opponent of established religion and of religious intolerance. The works of satire and rational criticism that established him as the leader of the Enlightenment include his tales "Zadig" and *Candide*, his *Lettres philosophiques* and *Dictionnaire philosophique*, and innumerable pamphlets, essays, and historical studies.

WIELAND, *Christoph Martin* (1733–1813): German writer of poetry, fiction, and criticism expressing rationalistic Enlightenment views. He tried to improve the flexibility and grace of the German language. His novel *Agathon* (1766–7) draws on many of the views of the British moralists.

WOLFF, *Christian, Freiherr von* (1679–1754): German philosopher and mathematician. He was the most influential philosopher of the early German Enlightenment. In works on logic, metaphysics, ethics, politics, and natural philosophy he systematized and expanded the views of Leibniz (see above). His views are discussed in the Introduction to this volume.

XENOPHON (c. 428 – c. 354 B.C.): Greek aristocrat, general, and writer. An Athenian general who was exiled to Sparta for many years, he returned to Athens at the end of his life. One of the most prolific writers of antiquity, his works include *The Spartan Constitution*, the *Anabasis*, the *Apology, Socratic Memorabilia, Oeconomicus*, and the *Symposium*.

YOUNG PRETENDER (Charles Edward) (1720–1788): The last serious Stuart claimant to the British throne, and leader of the unsuccessful Jacobite rebellion of 1745–6. Grandson of the exiled Catholic King James

II, he landed in Scotland in July 1745 with a small invasion force aiming to reclaim the crown. They raised a Highland revolt and marched into England toward London, but were outnumbered, forced to retreat, and finally defeated by the British forces. Charles Edward escaped to France in 1746 and subsequently became a national hero of Scotland.

ZENO (334–262 B.C.): Greek philosopher of Citium in Cyprus, who founded Stoicism (see above).

German-English glossary

This list is almost entirely confined to words of German origin. It omits cognate forms, e.g., verbs, and adaptations from Latin – *Moralität, Malevolenz,* etc. – which self-evidently resemble their counterparts in English.

Abbitte:	apology
Aberglaube:	superstition
Abgötterei:	idolatry
Abhaltung:	restraint
Abscheulichkeit:	abhorrence, aversion
Absicht:	intent
Abtragung:	discharge (of debt)
Abwürdigung:	degradation
Achtsamkeit:	vigilance, watchfulness
Achtung:	respect
Anbetung:	prayer, worship
Andacht:	devotion
Andächtelei:	zealotry
angenehm:	pleasant
Anhänglichkeit:	affinity, attachment
Anlockung:	inducement
Anmassung:	pretension
Anmut:	charm, comeliness
Annehmlichkeit:	amenity
Anschauung:	intuition
Anspruchslosigkeit:	unpretentiousness
Anständigkeit:	decorum
Anstoss:	stumbling-block
Antrieb:	impulse, incentive
Arbeitsamkeit:	diligence, industry
Arglist:	cunning
Armut:	poverty
Artigkeit:	civility
Aufgeblasenheit:	conceit
Aufopferung:	sacrifice
Aufrichtigkeit:	honesty

475

Aufschneiderei:	bragging
Ausübung:	exercise, execution
Barmherzigkeit:	compassion
Bedingung:	condition
Bedürfnis:	need
Beerbung:	inheritance
Befehl:	order
Befriedigung:	satisfaction
Befugnis:	authority, entitlement
Begebenheit:	occurrence
Begehrung:	desire
Begehrungsvermögen:	faculty of desire
Begierde:	desire
Begnadigung:	pardon
Beharrlichkeit:	persistence
Behutsamkeit:	caution
Beifall:	approval, assent
Beistand:	counsel, help
Bekehrung:	conversion
Bekenntnis:	confession
Belehrung:	instruction
Beleidigung:	injury
Belohnung:	reward
Beobachtung:	observance
Berauschung:	intoxication
Beschaffenheit:	constitution, nature
Beschäftigung:	occupation
Bescheidenheit:	modesty
Beschimpfung:	affront
Beschluss:	resolution, resolve
Beschwerlichkeit:	hardship
Besitz:	possession
Besorgnis:	apprehension
Beständigkeit:	steadiness
Bestechung:	bribery
Bestimmung:	determination
Bestrafung:	punishment
Betrübnis:	distress
Betrug:	betrayal, cheating
Beurteilung:	judgement
Beweggrund:	motivating ground
Bewegungsvermögen:	motor capacity
Bilderdienst:	idolatry

Bildung:	training
Billigkeit:	equity, fairness
Billigung:	appraisal
Blutdürstigkeit:	bloodthirstiness
Bonität:	goodness
Bösartigkeit:	malignity
Bosheit:	wickedness
bühlerisch:	amorous, ingratiating
Büssung:	penance
Demut:	humility
Dienst:	service
Dienstaufkündigung:	dismissal from service
Dienstbefliessenheit:	helpfulness
Dijudication:	appraisal, decision
Dreistigkeit:	insolence
Duldsamkeit:	indulgence
Ebenbild:	likeness
Ehe zur linken Hand:	morganatic marriage
Ehrbarkeit:	honorableness
Ehrbegierde:	ambition, craving for honour
Ehre:	honour
Ehrerbietung:	veneration
Ehrfurcht:	awe, reverence
Ehrlichkeit:	honesty
Ehrsüchtigkeit:	ambition
Eidesleistung:	oath-taking
Eifer:	zeal
Eifersucht:	jealousy
Eigendünkel:	self-conceit
Eigennutz:	self-interest
Eigensinn:	self-will
Eigentum:	property
Einbildungskraft:	imagination
Einstimmung:	consent
Eitelkeit:	vanity
Ekel:	disgust, revulsion
Elend:	wretchedness
Empfänglichkeit:	receptivity
Empfindung:	feeling, sensation
Entbehrlichkeit:	doing without, frugality
Entbehrung:	abstinence
Enthaltsamkeit:	temperance

Entledigung:	absolution
Entsagung:	renunciation
Entschädigung:	requital
Entschluss:	decision
Erbauung:	edification
Erdichtung:	fabrication
Erfahrung:	experience
Ergänzung:	fulfilment
Ergötzlichkeit:	diversion
Erhabenheit:	sublimity
Erhaltung:	preservation
Erkenntlichkeit:	gratitude
Erkenntnis:	knowledge
Erlaubnisgesetz:	permissive law
Erniedrigung:	abasement, demeaning
Ersatz:	compensation
Erstattung:	requital
erweiternd:	ampliative
Erwerbung:	acquisition
Erziehung:	education
Fähigkeit:	capacity, talent
Fasslichkeit:	comprehensibility
Faulheit:	laziness
Feigheit:	cowardice
Feindschaft:	enmity
Feindseligkeit:	enmity, hostility
Festigkeit:	firmness
Festsetzung:	decision
Filz:	stinginess
Frechheit:	impudence
Freiheit:	freedom
Freimütigkeit:	candour
Freundlichkeit:	friendliness
Freundschaft:	friendship
friedfertig:	peace-making
friedliebend:	peace-loving
Fröhlichkeit:	cheerfulness
Frömmelei:	bigotry
Frömmigkeit:	godliness, piety
Frömmler:	hypocrite
Fürwahrhaltung:	presumption

Gebot:	command
Gebrechlichkeit:	frailty
Geduld:	patience
Gefälligkeit:	complaisance
Gefrässigkeit:	gluttony
Gefühl:	feeling, sensation
Gehorsamkeit:	obedience
Geisselung:	scourging
Geiz:	avarice, miserliness
Gelehrsamkeit:	learning
Gelindigkeit:	gentility
Gemächlichkeit:	indolence
Gemüt:	mind
Gemütsbewegung:	emotion
Genauigkeit:	punctiliousness
Genügsamkeit:	sufficiency
Gerechtigkeit:	rectitude
Gericht:	sentence, verdict
Geringfügigkeit:	insignificance
Geschäftigkeit:	busyness
Geschicklichkeit:	skill
Geschlechtsneigung:	sexual impulse
Geschliffenheit:	politeness
Geschmack:	taste
Geselligkeit:	sociability
Gesetz:	law
Gesetzgebung:	jurisdiction, law-giving
Gesetzmässigkeit:	lawfulness
Gesinnung:	disposition
Gesprächigkeit:	garrulity
Geständnis:	admission
Gewahrsam:	custody
Gewalt:	power
Gewalttätigkeit:	brutality, violence
Gewissen:	conscience
Gewissenhaftigkeit:	conscientiousness, scrupulosity
Gewissensbiss:	pangs of conscience, remorse
Gewohnheit:	custom, habit
Giftmischerei:	poisoning
Glaube:	belief, faith
Glaubwürdigkeit:	credibility
Gleichgültigkeit:	indifference
Gleichheit:	equality

Gleichmütigkeit:	equanimity
Gliedergemeinschaft:	conjugal relation
Glückseligkeit:	happiness
Gottseligkeit:	godliness
Grausamkeit:	cruelty
Grausen:	horror
Grobheit:	coarseness
Grossmut:	generosity, magnanimity
Grübelei:	brooding
Gunst:	favour, grace
Gunstbewerbung:	courting favour
Gutartigkeit:	benignity, kindheartedness
Güte:	goodness
Gütigkeit:	benevolence, kindliness
Habsucht:	avarice, cupidity
Hahnrei:	cuckoldry
Handlung:	act, action
Hang:	inclination, tendency
Härte:	severity
Hartherzigkeit:	hardheartedness
Hass:	hatred
Heiligkeit:	holiness
Heiterkeit:	cheerfulness
Heuchelei:	hypocrisy
Hindernis:	impediment
Hinlänglichkeit:	adequacy, sufficiency
hinterlistig:	cunning, insidious
Hochachtung:	reverence
Hochmut:	pride
Hoffart:	haughtiness
Höflichkeit:	civility
Inbegriff:	totality
Jachzorn:	hot temper
Kaltblütigkeit:	cold-bloodedness
Kaltsinnigkeit:	frigidity
Kargheit:	parsimony
Ketzerei:	heresy
Keuschheit:	chastity
Kleinmütigkeit:	despondency
Klugheit:	prudence

480

Kränkung:	injury
Kühnheit:	boldness
Kunstfähigkeit:	artistic skill
Kunstweisheit:	artistry
Laesion:	injury
Lässigkeit:	indolence
Last:	vice
Lasterhaftigkeit:	villainy
Lauterkeit:	integrity
Leckerhaftigkeit:	daintiness
leichtgläubig:	credulous
Leichtigkeit:	ease, readiness
Leidenschaft:	passion
Leidlichkeit:	toleration
Leutseligkeit:	affability, courtesy
Liebe:	love
Lieblichkeit:	amiability
Lieblosigkeit:	callousness
Lossprechung:	acquittal
Lügenhaftigkeit:	mendacity
Lust:	pleasure
Lüsternheit:	greediness
Luxuries:	luxury, sumptuousness
Luxus:	self-indulgence
Maasstab:	standard, yardstick
Mässigkeit:	moderation, temperance
Menschheit:	humanity
Menschlichkeit:	humaneness
Mercurius:	right to sell
Meuchelmord:	assassination
Missbehagen:	discomfort, feeling unwell
Missfallen:	aversion, misliking
Missgunst:	enviousness, grudging
Missgünstigkeit:	jealousy
Misstrauen:	mistrust
Mitgefühl:	sympathy
Mitleid:	pity
Mittel:	means
Munterkeit:	vivacity
mürrisch:	morose
Musse:	leisure
Müssigkeit:	idleness

Mutlosigkeit:	timorousness
Mutwillen:	mischief, wantonness
Nachahmung:	copying
Nacheiferung:	emulation
Nachfolge:	imitation
Nachgeben:	compliancy
Nachlässigkeit:	negligence
Nachsicht:	leniency
Nachteil:	damage, detriment
Narrheit:	folly
Neid:	envy
Neigung:	inclination
Niederträchtigkeit:	self-abasement
Notdurft:	necessity of life
Notfall:	emergency
Nötigung:	constraint, necessitation
Notwendigkeit:	necessity
Nutzen:	utility
Obergewalt:	supremacy
Oberherrschaft:	command, governance, mastery
Obrigkeit:	authority
Obtrectation:	disparagement
Offenbarung:	revelation
Offenherzigkeit:	frankness
Ohrenbläser:	scandalmonger, slanderer
Peinlichkeit:	carefulness
Pflicht:	duty
Pöbel:	rabble
Pravität:	depravity
Probierstein:	touchstone
Pünktlichkeit:	punctiliousness
Rabulist:	pettifogger
Rachbegierde:	vengefulness
Rache:	revenge
rächend:	retributive
Rechthaberei:	dogmatism
Rechtschaffenheit:	righteousness
Rechtsgenugtuung:	quittance, satisfaction
Rechtskräftigkeit:	legality
Rechtsmässigkeit:	lawfulness

Redlichkeit:	honesty
Regel:	rule
Regellosigkeit:	lawlessness
Regelmässigkeit:	regularity
Reinigkeit:	cleanliness
Reinlichkeit:	purity
Reiz:	attraction, charm, incentive
Richtschnur:	guideline
Roheit:	crudity
Ruchlosigkeit:	impiety, infamy
Rüge:	censure, reprimand
Sanftmut:	mildness
Schadenfreude:	malicious glee
Schädlichkeit:	injuriousness
Schamhaftigkeit:	bashfulness, diffidence, modesty
Schändlichkeit:	infamy
Schätzung:	esteem
Schicklichkeit:	propriety
Schlauigkeit:	cunning, shrewdness
Schmälerung:	diminution, infringement
Schmarotzer:	parasite, sponger
Schmeichelei:	flattery, ingratiation, sycophancy
Schüchternheit:	diffidence, shyness
Schuldigkeit:	guilt, indebtedness, liability
Schwärmerei:	enthusiasm, fanaticism
Schwatzhaftigkeit:	chattiness
Schwelgerei:	revelry
Schwermütigkeit:	morbidity
Selbstängstigung:	self-anguish
Selbstbeherrschung:	mastery
Selbsterforschung:	self-examination
Selbstgunst:	self-favour
Selbstliebe:	self-love
Selbstmord:	suicide
Selbstprüfung:	self-testing
Selbstschätzung:	self-esteem
Selbstständigkeit:	self-sufficiency
Selbstsucht:	self-seeking
Selbstverläugnung:	self-denial
Selbstzufriedenheit:	self-satisfaction
Seligkeit:	blessedness
Sinnlichkeit:	sensibility
Sittlichkeit:	morality

483

Sittsamkeit:	modesty
Sonderling:	eccentric
Sparsamkeit:	thriftiness
Spötterei:	mockery, scoffing
Sprachhaftigkeit:	loquacity
Sprachlosigkeit:	taciturnity
Stolz:	pride
Strafbarkeit:	punishability
Straffälligkeit:	culpability
Strafgerechtigkeit:	punitive justice
Strenge:	rigour
Tadel:	blame, censure
tadelhaft:	blameworthy
Täuschung:	deception, delusion
Tierheit:	animality
Tollkühneit:	recklessness
Torheit:	stupidity
Trägheit:	indolence
Treulosigkeit:	betrayal, faithlessness
Trieb:	urge
Triebfeder:	motive
Trost:	consolation
Tugend:	virtue
Überdrüssigkeit:	satiation
Übereinstimmung:	agreement, conformity
Übermut:	insolence
Übertretung:	transgression, violation
Unachtsamkeit:	inattention
Unbehutsamkeit:	improvidence
Undankbarkeit:	ingratitude
Uneigennützigkeit:	disinterestedness
Ungefähr:	accident
Ungemächlichkeit:	discomfort
Ungerechtigkeit:	injustice
Ungeschliffenheit:	uncouthness
Unmässigkeit:	intemperance
Untätigkeit:	idleness
Unterlassung:	delinquency, omission
Unterwürfigkeit:	servility, submission, subordination
Unvereinbarkeit:	incompatibility
Unversöhnlichkeit:	implacability
Unverträglichkeit:	quarrelsomeness

Unvorsichtigkeit:	inadvertence
Unwillen:	indignation, resentment
Unwillfährigkeit:	disobligingness
Unwissenheit:	ignorance
Unzerstörlichkeit:	indestructibility
Üppigkeit:	excess, lordliness, luxury
Ursache:	cause
Urteil:	judgement
Verachtung:	contempt
Veränderlichkeit:	mutability
Verantwortung:	responsibility
Verbindlichkeit:	obligation
Verbrechen:	transgression
Verbundenheit:	obligation
Verdacht:	suspicion
Verderben:	corruption
Verdienst:	merit, service
Verdrehung:	quibbling
Verdruss:	chagrin
Verehrung:	reverence
Verfassung:	constitution
Verfolgung:	persecution
Vergeltung:	repayment
Vergnügen:	pleasure
Vergütigung:	restitution
Verhalten:	behaviour, conduct
Verhältnis:	relationship
Verheissung:	promise
Verherrlichung:	glorification
Verjährung:	long custom
Verläumdung:	calumny
Verlegenheit:	embarrassment
Verletzung:	infringement
Vermessenheit:	presumption
Vermischung:	intercourse
Vermögen:	capacity, means
Vernachlässigung:	neglect
Vernunft:	reason
Vernünftelei:	ratiocination
Verschlagenheit:	craftiness
Verschwendung:	extravagance
Verschwiegenheit:	secretiveness
Versoffenheit:	drunkenness

Versöhnlichkeit:	conciliation
Versprechen:	promise
Verstand:	understanding
Verstümmelung:	mutilation
Versuchung:	temptation
Vertrag:	contract
Verträglichkeit:	peaceableness
Vertragsamkeit:	conciliation
Vertrauen:	trust
Vertraulichkeit:	intimacy
Verwahrlosung:	neglect
Verwerfung:	abjuration
Verzagtheit:	despondency
Verzärtelung:	pampering
Verzeihung:	forgiveness, pardon
Verzweiflung:	despair
Völkergerechtsam:	national prerogative
Vollkommenheit:	perfection
Vorsatz:	purpose, resolution
Vorteil:	advantage
Vorurteil:	prejudice
Vorwitz:	forwardness
Vorwurf:	reproach
Vorzugsgeist:	presumptuousness
Wackerheit:	bravery
Waghalsigkeit:	foolhardiness
Wahrhaftigkeit:	genuineness
Wahrheitsliebe:	truthfulness
warnend:	deterrent
Wegwerfung:	forfeiture, self-abasement
Weichlichkeit:	flabbiness
Weichmütigkeit:	tenderness
Widerruf:	retraction
Widerwillen:	aversion, repugnance
Willigkeit:	willingness
Willkür:	choice
Wissgebierde:	curiosity
Wohlanständigkeit:	seemliness
Wohlbefinden:	well-being
Wohlgefallen:	satisfaction
Wohltäter:	benefactor
Wohlwollenheit:	goodwill
Wollust:	voluptuousness

Würde:	dignity, worth
Würdigkeit:	worthiness
Zaghaftigkeit:	timorousness
Ziererei:	affectation
Zierlichkeit:	address, elegance
Zorn:	anger
Zufälligkeit:	contingency
Zufriedenheit:	contentment
Zulässigkeit:	permissibility
Zulassung:	toleration
Zurechnung:	imputation
Zurechnungsfähigkeit:	accountability
Zürnen:	anger
Zurückhaltung:	reserve
Zusammenpassung:	compatibility
Zuschreibung:	ascription
Zuträger:	tale-bearer
Zuträglichkeit:	utility
Zuverlässigkeit:	reliability
Zwang:	coercion, compulsion
Zwangsmittel:	constraint
Zweck:	end, purpose
Zweckmässigkeit:	purposiveness

English-German glossary

abasement:	Erniedrigung
abhorrence:	Abscheulichkeit
abjuration:	Verwerfung
absolution:	Entledigung
abstinence:	Enthaltsamkeit
accident:	Ungefähr
accountability:	Zurechnungsfähigkeit
acquisition:	Erwerbung
acquittal:	Lossprechung
action:	Handlung
address:	Zierlichkeit
adequacy:	Hinlänglichkeit
admission:	Geständnis
advantage:	Vorteil
affability:	Leutseligkeit
affectation:	Ziererei
affinity:	Anhänglichkeit
affront:	Beschimpfung
agreement:	Übereinstimmung
ambition:	Ehrbegierde, Ehrsüchtigkeit
amenity:	Annehmlichkeit
amiability:	Lieblichkeit
amorous:	bühlerisch
ampliative:	erweiternd
anger:	Zorn, Zürnen
animality:	Tierheit
apology:	Abbitte
appraisal:	Billigung, Dijudication
apprehension:	Besorgnis
approval:	Beifall
artistry:	Kunstfähigkeit, Kunstweisheit
ascription:	Zuschreibung
assassination:	Meuchelmord
assent:	Beifall
attachment:	Anhänglichkeit

attraction:	Reiz
authority:	Befugnis, Obrigkeit
avarice:	Geiz, Habsucht
aversion:	Abscheu, Missfallen, Widerwillen
awe:	Ehrfurcht
bashfulness:	Schamhaftigkeit, Schüchternheit
begrudgement:	Missgunst
behaviour:	Verhalten
belief:	Glaube
benefactor:	Wohltäter
benevolence:	Gütigkeit, Wohlwollen
benignity:	Gutartigkeit
betrayal:	Treulosigkeit
bigotry:	Frömmelei
blame:	Tadel
blameworthy:	tadelhaft
blessedness:	Seligkeit
bloodthirstiness:	Blutdürstigkeit
boldness:	Kühnheit
bragging:	Aufschneiderei
bravery:	Wackerheit
bribery:	Bestechung
brooding:	Grübelei
brutality:	Gewalttätigkeit
busyness:	Geschäftigkeit
callousness:	Lieblosigkeit
calumny:	Verläumdung
candour:	Freimütigkeit
capacity:	Fähigkeit, Vermögen
cause:	Ursache
caution:	Behutsamkeit
censure:	Rüge, Tadel
chagrin:	Verdruss
charm:	Anmut
chastity:	Keuschheit
chattiness:	Schwatzhaftigkeit
cheating:	Betrug
cheerfulness:	Fröhlichkeit, Heiterkeit
choice:	Willkür
civility:	Artigkeit, Höflichkeit
cleanliness:	Reinigkeit
coarseness:	Grobheit

489

coercion:	Zwang
cold-bloodedness:	Kaltblütigkeit
comeliness:	Anmut
command:	Gebot, Oberherrschaft
compassion:	Barmherzigkeit, Mitleid
compatibility:	Zusammenpassung
compensation:	Entschädigung, Ersatz
compliance:	Gefälligkeit
compliancy:	Nachgeben
comprehensibility:	Fasslichkeit
compulsion:	Zwang
conceit:	Aufgeblasenheit, Eigendünkel, Hoffart
conciliation:	Versöhnlichkeit, Vertragsamkeit
condition:	Bedingung
conduct:	Verhalten
confession:	Bekenntnis
conformity:	Übereinstimmung
conjugal relation:	Gliedergemeinschaft
conscience:	Gewissen
conscientiousness:	Gewissenhaftigkeit
consent:	Einstimmung
consolation:	Trost
constitution:	Beschaffenheit, Verfassung
constraint:	Nötigung, Zwangsmittel
contempt:	Verachtung
contentment:	Zufriedenheit
contingency:	Zufälligkeit
contract:	Vertrag
conversion:	Bekehrung
copying:	Nachahmung
corruption:	Verderben
counsel:	Beistand
courtesy:	Höflichkeit, Leutseligkeit
courting favour:	Gunstbewerbung
cowardice:	Feigheit
craftiness:	Verschlagenheit
credibility:	Glaubwürdigkeit
credulity:	Leichtgläubigkeit
crudity:	Roheit
cruelty:	Grausamkeit
cuckoldry:	Hahnrei
culpability:	Straffälligkeit
cunning:	Arglist, Hinterlistigkeit, Schlauigkeit
cupidity:	Habsucht

curiosity:	Wissbegierde
custody:	Gewahrsam
custom, long:	Verjährung
daintiness:	Leckerhaftigkeit
damaging:	nachteilig
decision:	Dijudication, Entschluss, Festsetzung
decorum:	Anständigkeit
degradation:	Abwürdigung
delinquency:	Unterlassung
delusion:	Täuschung
demeaning:	Erniedrigung
depravity:	Pravität
desire:	Begehrung, Begierde
despair:	Verzweiflung
despondency:	Kleinmütigkeit, Verzagtheit
determination:	Bestimmung
deterrent:	warnend
devotion:	Andacht
diffidence:	Schamhaftigkeit, Schüchternheit
dignity:	Würde
diligence:	Arbeitsamkeit
diminution:	Schmälerung
disadvantage:	Nachteil
discharge (debt):	Abtragung
discomfort:	Missbehagen, Ungemächlichkeit
disgust:	Ekel
disinterestedness:	Uneigennützigkeit
dismissal:	Dienstaufkündigung
disobligingness:	Unwillfährigkeit
disparagement:	Obtrectation
disparaging:	nachteilig
disposition:	Gesinnung
distress:	Betrübnis
diversion:	Ergötzlichkeit
dogmatism:	Rechthaberei
doing without:	Entbehrlichkeit
drunkenness:	Versoffenheit
duty:	Pflicht
ease:	Leichtigkeit
eccentric:	Sonderling
edification:	Erbauung
education:	Erziehung

elegance:	Zierlichkeit
embarrassment:	Verlegenheit
emergency:	Notfall
emotion:	Gemütsbewegung
emulation:	Nacheiferung, Nachfolge
end:	Zweck
enjoyment:	Genuss
enmity:	Feindschaft, Feindseligkeit
enthusiasm:	Schwärmerei
entitlement:	Befugnis
envy:	Missgunst, Neid
equality:	Gleichheit
equanimity:	Gleichmütigkeit
equity:	Billigkeit
esteem:	Schätzung
excess:	Üppigkeit
execution:	Ausübung
experience:	Erfahrung
extravagance:	Verschwendung
fabrication:	Erdichtung
faculty of desire:	Begehrungsvermögen
faith:	Glaube
faithlessness:	Treulosigkeit
fanaticism:	Schwärmerei
feeling:	Gefühl
feeling unwell:	Missbehagen
firmness:	Festigkeit
flabbiness:	Weichlichkeit
flattery:	Schmeichelei
folly:	Narrheit
foolhardiness:	Waghalsigkeit
forfeiture:	Wegwerfung
forgiveness:	Verzeihung
forwardness:	Vorwitz
frailty:	Gebrechlichkeit
frankness:	Offenherzigkeit
freedom:	Freiheit
friendliness:	Freundlichkeit
friendship:	Freundschaft
frigidity:	Kaltsinnigkeit
frugality:	Entbehrlichkeit, Genügsamkeit
fulfilment:	Ergänzung

garrulity:	Gesprächigkeit
generosity:	Grossmut
gentility:	Gelindigkeit
glorification:	Verherrlichung
gluttony:	Gefrässigkeit
godliness:	Gottseligkeit
goodness:	Bonität, Güte
goodwill:	Wohlwollenheit
governance:	Oberherrschaft
gratitude:	Dankbarkeit, Erkenntlichkeit
greediness:	Lüsternheit
grudging:	Missgunst
guideline:	Richtschnur
guilt:	Schuldigkeit
habit:	Gewohnheit
happiness:	Glückseligkeit
hardheartedness:	Hartherzigkeit
hardship:	Beschwerlichkeit
hatred:	Hass
helpfulness:	Dienstbeflissenheit
heresy:	Ketzerei
holiness:	Heiligkeit
honesty:	Aufrichtigkeit, Ehrlichkeit, Redlichkeit
honorableness:	Ehrbarkeit
honour:	Ehre
honour, craving for:	Ehrbegierde
honour, love of:	Ehrliebe
horror:	Grausen
hot temper:	Jachzorn
humaneness:	Menschlichkeit
humanity:	Menschheit
humility:	Demut
hypocrisy:	Heuchelei
hypocrite:	Frömmler
idleness:	Müssigkeit, Untätigkeit
idolatry:	Abgötterei, Bilderdienst
ignorance:	Unwissenheit
imagination:	Einbildungskraft
imitation:	Nachahmung
impediment:	Hindernis
impiety:	Ruchlosigkeit

implacability:	Unversöhnlichkeit
improvidence:	Unbehutsamkeit
impudence:	Frechheit
impulse:	Antrieb
imputation:	Zurechnung
inadvertence:	Unvorsichtigkeit
inattention:	Unachtsamkeit
incentive:	Antrieb, Reiz
inclination:	Hang, Neigung
incompatibility:	Unvereinbarkeit
indebtedness:	Schuldigkeit
indestructibility:	Unzerstörlichkeit
indifference:	Gleichgültigkeit
indignation:	Unwillen
indolence:	Gemächlichkeit, Lässigkeit
inducement:	Anlockung
indulgence:	Duldsamkeit
industry:	Arbeitsamkeit
infamy:	Ruchlosigkeit, Schändlichkeit
infringement:	Schmälerung, Verletzung
ingratiation:	Schmeichelei
ingratitude:	Undankbarkeit
inheritance:	Beerbung
injury:	Beleidigung, Kränkung, Laesion, Nachteil, Schädlichkeit
injustice:	Ungerechtigkeit
insidious:	hinterlistig
insignificance:	Geringfügigkeit
insolence:	Dreistigkeit
instruction:	Belehrung
integrity:	Lauterkeit
intemperance:	Unmässigkeit
intent:	Absicht
intercourse:	Vermischung
intimacy:	Vertraulichkeit
intoxication:	Berauschung
intuition:	Anschauung
jealousy:	Eifersucht, Missgunst
judgement:	Beurteilung
jurisdiction:	Gerichtsbarkeit
justice:	Gerechtigkeit

494

kindheartedness:	Gutartigkeit
kindliness:	Gütigkeit
knowledge:	Erkenntnis
law:	Gesetz, Recht
lawfulness:	Gesetzmässigkeit, Rechtsmässigkeit
lawgiving:	Gesetzgebung
lawlessness:	Regellosigkeit
laziness:	Faulheit
learning:	Gelehrsamkeit
legality:	Rechtskräftigkeit
leisure:	Musse
leniency:	Nachsicht
liability:	Schuldigkeit
likeness:	Ebenbild
long custom:	Verjährung
loquacity:	Sprachhaftigkeit
lordliness:	Hochmut, Üppigkeit
love:	Liebe
luxury:	Luxuries
magnanimity:	Grossmut
malice:	Bosheit
malicious glee:	Schadenfreude
malignity:	Bösartigkeit
mastery:	Beherrschung, Oberherrschaft
means:	Mittel, Vermögen
meekness:	Demut
mendacity:	Lügenhaftigkeit
merit:	Verdienst
mildness:	Sanftmut
mind:	Gemüt
mischief:	Mutwille
miserliness:	Geiz
misliking:	Missfallen, Missgunst
mistrust:	Misstrauen
mockery:	Spötterei
modesty:	Bescheidenheit, Schamhaftigkeit, Sittsamkeit
morbidity:	Schwermütigkeit
morganatic marriage:	Ehe zur linken Hand
morose:	mürrisch
motivating ground:	Beweggrund

495

motive:	Triebfeder
motor capacity:	Bewegungsvermögen
mutability:	Veränderlichkeit
mutilation:	Verstümmelung
national prerogative:	Völkergerechtsam
nature:	Beschaffenheit
necessitation:	Nötigung
necessity:	Notwendigkeit
necessity of life:	Notdurft
need:	Bedürfnis
neglect:	Vernachlässigung, Verwahrlosung
negligence:	Nachlässigkeit
oath-taking:	Eidesleistung
obedience:	Gehorsamkeit
obligation:	Verbindlichkeit, Verbundenheit
observance:	Beobachtung
occupation:	Beschäftigung
occurrence:	Begebenheit
omission:	Unterlassung
order:	Befehl
pampering:	Verzärtelung
pang (of conscience):	Gewissensbiss
parasite:	Schmarotzer
pardon:	Begnadigung, Verzeihung
parsimony:	Kargheit, Sparsamkeit
passion:	Leidenschaft
patience:	Geduld
peace-loving:	friedliebend
peace-making:	friedfertig
peaceableness:	Verträglichkeit
penance:	Büssung
perfection:	Vollkommenheit
permissibility:	Zulässigkeit
permissive law:	Erlaubnisgesetz
persecution:	Verfolgung
persistence:	Beharrlichkeit
pettifogger:	Rabulist
piety:	Frömmigkeit
pity:	Mitleid
pleasant:	angenehm
pleasure:	Lust, Vergnügen

poisoning:	Giftmischerei
politeness:	Geschliffenheit, Höflichkeit
possession:	Besitz
poverty:	Armut
power:	Gewalt, Macht
prayer:	Anbetung
prejudice:	Vorurteil
preservation:	Erhaltung
presumption:	Fürwahrhaltung, Vermessenheit
presumptuousness:	Vorzugsgeist
pretension:	Anmassung
pride:	Hochmut, Hoffart, Stolz
promise:	Verheissung, Versprechen
property:	Eigentum
propriety:	Schicklichkeit
prudence:	Klugheit
punctiliousness:	Genauigkeit, Peinlichkeit, Pünktlichkeit
punishment:	Bestrafung
punitive justice:	Strafgerechtigkeit
purity:	Reinlichkeit
purpose:	Vorsatz, Zweck
purposiveness:	Zweckmässigkeit
quarrelsomeness:	Unverträglichkeit
quibbling:	Verdrehung
quittance:	Rechtsgenugtuung
rabble:	Pöbel
ratiocination:	Vernünftelei
readiness:	Fertigkeit, Leichtigkeit
reason:	Vernunft
receptivity:	Empfänglichkeit
recklessness:	Tollkühnheit
rectitude:	Gerechtigkeit
regularity:	Regelmässigkeit
relationship:	Verhältnis
reliability:	Zuverlässigkeit
remorse:	Gewissensbiss
renunciation:	Entsagung
repayment:	Vergeltung
reproach:	Vorwurf
repugnance:	Widerwille
requital:	Entschädigung, Erstattung

resentment:	Unwille
reserve:	Zurückhaltung
resolution:	Beschluss, Vorsatz
resolve:	Entschluss
respect:	Achtung
responsibility:	Verantwortung
restitution:	Vergütigung
restraint:	Abhaltung
retraction:	Widerruf
retributive:	rächend
revelation:	Offenbarung
revelry:	Schwelgerei
revenge:	Rache
reverence:	Hochachtung, Verehrung
revulsion:	Ekel
reward:	Belohnung
right:	Recht
right to sell:	Mercurius
righteousness:	Gerechtigkeit, Rechtschaffenheit
rigour:	Strenge
rule:	Regel
sacrifice:	Aufopferung
satiation:	Überdrüssigkeit
satisfaction:	Befriedigung, Wohlgefallen
scandalmonger:	Ohrenbläser
scoffing:	Spötterei
scourging:	Geisselung
scrupulosity:	Gewissenhaftigkeit
secretiveness:	Verschwiegenheit
seemliness:	Wohlanständigkeit
self-abasement:	Niederträchtigkeit, Wegwerfung
self-anguish:	Selbstängstigung
self-conceit:	Eigendünkel
self-denial:	Selbstverläugnung
self-esteem:	Selbstschätzung
self-examination:	Selbsterforschung
self-favour:	Selbstgunst
self-indulgence:	Luxus
self-interest:	Eigennutz
self-love:	Selbstliebe
self-mastery:	Selbstbeherrschung
self-satisfaction:	Selbstzufriedenheit
self-seeking:	Selbstsucht

498

self-sufficiency:	Selbstständigkeit
self-testing:	Selbstprüfung
self-will:	Eigensinn
sensation:	Empfindung
sensibility:	Sinnlichkeit
sentence:	Gericht
service:	Verdienst
servility:	Unterwürfigkeit
severity:	Härte
sexual impulse:	Geschlechtsneigung
shrewdness:	Schlauigkeit
skill:	Geschicklichkeit
slanderer:	Ohrenbläser
sociability:	Geselligkeit
spendthrift:	Verschwender
sponger:	Schmarotzer
standard:	Maasstab
steadiness:	Beständigkeit
stinginess:	Filz
stumbling-block:	Anstoss
stupidity:	Torheit
sublimity:	Erhabenheit
submission:	Unterwürfigkeit
subordination:	Unterordnung
sufficiency:	Genügsamkeit, Hinlänglichkeit
suicide:	Selbstmord
superstition:	Aberglaube
supremacy:	Obergewalt
suspicion:	Verdacht
sycophancy:	Schmeichelei
sympathy:	Mitgefühl
taciturnity:	Sprachlosigkeit
tale-bearer:	Zuträger
taste:	Geschmack
temper, hot:	Jachzorn
temperance:	Mässigkeit
temptation:	Versuchung
tenderness:	Weichmütigkeit
thrift:	Sparsamkeit
timorousness:	Mutlosigkeit, Zaghaftigkeit
toleration:	Leidlichkeit
totality:	Inbegriff
touchstone:	Probierstein

training:	Bildung
transgression:	Übertretung, Verbrechen
trust:	Vertrauen
truthfulness:	Wahrhaftigkeit, Wahrheitsliebe
uncouthness:	Ungeschliffenheit
understanding:	Verstand
unpretentiousness:	Anspruchslosigkeit
urge:	Trieb
utility:	Nutzen, Zuträglichkeit
vanity:	Eitelkeit
veneration:	Ehrerbietung
vengefulness:	Rachbegierde
verdict:	Gericht
vice:	Laster
vigilance:	Achtsamkeit
villainy:	Lasterhaftigkeit
violation:	Übertretung
virtue:	Tugend
vivacity:	Munterkeit
voluptuousness:	Wollust
wantonness:	Mutwille, Üppigkeit
watchfulness:	Achtsamkeit
well-being:	Wohlbefinden
well-doing:	Wohltätigkeit
well-wishing:	Wohlwollen
wickedness:	Bosheit
willingness:	Willigkeit
worship:	Anbetung
worth:	Wert, Würde
worthiness:	Würdigkeit
wretchedness:	Elend
zeal:	Eifer
zealotry:	Andächtelei

Name index

Subject index

abnegation, 58
abstinence, 162–4, 389–91
adiaphora, 134, 235, 276–8, 285, 314, 362
adultery, 160, 379, 398
aesthetics, xix, 225, 267
affability, 24, 181–2, 207
affection, 155–6, 182
age, 217–18, 220
agency, 312–15
alms-giving, 209, 299, 351, 399, 431
altruism, 3–4, 30, 299–300, 402
ama optimum quantum potes, 59
analogon rationis, xxvii, 21
anger, 416–17
animals, 60, 125–7, 147, 156, 160–1, 177, 198, 212–13, 218, 234, 262, 281, 373, 377, 381, 404, 434–5
anthropology, 42, 217, 226–7
apostasy, 121
appetite, 155–6, 167
arrogance, 135–6, 211, 354–5, 364, 366, 400–1, 413, 424, 433, 447–8
asceticism, 152, 310, 374–5, 387
atheism, 7, 32, 99–100, 111, 208–9, 291–2, 439
autonomy, 246, 262, 266–7, 270–1
avarice, 169–71, 394
awe, 15, 438, 444

backbiting, 211
beauty, 13–14, 23–4, 214, 432
Bedouins, 240, 457
begging, 351, 424, 431
belief, 96, 102–5, 327, 358–9, 441, 445
benevolence, 13–14, 24, 70, 177–80, 192, 364, 367, 381, 407, 413, 443–4
blessedness, 21, 47, 181, 259, 382–3, 392, 420
body, duties to, 144, 151–2, 157, 341–2, 349, 367, 371–2, 382

casuistry, 134, 235, 312, 362, 428
caution, 141–2, 410, 414–15, 418
censure, 205–7, 414, 430–1
chastity, 377
children, 160, 195, 198, 212, 217–20, 312, 331, 379, 381, 398, 403–4, 417, 421–2

choice, 234–5, 258, 261–3, 267, 273, 368
Christianity, xx, 9–10, 46–7, 91–2, 103, 192–3, 229, 354–5, 359, 429, 450–1
cold-bloodedness, 24, 182–3, 321, 404, 415
compassion, 25, 128
complaisance, 207
compulsion, 59–65, 74, 191–2, 218, 236–8, 282–9, 365–6
concubinage, 158–60, 378, 380
conscience, xxi, 4, 11, 18–19, 47, 88–9, 118, 130–5, 192, 241, 325, 327–8, 357–64, 448
consequences, imputable, 315, 319, 361–2
consequentialism, 235–6, 245, 257
contempt, 173–4, 177, 211–12, 311, 351, 375–6, 381, 393, 398, 400–1, 417, 426, 434
contentment, 142–3, 154, 162–4, 228, 242, 366, 382–8, 392, 402
contract: of service, 343–4; social, 338–9
courtesy, 182, 207, 210, 426
cowardice, 27, 146, 150, 219, 390, 427
crimina carnis, 124, 127, 146, 153, 160–2, 373, 381, 420, 425
cruelty, 212–13, 219, 311, 404, 434–5
cuckoldry, 342
custom, 91, 176, 240–1, 344–5, 433
Cynicism, 45–6, 152, 164, 228, 254–5, 387, 460
Cyrenaicism, 385, 460

daintiness, 374
death, 149–50, 196, 311, 347, 370–1, 375
debt, 123, 351
decorum, 259, 365, 432–3
deism, 439
despondency, 351, 355
destructiveness, 213, 219, 434
determinism, 268–71
devotion, 102, 104, 111, 119, 168–9, 444, 452
Dippelianism, 442
discipline, 151–2, 162–5, 218–21, 391–2
dispositions, 90–1, 97, 104, 112–13, 128, 130, 332–3, 335
dogmatism, 210